Feasting on the Word

Editorial Board

Feasting on the Word

Preaching the
Revised Common Lectionary

Year C, Volume 3

DAVID L. BARTLETT and BARBARA BROWN TAYLOR

General Editors

WESTMINSTER
JOHN KNOX PRESS
LOUISVILLE · KENTUCKY

Scripture quotations from the New Revised Standard Version of the Bible are copyright © 1989 by the Division of Christian Education of the National Council of the Churches of Christ in the U.S.A. and are used by permission. All rights reserved. Scripture taken from the Contemporary English Version (CEV). Copyright © The American Bible Society 1995. All rights reserved.

Book design by Drew Stevens
Cover design by Lisa Buckley

First edition
Published by Westminster John Knox Press
Louisville, Kentucky

This book is printed on acid-free paper that meets the American National Standards Institute Z39.48 standard. ∞

PRINTED IN THE UNITED STATES OF AMERICA

10 11 12 13 14 15 16 17 18 19 — 10 9 8 7 6 5 4 3 2

Library of Congress Cataloging-in-Publication Data

Feasting on the Word : preaching the revised common lectionary / David L. Bartlett and Barbara Brown Taylor, general editors.
    p. cm.
  Includes index.
  ISBN 978-0-664-23102-6 (v. 7 alk. paper)
  ISBN 978-0-664-23101-9 (v. 6 alk. paper)
  ISBN 978-0-664-23100-2 (v. 5 alk. paper)
  ISBN 978-0-664-23099-9 (v. 4 alk. paper)
  ISBN 978-0-664-23098-2 (v. 3 alk. paper)
  ISBN 978-0-664-23097-5 (v. 2 alk. paper)
  ISBN 978-0-664-23096-8 (v. 1 alk. paper)
  1. Lectionary preaching.   2. Common lectionary (1992)   I. Bartlett, David Lyon, 1941–
II. Taylor, Barbara Brown.
  BV4235.L43F43 2008
  251'.6—dc22

                                 2007047534

Contents

Publisher's Note

Feasting on the Word: Preaching the Revised Common Lectionary is an ambitious project that is offered to the Christian church as a resource for preaching and teaching.

The uniqueness of this approach in providing four perspectives on each preaching occasion from the Revised Common Lectionary sets this work apart from other lectionary materials. The theological, pastoral, exegetical, and homiletical dimensions of each biblical passage are explored with the hope that preachers will find much to inform and stimulate their preparations for preaching from this rich "feast" of materials.

This work could not have been undertaken without the deep commitments of those who have devoted countless hours to working on these tasks. Westminster John Knox Press would like to acknowledge the magnificent work of our general editors, David L. Bartlett and Barbara Brown Taylor. They are both gifted preachers with passionate concerns for the quality of preaching. They are also wonderful colleagues who embraced this huge task with vigor, excellence, and unfailing good humor. Our debt of gratitude to Barbara and David is great.

The fine support staff, project manager Joan Murchison and compiler Mary Lynn Darden, enabled all the thousands of "pieces" of the project to come together and form this impressive series. Without their strong competence and abiding persistence, these volumes could not have emerged.

The volume editors for this series are to be thanked as well. They used their superb skills as pastors and professors and ministers to work with · writers and help craft their valuable insights into the highly useful entries that comprise this work.

The hundreds of writers who shared their expertise and insights to make this series possible are ones who deserve deep thanks indeed. They come from wide varieties of ministries, but they have given their labors to provide a gift to benefit the whole church and to enrich preaching in our time.

Westminster John Knox would also like to express our appreciation to Columbia Theological Seminary for strong cooperation in enabling this work to begin and proceed. Dean of Faculty and Executive Vice President D. Cameron Murchison welcomed the project from the start and drew together everything we needed. His continuing efforts have been very valuable. Former President Laura S. Mendenhall provided splendid help as well. She made seminary resources and personnel available and encouraged us in this partnership with enthusiasm and all good grace. We thank her and look forward to working with Columbia's new president, Stephen Hayner.

It is a joy for Westminster John Knox Press to present *Feasting on the Word: Preaching the Revised Common Lectionary* to the church, its preachers, and its teachers. We believe rich resources can assist the church's ministries as the Word is proclaimed. We believe the varieties of insights found in these pages will nourish preachers who will "feast on the Word" and who will share its blessings with those who hear.

Westminster John Knox Press

Series Introduction

A preacher's work is never done. Teaching, offering pastoral care, leading worship, and administering congregational life are only a few of the responsibilities that can turn preaching into just one more task of pastoral ministry. Yet the Sunday sermon is how the preacher ministers to most of the people most of the time. The majority of those who listen are not in crisis. They live such busy lives that few take part in the church's educational programs. They wish they had more time to reflect on their faith, but they do not. Whether the sermon is five minutes long or forty-five, it is the congregation's one opportunity to hear directly from their pastor about what life in Christ means and why it matters.

Feasting on the Word offers pastors focused resources for sermon preparation, written by companions on the way. With four different essays on each of the four biblical texts assigned by the Revised Common Lectionary, this series offers preachers sixteen different ways into the proclamation of God's Word on any given occasion. For each reading, preachers will find brief essays on the exegetical, theological, homiletical, and pastoral challenges of the text. The page layout is unusual. By setting the biblical passage at the top of the page and placing the essays beneath it, we mean to suggest the interdependence of the four approaches without granting priority to any one of them. Some readers may decide to focus on the Gospel passage, for instance, by reading all four essays provided for that text. Others may decide to look for connections between the Hebrew Bible, Psalm, Gospel, and Epistle texts by reading the theological essays on each one.

Wherever they begin, preachers will find what they need in a single volume produced by writers from a wide variety of disciplines and religious traditions. These authors teach in colleges and seminaries. They lead congregations. They write scholarly books as well as columns for the local newspaper. They oversee denominations. In all of these capacities and more, they serve God's Word, joining the preacher in the ongoing challenge of bringing that Word to life.

We offer this print resource for the mainline church in full recognition that we do so in the digital age of the emerging church. Like our page layout, this decision honors the authority of the biblical text, which thrives on the page as well as in the ear. While the twelve volumes of this series follow the pattern of the Revised Common Lectionary, each volume contains an index of biblical passages so that all preachers may make full use of its contents.

We also recognize that this new series appears in a post-9/11, post-Katrina world. For this reason, we provide no shortcuts for those committed to the proclamation of God's Word. Among preachers, there are books known as "Monday books" because they need to be read thoughtfully at least a week ahead of time. There are also "Saturday books," so called because they supply sermon ideas on short notice. The books in this series are not Saturday books. Our aim is to help preachers go deeper, not faster, in a world that is in need of saving words.

A series of this scope calls forth the gifts of a great many people. We are grateful first of all to the staff of Westminster John Knox Press: Don McKim, Jon Berquist, and Jack Keller, who conceived this project; David Dobson, who worked diligently to bring the project to completion, with publisher Marc Lewis's strong support; and Julie Tonini, who has painstakingly guided each volume through the production process. We thank Laura Mendenhall, former President of Columbia Theological Seminary, and Columbia's Dean, Cameron Murchison, who made our participation in this work possible. Our editorial board is a hardworking board, without whose patient labor and good humor this series would not exist. From the start, Joan Murchison has been the brains of the operation, managing details of epic proportions with great human kindness. Mary Lynn Darden, Dilu Nicholas, Megan Hackler, and John Shillingburg have supported both her and us with their administrative skills.

We have been honored to work with a multitude of gifted thinkers, writers, and editors. We present these essays as their offering—and ours—to the blessed ministry of preaching.

David L. Bartlett
Barbara Brown Taylor

A Note about the Lectionary

Feasting on the Word follows the Revised Common Lectionary (RCL) as developed by the Consultation on Common Texts, an ecumenical consultation of liturgical scholars and denominational representatives from the United States and Canada. The RCL provides a collection of readings from Scripture to be used during worship in a schedule that follows the seasons of the church year. In addition, it provides for a uniform set of readings to be used across denominations or other church bodies.

The RCL provides a reading from the Old Testament, a Psalm response to that reading, a Gospel, and an Epistle for each preaching occasion of the year. It is presented in a three-year cycle, with each year centered around one of the Synoptic Gospels. Year A is the year of Matthew, Year B is the year of Mark, and Year C is the year of Luke. John is read each year, especially during Advent, Lent, and Easter.

The RCL offers two tracks of Old Testament texts for the Season after Pentecost or Ordinary Time: a semicontinuous track, which moves through stories and characters in the Old Testament, and a complementary track, which ties the Old Testament texts to the theme of the Gospel texts for that day. Some denominational traditions favor one over the other. For instance, Presbyterians and Methodists generally follow the semicontinuous track, while Lutherans and Episcopalians generally follow the complementary track.

The print volumes of *Feasting on the Word* follow the complementary track for Year A, are split between the complementary and semicontinuous track for Year B, and cover the semicontinuous stream for Year C. Essays for Pentecost and the Season after Pentecost that are not covered in the print volumes are available on the *Feasting on the Word* Web site, www.feastingontheword.net.

For more information about the Revised Common Lectionary, visit the official RCL Web site at http://lectionary.library.vanderbilt.edu/ or see *The Revised Common Lectionary: The Consultation on Common Texts* (Nashville: Abingdon Press, 1992).

Feasting on the Word

Genesis 11:1-9

¹Now the whole earth had one language and the same words. ²And as they migrated from the east, they came upon a plain in the land of Shinar and settled there. ³And they said to one another, "Come, let us make bricks, and burn them thoroughly." And they had brick for stone, and bitumen for mortar. ⁴Then they said, "Come, let us build ourselves a city, and a tower with its top in the heavens, and let us make a name for ourselves; otherwise we shall be scattered abroad upon the face of the whole earth." ⁵The LORD came down to see the city and the tower, which mortals had built. ⁶And the LORD said, "Look, they are one people, and they have all one language; and this is only the beginning of what they will do; nothing that they propose to do will now be impossible for them. ⁷Come, let us go down, and confuse their language there, so that they will not understand one another's speech." ⁸So the LORD scattered them abroad from there over the face of all the earth, and they left off building the city. ⁹Therefore it was called Babel, because there the LORD confused the language of all the earth; and from there the LORD scattered them abroad over the face of all the earth.

Theological Perspective

If this story appeared anywhere other than the Bible, and if the names of the teams involved were almost anything other than "the whole earth," on the one hand, and "the LORD," on the other, we would recognize it immediately. It is a rumble, a show-down, a battle between two teams on an only apparently level playing field "in the land of Shinar." "Come, let us build ourselves a city!" shouts one team. "Come, let us go down, and confuse their language!" counters the other. The huddles break. The lines form. And the game is on. Only this is worse than David vs. Goliath. One team kneels; the other runs off in confusion. The contest is over before it starts. What kind of story is this, and what does it have to say about God and us?

First, it is important to hear this story at its most basic level as God *vs.* humanity. This is not a story we like to hear or tell. We have "the whole earth" lined up on one side and "the LORD" and the heavenly community on the other. The groups have opposing game plans: one side wants to build a city and a tower with its top in the heavens, and the other side wants to thwart this project and rout the opposing team. Usually in the Bible the terms are not so stark; there is at least one holdout on the human team—like Noah or Moses or the people of Israel. And most of the time the opponents of God

Pastoral Perspective

In Genesis, the story is that people were multiplying at a great rate. They were a fine and wonderful people, but they were also a scared people. They were afraid of being scattered to the farthest reaches of the known world. So they decided to build a huge city, a fortress for themselves and for their God.

God saw that they were one people and had only one language. God was concerned about the possibility of the people not learning anything new, since they already seemed to be a nice homogeneous community. God was concerned about the hubris of the people speaking for God. So God decided to add diversity to the mix. God made it so people did not understand one another. The people stopped building that great city, and they scattered themselves over the earth. Their diversity made it either impossible or highly unlikely that they would work together again.

Ever since, Babel has come to represent individualism. The nature of capitalism comes from Babel. Each individual has the right to make a profit. All individuals have the right to better themselves.

Our Babel component is our First-Worldness, our materialism, our economic and military domination. Our Babel component is everything that built up the Berlin wall, the Israel/Palestine wall, the U.S./Mexico wall, the disputes between Pakistan and India, the former rifts in Ireland and Northern Ireland, the

Exegetical Perspective

The traditional understanding of this passage is that it describes human arrogance in attempting to build a tower reaching to the sky and God's punishment of the perpetrators, confusing their language and dispersing them so that they cannot attempt such a project again. Several recent commentators have called this understanding into serious question, and their alternate understanding will be presented in this essay.[1]

The story of Babel in fact deals with the origins of cultural difference, not with pride and punishment. The first half of the pericope deals with human activity (vv. 1–4). The second half describes God's activity (vv. 6–9), after God had descended to inspect what was going on (v. 5). The author describes a primeval time when everyone spoke the same language and used the same vocabulary (vv. 1, 6). The goal of the building project was to keep the community in one place, lest they be scattered over the surface of all the earth (v. 4). Hence the people with one language wanted to stay in one place. Building a tower was only a means to this end, and we learn in verse 8 that the people stopped building the city, with no mention of the tower at all. The

1. The best statement of this position is by Theodore Hiebert, "The Tower of Babel and the Origin of the World's Cultures," *Journal of Biblical Literature* 126 (2007): 59–81.

Homiletical Perspective

The preacher will probably pair this text with Acts 2 in order to compare and contrast how God is at work in human communication in the two stories, but the preacher is also free to address the Babel story alone, listening for gospel springing from this strange story.

To begin, it is helpful to clear away a few impediments to congregational understanding of this text. Listeners could be reminded that this is part of the "prehistory" of the Bible, used by ancient believers as an explanation for the existence of different languages and peoples. Along the same lines, congregants paying close attention to the wording in the Bible may notice God's plan to act, expressed in the words "Let *us.*" This is a reference not to polytheism but to the heavenly court.

Finally, at first hearing, God may seem petty and defensive (worried about humanity's power and responding with divine obfuscation and dispersion). But this obstacle to congregational understanding presents the preacher with an opportunity to be playful at the beginning of the sermon by painting absurd pictures of a God who is threatened and then vengeful toward these out-of-control human beings. "Uh-oh, humanity is at it again. Better quash this before things really get out of hand." After having some fun imagining the implications of a God who

Genesis 11:1-9

Theological Perspective

have names that set them apart, like Satan or Caesar or the enemies of Israel. But here, theologically, it is the whole of humanity vs. God.

The progression (or "digression") from Genesis 3 to 11—from Adam and Eve to Cain and Abel, through the flood toward Shinar—reminds us that not only are there times when humanity falls short and misses the mark, but there are times, or at least there is a time, when all of humanity takes action that runs directly counter to God's intentions. God's purposes are moving in one direction; humanity's purposes are moving in another. Though God usually takes action to clarify and gather, there are times when humanity forces God to do the opposite: to confuse and to scatter. Calvin writes: "For as soon as mortals, forgetful of themselves, are inflated above measure, it is certain that, like the giants, *they wage war with God.*"[1] It is one thing to confess that we are like lost sheep who have wandered from God's ways, wasted God's gifts, and forgotten God's love. It is another thing, in the words of a less-used prayer of confession, to make those verbs more active and confrontational: "We have not done your will, we have broken your law, we have rebelled against your love."[2] Again, as the structure makes clear, this is a rumble, a head-to-head fight between humanity and God.

So, second, and now more pressing, why does humanity's call to build provoke the Lord's summons to scatter? Here is where the genius and the mystery of Genesis 11 come forward most powerfully.

Like most biblical rebellions (think Israel's desire for a king or the disciples' rejection of Jesus), the story begins innocently enough. They make bricks and burn them thoroughly—a project that provokes no heavenly response. This is no story against technology per se. They make plans for a city and a tower "with its top in the heavens"—an application of technology on a scale and for a purpose that we will perhaps encounter again ("there was a ladder set up on the earth, the top of it reaching to heaven," Gen. 28:12). This is no story against all "heaven storming" of all kinds. Then come the motivation ("let us make a name for ourselves") and the fear that drives it ("otherwise we shall be scattered abroad upon the face of the whole earth"); and the battle is on. What is possible only for God—the granting of a name, by which humanity's fundamental fears might be eased,

1. John Calvin, *Genesis*, trans. John King (Grand Rapids: Baker Book House, 1989), 324, emphasis added.
2. *Book of Common Worship* (Louisville, KY: Westminster/John Knox Press, 1993), 89.

Pastoral Perspective

plethora of denominations that seek unity only by throwing others out. Our Babel component is the fact that most Americans can only speak one language and we expect others to learn ours.

We are addicted to Babel. We grew up believing that Babel is the God of true spirituality. Rugged individualism is the stuff of Babel. Individual thought is the stuff of Babel.

Babel is not all bad. From our Babel component we get cultural diversity. We get to push ourselves outside of our own understandings. We get humor and most things that are fun in this world.

But Babel is also what makes injustice thrive. Babel is what makes a distinction between rich and poor. Babel is what makes people think they can own other people. Babel is what makes people think they can condemn other people. Babel is what makes enemies. Babel is what makes wars to happen. Babel is often lived out in individual and corporate sin, because we tend not to look to God, but to ourselves for the ultimate answers. And what we end up with is confusion. None of us speak the same language anymore. We all have a Babel component.

Pentecost is a snapshot of the opposite. The Holy Spirit comes to everyone—the intellectual and the unsophisticated, the committed and the apathetic, the fundamentalist and the pagan, the man and the woman and those in between—and for an instant, they all speak the same language.

Right after Pentecost, the early church changed the way they did things. They got rid of their class distinctions. They held all of their money together and gave it out as people needed it. The *kairos* of God came and they saw the world in a different way. The Spirit moved among them and they no longer saw each other as people to be suspicious of, but as fellow children of God. They had a new freedom, and chance to be a different kind of community. They did not have to go back to Babel.

It would not last. Babel was too familiar. A few short chapters later in the book of Acts, members of the early church fought against each other as some said that it was better for the new foreign converts to be circumcised and stick to the tired old dietary laws of the Jewish culture.

The people on the *Titanic*, the rich and the poor, all knew the experience that changed their lives. It was an equal-opportunity iceberg. The economic and ethnic diversity on the ship for an instant was eradicated by the fact that they all experienced the iceberg and their oceanic cruise was to come to an end. After a moment of Pentecost, they reverted to

tower with its top in the sky merely demonstrates the magnificence of the city, and there is no explicit mention of pride in this passage.

In the Bible in general, making a name for oneself is never used to describe self-centeredness or pride. Rather, making a name implies an act of establishing an identity that will endure. Hence, building a city and making a name are only means to perpetuate a single culture—the human race speaking one language and living in one place.

When YHWH descends to see the city and the tower (v. 5), the narrator is merely describing the typical, two-tiered biblical universe, without any hint that YHWH had to descend because the tower was so tiny. YHWH does not comment directly on the city with its tower, let alone accuse the builders of pride, but merely notes that there is one people with one language—that is, they have cultural uniformity. YHWH adds: "This is what they have begun to do, and now all that they plan to do will be possible for them" (v. 6, my trans.). There is no indication that the people are harboring some kind of sinister plan as the NRSV implies: "This is only the beginning of what they will do." What did they plan to do? That was well described in the first four verses: Making bricks and building a city with a tower in hopes of not being dispersed across the earth.

The plural pronouns in verse 7 indicate YHWH's invitation to members of his divine council to join him in his actions: "Let us go down and let us mix there their language" (my trans.). More neutral choices of verbs in verses 7–8 reinforce the alternate interpretation of this passage that we are advocating. Instead of YHWH confusing their language, it is better to read that YHWH mixed their language there. YHWH's words, "Come, let us mix their language" (v. 7), echo the earlier words of the people, "Come, let us make bricks and build so that we will not be dispersed" (vv. 3–4). The mixing of languages becomes punishment only if the building project was an act of defiance and pride that demanded retribution from God. As we have seen, that motivation is *not* stated in the text.

Instead of YHWH scattering the people, it is better to translate "YHWH dispersed them from there over the surface of all the earth." This dispersal reverses the people's desire to stay in one place (v. 4), but is not punishment. As a result, they stopped building the city (v. 8b). The tower, so central to the traditional understanding of this text, is not even mentioned.

The last verse of the passage is a popular etiology of the name Babylon. The name "Babylon" (*babel*)

would act this way, then the preacher can turn and say, "Of course, we are not dealing with a scared, tyrant god; we are dealing with the Lord who is good in mysterious ways."

Briefly, here are a few issues raised by the text. The mortals (literally "children of Adam," God's human being formed from the dust) decide that the way to make a name (or it may be translated "reputation") for themselves is by burning clay bricks and building a city and a tower soaring to the heavens. In other words, "We are made from dust. So let us make a name for ourselves with dust." Hardly an auspicious beginning. Their rationale for building this city and tower is that they are making a name for themselves and they want to protect themselves from being scattered all over the earth. They assume that making "a name for ourselves" is what brings people together, when in fact such self-seeking often has the opposite effect.

Meanwhile, God comes down to take a look at humanity's handiwork, and God is not impressed. God says, "This is just the beginning. Nothing they can imagine will be impossible for them." (It can also be translated as, "nothing will enclose them or limit them"). So God says, "Let us go down and confuse [it can also be translated "enclose"] their language so they will not understand one another's speech." So God scatters the people and confuses their language and the building project is abandoned. The entire Babel enterprise is marked by irony, anxiety, and idolatry.

However, God's response does not have to be viewed merely as a punishment; it can be seen as a series of gifts received differently by different groups of people. To affluent and competitive people and congregations, God's invitation is to slow the feverish pace of life and to rest in the assurance of God's love that is given, not earned. To poor, marginalized people and congregations, God's promise is that our ultimate value does not depend upon our building gleaming cities and towers of achievement but upon God's dazzling and soaring love. In essence, one of the great gifts of this story read on Pentecost is to lift up the larger theme of vocation. We Christians constantly need to be reminded that we do not have to make a name for ourselves, because, as Jesus said, our names are already "written in heaven" (Luke 10:20). Instead, we are called and empowered to use our lives to bring glory to God. As the great preacher William Sloane Coffin wrote, "Our business in life is less to make something of

Genesis 11:1-9

Theological Perspective

and around which humanity's necessary unity might be achieved—becomes here a project for humankind, independent and counter to the gifting of God. Now the game is engaged, and the outcome established—for our own sakes! The scattering we sought to avoid becomes the judgment the Lord must render so that our desire for a name and our dreams of security will remain on a *proper* versus a *rebellious* track.

Theologian Reinhold Niebuhr has written powerfully on anxiety as the true source of our sin, especially in our best efforts: "The will-to-power is thus inevitably involved in the vicious circle of accentuating the insecurity which it intends to eliminate. . . . It seeks a security beyond the limits of human finiteness and this inordinate ambition arouses fears and enmities which the world of nature does not know. . . . The will-to-power is in short both a direct form and an indirect instrument of the pride which Christianity regards as sin in its quintessential form."[3]

So, third, and finally, much of the power of this showdown in Shinar comes from its contrast with other stories that move in the opposite direction, where the heavenly team comes down not in opposition to humanity, but in order to gather humanity, give it a name, and grant it a project on which it can work together in a good and redeeming way. Not only is this story of a showdown followed by the story of the Lord gathering a family to go out in order to bless all the families of the earth, but it is paired in the lectionary with the story of Pentecost. Here the scattered peoples come together around an upper room where some of those named as Christ's followers have been gathered by the Spirit. What proved impossible for an anxious humanity now becomes possible for God's gracious Spirit. And a whole new kind of rumble begins.

RICHARD BOYCE

Pastoral Perspective

familiar Babel by making distinctions, rich vs. poor, women vs. men, and so on.

In the early church, there was much confusion as to who was to receive the gift of the Holy Spirit. Paul, talking about the different gifts that we have, says that some have received the gift of tongues, some the gift of prophecy, still others the gift of teaching, and others the gift of evangelism (1 Cor. 12:8–10). They revisited Babel by trying to declare which gift of the Spirit was the best one.

We are children of Pentecost and children of Babel. We long for the ideal of Pentecost, but we revisit the comfort and predictability of Babel.

We come from very different walks of life. We are different ages, races, genders, and affectional orientations. We have achieved different educational levels. Different life experiences shape us. Sometimes, when we talk to each other, it is like we are talking in different languages. We live in Babel. We work in Babel. We breathe Babel. We are the children of Babel.

Explore with your congregation those things that they value about diversity. We all have a Babel component. Recognizing that is one of the best ways we can truly celebrate the unity in diversity that is the feast of Pentecost.

When we experience *kairos* events—often in response to a crisis—we are of one mind. We all speak the same language. And for a while, we do what redemptive communities normally do, as we help people in their healing. These Pentecost experiences don't always last. They don't last because we have a strong Babel component that causes us to confuse our language and get everything mixed up. Our Babel component, however, also causes us to ask the right questions, to wonder if everyone is really being heard. Our Babel component makes Pentecost meaningful.

DOUGLAS M. DONLEY

---

3. Reinhold Niebuhr, *The Nature and Destiny of Man* (New York: Charles Scribner's Sons, 1964), 1:192.

means something like "the gate of God," but here the name is explained as the place where YHWH mixed (*balal*) the language of the entire earth. The Bible viewed Mesopotamia and Babylon as the cradle of civilization. Elsewhere Genesis views the city of Ur in southern Mesopotamia as the homeland of Abraham's family. Genesis 11 does not present Babylon as the symbol of empire or offer a critique of it in this capacity. Rather, the story describes Babel as the point of origin of the world's different cultures.

Genesis 11 is customarily assigned to the Yahwist or J source. The Priestly source (P) also speaks of dispersion and cultural differentiation after the flood: "Be fruitful and multiply, and fill the earth" (Gen. 9:1, 7). The description of each of the sons of Noah in the priestly table of nations (Gen. 10) has a summary statement after listing a son's descendants. After Japheth's descendants, for example, we read: "These are the descendants of Japheth in their lands, each with its own language" (Gen. 10:5, my trans.; cf. vv. 20, 31). In P, the spread of culture is a natural consequence of reproduction and growth; but in J's story of Babel, the people's desire to stay together and preserve a single culture is held up against God's intention to disperse them and to diversify their languages and their cultures.

Cultural diversity is the consequence of God's design for the world, not the result of God's punishment of it. In this story the people desire uniformity, and God desires diversity. In a sense, both desires are good. Humans need identity and cultural solidarity, but it takes divine intervention and initiative to bring about the extravagant array of the world's cultures. The story embraces cultural solidarity and cultural difference and acknowledges the value of both. In the traditional understanding of this story, cultural difference is devalued and seen as a source of confusion and a curse upon the human race, even a judgment of God. The new, alternative understanding values difference highly and explains it as God's aspiration for the new world after the flood.

RALPH W. KLEIN

ourselves than to find something worth doing and losing ourselves in it."[1]

Another precious gift of this story is the implication that God uses humanity's city and tower building as the occasion to fashion a diverse humanity, flung like a divine sower's seed all over the planet. Apparently God is uninterested in a people united for the purpose of assuring their own fame and safety. Rather, could it be that God relishes having a world full of faithful people of different colors, sizes, shapes, ideas, and languages? As writer Annie Dillard puts it, "the creator loves pizzazz."[2]

Yet another direction for preaching would be to explore how God, the Creator of heaven and earth, is the one who acts in ways beyond our understanding and containing. This is no "User Friendly," "Seeker Friendly," or "cuddly" God we can be buddies with. This is a God who, with a word, may decide to scatter our neat existential architectural drawings to the wind and blow our carefully planned lives into something we had never imagined. Who wants to tangle with this God? Well, we do, but we do so aware of Babel's product packaging: "Warning—This God may turn your life upside down." So as we struggle with this God, we would be well-advised to say our prayers in the process. As we pray to this God, we might celebrate not only what God gives, but what God does not give. Here is a God who blesses humanity by *limiting* humanity. We are all just passing through this life, merely dust, limited in the amount of good and evil we can do, but also given the priceless opportunity for God to work in us for the glory of God. Who could ask for more?

JEFF PASCHAL

---

1. William Sloane Coffin, *Credo* (Louisville, KY: Westminster John Knox Press, 2004), 126.
2. Annie Dillard, *Pilgrim at Tinker Creek* (New York: Harper Perennial, 1988), 137.

Psalm 104:24-34, 35b

²⁴O Lord, how manifold are your works!
    In wisdom you have made them all;
    the earth is full of your creatures.
²⁵Yonder is the sea, great and wide,
    creeping things innumerable are there,
    living things both small and great.
²⁶There go the ships,
    and Leviathan that you formed to sport in it.

²⁷These all look to you
    to give them their food in due season;
²⁸when you give to them, they gather it up;
    when you open your hand, they are filled with good things.
²⁹When you hide your face, they are dismayed;
    when you take away their breath, they die
    and return to their dust.

Theological Perspective

Pentecost may seem like a strange time to examine God's work of creation, extolled in the closing verses of Psalm 104. After all, at Pentecost the Spirit is poured out, the church is birthed, and God's judgment at Babel is overcome. Furthermore, physical creation is not featured in Acts 2. Yet the psalmist's reflections about God's relationship to creation highlight a number of theological themes more fully manifest in the church and its birth at Pentecost.

In verse 24 the psalmist exclaims: "O Lord, how manifold are your works! In wisdom you have made them all; the earth is full of your creatures." Creation exhibits great biodiversity, which the psalmist describes in verse 25: "Yonder is the sea, great and wide, creeping things innumerable are there, living things both small and great." The manifold nature of creation is not observed only in plant and animal species; we see it throughout all creation itself. From the uniqueness of every snowflake, to the specific configuration of each sea coral plant, to the iris of every mammal's eye—God makes no two things exactly alike. Creation displays a profound diversity even amid similarity.

This abundance of creatures is an expression of, and testimony to, God's wisdom. "In wisdom you have made them all," the psalmist says (v. 24). This complexity and variety of life bears witness that

Pastoral Perspective

On Pentecost, we celebrate the event of the Holy Spirit descending to the faithful, allowing them both to speak and to be understood by the many peoples of the world. With tongues of fire and a great rushing wind, the Spirit opens the mouths of disciples and the ears of the gathered crowd. If one of the powerful implications of Pentecost is that God's Word transcends all of the great human barriers—language, understanding, race, nationality—other passages in the Bible encourage us to imagine God's Word moving out even farther, indeed through the whole of creation.

The inclusion of Psalm 104 in the Pentecost texts, for example, reminds us that human beings aren't the only creatures in the kingdom. The psalm tells us that God's word is translated beyond our human tongues and ears both to and through all creation. "Rocks and trees, skies and seas,"[1] and all the creatures therein have their place in the choir. The refrain of verse 35b, "Bless the Lord, O my soul," is sung by all the works of God, each in its own voice. Humanity does not sing a solo. If translation is the Spirit's primary Pentecost gift, we who persevere in translation must learn to speak and to hear more

1. From Maltbie D. Babcock, "This Is My Father's World," in *The Worshipbook* (Philadelphia: Westminster Press, 1970), #602.

[30]When you send forth your spirit, they are created;
and you renew the face of the ground.

[31]May the glory of the LORD endure forever;
may the LORD rejoice in his works—
[32]who looks on the earth and it trembles,
who touches the mountains and they smoke.
[33]I will sing to the LORD as long as I live;
I will sing praise to my God while I have being.
[34]May my meditation be pleasing to him,
for I rejoice in the LORD. . . .
[35b]Bless the LORD, O my soul.
Praise the LORD!

Exegetical Perspective

Like Psalms 8, 9, and 139, Psalm 104 is a psalm of creation, celebrating the work of YHWH in the created order. Psalm 104 brackets its poetic praise of creation with a repeated phrase in verse 1 and verse 35 that it shares only with Psalm 103, "Bless the LORD, O my soul." Beginning and ending with the imperative "Bless!" which generally means to bow the knee (here before YHWH), sets a context of praise, adoration, and veneration by the creature for the Creator. Concepts of the soul that suggest it is only a part of the human person run up against the Hebrew concept of soul (*nephesh*), which is much more suggestive of the wholeness of a living creature. The call here is for the whole person to enter into praise of God. Perhaps playing with echoes of Genesis 2, the psalmist implores the creature into whom God has breathed life (*nephesh*, in Gen. 2:7) to expend breath in the praise of God.

The first twenty-three verses of the psalm focus on the work of God in creation, from setting the earth on its foundation (v. 5), to providing flowing water (vv. 10–13), to causing vegetation to grow for food (v. 14). Beginning with verse 24, the lectionary passage opens with a summary verse that captures the preceding images in one all-encompassing statement celebrating everything as the creative work of God: "how *manifold* . . . made them *all* . . . is *full*."

Homiletical Perspective

Psalm 104 is considered too lengthy to be read in its entirety as part of a liturgy, but nevertheless the preacher will want to make some nod in the direction of the poem's literary integrity. The psalm as a whole is a sweeping, magnificent hymn to God the Creator, and it is laid out (mimicking the creation?) in a particular, orderly fashion. After the initial words of praise (v. 1), verses 2–4 enumerate the wonders of the sky. Verses 5–9 continue with appreciation for the earth. Verses 10–13 celebrate water, verses 14–18 vegetation, and verses 19–23 the moon and the sun. The lectionary portion, then, turns its attention, successively, to the sea (vv. 24–26), the gift of life (vv. 27–30), and finally the glory of YHWH (vv. 31–35). There is, of course, plenty in this segment to occupy the preacher, but the congregation's appreciation for the psalm will be heightened if it is aware of the ways in which the entire poem mirrors the creation accounts of Genesis, and further enhanced if listeners can somehow feel or experience the buildup of the preceding verses. Homiletically, it is desirable to convey something of the momentum of the psalm and the catalog of wonders that teem through the first twenty-three verses so that when the congregation turns its attention to verse 24, there is already a sense of excitement, energy, and wonder.

Psalm 104:24-34, 35b

Theological Perspective

God's "understanding is unsearchable" (Isa. 40:28). Thus the diversity displayed in God's manifold works is the revelation of God's wisdom in creation—indeed, God's signature upon this world.

The diversity manifested in the church serves the same purpose as in creation: to reveal the wisdom of God. In Ephesians 3, Gentiles are included with the Jews as "fellow heirs, members of the same body, and sharers in the promise in Christ Jesus through the gospel" (v. 6). Paul explains this as "the plan of the mystery hidden for ages in God who created all things; that through the church *the manifold wisdom of God* might now be made known" (vv. 9–10 RSV, emphasis added). For Paul the church reveals God's "manifold wisdom" by the diversity it displays. Christ's call to preach the gospel "to all nations" (Mark 13:10) is also a call for the church to reflect the ethnic diversity found among the Gentiles. Since all revelation of God's wisdom is grounded in the person of Christ (1 Cor. 1:24, Col. 2:3) it makes sense that the church as Christ's body has the task to "make known" God's manifold wisdom to the world.

For creation to bear witness to God's wisdom through its diversity requires that God have a personal relationship with each of God's creatures. This is indeed the focus of the psalmist's reflections in Psalm 104:26–30. God *personally* feeds the sea creatures by hand. These in turn respond to God, recognizing God's provision and thus "looking" to God "to give them their food." They depend personally upon God in every way. When God's face turns away, they are "dismayed"; when they die, it is because God removes their breath; and when God's *ruach* (breath/wind/Spirit) is sent forth, "they are created." The psalmist's point is that their birth, death, and very existence are a result of God's personal and sovereign action.

As in Psalm 104, Pentecost manifests God's personal and sovereign action. When the Old Testament imagery of God's *ruach* appears in Acts 2, the church is created. The third person of the Trinity is personally sent "from heaven" when "there came a sound like the rush of a violent wind." Acts declares the Spirit rests "on each of them" appearing as "divided tongues, as of fire." As a result, "all of them were filled with the Holy Spirit," speaking "in the native language" of "every nation under heaven," testifying concerning "God's deeds of power" in Christ (vv. 2–6, 22). Not only is each of the 120 believers personally anointed with the Holy Spirit; as soon as this divine action transpires, ethnic diversity appears representatively through the multiple

Pastoral Perspective

languages than all the God-fearing people of Jerusalem.

God's voice came through a great wind. Listen. Can you hear it now? Listen to the sounds of the wind. Listen to the beating wings of birds. Listen to the rustling trees. Listen to the creaks and groans of building floors. Listen to the pops of expanding woodwork as your house breathes in the warmth of summer. Listen to mountain streams carving their way down a hillside. Listen to still lakes wrapped in morning mist. Listen to the gravel beneath your car wheels. Listen.

All creation sings God's praise. All creation. If the Spirit can speak through tongues of flame, it can speak through all things that the flames of creation have brought into being. We humans may be able to speak God's word in a few hundred languages, but the earth and all that is within it echo God's holy name in a trillion different tongues. We might then ask, as did the people of Jerusalem, "How can this be?" and "What does this mean?"

It is one thing to get outside for a few days while on a summer vacation. It is quite something else to attempt to be in harmony with nature's voices. Too often we observe nature with the passive admiration of a back-pew worship attender. We nod at a beautiful sunset and think, "Nice job, God," in the same way people leaving worship shake the preacher's hand and say, "Nice sermon (what was it about?)." That nature and its Creator put forth so much effort at communicating praise only to have it fall on distracted human ears must be particularly insulting. Leviathan frolics, but an angry Leviathan —annoyed at being ignored, taken for granted, or dismissed as inconsequential—is to be feared. We humans are not nature's masters; at best we are cohorts, in tragedy its victims; and at worst we are its destroyers. As in human communications, when we forsake negotiation with nature in favor of brute force, all parties are injured. Learning to communicate with creation takes time. Listening takes work. Uniting in praise takes translation.

How do we engage in communication with nature? Most of us are aware of the need to reduce, reuse, and recycle. We know our carbon footprints should be downsized. But how many of our churches actively lead the way? Are we content to follow civic and economic bandwagons? Should we who pray "May the glory of the LORD endure forever" (v. 31) not continually strive to outdo each other in acts of ecofriendly praise? If God's glory in creation knows no bounds, should we stop at installing compact

Exegetical Perspective

God's creation abounds in its sheer infinite variety, yet equally astonishing are its complex structure and harmony, also formed by God. So the psalmist honors God's wisdom (*hokmah*) in creation, drawing on a vast tradition in the OT that praises God as both "artisan and architect."[1]

This dual nature of God's creative work plays itself out in the following verses. The artistic imagination of God expressed in God's creatures encompasses even taming and demythologizing other seeming powers in the ancient world. In many surrounding cultures, the sea represented the power, even the "god," of chaos, which threatened to destroy created order. Yet here the "sea" is simply another of God's created works (cf. Gen. 1). Despite being "great and wide" and "full of innumerable creatures," the sea is like the creatures playing there, formed by the handiwork of God. Even another form of the chaos sea god/monster Leviathan is merely an ocean-going plaything for God (v. 25).

The portrait of God as architect finds celebration through a series of images lined up in classic Hebrew parallelism (vv. 27–30). Following the simple pattern of saying one thing and then saying it again slightly differently (both in form and nuance), verse 27 opens as another summary statement followed by a series of parallel statements that together paint a poignant portrait of God's design for creation's provision. Verse 27 repeats the earlier emphasis on "all," as everything looks for the basic necessity of food from God at its appointed time. God created not only living creatures that inhabit the earth, but the structure of creation that provides for their ongoing life. The nature of God's providential care focuses on God's open hands, which give to creation, followed by creation's open hands filling themselves with God's gifts. Antithetically, the opposite parallel proves true. When God hides God's face and takes away their breath (*ruach*), creatures struggle and perish, returning to their original dust (cf. Gen. 2).

Canonically, verbal echoes reverberate between Psalm 104 and Genesis 1–2. The Genesis 2 image of living beings (*nephesh*) formed into creation by God breathing life into inanimate dust finds reversal here as breath (*ruach*) removed leads to disintegration into dust. Creation is utterly dependent on the nurturing care of its God, without which it simply dissolves away. Finally, these parallel images reach culmination in the movement of God's Spirit

1. J. Clinton McCann, "The Book of Psalms," *New Interpreter's Bible* (Nashville: Abingdon Press, 1996), 4:1098.

Homiletical Perspective

The themes of the remaining three segments—the sea, the gift of life, the glory of God—may be taken in turn but should not be disconnected from one another. That more schematic approach would make things easier for the preacher but would cheat the congregation of the richness that is inherent in the psalm's gestalt. Each part of the creation depends on the other parts for meaning (how can there be a sea without land or sky?), and all depend on the hand of God that formed it as a living whole. One might, if the cultural and theological situation of the congregation allows, consider raising the concept of Gaia, which hypothesizes that the living and nonliving components of earth function as a single system and that, according to some, the entire creation should be understood as a single organism. Whether or not one believes that these ideas are compatible with Christian theology, they present a rich perspective from which to rethink our relationship to the created order.

"Yonder is the sea," the psalmist chants, though it is unlikely that many of Israel's people had actually seen anything like the expanses of water which we call seas or oceans today. Even so, the image of the sea had great mythic power. Elsewhere in the psalms, the sea is the chaos from which the creation arose . . . or the chaos into which it sinks in the experience of human beings who are in great distress. It is a trackless, orderless void. In this psalm, however, the sea has been domesticated. Rather than being seen as a primeval chaos, here the sea is understood to be a vast, fecund medium in which myriad "creeping things" dwell, "living things both small and great." Humans have a place there too, in their ships, and in this text there is not even a hint of danger there. One sees the ships going about over this sea, unmolested by storm or ill current. So complete is God's power over this realm that even Leviathan, the great and (elsewhere) treacherous sea monster, is like a pet with whom one makes "sport."

The crescendo of the psalm is building now. The earlier verses that came before our present reading, followed by the passage about the sea, set the stage for a penultimate theme: the gift of life itself. This is no ordinary gift from which, once given, the Giver fades away. Here the Giver is a constant, necessary, and providential presence. These verses have a compelling cadence, a rhythmic insistence that all life is perpetually contingent on God's grace. When God is giving food and breath, we creatures are "filled with good things." When God's face is hidden, when breath and food are taken away, all things

Psalm 104:24-34, 35b

Theological Perspective

languages these people speak. This diversity displayed at the church's birth occurs for one purpose: to preach the gospel *to all nations* and thereby participate in the *personal* and *sovereign* work of the Holy Spirit in bearing witness to Jesus Christ.

In the closing verses of Psalm 104, the psalmist's reflections are elevated to doxology: "May the glory of the LORD endure for ever; may the LORD rejoice in his works" (v. 31). The psalmist's response should not be surprising. Whenever God's personal and sovereign nature and wisdom are made manifest, God's glory is also in view. Creation's manifold diversity *requires* the psalmist to extol the glory of God, because this diversity *is* an expression of God's wisdom and therefore *reveals* God's glory.

Because creation's majesty inspires doxology, we are required to be good stewards of creation, protecting natural habitats so that the biodiversity of our world may thrive. We serve God's glory by not allowing creation's witness to God's wisdom to become muted.

As with creation, the church was made for the glory of God. However, unlike creation the church will share personally in Christ's glory (2 Thess. 2:14). This glory is complete not only when the church displays "the harvest of righteousness" (Phil. 1:11), but also when her people come "from every tribe and language and people and nation" (Rev. 5:9). So important is this later point that Jesus declares in Matthew 24:14 that the eschaton will not commence until the gospel is preached "to all the nations." As Pentecost reveals, the Great Commission is not an option, but a necessity.

The psalmist's reflections on God's wisdom personally revealed through God's manifold works of creation finds its ultimate consummation in God's new creation, the church. In Revelation the heavenly chorus moves from praising God as creator of "all things" (4:11) to singing a "new song" celebrating God as redeemer of those "from every tribe and language and people and nation" (5:9). Both songs show the diversity manifested in God's two great works are worthy of praise. Furthermore, the diversity commenced at Pentecost is not lost in the eschaton, but becomes an expression of the glory the nations bring into the kingdom (Rev. 21:26). Indeed, Psalm 104 possesses theological themes magnified in the church and at Pentecost.

BONNIE L. PATTISON

Pastoral Perspective

fluorescent lightbulbs, or should we continue to glorify God through participation in government decisions? Some might argue these are political matters in which the church should not meddle. On the other hand, it could be that the church has ceded its care of creation to political and market forces. Becoming actively "green" out of respect for the Creator is an act of praise. However important our actions may be, though, surface action is not true communication.

At its root, translation is an act of humility. Anyone who has tried to learn a new language understands the tremendous effort involved. Hours of discipline and practice are required. Even when one becomes fluent, there is still a gap of translation from one language to another that requires nuanced skill, fresh familiarity, and agile thinking. So it is in all relationships. All relationships require skill, familiarity, and thought. Wives and husbands, children and parents, church members and pastors—if any of us expect to keep our communication fruitful, we must dedicate ourselves to the art of translation. Translation is not magic. The gift of the Spirit on Pentecost was miraculous, but not magical. It took effort on behalf of the disciples to convince the people that they truly were hearing the Word. It took patience on behalf of the listeners to discern the truth. So it is with us as we attempt to move from bystanders to friends of nature, translators of its praise, and partners in its glory.

Verse 34 prays that our "meditation may be pleasing" to the Lord. Surely we would hope that our meditation upon the vast glory of creation would be acceptable to God and a benefit to our souls. On Pentecost Sunday, we are especially called to pray that our *translation* might be pleasing to God. On this day it is not enough to simply meditate. Rather, this is the day to put our meditation to work, to raise our voices and declare our solidarity with all creation, of which we are but one important, but fleeting part.

JAMES MCTYRE

Exegetical Perspective

(*ruach*), whose presence means creation, individually and structurally, occurs (*bara'*, a word reserved in the Hebrew Scriptures for the unique work of God, e.g., Gen. 1:1). The psalm poetically states the dependence of *all* creation on the face of God. When God faces creation and breath/Spirit (*ruach*) goes forth, creation comes into proper being and exists in proper relationship. When God's face turns away, creation moves to oblivion.

These descriptions of God's creative power and care move the psalmist to break forth in praise and doxology in the remaining verses of Psalm 104. God's glory (*kabod*) symbolizes God's presence and rule, which is highlighted further by the theophanic language of smoke and trembling in verse 32 (see Exod. 19:1ff., 1 Kgs. 19:11). Wishing that God's glory would continue forever, the psalmist also desires that God will continually delight in God's own works as well. John Calvin notes that "the stability of the world depends on this rejoicing of God in his works."[2] Finally, the psalmist's praise now joins God's joy and delight in a new round of lifelong singing (vv. 33–34).

Intriguingly, the lectionary leaves out a brief mention of the wicked that occurs in verse 35. While it may seem disjunctive to the flow of the psalm, the prophets (e.g., Jer. 4:21–26, Hos. 4:1–3) suggest that human sinfulness proves to be one of the deep threats to God's created order and God's creatures. While this psalm primarily focuses on all creation joining in the praise and joy of its creator God, there is here a moment of tragic truth; creation is threatened and can be undone. So here, albeit very briefly, is a hope that a genuine threat to creation will be removed as another piece of the providence of God. "For human beings who turn away from God, do not praise him, but live conscious of only self and in self-reliance there is no longer room in the vast realm of joy, order, and dependence directed to God."[3] The psalm does not stop there, however, as in the end it goes back to the beginning. The living creature (*nephesh*) who has breath (*ruach*) breathed into it by God is to expend that breath in lifelong praise.

THOMAS W. WALKER

Homiletical Perspective

"return to their dust." There is a great homiletic opportunity here. One might, for instance, seek to emulate the cadences and rhythms of verses 27–30 in a sermonic passage that elicits, not only by its words but by its form, the understanding that we exist only by virtue of the "daily bread" that God provides— and, one might add, this is far from being news that is disturbing. What in the world would we rather be dependent on? Our own goodness and ingenuity? The whims of impersonal nature? No, since we are necessarily dependent, it is good to be dependent on God, who is faithful in all things.

No wonder, then, that the psalm erupts, in its final verses, into rapturous song about God's glory. Here, it becomes personal. *I* will sing to the Lord. *I* will sing praise to God. The psalmist (and we are all the "I" here) is swept up in gratitude, awe, wonder, and joy. Sadly, however, the lectionary omits verse 35a, which brings a note of reality and humanness to the text. Nevertheless, the writer's intent is intact: a survey of all creation and the resultant glory ascribed to God.

This passage lends itself to a sermon on environmentalism, though it would have to be one in which the political implications rise directly and seamlessly from a theological understanding, namely, that the creation we are needing to save is none other than the handiwork of God. The preacher may not exploit the psalm for a political end but may, with integrity, explore the psalm for prompts that will inspire such love for creation that listeners will be moved to positive action on its behalf.

JAMES GERTMENIAN

2. John Calvin, *Commentary on the Book of Psalms*, trans. James Anderson (Grand Rapids: Baker Book House, 1989), 170.
3. Hans-Joachim Kraus, *Psalms 60–150: A Commentary*, trans. Hilton C. Oswald (Minneapolis: Augsburg Fortress, 1989), 304.

Acts 2:1-21

¹When the day of Pentecost had come, they were all together in one place. ²And suddenly from heaven there came a sound like the rush of a violent wind, and it filled the entire house where they were sitting. ³Divided tongues, as of fire, appeared among them, and a tongue rested on each of them. ⁴All of them were filled with the Holy Spirit and began to speak in other languages, as the Spirit gave them ability.

⁵Now there were devout Jews from every nation under heaven living in Jerusalem. ⁶And at this sound the crowd gathered and was bewildered, because each one heard them speaking in the native language of each. ⁷Amazed and astonished, they asked, "Are not all these who are speaking Galileans? ⁸And how is it that we hear, each of us, in our own native language? ⁹Parthians, Medes, Elamites, and residents of Mesopotamia, Judea and Cappadocia, Pontus and Asia, ¹⁰Phrygia and Pamphylia, Egypt and the parts of Libya belonging to Cyrene, and visitors from Rome, both Jews and proselytes, ¹¹Cretans and Arabs—in our own languages we hear them speaking about God's deeds of power." ¹²All were amazed and perplexed, saying to one another, "What does this mean?" ¹³But others sneered and said, "They are filled with new wine."

¹⁴But Peter, standing with the eleven, raised his voice and addressed them, "Men of Judea and all who live in Jerusalem, let this be known to you, and listen

Theological Perspective

On Pentecost, the awesome power of God is revealed seven weeks after the death and resurrection of Jesus. A disheveled and mournful band of eleven gathered in the home of one of the disciples. They came together as the group with whom Jesus had had intimate time; this is the group who lived everyday life with Jesus. They understood that Jesus the human had supernatural connection with the God of their ancestors Abraham, Sarah, and Hagar as well as Isaac and Rebecca. These disciples believed that the son of Joseph and Mary was Emmanuel—the living Christ. Although they were dispersed, they decided to gather early in the morning to worship. They wanted to support each other because they were a religious minority and lived a faith that the majority in Galilee did not.

As the eleven worshiped, there was a noise so loud that it could not be ignored. So startled were they that they lost control of themselves—their sensory systems were flooded with adrenaline so that their minds and bodies processed intensely the sound, energy, and feeling of the coming of the Holy Spirit. She had come as Jesus had promised, and it was an experience rather than something cognitive. Rational theological reflection could not adequately explain the knowledge conveyed in this sensory event. All of the disciples were filled with the Holy

Pastoral Perspective

In the 1990s, the late Arthur Schlesinger Jr., the historian and public intellectual, raised a concern about the looming Balkanization of American society. Tribal interests and ethnic identities, he feared, would unravel the fragile bonds of unity in culture. People of differing ethnicities, races, and languages crowded together onto the same small plot of real estate spelled trouble with a capital *T* for Schlesinger. He feared the kind of social disintegration that occurred in the former Yugoslavia and led to ethnic cleansing. "Unless a common purpose binds them together, tribal hostilities will drive them apart," he wrote.[1]

In light of tensions around the world, Schlesinger's concerns must be taken seriously. In light of today's text, however, his concerns need not paralyze us in anxiety or restrain us from both taking seriously and celebrating the rich diversity of God's world.

The text startles us with a scene of almost unimaginable liveliness verging on chaos: sound like the rush of a mighty wind filled the whole house; tongues of fire appeared among the people; and as the crowd was filled with the Spirit of God, they spoke a cacophony of languages. Galileans, Parthians,

1. Arthur Schlesinger Jr., *The Disuniting of America: Reflections on Multicultural Society* (New York: W. W. Norton & Co., 1992), 10.

to what I say. [15]Indeed, these are not drunk, as you suppose, for it is only nine o'clock in the morning. [16]No, this is what was spoken through the prophet Joel:

[17]'In the last days it will be, God declares,
that I will pour out my Spirit upon all flesh,
and your sons and your daughters shall prophesy,
and your young men shall see visions,
and your old men shall dream dreams.
[18]Even upon my slaves, both men and women,
in those days I will pour out my Spirit;
and they shall prophesy.
[19]And I will show portents in the heaven above
and signs on the earth below,
blood, and fire, and smoky mist.
[20]The sun shall be turned to darkness
and the moon to blood,
before the coming of the Lord's great and glorious day.
[21]Then everyone who calls on the name of the Lord shall be saved.'"

Exegetical Perspective

Outside of the birth and passion narratives of the Gospels, Acts 2 is one of the most familiar passages of Scripture. As with all familiar narratives, Acts 2 has been retold so often and with so many elaborations that it is often difficult to remember what the author of Luke–Acts actually wrote. Yet this passage is key to Luke's assertion that the early Christians would bear witness to the resurrected Christ "in Jerusalem, in all Judea and Samaria, and to the ends of the earth" (Acts 1:8). As a result, it is helpful to review some of the most important aspects of the text, as we prepare to retell the story for future generations.

First, the timing of the story is crucial. The feast of Weeks, Shavuot—or Pentecost as it comes to be called in later generations (cf. Tobit 2)—is the third of the three great festivals of Judaism (Deut. 16). Shavuot was a joyful festival, in which the firstfruits of the harvest would have been given to God. The timing of the story may have reminded Luke's readers of Jesus' declaration that "the harvest is plentiful, but the laborers are few" (Luke 10:2). It may have connected them to the Joel passage that Peter later quotes, for in Joel a precursor to the outpouring of the spirit is the harvest: "the threshing floors shall be full of grain" (Joel 2:24a). More importantly, Shavuot is the celebration of the giving of the Torah, in particular the Ten Commandments,

Homiletical Perspective

In order to have a "conversation" (the root meaning of "homiletical") with a congregation about the Christian Pentecost, the preacher first must decide what the story is about. Is it about birthing or about broadening? Should the hymn of the day be "Happy Birthday" or "In Christ There Is No East or West"? Is this story about the birthday of the church, or is its intent broader—to tell us, as Frederick Faber's hymn says, that "the love of God is broader than the measures of our mind"? How the preacher answers will determine how the preacher preaches.

Happy Birthday. Luke begins his Gospel with the birth of baby Jesus. He begins Acts with an event popularly thought of as the birth of the body of Christ. One of the few hymns that speaks of that Pentecost Day as a birth day says:

> The Spirit *brought to birth*
> The church of Christ on earth.[1]

Whether or not Luke intended us to read his stories of the birth of Jesus and the birth of Christ's church in neat literary parallel, he clearly did intend to place both stories within the context of a family—a family

1. Fred Pratt Green, "Let Every Christian Pray," copyright © 1971 by Hope Publishing Co., Carol Stream, IL 60188.

Acts 2:1-21

Theological Perspective

Spirit. Not one was excluded. No mortal could engineer the vivacity of the coming of the Holy Spirit sent by the awesome God of Jesus Christ.

African Initiated Churches (AICs) on the continent of Africa know about the coming of the Holy Spirit. Members of St. John's Apostolic Faith Mission Church in Guguletu, an African township in Cape Town, South Africa, expect the Holy Spirit each time they gather as a community in worship. The core of St. John's ministry is healing, and members worship four times a day seven days a week to advance the healing of its members. AICs attract the poorest of the poor in social systems that perpetuate poverty. Women and men in AICs have total reliance on God—the God who predated the arrival of Christian missionaries. They understand Jesus to be one of their ancestors who came so they could have life more abundantly. These members who worship in their homes, just as the original disciples did, carry on the tradition of Jesus' promise: "God will send the Holy Spirit." The members of St. John's know that they cannot engineer the coming of the Holy Spirit, so they wait in anticipation of its coming. When it appears, individuals say things like, "I was not myself. I do not remember what I said or did when the Holy Spirit came upon me." Believers at St. John's in Guguletu, like the believers in Galilee on the day of Pentecost, speak languages they do not know.

What does it mean when human beings fluently speak languages they do not know and that native speakers recognize? In Jerusalem that day there were religious adherents who came for ceremonies marking an important season in their faith. Many were practicing Jews who came from distant places all over the world. God chose to send the Holy Spirit at the peak season, when large numbers of international visitors were in Jerusalem. Pilgrimages to the Holy City were very significant; thus, the coming of the Holy Spirit into this context demonstrates God's power. Why? Adherents of other religions came to the house where the disciples had gathered because of the unnatural circumstance; hurricane-like winds and flashes of fire upon the heads of the disciples who spoke in perfect dialect the languages of those who had journeyed from afar to Jerusalem. Those who watched could not explain rationally what was taking place. It was absurd to hear eleven people from Galilee speaking the local languages of Asia Minor, Egypt, Libya, Rome, and other places. Visitors to Jerusalem who heard their languages spoken were hearing about the mighty miracles of the God of Jesus Christ.

Pastoral Perspective

Medes . . . a roll call of peoples all represented in the crush of humanity as the winds of God's Spirit blew and the ecstatic fire spread.

At the heart of this text, however, we do not find a historian terrified about diversity, but witnesses "bewildered," then "amazed and astonished," because each person heard and understood what was said in his or her own language. In a breathtaking reversal of the story of the tower of Babel, when proud humanity was divided by the plurality of languages (Gen. 11:1–9), Pentecost represents the inbreaking of God's purposes for all humanity, bringing humanity together in understanding, despite their differences. Even as Genesis begins with the stunning good news that humanity was created in the image of God (Gen. 1:26–27) and that our highest purpose lies in trusting God—a trust violated in inappropriate self-confidence and independence at Babel—Pentecost tells us the good news that our humanity, ruined and distorted in our distrust, has been restored in Jesus Christ. The Spirit that animated his life, that united him to God the Father and empowered him to be fully the human image of God, is now shared with us. Thus the cacophony of voices becomes a chorus of praise, babble becomes communication, and community is fashioned out of potential adversaries.

Not everyone, even on the day of Pentecost, was convinced that a good thing was happening among those who were caught up in the Spirit of God. Some, in their amazement, were ready to attribute the ecstasy to God, while others simply thought the disciples and other visitors were drunk. When Peter stood to preach, at the climax of this scene, he moved quickly to disabuse those who were muttering: "They are drunk with new wine." No, said Peter, these people are not drunk. They are the living fulfillment of the long promise of God. God's Word is being heard, God's Spirit is being shared, and God's communion is being brought into existence among humanity here and now.

The prophetic poetry of Joel is pressed into the service of a new vision made necessary by God's incarnation in Jesus of Nazareth and God's coming among the people of the Spirit. The perils of Balkanization are abundantly real, terrifyingly real: genocide, under the euphemism of ethnic cleansing, lurks under the mantle of religious and tribal purity; fanatic nationalism, under the misnomer of patriotism, lures even the most settled souls and devoted spirits of fellow citizens. And so people fear difference, otherness, the strangeness of the stranger. But the real threat of Balkanization lies not in the differences that God

from Sinai. Luke is likely making a parallel here: just as for Jews the exodus revelation signals the birth of the chosen people of God, for Christians the Pentecost narrative in Luke, the outpouring of the Holy Spirit, signals the birth of the church.

In addition to timing, careful attention should be paid to those involved in Luke's narrative. There are two large groups, the first designated by the words "they were all together in one place" (Acts 2:1). By "all" it is likely that the author is referring to the entire community of Christians, which at Pentecost numbered "about one hundred twenty persons" (Acts 1:15). These would have included women *and* men, the Twelve, and the many other unnamed, faithful followers of Jesus. All of these receive the Holy Spirit; all are given the gifts of speaking in other languages. This follows a pattern that will reoccur in Acts, that the Holy Spirit has a tendency not to discriminate based on human standards (see especially, Acts 10).

The second large group is denoted as those "living in Jerusalem" (Acts 2:5, 14). These were immigrants (not pilgrims as it is often preached) who had emigrated from areas of the Roman Empire to the north, east, south, and west of Jerusalem. As subjects of Rome, all of them would have spoken Greek, the language of the Roman military and of commerce for much of the early imperial period. They were also multilingual, speaking languages of their natal lands also.

Without a clear understanding of who these people were, it is possible to miss what is actually going on when the Jesus followers receive the Holy Spirit. They do not speak in "spiritual languages" as in 1 Corinthians 12–14. Rather, they speak the natal languages of these immigrant peoples; and they tell of the glories of God, not in the language of the empire but in the languages of the people subject to empire. Note: this phenomenon cannot be understood as a reversal of Babel (Gen. 11), as is often preached. The Genesis narrative of Babel explains the creation of multiple languages; and its reversal would have been the creation of one unifying language. Rather than requiring of all of the people to speak one language, Pentecost gives power to the band of Jesus followers to speak the languages of the world, to tell the gospel in every language. The early church was to bear witness to the ends of the earth in the languages of the people of the world; on the day of Pentecost, Christianity became a religion with a divine sanction to multilingualism and to translation.

Finally, it is helpful to pay close attention to the explanation for the phenomenon given by Peter. In

of faith. Luke grounded both the birth of Jesus and the birth of the church in the family story about what God was *already doing* in his covenant with generations of Jewish people. Every Bible is a family Bible. And the family in view that Pentecost is that of Abram and Sarai (Gen. 12:1–3), in whom God promised "all the families of the earth shall be blessed."

But not all the families of the earth have been blessed. History is replete with examples of what has happened when the body of Christ has separated itself from the people of God by its words or actions. Marcion's heresy is still alive in practical ways in the lives of many Christians who live uncomfortably with the question of how God's blessing extends (or does not extend) to non-Christians, including Jews. Pentecost is an ideal day on which to raise this issue.

One way to do that is to think of the Acts of the Apostles, recording the growth of what we know as the church, as "The Act of the Holy Spirit." The same "wind" that blew "in the beginning" (Gen. 1:1–2) was blowing in a mighty way on the day of Pentecost. God's Word was still creating. And so Peter in his sermon spoke of God's continuing to keep covenant with the family of Abram and Sarai, in the life, death, and resurrection of the one "born to give us second birth"; who has poured out his Spirit (Acts 2:33) *in fulfillment of "the [Hebrew] scriptures"* (Luke 24:45–49).

Liturgically, then, instead of lighting birthday candles on Pentecost, we should light the Christ candle and sing, in the words of Ruth Duck:

> Arise, your light is come!
> The Spirit's call obey;
> Show forth the glory of your God,
> Which shines on you today.[2]

Broadening. If Peter had had Ruth Duck's hymn at hand, he might well have answered his hearers' question "What should we do?" (v. 37) by singing "Arise, your light is come!" Instead he preached the first Christian sermon. Unlike the lesson, however, his sermon does not end with, "Everyone who calls on the name of the Lord shall be saved" (v. 21). Peter preached on, grounding his message on that first *Christian* Pentecost in the resurrection of Jesus *and* in the Hebrew Scriptures. As he did, the words of Joel and Isaiah (vv. 17–21) took on broader meaning. God's promise, throughout the Hebrew Scriptures, was interpreted by Peter to be for "everyone whom the Lord our God calls to him" (v. 39).

2. Ruth Duck, "Arise, Your Light Is Come!" copyright © 1992 by GIA Publications. Used by permission.

Acts 2:1-21

Theological Perspective

Some mocked the eleven. There was no plausible explanation for what happened. It makes sense that a few people found relief by saying that the disciples were drunk. Such talk provided comic relief in making fun of their inappropriate behavior. But Peter the disciple, the Jesus confessor and the Jesus denier, the Rock, came forward to speak to the crowd. He preached on this occasion of the birth of the church. What did Peter say? By drawing upon the Jewish prophetic tradition Peter showed that he too was a Jew, he knew the foundational texts and was calling the name of one of their ancestors. Peter was calling upon Jewish history and so people in the crowd could identify with, rather than discount, him. In fact, Peter told the crowd that more than three centuries ago Joel spoke about the very moment that was occurring. In other words, God is a God of history. Peter was able to give chapter and verse about the coming of the Holy Spirit in the Hebrew texts.

They are words of prophecy: the Holy Spirit will come upon *all* of my servants. Again, no one is excluded. Freedom will come for all who serve; liberation and salvation is available for all who are disciples. As in that time, Joel's words mean disciples of Jesus include all who believe in the Christ who promised the gift of the Holy Spirit, continuously adding to the church created by an awesome God. Those who believed Jesus was the Christ joined the church that day, for it was birthed by an incredible God.

LINDA E. THOMAS

Pastoral Perspective

has woven into all parts of God's creation, including humanity. The great danger of Balkanization lies in any group's lust to power over others, its insistence that its identity alone reflects God's nature and God's way, its demand that the otherness of others be erased from the pages of history or from the face of the earth.

What was lost upon generations of persons of faith is recovered in the pages of the Acts of the Apostles, that the image of God is not something that adheres to the singular individual, as though God were a windowless monad, singular and distant, in whose image we were created in arrogant isolation. The image of God in which we were created is the image of the triune God of grace, as G. K. Chesterton observed, "a God of Love against a God of colourless and remote cosmic control." When we say God the Trinity, we are saying that God is in God's own being, a "Holy family."[2] In the image of the God who, as Father, Son, and Holy Spirit, is eternal and living community, differentiated in person, united in love, we are ourselves created for community, and never fully live in God's image until we live in communion. Communion assumes difference—not uniformity, not conformity to a single idealized form of life, or nationality, or ethnicity, or tribe.

Peter's sermon reminds us of the promise of God—prophesied, envisioned, dreamed of, and longed for from long ages hence—that the Spirit, the living presence of the eternal God, would pour down upon all humanity, and "then everyone who calls on the name of the Lord shall be saved," in whatever languages they may use, by whatever names they may be called. Peter conjures up Joel's vision of heavenly portents and earthly wonders, sun turned to darkness and moon to blood, signs of the coming of the Lord's great and glorious day, the day that, Peter will soon tell this crowd, has already dawned in Jesus Christ, the same Christ whose Spirit blows through the house in which they are standing, whose fiery love created a community where only strangers stood before.

MICHAEL JINKINS

---

2. G. K. Chesterton, *The Everlasting Man* (London: Hodder & Stoughton, 1925), 262.

Day of Pentecost

Exegetical Perspective

quoting Joel, Peter is announcing the end of this present age and the beginning of the age to come, the age of the reign of God. For Peter—and for Luke, who tells his story—the unusual tongues of fire and abilities of speech are signs that God's reign is immanent, that God will ultimately redeem God's people.

This is both a political assertion and an eschatological one. Politically, it is likely that Luke is making a treasonous prediction of the eventual divine overthrow of the Roman Empire. The Joel passage was written at a time of occupation; as part of the same prophecy, Joel wrote, "I will remove the northern army far from you, and drive it into a parched and desolate land" (Joel 2:20). Luke, writing after the Roman siege of Jerusalem, must surely remember these promises as he puts Joel into Peter's mouth.

The assertion is also eschatological, for it points to the end of the age in which Peter is speaking and Luke is writing. Luke affirms that on that particular Pentecost—when all Jesus' followers, named and unnamed, women and men, young and old, were given the power of the Spirit of God to bear witness in every language of the good news of Jesus Christ—the coming of the day of the Lord is beginning. While we do not yet see the fulfillment of that promise, as we retell the story of Pentecost one more time, we remember that, according to Luke, it will surely come.

MARGARET P. AYMER

Homiletical Perspective

Those who sneered and said of the apostles, "They are filled with new wine" (v. 13), were right! *They were!* The consequences of that, described in Jesus' parable about putting new wine into old wineskins (Luke 5:36–39), were not lost on those who heard that Pentecost "babble" any more than they were on those who crucified Jesus. The tongues were not unintelligible glossolalia, but a clear message that all heaven was bursting out singing for all the world to hear, that "in Christ there is no east or west"!

The day of Pentecost occurred just seven weeks after those who were opposed to Jesus had ended this "nonsense" with crucifixion; but now, for some, their worst nightmare was coming true. This broadening understanding of God's love would grow, as it did "that day [by] about three thousand persons" (v. 41) as the "divided tongues" (v. 3) spoke with one voice about "God's deeds of power" (v. 11) in the languages of "every nation under heaven," (v. 5) of "all the families of the earth."

It is unfortunate that "tongues, *as of* fire" (v. 3) has been so loosely understood as "tongues *of* fire." The divided tongues were not "fire" and perhaps better represent the divided tongues, or languages, of Babel. That Pentecost, each of the apostles, traditionally representing the twelve tribes of Israel, received the ability to speak in the tongue of another nation—a foreshadowing of things to come. Babel, signifying tongues that divided people one from the other, was undone in the speaking of God's Word to everyone. In "[their] own languages" they heard "them speaking about God's deeds of power" (v. 11); they heard that "the love of God is broader than the measures of our mind."

Wulfert de Greef writes:

> The God of Israel is now also the God of the nations. . . . [However,] the fact that the nations are also now included among God's people does not imply that Israel's importance is in any way diminished. Calvin observes that God's care for us as Gentiles implies that he has joined us together with the Jews. We have been united with the descendants of Abraham into one body. We are together with Israel, the people of God.[3]

RICHARD L. SHEFFIELD

---

3. Wulfert de Greef, "Calvin as Commentator on the Psalms," in *Calvin and the Bible,* ed. Donald K. McKim (New York: Cambridge University Press, 2006), 95.

John 14:8-17 (25-27)

⁸Philip said to him, "Lord, show us the Father, and we will be satisfied." ⁹Jesus said to him, "Have I been with you all this time, Philip, and you still do not know me? Whoever has seen me has seen the Father. How can you say, 'Show us the Father'? ¹⁰Do you not believe that I am in the Father and the Father is in me? The words that I say to you I do not speak on my own; but the Father who dwells in me does his works. ¹¹Believe me that I am in the Father and the Father is in me; but if you do not, then believe me because of the works themselves. ¹²Very truly, I tell you, the one who believes in me will also do the works that I do and, in fact, will do greater works than these, because I am going to the Father. ¹³I will do whatever you ask in my name, so that the Father may be glorified in the Son. ¹⁴If in my name you ask me for anything, I will do it.

Theological Perspective

There are so many theological themes in this particular passage that, even though each is related to the doctrine of the Holy Spirit, it is difficult to know where to start. Philip's request to be shown the Father (v. 8) is as good a place as any. Just how is God to be known? The answer given by Christ—namely, that he (and by implication no other) is the way to the truth of God and the life of God (v. 7)—presents the reader not only with the question of revelation but also with the question of other religions and other ways of knowing God. The justification for the hotly contested assertion that Jesus is "the way, the truth, and the life" is that he is "in the Father" just as the Father is in him (vv. 10a, 11a). This claim in time gave rise to a fully developed doctrine of the incarnation.

Moving through the chapter, other doctrinal issues emerge. The relation between Christ's person and his works (v.11b), the power of the ascended Christ at work in the church (v. 12a), the nature of Christ's coming again (vv. 18b–19), and the efficacy of prayer (v. 14) are but a few of them. However, one theme, the presence of the Holy Spirit in the church, ties them all together.

Mention of the Holy Spirit, the subject of this particular feast, does not appear overtly until verse 16. There Jesus promises that the Father will send

Pastoral Perspective

John 14 raises and responds to a pastoral concern that arose early on within the Christian community and continues to this day: What happens when Jesus, the founder of the community, is no longer around? Is the community left on its own, with no access to his presence or transformative power? The author of John's Gospel and our observance of the Day of Pentecost respond to that concern by reminding the community of Jesus' assurance that, when he has gone, another Advocate will come, "the Holy Spirit, whom the Father will send in my name" (v. 26).

On other occasions the preacher might focus on the promises of Jesus in verses 12–14, exploring especially what it means to ask the Father in Jesus' name (v. 14) or what it could possibly mean that the works of those who believe in Jesus will exceed his own (v. 12); but the proper focus on the Day of Pentecost is surely the promise of the text regarding the presence and activity of the Holy Spirit within the Christian community.

Given the individualism prevalent in both culture and church, the preacher should take pains to say that the community is the primary concern of the text. The lesson is part of Jesus' Farewell Discourse to the community of his disciples, and John wants the ongoing community of disciples to have confidence that, because of the presence of the

¹⁵"If you love me, you will keep my commandments. ¹⁶And I will ask the Father, and he will give you another Advocate, to be with you forever. ¹⁷This is the Spirit of truth, whom the world cannot receive, because it neither sees him nor knows him. You know him, because he abides with you, and he will be in you. . . .

²⁵"I have said these things to you while I am still with you. ²⁶But the Advocate, the Holy Spirit, whom the Father will send in my name, will teach you everything, and remind you of all that I have said to you. ²⁷Peace I leave with you; my peace I give to you. I do not give to you as the world gives. Do not let your hearts be troubled, and do not let them be afraid."

Exegetical Perspective

This passage is located in the heart of the first half of the Farewell Discourse in John. The author describes no formal institution of the Eucharist, but instead offers a final dialogue between Jesus and his disciples; perhaps it is better described as a monologue with prompts from his disciples. This particular passage begins with Philip's prompting to "show us the Father." It follows a statement of Jesus about his ultimate destiny (going to the Father) and his desire to take the disciples with him, "so that where I am, there you may be also" (14:3). Thomas interrupts Jesus after he says, "You know the way to the place where I am going," by asking, "How can we know the way?" (14:5). This allows Jesus to say his famous, "I am the way, and the truth, and the life" saying and to claim that the disciples have seen the Father.

Jesus chastises Philip for his question. If this were an accurate, factual record of a real conversation, then one might say that Philip has missed one of the main points of Jesus' presence and is rightly chastised. Since this is a literary construction, Philip's question is better described as a classic case of Johannine "misunderstanding"—a literary device used by the author to move the discourse to another topic or deeper into the topic at hand. It is like the converse of the Socratic method. Where Socrates would ask a series of questions that would allow his

Homiletical Perspective

This pericope contains so many highly charged theological statements that the preacher might tend to make the sermon into an essay on the Trinity, guaranteed to put most people to sleep. Believers should be encouraged to think deeply about such things, but most are not ready for twenty minutes of such instruction. Therefore, it is important to notice also the people and interpersonal dynamics reflected in the text. It often helps to read this sort of narrative aloud to try to vocalize the dynamics in different ways.

The Gospels usually show Peter as the one who opens his mouth first or does impetuous things, like jumping out of boats. John shows Peter doing his characteristic thing in 13:37, just before our lesson for today. However, following that account, it is first Thomas and now Philip who ask the leading questions. I pushed some students working with this text to describe a connection between something in the text and a common experience. One of them said, "Everybody has had the experience of saying something and immediately regretting it." We agreed that the way Jesus responds to Philip's question could have made Philip feel just that way. Yet the teaching of Jesus that follows Philip's question is for all believers, not just for the foot-in-mouth crowd. Perhaps the big surprise in this text is how long it

John 14:8-17 (25-27)

Theological Perspective

"another Paraclete," that is, another advocate or intercessor, Jesus himself being the first one. The other Paraclete is named the Spirit of truth, and Jesus promises that this counselor will "be with you [the disciples] forever." The second overt reference to the gift of the Spirit comes in verse 26. There, Jesus assures the disciples that the Father will send the Paraclete "in my name." He goes on to say that when the Holy Spirit comes he "will teach you [once more, the disciples] everything, and remind you of all that I have said to you."

It is perhaps best to begin with the work of comfort, since comfort is the issue that frames the entire passage. Jesus begins this dialogue with the disciples by commanding them not to allow their hearts to be troubled, and he ends it with the same command. (14:1, 27b) The disciples are troubled because Jesus has announced both his own death and that of Peter (13:36). To the disciples, an announcement of this sort can mean only the triumph of Satan and their own bereavement. The comfort Jesus offers is another *paraklētos* like himself who will be with them. Jesus will be present with the disciples through the Spirit. In a real sense he will live in them even though he is absent in body (14:18–19). The Spirit is a comforter because, through the Spirit, Jesus, though he is now with the Father in glory, still stands alongside the disciples.

The nature of the Spirit's presence, however, is not ill or vaguely defined. It serves a particular purpose, namely, to remind the disciples of all that Jesus taught them and to explain to them the meaning of all that Jesus has said and done (v. 26b). In this passage, the function of the Spirit is largely sapiential. However, the Paraclete does not teach new truths or do things clearly different from the sorts of things Jesus has done. The presence of the Paraclete brings *Jesus* to mind, and it is *Jesus* who is the way, the truth, and the life. This sense the Paraclete is the Spirit of truth; that is, the Spirit always bears witness to Jesus, who is the truth.

For this reason the church has always held that to separate the Spirit from Christ is a grave theological error. Karl Barth summarized this well-established but frequently challenged view: "But the Holy Spirit distinguishes himself from any other spirit by his absolute identity with the person and work of Christ. . . . All that is Spirit proceeds from Jesus and results in him."[1] Barth was on firm ground. The

---

1. Karl Barth, *The Faith of the Church: A Commentary on the Apostles' Creed* (London: Fontana Books, 1960), 109–10.

Pastoral Perspective

Advocate, there is not, and will not be, any loss of the presence or power of Jesus.

There is, however, the problem represented by Philip (v. 9): the Christian community of the disciples, despite having been privy to the story of Jesus, having heard his teaching, and having been a guest at his table, either does not "know" Jesus, has not begun to fathom how he is the essential and ultimate disclosure of "the Father," or is in danger of amnesia, of forgetting what at one time it did know. Thus the promise of the presence of "the Spirit of truth," who is in the community (see the alternative rendering of v. 17, "among you") and who "will teach you everything, and remind you of all that I have said to you" (v. 26).

More than a mere recollection is involved. The community will be helped both to remember all that Jesus has said—the totality of his teaching, the hard as well as the more comfortable parts—and to discover what it all means in the constantly changing circumstances in which the church finds itself. How critically important it is for the community to hear and trust the promise: when it comes to the meaning of Jesus' life and teaching, the community can expect new conviction and fresh clarity.

All of which is related to the Christian practices of teaching and worship. In its teaching—whether of children, newcomers to the community of faith, or those who have been around for a long time—the church tells the story of Jesus and calls to mind his teaching. But it is the Spirit of truth who aids the community to "know" what the story means and to make connections between the old, familiar (and unfamiliar) words and the new reality. So, too, with the church's liturgical practices: the story is rehearsed, and, because of the presence of the Spirit of truth, all that Jesus has said comes alive.

The concern of the text, however, is not remembrance for its own sake, not even remembrance that leads to fuller understanding. Remembering is for the sake of *faithfulness*. The concern of the text is a community whose life is obedient to Jesus, a community that proves its love for Jesus by keeping his commandments (v. 15). John seems to believe that it is within obedient Christian communities that the Spirit comes (vv. 15–16; see also v. 23). The text as a whole also suggests that, apart from the presence of the Spirit of truth, it is all too easy, in times of testing (whether externally, as in 9/11, or internally, as when congregations or denominations are threatened with schism), for the Christian community to forget the teaching and example of

interlocutor to discover "the correct" way of thinking on the topic, the author of John has Jesus' interlocutor ask a question that betrays ignorance or misunderstanding, so that Jesus then has the opportunity to correct the misunderstanding while at the same time revealing something new or describing something in more detail.

In this case, the question prompts Jesus to describe the nature of his relationship with the Father more specifically, namely, that of mutual indwelling. The purpose of this passage is not to express a Trinitarian theology but to describe the effects of Jesus' advent and presence on his community of followers, even after his death. The author wants to articulate an experience of God's presence in Jesus and in the community by using "mystical" language of being "in God." Because Jesus acts both as a teacher (13:13) from outside the community (having come down from heaven) and as its leader and friend from within the community (13:12–15), the mutual indwelling between Jesus and the Father acts as window into the divine life for the community. Jesus is how the community sees the Father, because, for John, the Father actually dwells within Jesus and seemingly directs his speech and actions, or at least "does his works" through Jesus.

The major difficulty with this from a metaphysical perspective is the relationship between Jesus' will and the Father's will. Does Father's will replace Jesus' will because the Father dwells in Jesus? This became one of the many difficult questions for later church fathers during Trinitarian debates about the nature of the three persons of the Trinity. However, this does not seem to be John's concern; rather, he is interested in asserting to his community, and thus encouraging them, that through their experience of Jesus they have access to the Father because of the interrelationship and connection between the Father and Jesus. One of the major benefits of this relationship, besides the window to the Divine that the community has in Jesus, is that by Jesus going to Father the community will have an advocate in heaven, due to their connection with Jesus (14:13–14). This language and this concept parallel the Paraclete being sent to the community. Where Jesus is an advocate for the community in heaven, the Paraclete is an advocate for the community on earth. All of this advocacy language assumes a certain understanding of *paraklētos*.

There has been a long scholarly debate about the meaning of *paraklētos*, the word that John uses in 14:25 for the Holy Spirit. The most likely meaning of

took for a disciple to ask to see God. We might all secretly wish to see God, but it is unlikely we would ask anyone to show God to us until we were convinced that that person could actually show the Father. After all, even Moses was granted only a glimpse of God's back. We could well meditate on just what it is that Philip might have expected with such a question.

The Gospels deal extensively with seeing and believing—especially John, where light and darkness, sight and blindness, provide symbols of the contrast between belief and unbelief. What Philip means by seeing the Father and what Jesus means by it could make an interesting and helpful contrast in a sermon. This connects nicely to Jesus' statement in his prayer in John 17:20: "I ask not only on behalf of these [who see me], but also on behalf of those who will believe in me through their word." The connection we have with Jesus is what we call faith, and it is not based on sight. In that sense, seeing is *not* believing; rather, seeing obviates the necessity of believing.

The primary concern of the passage is not seeing God, but the intimacy of Jesus' relationship with God and what that means for Jesus' followers. So what Philip gets in response to his question is a discourse on the relationship between the Father and the Son, and this leads to the promise of the Paraclete/Advocate—another divine figure. This promise of divine power is also a promise that this powerful presence will enable disciples of Jesus to accomplish great things. When we think of "great things," too often we think of what we call miracles; but an objective look should show us that the followers of Jesus have actually accomplished more than he could. Jesus was limited in space and time—one person at one relatively small place in one brief lifetime; but his many followers have gone around the world for 2,000 years, healing, comforting, converting, and generally making life better for people. There have, of course, been negative outcomes too; but by and large the church of Jesus Christ has brought the presence and power of God to bear on the plight of humanity. As long as we can do it in the name of Jesus and for the glory of God, our works of love will be a positive influence in the world.

"If you love me": these words should always be kept in close relationship with "you will keep my commandments." Too often in our cultures, love is understood as a soft sentiment that leans toward permissiveness. Our desire to lock God into this understanding of love fits nicely into the contemporary interest in spirituality, but it does not describe

John 14:8-17 (25-27)

Theological Perspective

implication of this passage is that any claim that the Spirit is teaching a new thing can be accepted as true only if it coheres with what Christ himself taught and did.

A final theological theme to note is the close relation in this passage between Jesus, the Father, and the Paraclete. It would be an error to use this particular section of John's Gospel as proof of later developments in the doctrine of the Trinity. In the Gospel of John, relations between the Father, Son, and Spirit are understood first of all in relation to the mission of Jesus rather than in relation to the inner life of God. Thus here Jesus asks the Father, who is Spirit (4:24), to send the Spirit in his (that is, Jesus') name (14:16, 26), so that through the Spirit he will remain always in and with the disciples (14:18–19). It would be a mistake to use this passage as a way to sort out the argument between East and West over the single or double procession of the Spirit. It would, however, be most appropriate to exposit it in a way that makes clear that disciples in every age need not be troubled by the physical absence of Jesus or by the tribulations they might face in his name or by the sense that they are left alone. Our hearts are not to be troubled, precisely because Jesus has asked the Father to send us a Paraclete who will be with us, who will teach us all things about Christ, and who will bring Christ to our remembrance.

PHILIP TURNER

Pastoral Perspective

its Lord and fall into cowardly silence or outright disobedience.

The intent of John 14 is to form a community of believing and obedient people, a community that is confident in the disclosure of God that has come in the person of Jesus and that depends on the leadership of the Spirit of truth to keep it obedient and productive in its life. The community intended by the text will not be satisfied with bowling leagues, sewing circles, and yoga classes, or even with therapy sessions or Bible study classes, but will be led to do "works" similar to those of Jesus: befriending the outcasts, healing the sick, speaking up for the marginalized, housing the homeless, feeding the hungry, and speaking truth to and about the empire. Because the community remembers, because it is helped by the Spirit to "know" its Lord, because it is obedient to Jesus' commands, because it is doing his works, and because of the presence and power of the Spirit in its life, it will be a nonanxious presence in an anxious, fearful age; it will have the peace the world cannot give (v. 27) or take away.

A Pentecost observance using John 14 as its focus will be softer, quieter, more reflective than one focusing on Acts 2. The liturgy will be less flashy and less flamboyant, the hymns and prayers more reflective. It may well be, however, that the day will be more in touch with the concerns of the people who gather to celebrate the day, and more encouraging to a community that seeks direction and empowerment so as to be faithful.

EUGENE C. BAY

Exegetical Perspective

the rare word in this context is "advocate," as in a forensic situation. John's understanding of judgment is not placed within an apocalyptic setting like that reflected in the literature of apocalyptic movements within Judaism of the time (including those associated with Paul and the other canonical Gospels). Rather, his ideas about judgment have a clear forensic overtone; the Paraclete acts as the advocate for the accused, in this case, the community. What is interesting about John is that the roles necessary for a typical courtroom trial are not always distinctly associated with particular characters in the Gospel. So it is unclear against whom the community needs advocacy. There is the unspecific "the world," but John is not more specific than that.

Whatever the most likely meaning of *paraklētos* is, it must be conditioned by the context of its use in verse 26. Here, the Paraclete will (1) be sent by the Father in Jesus' name, (2) teach the community "everything," and (3) remind the community of all that Jesus has said to them. Roles 2 and 3 are closely related to each other because, in the ancient world, learning is oftentimes configured as recollection, especially in a Platonic system. In any case, John draws a clear connection between the work of Jesus (sent from the Father/heaven, abiding among/within the community, teaching the community about the works of the Father) and the work of the Paraclete (sent from the Father in Jesus' name, abiding within the community [14:17], and teaching the community about the ways of Jesus, which were all about the works of the Father). So there is a functional equivalence between Jesus' earthly presence among the community and the continuing presence of the Paraclete among the community. The *parakletos* for John is the ongoing presence of Jesus while he is physically absent from the community. For John, Jesus is never really absent from the community, because he is present through the Paraclete.

STEPHEN P. AHEARNE-KROLL

Homiletical Perspective

the God portrayed in the Bible. Grace, compassion, and love as divine attributes are always linked in Scripture with the divine demand for righteousness, holiness, and obedience. The preacher should look carefully at the textual evidence on verse 15, since many of the ancient manuscripts have the word translated "you will keep" as an imperative. Whether Jesus is commanding obedience or stating obedience as an expected characteristic of his followers will make a big difference in a sermon. This same connection between love of Jesus and keeping his word is repeated in verses 21 and 23, so it plays a vital role in the passage.

The main thrust of the paragraph beginning with verse 18 is the continuing divine presence in the life of the followers of Jesus. As is true in other texts (see Rom. 8:9–11) the New Testament presents divine presence as a promise or fact, but does not systematize it. There is a mix of God's presence, Christ's presence, and the advocacy and teaching of the Holy Spirit. This should stand as a warning to the preacher not to try to get too systematic in describing the functions of the Godhead in the life of the believer. What we need to hear and rely on is the general promise: "I will not leave you orphaned."

All of this leads up to the very familiar verse 27—the promise of the peace of Christ. A sermon on the breadth of implications of the Hebrew concept of *shalom* could help believers realize that peace is more than the absence of hostilities. Jesus' words "not . . . as the world gives" offer the preacher a contrast that should work well in preaching to a contemporary congregation. The fears that disturb our peace are too often fleeting and superficial, and Jesus promises a deep peace that will not only give us rest but also motivate us to the adventure of the Christian life.

BRUCE E. SHIELDS

Proverbs 8:1-4, 22-31

¹Does not wisdom call,
  and does not understanding raise her voice?
²On the heights, beside the way,
  at the crossroads she takes her stand;
³beside the gates in front of the town,
  at the entrance of the portals she cries out:
⁴"To you, O people, I call,
  and my cry is to all that live.
. . . .
²²The Lᴏʀᴅ created me at the beginning of his work,
  the first of his acts of long ago.
²³Ages ago I was set up,
  at the first, before the beginning of the earth.
²⁴When there were no depths I was brought forth,
  when there were no springs abounding with water.

Theological Perspective

Where do we go to find God? Or better, where in the world does God seek us out? These are questions that go to the heart of the doctrine of revelation, and they rumble beneath all the varied verses of Proverbs, including these selected for Trinity Sunday. Proverbs stands out in the biblical canon both for the places it points toward, and those it does not.

God's Wisdom Calls to All. In a world of competing religious voices, many would say the best way to be "wise" is to delve into the revealed Scriptures of all the world's faiths. The more particular, the better. Truly to find any wisdom that one might designate with a capital *W*, the seeker must be willing to journey to temple, synagogue, and ashram to hear the particular words that the Divine has revealed to particular peoples within their own particular faith and practice.

Proverbs, at least at first glance, provides a countermodel for the seeker of wisdom. Wisdom calls out to "all that live," not so much from the heart of all the world's revealed religions, as from those public spaces available and accessible to all: the heights, beside the way, beside the gates (our schools and courts and public spaces set aside for public functions). Though there are competing voices coming from these same locales (especially the far

Pastoral Perspective

This passage in Proverbs personifies Wisdom, and here on Trinity Sunday we can see in this personification of Wisdom a depiction of the Holy Spirit. But Wisdom is often lost in our discussions of the Holy Trinity. When look at the Godhead, we focus so much more on the first two persons of the Trinity. This scripture is about the third person and offers us a much more personal explanation of her identity, purpose, and continuing presence in our lives. Through the lens of Proverbs 8, Wisdom becomes more than simply the nondescript sustainer; she becomes the Advocate highlighted by John's Gospel. Wisdom is the Holy Spirit personified. Reclaiming this aspect of the Holy Spirit can be an illuminating and liberating exercise.

We all have human wisdom. Call it intuition, call it life experience—we all have wisdom. Wisdom often exists beneath our consciousness. In a secular sense, wisdom is the sum of our experiences, the perspectives and insights that are part of our core being. Why can't this form of wisdom be seen as an aspect of God's presence in our lives? As we are innately wise, so are we innately connected with God.

We need Wisdom's presence and voice. We need to hear her beauty, acknowledge her integrity, appreciate her fresh perspective. On Trinity Sunday, helping people to remember their own wisdom

^{25}Before the mountains had been shaped,
  before the hills, I was brought forth—
^{26}when he had not yet made earth and fields,
  or the world's first bits of soil.
^{27}When he established the heavens, I was there,
  when he drew a circle on the face of the deep,
^{28}when he made firm the skies above,
  when he established the fountains of the deep,
^{29}when he assigned to the sea its limit,
   so that the waters might not transgress his command,
  when he marked out the foundations of the earth,
^{30} then I was beside him, like a master worker;
  and I was daily his delight,
   rejoicing before him always,
^{31}rejoicing in his inhabited world
  and delighting in the human race.

Exegetical Perspective

Proverbs 8, from which these two excerpts are taken, can be outlined as follows:

1–5 Wisdom's introduction of herself and her address to humankind

6–21 Wisdom's virtues (vv. 6–11 the value of her words ["Take my instruction instead of silver," v. 10]; vv. 12–16 the role of Wisdom in ordering society ["By me kings reign, and rulers decree what is just," v. 15]; vv. 17–21 the value of Wisdom's gifts to humankind ["endowing with wealth those who love me," v. 21])

22–31 Wisdom and creation (vv. 22–26 the origin of Wisdom before God's creative acts; vv. 27–31 Wisdom's role in creation; cf. Prov. 3:19–20)

32–36 Wisdom's promise of happiness for those who listen to her

Wisdom is feminine in Hebrew and speaks as an individual entity. Scholars are divided on whether Wisdom is merely a personification of one of God's attributes or is presented as a hypostasis, an independent personal being. Such hypostases cannot be separated from God's being, and yet they are not identical with it. Other Old Testament examples of hypostases are the word of the Lord and the name of the Lord. See especially the role of the divine word in the exodus story as recorded in Wisdom 18:15–16: "Your all-powerful word leaped from heaven, from

Homiletical Perspective

This is a wonderful text for preaching, a good change of pace from our tendency to preach from overly familiar parts of the Bible. We begin with the fascinating image of Lady (or Teacher) Wisdom standing up and hollering an invitation for us to come to her. Wisdom cries out "on the heights, beside the way, at the crossroads . . . beside the gates . . . at the entrance of the portals"—she seems to pop up almost everywhere, beckoning us to something infinitely better than the seductive invitation of the adulterer in the previous chapter. What blessing does Wisdom have to offer? We shall see.

The lectionary skips verses 5–21, and we hear Wisdom lifting up her voice again in verses 22–31, where it is as though Wisdom is establishing her credentials. She tells us of her age and her constancy. In verse 22 she promises, "The LORD created me at the beginning of his work, the first of his acts of long ago." In verse 24 she elaborates, "When there were no depths I was brought forth." The Hebrew verb for "brought forth" may also be translated as "whirl, dance, or writhe." Can we imagine Wisdom whirling, dancing, writhing forth? What is more, in verse 30 Wisdom says of her time with God at creation, "I was beside him, like a master worker." In essence, Wisdom says, "I am not a Jill-Come-Lately. You can trust me. After all, I have been with God from the

Proverbs 8:1-4, 22-31

Theological Perspective

more seductive voice of "Lady Folly"), those who would be found by this wisdom need not separate themselves from the world or mistrust any voice that can be heard in public places. The voice of this particular wisdom is one that cries out to all Homo sapiens—especially from those places open to all. This is "general revelation" at its best:

> If the Christian faith claims to speak of the truth, it must have some correspondence with the truth we can learn from the natural sciences, philosophy, modern psychology, and the attempts of artists to grasp the mystery of life. . . . God is not the prisoner of the Christian church. We must expect him to be present and at work also outside the sphere of those who know about and depend on Christ and the Bible.[1]

Wisdom as the Architect of God's Creation. The fact that Wisdom (now personified) can be found by all human beings in those public places where all people gather is far from accidental. Indeed, Wisdom's fingerprints are all over God's creation because Wisdom was there when everything in this world began: "then I was beside him, like a master worker [or architect]; and I was daily his delight, rejoicing before him always, rejoicing in his inhabited world and delighting in the human race" (vv. 30–31).

Just as the trained eye can see the evidence of an individual architect in the design of a particular building, just as the trained ear can hear the patterns of a particular composer in the movements of a specific piece of music, just as the trained heart can sometimes sense the inclinations and leanings of a particular teacher in what the students learn, so "the heavens are telling the glory of God; and the firmament proclaims his handiwork" (Ps. 19:1) and, we might add, the touches of God's architect, Wisdom. As John Calvin poetically put it: "Wherever you cast your eyes, there is no spot in the universe wherein you cannot discern at least some sparks of his glory. You cannot in one glance survey this most vast and beautiful system of the universe, in its wide expanse, without being completely overwhelmed by the boundless force of its brightness."[2]

Wisdom Now Embodied in Jesus Christ.
Nevertheless, the Wisdom available in nature and in the public square will only go so far, even if Wisdom

Pastoral Perspective

alongside divine Wisdom would be a real blessing. It is also important to observe that Proverbs presents Wisdom, Sophia, as a female. For some people, hearing about a feminine aspect of the Divine will be shocking. Proverbs certainly gives Wisdom feminine attributes, while John's Gospel, by identifying Wisdom with the Word, the *logos*, seems to make her male (John 1:1). For female congregants this identification with the Godhead could be a very liberating insight.

Wisdom takes her stand (v. 2) and proclaims, "To you, O people, I call, and my cry is to all that live" (v. 4). Wisdom is the speaker who not only explains who God is, but reminds us of who we seek to be. Wisdom speaks to everyone, and every one of us has a piece of Wisdom in our souls, if we just pay close enough attention. Do you pay enough attention to the wisdom you have around you? How do you recognize wisdom? Does the wise one have wisdom based upon experience, or education, or a combination of both? What about the wisdom of a child? Might it be more pure than the wisdom of an older "sage"?

The poetry of Proverbs reminds the hearers that Wisdom was created by God at the very beginning (v. 22). Wisdom was no afterthought. She was there at the beginning, witnessed all of creation, and worked alongside God as a master worker (v. 30). The poem is a beautiful depiction of creation and would be a fine poetic midrash on the first chapter of Genesis. The point is that Wisdom was there. She was always there. She is always here too.

This Scripture is about Wisdom's identity. It shows where she was, who she was, how she was helpful, what her manner of support and companionship was with God. It would be a great asset to explore with the congregation what companionship we have with God. In what ways do we support God? How do we back up God? How do we witness God's creative work? More than that, how do we participate in the creative process? What do we create? What relationships do we help to mold? What choices do we make? What part of the Wisdom of God are we willing to claim for ourselves?

Wisdom is a helper to God. She was beside God as a master worker (8:30). She was cocreating with God. The preacher may want to explore with the congregation the ways in which we cocreate with God. What piece of creativity do we claim? Could we be so audacious as to claim that our creating is divinely inspired? Poets, musicians, artists, even preachers claim that their work is inspired by God. Why can't the parishioners hearing this sermon also

---

1. Shirley C. Guthrie, *Christian Doctrine* (Richmond: CLC Press, 1968), 68–69.
2. John Calvin, *Institutes of the Christian Religion*, ed. John T. McNeill, trans. Ford Lewis Battles (Philadelphia: Westminster Press, 1960), 1.5.1.

Exegetical Perspective

the royal throne, into the midst of the land that was doomed, a stern warrior carrying the sharp sword of your authentic command, and stood and filled all things with death, and touched heaven while standing on the earth." In these days when we struggle to describe God in gender-neutral ways without undercutting Trinitarian beliefs, it is important to know that in antiquity there were efforts to describe beings "in the vicinity of God," that is, hypostases, that were considered feminine.

In the first excerpt (vv. 1–4) Wisdom invites all humanity to listen to her. Her specific admonition, in verses not included in this pericope, is for humans to acquire for themselves prudence, intelligence, instruction, and wisdom (vv. 5–11). In the previous chapter of Proverbs, by contrast, the author urges readers to shun the "Strange Woman," whose words are folly.

Two translation difficulties in verses 22–31 have exercised scholars over the centuries and even today. Did the Lord "create," "acquire," or "possess" Wisdom as the first of God's acts of old (v. 22)? Most scholars today prefer one of the first two choices in preference to "possess" (used in the KJV and the Vulgate), since the verbs in verses 22–25, dealing with Wisdom's genesis, refer to one-time action, whereas possession is an ongoing phenomenon. In the fourth century CE, the choice of a translation for this verb separated Arians from orthodox Christians. Following the Septuagint, the Arians preferred "created" and concluded that Christ was not God in the same sense that the Father was, since there was a time when Christ did not exist. The orthodox party preferred a translation of "possessed" (reflected in a variant reading in the Septuagint) or "begat"; this led to the statement in the Nicene Creed that Christ was "begotten, not made." Athanasius argued that what was created was not Christ but his position as the first of God's ways. These points are moot when we do not attempt to equate the figure of Wisdom with Christ, but instead interpret the figure of Wisdom in its Old Testament context.

The second translation problem, in verse 30, is equally difficult but perhaps not so crucial. Was Wisdom beside God as a master worker, as a faithful companion, or as a ward or nursling? Recent commentators have also suggested a translation of "sage," "I was near him, growing up" or, somewhat periphrastically, "I was with YHWH as an architectural associate at the creation of the world." One scholar even proposed that Wisdom was with YHWH and that YHWH was the master worker.

The chronological priority of Wisdom's coming into existence before other creative acts is spelled out

Homiletical Perspective

very beginning. In fact, I was God's helper, working right beside the Creator. My references are impeccable. Listen when I speak."

Then in verses 30–31 Wisdom shouts a final surprising claim: "I was daily his delight, rejoicing before him always, rejoicing in his inhabited world and delighting in the human race." This is not at all the way we expected Wisdom to look! When we say the word "wisdom," don't we often imagine a stern, tight-lipped person, a killjoy, or a solemn judge in black robe? But that is not the picture of wisdom here. Wisdom is not dour drudgery; Wisdom is joyous laughter, dance, and play. And to top it off, Wisdom rejoices in *us*, in humanity.

How might the rhetorical form of this text inform preaching? The book of Proverbs itself tends to deal not in shades of gray but in absolutes, clear right and wrong. For example, chapter 7 (the enticing call of the adulterer) is followed by chapter 8 (the call of Wisdom). One option for preaching on this text would be to paint a study in contrasts. As sympathetically, but also as truthfully, as possible, the preacher might contrast "lifestyles of the foolish" with lives lived in the richness of God's Wisdom. The difficult challenge of preaching a study of contrasts is to avoid an unfair and unsympathetic caricature of those who are behaving foolishly, while also remembering our own sin and foolishness.

Another option Proverbs 8 offers is to use personification in all or part of the sermon. This approach is especially powerful for ending a sermon. Here is one illustration for today's reading:

> I was out shopping yesterday, and whom did I run into? Wisdom. Yeah, there she was. She called me over and we began talking, Wisdom and I. Then, I went down to the courthouse, and there she was again, making a plea for justice in some dingy courtroom where somebody had been unjustly accused. After that, I dropped by the school, and she had gotten there before me, calling for students and teachers alike always to seek truth. Then I went for a walk in the woods, moving along the trail in quiet meditation. Wisdom snuck up on me and said, "Now that we are alone, I have something I want to share with you, a present I want you to enjoy. You know, I have been around a long time, really before the beginning of time. I have been whirling and dancing with God all along. I am God's delight, laughing and playing. I want you to know the lightness of spirit and gladness that come when you welcome me. Will you set aside those thoughts, words, and deeds that make life heavy and sad for you and others? Will you come

Proverbs 8:1-4, 22-31

Theological Perspective

is listened to. Just as Psalm 19 links the revelation available through nature to the revelation available through the law (Ps. 19:7–13), and just as the "light of nature" must be supplemented by Holy Scripture in order "to give that knowledge of God, and of his will, which is necessary unto salvation" (Westminster Confession, in *Book of Confessions* [Louisville, KY: Office of the General Assembly, 1999], 121), so finally the Wisdom reflected in her who was created at the beginning of God's work (Prov. 8:22) must be placed in concert with the Wisdom embodied in him who was around before such creation began (John 1:1). This is known theologically as "special revelation," God's truth revealed in Scripture and through Christ.

Here, right here, is where the playful dance of delight between God and Wisdom celebrated in Proverbs 8 might be joined by the playful delight inherent in the Godhead, leading to a truly Trinitarian experience of worship on this particular Trinity Sunday. For rather than pitting the knowledge of God available through general revelation against the knowledge of God available through special revelation, the deeply personal and communal knowledge of God revealed in Jesus Christ helps us accurately see the fingerprints of this God's architect in the large and small events of all our lives. One writer, in an article on Trinitarian spirituality, puts it in this proverbial way: "On the road of life there are innumerable occasions for us to stand at the corner of 'Mystery' and 'Mundane' and see God at work in the course of an ordinary day. The love and beauty of the Divine Trinity is embedded in every moment of our lives, could we but see; and to see, we have only to look."[3] According to Proverbs 8, we have only to listen—wherever and whenever Wisdom calls.

RICHARD BOYCE

Pastoral Perspective

claim such connection with God in their own creative endeavors?

Ask what people have made that made them the most proud: a meal, a garden, a vocation, a perspective, a child, a sense of recovery, a vital church community, an inspired mission. These things were created with your own wisdom, and with an aspect of the Wisdom that is part and parcel with God. Do you see yourself alongside God in the creative process?

People need to trust God, but they also need to trust their own wisdom. A preacher might ask people about the wisest people they know. What makes them wise? What attributes do they share with the Godhead? What do you emulate about them?

Too many people speak for God these days. God is invoked in presidential campaigns. God is trumpeted in pious ways to show how one is purer than another. God's name is used to fight wars and to make enemies. Somehow, Wisdom does not lend itself to such abuse. Wisdom is an intuitive posture of truthfulness. Wisdom is a propensity to see things clearly. Wisdom is an ability to discern right from wrong. It is an ability to see through the facades of those who use religion for personal gain. Wisdom gives life. Reclaiming this aspect of the Godhead would be a refreshing change in our political, social, and even religious landscape.

I thank God for Wisdom. She is the great sustainer. We all need Wisdom that does not spout platitudes but gets deeper and sustains us during the darkest nights of our souls. This is another aspect of God too often overlooked and intellectualized. When you are feeling lost and alone, remember that your wisdom is connected with a Wisdom that has been there since the beginning of creation. It urges you forward. It calls you to claim your own true self. It sets you free to become the child of God you were called to be.

DOUGLAS M. DONLEY

---

3. Steve Shussett, "The Intersection of Mystery and Mundane," *Hungryhearts* 16 (Spring 2007): 6.

poetically in verses 22–26. Since Wisdom literature in the Old Testament often associates Wisdom with age, Wisdom's early existence authenticates her wise reputation.

In verses 27–31 we learn that Wisdom was present with YHWH during his various acts of creation. This interpretation may lie behind the famous painting by Michelangelo in the Sistine Chapel in the scene where God reaches out a finger to give life to the inert Adam. In the crook of God's left elbow is a woman who accompanies him in this creative activity. Others associate this woman with Mary.

God's Wisdom in creating is shown by features of the sky, waters, and land. The sea normally stays within its boundaries so that flooding does not occur, and the earth is set on a firm foundation despite occasional earthquakes (v. 29). It is not so much the skies that YHWH strengthened, as our modern translations suggest, but probably the high cirrus clouds that God energized to remain suspended above the earth (v. 28). Similarly God gave "the fountains of the deep" (that is, springs) power to surge up perpetually.

Verses 30–31 speak of the mutual joy experienced in each other by YHWH and Wisdom. YHWH delighted in Wisdom, and Wisdom in turn always rejoiced in YHWH's presence. Wisdom, and therefore YHWH, always rejoices in the created world and especially in the human race. While Western theology in particular has often given strong emphasis to the fallen condition of humanity, Wisdom literature generally speaks of God's delight in humans and presents them as God's trusted creatures, for whom God has high expectations.

The personification of Wisdom in Proverbs 1:10–33 and in this chapter also appears in later, apocryphal books of the Old Testament. In Sirach 24, Wisdom, which came forth from the mouth of the Most High, sought to find a home and eventually settled, at God's command, in Jerusalem. In Sirach 24:23, the author identifies Wisdom as the book of the covenant of the Most High God, that is, the Torah or the Pentateuch (cf. Baruch 3:9–4:4). In the New Testament, Christ, especially in his role as creator, is described as the Word or the wisdom of God. Many of the features of the "Word made flesh" are described in terms of personified Old Testament Wisdom (John 1:1–3, 10; Col. 1:15–20; Heb. 1:2–3; 11:3).

RALPH W. KLEIN

and laugh and play with me? Will you come and dance with me? Will you?"

Of course, the preacher is considering Wisdom on Trinity Sunday, one of the few Sundays in the liturgical year devoted primarily to reflection on one of the doctrines of the church. Though Proverbs 8 provides no explicit instruction on this doctrine, how might it speak to and expand our understanding of the Trinity? First, the image of Wisdom as God's helper reminds us of the reciprocity of the Trinity—Father, Son, and Holy Spirit giving and receiving within the very being of God. Even more, the description of Wisdom in verses 24 and 25— "brought forth" (whirling, dancing)—calls to mind the Eastern Church's emphasis on the Trinity as perichoresis, literally "dancing around." So we do not worship a stingy God who grudgingly gives gifts and who grants forgiveness as a divine grump. Not at all. The triune God is a joyous, dancing God who pours out overflowing gifts to humanity with gladness. As author Kathleen Norris puts it, "In the Orthodox tradition, the icon of Wisdom depicts a woman seated on a throne. Her skin and her clothing are red, to symbolize the dawn emerging against the deep, starry blue of night."[1] With all her beauty and grace, Wisdom invites us all to walk, laugh, play, and dance into the light of God's new day.

JEFF PASCHAL

---

1. Kathleen Norris, *The Cloister Walk* (New York: Riverhead Books, 1996), 1.

Psalm 8

[1]O Lord, our Sovereign,
   how majestic is your name in all the earth!

You have set your glory above the heavens.
[2] Out of the mouths of babes and infants
   you have founded a bulwark because of your foes,
   to silence the enemy and the avenger.

[3]When I look at your heavens, the work of your fingers,
   the moon and the stars that you have established;
[4]what are human beings that you are mindful of them,
   mortals that you care for them?

Theological Perspective

In Psalm 8, David bursts forth in praise as he gazes upon the vast splendor of the heavens God created: "O Lord, our Sovereign, how majestic is your name in all the earth!" David's adoration is inspired by his recognition of a fundamental paradox: How can God, whose glory is set "above the heavens," whose fingers establish the moon and stars (v. 3) in their place, be "mindful of" humanity (v. 4)?

David's awe is not difficult to understand. Few fields of learning are more daunting than astronomy. The lens of a telescope awakens our soul to the sheer enormity of God's creation. Our galaxy alone is spread over a 100,000-light-year expanse and is estimated to be one among millions in the universe. As David wrote Psalm 8, his eyes saw only .001 percent of the 100 billion stars in our Milky Way. Indeed, our understanding the heavens confronts us with two important thoughts: the incomprehensible greatness of our Creator and our own very small and inconsequential stature in the universe.

If contemplating the heavens reveals to us our smallness, what then is the answer to David's bold question: "What is humanity?" Scripture reveals that God has dignified man and woman by placing the divine image in them, making them "a little lower than God" and thus crowning them "with glory and honor" (v. 5). This royal coronation is manifested in

Pastoral Perspective

The well-known hymn "Holy, Holy, Holy" sings, "God in three persons, blessed Trinity." Less well known, though, and even less understood is what this hymn truly means. How can God be three persons? Why is the Trinity blessed? Our hearts sing what our minds cannot grasp. We sing of things too wonderful for ourselves.

Psalm 8, another example of singing what our minds cannot fathom, is a beloved psalm of praise to the mystery and wonder of God's holiness. Anyone who has stared at the starlit sky or listened to children at play can sense the psalm's truth. Any who have experienced God's undeserved, unsolicited mercy hear their own voice in the psalm's gentle amazement. God's holiness flows from its words. Yet the psalm is so much more than the sum of its parts. An exegesis of dissection strips the music from this word of God. As with all great pieces of art, this psalm is to be appreciated, not understood.

So it is quite fitting that Psalm 8 and the Trinity are bound together this Sunday. Two mysteries that evoke wonder instead of explanations harmonize well. We cannot fully comprehend how the three persons of the Trinity independently coexist. Nor can we fully understand how the lips of infants sing praise. Yet we know they do. We know beyond our

⁵Yet you have made them a little lower than God,
  and crowned them with glory and honor.
⁶You have given them dominion over the works of your hands;
  you have put all things under their feet,
⁷all sheep and oxen,
  and also the beasts of the field,
⁸the birds of the air, and the fish of the sea,
  whatever passes along the paths of the seas.

⁹O LORD, our Sovereign,
  how majestic is your name in all the earth!

Exegetical Perspective

Boundaries and Borders. At the beginning of creation God created boundaries and borders, according to Genesis 1 (and assorted other OT texts). Night is separated from day, earth from sky, dry land from water. Proper limits are set and borders erected. In the midst of the bounded waters above and waters beneath, God forms a safe place for creation to flourish and appoints a particular creature, one made in God's own image, to be God's viceregent in this safe and bounded place.

As the first psalm of praise in the book of Psalms, Psalm 8 celebrates the boundary-forming nature of God and the significance of those boundaries for human beings. Psalm 8 differs from the "typical" psalm of praise because it lacks an invitation to praise and the reasons for praise that usually begin this type of psalm. Here, however, the first verse of the psalm sets a boundary, as well as the theme and tone, for all that follows: "O LORD, our Sovereign, how majestic is your name in all the earth!" While the mention of God's name seems a step removed from the mention of God directly, the unique power of the name in the ancient Near East is well documented. Names conveyed presence and the "nature, power, and reality"[1] of their bearers, especially in relation to their divine

1. Tryggve N. D. Mettinger, *In Search of God: The Meaning and Message of the Everlasting Names* (Philadelphia: Fortress Press, 1988), esp. 1–11.

Homiletical Perspective

This psalm begins and ends with pure praise for God, and the preacher, before attending to the content of the middle verses, will do well to help hearers locate themselves in that attitude of adoration, without which the text as a whole is meaningless. This will be done not so much by instruction *about* praise (as though it were something to be taught) or by exhortation *to* praise (as though it were something that could be ordered) but by stimulation of the congregation's imagination *in* praise, that is, by helping listeners recognize in themselves the tidal pull of praise, its artesian inevitability as a human response to God, a response that can be dammed up only at huge expense to the soul. We are made for praise, meant for praise, and the preacher who wants to elicit or expose the power of this psalm will begin by leading hearers to that place in themselves where praise rises up naturally.

The liturgical and cultural context, of course, will determine how this is done, but in any case it will involve richly narrative reminders of situations where gratitude or adoration was expressed instinctively: the receipt of a great and unexpected gift, the experience of a community delivered from some imminent peril, the realization of God's presence, the exposure to art that is not simply good but sublime. Praise, of course, is not *always* instinctual—it may be

Psalm 8

Theological Perspective

the way God has "given them dominion" over all of God's works and has "put all things under their feet": "sheep," "oxen," "beasts of the field," "birds of the air," "fish of the sea" (vv. 6–8).

David's meditations on Genesis 1, however, raise the question: What does it reveal about our God that God would choose to place God's image in the small, apparently inconsequential joint humanity of man and woman? Stated another way, why—when so much else God created in the universe clearly displays God's power, glory, wisdom, and greatness—would God confer the divine image upon humanity?

The writer of Hebrews begins to unfold the answers to these questions in Hebrews 2:5–9. After quoting most of Psalm 8, he points to its christological fulfillment: "We do see Jesus, who for a little while was made lower than the angels, now crowned with glory and honor because of the suffering of death, so that by the grace of God he might taste death for everyone."

According to Hebrews, the psalmist's question, "What is humanity?" may be answered most fully in the person of Christ: Christ alone circumscribes true humanity. Christ alone reveals God to us in human flesh. Christ alone is the archetype from which humanity is patterned.

We are invited by the author of Hebrews to read David's thoughts on Genesis through a christological lens. When we do this, we see that God's subordination of the beasts of the fields, birds of the air, and fish of the sea to man and woman at creation pictures a much bigger drama played out in the life, death, and resurrection of Christ. Just as God crowned the first man and woman "with glory and honor" and "put all things under their feet," the writer of Hebrews makes clear, this divine act that David ponders is ultimately patterned after Christ, on whom ultimate glory and honor is bestowed because of his suffering and death. Thus, according to Hebrews 1:3, Christ *is* "the reflection of God's glory" and bears "the exact imprint of God's very being." Therefore it is *Christ's image* that we were actually created to bear.

As central as this teaching is to our faith, Hebrews' interpretation of Psalm 8 fails to resolve our initial question while it deepens the paradox David initially saw: namely, why does God choose most fully to reveal God's self in creation by joining the second person of the Trinity to small and insignificant humanity through the incarnation of Jesus Christ? According to Scripture's witness, the answer is found in the trinitarian life of God and revealed to us through Christ's person and work.

Pastoral Perspective

ability to know. We believe. These mysteries, the Trinity and Psalm 8, help our unbelief.

By this point in our church and social calendars, Easter is long gone. Whatever brief and ceremonious observance of the resurrection might have been held in our churches has been shoved off the pages of the datebook. Life goes on. Why? What purpose propels the trajectory of the life that goes on and on and on? By Trinity Sunday we have practically forgotten Easter's glory. Perhaps one reason Easter does not command our attention fifty-seven days later is that on Easter Sunday we try too hard to explain that which is too wonderful for us. With the precision of medical examiners we expect to solve the mystery of God's presence. Instead of bathing in glory, we expect the automatic cleanliness of outlined prose. Slightly more than a month and a half later, the answers have aged not so well. Trinity Sunday and Psalm 8 are poetic correctives.

Not even the most gifted preacher can fully explain the force behind the life that goes on and on and on. The meticulously crafted Easter sermon, sadly, is often forgotten by Easter dinner. Yesterday's satisfactory explanations dissolve in today's troubles. Life defies explanation. Yet there is wisdom, there is understanding. Sometimes these come through articulation, but most often they are felt through inspiration. The heart knows what minds suppose.

"What are human beings, that you are mindful of them?" (v. 4) Notice how in the psalm this question is an answer. Instead of acting as a topic sentence, this question is the response to the psalmist's sense of wonder, after he or she has considered the awesome, vast expanse of the Creator's reach. Verse 4 is not a question to be answered; it *is* the answer. It is the prayer of the Breton fishermen: "O God, thy sea is so great and my boat is so small." It is the prayer of a teacher going forth to an unruly class. It is the prayer of anyone with both a daunting task and sense of perspective. The prayer, the answer, the response to creation's immensity is, all at the same time, a whispered "Thank you," a dumbstruck "Wow," and a shouted "Help me!" The psalmist's answer is at least three things in one.

God is so great and we are so small. Yet God in three persons chooses to be known. God chooses a relationship with us that goes on and on and on. Why? Why does a parent choose to love a rebellious child? Why sacrifice riches to help the poor? Why preserve wilderness for the flocks and herds and beasts of the field when we know land could be put to more productive use? Sometimes we can explain

Exegetical Perspective

bearers (see Deut. 14:23; 16:2, et al., where the place where God's name dwells is used symbolically for the Jerusalem temple to suggest God's presence there). The repetition of this verse at the end of the psalm (v. 9) serves to enclose the remaining verses in the sovereignty of God's rule. God's majesty, God's rule, forms the framework that is filled by verses 2–8.

Moving inside the framing construction, the remainder of verse 1 and beginning of verse 2 offer translation difficulties with regard to the "mouths of infants"; either they are joining in praise of God, or they are vessels of God's defeat of chaotic forces that threaten the created order.[2] In either case, the psalmist has begun to describe the arena in which the majesty of God's name is demonstrated. In verse 3, the psalmist shifts the frame of reference, moving from a general cosmic stage toward the psalmist's own observation of that same cosmos, "When I look at . . ." Again with echoes of Genesis 1, all creation is laid out as God's handiwork. Seemingly powerful forces that ruled the skies (moon and stars) and were thought by neighboring cultures to be gods are reduced to the work of God's fingers. Yet, even with this reduction, the psalmist stands in awe of the vastness and wonder of creation, awe we may feel gazing at a starlit sky from a mountaintop or standing on the ocean shore.

In the midst of the vastness of God's creative glory, the psalmist moves quickly to the center of the boundaries, both literally in the structure of the psalm and symbolically, by asking a series of brief questions: "What are human beings that you are mindful of them; mortals that you care for them?" (v. 4). Even though the Hebrew of these verses is singular and can properly be understood as a reflection of an individual with individual concern, most translations treat this verse as a collective understanding of the nature and lot of all human beings. This generalizing also occurs as verbs used to describe God's action in the exodus, Israel's primal event, which would be very familiar to an ancient Israelite—"to be mindful" (*zkr*, "to remember"; see Exod. 2:23–25 et al.) and "to care for" (*pqd*, "to visit, give heed"; see Exod. 3:16; 4:31)—are used here for this unnamed individual, representative of human creatures before their creator. Of all created wonders, God remembers and pays particular heed to the human creature; given the exodus connections of the verbs used here, this may suggest that God's singular

2. J. Clinton McCann, "The Book of Psalms," in *New Interpreter's Bible*, vol. 4 (Nashville: Abingdon Press, 1996), 711.

Homiletical Perspective

elicited, nurtured, cultivated, even willed—but examples of praise that flows without prodding or rehearsal, praise that erupts naturally, will serve best to help a congregation be in touch with the spirit of the psalm. One thinks of the drawn breath that comes at the first sight of some great natural wonder, the expelled sigh that lovers know, the guttural joy when a friend comes in the door after a too-long separation.

Verse 2 leads us in the right direction: the praise that comes from "babes and infants" is held up as the example. This kind of gratitude/adoration, which is neither premeditated nor studied but comes as naturally as the cry of a newborn, is the model to be followed; not incidentally, this constitutes the best "bulwark" against the "enemy and the avenger." Natural praise, it should be noted, is not necessarily exuberant, enthusiastic, or ecstatic. The key is that it springs up from the center of our being; whether it gushes at the surface or flows quietly is of little consequence.

Once the basic heft, shape, and dynamic of praise is established, the preacher can move to capture the more subtle ideas that flow from the middle verses of the text. Immediately, though, there is a danger here. The images of verse 3 (heaven, moon, stars) are so pungent as to be distracting; it is easy—too easy—to hear or preach this psalm as though it were a paean to nature, a hymn about creation's beauty. Verses 4 and 5 pose a similar trap that can draw the preacher into a breathless essay on the nobility of humankind. In either case, the value of the psalm would be lost. The subject of the text (and of our praise) is not the creation but the Creator. It is not humankind per se, but rather the One who endows humans with qualities that are "a little lower than God."

Verses 3 and 4 are a question that the rest of psalm makes no immediate attempt to answer. The homiletic challenge is for the preacher to show the same restraint as the psalmist. That is, we should not try to solve the question of God's inexplicable care for humankind but rather let its penetrating poignancy touch us and the congregation in such a way that we, with the psalmist, are caught in wonder about this Creator who exhibits such unearthly grace. It does not matter if nothing else comes of the sermon; if people leave the church in a state of happy bewilderment about God's grace ("Who are we, that God is so good to us?"), the purposes of the psalmist and the preacher will have been served. This is, it might be noted, the positive side of the anguished cry "Why me?" that we sometimes raise when we are suffering.

Psalm 8

Theological Perspective

Among the most important things Christ proclaims in the Gospels is his relationship to the Father. In John 14:8–11 he responds to Philip's request to "show us the Father" with this amazing declaration: "Whoever has seen me has seen the Father. . . . Do you not believe that I am in the Father and the Father is in me?" Jesus explains that the works he does *are* the works of the Father who dwells in him. In other words, *the image* that the Son bears is that of the Father; thus the Son's work is intended to *reveal* the person of the Father. Furthermore, Jesus explains in Matthew 11:27 that "no one knows the Son except the Father, and no one knows the Father except the Son and anyone to whom the Son chooses to reveal him." In Matthew 11:29 Jesus instructs his hearers, "Learn from me; for *I am gentle and humble in heart.*" One of the things the divine act of creating humanity after the image of God reveals is that we have a humble God. The divine revelation of the Father to us through the incarnation, life, and death of the Son is one great demonstration of the humility of our God.

Gazing up at the heavens, David stood in amazement before a God who both could hang magnificent orbs in the sky and also be mindful of humanity. A millennium later, the second person of the Trinity entered David's lineage through the power of the Holy Spirit to reconcile humanity to our heavenly Father. Hours before his death Jesus explains the significance of this to his disciples by speaking about the work of the Spirit: "He will glorify me, because he will take what is mine and declare it to you. All that the Father has is mine. For this reason I said that he will take what is mine and declare it to you" (John 16:14–15). As Christ revealed the Father, it is now the Holy Spirit's task to take what Christ humbly revealed and manifest it through us. Thus it is by the power of the Spirit that we cry with the humility of a child, as Jesus did, "Abba! Father!"

BONNIE L. PATTISON

Pastoral Perspective

our reasons with scientific evidence, but sometimes there is no reasonable answer. Why does God continually choose to love us, knowing who we are, knowing the smallness of our minds? Do we really need an answer? Or is it enough to respond, "Thank you," "Wow," and "Help me!"?

Our lives are driven by the quest to find solutions. We think that if we can make a little more money, our problems will disappear. If we can get our children in the right schools, they will be contented fifty years later. If we can only do *this*, then *that* will be fixed; but the amount of this and that keeps growing. There are always answers we have not considered and questions we have forgotten to ask. The life built around answers is a life propelled by anxiety. Either we live in disappointment when yesterday's answers are rendered obsolete, or we live on guard, protecting today's answers from tomorrow's destruction. The psalmist calls us to live not by anxiety but by wonder.

What if questions replaced answers as the driving force of life? What if wonder became more important than solutions? What if, instead of trying to solidify our formulaic descriptions of God, we sang with the angels, "Holy, holy, holy!"? Would comfort with questions paradoxically bring us less anxiety than the endless search for resolution? Would our families, churches and nations fight less and praise more? Who knows?

In Psalm 8, questions and praise peacefully coexist. It is possible to have questions and doubts, and still believe. Even more, between the questions and praise, there is purpose to life. God has made human beings little less than angels in order to care for all things under heaven. On the day we speak of the mysterious union of God the Father, Son, and Holy Spirit, we are guided by this psalm in its lyrical union of questions, praise, and purpose. While three things in one may be difficult to explain, they can be understood.

JAMES MCTYRE

focus is an incredible gift (see Job 7:17–21, however, where this individualized attention is seen by Job as oppressive).

Continuing, the psalmist confirms that God's attention is gift, by using two images that yet again echo canonically in the creation story in Genesis 1. First, humans literally "lack little from God" ('*elohim*), which is typically translated either "made them little lower than God" (NRSV) or "a little less than the angels" (KJV). It does not take much imagination to envision being "created in God's image" (Gen. 1:26–27), poetically described here, as lacking little from God, being made a little less than God. Compounding the imagery of Genesis 1 is the second attribute given to humanity: they are royalty, kings and queens. With the royal imagery of being "crowned with glory and honor," the human creature is to "rule"(*mashal*, here in Ps. 8:6, compared to *radah*, in Gen. 1:28) over the rest of the living creatures in God's world. Here, the echoes of Genesis 1 ring clearly as the creature created in the image of God is to rule the earthly created order as God rules the cosmos. Jewish scholar Jon Levenson points out, "[God] has appointed humanity to be [God's] viceroy, the highest ranking commoner, as it were ruling with the authority of the king. The human race is YHWH's plenipotentiary, [YHWH's] stand-in."[3]

Completing the psalm with the repeated phrase of the majesty of God's name, the psalmist frames humanity's role within the rule of God. Human beings are little less than God, crowned with glory and honor, and are to rule over the created order. They do this, however, only *in the midst*, surrounded and bounded by God's rule. Symbolically, the psalmist asserts the place and role of humanity, the ruling of creation, but also limits that authority by the majesty and glory of God.

THOMAS W. WALKER

Here the psalmist exclaims on behalf of humans who are happily stunned by our favored place in the created order, "Why us? Why has God treated us so well?" It would be theologically perilous to suggest that the God who is the author of our glory is also the author of our suffering, but neither is it inappropriate to hint at the unfathomable sovereignty of the Creator in which humankind's weal or woe must ultimately rest.

There will be, of course, in our ecologically precarious world, some question about the meaning of human "dominion" over the created order (vv. 6–8). Put together with the creation accounts in Genesis, these verses are ripe for misuse and all sorts of rationalizing mischief. The psalmist's idea here is surely not to invite despoilment of what God has made. The faithful response to God's grace in honoring humankind with such "dominion" is not hubris ("It's all ours to do with as we wish") but humility ("How amazing that we are entrusted with such gifts!"). In its original setting the psalm cannot be referring to a manipulative dominion, such as is possible with modern technology, but a spiritual dominion that draws its power from humankind's primary relationship with God. This exposes an underlying tension in the text, a fine balance between the experience of surpassing worth that God has invested in us and the experience of profound contingency that is the only possible response to the fact of God's sovereignty. Human beings delicately tread the mysterious frontier between earth and heaven, partaking of each, claimed by both. The preacher's task in unfolding this psalm is to create for worshipers a way into that liminal territory where they may find their truest worth and purpose in living lives that, by their nature, are instruments of praise to God.

JAMES GERTMENIAN

---

3. Jon D. Levenson, *Creation and the Persistence of Evil: The Jewish Drama of Divine Omnipotence* (Princeton, NJ: Princeton University Press, 1988), 113–14.

Romans 5:1-5

[1]Therefore, since we are justified by faith, we have peace with God through our Lord Jesus Christ, [2]through whom we have obtained access to this grace in which we stand; and we boast in our hope of sharing the glory of God. [3]And not only that, but we also boast in our sufferings, knowing that suffering produces endurance, [4]and endurance produces character, and character produces hope, [5]and hope does not disappoint us, because God's love has been poured into our hearts through the Holy Spirit that has been given to us.

Theological Perspective

So now, since we have been made right in God's sight by faith in God's promises, we can have real peace with God because of what Jesus Christ has done for us. Because of our faith, he has brought us into this place of highest privilege where we now stand. We confidently and joyfully look forward to becoming all that God has had in mind for us to be.

We can rejoice, too, when we run into problems and trials, for we know that they are good for us—they help us learn to be patient. Patience develops our strength of character and helps us trust God more each day until finally our hope and faith are strong and steady. We are then able to hold our heads high, no matter what happens, and confidently know that all is well. We know how dearly God loves us, and we feel this warm love within us because God has given us the Holy Spirit to fill our hearts with God's love.

Today is Trinity Sunday, the first Sunday after Pentecost, and Paul gives assurance to the church of Rome that God's promises are fulfilled through Jesus' ministry, death, and resurrection, as well as the Holy Spirit. How does Paul get his message across? First, he explains the real peace they or we can have with God as a result of our faith in God. We are whole in God's sight because no matter what others say and do, no matter what happens to us and

Pastoral Perspective

The most dynamic section of Dante's *Divine Comedy* is *Purgatorio*. The damned in hell lie in the misery of everlasting separation from God. The blessed of heaven bask eternally in God's presence. The souls in purgatory are, as the name implies, being purged of all that separates them from God, so Dante's tour guide says:

> I have shown him the guilty people. Now I mean
> to lead him through the spirits in your keeping,
> to show him those whose suffering makes
> them clean.[1]

What if purgatory is not a place? What if purgation is a process through which God makes us whole? Then we have arrived at the wisdom of this text from Romans.

So often we think of our deliverance from the powers of sin purely retrospectively, as liberation from sin's consequences, and Paul does devote a well of ink to this subject. But there is also a prospective aspect to our liberation, as Paul tells us: "Therefore, *since* we are justified by faith, we have peace with God through our Lord Jesus Christ, through whom we have obtained access to this grace in which we

1. Dante Alighieri, *The Purgatorio*, trans. John Ciardi (New York: Mentor, 1961), 33.

Exegetical Perspective

Romans 5:1–5 is an interconnected set of three arguments, the centerpiece of which is the series of interlocking assertions in 5:3b–5a. Key to these assertions is the word *kataiskynō* at the beginning of verse 5. The NRSV translates *kataiskynō* as "disappoint" ("hope does not disappoint us"), but a better translation of this word, especially in light of the cultural context of Paul's Letter to the Romans, is "disgrace" or "put to shame." The New Testament writers all wrote in a cultural milieu governed by honor and shame; honor was to be sought at all costs, and shame, particularly public shame, was to be avoided. As Philip Esler, and others before him, have noted, "to be dishonored publicly by some event, person, or . . . group affiliation with unique beliefs and practices was a grievous social ill."[1] What Paul is addressing in Romans 5 is a matter not of Christian disappointment but of the real possibility of the public shaming of the Roman church.

Paul begins verse 3 with the unlikely assertion "we boast in the afflictions" or "we boast in our sufferings" (NRSV). Within a Deuteronomic worldview, one would never boast in one's sufferings, for such were seen to be a sure sign of

1. Philip F. Esler, *Conflict and Identity in Romans: The Social Setting of Paul's Letter* (Minneapolis, Fortress Press, 2003), 139.

Homiletical Perspective

"Don't waste the pain!" A friend said that to me in the midst of a difficult personal situation. Other "friends" have said to me in the midst of difficult workouts at the gym, "No pain, no gain!" The latter seems to suggest pain is good—at least for muscles. The first suggests that good will come of pain or suffering in life, if we do not waste some opportunity it gives us. Is either, however, what Paul meant when he wrote to the Roman church, "*We boast in our pain*; for in the end pain produces hope!" (vv. 3–4)? Is the "audacity of hope" (the title of a book by Barack Obama) for Paul that pain is the prerequisite for hope, or something different? Since he goes on to say that hope is founded on God's love that is *given to us*, Paul clearly means more than a simple formula suggesting that suffering → endurance → character → hope. At a minimum the formula is descriptive, not prescriptive.

"No Pain, No Gain!" This truism, most commonly associated with physical exercise, asserts that aches and pains are somehow the way to bigger or stronger muscles, but athletic trainers now say, "Not true!" Muscle pain may well be a warning of overuse or physical damage. "No pain, no gain," though, is much older than pursuit of the American dream. The seventeenth-century English poet Robert

Romans 5:1-5

Theological Perspective

around us, we believe in God's promises. Real peace is not something we automatically wake up with in the morning. Real peace with God is a verb. It is more often a sweat-blood-and-tears process that requires of us an active cultivation of our relationship with God. It means having constant contact with God; thus, each person has to construct how she or he will build, maintain, and sustain her or his relationship with God.

For some people, it may be intentionally taking some part of the day to pray (e.g., talk to God and meditate or listen to God). For others, it may mean taking a walk in the city and noticing God's active presence in the hustle and bustle of life. For yet others, it may be giving service in a soup kitchen and seeing God's face in those coming to get food. For those who are partners or parents, it may mean building a culture of peace between family members where anger or frustration or apathy have permeated relationships. For young adults in high school or college, it may mean noticing that peers from other cultural backgrounds are being treated differently and that their learning community could intentionally build practices of welcome, inclusion, and acceptance. For those in church leadership, it may entail attempting to negotiate peace between warring parishioners over the direction of the congregation's mission. Such courageous leaders within Christian communities may help to resolve genuine fears and distrust that has been festering between parishioners over generations. Each of us must make a decision intentionally to seek peace, real peace with God and real peace with our neighbor.

Paul reminds the Christians in Rome of what Jesus Christ has done for us. Jesus died for us, and on Trinity Sunday we remember that God came humbly into the world as a vulnerable little baby in the person of Jesus Christ. Because God in Jesus Christ died for us, we are guaranteed life beyond the present one we are experiencing. This knowledge that eternal life begins now is another part of having real peace with God. God promises eternal life through Jesus Christ. Moreover, Paul tells the believers in Rome that because they believe that Jesus is the Son of God, God brings them to a place of highest privilege and they stand there presently. So whatever their place or station in life, in whatever circumstance they find themselves, they can rest assured that God gives them special honor and freedom now. Because of this, they can boldly and merrily anticipate developing into the complete person God always intends for them and for us to be. Following Paul's message to the Romans

Pastoral Perspective

stand; and we boast in our hope of sharing the glory of God" (vv. 1–2). Instead of transporting us directly to celestial spheres, Paul takes us into the purgation that is necessary for us to become whole. We are forgiven, yes! But we are being made whole, even now. We are being made whole—through our sufferings.

We are not likely to brag about this aspect of our faith, though Paul encourages us to "boast in our sufferings" (vv. 3). Most Protestants, especially of the contemporary North American variety, are uncomfortable with anything that smacks of suffering. We are likely to portray such faith as medieval, masochistic, even sadistic (depending on which end of the whip we think we are on). Paul is not so squeamish or so unrealistic. "If the Lord chooses to make nothing of our transgressions, then they are nothing," writes Marilynne Robinson in her novel *Gilead*, "or whatever reality they have is trivial and conditional beside the exquisite primary fact of existence. Of course the Lord would wipe them away, just as I wipe dirt from your face, or tears."[2]

When the Lord cleans these smirches from God's good creation, sometimes the trial of cleansing is more like a refiner's fire than a bubble bath. "Suffering produces endurance, and endurance produces character, and character produces hope, and hope does not disappoint us, because God's love has been poured into our hearts through the Holy Spirit that has been given to us" (vv. 3–5). In this text, Paul becomes the tour guide of purgation, if not purgatory, introducing us, in Dante's words, to "those whose suffering makes them clean." We must all pass this way, because there is in all of us that which must be cleaned away—if necessary, burned away—by the searing love of God, the Holy Spirit, who has been poured into our hearts.

It is perhaps strange to think of the love of God—the Holy Spirit, *the love that is God*, the love that binds the Father and the Son in one—as fire, but this is the significance of those tongues of fire the crowds witnessed on Pentecost. Perhaps no one has understood this reality better than George MacDonald, the nineteenth-century Scottish preacher and author of fairy tales such as *The Princess and the Goblin*. MacDonald spoke of the love of God as the fire that is God's "essential being," the "creative power" of God that is unlike any earthly fire, in that it burns only at a distance. The farther

2. Marilynne Robinson, *Gilead* (New York: Farrar, Straus & Giroux, 2004), 190.

Exegetical Perspective

God's displeasure (thus Job's friends). There is, further, a political double entendre, for *thlipsis* may also be translated "oppression." While there was no empirewide oppression of Christ-followers during Paul's day, most scholars believe that the church in Rome to which Paul is writing lived through the Claudian expulsion of the Jews from Rome. In a smaller sense, the turning away from family gods and family worship practices to the worship of YHWH would have caused conflict among Gentiles, just as the turning toward Jesus as Messiah would have caused conflict among YHWH worshipers. Both of these could have been the basis for family and local community-based affliction, or perhaps even oppression. Such actions, whether on the local or imperial level, would have been intended to shame the worshipers of YHWH, especially those who were also followers of Jesus. Paul argues against the shame that such experiences were supposed to cause; instead, he asserts that oppression creates patience, which creates character, which creates hope. Contrary to the intentions of the exterior oppressive forces, hope does not disgrace, does not put Paul's readers to shame.

The focus on shame is key, because without it, one misses both the meaning of the interlocking phrases at the heart of the pericope and the rationale behind the argument of the vindication or justification (*dikaiōthentes*, v. 1) of the Roman church. The use of the legal term "vindication" also speaks to questions of shame. The community is, in essence, on trial, both because of its trespass of Torah (an internal reality caused by the presence of Gentiles among them) and its experience of oppression (an external reality). These can be understood in a causative relationship, the internal trespass causing the external affliction or oppression. Such a visible sign of God's displeasure should be the basis of community-wide shame.

Paul argues that, rather than being subject to shame-making oppression or affliction, the community is vindicated by its faithfulness (*pistis*) to the one who "raised Jesus our Lord from the dead" (Rom. 4:24). This vindication is accompanied by other evidence of divine favor. Through Jesus Christ, the Roman church has peace with God and access into the grace of God. Through the gift of the Holy Spirit, it also has had the love of God poured into the hearts of its members. All of this underscores that, Deuteronomic theology notwithstanding, the affliction or oppression of the Roman church is not the result of divine displeasure and should not,

Homiletical Perspective

Herrick, an Anglican priest, wrote a poem called "No Pains, No Gains."

> If little labour, little are our gains;
> Man's fortunes are according to his pains.[1]

Paul was writing to Rome about more than a formula for bigger muscles or greater success. Paul's view is closer to that of my friend who in a time of trouble said to me, "Don't waste the pain!" The pain was a given; the only question was what I would do with it.

"Don't Waste the Pain!" Peter L. Steinke says, "We 'waste' suffering if we gloss over, deny, avoid, or neglect its message. . . . If, however, we can learn from pain it is not wasted but *a source of life and health.*"[2]

The letter to Rome, written toward the end of Paul's life and ministry, can be viewed as a summary of what he had learned of faith and hope and love through his own suffering (if only with insufferable congregations like the one in Corinth). He had suffered much and would again before his death a few years later in Rome. His "formula" for hope describes what he learned from his pain—not that suffering is desirable or to be pursued, or to be wished on anyone, but that when pain comes, and it will, denial and avoidance are a "waste." Life and health, hope, can come, even in the midst of suffering, out of our learning to endure (v. 3 KJV, "patience") and growing in character (v. 4 KJV, "experience"), says Paul.

That one can find hope, even give hope, in the midst of pain and suffering, is seen in the lives of those saints who show us how. One such saint was Mother Teresa. Varahagiri Venkata Giri, former president of India, said of her: "In our present-day troubled world, incessantly plagued by conflict and hatred, the life that is lived and the work that is carried out by people like Mother Teresa bring new hope for the future of mankind."[3] To live such a life and do such a work demands endurance and character learned in living with pain and suffering, our own or that of others. It also demands and at once "produces hope" (v. 4).

Hope thus produced, however, is not just the result of "being hopeful," or "wishful thinking," or

---

1. Robert Herrick, *The Hesperides & Noble Numbers: Vol. 1 & 2*, ed. Alfred Pollard (London: Lawrence & Bullen, 1898), 2:66.
2. Peter L. Steinke, *Healthy Congregations: A Systems Approach* (Herndon, VA: Alban Institute, 2006), 52.
3. Quoted by Professor John Sanness, chair of the Norwegian Nobel Committee, in his speech awarding the Peace Prize for 1979 to Mother Teresa.

Romans 5:1-5

Theological Perspective

means that becoming all God intends for us to be begins *now*. This too is part of the real peace we have with God.

Paul continues his message to the Romans with words about life's challenges and hardships. When we face problems, guess what? We can rejoice and say, "Bring them on!" Paul takes the sting out of problems. He deflates them by saying that they are good for us. The strains and frictions in life help us grow stronger and build our character, especially our patience—the capacity to have endurance, staying power, resilience, and fortitude. Having these characteristics is what is required of us to live without complaint, but we can do this only if we develop an abiding sense of the presence of God. The more we cooperate with the reality of God in our lives, especially during times of trouble, the stronger our hope and faith become. Then a marvelous thing happens: we have the ability to hold our head high, no matter what comes our way. Even in a storm we know that all is well, because we are convinced of the utter love of God. Moreover, we feel God's warm love throughout our bodies, because God so powerfully and gracefully gave us the Holy Spirit to fill our hearts with love. This same God enables us to walk confidently through the joys and sorrows of life with Jesus, who helps us carry our cross every day and night. God as a community of persons (Trinity) assures us that we can love and be loved under exceptional conditions.

LINDA E. THOMAS

Pastoral Perspective

away from God we are, the more terribly this fire burns us; and the closer we draw to God, the more "the burning begins to change to comfort."[3]

Paul welds together the high mysticism of the spiritual life and the common pragmatism of those who stand with both feet planted firmly on the ground. The life we live—with families and friends and strangers, amid gossip and good news and bills to pay—is rich in eternal significance. God does not forgive us our misdemeanors and sins as we sit among the clouds, but while we go about the business of ordinary life. God does not reserve our spiritual transformation to the afterworld, but delivers it with the morning paper to our front door. To claim, as we do, that we are baptized in the name of the Father, the Son, and the Holy Spirit is to claim no less than this: We are washed, cleansed, in fire water, and henceforth we drip the holy stuff wherever we go. We track it into every room of our lives and out into the world.

There is one thing more we must say. Paul does not provide us here with a general rule, an old adage of inevitability. Paul does not say that whenever the world breaks us, we will inevitably heal back stronger. Paul does not—indeed, Paul cannot—make such a general statement. It is simply not true. Some who suffer are broken for good, and they do not get well again. Paul is no magician, nor does he advocate a simpleminded optimism. What Paul does promise is that our suffering need never be wasted. Because we belong to God in Christ, because God has poured his love into our hearts, that which we suffer can produce patient endurance. This endurance can form the character of the God who gives God's self away for us all, and this character produces hope, hope that will never disappoint because God is more faithful than we can ever imagine.

MICHAEL JINKINS

---

3. George MacDonald, *Creation in Christ*, ed. Rolland Hein (Wheaton, IL: Harold Shaw Publishers, 1976), 86.

therefore, cause the Roman church shame. Rather, all evidence to the contrary, the church is awash in the gifts of God and, despite its affliction or oppression, is filled with divine favor and love.

Paul thus is reframing the way in which the Roman church should understand itself with relationship to God and, as a result, to the oppressive world. Rather than hiding itself in the face of oppression, the Roman church, Paul argues, is to stand and to boast. It is to boast in its hopes and to boast in its afflictions. To boast in its hopes is to affirm again the glory of the God upon which the church stands—the glory of the God who raised Jesus Christ from the dead and who through the power of the Holy Spirit has poured love into the church. Such boasting makes sense, for it speaks to the honor bestowed upon the church by the God of heaven and earth. Surely one could not garner more honor than to be vindicated by one's faithfulness to the God of the cosmos. In the face of such honor, Paul can assert, like Isaiah before him, "Do not fear, for you will not be ashamed; do not be discouraged, for you will not suffer disgrace" (Isa. 54:4).

Paul not only reframes the social dishonor the church was experiencing; he also reframes the church's response. Rather than being deterred by its afflictions or oppressions, the Roman church is to stand and to boast in them. Its afflictions are a sign, not of the displeasure of God, but of the faithfulness of God's beloved people. Such a stance is based on hope, a hope that emerges out of such suffering, the very hope in which the church stands, the hope of the glory of God. And that hope—built upon patience and character—will not shame us, despite every attempt of affliction or oppression to do just that.

MARGARET P. AYMER

how much we hurt. Hope happens because—as Paul wrote, again about suffering—"we know that all things work together for good for those who love God" (Rom. 8:28), even bad things like suffering and pain. Hope is not something we "work out" but something we take in. "And hope does not disappoint us, because God's love has been poured into our hearts through the Holy Spirit that has been given to us" (5:5). Our faith (endurance and character) and God's love, freely given, are the substance of hope.

If that sounds familiar, it is. Paul wrote to the church in Corinth, "Faith, hope, and love abide, these three; and the greatest of these is love" (1 Cor. 13:13). Paul's "words for weddings" are really words for life. In similar words, Paul called the church at Rome to be faithful, knowing that in their faithfulness they would discover God's faithfulness, God's love, at work among them, and out of that could find hope in any and every circumstance of life. Our faith is not a matter of earning God's love, but of discovering God's faithfulness in loving us always. In this, said Paul, we can boast! "We boast in our hope of sharing the glory of God" (Rom. 5:2). "And not only that, but we also boast in our sufferings" (v. 3).

"To boast," in English, though, is somewhat misleading. It can connote becoming braggarts and full of self pride. Clearly Paul does not intend that. The archaic synonyms "glory" (KJV) and "exult" perhaps convey Paul's meaning better: We glory, we exult, in our hope and even in our sufferings. Perhaps the NIV says it best: "We rejoice." What more could we ask, in the midst of the pain and suffering that beset us all, than to find joy!

RICHARD L. SHEFFIELD

John 16:12-15

¹²"I still have many things to say to you, but you cannot bear them now. ¹³When the Spirit of truth comes, he will guide you into all the truth; for he will not speak on his own, but will speak whatever he hears, and he will declare to you the things that are to come. ¹⁴He will glorify me, because he will take what is mine and declare it to you. ¹⁵All that the Father has is mine. For this reason I said that he will take what is mine and declare it to you."

Theological Perspective

It is not difficult to see why this particular passage has been appointed as the Gospel for Trinity Sunday. It plainly addresses the relation between the Father who is said to have all that belongs to the Son, and the Son who is said to have all that belongs to the Father, and the Spirit (of truth) who takes what belongs to the Son and declares it to the disciples (John 16:15; cf. 16:13). Not surprisingly, the church fathers wrestled with the issue of the interrelation among these three "persons," each of whom they believed to be God.

In struggling with this issue, the early church articulated the defining marker of God by which Christians find their own identity, the doctrine of the Holy Trinity. According to this doctrine, there is one God in whom there are three "persons" who share one "substance." Further, according to this doctrine, God has a name that denotes those persons—Father, Son, and Holy Spirit. Accordingly, when Christians pray, typically they address the Father, through the Son, in the Spirit. In like manner, when they proclaim the good news of God in Christ, they do so in the name of God: Father, Son, and Holy Spirit.

This way of addressing God is currently the subject of heated theological debate. Is it right and good to address God with such a gender-specific

Pastoral Perspective

If the preacher has in mind for Trinity Sunday an instructional sermon on the doctrine of the Trinity, there are more suitable texts than John 16:12–15. While there is in verse 15 a vague reference regarding the Spirit's relation to the Father, the passage mostly concerns the activity of the Spirit in advancing the teaching ministry of Jesus, specifically in facilitating within the Christian community a mature appreciation of the revelation brought by Jesus.

In John's Gospel, that revelation is given less to individuals and more to the community of Jesus' disciples, and in verses 12–15 it is within the community that the Spirit works. In a culture of individualism, the preacher will need to emphasize that the promise of the text is not that the Spirit will enhance an individual's mystical relationship with Jesus. The beneficiary of the Spirit's activity is the community, which will be led "into all the truth" (v. 13).

The word "truth" will require interpretation by the preacher. Worshipers will be inclined to understand "truth" as the equivalent of "facts," or perhaps as a reference to wisdom. But in John's Gospel, "truth" is a reference to Jesus, who is "the truth" (14:6). So the "truth" into which the community is to be guided has to do with Jesus himself, providing both greater clarity about all that he has said and deeper conviction regarding who he is.

Exegetical Perspective

This passage continues the Farewell Discourse, from which the Gospel reading for Pentecost was taken. In many ways, it continues the same discussion about the nature of the relationship among Jesus, the Father, and the Spirit that was discussed in the Pentecost exegetical essay. In particular, for John there is a functional equivalence between Jesus and the Spirit, because the Spirit is sent from the Father, abides within the community (14:17), and teaches the community about the ways of Jesus, which were all about the works of the Father (one of Jesus' main functions). So the Spirit functions as the presence of Jesus for the community after his death and resurrection. It is important to remember that John is not engaging in an ontological discussion about the nature of the three persons of the Godhead, like later Trinitarian formulations. He is trying to express in relational terms the experience of the Divine he and his community have shared.

The passage at hand talks about the Spirit in slightly different terms than in the Pentecost passage. With the epithet "Spirit of truth," John adds another function for the Spirit, namely, to "guide you into all the truth" (16:13). This is not unlike the language used for God throughout the book of Isaiah, especially in 2:3 ("Many peoples shall come and say, 'Come, let us go up to the mountain of the LORD, to the house of

Homiletical Perspective

As a great teacher Jesus was aware of what his pupils were able to take in. Such attention to the hearers is important in any kind of communication. It is especially important in preaching. This text is relatively short, but it appears in a context of an extended time of teaching—both example and precept for the disciples in the upper room. A primary challenge for the preacher here is finding something in the text or its context that the hearer will be able to relate to. This point of contact might be positive (an intimate conversation in a small group setting) or negative (a story from two millennia ago that appears to be irrelevant to life in the twenty-first century). In either case, the preacher who identifies a point of contact will have some idea of where the hearers are, at the beginning of the sermon, relative to the text and also relative to the Holy Spirit, who is the primary content of Jesus' teaching here. This should point to a way of beginning the sermon and perhaps a way of ending it.

The next big question should be, What does Jesus teach here about the Holy Spirit that my hearers need to understand? The title "Spirit of truth" is peculiar to John and it does not appear in this form in the Hebrew Scriptures. It does appear in the pseudepigraphic *Testament of Judah*, chapter 20, where it is contrasted with the spirit of error, but Jesus' use of it here appears to be original. Jesus not

John 16:12-15

Theological Perspective

appellation? Might it not be more inclusive to substitute a more generic set of appellations such as *creator, redeemer,* and *sanctifier*? The theological issue before the churches is whether the substitution of *functional* terms such as these can in fact serve adequately, either as terms of address or as denotations of the nature of the relation among the three persons.

No matter how one comes down in this debate, for all Christians there is a Trinitarian structure that defines both the prayer and the proclamation of the church. Nevertheless, one must still address the question of how the three persons denoted by this structure are related one to another. In the centuries after the writing of the New Testament, different answers were given to this question by the Eastern and Western churches. The Western church held that the Spirit proceeds from the Father and the Son, while the Eastern church insisted that the Spirit proceeds from the Father only. The Western version seeks to make clear that the Son gives the Spirit to the church. The Eastern version, in order to make clear that there is but one God, insists that both the Son and the Spirit issue from God the Father, but in different ways. The Father *begets* the Son, but the Spirit *proceeds* from the Father.

Early commentators on this passage interpreted it in a way that supports the Eastern view. Augustine comments on John 16:13c in this way:

> It is the Father only who is not of another. For the Son is born of the Father, and the Holy Spirit proceeds from the Father. But the Father is neither born of, nor proceeds from another. And yet this should not occasion in human thought any idea of disparity in the supreme Trinity. For the Son is equal to him of whom he is born just as the Holy Spirit is equal to him from whom he proceeds.[1]

Support can be found in John's Gospel for the positions of both the East and the West. In support of the Western position, one can cite John 16:7 that says Jesus will send the Paraclete. On the other hand, John 14:16 and 26 say that it is the Father who sends the Spirit. More recent interpretation of the passage supports the Eastern view. John 16:15 suggests that John believed that in a final sense the Father is the source of both Jesus and the Spirit.

The main focus of John's Gospel is, however, not on the interrelations of the three persons within the life of God. Rather, it is on what has come to be called

1. Augustine, *Tractates on the Gospel of John*, 99.4, *Nicene and Post-Nicene Fathers* 17:382.

Pastoral Perspective

Worshipers will have little difficulty relating verse 12 to their own experience. Examples abound of someone having more to say than listeners are able to bear, either because they lack the capacity to understand or because it is too painful. Parents have more to say about a multitude of things that their younger children cannot yet bear to hear. Adolescents have things to say that adults, including parents, cannot bear. So too with teachers and students, and pastors and people! There are things to be said about suffering, or terminal illness, or grief, or childbirth, or working on an assembly line, or war, or destructive acts of nature such as hurricanes, floods, and tornadoes, that cannot be borne, cannot be understood, by those who have not themselves had the experience.

It is, the text is contending, much the same within the Christian community. Clearly such was the case within the community gathered about Jesus on the eve of his death. Not just in John, but also in the other Gospels, especially Mark, there is much that Jesus has already said that the disciples do not comprehend or cannot bear: references to his impending suffering and death, for example, and his call to service. What the disciples do not possess, and will not possess until Pentecost and after, when the Spirit of truth has guided them "into all the truth," is primarily the meaning of the revelation that is Jesus himself.

So too with every Christian community since: Jesus has said more than we can bear, and regarding the meaning of his words, his ministry, his life, death, and resurrection, we are still far from grasping the "truth." There may be some Christian communities where even this word will be hard to bear, so self-assured are they that they already have "all the truth." The preacher should speak it nonetheless.

What the text wants most to do is encourage within the community an openness to fresh encounters with the revelation of Jesus. John intends to shape a community that is receptive to Spirit-guided growth. It is not that there will be new "truth" beyond that of "the Word made flesh"; John cannot imagine that. But he can and does imagine that the message of Jesus and the meaning of Jesus will require ongoing interpretation. John imagines a Christian community that is not locked into the past but understands what Jesus means for its own time. He anticipates that changing circumstances and the emergence of new questions—stem cell research, for example, or the ability to prolong life by artificial means, or growing religious pluralism—will require the community to think afresh.

the God of Jacob; that he may teach us his ways and that we may walk in his paths.' For out of Zion shall go forth instruction, and the word of the LORD from Jerusalem") and in 30:20–21 ("Though the LORD may give you the bread of adversity and the water of affliction, yet your Teacher will not hide himself any more, but your eyes shall see your Teacher. And when you turn to the right or when you turn to the left, your ears shall hear a word behind you, saying, 'This is the way; walk in it'"). Furthermore, the Spirit will "speak whatever he hears, and he will declare to you the things that are to come" (John 16:13).

These two functions bear a striking resemblance to prophetic speech and action. The prophets of Israel do not speak their own words, but those of God. They also speak about things that will happen, not as soothsayers, but as ones knowledgeable about the workings of the world because of their connection with God. John is playing with these concepts in his configuration of the Spirit; the result is that the Spirit acts as the conduit for the word of God for the community, guiding them in truth and pointing the community in the proper direction for the future.

The next two verses get at the heart of the relationship among the Spirit, Jesus, and the Father. Verse 14 talks about the Spirit glorifying Jesus by taking "what is mine and declar[ing] it to you." While it is not unusual for John to talk about glorification of Jesus in explicit terms, he usually associates Jesus' glorification with "the hour" of Jesus' death. All through the first half of the Gospel, John speaks of Jesus' "hour" as not yet having come. When it does come, John associates his glorification with his death (12:27–36 [where the image of being "lifted up from this earth" is used, which is not his resurrection but his crucifixion]; 13:31–35 [where Jesus proclaims that the Son of Man has been glorified, right after Judas leaves after being revealed as the one who will hand Jesus over]). There are some other references to God glorifying Jesus (8:54; 12:43), and one of the Son of God being glorified through Lazarus's illness and death (11:4); but Jesus' ultimate glorification is not at the resurrection but in the crucifixion, where the "glory as of a father's only son" (1:14) is fully revealed. For John, Jesus embodies the Father's love because he lays down his life for his friends, thus revealing God's glory. In his death Jesus is glorified because God is glorified—part of the reciprocal relationship that they share.

Verses 14–15 express the heart of the interrelationship among the Spirit, Jesus, and the

only draws on his heritage; he expands on that heritage. The Trinity always offers us, like the disciples, much more thought than any of us can understand.

We all need to be fed such learning gradually, so it is important to decide just what bit of information is most important for the pastor to share with members of his or her congregation. This is where the preacher's pastoral sensitivities inform the development of the sermon. Through pastoral experience and imagination the preacher should be able to determine whether the question of divine truth (v. 13) or the glorification of Christ (v. 14) or the interrelationships of the members of the Trinity (the whole pericope) or the Spirit's work in maintaining relationships among the followers of Jesus (v. 15) is most pressing. Perhaps some combination would be helpful, such as the relational aspects of divine revelation. In preaching on a text like this that skims the surface of deep doctrinal issues, it is important to develop a tight focus for a sermon, so as not to overburden the hearers, but rather to give them something to challenge their thinking and acting.

One such tight focus could be that truth is relational. Some people define truth in terms of statements of fact or propositional affirmations; others like to say that there is no such thing as "capital-*T* truth." What people hunger for today is the kind of truth that flows out of relationships and helps to develop and cement relationships. Here a statement by Jesus affirms a truth that comes out of the relationship of Father, Son, and Spirit and that is given to persons related to Father and Spirit through the Son.

Furthermore, Jesus points out that this truth will bring glory to him. This aspect of relationship is of special importance in cultures like our Western culture that glorify the individual. Such individualism prompts people to evaluate nearly every experience and every relationship in terms of what it does for me. Marriages flounder because the perceived needs of one or both partners are not being met. People even choose churches on the basis of how a given congregation's program, worship service, preacher, or property fit their individual tastes and desires. The relational model shown in our text points to how truth will glorify Christ—a much more adequate criterion for evaluating any decision of life. Too often overlooked in our preaching is the fact that Jesus communicates in such a way as to point people to God, and here Jesus assures us that the Holy Spirit will communicate in such a way as to point people to

John 16:12-15

Theological Perspective

"the economic Trinity"—the way in which the Father, Son, and Holy Spirit relate one to another in respect to the creation, preservation, and perfection of the world. In John 16 the emphasis falls particularly on the role of the Holy Spirit in interpreting to the disciples (and therefore to the church) the way in which Jesus is "the way, and the truth, and the life" (14:6) that lead to the Father. In this particular section of John, the Spirit proves to the disciples that the world was wrong to condemn Jesus and that the forces of evil have been defeated. The Spirit then empowers them to go to the world to proclaim the real truth about both Jesus and the world. In this way, the Spirit continues the work of Jesus within the world after he "has gone to the Father."

At this point, the passage raises another thorny theological problem. When John indicates that the Spirit has things to say that the disciples at present cannot bear, or when he says that the Spirit will declare things to come (16:12–13), does he refer to things additional to those Jesus has revealed? Is there an unfolding truth in some way not contained in God's revelation in Christ? This passage, however, provides little support for the idea of new revelations. In 15:15 Jesus says, "I have made known to you everything I have heard from my Father." In the light of this saying, the more likely meaning of 16:12–13 is that only after Jesus' resurrection will the full meaning of his life and teaching become clear. In short, the relation of the persons of the Trinity as portrayed by John is that Jesus makes known the Father, and the Spirit interprets what Jesus had made known about the Father to the disciples and to the church.

PHILIP TURNER

Pastoral Perspective

John is confident that, relying on the guidance of "the Spirit of truth," the community will be led where it needs to go. Where the community needs to go is not merely to a deeper intellectual understanding of Jesus' revelation, but to a life of conformity with his life and teaching. The community John seeks to form is not only one that has the right understanding or is orthodox regarding what it believes, but one that corresponds morally and ethically with Jesus, cares about the things Jesus cares about, and carries out the kind of ministry that reflects Jesus' ministry.

John is confident that such a community is possible because of "the Spirit of truth" whose ministry it is to "guide" the followers of Jesus "into all the truth" (v. 13). The text seeks to instill a similar confidence into the church of every time and place. The Spirit will come, not with new truth, not with a new revelation, but to glorify Christ (the Son) by taking the message and meaning of Jesus and declaring it, enabling the community to receive and obey it.

The community can face the future with confidence because the Spirit will "declare . . . the things that are to come" (v. 13). The promise is not that the community will have advance knowledge of future events, but that it will be able to grasp the meaning of Jesus' revelation and remain faithful, no matter what the circumstances.

The reference in the text to the Spirit as one who "will guide [the community] into all the truth" is consistent with the method of Jesus, who sought to persuade and refused to coerce or impose, and should serve as an example to congregations and their leaders. Preachers, especially, so as not to be in conflict with "the Spirit of truth," would do well to think about what it means to "guide" their people into a deeper appreciation of the meaning of Jesus and into a greater conformity with his life and ministry.

EUGENE C. BAY

Exegetical Perspective

Father. In verse 14, the Spirit will glorify Jesus, "because he will take what is mine and declare it to you." In verse 15 we learn that "all that the Father has" is Jesus'. So the Father gives everything to Jesus, and then the Spirit "takes" what is Jesus' and declares it to the community. The Greek for "take," *lambanō*, can also mean "receive." Taken with this nuance, there is a mutual giving and receiving among the Spirit, Jesus, and the Father that constitutes their relationships, and what they give is "all that the Father has" (v. 15). There is no holding back. One can understand why the Farewell Discourse was such rich fodder for later Trinitarian formulations.

Where does the community come into play here? They are the recipients of "all that the Father has," which has been passed around from the Father to Jesus to the Spirit. Their relationship, however, is not closed off within the divine reality; rather, it emanates to the community who, for John, share in the life of the Divine through the ongoing presence of the Spirit. In the Pentecost passage from last week, John claims that the Spirit will teach the community everything and remind them of what Jesus said. Here, the Spirit "declares" or proclaims (*anaggellō*) what is Jesus' (all that the Father has) to the community. The Spirit is now the source of the divine life that was available to the community when Jesus was present. And as with the relationship among the Father, Jesus, and the Spirit, nothing is held back from the community. For John, the community has access to the fullness of the divine life—everything that the Father has—because they have loved Jesus and believed that he came from God (16:27).

STEPHEN P. AHEARNE-KROLL

Homiletical Perspective

Christ. Unselfishness is an important but neglected characteristic of the Trinity. We talk about God in "omni" terms—omniscience, omnipotence, omnipresence—but rarely do we hear about God's unselfishness. Such a sermon could be refreshing.

With the question, Does this truth glorify Christ? comes the question, How can I communicate this truth in a way that glorifies Christ? Truth never just appears or just lies there. Truth is always communicated somehow, and the *how* too often negates the *what* of the truth. The terms for communication in these verses are instructive. Jesus has more to *say* to them. The Spirit of truth will *guide* them into all truth. That Spirit will not *speak* from himself (or on his own) but will *speak* what he hears. He will *declare* the things to come. He will take (or receive) what belongs to Christ and *declare* it to them. This last statement appears in both verse 14 and verse 15. A close study of these terms in their contexts should lead to a helpful sermon on communicating the truth—both sending and receiving—and humility would play a vital role in both the structure and the content of the sermon. The day is gone when the preacher was expected to have all the truth in a neat package. People need to know that we are all involved in the search for truth. We have a dependable guide in the Holy Spirit along with the word of God; but full comprehension (we "know only in part," 1 Cor. 13:12) awaits the consummation of all things.

BRUCE E. SHIELDS

PROPER 3 (SUNDAY BETWEEN MAY 22 AND MAY 28 INCLUSIVE)

Isaiah 55:10-13

¹⁰For as the rain and the snow come down from heaven,
   and do not return there until they have watered the earth,
  making it bring forth and sprout,
   giving seed to the sower and bread to the eater,
¹¹so shall my word be that goes out from my mouth;
  it shall not return to me empty,
  but it shall accomplish that which I purpose,
   and succeed in the thing for which I sent it.

¹²For you shall go out in joy,
  and be led back in peace;
 the mountains and the hills before you
  shall burst into song,
  and all the trees of the field shall clap their hands.
¹³Instead of the thorn shall come up the cypress;
  instead of the brier shall come up the myrtle;
 and it shall be to the LORD for a memorial,
  for an everlasting sign that shall not be cut off.

Theological Perspective

In our time we are all too aware of nature's unpredictability. Hundred-year droughts and floods seem to come every couple years. Tsunamis crash into subcontinents with little warning. New viruses and microorganisms show up out of nowhere and wreak destruction on human and animal populations. We might not immediately turn to nature for metaphors of predictability and trust.

The exiles to whom the prophecies of Second Isaiah were directed knew that nature could surprise as well as soothe. Dust storms could blow up on the desert. Whirlwinds could break out in the forests. Droughts could go on for days or years, so that fig trees withered, and grapes died and dried out on the vine.

The key to the metaphor in this passage, therefore, is not the unpredictability of how nature might "arrive," but rather the certainty of certain "effects" when it does. Anyone who has seen a time-lapse film of the arrival of the first rivulets of water in a wadi that has long been dry knows the inevitability that the prophet now celebrates. Seeds long dormant split and send out roots. Insects and microorganisms that were hidden or buried burst forth from the ground. Plants attract birds that attract animals that attract more animals still—and soon a place that was empty and void is teeming

Pastoral Perspective

Living through the cold gray of February is an act of faith. Our seasonal affective disorder is in overdrive. The groundhog's shadow gives us little comfort as we wait out the month. The snow is as high as an elephant's eye, and it has long lost its romance. We can be thankful that, just as Epiphany transitions to Lent, spring is right around the corner. In the springtime, a wonderful metamorphosis occurs. What was once frozen, brown, and lifeless comes alive. Grass begins to turn green, and the long slumbers of winter begin to rub the sleep out of their eyes. Spring is full of hope and surprises, such as the sprouting of bulbs planted in the once-frozen earth. One never knows what will survive the winter's cold.

Isaiah 55:10–11 speaks of God's spirit watering us like a springtime garden. Just as plants receive their life from God, we too receive our life and purpose from the wonderful God who creates, redeems, and sustains us all.

Isaiah is getting at something even more powerful than simple growth and rebirth. Just as the rain comes down and does not go up without nourishing seeds, so too God's word will reach this people and will remain until it bears fruit in people.

This Scripture closes the section known as Second Isaiah, chapters 40–55, written to the people who had seen Jerusalem fall and were now living in Babylonian

Exegetical Perspective

This pericope closes out the document that has become known as Second Isaiah (Isaiah 40–55). While the original prophet Isaiah lived in the late eighth century in Jerusalem and was responsible for most of the materials in Isaiah 1–39, Second Isaiah lived two centuries later, during the Babylonian exile, and in Babylon. Because Second Isaiah knows of the rise of Cyrus, but has not experienced the decree of Cyrus allowing the Jews to return home, he is dated in the mid to late 540s BCE. Second Isaiah's message is characterized by a lyrical affirmation that the exile will soon come to an end.

Second Isaiah begins with the announcement that a highway is to be built from Babylon to Jerusalem on which the exiles will return home. There the glory of YHWH will be revealed, and all humanity will see this epiphany at the same time (40:1–8). This wonderful news was far beyond the exiles' expectations and hard to believe, and therefore this announcement is backed up by references to the promise or word of YHWH: "For the mouth of YHWH has spoken" (40:5); "The word of our God will stand forever" (40:8).

These twin themes of a new exodus and the surety of the promise of God reappear in this final pericope of Second Isaiah. The new exodus and the word of God are an *inclusio*, or bookends, around this prophet's

Homiletical Perspective

Through the prophet Isaiah, God speaks to Israel in exile. Here, in chapter 55, God comforts a people whose carefully planned lives have been obliterated, a people who wonder how they can sing God's song in a strange land. The people question, "Has God abandoned us?" Maybe they even ask, "Is God simply not strong enough to save us?"

To these implicit questions, God speaks an emphatic and beautiful answer. God declares God's word will be utterly successful, because God gives life and life is returned to God. It is as though God preaches a children's object lesson: "OK, kids. You know how it works. You have seen the rain and snow fall from heaven. They saturate the earth and cause the earth to bear grain, sprout seed for the sower and bread for those who eat. In other words, you have seen how I provide for present *and* future abundance. That is how my word is too. I do not speak without reason, and my word does not go out and come back to me empty. My word is going to do what I want it to do and succeed in the thing I sent it to do."

The social location of our congregations has a tremendous effect on how this text is heard and interpreted. Worldwide, there are numerous churches that face violent persecution and oppression. To them this text speaks a clear and vigorous word: God is stronger than what you are facing; keep the faith.

Isaiah 55:10-13

Theological Perspective

with life and possibilities because of the rain that has watered the earth. Some powers, once unleashed, cannot be brought back. They hasten to their purpose, or end.

God's Word Has Gone Out. Isaiah 40 and Isaiah 55 serve as bookends for this section of Isaiah's prophecy. While Isaiah 40 is full of the summons to speak ("A voice says, 'Cry out!' And I said, 'What shall I cry?'" Isa. 40:6; "Get you up to a high mountain, O Zion, herald of good tidings; lift up your voice with strength, O Jerusalem, herald of good tidings," Isa. 40:9), Isaiah 55 moves forward to the effects of this speech once uttered. The first bookend serves to encourage the speaker to lift the voice with courage and strength. The second bookend bears witness to the results of this voice once unleashed. Just as the tongue wrongly used is like a small fire let loose that consumes a great forest (Jas. 3:5), so the words of God's promise, once they are uttered, set in motion changes that reconfigure the entire cosmos. If Isaiah 40 serves to recruit the preacher or teacher for the pulpit or classroom, Isaiah 55 grants them the confidence to stay there.

God's Word Will Create Its Effect. How certain are our assumptions about cause and effect? Drop a stone, and it will fall. Put a match to paper, and it will burn. Flip a switch, and electricity will flow. But there are places (outer space with the stone) and situations (dampness with the paper) where these certainties fail. Also, with the stone, the paper, and the switch, *we* exercise some degree of control (e.g., *we* flip the switch). In Isaiah 55, though, the rain's effect is assumed to be both assured and out of our control. Though the messenger may seem to be in control of the message, Scripture is full of examples of words being brought without human assistance (by angels and other nonhuman creatures) and threats of other parts of creation being drafted for use if we humans should fail (e.g., the stones in Luke 19:40). Isaiah 55 challenges us to trust a power even more predictable than gravity on a stone—the power of God's word (here, concerning return from exile) to accomplish its purpose.

That Effect Will Be Surprising in the Natural as well as the Human Realm. We seem to assume that God's heaviest lifting might be to inspire surprising effects in nature, not the human heart. The word "supernatural" witnesses to this way of seeing and understanding. Scripture, however, assumes almost

Pastoral Perspective

exile. The experience of the people Second Isaiah wrote to was not unlike the experience of the ancestors of many of the people gathered in our congregations who were yanked from their homes and their families in Africa and forced to work as slaves on the plantations of North America and the West Indies.

Second Isaiah gives hope to the people who must try to sing the sacred songs in a strange land. In exile and despair, Isaiah preaches a word of hope. Too many of us have lost hope and see the future as nothing but bleak. In our despair, we fear that elections hold no real hope, just a break in the monotony of the constant struggle to make ends meet. We worry about rising prices, continually foreign technologies, losing what little we have at the hands of another more qualified or better connected. We fear that no matter how hard we work, we will be constantly one step behind and out of luck.

Handel used the opening of Isaiah 40 to begin his wonderful oratorio *Messiah*: "Comfort ye my people, saith your God; speak ye comfortably to Jerusalem, and cry unto her, that her warfare is accomplished, that her iniquity is pardoned" (Isa. 40:1 KJV). Second Isaiah is where all of the Servant Songs come from—the songs that point to a Messiah who will lead the people out of their darkness into great light. Is it any wonder that Isaiah was Jesus' favorite scroll?

So to a people who are in a strange land, with a strange language, with laws and religious beliefs that seek to squelch any kind of integrity that they may have at their disposal, God through Isaiah speaks these words of comfort and hope:

> You shall go out in joy,
> and be led back in peace;
> the mountains and the hills before you
> shall burst into song,
> and all the trees of the field shall clap their hands.
> (Isa. 55:12)

Jesus once said that rocks and stones would sing if the powers of this world tried to shut down the word of God. Can you just imagine trees applauding the works and the wonders of God?

Isaiah goes on:

> Instead of the thorn shall come up the cypress;
> instead of the brier shall come up the myrtle;
> and it shall be to the Lord for a memorial,
> for an everlasting sign that shall not be cut off.
> (Isa. 55:13)

Can you imagine something positive that will not end? Paul said that prophecies, tongues, and

Exegetical Perspective

words. Isaiah 55:10–11 contains words of assurance about the word or promise of YHWH. Rain and snow fall from the sky to the earth, but they do not merely bounce directly back to the sky. Instead, they soak into the ground and make possible the productivity of agriculture. The farmer gets seed for the following year, and all who are dependent on the farmer's efforts—the eaters—get bread or food in general.

"That's the way it is with my word," YHWH affirms. It too does not just return to me like a boomerang; it does not come back empty. The metaphors here are quite vibrant and anthropomorphic, even mixed. The "word" is speech that comes from YHWH's mouth; this word from YHWH's mouth does not come back "empty-handed" (a possible rendering of the word "empty" in v. 11). Rather, like the rain and snow, this word causes things to happen.

What those "things" are is spelled out in verses 12–13. The previous two verses had been spoken objectively by YHWH, but now YHWH or the prophet himself addresses Israel directly and personally (the word "you" in this verse is in the plural). The first lines describe the new exodus. It will be a joyous occasion, a peaceful one. "Peace" may indicate a lack of violence, but it more likely refers to the completeness of this restoration and its fullness. All creation will join in the celebration. Inanimate nature in Second Isaiah is sympathetic with God's redemptive activity:

> Sing, O heavens, for YHWH has done it;
>   shout, O depths of the earth;
> break forth into singing, O mountains,
>   O forest, and every tree in it!
> For YHWH has redeemed Jacob,
>   and will be glorified in Israel.
>   (Isa. 44:23)

Mountains and hills occasionally serve in the Bible as witnesses to God's words or actions ("Hear, you mountains, the controversy of YHWH," Mic. 6:2). Here in verse 12 the mountains and hills also break forth into songs of praise and thanksgiving. One is reminded of Psalm 114: "When Israel went out from Egypt, . . . The mountains skipped like rams, the hills like lambs" (vv. 1, 4). Now in Second Isaiah we also read that the trees will give Israel a standing ovation on its return to Jerusalem. Only a pedant would argue that trees do not have hands for clapping. The psalmist too saw nature actively praising God in ways normally attributed only to humans: "Let the floods clap their hands; let the hills sing together for joy" (Ps. 98:8).

Homiletical Perspective

Most U.S. congregations do not typically think of themselves as being "in exile." Our situation seems comfortable and easy, yet the forces we face are insidious. We live in a culture that is subtly, and sometimes not so subtly, antithetical to our faith. Writer and Christian Annie Dillard actually felt she had to explain to an interviewer for the *New York Times Magazine*: "Just because I'm religious doesn't mean I'm insane."[1] In addition to society's largely hidden hostility to our faith, many American Christians themselves live with only shadows of faith, their fragmented lives characterized by loss of meaning and quiet despair, a sense of emptiness filled with busyness and entertainment. Underneath, the implicit question is asked: "Has God abandoned us? Are our problems too big for God to solve?" Poor God, barely getting by. Poor God, the world was just too much.

God will have none of this silliness. God's word does not just scrape by, barely eking out God's will, hardly able to overcome evil. No. The Hebrew in the second half of verse 11 is quite expressive. Literally, God's word "shall accomplish *what I delight in* and cause to prosper the thing for which I sent it." For Christians, the promise that God's word will bring about God's delight reminds us of Jesus' baptism, when the voice from heaven declared, "This is my Son, the Beloved, with whom I am well pleased [or we might translate "with whom I am *delighted*"]" (Matt. 3:17).

What is the natural response to such a powerful, wonderful, and delightful word? One response is magnificent growth: "Instead of the thorn shall come up the cypress; instead of the brier shall come up the myrtle; and it shall be to the LORD for a memorial, for an everlasting sign that shall not be cut off" (Isa. 55:13). Rather than some scrub brush that is ugly, prickly, and short-lived, God's word is like a tree that is glorious, stately, and productive. In our mind's eye, can we see a multitude of Christian elders formed and re-formed over the decades by God's word? God's word changes lives.

A second response to God's word is a parade—a parade not just for God's people but a parade in which all creation takes part: "For you shall go out in joy, and be led back in peace; the mountains and the hills before you shall burst into song, and all the trees of the field shall clap their hands" (v. 12).

Preacher and writer Frederick Buechner recalls his days as a student at Union Theological Seminary in

---

1. Mary Cantwell, "A Pilgrim's Progress," *The New York Times Magazine*, April 26, 1992, 40; quoted by Paula J. Carlson in *Listening for God: Contemporary Literature and the Life of Faith* (Minneapolis: Augsburg Fortress, 1994), 132.

Isaiah 55:10-13

Theological Perspective

the opposite. Mountains that sing and trees that clap; cypress appearing where the ecosystem might dictate thorns, and myrtles sprouting up where the soil might point toward briers—these are tangible effects of God's word that are seen as no more miraculous than the seed and bread that spring forth following the rain (v. 10). What may be trickier is inspiring God's people to go out "in joy" and to be led back "in peace" (v. 12). Yet even here, Isaiah 55 claims a potency to God's word that boggles our minds and hearts. As Isaac Watts makes clear in his hymn "Joy to the World," the Lord's coming inspires not only the singing of "heaven and nature," but human songs as well:

> Joy to the world! The Savior reigns;
> Let us our songs employ;
> While fields and floods, rocks, hills, and plains
> Repeat the sounding joy, Repeat the sounding joy,
>   Repeat, repeat the sounding joy.

Nature, in this song and Isaiah's, joins in singing a song that the word of God has affected first in the human heart.

God's Word Will Last—with the World and with God. There is, however, already some hint that the effects of God's word on the human community may not last too long. Anyone who has read and studied the history of God's people on return from exile (a story that is reflected beneath the glorious poetry that follows in Isaiah 56) knows this fact all too well. And so, as God's word caused an effect in the skies following the flood ("I have set my bow in the clouds," Gen. 9:13), the misplaced cypress and myrtle function as effects in the desert—to jog the Lord's memory and remind God of the covenant made with this people that shall not be "cut off." While the effects of God's word once unleashed are sure and reliable, they are not long lasting in the human community, and only slightly more permanent in the natural world. But these effects are forever in the promise keeping of God. Yes, "the grass withers, the flower fades [and the faithfulness of God's people is even more transient!]; but the word of our God will stand forever" (Isa. 40:8).

RICHARD BOYCE

Pastoral Perspective

knowledge will end, but God's love will not ever end (1 Cor. 13:8). The church is God's love lived out in community. God's love will not end.

The church is a sign of hope in a world where many can see nothing but a bad economy, a rough road ahead, addiction, and misguided leadership. To the people in exile who had just about lost hope, God put together an everlasting sign, and it was good.

God nourishes us with rain and with the Word. When that happens, we cannot but bear fruit. The problem is that people do not realize that they are part of God's plan. They believe that they are alone—even some churchgoers. Thus the soil is not tended, and weeds grow up and choke the good plants. The church is the tiller of the good soil of hope, action, and justice in this world. Anything else is a weed.

What is the everlasting sign of God's love and hope if not the church? Even though the world's powers and principalities have worked against God's plan, the church stands as a beacon of hope and a repository of justice and compassion. Remind people about how the church has stood up on behalf of the outcast. There are plenty of examples: abolitionism, women's suffrage, the civil rights movement, the gay-lesbian-bisexual-transgender liberation movement. Remind people of the hope that the church has brought and how it remains a sign of hope for the world.

We are God's soil. Any good gardener knows that a seed is only as good as its soil. The church is the soil in which the seed grows. We worship and work to continue to make the ground fertile. We do it to praise God for what is growing and to weed out that which stands in God's way. When we take care of the church like a gardener, we bear witness to the everlasting sign of hope God has given to us in the body of Christ.

As we enter the spring, let us look for the new growth, and thank God for planting the seed and sticking with us until we bear fruit.

DOUGLAS M. DONLEY

Exegetical Perspective

New exodus is matched by a renewal of creation, its return to "peace" or wholeness (cf. 41:18–19; 43:19–20). Instead of thorns, cypress trees will sprout; instead of briers, myrtle will flourish. Myrtle is an evergreen bush that grows to a height of six to eight feet. One might have thought that after the new exodus the desert would return to its former condition, but now we read that the transformed desert will be kept in perpetuity as a commemorative park. The fact that this was not literally fulfilled does not diminish Second Isaiah's strong affirmation that "the word of our God will stand forever" (Isa. 40:8).

A better translation of the third line of verse 13 in NRSV might be: "All this will add to YHWH's reputation." That is, YHWH's accomplishment in the new exodus and the renewal of creation will only enhance YHWH's praiseworthy character. The fourth line of verse 13 confirms this: These actions will be "an everlasting sign that shall not be cut off."

What will allow human eyes to see these things clearly? The Old Testament lesson should have included verses 6–9. There the prophet urges the people to seek YHWH, and to return to God in repentance so that God will have mercy and abundantly pardon. Divine grace is no excuse for human complacency. Repentance and pardon can open minds to the ways of God. The expectations and promises in verses 6–13 are well beyond human imagining. God's thoughts and ways are higher than human thoughts and ways. Again the prophet uses a simple and clear metaphorical comparison. The sky is higher than the earth. Just so, God's ways and thoughts are higher than human ways and thoughts (vv. 8–9).

What is described in this pericope is an Old Testament epiphany, that is, a manifestation of YHWH's saving power. In the epiphanies that took place in the life and ministry of Jesus, the God of the Old Testament acted once more.

RALPH W. KLEIN

Homiletical Perspective

New York. In particular, he remembers Old Testament Professor James Muilenburg. Buechner writes,

> In his introductory Old Testament course, the largest lecture hall that Union had was always packed to hear him. Students brought friends. Friends brought friends. People stood in the back when the chairs ran out. Up and down the whole length of the aisle he would stride as he chanted the war songs, the taunt songs, the dirges of ancient Israel. With his body stiff, his knees bent, his arms scarecrowed far to either side, he never merely taught the Old Testament but *was* the Old Testament.[2]

Clearly, a sermon on this text will end with overflowing joy. What if the preacher followed Professor Muilenburg's example and paraded around the sanctuary? What if the preacher sang and led a parade around the sanctuary and invited the congregation to join with the singing mountains and hills and the clapping trees? Talk about a memorable sign. After all, if the mountains and hills sing at God's word and the trees clap their hands, what is to stop the congregation from belting out a song, cracking a smile, and laughing with the One whose will certainly and finally will be done?

The rhetorical form of this text lends itself to several possible preaching structures. It seems appropriate to prepare a sermon in the standard forms of "Not this, nor this, nor this, but this" or "This is a prevailing view, but here's the gospel's claim."[3] The preacher might paint pictures of how we sometimes worry that God is not strong enough or faithful enough and how we feel "in exile" ourselves. But then God's promise is sure; God's word will succeed, to God's delight.

JEFF PASCHAL

2. Frederick Buechner, *Now and Then* (San Francisco: Harper & Row, 1983), 15.
3. Thomas G. Long, *The Witness of Preaching* (Louisville, KY: Westminster John Knox Press, 2005), 128.

Psalm 92:1-4, 12-15

¹It is good to give thanks to the LORD,
    to sing praises to your name, O Most High;
²to declare your steadfast love in the morning,
    and your faithfulness by night,
³to the music of the lute and the harp,
    to the melody of the lyre.
⁴For you, O LORD, have made me glad by your work;
    at the works of your hands I sing for joy.

. . . .

¹²The righteous flourish like the palm tree,
    and grow like a cedar in Lebanon.
¹³They are planted in the house of the LORD;
    they flourish in the courts of our God.
¹⁴In old age they still produce fruit;
    they are always green and full of sap,
¹⁵showing that the LORD is upright;
    he is my rock, and there is no unrighteousness in him.

Theological Perspective

Psalm 92 was used on the Sabbath, a day the Israelites rested from their previous six days of labor, putting aside their millstones, setting down their plowshares, not harnessing their animals. This psalm teaches that the rest observed on the Sabbath is intended to contemplate works—God's works—and to engage in the worship they inspire. Thus the psalm is rightly titled "A Song for the Sabbath Day."

Though used in Israel's corporate worship, this psalm was written also to be sung personally to God by the worshiper. Here, as in all worship, God is the audience. Worshipers offer their hearts to God in gratitude and praise for God's daily provision. Thus the psalm's doxology expresses a song that frames not only the Sabbath but a person's entire day: "It is good to give thanks to the LORD, to sing praises to your name, O Most High; to declare your steadfast love in the morning, and your faithfulness by night" (v. 1).

Yet, before the psalmist directs his praise to the Lord, he declares to those around him that such gratitude "is good." To the casual observer, the reason seems all too obvious: "For you, O LORD, have made me glad by your work; at the works of your hands I sing for joy" (v. 4). The larger question, however, is, why does the psalmist have this response? What is it about God's works that inspires joy?

Pastoral Perspective

Around 8:00 a.m., a student walks across a college campus, his flip-flops clapping against his heels, his half-opened eyes half covered by a ball cap, his MP3 player plugged into his ears. He walks past strangers, unnoticed. He nods his head at the occasional student who nods a head in return. He's in his own little world. Especially at this time of morning, he likes it that way.

At the restaurant, her parents and older sister engage in what seems to her a totally useless conversation. Flipping open her phone beneath the table, she checks her e-mail, texts a friend about how incredibly boring her family is, and updates her social network status to "Enduring slow death." Of course, her parents and sister know what she is doing, but they do not comment, out of fear of scaring her away from the next family gathering. She knows this. She likes it that way.

Psalm 92 tells us that the righteous will flourish like the palm tree, that even in old age they shall still produce fruit, always being "green and full of sap" (v. 14). Yet to so many of the church's children and grandchildren, the "old" are fruitless, gray, and empty. Youthful music and technology serve not only to exacerbate a generational divide, but to isolate young people from each other. It's difficult to have a conversation with someone wearing

Exegetical Perspective

The superscription of Psalm 92 (not included above) is intriguing. It is the only psalm in the Psalter assigned to a particular day, as it is a "song" for the "Sabbath day." While the particular reasons for this assignment can only be speculated, Psalm 92 seems to play on images given for the Sabbath in Exodus 20 and Deuteronomy 5. In Exodus, the Sabbath is remembered as part of the orderliness of creation put in place by God at the dawn of time (Exod. 20:8–11). In Deuteronomy, the Sabbath is observed as part of God's redemption of Israel from the oppression of Pharaoh (Deut. 5:12–15). The language and movement of Psalm 92, a song of thanksgiving and praise, pick up both of these themes: the ordered nature of God's creation and God's deliverance from enemies like Pharaoh.

Psalm 92 begins with a declarative statement about what is good, the right and proper orientation for the world: doxology, that is, giving thanks and praise to God. Canonically, the word "good" is freighted through its repeated use in Genesis 1, as the "goodness" of creation is celebrated by the recurring phrase of God seeing that the new created order was "good" (Gen. 1:10, 12, 18, etc.). In Psalm 92, the psalmist begins with the declaration of the "goodness" of praising God, perhaps hinting that the proper order of creation centers on the praise of

Homiletical Perspective

Not all of the psalms were composed for liturgical purposes, but this one clearly was. Its intent is twofold: to explain the apparent success of the wicked and to encourage the righteous by means of promises and images of vindication. The former purpose will be lost if verses 5–11 are omitted, but the preacher may be assured that any facile argument about righteousness bringing certain reward will be met with tough resistance from thoughtful listeners. Those in the pews, who after all live in the world, will of their own accord raise the troubling question, "Why do evildoers flourish?" They will not settle for pietistic nostrums or for promises that fly in the face of experience. They want a faith that connects to the realities of their lives. The psalm addresses these personal concerns, but its liturgical setting lifts the issues beyond the personal to the realm of the universal. The psalmist wants worshipers to think— together—about questions that are played out in their individual lives but also reflect eternal realities.

The wonderful and characteristic parallelisms of verses 1–4 (thanks/praises, morning/night, love/faithfulness, music/melody, harp/lyre, glad/joy) suggest a rhetorical approach that will be difficult if undertaken, but rewarding if executed well. To build in one's hearers a growing intellectual and emotional response (as the psalmist does) calls for language

Psalm 92:1-4, 12-15

Theological Perspective

When the psalmist sings, "It is good . . . to sing praises to your name," it is because the works of God's hands demonstrate God's "steadfast love" and "faithfulness" (v. 2). In other words, the divine work of creation and redemption makes visible our invisible God. It manifests to us knowledge of God's nature that would otherwise remain hidden. Through God's acts, God is made known to us; as a result, our hearts respond in worship with praise and gratitude.

There is another reason why "it is good" to sing praises to God's name, a reason found in the answer to the question, why would God desire our praises? What happens in the greater divine economy of things when we offer our praise to God? What greater function do they fulfill?

In Psalm 22:3 David reveals why our praise is important to God. He declares that God is "enthroned on the praises of Israel." The Hebrew word *yashav*, translated here as "enthroned," is a common term. Ordinarily it means "sit," "dwell," "remain," or "inhabit." This means that our praise of God is more than just our personal opinion about God or our emotional reaction to God's works. No, praise is the very way God has chosen to dwell among us and be enthroned in our midst. When the church participates in the praise and adoration of God, God's invisible nature, God's very presence, is made visible in and through the praise and worship of God's people. Thus the prayer Christ taught his disciples to pray—"Your kingdom come. Your will be done, on earth as it is in heaven" (Matt. 6:10)—is answered whenever the church worships the Lord in praise and thanksgiving. Since the ruler's presence is made manifest in our praise, then in our praise we witness to the reality of God's kingdom come to earth. Thus together with the psalmist we proclaim, "It is good."

The psalmist's attention moves from a declaration of praise for God's steadfast love and faithfulness (vv. 1–4) to a declaration: the righteous "flourish like the palm tree, and grow like a cedar in Lebanon" because they "are planted in the house of the LORD" and therefore "flourish in the courts of our God" (vv. 12–13). Here the righteous reflect God's nature described in the opening verses of this psalm. Just as God's works reveal God's steadfast love and faithfulness, so the righteous who are planted in God's house remain faithful and steadfast in their love for God. Further, just as God dwells or is enthroned upon the praises of the faithful (Ps. 22:3), so also the faithful are "planted" or dwell "in the house of the LORD" (v. 13).

Pastoral Perspective

earphones and texting multiple other persons. Do they like it that way?

In contrast, the psalm appears to presuppose, not a sense of isolation, but a public conversation between music and its listeners, between the one who sings praise and the ones who hear and join in praising. The psalmist may sing in the first person, but one presumes the psalm is intended for public, corporate worship. It would be difficult to imagine the singer of this psalm wanting to be isolated in any way. The psalm is praise, unplugged and unhindered. Lute, lyre, and harp accompany and amplify the psalm so that all—even God—can hear and enjoy. Even early in the morning, even late at night, the singer wants the world to join in glorifying the totally righteous Creator God, but, given how long ago and far away the psalm was written, is it truly possible for us to join in its intended melodies?

As it has been and forever shall be, the music of one generation sounds like noise to another. When notes spill out of order, when rhythm breaks the anticipated beats, the brain in self-preservation shuts out the sound. Our minds have to be trained to understand, much less appreciate, the music of other generations and cultures. So when a teenager hears, "I sing for joy" (v. 4), what does this mean to her? What notes and tones run through her head? At what time of day or night is she prone to joy? Does she want to share this joy or absorb it in isolation? Do her songs of joy in any way resemble those of her grandparents? It is unfortunate that the lectionary passes over verses 5–11 of the psalm, which so well express the mood of those who despise the noise of the "unrighteous," however the noise or the unrighteous may be defined.

Psalm 92 offers an invitation to dialogue about how music conveys joy, as well as myriad other emotions. Is joy limited to the tones of harp, lute, and lyre, or can it be expressed through other instruments, perhaps those foreign to our ears? What do our favorite songs and musical genres say about us? What, if anything, might ancient Hebrew folk songs have in common with heavy metal rock? Given that all music was once new, what timeless themes are common to our songs?

The pastoral intent of this exploration is more than a lesson in music appreciation, although choir directors and organists might welcome the congregational enrichment. More than helping us learn to appreciate or tolerate the music of other generations, perhaps music can be the inroad to empathy that transcends the generations. Rather

Exegetical Perspective

God. The remainder of verse 1 restates the "right-ness" of doxology by reframing it to the singing of praises to God's name.

Given that this doxological posture is part of the "goodness" of the world, the psalmist declares the nature of God's goodness by describing the attributes of God that are praiseworthy. The psalmist calls upon a poignant pair of words, "steadfast love" and "faithfulness" (v. 2, *hesed* and *amunah)*, that occur throughout the psalms emphasizing God's enduring goodness and providential care, as primary descriptions of the character of God (see Pss. 36:6; 40:11; 88:11; 89:1, 2, 33, 49; 98:3; 100:5). These characteristics mandate praise from God's creatures at all times, through the day and through the night. This praise is melodious in nature, as the psalm suggests various musical instruments with which to accompany the continuous doxology.

Furthermore, it is the works of God that instigate the joy of the psalmist (v. 4–5). The work (*ma'aseh)* of God mentioned at the end of verse 4 and beginning of verse 5 can refer to both God's work of creation (Ps. 8:3) and God's work of salvation (Ps. 35:3).[1] Capturing echoes of the worship of Sabbath that celebrates the creative ordering work of God and observes God's redeeming exodus work, this simple word captures the manifold nature of God's activity that inspires the psalmist to this song of joy.

At this point, however, the lectionary skips over the central part of the psalm (vv. 5–11), where the focus of order and redemption moves into the realm of a contrast between the wicked and righteous, including the triumph of the righteous over the wicked. Through this excision, a significant comparison of the fates of the wicked and the righteous can be lost, a comparison that is similar to the opening lines of the Psalter in Psalm 1. This comparison, highlighted in verses 5–11, suggests that part of the orderliness of reality, supported by the faithfulness of God, is that the wicked, who seem to flourish (v. 7), will eventually be doomed and perish (v. 9). In fact, the psalmist moves on to rejoice in a particular act of redemption, which many suggest is the underlying impetus for this psalm of thanksgiving, that has seemingly reinforced God's created order of righteous prospering and confirmed God's saving activity (v. 11).

The lectionary resumes its selection in verse 12, where the contrast between the wicked and righteous comes to completion as the righteous are described

1. J. Clinton McCann, "The Book of Psalms," in *New Interpreter's Bible*, vol. 4 (Nashville: Abingdon Press, 1996), 1051.

Homiletical Perspective

and syntax that uses numerous small steps to traverse a large distance. Each point, each phrase, must advance the cause, but not too much. Verses 12–13, for instance, use the verbs "flourish," "grow," and "are planted," in turn before coming around again to "flourish." There is a spiraling rhythm here that builds excitement and draws the hearer (and even more, the cantor!) into a joyous and physical experience of the psalm. The aim is, finally, to help worshipers be able to join the psalmist in saying, "For you, O LORD, have made me glad by your work" (v. 4). One might even consider a "call and response" format in which the preacher enumerates the gifts of God and the congregation responds in each instance by reciting verse 4. This could be done earlier in the service or during the sermon itself, if the church's culture allows it.

In any case, the gladness that the psalm reflects is born of gratitude for God's steadfast love, for God's faithfulness, and for the work of God's hands. The psalmist invites the worshiper to drink deeply of this gratitude, and the preacher may help, not by instructing hearers to be grateful, but by eliciting gratitude through enumeration of God's saving and loving acts. These should reflect not only the providence of God toward individuals, but also the ways in which God has blessed the life of the community. At the same time, this approach of "counting your blessings" needs to be put in the context of a larger gratitude that is more than a response to particular favors or gifts. The relationship of humankind to the Eternal is, in its very essence, one of grateful worship. Ultimately, no ledger of gifts need be kept, no balancing of scores. God's sovereign and benevolent power infuses all existence; what else can mortals do but give thanks?

Verses 12–15 use familiar, natural images to describe the life of the righteous. The first two of these—"palm tree" and "cedar in Lebanon"—are iconic realities of the Middle East that are characterized by having deep, sturdy roots. A contrast is offered (lost if we omit vv. 5–11, particularly v. 7) with the condition of the "wicked," who "sprout like grass." Grass grows up quickly and is but briefly green; soon enough it is swept away. Palms and cedars, on the other hand, stand, unbowed, for ages. As these verses unfold, other rich, evocative images flow, particularly the comparison of the righteous to trees that are perpetually green and fruitful, even in old age. There is no hint here that the recompense for the righteous will come in an afterlife or on some other plane of being. The only argument being made is that in the long run the righteous will outlast the

Psalm 92:1-4, 12-15

Theological Perspective

Both the date palm and the cedar grow impressively tall in their old age. In verse 13, the psalmist states that the righteous "flourish" and "grow" because they abide with God. As the text implies, their roots are sunk deep into the temple's courts, thriving in spiritually rich soil of the Word and experiencing the abundant water of the Spirit. In the "courts" of the temple the righteous participate in offering their praises to God. Because the righteous are "planted" in God's house, the text implies that their worship of praise and gratitude is offered daily. Thus the psalmist observes, "In old age they still produce fruit; they are always green and full of sap, showing that the LORD is upright" and that "there is no unrighteousness in him" (vv. 14–15). The psalmist's language points forward to the example of "righteous and devout" Simeon and Anna, who "never left the temple but worshiped there with fasting and prayer night and day" (Luke 2:25, 37). Both were "planted in the house of the LORD," both were advanced in years but, spiritually speaking, were "still produc[ing] fruit" (Ps. 92:13–14).

The psalmist's description about the righteous is also portrayed in Jesus' teaching in John 15:4–5:

> Abide in me as I abide in you. Just as the branch cannot bear fruit by itself unless it abides in the vine, neither can you unless you abide in me. I am the vine, you are the branches. Those who abide in me and I in them bear much fruit.

The psalmist's picture is ultimately realized in Christ. Our union with Christ begins first with God's Word who becomes flesh (John 1:1, 14) and abides eternally in the humanity of Jesus of Nazareth through the union of the incarnation. Thus we are told to "abide" in Christ as a branch "abides in the vine." John tells us this union is accomplished through our obedience to Christ's word (John 14:24) and through the gift of the Holy Spirit, who, in turn, abides in us (John 14:17).

BONNIE L. PATTISON

Pastoral Perspective

than fearing what is fed to the ears of young people, perhaps we can invite them to bring new expression to age-old faith and doubt. Perhaps their text messages can illuminate the message of our sacred texts, and vice versa.

The imagery of the psalm begins with a singer, preparing to sing and then bursting forth in song. By its end, the psalm's images are trees and rocks, fruitful, unblemished, and unmovable. Thus the psalm draws us from private opinion to public proclamation to the enduring harvest of old age and timeless wisdom. The psalm itself moves from isolation to conversation to the God-given benefits of this transformation. As we look around our college campuses, our dinner tables, and our sanctuaries, where do we see the need to guide ourselves through this age-old path? What forms of isolation do we bring on ourselves or put upon each other because we fail to sing this psalm in our journeys of faith?

In a nursing home, in an Alzheimer's ward, a woman visits her father. He no longer recognizes her or remembers that he has had children. She speaks to him, comforts him, pats his hand, and hugs him. Despite her attempts to reach out, she cannot connect. With a sigh, she sits down in the chair beside his bed. Her mind wanders back through her years to a living room. To a song. So she sings. She sings a song she and her mother and he used to sing around the old family piano. She closes her eyes and sings. Halfway through the chorus, she realizes her father is singing too. Maybe she has stumbled upon an old favorite. Or maybe tones and rhythm express more than words. She sings. He sings. They sing for joy.

> For you, O LORD, have made me glad by your work;
> at the works of your hands I sing for joy. (v. 4)

JAMES MCTYRE

Exegetical Perspective

through images that suggest verdant fruitfulness. Without the skipped text, however, the power and poignancy of these images can be lost. Unlike the numerous and seemingly flourishing wicked who nevertheless are destined for destruction, the righteous "flourish" in such a way that they are secure and productive. At the beginning of the entire Psalter, Psalm 1 sets up a contrast between the righteous and wicked in which the righteous are "planted" by streams, yielding their fruit at the proper time, and the wicked disintegrate and dissolve away. Following that comparison, Psalm 92 suggests that the righteous flourish (see Prov. 11:28) and even weather the ravages of time as the fruitfulness and vitality extend even into old age. Part of this flourishing includes being firmly planted into God's house of worship, where worshipers routinely sing songs like this one that celebrate God's rule (v. 13).

While similar themes of the flourishing of the righteous and the eventual withering defeat of the wicked/enemy can be found in the wisdom tradition, most prominently in Proverbs, the overall thematic context of Psalm 92 ties this contrast to the creative and redemptive work of God. The order of creation is the fruitful thriving of the righteous, with redemption from the wicked seemingly ensuring the continuance of that order, particularly for the psalmist when threatened by enemies. In fact, the reality of this created order and the deliverance from that which threatens to undo it (the enemy) testify to the uprightness/righteousness of the Lord who "watches over the way of the righteous" while the "way of the wicked will perish" (Ps. 1:6).

God's creation of a right and just world with the concomitant redemptive work to save those who live according to God's order is solid, trustworthy, and true. God is as secure as a "rock," a theme that echoes throughout the Psalter, especially in relation to God's deliverance from enemies that threaten to undo the psalmist or creation (see esp. Pss. 28:1; 31:3; 62:7; 71:3; 95:1).

The final proclamation of the psalmist is that nothing "wicked" exists in God. God's created order is good, and where it goes astray, God works to restore it. The righteous recognize this goodness and contribute to it by offering songs of thanksgiving on the Sabbath for the God who creates, redeems, and guides them.

THOMAS W. WALKER

Homiletical Perspective

wicked. Whether this applies to righteous individuals or to a more generalized righteousness is a question worth exploring.

In any case, the promises inherent in this psalm present some significant homiletical challenges for the preacher. On the one hand, there will be the temptation to posit that justice for the righteous and the wicked will come after death, though there is nothing in the text to suggest this. On the other hand, there is the test of experience, which, on the face of things, does not always bear out the premise (or the promise) that both wicked and righteous will get their just rewards. On the surface, at least, of everyday reality, this does not seem to be true.

One solution, which will be satisfactory for some and less so for others, is to understand reward not as a consequence of an act but as a part of the act's inherent nature. It is the difference between saying, "If you do A, then you will get B," and saying, "If you are doing A, then B will already have become a reality in you." Being in sync with God's creative purposes is, indeed, its own reward; nothing else is needed.

The psalm's conclusion, in verse 15, is telling. The purpose of all of what has gone before (describing the rootlessness of the wicked and the endurance of the righteous) is to establish in the hearer's ear the righteousness of *God*, not the entitlement of righteous human beings. As in the Gospel of John, where the signs of Jesus point not only to themselves but to the power and glory of God, here the celebration of ultimate justice finds its deepest meaning not in the assurance it provides to mortals but in the acknowledgment of God's goodness.

JAMES GERTMENIAN

1 Corinthians 15:51-58

[51]Listen, I will tell you a mystery! We will not all die, but we will all be changed, [52]in a moment, in the twinkling of an eye, at the last trumpet. For the trumpet will sound, and the dead will be raised imperishable, and we will be changed. [53]For this perishable body must put on imperishability, and this mortal body must put on immortality. [54]When this perishable body puts on imperishability, and this mortal body puts on immortality, then the saying that is written will be fulfilled:

"Death has been swallowed up in victory."
[55]"Where, O death, is your victory?
Where, O death, is your sting?"

[56]The sting of death is sin, and the power of sin is the law. [57]But thanks be to God, who gives us the victory through our Lord Jesus Christ.
[58]Therefore, my beloved, be steadfast, immovable, always excelling in the work of the Lord, because you know that in the Lord your labor is not in vain.

Theological Perspective

Even though the *Left Behind* novels are consumed by millions of the devout, many people today in advanced technological societies are skeptical of apocalyptic scenarios. These novels tend to graphically depict the end times as imminent, violent, vengeful, and victorious for one faith community of true believers over all others. At the same time, both the Bible and the Qur'an include such apocalyptic symbols and stories, and they are not marginal to these Scriptures. Rather these remarkable texts are central to the plots of our holy books and full of divine promise to heal creation. Even a first-time reader of the Qur'an cannot ignore the extraordinary promise of resurrection of the dead, warnings of final divine judgment, and promises of mercy to all who believe in one God and obey the will of Allah as revealed by the prophets.

How can our faith become informed by these apocalyptic texts when we know the only certainties in this life are death, debt, and taxes? None of us has stood face to face with the risen Jesus and taken his photograph. Even Paul's conviction that Christ would return during his lifetime was falsified by history (15:51; cf. 1:7–8; 3:13–15; 4:4–5; 5:5; 7:29–31; 10:11; 1 Thess. 4:15; Rom. 13:11–12; 15:4). When we stand by the graves of our loved ones, when we remember millions of people slaughtered in

Pastoral Perspective

"Lo, I tell you a mystery!" (v. 51, RSV)

Seldom do we use the word "mystery" correctly. We use it to speak of a muddle, or a riddle, or something difficult to understand, or a point of illogic; but we seldom use the word "mystery" in its true, full-bodied sense.

Paul, however, does. A mystery is something beyond human comprehension—not just difficult to figure out, but impossible to understand. A mystery is not something that could be seen clearly with a little more light or a better lens, but something so holy, awesome, and inscrutable that, were we to turn every halogen lamp in the world on it and turn it every conceivable way under the best optics available, it would remain ultimately unknowable. In this sense, a "murder mystery" is a misnomer; it is just a story that resists an easy solution. The real mystery stories start with a creation out of nothing by a God who will not be named; climax in the coming into creation of creation's God in the form of a creature; and culminate in this incarnate God's crucifixion and resurrection from the dead. That's a mystery, and Paul knows it, which is why he says, "Lo, I tell you a mystery!"

It is appropriate to dwell upon this mystery today, when the lilies of Easter have wilted and the crowds have dispersed, and we have entered the long days

Exegetical Perspective

In much of 1 Corinthians 15, Paul outlines the central Christian belief in the resurrection of the dead. In a time of high and early mortality, both from disease and from Roman military might, it is not surprising that people were tempted to live without hope, and a belief in resurrection and eternal life faced opposition, even within an assembly of Christians founded by Paul. To such opposition, Paul provides a twofold response: first, a defense of his theology of resurrection (1 Cor. 15:1–34); second, a response to questions of the nature of the resurrected being (1 Cor. 15:35–50).

First Corinthians 15:51–58 serves as a summation of Paul's argument. The focus of his summation is contained in his opening statement: "Look, I am saying to you a mystery: we will not all sleep, but we will all be changed" (1 Cor. 15:51, my trans.). "We will not all sleep" (*pantes ou koimēthēsometha*) should be understood as a euphemism for "we will not all die," for the entirety of the chapter is concerned with matters of death and resurrection. The emphasis, however, rests neither on sleeping nor on dying, but on Paul's assertion that "we will all be changed" (v. 51). This impending change is at the heart of his resurrection theology.

The nature of the impending change, according to Paul, is that we mortals will put on immortality.

Homiletical Perspective

"When the trumpet of the Lord shall sound, and time will be no more . . ."—what then? "At the last trumpet" (v. 52), what happens to me and to those I love? What happens to "the quick and the dead"? The answer is no clearer to the average churchgoer in the twenty-first century than it was to those early churchgoers in Corinth in the first.

Disagreements within the Jewish tradition, between the Sadducees and the Pharisees, as to whether there was such a thing as resurrection at all were even more confusing for non-Jews, for whom the whole idea of "bodily resurrection" was philosophically and culturally ridiculous.

Paul wrote to Corinth, in part, to respond to the confusion there about the Hebrew hope for resurrection—a hope expressed by Martha when she said to Jesus after the death of her brother, Lazarus: "I know that he will rise again in the resurrection on the last day" (John 11:24). So before preaching Paul's *conclusion*, the preacher should consider Paul's *argument*, the whole of 1 Corinthians 15. Since the confusion in our pews is much the same as in Corinth, a sermon based on what the preacher (and the Bible!) means by "resurrection" just might help hearers clarify their belief and become more secure in their own understanding and assurance. Otherwise, Paul's declaration of victory (v. 54b), mocking of

1 Corinthians 15:51-58

Theological Perspective

genocidal conflicts and destroyed in natural disasters, the sting of death brings us to a grim sense of the brutal reality of life and death in this material world. There is no New-Age magic or technological fix that can recover the lives of millions already slaughtered over the centuries by blind nature and humankind.

So, like those Gentiles (and some Hellenized Jews) in the ancient Greco-Roman city of Corinth who came to believe in Paul's proclamation of a crucified and risen Messiah, we long for an escape from time, history, nature, and our bodies that someday will perish. We seek escape through various technologies to induce feelings of timelessness and out-of-body awareness: private methods of "spiritual" meditation, elite groups of the "spiritually" directed, or abuse of controlled substances. Or we search for the miracle diet, surgery, exercise regimen, or drug that will render our aging bodies timeless, with the sexual endurance of gods.

When we are confronted with Paul's gospel of a crucified and risen Messiah who appeared to numerous witnesses (15:1–11) but *not* as a disembodied ghost (15:44), we ask with the "someone" of 15:35: "How are the dead raised? With what kind of body do they come?" The *how* and *what kind of* questions belong to our late modern skeptical, scientific, medical age. Paul never directly answers them on our terms. His proclamation of the resurrection of Jesus' executed body and of all embodied lives is framed by ancient Jewish apocalyptic images (e.g., the "last trumpet" of 15:52) and a hopeful, extraordinary worldview that we find alien and esoteric.[1]

We go searching for answers to the *how* and *what kind of* questions in dialogues between scientists and theologians. This dialogue is necessary, creative, and revelatory. It is part of our worldview, proper to our age, and endlessly fascinating.

We also need another kind of dialogue, a dialogue that almost all Christians have avoided for most of our history.[2] This is a dialogue with Jewish history, life, and thought—with the Scriptures we call "Old," with rabbinic commentaries, with Judaism's deeply embodied way of life that refuses to escape from being creatures of the original Creator. For the ancient Israelites and living Jewish tradition, created life cannot be disembodied from God's good

Pastoral Perspective

after Pentecost. "Lo, I tell you a mystery!" Paul unfolds a tale of utter incomprehensibility, of death and resurrection, of transformation from mortal to immortality in the twinkling of an eye, of flesh that rots changing into imperishability. We are bound to confront this story where we live most of the time, without the bravado of Handel's "Hallelujah Chorus" to sustain us.

Thomas Lynch, the poet undertaker, quotes a worldly wise French philosopher, La Rochefoucauld: "Death and the sun are not to be looked at in the face."[1] Christianity does try to look death in the face, and Christianity sees only the mystery of resurrection. A major challenge we face as Christians is to get the analogy right when we speak of the resurrection. Many people think that resurrection is "like" or "analogous to" the resuscitation of a dead or apparently dead body. Thus every situation from the biblical story of Lazarus being brought back to life to the story of saving a child who has fallen through the ice in a skating accident becomes a resurrection analogy. In fact, as amazing as it is to resuscitate a dead or near-dead person and as miraculous as it was for Jesus to bring Lazarus back, these kinds of incidents do not get at the utter impossibility, the uniqueness, and the mystery of resurrection. Both Lazarus and the child will die again.

The analogy of resurrection is not resuscitation, but creation out of nothing. According to Paul, the body created out of nothing (the classical theological phrase is *creatio ex nihilo*) has continuity with the body that existed before death. So Paul plays a game of theological "Twister" for page after page with the Corinthians, and theologians ever after him have painted themselves into theo-logical corners. Finally the Nicene Creed throws up its hands and confesses simply, with eyes still smarting from looking too long into the light, "We look for the resurrection of the dead."

"Lo, I tell you a mystery!" Beyond belief, beyond the boundaries of mere possibility and impossibility, far from the shores of the conceivable, lies the realm of resurrection. That which God created out of nothing, God did not create in vain. That which God created out of nothing, God re-creates, resurrects from the dead.

Death, be not proud, though some have called thee
Mighty and dreadful, for thou art not so;
For those, whom thou think'st thou dost overthrow,

---

1. J. Christiaan Beker, *Paul the Apostle* (Philadelphia: Fortress Press, 1980). Cf. Joseph A. Fitzmyer, *First Corinthians*, Anchor Yale Bible Commentaries (New Haven, CT: Yale University Press, 2008).

2. Jon D. Levenson, *The Death and Resurrection of the Beloved Son* (New Haven, CT: Yale University Press, 1993).

1. Thomas Lynch, *The Undertaking: Life Studies from the Dismal Trade* (London: Vintage, 1998), 33.

Exegetical Perspective

This is so critical that Paul reiterates it five times in these eight short verses. Paul is convinced, as he has stated earlier in chapter 15, that "flesh and blood cannot inherit the kingdom of God, nor does the perishable inherit the imperishable" (v. 50). Thus, Christ-followers must "put on immortality" if they are to inherit an immortal kingdom. What such an immortality might look like, Paul does not venture to guess; but it will not be the same as our flesh-and-blood bodies; it will be, rather, a spiritual body (vv. 35–49).

If Paul, in telling this mystery, cannot fully depict the nature of the change, he makes its timing perfectly clear. For the change will happen "at the last trumpet." In the Hebrew Bible, the sounding of a trumpet puts the listener on alert. It can signal the advent of war and violence (Jer. 4:19), the beginning of a time of communal prayer and fasting (Joel 2:15), and the coming of a king (1 Kgs. 1:34). Often, too, the sounding of a trumpet signals the presence or the advent of God (Exod. 19:16–20; Ps. 47:5; Joel 2:1); Paul is principally referring to this kind of sounding. In referring to the "last" trumpet, he signals that such a sound will usher in the end of this age and the beginning of the age to come. This then is an eschatological mystery—a mystery about the end of our age and the beginning of the age of Christ. But in Paul's day, it must also have been understood in its military connotation, as the age of the coming of the one who would replace even the power of Rome itself, the coming of the one crucified by Rome, whom the Christians had the nerve to call Lord. Such a reversal is an important element of the mystery, for it underscores the commitment Paul had, not to the governing powers as they currently were, but to the ultimate governance of Jesus as Christ and thus as Lord.

What makes the change most significant is its impact: the defeat of the ultimate enemy, death. Paul's explication of this is so cryptic—and thanks to Handel's *Messiah* so familiar—that it is possible to miss his point. Paul's first assertion, "death is swallowed up in victory," hearkens back to the apocalyptic scene of divine restoration in Isaiah 25:6–8, in which Isaiah proclaims that God "will swallow up death forever." In quoting Isaiah, Paul even more firmly links the donning of immortality at the "last trumpet" to the fulfillment of the Isaian vision of the *yom YHWH* (Day of the Lord).

Immediately Paul shifts to the problem underlying the entire human condition: sin. This is what is being invoked in verse 55; for Paul is alluding to questions

Homiletical Perspective

defeated death (v. 55), and assurance that God gives *us* the victory (v. 57) may ring hollow or bring hurt to someone facing the death of a loved one or their own death.

The challenge, however, in dealing straight on with Paul's teaching on resurrection may be that it challenges us. It either challenges our personal belief or challenges the preacher to speak an unexpected truth to hearers for whom "resurrection" is a vague term synonymous with "life after death." Jesus was resurrected; but we die and our souls go to heaven—or so the average believer believes. As T. A. Kantonen puts it:

> Ask the ordinary churchgoer who inquires about life after death what he means by "life" and he is likely to give an answer which he thinks is self-evident to every Christian. Human life, he will say, has two parts, the life of the body and the life of the soul. The life of the body ends in death but the soul is immortal.[1]

Paul would have it differently. Yes, the life of the body ends in death; but immortality *of the body* begins in resurrection (v. 52). Paul's words spit in the face of death, and also in the face of *the grave* itself. The better translation of Paul's words is from the King James Version: "Death is swallowed up in victory. O death, where is thy sting? *O grave,* where is thy victory?" (vv. 54–55). Or, as an earthy old Easter hymn puts it: "*Low in the grave he lay,* Jesus my Savior . . . [but] Up from the grave he arose! With a mighty triumph o'er his foe; *He arose a victor from the dark domain.*" *He* arose, and so shall we! That is Paul's message.

The "victory" of God Paul proclaimed, though, is not of the spiritual over the physical, a common gnostic misunderstanding of his words "flesh and blood cannot inherit the kingdom of God" (v. 50), but over death. In becoming one with creation in the incarnation, God is renewing or re-creating creation itself. More precisely, "resurrection" is synonymous with "re-creation" rather than with immortality. "She is his new creation" is more than a phrase in "The Church's One Foundation." Paul wrote in 2 Corinthians, "If anyone is in Christ, there is *a new creation:* everything old has passed away; see, everything has become new!" (5:17).

Our euphemism for death, "to pass away," is in fact dead on. "To pass away" means "to go out of existence"—not to go "somewhere" else (or "fly

---

1. T. A. Kantonen, *Life after Death* (Philadelphia: Fortress Press, 1962), 6.

1 Corinthians 15:51-58

Theological Perspective

creation and God's generous provision of land and history in which dialogue and partnership occur. If there is any resurrection of the dead, it must include the transformation of all bodily life, in fact, the transformation of the entire cosmos. The Creator and Redeemer disclosed in ancient Israel's apocalyptic hope and in Jewish life down the ages to our time is a God who delivers her captives from oppression, is "a refuge to the poor," provides a feast for all nations, a God who "will swallow up death forever," "will wipe away the tears from all faces," and take away "the disgrace of his people" Israel (Isa. 25:1–10; cf. Isa. 25:8 and 1 Cor. 15:54b; also cf. Hos. 13:14 and 1 Cor. 15:55).

How did God raise the executed Jesus from the dead? *How* will God produce the new creation of resurrection life for the billions who have perished on earth? Though we have never measured the transformed body of the risen Jesus, we have seen the people named "Israel," the Jews, and the people called "church," the body of Christ (cf. 1 Cor. 3:16; 6:13–20; 10:17; 12:12–28). The lives and histories of these two peoples, past and present, provide adequate grounds for faith in the resurrection of the dead. The Israelite named Jesus, who appeared to his disciples as their crucified and risen Lord, now lives, moves, and has his being in the cruciform bodily life of the church in the world.

Resurrection is not a private spiritual high that I can enjoy in the security of my own privileged way of life. It is coming to live, die, and be transformed in the life of a people and a bodily world that God indwells as Creator-Provider and Redeemer. Every time we break bread and share the cup at the Lord's Table, or celebrate the baptism of an infant or adult, we participate in the pattern of life, death, and transformation that prefigures God's gift of resurrection life. The gracious God of Isaiah 25 is the power of the resurrection in 1 Corinthians 15. Since this God through the ages has sustained the people named Israel and the church, despite persecution, oppression, destruction, and temptation, Christians have reason to hope that we will come face to face with our Lord Jesus Christ and with all God's creatures in a renewed creation.

ROBERT CATHEY

Pastoral Perspective

Die not, poor Death, nor yet canst thou kill me.
. . . .
One short sleep past, we wake eternally,
And Death shall be no more; Death, thou shalt die.[2]

Auden, if anything, is even more personal than Donne when he writes:

Nothing can save us that is possible:
We who must die demand a miracle.[3]

When someone says that they cannot believe in the resurrection because it is an impossibility, contradicting logic and science, they are not far from understanding the whole point. But they need to press on. If we can believe that everything was created out of nothing, then believing that God can again create everything out of nothing is a piece of cake. Resurrection is a second, new creation, quite as inconceivable as the first. Anything more conceivable and less impossible would not be adequate. "We who must die demand a miracle." And so Paul writes, "Lo, I tell you a mystery!" "Death has been swallowed up in victory."

Perhaps we should pause, if only for a moment. While not taking away one whit from Paul's victory lap, perhaps we should note that even in God's victory over death, there is still a little sting left in the old scorpion's tail. Even a dead scorpion can still sting you. We may not feel the sting of death when we think of our own deaths, but death still stings us when we think of the death of those we love. Perhaps Paul understood this. He affirms our grief; we just do not grieve like those who have no hope. We have hope because we know that nothing entrusted to the God of creation and resurrection can be lost forever, even in death.

"Lo, I tell you a mystery!" I tell you a mystery, because nothing less will do.

MICHAEL JINKINS

---

2. John Donne, "Divine Poems, X," in *Poems of John Donne*, ed. E. K. Chambers (London: George Routledge & Sons, 1900), 1:162–63.
3. W. H. Auden, "For the Time Being," in *Collected Longer Poems* (New York: Random House, 1965), 138.

Exegetical Perspective

posed by the prophet Hosea before the conquest of Ephraim: "O Death, where are your plagues? O Sheol, where is your destruction? Compassion is hidden from my eyes" (Hos. 13:14). In Hosea, these questions are not a taunt of death's impotence, but the promise of impending death as a result of sin. If we understand this allusion, then it is easier to understand Paul's next assertion: "The sting that produces death is sin" (v. 56a, my trans.). Death's victory and sting are located, Paul asserts, in the reality of sin. Further, Paul argues—as in other places—that sin is empowered by "the law." Here the "law" may not be the Torah, as Paul argues in Romans, but rather the original Edenic law violated by Adam.[1] Thus Adam, the original law-breaker, by breaking the law empowers sin, which in turn becomes the sting that produces death: "for . . . all die in Adam" (v. 22a).

Only if one understands this sequence does Paul's reaffirmation in verse 57 of the victory that has "swallowed up" death and been given by God through Christ make any sense. For Paul's victory is not simply the resurrection of Christ; rather, it is the resurrection of the dead. The argument about eschatological resurrection is not simply a theological curiosity, but sits at the very heart of the importance of Jesus' resurrection.

For Paul's community, the consequence of this eschatological assertion should be, he argues, steadfastness in their faith and in their work. No trouble or toil is to be feared, not even the power of imperial Rome. For in the end, at the last trumpet, not even death will triumph. They will be changed to a form that death cannot touch, and given ultimate victory by God through Jesus Christ.

MARGARET P. AYMER

Homiletical Perspective

away"), but to go "nowhere" but the grave. According to Paul, all will "pass away" in the sense that "at the last trumpet . . . the dead [those who have passed away] will be raised imperishable, and we [who have not yet passed away] will be changed" (v. 52). The "old us" will pass away, as has already happened for those who have died, and all of us, who will all be "dead to sin" (Rom. 6:11), will put on immortality, a "new us." That, says Paul, is what it means to say that "God . . . gives us the victory through our Lord Jesus Christ" (v. 57).

Will it preach? If it does not, as Paul puts it earlier in his letter to Corinth, "then those also who have died in Christ have perished. If for this life only we have hoped in Christ, we are of all people most to be pitied" (1 Cor. 15:18–19). We are to be pitied because our death is not "when the soul is freed from the prison house of the body,"[2] as John Calvin said. Instead our death is as real and gruesome as the artist Grünewald depicted it. E. H. Gombrich wrote of the Isenheim altarpiece,

> Christ's dying body is distorted by the torture of the cross; the thorns of the scourges stick in the festering wounds which cover the whole figure. The dark red blood forms a glaring contrast to the sickly green of the flesh. By His features and the impressive gesture of His hands, the Man of Sorrows speaks to us of the meaning of His Calvary.[3]

In his letter to Corinth, though, Paul paints a different picture—a picture of the meaning of Jesus' resurrection for us. Death is still death, but Christ is risen! "When the trumpet of the Lord shall sound, and time will be no more, and the morning breaks eternal, bright and fair," Paul says, as the old hymn says, "I'll be there!" And so will we all, in resurrection.

RICHARD L. SHEFFIELD

---

1. Chris Alex Vlachos, "Law, Sin and Death: An Edenic Triad? An Examination with Reference to 1 Corinthians 15:56," *Journal of the Evangelical Theological Society* 47/2 (June 2004): 277–98.

2. John Calvin, *Institutes of the Christian Religion*, ed. John T. McNeill, trans. Ford Lewis Battles (Philadelphia: Westminster Press, 1977), 1.15.2.
3. E. H. Gombrich, *The Story of Art* (Oxford: Phaidon Press Ltd., 1972), 270.

Luke 6:39-49

³⁹He also told them a parable: "Can a blind person guide a blind person? Will not both fall into a pit? ⁴⁰A disciple is not above the teacher, but everyone who is fully qualified will be like the teacher. ⁴¹Why do you see the speck in your neighbor's eye, but do not notice the log in your own eye? ⁴²Or how can you say to your neighbor, 'Friend, let me take out the speck in your eye,' when you yourself do not see the log in your own eye? You hypocrite, first take the log out of your own eye, and then you will see clearly to take the speck out of your neighbor's eye.

⁴³"No good tree bears bad fruit, nor again does a bad tree bear good fruit; ⁴⁴for each tree is known by its own fruit. Figs are not gathered from thorns, nor are grapes picked from a bramble bush. ⁴⁵The good person out of the good

Theological Perspective

These verses provide the conclusion of the Sermon on the Plain, Luke's initial summary of Jesus' teaching. Their theological import can be gleaned only if related to the larger themes of that sermon. First, their ethical demands describe life in the kingdom of God (Luke 6:20). Second, Jesus addresses his teaching first to the disciples and so to the church (Luke 6:20). Third, the teachings from which these verses take their primary meaning concern love for one's enemies, readiness to forgive offenses, and refusal to make judgments about the lives of others while failing first to make a judgment about one's own life (Luke 6:27, 32, 35–37). Fourth, the ethical demands concerning forgiveness and judgment flow from the actions of God who has shown mercy to his own enemies (Luke 6:35–36; 23:34).

Luke 6:39–49 is introduced by a specific command: "Be merciful, just as your Father is merciful" (v. 36). This command puts on display the defining feature of Christian ethics, namely, the command "Love your enemies" (v. 27). The arrival of God's kingdom is marked by love seeking reconciliation. Life within the church is marked in the same way. For Luke, love that seeks reconciliation forms the very foundation upon which life in the kingdom of God is built. A failure on the part of the church to display such love will be judged, with the result that

Pastoral Perspective

The theme of these collected sayings of Jesus has to do with character, both how it is formed and how it is revealed. Individually and collectively, the teachings are relevant personally and interpersonally, within Christian communities and within the world of political discourse and decision making. The sayings are particularly apt for the Sunday that is near to the United States Memorial Day observance, when the norm for public discourse—perhaps even that of the pulpit—tends toward uncritical patriotism.

The text falls into three sections, each of which has pastoral dimensions, as does the lesson as a whole.

Verses 39–42 are concerned with blindness, especially to one's own faults and failures, resulting in self-righteous or hypocritical judgments of others. The warning is one that preachers themselves need to heed, lest their sermons become harangues about the sins of others, without any sense that they themselves share fully in human frailty, thus revealing that they are "blind guides" (v. 39).

This portion of the text suggests that a faithful life consists, not in flawlessness, but in the ability to be self-critical. The parable's teaching that our judgments can be so terribly skewed, exaggerated humor though it is, offers an important pastoral word, one that is relevant to interpersonal

treasure of the heart produces good, and the evil person out of evil treasure produces evil; for it is out of the abundance of the heart that the mouth speaks.

46"Why do you call me 'Lord, Lord,' and do not do what I tell you? 47I will show you what someone is like who comes to me, hears my words, and acts on them. 48That one is like a man building a house, who dug deeply and laid the foundation on rock; when a flood arose, the river burst against that house but could not shake it, because it had been well built. 49But the one who hears and does not act is like a man who built a house on the ground without a foundation. When the river burst against it, immediately it fell, and great was the ruin of that house."

Exegetical Perspective

This series of parables in Luke ends the Sermon on the Plain, a section that roughly parallels Matthew's Sermon on the Mount. Like Matthew, Luke starts his sermon with a list of beatitudes, but he also includes corresponding woes. This literary feature works to further the theme of social reversal begun in the opening chapters, especially in the Magnificat (1:46–55). Overall, Luke's sermon is more focused on justice for the poor and love of enemies than is Matthew's, and this fits with Luke's overall emphasis on the poor and on just relations between rich and poor.

The first cluster of sayings centers on blindness and includes the famous log/speck image that speaks directly to the self-righteous. The image is laughably hyperbolic; one cannot even imagine having a log in one's eye, not noticing it, and being audacious enough to point out a minor flaw in someone else. The image very clearly makes a laughingstock out of a person who would judge someone else when that person has clear issues with which to contend before passing judgment on another person. In a sense, however, the cluster of sayings also acts to remind the hearers of the social responsibility to point out blindness in one's neighbor. "Can a blind person lead a blind person?" Obviously not, but those who can see do have the responsibility to lead. Those who can see are obliged first to help a person who has a log in

Homiletical Perspective

Be careful, preacher. These three paragraphs offer you more than enough ammunition to blow out your whole congregation. It is too easy to attach names of folks you deal with regularly to the description of the person with the log in the eye, the bad tree that bears bad fruit, or the foolish builder. Preachers are well advised not to go for this easy, superficial application. The cheap shot should not be in the preacher's arsenal. Ezekiel 13, which includes (vv. 10–15) an earlier version of the story of the flood destroying the work of mortals (in this case, prophets), begins with a warning that only those prophets who have gone "into the breaches or repaired a wall for the house of Israel" (Exek. 13:5) have the right to speak the prophetic word to the people.[1]

The preacher must first hear these words of Jesus for himself or herself and only then attempt to preach them to others. Begin by hearing the words of Jesus for yourself. Read them aloud or listen to them read by somebody else. Do not hurry. Let the warnings sink in. Are you the blind guide? Do you sometimes put yourself above your teacher? Might you even learn something from the people you preach to? Do you find it easier to see the speck in

1. See the sermon "On Being a Prophet" by Elizabeth Achtemeier, in her *The Old Testament and the Proclamation of the Gospel* (Philadelphia: Westminster Press, 1973), 189–97.

Luke 6:39-49

Theological Perspective

the house intended to be God's house will fall, and, as Luke says, "the ruin of that house" will be "great" (Luke 6:49c).

For this reason, the members of the church are to take care that they are not led astray by teachers who do not understand that love and forgiveness are the basic markers of what Dietrich Bonhoeffer termed "life together" (vv. 39–40). Luke here provides his readers with a means of testing the leadership of the church. To what extent are these leaders fully taught? To what extent do their lives mirror the life of their teacher, Christ? Church order is not often discussed as a theological theme, but this passage from Luke clearly makes it so. If God is defined by love and mercy, and if the common life of the church is similarly defined, so also is the church's leadership.

The centrality of love and mercy to the life of both God and the church provokes the next question addressed by this passage. What stands in the way of showing love and mercy, particularly toward one's enemies within the fellowship of the church? By using the term "brother" (NRSV "neighbor") for the one to which correction is offered, Luke clearly has in mind disputes that arise between fellow believers (v. 42; cf. Matt. 18:15–20). What stands in the way of those disputes being settled? Quite simply, a focus on the fault of another that blinds a person to his or her own shortcomings! At a more profound level, the blindness comes from a failure to realize that God is judge of both you and the other person (v. 37) and that your condemnation of others will issue in your own condemnation before the judgment seat of God. At a more proximate level, a focus on the minor faults of others (the speck in your brother's or sister's eye) will blind you to the fact that you yourself have major faults (the log in your own eye). In addition to self-righteousness, the major fault is apt to be a failure to love and show mercy.

Deeply imbedded in this passage is the issue of how peace and order are to be maintained within the body of the church. Its message seems to be that the detection and correction of faults is possible only if there is within both the body and its leadership a profound sense of their own failings before God. Only then will it be possible to see clearly the faults that may plague the lives of other individuals and the common life of the church. One might say in summary that spiritual discernment grows out of the soil of profound humility before the clear-sighted eye of God.

A community of people in which the members habitually focus on their own vices and their own

Pastoral Perspective

relationships of all kinds—within marriages and families, among colleagues at work or school, and within congregations where accusations of faithlessness over issues of belief or practice have become all too common. The warning of the parable is especially apt when it comes to our national life, where, Reinhold Niebuhr observed, "nations will always find it more difficult than individuals to behold the beam that is in their own eye while they observe the mote that is in their brother's eye."[1] In the years since 9/11, both political leaders and ordinary citizens within the United States have been quick to condemn other nations, sometimes consigning them to an "axis of evil," without any recognition that our nation's own behavior may have contributed to the world's unfortunate condition.

The second (vv. 43–45) and third (vv. 46–49) portions of the lesson, each in its own way, encourage ministries from which come people of good character. Verses 43–45 in particular suggest that prior to the question, "What will I say, or what will I do?" is the question, "Who will I be?"

There are two points at which the preacher may want to argue a bit with the text. In the instance of the good tree/bad tree analogy, one may well ask if it is quite as simple as the saying seems to suggest. While good trees may produce only good fruit, even a very good human life will produce some bad fruit. The saying needs to be qualified by the acknowledgment that "no one is good but God alone" (Mark 10:18).

Verse 45 suggests that character is formed from the inside out. Well and good. But what is not accounted for, and needs to be, is the effect that practice has on the formation of character— something that *is* acknowledged in the last portion of the text, where the good person is one who not only hears the words of Jesus but does them. Christian practices not only are the consequence of character, but also help to form it. Those who practice generosity—whether in sharing possessions, welcoming strangers, offering forgiveness, or caring for "the least of these" (Matt. 25:40, 45)—will as a consequence likely become more generous persons.

In the verses making up the third portion of the text, the vision of both the faithful life and the life of the Christian community emphasizes the importance of not only hearing, but heeding the teaching of Jesus—of right behavior, not merely right belief. Those who hear *and* obey are the ones

1. Reinhold Niebuhr, *Moral Man and Immoral Society* (New York: Charles Scribner's Sons, 1932), 107.

his or her eye to see it, and then to help him or her remove it. How else would someone with a blind spot so large be able to see it and to remove it?

The second cluster of sayings flows from the first in the sense that the first has something to do with the need to look inside before passing judgment. The second cluster focuses on the inner disposition of a person and the interrelationship between the inner person (the heart) and the outer person (the actions). Luke focuses his attention on the heart of a person as the necessary foundation of proper action and speech. In ancient Mediterranean culture, the heart is not the seat of feelings, as it is in modern Western culture, but the seat of decision making, the place where reason and emotion meet. In that sense, it is the place where judgments and choices are made and from which proper action flows, similar to the way that ancient Stoics conceived of the ethical life as dependent upon proper formation of judgment or choice (*prohairesis*), which results in proper action and happiness (*eudaimonia*). Luke says that the good is produced from the good treasure of the heart. There is no insinuation that one is born with this treasure intact; rather, the implication is that the treasure needs to be gathered, collected, or formed. So there is the possibility of change. Stoics claimed something similar, that one becomes ethical by being properly educated and formed to make good decisions. The implication in Luke's saying is that one can be formed into a person that produces good things (speech, action, fruit).

The final cluster of sayings addresses the formative aspect of the person in the sense that Luke has Jesus tell a parable that gives some sense of how one is formed properly in order to produce the good, at least from Luke's perspective. The person who wants to be formed well should come to Jesus, hear his words, and act on them. This process forms a foundation from which the good life can be lived in a secure and stable way. Again, like Stoicism, where the proper and ongoing formation of one's opinions and judgments results in living according to God (which for Stoics is sometimes expressed as Nature), Luke envisions that the person who seeks after Jesus, listens to his words, and acts on them is properly formed and living according to God's ways. This results in the ability to withstand the storms of life without crumbling. It gives the individual the stability to live properly—at least in Luke's vision of what is proper—in the midst of strong contrary forces.

These parables, and the whole of the Sermon on the Plain, all have a strong social dimension; they are

another's eye than the log in your own? None of us likes to look deep into our own hearts, but of all people the preacher should practice the discipline of introspection regularly, so as to be aware of tendencies that produce bad fruit. If the foundations of our lives are not deep and strong, we will not be much continuing help to others, especially in storms. Furthermore, if we expect our congregations to hear such convicting words, we had better first hear them addressed to us.

If a preacher wants to tie this text together with the Gospel text for Trinity Sunday, the concept of truth would be a good connecting point. Truth in the Johannine literature includes what we now call integrity, that is, the correspondence between words and actions, between orthodoxy and orthopraxy. So this Lukan emphasis on integrity goes nicely with John's use of truth that comes from the internal unity of the Divine.

Perhaps by this time we have discovered the unifying issue in these paragraphs. The primary hint is in verses 37–38, where condemning attitudes are explicitly ruled out for the Jesus-follower. The preacher should then decide what direction the congregation most needs to go in reference to condemnation or judgmental attitudes. Does this touch on an internal problem in the congregation? Are there people condemning or judging fellow members of the body? Usually this happens in subtle ways. In the South, they say that one can condemn anybody if one begins with the words, "Bless his (or her) heart." One congregation I know overcame this debilitating tendency by declaring a Month of the Compliment. The members of this small congregation were challenged to give each person they saw on Sunday mornings a compliment. Just the practice of speaking positively to one another broke a chain of destructive criticism. However, problems of judgmentalism within the congregation are not the only possible application of these words.

Perhaps the congregation needs to hear a broader application. Perhaps we are too apt to fall into a sectarianism that almost instinctively condemns to hell people in different faith traditions. The refusal to do any cooperative serving with "those people" will isolate a congregation and do irreparable harm to the reputation of believers in the community. Too often this attitude becomes attached to partisan political distinctions. The terms *liberal* and *conservative* appear at least as often in the political arena as in theological circles. Racial or ethnic assumptions can also be damaging to the

Luke 6:39-49

Theological Perspective

flawed relations with both God and their neighbor would indeed be unusual. It would, however, be characteristic of life in Christ. The next theological theme that appears in this passage addresses the source of such an unusual form of personal and communal life. The source can only be internal. It can neither be imposed from without nor feigned from within. Only a good tree produces good fruit (v. 45).

How then is one to become the good person who from the good treasure of his or her heart produces good? The answer, Luke suggests, is to become cognizant of the mercy of God. Mercy received, he insists, asks for mercy to be shown (v. 36). Here the life of God is seen as a wellspring of goodness that flows through the life of those who follow God's Son and who seek to become like him (v. 40).

The basic questions of ethics concern what is good and right. Good is defined in this passage as love and mercy—qualities internal to the person. Where these are present, one knows that the person is good. Where they are not present, one has reason to suspect that one is facing evil (v. 45). Further, where these are not present in the individual and the church, Luke is clear that judgment follows. Thus our passage begins by stressing the centrality of love and mercy and concludes with a warning about the judgment that comes to those who call Christ Lord but do not do what he tells them. The passage ends, therefore, by asking us to contemplate the relation between divine love and mercy on the one hand and divine judgment on the other.

PHILIP TURNER

Pastoral Perspective

prepared to withstand the storms of life, while those who hear but do not heed are ill equipped to withstand the storms of life.

The preacher can help worshipers recognize that storms come in an almost infinite variety: personal storms in the form of sudden death, divorce, unemployment; economic storms in the form of recessions or runaway inflation; storms that come to entire nations as acts of terror or war. The storms come. They are part of life and take no account of whether one is good or evil, whether one is a committed Christian or a dedicated atheist. The rain falls on the righteous and the unrighteous (Matt. 5:45). Storms do not pick and choose among good and evil people; but, according to the text, they inevitably reveal the character of those to whom they come.

These verses provide opportunity for considering how the practice of worship relates to character formation. In worship, Christians regularly confess their own sins, acknowledge their own faults and failures, and are reminded therefore that their own eyes are not free of debris. In worship, the people of God encounter the prophets with their demands for justice and righteousness, listen to Jesus, and learn from the example of his life. In worship, hymns, prayers, and sermons do their work of Christian formation Sunday after Sunday after Sunday.

A powerful example of how the practice of worship helps to create people of courageous Christian character, whose trees produce good fruit and whose houses withstand terrifying storms, may be found in Philip Hallie's book *Lest Innocent Blood Be Shed*.[2] It is the story of how the people of the French village of Le Chambon, at great risk to themselves, shielded Jewish neighbors from the Nazi Holocaust. Their character was largely formed, Hallie believes, by their gathering, week after week, in the little church where they heard the Scriptures read, said their prayers, sang hymns, and, most importantly, listened to the preaching of Pastor Trocmé. The Christians of Le Chambon did what they did, Hallie concluded, because of who they were, and who they were was formed largely by their practice of worship.

EUGENE C. BAY

---

2. Philip Hallie, *Lest Innocent Blood Be Shed* (New York: Harper & Row, 1979).

Exegetical Perspective

not about the individual life, as understood in the modern, Cartesian sense of the introspective, "I think, therefore I am" person. Ancient individuals formed their identities in relationship to the social realms within which they existed more than modern individuals do. So, one was not Jesus, but Jesus of Nazareth, or not Simon, but Simon son of Jonah. Luke's parables here are at the heart of Jesus' teaching to the disciples about who is important and about the proper way to treat others, especially those who are traditionally low in status and most vulnerable. This fits very well with Israel's teachings of justice, which were much more about proper relationship with God and neighbor than about being individually virtuous. Central to a Jewish understanding of justice is care for the widow, the orphan, the stranger in the land, and the poor. These are all core relational values that Luke promotes in his Gospel by portraying Jesus as interacting with these people in just ways and teaching others to do the same through parables and other more direct teachings. This concern continues in the Acts of the Apostles in various ways, two examples of which are the sharing of goods among the early followers of Jesus (Acts 2:44–45; 4:32–35) and the creation of a group of people responsible for caring for the widows (6:1–6). So the parables at hand do not simply end the Sermon on the Plain; they conclude it, meaning that they capture and sum up the whole of the sermon that began with the beatitude, "Blessed are you who are poor, for yours is the kingdom of God" (6:20).

STEPHEN P. AHEARNE-KROLL

Homiletical Perspective

larger fellowship of believers. It will take more than a sermon or two to root out these attitudes of judgment, but a well-timed sermon, followed by opportunities for people to actually meet across such barriers, can go far toward healing the sickness of division. Loving the neighbor is not the only command of Jesus to which we tend to give lip service with little or no real acting, but it is not a bad place to start laying a firm foundation for the Christian life.

Perhaps this congregation needs to be reminded of the importance of simple integrity. Every conscientious Jesus-follower becomes aware all too often of failing to live out what we profess to believe. For this use of the text, it is important to recognize that there is a positive side of each of the challenges: "First take the log out of your own eye, and then you will see clearly to take the speck out of your neighbor's eye" (v. 42); "The good person out of the good treasure of the heart produces good" (v. 45); "I will show you what someone is like who comes to me, hears my words, and acts on them. That one is like a man building a house, who dug deeply and laid the foundation on rock; when a flood arose, the river burst against that house but could not shake it, because it had been well built" (vv. 47–48). Now we see that integrity is possible for the one who hears and acts on the words of Christ. It is important for the preacher not only to point out the faults of hearers, but also to point them to the power that will enable them to correct the faults and live a life that will glorify God.

So point out the faults of your hearers, if you must; but always do it with a tear, and always accompany it with a pointer to the divine power available to believers to help us do better.

BRUCE E. SHIELDS

1 Kings 18:20-21 (22-29), 30-39

²⁰So Ahab sent to all the Israelites, and assembled the prophets at Mount Carmel. ²¹Elijah then came near to all the people, and said, "How long will you go limping with two different opinions? If the LORD is God, follow him; but if Baal, then follow him." The people did not answer him a word. ²²Then Elijah said to the people, "I, even I only, am left a prophet of the LORD; but Baal's prophets number four hundred fifty. ²³Let two bulls be given to us; let them choose one bull for themselves, cut it in pieces, and lay it on the wood, but put no fire to it; I will prepare the other bull and lay it on the wood, but put no fire to it. ²⁴Then you call on the name of your god and I will call on the name of the LORD; the god who answers by fire is indeed God." All the people answered, "Well spoken!" ²⁵Then Elijah said to the prophets of Baal, "Choose for yourselves one bull and prepare it first, for you are many; then call on the name of your god, but put no fire to it." ²⁶So they took the bull that was given them, prepared it, and called on the name of Baal from morning until noon, crying, "O Baal, answer us!" But there was no voice, and no answer. They limped about the altar that they had made. ²⁷At noon Elijah mocked them, saying, "Cry aloud! Surely he is a god; either he is meditating, or he has wandered away, or he is on a journey, or perhaps he is asleep and must be awakened." ²⁸Then they cried aloud and, as was their custom, they cut themselves with swords and lances until the blood gushed

Theological Perspective

The vivid story of the contest between Elijah and the prophets of Baal offers a scathing indictment of idolatry that is relevant in every age. This razor-sharp satire dramatizes the uselessness of false religion and underscores the truth that Israel's God alone can work wonders. False gods are shown to be powerless and worthy of mockery, and the worship of false gods leads to the ruination of their devotees. Some contemporary readers may find inspiring the uncompromising rejection of idolatry here. Others may balk at the butchering of the prophets of Baal, a narrative development in line with the ruthless treatment of apostates and foreigners generally endorsed by the Deuteronomistic History.

However we read this story, it underscores the life-and-death stakes involved in cultural disputes over how to understand the Holy. Here we find both encouragement and admonition, directed not to outsiders (who would not have been listening to Israel's prophets or reading Israel's sacred literature in any case) but to those within the believing congregation. The encouragement: believers are not to despair when they experience God as hidden or absent; they are to trust that God will answer prayer. Beneath the encouragement is an unmistakable warning to those faithful who might have been

Pastoral Perspective

In front of the main chapel on the campus of Seattle University, there is a large pool and in the pool, a large rock. On that rock, pieces of wood that will serve for the "new fire" for the Easter Vigil are placed and lit.

In the dark, the water and rock blend as the fire soars, ever brighter. To the eyes of those who come to celebrate this liturgical "night of nights" for many Christians, the fire is a miraculous sight, its brilliant light duplicated on the water below. The people gathered in the night have long waited for this fire, which kindles their delight: the long dark winter will give way to the dawn of a new day.

Fire from out the water. Or so it seems.

The image echoes a saying from a fourth-century baptismal sermon of Gregory of Nyssa. Speaking about Elijah and the worshipers of Baal, Gregory said:

For he [Elijah] did not simply by prayer
bring down the fire from heaven
upon the wood when it was dry,
but exhorted and enjoined the attendants
to bring abundant water.

And when he had thrice poured out
the barrels upon the cleft wood,

out over them. ^{29}As midday passed, they raved on until the time of the offering of the oblation, but there was no voice, no answer, and no response.

^{30}Then Elijah said to all the people, "Come closer to me"; and all the people came closer to him. First he repaired the altar of the LORD that had been thrown down; ^{31}Elijah took twelve stones, according to the number of the tribes of the sons of Jacob, to whom the word of the LORD came, saying, "Israel shall be your name"; ^{32}with the stones he built an altar in the name of the LORD. Then he made a trench around the altar, large enough to contain two measures of seed. ^{33}Next he put the wood in order, cut the bull in pieces, and laid it on the wood. He said, "Fill four jars with water and pour it on the burnt offering and on the wood." ^{34}Then he said, "Do it a second time"; and they did it a second time. Again he said, "Do it a third time"; and they did it a third time, ^{35}so that the water ran all around the altar, and filled the trench also with water.

^{36}At the time of the offering of the oblation, the prophet Elijah came near and said, "O LORD, God of Abraham, Isaac, and Israel, let it be known this day that you are God in Israel, that I am your servant, and that I have done all these things at your bidding. ^{37}Answer me, O LORD, answer me, so that this people may know that you, O LORD, are God, and that you have turned their hearts back." ^{38}Then the fire of the LORD fell and consumed the burnt offering, the wood, the stones, and the dust, and even licked up the water that was in the trench. ^{39}When all the people saw it, they fell on their faces and said, "The LORD indeed is God; the LORD indeed is God."

Exegetical Perspective

Ahab, son of Omri, ruled over the northern kingdom of Israel from around 869 to 850 BCE. He is described in 1 Kings as more evil than all of his predecessors (1 Kgs. 16:30–33). He married Jezebel, daughter of King Ethbaal of Sidon, and under her influence introduced the worship of Baal into Israel. Baal was the Canaanite agricultural god, the giver of the rain that ensured the growth of crops.

Elijah the Tishbite was a prophet of YHWH, the God of Israel. The stories of his opposition to Ahab are told in 1 Kings 17–19 and 21. Today's Old Testament reading, as well as the following Sunday's text, are part of an extended story cycle concerning a drought in Israel. In 1 Kings 17:1, Elijah announced to Ahab the beginning of a drought, which would last for three years (17:1; 18:1). This drought was YHWH's judgment on Ahab and pointedly challenged the power and authority of Baal. Chapter 17 contains stories of how YHWH enabled Elijah to survive the drought and, in the process, provided deliverance for the widow of Zarephath and her son. Chapter 18 begins (vv. 1–19) with accounts of Ahab's response to the drought (seeking grass for his animals and searching high and low for Elijah) and Elijah's meeting with Ahab after three years of drought. The chapter ends with the coming of rain

Homiletical Perspective

In a time when it is imperative that people of different faiths respect each other rather than denigrate each other, how is the preacher to handle the story of Elijah and the prophets of Baal? How is the preacher to handle this text in which the themes "our prophet is better than your prophet," "our faith is better than your faith," and "our God is better than your God" seem to be the points of the story? In a diverse and pluralistic context, does this rather exclusive tale express any good news?

These questions make it clear that this text must be approached with humility and caution. These questions remind the preacher that our violence-plagued world certainly does not need people doing harm to each other because they feel their God is superior or because they feel their God has been offended.

In the city in which I live, a newspaper editor was murdered last week. The nineteen-year-old male who was arrested for the crime apparently was trying to prevent the editor from doing any further research into a religious group the young man was a part of, a religious group that may have been making money through fraud, conspiracy, and extortion. The young man told the police that he was a "good soldier."

1 Kings 18:20-21 (22-29), 30-39

Theological Perspective

tempted to practice syncretistic religion, that is, to hedge their bets by worshiping the Divine in multiple cultural manifestations. The warning: apostasy results in death.

Elijah's extravagant soaking of the altar with water underscores the thirst of YHWH's followers—both their literal thirst in that third year of drought and their spiritual thirst for a sign from their God. Beneath the surface of this narrative throbs the terrible fear of being abandoned by God. If the God of Israel cannot be shown to be active on behalf of the community of faith, then loyal believers will be left as victims of both drought and political powerlessness. The mighty Elijah appears here not simply as a prophet calling on his God, but as a figure of political dissent. He publicly shames the prophets whose role is to confirm the authority of King Ahab and Queen Jezebel. Under those two rulers, Israelite religious practice included the worship of the Phoenician god Baal-Shamem and the Canaanite goddess Asherah. Political alliances led to the syncretistic blending of ritual traditions, the intermarrying of Israelites with other ethnic populations, and ultimately—in the Deuteronomistic view—the pollution of God's holy people, whose spiritual mandate since Sinai had been to refrain from becoming like the nations all around them. Elijah's victory in the contest underscores the political impotence of Baal and, by extension, Baal's supporters. Thus this is a story of resistance: the prophet urges believers not to capitulate to cultural pressures that threaten to deform their identity as a covenant people set apart.

Augustine knew that our hearts are restless until they find their rest in God. Inevitably, idolatry lures believers. Our tendency to cling to sources of security that are not God leaves us looking by turns ridiculous and pathetic—the biting irony of the Elijah story requires candor about this. We frantically dance to appease powers that are not real; we try to ensure prosperity through things that cannot respond to us; we look for hope in things that cannot truly transform our lives. When we fail to recognize God as the source of our rest and our peace, we live our lives chaotically, on the edge of desperation. Seeking the Holy in profane places, we go limping through life with two different opinions (v. 21), as risible as the hopping prophets of Baal. Our idols may appear in various garbs, depending on the values and mores of our social contexts. A believer living in a gated suburban subdivision may be seduced by the blandishments of a materialist

Pastoral Perspective

he kindled at this prayer
the fire from out the water.[1]

In this reading we are faced with the contest between the worshipers of Israel's God and the prophets of Baal, god of the storms, nicknamed "the rider of the clouds," one of the many ironies in the story, for water was the problem: not enough of it in the land. The very name "Baal" conveys a sense of power: the "weather God," on whom agrarian peoples depended. Furthermore, Baal worshipers had the support of the politically powerful. Ahab and Jezebel had already sent some religious leaders running for their lives. There was more at stake here than a decision about which God to worship: life and death were in question. This event opens the door for preaching with an eye to the powerless among us and to those whose faith falters under life's burdens.

The scene is full of symbolic imagery: Elijah has the altar built of twelve stones, twelve jars of water poured in three batches, four jars each time, symbolic and meaningful numbers and actions. Like us, the people of Israel needed to remember who and whose they were in their helplessness.

Pouring water on the altar when praying for fire sounded incongruous, wasteful at best. The people knew that water and fire are opposing forces, one annihilating the other. Surprisingly, for God, unlike Baal, fire does come down. Eyesight here becomes great insight: Elijah's long night of powerlessness and despair is conquered by the fiery light of God. The fire reminds the people that evil will be conquered and that this God—unlike Baal—meets humans in the mountain of their distress, against powerful forces, in unexpected ways. Elijah could have sung today's psalm: "The LORD [is] greatly to be praised, he is to be feared above all gods" (96:4 RSV).

For Elijah and onlookers at Carmel, for Gregory in the fourth century, for those who gather in a dark Seattle night, and for all eager to hear good news, the story is the same: God is merciful and powerful enough to conquer evil and to redeem hopelessness. Today's readings reveal that Elijah (first reading), Paul (Epistle), and the slave and his master (Gospel) experienced the power and mercy of God in equal measure. Light in the night of human despair.

The Hebrew Scripture readings for today and the next four Sundays immerse us in the fears and the

---

1. "A Sermon for the Day of the Lights," in *Select Writings and Letters of Gregory, Bishop of Nyssa*, trans. William Moore, vol. 5, *Nicene and Post-Nicene Fathers*, 2nd printing (Peabody: Hendrickson, 1995), 522. "The Day of the Lights" refers to the Eastern church's name for the Sunday of the Baptism of the Lord.

Exegetical Perspective

to break the drought (18:41–46). Chapter 19 concludes this cycle with the story of Elijah's flight to Horeb to escape the wrath of Jezebel.

First Kings 18:20–39 is the center and the climax of the drought stories—a public contest between Elijah and the prophets of Baal, ultimately between YHWH and Baal. After three years without rain, Elijah told Ahab to assemble the people of Israel on Carmel, along with the prophets of Baal (1 Kgs. 18:17–19). The characters in the narrative are Elijah (and YHWH), the 450 prophets of Baal (and Baal?), and the people of Israel. The action of the narrative centers on Elijah and the prophets of Baal—and their respective gods. However, the most significant human characters are the people of Israel, who are called to witness the contest between the prophets and their gods and to make a decision about whom to worship—YHWH or Baal.

The structure of the narrative is as follows: Verses 20–24 describe the preparations for the contest. The people of Israel and the prophets of Baal were assembled by Ahab at Carmel (v. 20). Elijah addressed the people in v. 21, asking, "How long will you go limping with two different opinions?" Hedging their theological bets by serving *both* YHWH and Baal was unacceptable. They must choose whether to follow YHWH or Baal. Failure to choose between the two was, by default, a decision again serving YHWH. The people, however, did not answer. Then Elijah explained how the contest would work (vv. 22–24). He and the prophets of Baal would each prepare a bull for sacrifice on an altar and call upon their god. Whoever answered by fire, Baal or YHWH, was the true God.

The contest itself is described in vv. 25–38. First, the prophets of Baal prepared their sacrifice and called upon Baal (vv. 25–29). The preparations are described minimally in verse 26a. The bulk of the narrative details their efforts to call upon Baal (vv. 26b–29a). From morning until mid-afternoon (the time of the offering of oblation), they paraded around the altar, crying out to Baal and cutting themselves until they are covered with blood. Despite their persistent efforts, there was "no voice, no answer, and no response" (v. 29b).

Then it was Elijah's turn (vv. 30–38). The majority of this narrative focuses on Elijah's preparation of the offering (vv. 30–35). He built an altar with twelve stones (representing the twelve tribes of Israel), dug a trench around the altar, prepared the wood and the bull for the sacrifice, and then poured four jars of water over the offering and

Homiletical Perspective

In sorrow over the murder, in sorrow over the actions of the young man, in sorrow over the fact that he claimed religious motivation for his crime I wrote these words:

> It is imperative that every congregation and faith-based organization in our city rethink the way we use terms like soldier, warrior, army, conquer and battle. These militaristic terms are not helpful in conveying the need for our people to be peace-makers. They have proved to be subject to misuse in our murder-plagued streets. We need students of God, followers of God, and seekers of God. We can do without more soldiers of God.

I fear that the story of Elijah's confrontation with the prophet of Baal might motivate some young person to say, "I want to be strong like Elijah. I want to be brave like Elijah. I want to be faithful like Elijah. I want to be forceful like Elijah. I will defeat God's enemies the way Elijah defeated God's enemies. I will be a good soldier of God." Are my fears misplaced?

This story of Elijah and the prophets of Baal ends with the people confessing, "The LORD indeed is God; the LORD indeed is God" (v. 39). These words of fidelity, love, and passion are a fitting climax to a captivating competition. These words of commitment to God are fitting expressions of worship. These words are fitting articulation of our deeply held conviction that there is, in the end, one God.

It matters how we arrive at these words. It matters how we tell the stories from which they rise. It matters how we understand them. It matters how we use them. It can be a matter of life and death.

In handling this story, it is best to let it raise questions in our minds rather than attitudes of superiority in our hearts. The story begins with Elijah demanding of the people, "If the LORD is God, follow him; but if Baal, then follow him" (v. 21). Most readers of this text would respond, "We want to follow God. We want to follow God completely. We want to follow God only. But in our world there are so many voices claiming to be God's voice, so many ways claiming to be God's way, so many communities claiming to be God's people. It is hard. It is confusing. How do we distinguish between the things of Baal and the things of God?" On the road to confessing, "The LORD indeed is God," much discernment needs to go on. Christians in the early twenty-first century need to be identified by the amount of attention paid to discernment, rather than by their volume in proclaiming they have delineated that which is God and God alone.

1 Kings 18:20-21 (22-29), 30-39

Theological Perspective

culture that fosters addiction to high-end possessions. A believer living in a turbulent inner-city neighborhood may be tempted to seek security in a kind of gang solidarity that uses violence to reinforce group norms. But however we clothe our idols, they cannot save. We hear in the story of Elijah's victory a thunderous exhortation to seek peace and flourishing only in the one true God.

This story amplifies a theme that runs through Scripture: that God's purposes are furthered through the prophetic mediation of divine intervention in human life. Because false prophets are ever at hand to lead the people astray (e.g., Deut. 18:15–22; Jer. 28), discernment is essential if the believing community is to understand God's purposes aright. Is God among us or not? the Israelites asked in the wilderness (Exod. 17:7). Elijah shows us that God is indeed among God's people and will act. We are still a community in diaspora, and we need trustworthy prophetic voices. We need voices that can sound through the incessant clamor of consumerism, the self-indulgent murmurings of social narcissism, and the bitter divisiveness of contemporary politics, calling us away from our idols and back to the Holy One. Droughts of many kinds parch our cultural landscape. We are thirsty indeed for a God whose word can once again water the earth (Isa. 55:10–11) and bring forth fruitfulness in believers for the sake of the world.

Does God put God to the test? Yes, and with notable success. So this story may be seen to stand in tension with Jesus' admonition not to test God (Matt. 4:7//Luke 4:12, drawing on Deut. 6:16). Yet Elijah's prophetic contest and Jesus' endurance through temptation are not so different after all; the point is that trust in God, and God alone, will sustain the faithful. Elijah demonstrates decisively in the public arena that God answers the prayer of faithful intermediaries, a point that might well spur us to renewed intercessory efforts in our own prayer lives. More important, Elijah's decisive routing of the prophets of Baal clears the field in our theological imaginations, preparing us to understand with renewed clarity the promise of Jesus: "Trust in me, and you will not thirst" (John 6:35).

CAROLYN J. SHARP

Pastoral Perspective

faith of Elijah. With him we experience life and death, rebirth, wonder, and mystery. We are moved by God's favor toward the widow, the poor, the oppressed, and the hopeless. These texts follow Pentecost and Trinity, festival days when the church speaks and reenacts the manifestation of God as the fiery Spirit. Many Christians wear red to church on Pentecost; images of flames, symbols of the Spirit, hover about our worship places. Pentecost, for many churches, appropriately includes the sacrament of baptism. In baptism we reject evil and its power and confess Jesus as Lord. The coming of the Spirit is the birth of the church, and baptism is our birth into the church. We are baptized in the name of the Trinity. The wonder is that this is a gift of the Spirit given at our baptism.

Fire from out the water, or so it seems!
For at the font we pray:

Pour out your Spirit upon us and upon this
     water. . . .
May *all* who now pass through these waters
be delivered from death to life. . . .
Strengthen *them* to serve you with joy
until the day you make all things new.[2]
                              (Italics: name/s of baptized)

Elijah's story here serves as metaphor: our baptismal story moves us, the church, and the world from despair to joy, from darkness to light, and from death to life. God makes all things new to Elijah, to Gregory, to the people in a Seattle night, and to us. So, in the dark night of the soul, we remember our baptism and sing this hymn of the church:

Come down, O Love divine,
seek out this soul of mine
and visit it with Your own ardor glowing;
O Comforter, draw near;
within my heart appear
and kindle it, Your holy flame bestowing.[3]

We can say: remember your baptism, church, and give thanks; for at the prayer at your baptism, God kindled the fire. Old Gregory was right.

Fire from out the water.
So it *is!*

GLÁUCIA VASCONCELOS WILKEY

---

2. *Book of Common Worship* (Louisville, KY: Westminster/John Knox Press, 1993), 412.
3. Bianco da Siena (d. 1434); trans. R. F. Littledale, alt. In *The Presbyterian Hymnal* (Louisville, KY: Westminster/John Knox Press, 1990), 313.

Exegetical Perspective

wood—not once but three times, until the trench was full of water. He then offered a two-sentence prayer to YHWH (vv. 36–37). Following Elijah's prayer, fire consumed everything (v. 38).

The people's response to what they have witnessed is given in verse 39. They fell down to worship and confessed, "The LORD [YHWH] indeed is God; the LORD [YHWH] indeed is God."

The lectionary places verses 22–29 in parentheses, indicating that these verses are an optional part of the reading. Although omitting these verses does not affect the theological emphasis of the narrative (presented in vv. 21 and 39), the narrative structure and drama of the text are lost if they are not read. Verses 22–24 provide the setup for the contest, as well as the significance of its outcome: "the god who answers by fire is indeed God" (v. 24b; cf. the people's response in v. 39). Verses 25–29 describe the effort of the prophets of Baal, which is in dramatic contrast to that of Elijah (vv. 30–38), and which concludes with no answer from Baal (v. 29)—echoing the initial silence of the people of Israel in verse 21.

The theological question of this text, and indeed of the entire cycle of drought stories, is, Who is God—YHWH or Baal? Elijah told the people of Israel in verse 21 that a choice, a decision, must be made. To that point, Ahab and the people of Israel had refused to make a choice. They preferred to worship both YHWH and Baal, in hopes of receiving the blessings of both; but the claim of Scripture, of both the Jewish and Christian faith, is that YHWH alone is God. There are no other gods—only idols, without power, authority, or the ability to bless.

Even today we are tempted to give our loyalty, commitment, and worship to idols, alongside God. We may not acknowledge our behavior as worship, but when things such as financial security, self-gratification, or even family take priority in our lives over obedience and service to God, they indeed become idols—and we worship them.

MARSHA M. WILFONG

Homiletical Perspective

As the story progresses, Elijah prods the prophets of Baal to do more to get their God's attention. In response, "they cried aloud and, as was their custom, they cut themselves with swords and lances until the blood gushed out over them" (v. 28). We recoil from this imagery but we do well to ask, "What do we think we have to do to get attention, to get God's attention? Are there destructive practices we engage in, thinking they will cause God to look in our direction, to respond favorably to us?" Most preachers will need to look no further than the badge of honor that they wear—a badge of honor bearing the inscription "I am so busy"—to begin to answer this question.

In his closing plea to God, Elijah asks God to act so that the people will know "that you have turned their hearts back" (v. 37). This plea is an invitation to consider our belief, our trust, that God indeed is at work to turn our hearts to good, to love, to God. In our heads and in our hearts, do we believe that God is at work in this way, or do we believe that God got tired of us some time back? We may answer this question one way with our mouths but another in our outlook, actions, and attitude.

Elijah may be brash and arrogant; he may see the world in ways that we cannot. Nevertheless, at the very least we must admit that he is in a lively conversation with God, a conversation he believes it is our role, and God's will, to continue. We can continue that conversation with our affirmations and with our questions. We appreciate Elijah's model in this regard. We do well to recognize that we are not the only ones to value his contributions. He might be surprised by the diversity of people that honor his story.

H. JAMES HOPKINS

Psalm 96

¹O sing to the LORD a new song;
   sing to the LORD, all the earth.
²Sing to the LORD, bless his name;
   tell of his salvation from day to day.
³Declare his glory among the nations,
   his marvelous works among all the peoples.
⁴For great is the LORD, and greatly to be praised;
   he is to be revered above all gods.
⁵For all the gods of the peoples are idols,
   but the LORD made the heavens.
⁶Honor and majesty are before him;
   strength and beauty are in his sanctuary.

⁷Ascribe to the LORD, O families of the peoples,
   ascribe to the LORD glory and strength.

Theological Perspective

Many of us grew up with a strong sense that the God we worshiped was the creator of the earth and all its creatures. We understood that the God we worshiped is the only God, that everyone should recognize the power and glory of our creator. That meant that, for us, any other object of worship was an idol, and its worship should be condemned. To whatever extent we have held on to this understanding, or returned to it, most of this psalm is unproblematic. In a beautiful and powerful way it expresses the shared faith of the Abrahamic traditions.

For theologians, the situation has been somewhat different. Toward the end of the eighteenth century, the Scottish philosopher David Hume argued that we had no basis for positing that this world has a Creator. Even more important for Protestant history, the German philosopher Immanuel Kant agreed with him. Whereas Hume probably had no constructive interest in Christian theology, Kant did, and he proposed that affirmations about God be associated with human ethical experience rather than with ideas about the origins of the universe.

Especially in the German heartland of Protestant theology, the idea that a divine being, external to the world, had literally brought it into existence was abandoned. Indeed, any sort of interest in the relation of God to the natural order virtually

Pastoral Perspective

"O sing to the LORD a new song," exhorts the psalmist. The idea of singing a "new song" poses some challenges for today's world. Why should one sing a *new* song? Are the old songs not good enough? What are the new songs we are called sing to the Lord? What if we do not "sing" that well—maybe not literally, but in the way we "sing" to God through how we live our lives? These are some of the questions raised by this seemingly simple, but very provocative first verse.

There is a distinctly universal message embedded in the words of the psalm: "Declare his glory *among the nations*, his marvelous works *among all the peoples*. For great is the LORD, and greatly to be praised; he is to be revered *above all gods*. For all the gods of the people are idols" (vv. 3–5a). This proclamation of the universality of God's sovereign rule invites encounters with those of other faiths. Ecumenical and interfaith dialogues continue to be a growing need in our world. As the global community becomes a reality through technology and other means, how Christians relate to those of other faiths will be an ongoing issue. What does it mean to confess God's glory among the nations? How does one profess belief in the one true God in a way that deals respectfully with those who believe otherwise? How does one "say among the nations,

^{8}Ascribe to the L<small>ORD</small> the glory due his name;
  bring an offering, and come into his courts.
^{9}Worship the L<small>ORD</small> in holy splendor;
  tremble before him, all the earth.

^{10}Say among the nations, "The L<small>ORD</small> is king!
  The world is firmly established; it shall never be moved.
  He will judge the peoples with equity."
^{11}Let the heavens be glad, and let the earth rejoice;
  let the sea roar, and all that fills it;
^{12} let the field exult, and everything in it.
  Then shall all the trees of the forest sing for joy
^{13} before the L<small>ORD</small>; for he is coming,
  for he is coming to judge the earth.
  He will judge the world with righteousness,
  and the peoples with his truth.

Exegetical Perspective

Psalm 96, along with Psalms 40, 93, 95, and 97–99, is classified as an enthronement psalm. These psalms, all but one of which are located in Book 4 of the Psalter, celebrate YHWH as sovereign over the community of faith. Sigmund Mowinckel suggested that enthronement psalms were originally used in preexilic Israel during the New Year's festival, an annual commemoration of YHWH as victorious king over the earth. The biblical text provides no firm evidence of such a commemoration, although 1 Chronicles 16 incorporates a portion of Psalm 96 in the words sung by the Asaphites after the ark of the covenant was brought to the sanctuary in Jerusalem during David's reign.

People of faith today encounter Psalm 96 in Book 4 of the Psalter, and thus we may ask how we might understand it in its current canonical context. The Psalter is often called the "Hymnbook of the Second Temple," an apt designation. Was the hymnbook compiled in some purposeful way, or is it simply a miscellaneous collection? The shaping of the Psalter has been an ongoing subject of study during the past twenty years.[1] The consensus is that the Psalter's five books tell a story of ancient Israel that begins in the

1. See esp. J. Clinton McCann Jr., ed., *The Shape and Shaping of the Psalter*, JSOTSup 159 (Sheffield: JSOT Press, 1993), and Nancy L. deClaissé-Walford, *Introduction to the Psalms* (St. Louis: Chalice Press, 2004).

Homiletical Perspective

Have you ever been so happy that you could hardly contain yourself? One such time for me was the day I received my acceptance letter into seminary. I was a single young adult stuck in a dead-end job. I had felt a call into ministry and had thrown myself into the work of applying. Not much of a mystic, still I had prayed as I dropped my application into the mailbox. I so much wanted a change of life! For months, I waited and waited. When the acceptance letter came, I held in my hands on one sheet of paper my New Life. I danced around my studio apartment singing the only hymn I could remember by heart, the doxology: "Praise God from whom all blessings flow!"

Psalm 96 is a doxology, a song of ecstasy and praise. It is the ultimate summons to worship. It is a perfect combination of formal liturgical style and pulsing, authentic energy. "O sing to our God a new song! Sing to our God, all the earth!" The singer cannot keep her joy to herself. She wants the whole earth to join her singing!

Sometimes such joy is personal: a proposal of marriage, the birth of a child, news of a new job, an acceptance letter into college. Other times such joy is communal: the wedding itself, the baptism of a child, a new employer moving to town, the dedication of a new school building. I think of those

Psalm 96

Theological Perspective

disappeared from the leading forms of Protestant theology. Theology was reorganized around moral experience, religious experience, or simply biblical faith. The Bible was reinterpreted to center on God's covenant with Israel and subsequently the new covenant in Christ. It was often taught that the interest of biblical writers in nature expressed the continuation of Canaanite religion rather than the distinctive Yahwistic tradition.

In North America, many leading theologians followed the Germans, but others adopted a philosophical naturalism. In that context, a sense of God's work in the whole of nature was preserved. This point of view gained wider acceptance in the church as a result of the awakening around 1970 to the ecological crisis. There was widespread recognition that the preoccupation with human history had allowed Christians to ignore the consequences of human activity for the natural world. Later the World Council of Churches began speaking of "the integrity of creation," warning us not to tamper with that integrity in such a way as to bring about the disintegration of nature.

The psalmist does not think in these terms. The psalm takes nature seriously in another way. The natural world joins with human beings in the joy of existence and the praise of God for that existence. In the twenty-first century, we are trying to recover a sense of participation with other creatures rather than separation from them. Perhaps the vision of the psalmist will help: together with all creation we praise God.

The psalm ends with the assertion that the Lord is king and is coming in judgment. Interestingly, the mood is positive. Divine sovereignty gives assurance that the world is "firmly established." One feels that the judgment will bring justice, but there is no anxiety about possible punishment. Even the trees sing for joy at the coming of the Lord.

The same basic ideas can inspire quite different feelings. An emphasis on God's royal rule can lead one to resentment that the justice one would expect from such a rule is not forthcoming, or to self-condemnation from the belief that one's suffering must be a punishment for one's sins, or to a feeling of powerlessness from assuming that God calls all the shots. Feelings of this sort can follow from a primary emphasis on God as creator, king, and judge. But in this psalm—and quite often in Christian history as well—the same ideas provide grounds for security and joy, wonder at the magnificence of the world, and comfort in the

Pastoral Perspective

'The Lord is king'" (v. 10), without starting the next holy war?

One answer is to remind ourselves that this Lord is one who judges *all* peoples *with equity* (v. 10b). All of creation, even the seas and the trees of the forest, rejoices when this takes place. God's judgment is not about punishment, but about restoration of God's established order that brings life and fulfillment to God's creatures. Those longing for justice may hear God's judgment as a word of hope.

Another aspect of God's judgment is linked with the proclamation of God's truth. As verse 13 reminds us, God "will judge the world with righteousness, and the people with his *truth*." In this postmodern age, there continues to be a struggle for a shared understanding of truth. While the cynic may point to the emergence of "truthiness" in place of truth, there is still a longing for something genuine and unchanging. For many, the postmodern movement has left them without a "place" that feels firmly established. The fluidity of a postmodern world and the changing perspectives of truth feel uncertain, as if things are always moving and in flux, rather than being grounded in a place that "shall never be moved." The words of Psalm 96 speak to a thirst for something or someone to hold on to, a place or person of eternal grounding.

Verses 6–9 remind the hearer that the source of this grounding is found in God, who can be worshiped "in his sanctuary." In worship we find, or are found by, the "ground of our being," the one who not only *speaks* the truth, but *is* the truth. Those seeking such grounding in life tend to look for it in other places. Self-help books continue to make the journey for self-enlightenment sound like an entirely solitary expedition. This psalm reminds us that we find our way journeying *together* as we gather to worship the God who brings equity, justice, and truth.

While praise and doxology fill this psalm, such words do not seem to flow as easily in our age as in the time of the psalmist. Cynicism is more likely to be the expression du jour. Genuine praise is often confused with trying to affirm everything by helping everyone to feel good about themselves. This psalm invites us to go deeper, in search of an affirmation that is grounded in one's relationship with God. That relationship with God can then melt away the superficial affirmations that may trigger the cynicism of our day.

As a lectionary reading that is often placed on Christmas Eve or Christmas Day, Psalm 96 anticipates the coming of the one sent by God who

time of David's reign (Book 1), continues through the divided monarchy and the destruction of the kingdoms (Books 2 and 3), through the exile in Babylon (Book 4), and ends in the period of the return from exile and the rebuilding of the temple (Book 5).

The destruction of Jerusalem and the temple by the Babylonians in 587 BCE changed life forever for our ancestors in the faith. King and court, symbols of nationhood, of being, were gone forever. Only faith in YHWH remained to unite the people and give them identity. Psalm 96 in its canonical context, then, is part of the celebration of the reign of YHWH over the people in a new world, one without a Davidic king, one in which God would be sovereign.

Two parts make up Psalm 96, verses 1–6 and verses 7–13. Each consists of a call to praise (vv. 1–3 and vv. 7–12) and a reason for praise (vv. 4–6 and v. 13). In verses 1–3, six imperative verbs call the people to "sing" (vv. 1–2), "bless" (v. 2), "tell" (v. 2), and "declare" (v. 3). Verses 4–6 provide the rationale for the call to praise with descriptive phrases about YHWH. The call to the people and to all of creation resumes in verses 7–12, with imperatives and invitations to "ascribe glory" (vv. 7–8), "worship" (v. 9), "be glad" (v. 11), and "exult" (v. 12). The psalm's closing verse gives the final reason for praise to YHWH (v. 13).

Psalm 96's simple outline, however, belies its masterful rhetorical structure. In a subtle combination of repetition and assonance, the psalmist invites worshipers to join in the celebration of YHWH as sovereign over all people and all creation. The call to praise in verses 1–3 repeats the verb "sing" (*shir*) three times and sibilant (*s*) sounds echo the verb's acoustic beginning over and over—nine times in the three verses. Verse 1a's "new song" (*shir hadash*) occurs only seven times in the Hebrew Bible, four times in the Psalter. The descriptive word "new" does not denote a newly composed tune, but some new event—here the reign of YHWH. Thus the "new song" is not a new tune, but the next verse of the already-familiar song of God's redemptive acts on behalf of God's people.

The Hebrew word *ki*, "for, because," occurs at the beginnings of verses 4 and 5, introducing descriptive phrases that give the reasons the people should sing a "new song" to YHWH as sovereign. In verse 4, "for" introduces statements about YHWH's greatness and reverence. Verse 5's "for" introduces a statement that contrasts YHWH with the gods of the peoples. The basic meaning of the word "idols" (*'elilim*) in

famous black-and-white photographs of the end of World War II, with crowds of New Yorkers singing, dancing, and kissing in the streets. "O sing to our God a new song! Sing to our God all the earth!"

Perhaps Psalm 96 was written in response to some great victory, or the royal proclamation of a New Deal that would save a lot of people from hardship. It was a communal ecstasy, a communal celebration. "Sing to our God! Bless God's name! Tell of God's salvation from day to day!" There is an invitation to tell others—other people, other nations—the good news of God. "Declare God's glory among the nations, God's glorious works among all nations."

Scholarship informs us that this psalm was used for the annual New Year's worship in which the Hebrews/Jews renewed their covenant together and celebrated God as their sovereign. Imagine pilgrims coming in all directions from the twelve tribes and assembling at the temple in Jerusalem. By celebrating the identity of their God, they simultaneously celebrate their own identity as a covenant people. The poetry of the psalm perfectly blends the God of creation and the God of history.

Notice the ecological sensibility woven into the psalm. Sometimes we get so used to hearing Scripture read in the context of our world that we subconsciously assume that its context is like our context and thus fail to let the text teach us. Instead of a North American suburban setting, imagine this psalm spoken in a Native American setting, which would be closer to the Hebrews' tribal reality. "Let the heavens be glad! Let the earth rejoice! Let the sea roar, and all that fills it! Let the field exult, and everything in it! Then shall all the trees of the forest sing for joy before our God!" (vv. 11–13a). We are woven into nature, not separate from it. When we worship, the forest is the choir.

But the God of creation is also the God of history, who works among the peoples, performing saving deeds from day to day. That there are other gods and goddesses is acknowledged, and not in an entirely pejorative way. But YHWH, God of *life* and *love*, *justice* and *peace*, is enthroned as sovereign above all other deities. Imagine the pilgrim worshipers acting this out on New Year's Day, crowning YHWH and putting God on their throne.

What if we were to act this out in a worship service? What would it look like? Instead of tribes we could gather in neighborhood groups and approach our sanctuary like pilgrims. "O families of the peoples, ascribe to our God the glory due God's

Psalm 96

Theological Perspective

assurance that we are in good hands, that justice ultimately rules.

The psalmist may have had in mind that justice was related to the Jewish law, but the law is here not mentioned. It seems instead that the recognition of God as creator of all things evokes worship, and that the outcome of this worship leads to the righteousness God wants. As in Paul, it seems that all the nations can recognize the Creator and share in worship. All the nations can rejoice that the Lord comes to bring justice. The discovery that the God of Israel is the creator of all does not lead to self-congratulation by Israel and the condemnation of others for their worship of idols. The psalmist expects all to worship the one universal God, the creator of all, and to live righteously.

Even today, as we try to understand ourselves in the context of religious diversity, this spirit seems admirable. The psalmist lived in a context where every community and group had its gods. When we compare his response to the attitudes of those representatives of the Abrahamic traditions who condemn one another, we can marvel that so long ago at least some of our religious ancestors were far more enlightened and charitable.

Today our theological task is more complex. We know that there are deeply thoughtful and spiritually sensitive people who do not want to orient their lives through worship to a transcendent creator and sovereign deity. Whereas it is hard for us to read this psalm without celebration and joy, it does not speak to them. Some of them seek serenity and compassion through a profound realization of who they are in their interconnection with all things. Their rituals and meditation are oriented to the achievement of this realization. They may resonate to this psalm's sense of human sharing with the rest of creation, but the note of praise is not relevant for them. Can we find ways to be as open to them as the psalmist was to the "nations" of his day?

JOHN B. COBB JR.

Pastoral Perspective

will bring equity, justice, and a life filled with grace and truth. The echoes of these Advent and Christmas expectations color the way we hear the psalm. Removed from those liturgical constraints, these words of praise and proclamation that invite us to sing new songs still have their place. They may challenge us to think about the songs we sing with our own lives.

From time to time we may talk about a certain melody being "our song." What "song" would we say characterizes our lives? Would it be a "new" song of hope? Would it be more like the blues? One could describe the blues as a "secular gospel." Conversely, the gospel songs might be described as the blues *with hope*. Gospel music, whose roots are intertwined with those of the blues, acknowledges the genuine sufferings in life, *but always in the context of hope*. There is a better day coming! And the words of a "new" song like "We Shall Overcome" sow the seeds of hope in the very act of singing the song. The proclamation of the truth that brings security and justice is manifested as the words are sung. Singing itself becomes an expression of realized eschatology reflecting the inbreaking of God's reign into the here and now.

Psalm 96 invites us at least to try singing a new song. It does not have to be perfect. Given our humanity, it probably will not be. We may not think that we can sing this new song very well. Do not worry—others are there with us to help us find the right notes. Together we can sing the "new" songs of hope that not only remind us of what God is doing but become the instrument that God uses to make the hope a reality!

C. GRAY NORSWORTHY

Exegetical Perspective

verse 5 is "insignificant, vain, useless." Its use here is an obvious play on words with *'elohim*. Verse 4b states that YHWH is to be revered above "all the gods" (*'elohim*), suggesting the existence of other gods, but verse 5's "the gods (*'elohim*) of the peoples are idols (*'elilim*)" unequivocally states that YHWH is the only God.

Verses 7–8 resume the call to the faithful to praise with a threefold imperative "ascribe [*habu*] to YHWH," paralleling verses 1–2's threefold imperative "sing." The acoustic beginning of "ascribe"—*habu*—continues in verse 9's call to "worship" (*hishtakhvu*) and "tremble" (*hilu*).

The theological center of Psalm 96 is verse 10. Here the psalmist calls the faithful to "say among the nations, 'YHWH is king.'" The simple affirmation leads to the next: the world is firmly established. The repetition of sounds found in verses 1–3 and verses 7–9 continues in verses 11–12, using a series of verbal forms beginning with the Hebrew letter *yod* in an invitation to all creation to join in the "new song" to YHWH. Verse 11 calls on the heavens to "be glad" (*yishmekhu*) and the sea to "roar" (*yir'am*), and verse 12 invites the field to "exult" (*ya'aloz*) so that the trees may "sing for joy" (*yerannenu*).

Psalm 96's pattern of repetition continues in its closing words in verse 13. The psalm singer states twice in rapid succession "for he is coming" [*ki ba'*]. "Is coming" translates a verb (*ba'*) that can be rendered by a number of English verbal forms, including "is coming," "has come," and "comes." The Hebrew form indicates an act that has already taken place and/or an act that is ongoing at the present time. Thus YHWH the sovereign ruler is presently on the earth, judging the world with righteousness and people with truth.

Psalm 96 conveys a powerful message in both its content and form. The psalm singer combines powerful words with powerful rhetoric in celebration of YHWH as sovereign over all the earth.

NANCY L. DECLAISSÉ-WALFORD

Homiletical Perspective

name (Life, Love, Justice, and Peace). Bring an offering and come into God's courts" (v. 8). Just for one Sunday, we could use our Communion table as a throne. What symbols could we use as we processed into the sanctuary to enthrone YHWH as the sovereign of our lives, both personal and communal? I think of an olive branch, the scales of justice, a huge St. Valentine's heart, perhaps many flags from diverse nations, or that picture of the whole earth taken from outer space. We also would each bring a personal offering, something emblematic of ourselves and/or our family of origin or family of choice to put before the throne.

The ancient Israelites, of course, would process in behind the ark of the covenant, their major symbol of the presence of God, which also symbolized their covenant with one another. What can we use as a symbol or symbols of our covenant together as a church community? Often we think of our church building as the symbol of our faith community, but let us think outside of that box. What might serve as symbols of our spiritual community? Perhaps the neighborhood groups could each think of a "tribal" symbol of what our church means to them.

What of the worship service itself? "O sing a new song!" Perhaps we could sing a new hymn, such as "Bring Many Names" or "I Come with Joy, a Child of God, Forgiven, Loved, and Free" by Brian Wren. Perhaps as part of the prayers we could all shout out, like popcorn popping, words that we ascribe to the nature of God——life, love, justice, peace. The sermon might be about what it means for God to judge the world, its nations and peoples, with "righteousness" and "truth," and why that is not something to fear, but something to enjoy. "Sing for joy before our God, for God is coming to judge the earth with righteousness and truth!"

DANIEL M. GESLIN

Galatians 1:1-12

¹Paul an apostle—sent neither by human commission nor from human authorities, but through Jesus Christ and God the Father, who raised him from the dead—²and all the members of God's family who are with me,

To the churches of Galatia:

³Grace to you and peace from God our Father and the Lord Jesus Christ, ⁴who gave himself for our sins to set us free from the present evil age, according to the will of our God and Father, ⁵to whom be the glory forever and ever. Amen.

⁶I am astonished that you are so quickly deserting the one who called you in the grace of Christ and are turning to a different gospel—⁷not that there is another gospel, but there are some who are confusing you and want to pervert the gospel of Christ. ⁸But even if we or an angel from heaven should proclaim to you a gospel contrary to what we proclaimed to you, let that one be accursed! ⁹As we have said before, so now I repeat, if anyone proclaims to you a gospel contrary to what you received, let that one be accursed!

¹⁰Am I now seeking human approval, or God's approval? Or am I trying to please people? If I were still pleasing people, I would not be a servant of Christ.

¹¹For I want you to know, brothers and sisters, that the gospel that was proclaimed by me is not of human origin; ¹²for I did not receive it from a human source, nor was I taught it, but I received it through a revelation of Jesus Christ.

Theological Perspective

The specific issue that compels Paul to write this letter to the community in Galatia is whether non-Jews must take on Jewish practices in order to become Christians. Very quickly, non-Jews completely dominated Christianity, and the question eventually became whether Jews were saved at all. At the time Galatians was written, however, Paul was opposing some of Jesus' closest friends and family by including non-Jews among the faithful. For many in the earliest Christian community, it was virtually unthinkable to excise Jewish practices from Christian community. This would mean a sacrifice of the customs that had held the Jewish people together over many centuries and through terrible persecutions. It would mean betraying their heritage, martyrs, and a whole universe of values, practices, and authorities. For most of the original followers of Jesus, being "Christian" meant a particular way of being Jewish, but Paul, in his wanderings in the eastern part of the empire, discovered among non-Jews a particular susceptibility to his teachings about Jesus. A sprinkling of small communities sprang up where he traveled, united not by any of the typical demarcations of the Roman Empire, but by a vision of a new life conveyed to them through the message of a dying and rising Lord of love.

Paul's impulse to spread Christianity outside of Judaism proved decisive for the history of the

Pastoral Perspective

This is the only letter in which the apostle Paul forgoes the customary prayer of thanksgiving that follows the opening greeting. In some of his epistles, Paul goes on for a paragraph or two expressing appreciation. He is often effusive in his praise, but not for these fledging congregations in Galatia. By the time we get to verse 6, their founding pastor launches into a feisty rebuke, calling into question the beliefs and behaviors of these mission churches. He is "astonished" at their fickleness. Far from pastoral, the tone is irritated, cranky.

Were it not for the assigned lectionary reading holding our feet to the fire, contemporary congregations would be tempted to avoid this text. It would be easy enough to justify: We have simply intercepted mail that is not addressed to us. We can write it off as a personal matter between Paul and the Galatians—except it *is* God's word to us. And in fact the text can help us address a number of impulses or attitudes that hamper the spiritual health of present-day congregations.

Apathy-ism. One prevailing threat to congregational vitality today is not so much a blatantly anti-God atheism as a passionless apathy-ism. The gospel of Jesus Christ often operates less as the radical and

Exegetical Perspective

Surprising Salutations. To readers in the twenty-first century, the urgency and indignation of Paul's Letter to the Galatians leap out, with the exclamation "You foolish Galatians!" of 3:1 and the intemperate wish of 5:12. Paul's earliest readers, by contrast, may have suspected that something was up as early as the opening line. Typically, letters began by directly identifying the writer and the addressee: "Bethany to Suzanne. Greetings!" as Paul does in 1 Thessalonians. Paul elsewhere embellishes these identifications (see 1 Cor. 1:1; 2 Cor. 1:1; Phil. 1:1), but nowhere else is the embellishment cast first of all in negative terms: "sent neither by human commission nor from human authorities" (v. 1). Paul is emphatically not writing with the authority or approval of any human judicatory.

To readers schooled in the hermeneutic of suspicion, this denial has about it a strong scent of defensiveness, and Paul may well be on the defensive here. Yet this denial more importantly underscores what follows: Paul serves "through Jesus Christ and God the Father, who raised him from the dead" (v. 1). How this commission came from God, Paul explains (however tersely) a bit later in the letter, but here he identifies it with a synopsis of the gospel message. The astonishing heat of this letter should not prevent readers from understanding that Paul is up to far

Homiletical Perspective

"Edith! Get in here! I'm having to defend God all by myself!" is the terrified cry of Archie Bunker when he found himself alone with son-in-law Mike (a.k.a. Meathead), the household's village atheist.[1] Every preacher has sympathized at some time with both Archie and the apostle Paul in their single-handed defense of the faith against despisers and detractors. While Archie defends against one who says there is no God, Paul must contend against those who seem bent on effectively reconfining God's people to an old box from which Paul and his fellow converts have been freed by the grace of Christ.

The opening words of Paul's epistle to the Galatian churches establish immediately that Paul is eminently qualified for the task that is before him. Far from needing a spouse in the next room to come to his aid, Paul knows that his divine commissioning and provisioning has equipped him to face this severe challenge. Paul whips through the customary pleasantries, ready to leap directly into the fray. "I am astonished!" he begins, setting the pattern of mincing no words in this harsh epistle-long rebuttal to the Jewish Christian missionaries who have set about correcting Paul's "errors" of theology and praxis with which he midwifed the Galatian churches.

1. *All in the Family*, CBS sitcom from 1971 to 1979.

Galatians 1:1-12

Theological Perspective

church. Like Christians encountering Islam, few Jews beyond those initial followers of Jesus found the new Christian *religion* particularly compelling. The real audience for the gospel was not the Jews, who had access to God through Torah, but Gentiles. The deeper issue for contemporary Christians remains Paul's heretical notion that faith relativizes even the most precious parts of a religion's authorities and practices.

In order to extend Christianity to outsiders, Paul makes a passionate case for the radical inclusivity of the gospel of Jesus Christ. Jewish practices are not to be understood as essential to Christian community. It is not the case that Jews, Christian or otherwise, were ignorant of God as compassionate and gracious. Nor is it the case that they believed they could "earn" salvation through works. This is a calumny attributed to them by later Christians. Paul does not think that Jewish Christians betrayed the gospel by continuing their traditional practices. The problem was more subtle. Christ is a doorway through which anyone can enter at any time, not because belief is a new "work" or Christianity a new "law."

The gospel is the unbearably good news that divine love anticipates us, surrounds us, precedes us; anything that serves as an obstacle to our awareness of this love is "accursed." The nature of the Divine is to be love, and the great conversion of faith is to let this love live in us. For Paul, the gospel makes every religious, civil, and social authority secondary to confidence in the intimate love of God manifest in Christ. If one is Jewish, one need not stop being a Jew. If one is a slave, one need not wait for legal ransom to be Christian. One's status and condition do not need to be altered in order to be invited into divine love. The death of Christ reveals that this love is unconditional. Through this revelation, the logic of our "evil age," so fascinated by power, might, prestige, and hierarchical authorities, is broken. Christians lived outside of the claims of empire, loyal and devoted to a completely different logic and power. The difficult and even unbearable shadow side of this love is that no authority, practice, or social hierarchy deserves our deepest loyalty.

In both Corinth and Galatia, Paul resisted teachers who privileged a particular practice as essential to Christian life. In Galatia, it was Jewish custom; in Corinth it was prophecy. Although the debate was over different practices, the underlying problem was similar. It is not that Paul stands in the middle mediating between law and prophecy; rather, he challenges the kind of piety that makes anything

Pastoral Perspective

motivating center in the lives of believers, and more like a hobby to dabble in on the side at their convenience.

Paul's rebuke rattles this passive status quo; his intensity bursts the bubble of our spiritual indifference. He is passionate about the gospel, about what God has done in Jesus Christ—"who gave himself for our sins to set us free from the present evil age" (v. 4). While terms like "sin" and "evil age" may strike us as unfashionable, perhaps evoking images of fanatical TV preachers, or sounding hopelessly archaic in our scientifically sophisticated world, we are challenged to grapple afresh with their meaning in the church today.

Pluralism. After 9/11 we not only became acutely aware of a world filled with pockets of religiously fueled fanatics; we also began to seek to understand and make room for the different other, valuing tolerance for various worldviews, resulting fortunately in increased sensitivity, humility, and respect. Some Christians, sometimes arguing from a basic conviction that we are to love even our enemies, are increasingly loath to draw lines that call into question or exclude others, whether inside the church (intra-Christian) and outside the church (interfaith). Who are we to judge?

Paul, however, appears to be drawing one such line within the church: "I am astonished that you are so quickly deserting the one who called you in the grace of Christ and are turning to a different gospel—not that there is another gospel, but there are some who are confusing you and want to pervert the gospel of Christ" (vv. 6–7). Due to a prevailing pluralistic impulse, these may be difficult words to hear today, but apparently a perversion of the gospel can develop that is outside the bounds, a subbiblical Christology that calls into question the very faithfulness and legitimacy of those who espouse it. Paul nearly comes unglued here because some followers of Jesus have lost their way; they have compromised the uncompromisable.

In addition to his rebuke, Paul states that anyone who perverts the gospel—including himself or any other messenger from God—should be summarily cursed. Clearly Paul is not promoting allegiance to himself here. Rather, he argues for allegiance to the unadulterated gospel of Jesus Christ—who by his life, death, and resurrection is the unique and only Savior of the world. Believing whatever one wants, as long as one is sincere, is not enough. Sometimes a line has to be drawn—although knowing where to

Exegetical Perspective

more than a defense of his own position; he is in the act of re-preaching the gospel to congregations he believes have been disastrously misled.[1]

The sheer size of God's action in Jesus Christ comes into view in verses 3–5. Again the standard greeting—which in Paul's other letters is simply "Grace to you and peace from God our Father and the Lord Jesus Christ" (except for "Grace to you and peace" in 1 Thess. 1:1)—is here elaborated in two ways. First, Jesus "gave himself for our sins" (v. 4). Paul frequently identifies Jesus' death in this way, as Jesus' own action accomplished on behalf of humankind. Familiar as this statement may be, it bears noting that Paul does not reach for a sociological or political interpretation of Jesus' death but for a theological interpretation.

That theological interpretation takes on a larger horizon in the second elaboration, when Paul adds that Jesus' death was "to set us free from the present evil age" (v. 4). That Jesus died on behalf of human sinfulness is susceptible to individualistic, even sentimental, renderings, in which individual sins are listed in lurid (and therefore fascinating) details. But for Paul "our sins" are not occasions for spiritual exhibitionism but are symptoms of a larger crisis, "the present evil age." Unlike Luke, who favors the language of repentance and forgiveness (as in Acts 2:38), Paul does not say that Jesus' death brought about forgiveness. Instead, Jesus' death "set us free." For Paul, sinful behavior is a symptom of humanity's captivity, and humanity can be rescued only by God's action. The ascription of glory in verse 5 is no mere formality, but a fitting response to God's action.

No Other Gospel. Again following the custom of the day, Paul's letters typically include a thanksgiving, even in 1 Corinthians, where he gives thanks for the same spiritual gifts that have turned into a battleground (1 Cor. 1:6–7). Paul's distress about the Galatian congregations prevents him from offering some euphemism that might serve as a foot in the argumentative door. Instead, he accuses the Galatians of "deserting" God's call and turning to "a different gospel" (v. 6).

Only later in the letter do the lines of this "different gospel" come into view. Some other Christian teachers[2] have arrived in the Gentile Galatian congregations and have taught them that the gospel they heard from Paul was only part of the

1. J. Louis Martyn, *Galatians*, Anchor Bible (Garden City, NY: Doubleday, 1997), 22.
2. Ibid., 18.

Homiletical Perspective

In Paul's passionate defensiveness, you can hear a loving parent's bewildered and angry cry at how quickly and easily the child has put aside the many years of wise and patient upbringing, taking to paths and practices utterly at odds with the lessons of home. "Well," one could offer to a parent or Paul, "you gave them their wings, and . . . now they fly." The great irony here is that the Galatians' new freedom has, Paul believes, opened them to being rebound by the old strictures of Jewish law.

Paul left the fledgling church with a gospel that emphasized the new creation brought about through the cross—the sacrificial and atoning death—of Jesus Christ. In that new creation, so much is new and transformed, and so much of the *particularity* of the old is simply left behind. The old Jewishness marked by peculiarly Jewish cultic practices, including male circumcision, has been utterly subsumed by the event of the cross. The essence of God and the grace of the Christ event are simply not contained by the cultic practices of the faith of Paul's upbringing. They are not vessels or means to the grace of Christ; they are, in fact, utterly irrelevant in the context of this non-Jewish Christian setting. Moreover, they stand in the way of Christ's grace. The perverters of the gospel who followed Paul are not wrong on just the *nuances* of the gospel, Paul claims; they are presenting a *whole new "gospel."* It is a term Paul uses loosely and advisedly, knowing there is little "good news" in a system of belief that reverses the freedom of Christ, saps the strength of the Spirit, and relocks the shackles of the law.

Pity the clay-footed preacher who ascends the pulpit each week with less certainty than Paul would seem to demand. It is fair to wonder: Is the "gospel" we preach faithful to that first received by the Galatians? (How would a Pauline epistle to *us* sound, one wonders?) We might try to imagine the first hearing of Paul's angry epistle. Do the reader and listeners know what kind of apostolic fireworks await them? This writer has heard his own children ask: "Why are you so *mad*? What did I *do*?" We might find ourselves wishing to offer a sympathetic word and pastoral presence to these new Christians as their ears receive Paul's scalding, invective-laden blast.

As preachers *and* pastors, we may fear that Paul is the kind of parent whose tutelage would seem to encourage nervous mistakes. This writer studied piano for a time with an overwrought perfectionist who took to swatting the slouching wrists of his young pupil. Under his teaching, his student's regression was astonishing. Yet, if Paul was conscious

Galatians 1:1-12

Theological Perspective

other than the graciousness of divine love a marker of the gospel. Jewish customs are consistent with faith; Gentile prophecy is consistent in faith. But limiting divine grace to these or anything else is not consistent with faith. Love makes one a Christian. It is love that justifies, that makes us right. That love is not conditioned by anything but God's own self-initiating love for humanity. If we miss this, for Paul, we miss everything.

We have to choose between our loyalty to familiar and stabilizing structures and the priority of the gospel. For Paul, faith is opposed to even the most precious and divinely sanctioned traditions. Faith is a faithful abandon that frees us from the "present evil age." This freedom is accomplished by the gift of Christ, which reveals that every single human being is an object of divine love. In setting up obstacles to this free justification, we desert and pervert the gospel. Paul puts us in the terrible position of either being heretics to tradition by opening our hearts to the whole wretched, sinful mass of humanity or being heretics to the gospel by clinging to religious norms.

The shocking significance of Paul's understanding of faith loses none of its difficulty over the centuries. Christianity became a religion no less committed to its traditions than was Judaism. It is no easier for Christians to die to "the present evil age" than it was for first-century Jews and Gentiles. It is useful for us, like Paul, to consider ways in which we have allowed other allegiances to displace our faith, ways in which we put up obstacles by demanding something other than raw devotion to the foolish, countercultural priority of love.

WENDY FARLEY

Pastoral Perspective

draw the line, or deciding who gets to draw the line, is notoriously difficult!

Perhaps the eminent twentieth-century theologian Karl Barth points us in the right direction as we negotiate our way across this christological landscape, dotted with the land mines both of an easy pluralism and of an equally dangerous rigid fundamentalism. At the conclusion of a lecture series at Princeton Seminary back in the early 1960s, Barth was asked if God was revealed in other religions too, or in Christianity only. Barth is reported to have said: "God is not revealed in any religion—*including Christianity*. God is revealed through his Son, Jesus Christ."

Consumerism. Today people are fundamentally consumers: they want what they want when they want it, even in the church. If they do not like what is happening or what they hear, they leave and start shopping for a better deal. Meanwhile, the pressure is constantly on preachers to increase attendance, to raise the budget, to grow a church—to do whatever it takes to improve market share. Be nice; be funny; make promises; do not offend. There is an inordinate desire for approval, for applause, for appreciation on the part of pastors today. To Paul's question, "Am I seeking human approval, . . . am I trying to please people?" (v. 10), many preachers today would have to answer, in all honesty, yes. When preachers are captive to public opinion, when churches too easily become purveyors of gospel gimmicks, offering the religious goods and services people want, what is sacrificed is the ability to be a slave of Christ in service to his unchanging gospel.

Alas, occasionally congregations experience a renewed longing to be faithful, or give voice to the plea, If only we could be like the early church today! Paul's Letter to the Galatians reminds us we are! Like the churches in Galatia, our congregations are often marked by conflict and theological confusion, and we busily doctor the gospel, concocting alternative Christologies. This is one Sunday it might make sense for the confession of sin to come after the text and sermon, immediately followed by the affirmation that Christ alone breaks the power of reigning sin, and sets the captives—preachers, congregants, and congregations—free!

HEIDI HUSTED ARMSTRONG

story. In order to participate fully in the gospel, they would need to be circumcised and keep the law of Moses. Paul's adamant rejection of this claim is worked out in the letter, but here it is denounced as a perversion of the gospel. To a generation trained in the language of inclusivity, Paul's language will seem grossly intolerant. Yet Paul's gentle words about other Christian preachers in Philippians 1:15–18 and the welcoming stance he takes toward differences in Romans 14:1–15:13 suggest that this is something other than knee-jerk rejection of alternative views. Paul is convinced—for reasons that will come clear later in the letter—that nothing less than the gospel itself is on the line in these congregations, and they must understand that the gospel means God's actions in Jesus Christ and nothing else. The repeated anathema of verses 8 and 9 concludes this point with a fierceness at least the equal of the language of 5:12.

A Servant of Christ. The remainder of the lection returns to the initial announcement of verse 1 concerning the divine source of Paul's gospel. Verse 10 suggests that the teachers have employed some smear tactics, cleverly whispering among the Galatian congregations that Paul offered them "gospel light," a watered-down instruction designed to win them over and secure their goodwill. Paul adamantly rejects the charge and then moves in verses 11–12 to an expanded restatement of verse 1 that introduces the major point of chapters 1–2. Paul received the gospel from Jesus Christ alone and from no human source. Again a glance at Paul's writings elsewhere is helpful, since he otherwise takes a positive stance toward Christian tradition (1 Cor. 15:1–3) and reminds others of his own role in passing along the gospel. There is nothing wrong when women or men teach others the content of the gospel, but it seems that Paul has again been undermined by the rumor that he is not a "real" apostle, that his authority is secondary. More important, the gospel has its origin in Jesus Christ; whatever work there is of teaching and preaching, the gospel is, as Paul has already affirmed in the salutation, "through Jesus Christ and God the Father."

BEVERLY ROBERTS GAVENTA

of the potential damage his angry diatribe might cause to the tender Christians, he clearly believed the greater risk was that the teaching of the Jewish Christian missionaries would supplant Paul's original teaching. In the poem "The Road Not Taken," Robert Frost notes the natural human tendency never to return to roads once considered and then abandoned: "knowing how way leads on to way, I doubted I should ever come back."[2] If this regression and perversion of the gospel was not arrested, Paul rightly believed, there might be no returning, no recovery of the true gospel, and no salvation from the deadly dangers of any false gospel.

Yet one wonders: what instructions did Paul leave behind as to the minutiae of the gospel he espoused? Many new parents, upon leaving the hospital with their firstborn, find that the painstaking advice of the birthing room nurse has vanished and they are left to fend for their child with whatever their frazzled wits provide. One may feel a bit for the Galatians, whose birth parent has gone on to other birthings, leaving them vulnerable to whatever postnatal care and guidance others can provide in Paul's absence.

In a sermon William Sloane Coffin once spoke of the tendency to "defend ourselves, defending God." Paul's Epistle to the Galatians fairly bristles with his defensiveness. Surely his own credibility is at stake as much as the purity and truth of the gospel. Surely the danger of every sermon is an insufficient differentiation between preacher and gospel. It is often a fine line, and Paul we are not. Utter clarity of the difference between the message and the messenger is essential. Nevertheless, each time we stand to preach, we like Paul will invariably be seen as part messenger, part message; and like Paul, our own pastoral credibility will have a lot to do with the gospel that is preached and heard—then embraced or rejected. This is an enormous burden for any one preacher and any one sermon to bear.

GREGORY H. LEDBETTER

---

2. Robert Frost, "The Road Not Taken," in *Robert Frost's Poems* (New York: Pocket Books. 1971), 219.

Luke 7:1-10

¹After Jesus had finished all his sayings in the hearing of the people, he entered Capernaum. ² A centurion there had a slave whom he valued highly, and who was ill and close to death. ³When he heard about Jesus, he sent some Jewish elders to him, asking him to come and heal his slave. ⁴When they came to Jesus, they appealed to him earnestly, saying, "He is worthy of having you do this for him, ⁵for he loves our people, and it is he who built our synagogue for us." ⁶And Jesus went with them, but when he was not far from the house, the centurion sent friends to say to him, "Lord, do not trouble yourself, for I am not worthy to have you come under my roof; ⁷therefore I did not presume to come to you. But only speak the word, and let my servant be healed. ⁸For I also am a man set under authority, with soldiers under me; and I say to one, 'Go,' and he goes, and to another, 'Come,' and he comes, and to my slave, 'Do this,' and the slave does it." ⁹When Jesus heard this he was amazed at him, and turning to the crowd that followed him, he said, "I tell you, not even in Israel have I found such faith." ¹⁰When those who had been sent returned to the house, they found the slave in good health.

Theological Perspective

At first glance, this story of the healing of the centurion's slave seems to be a miracle story, but by the end it is clear that the centurion's faith in Jesus is at the center of the narrative. Through Jesus' long-distance encounter with the centurion, Luke addresses both soteriological and christological questions. How does one become part of the people of God? Further, who is Jesus, and what does God intend to accomplish through him?

The centurion belonged to the militia of Herod Antipas. He was likely one of the God-fearers, non-Jews who were attracted to Judaism because of its monotheism and ethical teachings. While they attended Jewish liturgical services and kept the major commandments, including a respect for the separation of Jews from non-Jews (see Acts 10:28), they were reluctant to abandon their ethnic group by taking the final step of circumcision. The Christian message found a vibrant response among such Gentiles, for according to Luke, they could belong fully to the people of God by faith in Jesus together with obedience to the ethical requirements of the law of God.

The centurion demonstrates the love and compassion which stand at the heart of the law. He loves *foreigners*, the Jews of his town, and acts as their benefactor, funding their synagogue's

Pastoral Perspective

On the surface, this busy collage of scenes ultimately relays a message about one man's faith and another's healing. The community does such an excellent job of speaking for the centurion we hardly realize that Jesus never actually encounters either him or his servant. The appearance of these communal voices is not merely a chorus intended to deliver a message while two of the central characters bide their time offstage. Rather, the community itself is a central part of the message.

The centurion seems to understand that he will need the help of his community if he is to convince Jesus to heal his servant. He calls first upon a group of Jewish elders to bear witness that he is worthy in character. The officer's request of these elders: convince this man Jesus to come "heal my servant." Clearly there is strong bond between the soldier and the Jewish community. He was responsible for building the synagogue; but make no mistake, he is much more than just a benefactor, for the elders state that he "loves our people." Moved, or at least intrigued by their plea, Jesus begins to follow them.

In spite of the risk that the elders or his friends might leave out some very important detail that would prove his worthiness, the centurion resists the impulse to rush toward Jesus and plead his own case. Rather, he sends a group of friends who search out

Exegetical Perspective

In Luke 4:18–19 Jesus announces his mission and the marks of his ministry. Divinely anointed, he is the harbinger of the Lord's favor, the preacher of liberation, the bringer of healing, and the bearer of good news to the poor. Immediately after this, Luke reports the rejection of Jesus' claims by his hometown (4:23). Jesus responds by reminding them that a prophet is not accepted by his own and reminds them of the treatment of Elijah and Elisha, referring specifically to Elijah's healing of the Zarephath widow's son and Elisha's cleansing of Naaman's leprosy (4:25–27). Luke returns to those motifs and to the truth that God's purposes will not be thwarted. Like Elijah and Elisha, Jesus will take his message to those who will heed it. Luke uses this episode, together with the following story about the widow from Nain, to show that God's favor extends to all, transcending social and cultural boundaries.

Up to the Sermon on the Plain (6:17–49), Luke follows the literary order of Mark 1–3. However, beginning with the sermon he diverges from Mark's order, not returning to it until 8:4. Although this section, often called "The Little Interpolation," shares content with Matthew's narrative, much of the material is Luke's and reflects Luke's ideas, interests, and concerns. In particular, Luke draws attention to Jesus as an eschatological prophet, the scope of his

Homiletical Perspective

Have you ever gone to a party where you were not invited? This happened for me a number of years ago. I had been invited to an early evening reception for a board on which I served. The host was new to the community, and I had not previously visited her home. Following the directions on the printed invitation, I pulled up uncharacteristically early in front of a stately home in an unfamiliar neighborhood and parked. The address was not posted on the house, but the host had described the house to me. Walking up to the front door, I rang the bell. Seeing others in the kitchen I walked in and through to the back of the house, and introduced myself to those gathering for evening refreshment. After a few minutes of chitchat, it dawned on me that they had no idea what I was doing in their kitchen. "This is not the Smith house, is it," I said.

"No," they replied. "The Smiths live next door." Each of them had been afraid to ask me why I was intruding, for fear that one of the other family members had invited me to their table and forgot to mention it.

The Gospel lectionary texts for this week and the next two weeks might be described as stories of unexpected guests and God's surprising graciousness. In each pericope, a guest receives some form of hospitality, though none was required in the circumstance.

Luke 7:1-10

Theological Perspective

construction. He also loves *his neighbor*, his servant, in a fashion which foreshadows the Good Samaritan (10:25–37). The servant, who is not just ill but near death, is "valuable" to him (v. 2). Perhaps the meaning is financial, yet Luke likely intends a personal meaning beyond the functional, for the centurion is described as having "friends," *philoi*, a word rare in the New Testament (v. 6). The centurion fears the loss of a valued interpersonal relationship. Together, verses 2–6 describe a man who is hospitable, generous to those around him, compassionate toward those weaker than him, and kind toward those of different ethnic groups—thus fulfilling the law and Jesus' ethical commands in the Sermon on the Plain (6:17–49).

Along with love toward others, the centurion has faith in Jesus (vv. 6b–9). He calls Jesus by the title "Lord," which a Christian reader would recognize as a sign of faith (*kyrios*, v. 6). Further, while people in antiquity believed in miraculous healings, they thought direct contact with the person mediating divine healing power was necessary (see 5:17, 6:19). In contrast, the centurion believes Jesus' commanding word, even from a distance, is sufficient to heal his slave. The centurion does not trust in Jesus' magical abilities; he trusts in Jesus' person, perceiving in Jesus an authority which places him above lower earthly elements (*exousia*, v. 8; cf. 4:6–8). Analogous to the centurion's own authority over his soldiers, when Jesus gives a command, the word is carried out with full effect. It is this deep level of trust in Jesus' person and authority by the centurion which Jesus finds "amazing," his praise bringing the narrative to its climax (v. 9).

The centurion's exemplary unity of *love* and *faith*, praised by Jesus, presents a potential challenge to Protestant readers. Pelagians, and later some feminist scholars, have used this centurion and the later Cornelius (Acts 10) to argue against Augustine's contention that "God alone" and "grace alone" bring a person into the people of God. In the story, Jesus appears "surprised" at the centurion's obedience and faith—piety which Jesus did not initiate (v. 9). Following the Protestant exegesis concerning the saints, Luther argues that God's grace brings about the centurion's faith, while Calvin says Christ healed the centurion spiritually before healing the servant.[1]

---

1. Cf. Martin Luther in Christian G. Eberle, *Luthers Evangelien-Auslegung: Ein Kommentar zu den vier Evangelien*, 2nd ed. (Stuttgart: S. G. Liesching, 1877), 364–69; and John Calvin, *A Harmony of the Gospels Matthew, Mark and Luke*, trans. Morrison (vols. 1, 3) and Parker (vol. 2), Calvin's Commentaries 1–3 (Edinburgh: Oliver & Boyd, 1972), 247.

Pastoral Perspective

Jesus to deliver the message "do *not* come to me, for I am unworthy"; he is an officer who commands others to do his bidding—sometimes, we suspect, in difficult or terrible circumstance. With this we reach what seems to be the climactic moment when the centurion's faith reveals itself: "Only speak the word and my servant will be healed" (v. 7 NIV). The officer's intentions are dramatic, and Jesus recognizes them as such. "Not even in Israel have I found such faith," he says (v. 9). We are left to wonder how the servant feels to be on the receiving end of such heroic efforts. The healing itself, witnessed as a final act by the group of friends, comes almost as an afterthought.

Before moving farther, we must struggle with the difficult and offensive notion that two of the central characters in this story are a slave and his master. When the centurion states that his is a "slave whom he valued highly" (v. 2), we are unsure if it is meant to be a practical comment on the value of his property as the social status might imply or a gentler notion of a compassionate heartfelt plea on behalf of a servant of strong character whom the soldier admires. Regardless, while this relationship may rightly stir us against the social injustice represented here, we ought not to lose sight of the notion that the centurion is *speaking on behalf of one who has no voice in society*. When our faith is enacted on behalf of another, it celebrates our web of human connectedness, especially in times of illness and tragedy. This is the imperative of faith living in the world.

The sense of connectedness begins when the Jewish leaders testify to the soldier's worthiness by lifting up how he has been accountable to the larger community. "He has loved our people, they say; further, he has built our synagogue" (v. 5, my trans.). Both of these are expressions of affection and care offered by a military officer who is under no obligation but does so out of some deep connectedness to the people. Love and commitment become central tenets of accountability to the community.

This story challenges the perception that faith can remain a solitary endeavor. We in the West especially are culturally conditioned to believe that the greater strength is found in individual fortitude. Spiritually this manifests itself in the desire to categorize faith as private and personal, rather than a public matter. Intellectually we appreciate the value of helping others, but too often we do not want to get involved. To be on the receiving end of such generosity can make us feel vulnerable, shamed, or burdened by the obligation to return the kindness in a like manner.

appeal, and the contours of faith that accepts him as God's agent. These concerns can be seen in the text's structure: it opens and closes with examples of genuine faith in Jesus (7:1–10, 36–50), which bracket passages revealing Jesus as God's eschatological agent (7:11–17, 18–35).

The passage begins with the interesting phrase "after all of his words had filled the people's ears" (v. 1, my trans.), connecting it to 6:46–49, where faithfulness is defined as both hearing and doing. A centurion, who has heard of Jesus (v. 3), demonstrates that sort of faith by acting on it. A delegation of Jewish elders approaches Jesus on behalf of a Roman centurion whose servant is gravely ill. The elders commend the centurion to Jesus because of his patronage of their synagogue and because he has shown respect for their religion (v. 4). Luke makes obvious allusions to the story of Elisha's healing of Naaman (2 Kgs. 5:1–14). In both stories, a Gentile with military rank requests miraculous healing from a prophet of Israel's God, the exchange between prophet and requester occurs through emissaries rather than face to face, and the healing is effected at a distance. There are differences however. While Naaman initially rejects Elisha's instructions, the centurion, appreciating Jesus' stature, is willing to follow whatever Jesus instructs. The contrast is important for Luke. While Jesus is a prophet like Elisha, he is also more. He is the great prophet whom God has raised among his people (v. 16). His immediate and unqualified acceptance by the centurion makes this clear.

Of importance are the contrasting delegations sent by the centurion. The first, as we have seen, is made up of Jewish elders from a local synagogue. Because of the cultural and religious divide between Gentile and Jew, the centurion does not presume to approach Jesus directly, but only through these intermediaries, who present the centurion as "worthy" (v. 4). The second delegation is composed of the centurion's friends (v. 6). Luke has them speak in the first person, thus expressing the centurion's own voice. In contrast to the first delegation, the second stresses the centurion's lack of worthiness and requests that Jesus not come to his house.

The centurion is not denying what the elders have said, but he changes the elements of evaluation. He recognizes the difference between himself and Jesus. Superficially, the centurion's statement can be taken as another instance of his appreciation of Jewish sensibilities. He does not approach Jesus, and he asks Jesus not to enter his house, because he realizes that

The context of these stories is that Jesus finished his teaching on a level place to a great crowd of his disciples and a great multitude of people. He then entered Capernaum, where, in the first of these stories, the text for this week, a centurion of the Roman army heard that Jesus was coming. Jesus' reputation must have preceded him. The centurion was an outsider who would not have received an invitation to party with Jesus, yet he had a particular dilemma. One of his servants, a favored slave, was quite ill. Not so bold as to walk directly into Jesus' living room uninvited, he sent word through the Jewish elders that he would like to have Jesus come to heal this important member of his household.

"When Jesus heard this he was amazed at him, and turning to the crowd that followed him, he said, 'I tell you, not even in Israel have I found such faith.' When those who had been sent returned to the house, they found the slave in good health" (vv. 9–10).

Jesus healed the slave from a distance, that the faith of the centurion, who was outside the house of Israel, might be confirmed. Jesus turned on its head the prevailing understanding of who was invited to the welcome table, by his willingness to restore health based not on who held the printed invitation, but on who by faith was willing to walk through God's front door of mercy.

This text is troubling in several ways. First, we struggle with the fact of first-century life, that the centurion had a slave, however beloved. The Talmud describes various forms of servant status among Jews from about 200 BCE to 400 CE. Relationships in Roman households were prescribed by household tables that spelled out the lines of responsibility and authority among various servants and family members. The centurion was accustomed both to commanding a company of soldiers and to standing at the head of the household that was structured according to custom and law.

Although slavery in the first century was quite different from the chattel slavery of eighteenth- and nineteenth-century America, our sense of justice makes the hair rise on the back of our necks when we consider the inequity of relationship evoked by this image. Yet this inequity in power and authority testifies to Jesus' authority when the centurion compares his status before Jesus to that of a slave. The centurion makes it clear to Jesus that the beloved slave follows orders as a servant in his household. The centurion compares himself to the beloved slave: "As I order my slave with authority, so you can command it for me."

Luke 7:1-10

Theological Perspective

However, beyond questions of faith's origin, Luke portrays faith as situated within a community of hospitality in which God and others are embraced. The centurion both trusts personally in Jesus and uses his power to support others in his community. The story's coherence with the Reformation insistence that we are "saved by grace through faith alone" is seen in the centurion's unconditional clinging to Jesus' word as having saving power and in his humility before Jesus. The centurion may stand over his slave, yet he is wordless and powerless in relation to the illness. Further, he knows he is unworthy of Jesus' presence with regard to God's law (cf. 17:10). He becomes worthy by believing he is not (cf. 9:24) and holding fast to Jesus. Finally, his faith is proleptic; he believes in Jesus' power and authority, but does not yet know fully who Jesus is, revealed in cross and resurrection (Luke 22–24).

Who is this Jesus to whom the centurion clings? On the most obvious level, Jesus is *a healer*. He is filled with God's compassion and like a "physician" (5:31) acts to free people of demons (4:31–37, 41) and to cure people of leprosy, paralysis, and other diseases (5:12–32; 4:38–40).

However, he does these exorcisms and healings as *a prophet of Israel*. In this story, Jesus performs an act that clearly points back to an earlier prophet's cleansing of Naaman the Syrian general (see 4:27; 9:19). Naaman, also a non-Jew, had sought help from Elisha, who healed Naaman's leprosy with imperative words without their meeting (2 Kgs. 5:1–14). As before, so here, a person sent by God heals a non-Jew so that all may see "that there is a prophet in Israel" (2 Kgs. 5:8).

At the deepest level, Jesus is greater than the Old Testament prophets and John the Baptist. He is *the hoped-for Jewish Messiah of God*, the one "filled with the power of the Spirit" to proclaim the inbreaking visitation of God in saving judgment and grace (see 9:18–20; 4:14, 18–21). As in the earlier exorcisms and healings, Jesus' spoken word (7:7) has the power of YHWH's word to subdue death-dealing forces, a power revealed in the story's end: "When those who had been sent returned to the house, they found the slave in good health" (7:10).

GREGORY ANDERSON LOVE

Pastoral Perspective

As I write this essay, for survivors of southern Sudan's brutal civil war, connectedness to each other is a matter of survival. Many families are now returning to their homeland, some after as many as fifteen years in refugee camps. The comprehensive peace agreement signed in 2005 has stopped the shooting but it has done nothing to restore health and livelihood among the Dinka people.[1] They are held accountable to each other by a long tradition of communal responsibility. Food and medicine are very limited and the only medical doctors are located miles from the rural villages. Like the servant in this story, the Dinka depend especially upon those in the community to speak on their behalf in search of healing. At times this means negotiating with local officials for assistance or seeking money from family members resettled abroad. For many it means carrying a frail body to the village church and gathering literally to speak to Jesus on behalf of healing.

Whom do we turn to when available resources fail us or are depleted? Often we cling to a stoic sense of private faith that longs to call out to others for prayer at the bedside vigil or in moments of desperate need. Sometimes it is the simple burden of everyday life that urges us to call out to another. When we finally do reach out, too often we do so with a sense of shame or failure that our faith is not strong enough to go it alone. Indeed, the roots of one's faith are embedded deeply within the individual heart. But a *lived faith* must recognize itself as part of the world. We require the larger community, especially the community of faith, to speak with us and for us—to name what is just and hold us accountable. It is this faith that helps us to encounter the joys, challenges, and tragedies of life and reconcile the unpredictable nature of each with the grace of Jesus Christ.

M. JAN HOLTON

---

1. The Dinka tribe is one of the largest in southern Sudan.

Exegetical Perspective

Jesus would risk ritual pollution by coming in contact with a Gentile. However, the reason that the centurion offers for his unworthiness is not based on his religious status, but the qualitative difference between Jesus' authority and his own. Through military experience the centurion has learned the marks of authority and the chain of command. His life has been one of giving and receiving orders, and he understands the power vested in them (v. 8). Having heard of Jesus' miraculous power, he recognizes the authority Jesus possesses. The centurion knows that this one, as the designated representative of God, has been vested with God's power over the creation.

The centurion also knows that his authority is derived from those he represents. Thus, when he says, "Go," his subordinates go, and when he orders them "Come," they come. By analogy he knows that if his power, derived from human authority, can direct human will, then the one whose power is derived from God is capable of even more. Just as the centurion effects change with a simple order, he realizes that Jesus can heal his servant by merely uttering the word (v. 7). And indeed this is what happens (v. 10). Luke thus shows that the healing power of God is not bound by space or limited to those who are recognized as God's people. It is available to all without exception. The centurion has understood this, and in his recognition of Jesus' status as God's representative he allows that power to become evident. It is for this reason that Jesus commends his faith (v. 9).

Luke not only records Jesus' sanction; he also notes his amazement at finding faith in a non-Jew. Sadly, it is in an outsider, not Israel, that he discovers someone with genuine faith. However, the story also holds out hope that such faith can be found in Israel. Luke notes that when he commends the centurion, Jesus turns to the crowd who had followed him. In doing so, he holds him up as an exemplar, thus allowing for the possibility that they will emulate this faith and allow the power of God's favor to extend to them as well.

STEVEN J. KRAFTCHICK

Homiletical Perspective

The second problematic issue in this text is that it sounds initially as if the centurion was worthy to receive this blessing. His worthiness came not from his membership in the house of Israel, but from the fact that according to the Jewish elders, "[He] built our synagogue for us" (v. 5). Though not a Jew, he was clearly sympathetic, even supportive of Jews. Does this imply that the one who contributes the most money is worthy of Jesus' attention?

Jesus turned on its head the conventional custom of bestowing greater honor on the wealthy. He healed the slave of the centurion, not because he gave a great deal of money, but because he exhibited a great deal of faith. This situation gave Jesus the opportunity to demonstrate that faithfulness did not depend on membership in the club (house of Israel), on social status (free slaveowner), or on economic status (those who make greater financial contributions). In it he demonstrated to the Jewish elders that they were asking the wrong questions about righteousness.

Finally, Jesus healed the least powerful one of all. As the centurion was an outsider by position and culture, to a much greater extent the servant of his household was outside the central area of Jesus' concern. The slave lived on the margin, without voice or vote in what became of him. He served, dependent upon the generosity of his boss to provide for him, in sickness as well as health. The centurion could have treated him as disposable, replacing him with someone more able-bodied.

Jesus, through his healing of the centurion's slave through faith, extended God's graciousness to the least member of this culture. By so doing, he taught the disciples and the elders that God's saving grace extends to the uninvited guest. The ones we consider to be gate-crashers unworthy to attend the party are the very ones offered God's provision regardless.

VERLEE A. COPELAND

1 Kings 17:8-16 (17-24)

⁸Then the word of the LORD came to him, saying, ⁹"Go now to Zarephath, which belongs to Sidon, and live there; for I have commanded a widow there to feed you." ¹⁰So he set out and went to Zarephath. When he came to the gate of the town, a widow was there gathering sticks; he called to her and said, "Bring me a little water in a vessel, so that I may drink." ¹¹As she was going to bring it, he called to her and said, "Bring me a morsel of bread in your hand." ¹²But she said, "As the LORD your God lives, I have nothing baked, only a handful of meal in a jar, and a little oil in a jug; I am now gathering a couple of sticks, so that I may go home and prepare it for myself and my son, that we may eat it, and die." ¹³Elijah said to her, "Do not be afraid; go and do as you have said; but first make me a little cake of it and bring it to me, and afterwards make something for yourself and your son. ¹⁴For thus says the LORD the God of Israel: The jar of meal will not be emptied and the jug of oil will not fail until the day that the LORD sends rain on the earth." ¹⁵She went and did as Elijah said, so that she as well as he and her household ate for many days. ¹⁶The jar of meal was not emptied, neither did the jug of oil fail, according to the word of the LORD that he spoke by Elijah.

Theological Perspective

In a world riven by conflict and urgent need, we thirst for miracles. The story of Elijah and the widow of Zarephath dramatizes the miracle of divine compassion that unfolds when we dare to invite the prophetic word into our midst.

First Kings 17 offers us no fewer than three miracles in twenty-four verses, in a series of vignettes that increase in narrative intensity. The scene is set in 17:6–7, where we see the first miracle: ravens bring bread and meat to Elijah in the morning and in the evening. Many cultures tell of infants, saints, and warriors who are nurtured in the wilderness by feral creatures that normally would represent a threat to humans. The wilderness is a place of testing, as Abraham knew. It is a place of struggle and unexpected gift, as Moses knew. For those who venture into the wilderness, it is a place to meet God. God calls from a flaming bush (Exod. 3); God thunders from atop Sinai (Exod. 19). God's glory illumines the wilderness, leaving Moses's face radiant with the terror and wonder of it (Exod. 34:29–35).

When Elijah emerges from the wilderness, we are alarmed, for he is a wild man (see 2 Kgs. 1:8). In the storytelling of many cultures, the figure of the wild man is set over against cultured society and the conventions of civilization. Think of Enkidu from the Epic of Gilgamesh, Samson and John the Baptist

Pastoral Perspective

"The widow, the orphan, and the stranger." These words or categories appear many times in the Scriptures grouped as one social class of voiceless people. Why? What was the thread that united those categories of people? Is it possible that a system of laws designed to protect these people, a system forged under the guidance of the God who is decidedly in favor of the voiceless, nevertheless keeps these very people locked in a perpetual second-class position?

Indeed widows, orphans, and strangers were the poorest of the poor of Elijah's days. Being a widow also meant her child was considered an orphan, the father figure bearing more societal weight than a mother. Widows, orphans, and strangers had this in common: they did not count on the protection offered by a citizen adult male in their family. Thus they were poor and powerless; life was miserable. Much in the OT lets us know of God's care for them, but what kept them powerless?

In North America today there are many laws protecting vulnerable ones. Not strong enough or empowering enough, these laws are attempts in the direction of care for the weak. Are some of these laws also keeping justice at bay? Are we as a nation and as individuals more interested in doing charity than enabling justice for all? Such a thing happened in Elijah's days.

¹⁷After this the son of the woman, the mistress of the house, became ill; his illness was so severe that there was no breath left in him. ¹⁸She then said to Elijah, "What have you against me, O man of God? You have come to me to bring my sin to remembrance, and to cause the death of my son!" ¹⁹But he said to her, "Give me your son." He took him from her bosom, carried him up into the upper chamber where he was lodging, and laid him on his own bed. ²⁰He cried out to the LORD, "O LORD my God, have you brought calamity even upon the widow with whom I am staying, by killing her son?" ²¹Then he stretched himself upon the child three times, and cried out to the LORD, "O LORD my God, let this child's life come into him again." ²²The LORD listened to the voice of Elijah; the life of the child came into him again, and he revived. ²³Elijah took the child, brought him down from the upper chamber into the house, and gave him to his mother; then Elijah said, "See, your son is alive." ²⁴So the woman said to Elijah, "Now I know that you are a man of God, and that the word of the LORD in your mouth is truth."

Exegetical Perspective

Today's reading is part of the narrative cycle in 1 Kings 17–19 that tells of the confrontation between King Ahab of the northern kingdom of Israel and Elijah the prophet. Under the influence of his wife Jezebel, Ahab introduced into Israel the worship of the Canaanite god Baal. One of Baal's attributes was giving rain to nurture the crops. (For a fuller discussion of 1 Kgs. 17–19, see essay on 1 Kgs. 18:20–39, pp. 75–79).

Chapter 17 begins with Elijah's announcement of a drought to Ahab (v. 1). The fact that Baal was responsible for rain makes this announcement a direct challenge to Baal's power and a judgment against Ahab's support of Baal. Having confronted Ahab with this word of YHWH, Elijah is forced to flee.

The rest of chapter 17 contains three stories of Elijah's experiences as he hides from Ahab during the drought. In verses 2–7, YHWH sends Elijah to the Wadi Cherith, east of the Jordan. There the ravens feed him, and he drinks from the wadi until it dries up. In verses 8–16, Elijah is fed by a widow of Zarephath. In verses 17–24, he revives the widow's desperately ill son.

All three stories are prophet legends, designed to praise the prophet's good qualities and to establish the prophet's legitimacy. In all three stories God provides a miracle to sustain life in a situation where

Homiletical Perspective

The relationship between the kings of Israel and the prophets of God is a storied one. The kings seemed to value—indeed, need—their prophets. They seemed to sense that God liked to be in touch with them. They just did not appreciate the fact that sometimes the prophets' message was, "O Great King, O mighty ruler before whom mere mortals tremble, God has a word for me to speak to you. It is a hard word, for God is not exactly pleased with you. There is a price to be paid for your dance with unrighteousness. There is score to be settled for your embrace of injustice. God is merciful, yet God is just. Beware, for God is no respecter of persons." Yes, the prophets often found themselves in awkward positions, perpetually asked to bite the hand that fed them. This, of course, led to a life of bold pronouncements, interspersed with lingering questions. Sound familiar?

Elijah the Tishbite was the prophet of God when Ahab was king of Israel. The Bible tells us that "Ahab did more to provoke the anger of the LORD, the God of Israel, than had all the kings of Israel who were before him" (1 Kgs. 16:33). We can be sure that Elijah fully expected to spend a lot of time delivering Ahab his failing grades from God and a lot of time running for cover and fearing for his life. In other words, he could anticipate a life of bold pronouncements followed by lingering questions.

1 Kings 17:8-16 (17-24)

Theological Perspective

in the Bible, and Tarzan in contemporary Western culture. One theological implication here is that the prophetic word cannot be tamed. The wild Elijah approaches a widow at Zarephath. Her vulnerability underscores the risk that the word of God presents to those who confront it. The potential danger that the widow faces when she meets an unkempt stranger from the wilderness is clear, but she is dangerous to him as well. In stories of wild men drawn into civilization, often women serve as lure and civilizing force. Our text is careful to note that she is Sidonian—of the same ethnicity as Jezebel, who will become Elijah's most potent nemesis. Risk abounds as Elijah steps through the liminal space of the gate at Zarephath. Will he harm her? Will she tame him? We hold our breath, alert and tense.

The emphasis on hospitality increases the dramatic tension in the narrative. Elijah demands water and food from this desperate woman, whose family is at the point of starvation. Now comes the second miracle: her jar of meal and jug of oil are miraculously replenished, day after day. Those who dare to host the wild divine word in their midst are saved from disaster. We are relieved. The story continues; this was only a feint toward closure, and our anxiety mounts once again. The wild-man prophet lingers in the heart of this community. Does another crisis loom?

Indeed it does. The son of the widow dies, and she names the darkest dread that a community can harbor about its prophets: has the presence of Elijah brought the terrible wrath of God upon her? Rather than defend himself, Elijah challenges God on her behalf. Elijah is interceding: imagine not meek hands folded in quiet prayer, but the fierce raging of a wild man. His God has killed the only child of the woman who has been kind to him. This wrenching loss cannot go unaddressed—not here, not in this fragile community that has been brave enough to host the divine word in its midst.

God listens to the voice of Elijah.

The widow's cry, "Now I know ['atah zeh yada'ti] that you are a man of God, and that the word of the LORD in your mouth is truth" (v. 24), echoes the confession of another outsider, Jethro of Midian, when he saw that God redeemed Israel from slavery: "Now I know ['atah yada'ti] that the LORD is greater than all gods, because he delivered the people from the Egyptians" (Exod. 18:11). Her cry echoes the angel's confession after Abraham bound Isaac: "Now I know ['atah yada'ti] that you fear God, since you have not withheld your son, your only son, from me" (Gen.

Pastoral Perspective

In our story we find a widow and her child—strangers to Elijah, Elijah also a stranger to them. Elijah is physically thirsty and hungry, but, as a fugitive from the anger of King Ahab, he is also emotionally distressed. The widow, a loving mother, is thirsty and hungry, but not only for food and water. She earnestly desires a voice that can be heard and fullness of life for her and her son. We know Elijah's name. We do not know the names of the woman or the child—something common in biblical narratives, yet another sign of injustice. Women and children were, more often than not, referred to as the wife or child of male adults, in those days the only ones with any power in social and religious life. The laws of the land kept things that way. Some of us know how that feels.

No wonder Isaiah clamored:

Ah, you who . . . write oppressive statutes,
to turn aside the needy from justice,
    and to rob the poor of my people of their right,
that widows may be your spoil,
    and that you make the orphans your prey!
(Isa. 10: 1–2)

Too many around us are that widow or that child, literally or figuratively. Too many around us feel lost, hopeless, hungry, and thirsty for something beyond the tangibles of daily living, for more than meager leftovers, scraps of food, love, and justice. Many feel that there is simply no one willing to empower them with healing and grace. The image of a widow also stands for all manner of poor people in the Bible; the psalms are full of such imagery. We see widows in Gospel narratives like today's story of Jesus' encounter with a grieving widow. Widows are also metaphors for spiritual or emotional poverty. Are we not all poor before God? We are all indeed needy, widow, orphan, and stranger in spirit. Yet our trust in God leads us to sing with the psalm of the day:

Praise the LORD. . . .
who executes justice for the oppressed;
who gives food to the hungry. . . .
watches over the strangers;
upholds the orphan and the widow.
(Ps. 146:1, 7, 9)

We first know ourselves to be the poor, and God is on the side of the poor.

The stranger woman and her child feed Elijah and receive him, glad of the miracle of unending food for life, and oil for healing and light. Then the child dies. The widow's grief is beyond the normal

death threatens. In the process, Elijah's vocation and power as God's prophet are confirmed.

The last two stories in chapter 17 comprise today's lectionary reading. The primary reading is verses 8–16. Verses 17–24 are an optional extension. The two stories belong together in the sense that the characters remain the same in both. However, each story can stand alone as a coherent unit. It is possible that verses 17–24 were included because today's Gospel reading, Luke 7:11–17, is the story of Jesus raising the son of the widow of Nain. The preacher could focus on the miraculous feeding, the miraculous healing, or the entire interaction between Elijah and the widow.

The structure of verses 8–16 is an interplay of words spoken by one character followed by the response of another character. The stage is set with YHWH's command to Elijah to go to Zarephath, where YHWH has commanded a widow to feed him (vv. 8–9). Elijah obeys, going to Zarephath, where he finds a widow gathering sticks (v. 10a). He requests that she bring him water to drink (v. 10b), and she obeys, setting out to bring the water (v. 11a). Elijah calls to her again, asking for bread (v. 11b). This time the widow protests the request, explaining to Elijah that she has only enough meal and oil to prepare a last meal for herself and her son (v. 12). Elijah reassures her, asks her to feed him first, and proclaims the word of YHWH that the meal and the oil will not fail until YHWH sends rain again (vv. 13–14). The widow obeys, and they all eat for many days (v. 15). The narrative ends with confirmation of YHWH's word concerning the unfailing supply of meal and oil (v. 16).

Elijah is sent by God right into enemy territory: Sidon is the home of Jezebel and the land of Baal. Moreover, God's provision for Elijah's survival during the drought-induced famine is an unlikely choice. She is a widow, left to her own meager resources, with no support from family and with a child to care for. The famine makes her situation even more desperate. She has only "a handful of meal," "a little oil," and "a couple of sticks" with which to prepare a last meal for herself and her son (v. 12). The widow's initial protest to Elijah's request for bread makes clear that she is unaware of YHWH's command for her to feed Elijah. However, she ultimately accepts Elijah's assurance and acts in trust of YHWH's word.

This story speaks of the obedience and trust of Elijah and the widow. It also proclaims the extent of YHWH's power and grace. Even in the home

As this text begins, Elijah has only recently informed Ahab that his actions have brought a drought upon Israel. This drought will not be lifted except upon God's command. After he delivers this message, God tells Elijah to hide in the Wadi Cherith. The wadi seems to be a pleasant enough place. There is water to drink, and "ravens brought him bread and meat in the morning, and bread and meat in the evening" (1 Kgs. 17:6a). The problem is that because of Ahab's wickedness God has brought a drought on Israel. That drought falls on the just and the unjust. It falls on the Wadi Cherith. It falls on Elijah, who was hiding there. Elijah needs another option. He needs a plan B.

God's plans, particularly God's plan Bs, are always very interesting. They leave us scratching our heads, wondering if we heard God right and wondering if God knows what God is doing. Since there is no water in the wadi, and it does not look as if this is going to change in the foreseeable future, God says to Elijah, "Go now to Zarephath, which belongs to Sidon, and live there; for I have commanded a widow there to feed you" (1 Kgs. 17:9). We don't know if Elijah knew much about Zarephath or Sidon. We know that he would not have been optimistic about a widow feeding him. In the best of times, most widows lived a very tenuous existence. In a time of drought, their need would have been even more pronounced. We cannot blame Elijah if he mutters to himself, "I would rather trust the ravens than depend on the widow. Does God know what God is doing?"

It probably does not help Elijah's confidence much when, upon arriving in Zarephath, he sees the widow gathering sticks, an act not exactly synonymous with wealth and financial security. Maybe because he is tired, thirsty, and hungry, or maybe to assess how bad her situation is, Elijah asks the widow for a drink of water and little bite of bread. How his chest must tighten when he hears her reply, "As the LORD your God lives, I have nothing baked, only a handful of meal in a jar, and a little oil in a jug; I am now gathering a couple of sticks, so that I may go home and prepare it for myself and my son, that we may eat it, and die" (1 Kgs. 17:12). "Oh no," Elijah must be murmuring, "It's worse than I thought, it's as bad as it can be. God, don't you have a plan C?"

Of course, these are not the words that come out of Elijah's mouth. Instead of voicing his questions, Elijah makes a bold pronouncement, that the widow should go ahead and make him a meal and that God will see to it that her jar of meal will not be emptied and her jug of oil will not run out. Where does

1 Kings 17:8-16 (17-24)

Theological Perspective

22:12). Because of the wild intercession of Elijah, the exodus unfolds anew and God halts the sacrifice of the beloved. Once again we are delivered. Once again we praise a God whose love defeats death.

Elijah shows God's compassion to those who dare to host the prophetic word. Most striking in this story is not the resurrection of the boy but the intimacy of prophetic presence. The Israelite wild man dwells with the Sidonian widow in abject poverty, not just briefly but for years. His choice to be present with her shows us how we may embody the prophetic word in our own lives: in intimate solidarity with those at risk.

The intertestamental book of Sirach lionizes Elijah as "a prophet like fire" (Sir. 48:1). Elijah's prophetic witness burns like fire through the constraints of our spiritual imagination. God's word is truth, and it is mighty. Boundaries between insider and outsider are as nothing, the desperation of famine is as nothing, before the prophetic word of God's abundant mercy. There is nothing stronger than the wild compassion of God. In welcoming the prophet, we learn that God's power is among us not for judgment but for life.

In the story of the transfiguration (Luke 9:28–36; Matt. 17:1–8), we see Jesus conferring with Moses the lawgiver and Elijah the wild-man prophet. Moses and Elijah together ratify a gospel that is all radical obedience and ferocious compassion. When we dare to host the prophetic word, we are transformed. For we encounter a God who delivers the powerless, a God whose word yields inexhaustible abundance, a God whose compassion is stronger than death. Elijah's prophetic word points to the One who is the way, the truth, and the life. Host that word, know the truth, and live.

CAROLYN J. SHARP

Pastoral Perspective

grief of a mother: she knows that without a male adult in her life she will be kept at a level of dependency even more profound than her current situation. Her son was hope for her later years, and now hope is gone. Elijah pleads with God, covers the boy's body with his own—symbolizing God's care for the whole person—and hope and life return to the widow and child.

We are that widow today, but God's countercultural favor and actions on behalf of the poor, love beyond measure, are also in our midst today. See signs of mercy in our Sunday assemblies: in the font, good news of life in unending water; in the anointing, good news of healing and light in unending oil; in the pulpit, good news of justice and salvation in unending Word, Jesus Christ; in the Table, good news of life, grace, and joy in unending bread and wine. All these things are set out for all.

We are the voiceless widows. We are the silenced orphans. We are the homeless strangers. Some translations of the Scriptures refer to strangers as "aliens," today a pejorative, wounding word applied to many wanderers among us; but we are the poor, wayfaring strangers. We die, but God covers us with life, then sends us forth, surprised, to be Elijah. We must not remain silent while political and religious laws keep the poor in our midst locked in poverty and oppression. To strangers who escape a land of known despair and seek a new land of unknown hope, we with God become their shelter. In God's name, we like the widow bring water, oil, bread, and wine for the lost, oppressed, poor, and forgotten. Surprised by joy, we receive life from their hand, for God promises that when we receive the stranger and the poor, we may be receiving angels without knowing it (Heb. 13:1–2).

We first know ourselves to be the real poor. God is on the side of the poor.

GLÁUCIA VASCONCELOS WILKEY

territory of Baal and Jezebel, YHWH is in charge. Even to a poor and desperate widow, who is not one of YHWH's own people Israel, YHWH offers life.

In verses 17–24, the predicament is the illness of the widow's son. This illness "was so severe that there was no breath left in him" (v. 17). The text does not necessarily indicate that the child is dead, but certainly the illness is serious enough that he is on the verge of death.

In addition to the son, a passive participant throughout the story, the characters are Elijah, the widow, and YHWH. The narrative unfolds in three scenes: verses 18–19, the widow and Elijah; verses 20–22, Elijah and YHWH; and verses 23–24, Elijah and the widow.

In the first scene the widow blames Elijah for her son's illness (v. 18). She believes that this illness is divine punishment for some sin of hers, and that the presence of Elijah, man of God, in her house has brought her (and her sinfulness) to God's attention. Elijah's response is to take the child from her, carry him upstairs to his own bed (v. 19).

In the second scene Elijah offers a prayer of lament to YHWH (v. 20). His complaint is that YHWH has caused this calamity—"killing" the widow's son despite the fact that she has saved Elijah's life at YHWH's command (vv. 8–16). Elijah then stretches himself out upon the child three times and concludes his prayer with a petition for YHWH to revive him (v. 21). YHWH hears Elijah's prayer, and the boy is revived (v. 22).

In the third scene Elijah takes the revived child back to his mother (v. 23). The widow's response is a confession of faith (v. 24). This confession is not directly about YHWH, but about Elijah's identity as YHWH's prophet (v. 24). In the context of the entire chapter, this affirmation applies not only to the child's revival and to the unfailing food supply (vv. 14–16), but also to Elijah's initial announcement of the drought to Ahab (v. 1).

MARSHA M. WILFONG

Elijah find the confidence to speak so boldly and back up his words with deeds?

I know this. I know that Rufus Watson loved this story. Rufus, who lived to be ninety-nine years old, was born in Texas, the son of former slaves. He served his country in the military. He pitched in the Negro professional leagues. He made some money investing in real estate. He witnessed lynchings and spent a lifetime wondering how people commit such atrocities and still go to church and call themselves Christians.

He found comfort in the story of Elijah and the widow. He said if his life was not proof enough, this story showed that God meets people at the bottom of the barrel. "That's where God meets us, Jim, at the bottom of the barrel. God meets us when we've gone so low that all we can do is look up." If Rufus trusted God to meet him at life's low points, if Elijah trusted God to meet him at life's low points, if God met Elijah and the widow at the point where the grain, oil, and rain were running out, I guess we are well advised to do the same. We can hold on to our questions. They are not inconsequential or invalid. Elijah probably held on to his. He just spoke his faith and backed up his words with actions.

Of course let's not forget about Ahab—fuming about Elijah's impudence, wishing someone would do something to make it rain. We could always put our trust in him.

H. JAMES HOPKINS

Psalm 146

¹Praise the LORD!
  Praise the LORD, O my soul!
²I will praise the LORD as long as I live;
  I will sing praises to my God all my life long.

³Do not put your trust in princes,
  in mortals, in whom there is no help.
⁴When their breath departs, they return to the earth;
  on that very day their plans perish.

⁵Happy are those whose help is the God of Jacob,
  whose hope is in the LORD their God,
⁶who made heaven and earth,
  the sea, and all that is in them;
  who keeps faith forever;

Theological Perspective

Psalm 146 carries forward much of the spirit and thought of Psalm 96. It differs chiefly in that it has much less to say about the natural world, although it is equally clear that God is the creator of both heaven and earth. It focuses instead on the relation between God and human beings. Here it sets up a sharp contrast between mortal rulers and the everlasting God. If we attach ourselves to the former, we will be left with nothing when these rulers die; but God endures always.

Although the point is not made explicitly, it is also clear that God's work in the world is quite opposite to that of worldly powers. God executes justice for the oppressed, feeds the hungry, and sets the prisoner free. Presumably the oppression is by powerful humans who so order society that some people are hungry and who imprison others. As the psalm proceeds, it is the blind, the bowed down, the widow, and the orphan whom God supports. In other words, God directs God's work to support just those who are the victims in human society.

In short, this psalm is an expression of the liberation theology that many have found in the Bible. Its primary understanding of God is as supporting the weak against the strong, the oppressed against the oppressor. This is not the only theme in the Bible, but this theme has made the

Pastoral Perspective

Psalm 146 begins and ends with doxology. Praising God is something we all know we need to do. Praising God throughout our lives, and especially *singing* praise, is good for our souls. However, after the first few verses the psalmist quickly changes the tone by bringing praise (which may be seen as a somewhat otherworldly activity) into the realm of present struggles. How does one live out the doxological life when facing the realities of oppression, imprisonment, blindness, and feeling "bowed down"? And perhaps more important, *who* will help us face these challenges?

The psalmist cautions against putting one's "trust in princes." Yet that may be a temptation for all who seek help. In Colette Dowling's book *The Cinderella Complex*,[1] the author takes the fairy tale of the prince who rides in to rescue the woman in distress as a metaphor for the tendencies in some women to seek for a male rescuer. Dowling suggests that this is a flight from independence and responsibility. While this may be true, the idea of looking for a "prince" to swoop in and rescue us may not be gender specific. All of us tend to look for someone to take care of our needs, and this is particularly true when

---

1. Colette Dowling, *The Cinderella Complex: Women's Fear of Independence* (New York: Simon & Schuster, 1990).

7 who executes justice for the oppressed;
   who gives food to the hungry.

The LORD sets the prisoners free;
8 the LORD opens the eyes of the blind.
The LORD lifts up those who are bowed down;
   the LORD loves the righteous.
9The LORD watches over the strangers;
   he upholds the orphan and the widow,
   but the way of the wicked he brings to ruin.

10The LORD will reign forever,
   your God, O Zion, for all generations.
   Praise the LORD!

Exegetical Perspective

Psalm 146 begins the Psalter's final doxological section: Psalms 146–50. Each psalm begins and ends with "praise YHWH" (*hallelu yah*), a firm acknowledgment of the position of YHWH within creation and within the life of the faithful. This section stands in stark contrast to the Psalter's beginning. In Book 1, psalms of lament dominate (59 percent), while in Book 5, the majority are psalms of praise (52 percent). The Psalter moves from lament to praise, a movement that reflects its "plot line."

The book of Psalms is often called the "Hymnbook of the Second Temple," an apt description. Many scholars believe that the Psalter was not just a haphazard collection of hymns, but that it was purposefully shaped to tell a story.[1] The five books of the Psalter tell a story of ancient Israel that begins with David's reign (Book 1), continues through the divided monarchy and the destruction of the kingdoms (Books 2 and 3) and through the exile in Babylon (Book 4), and ends in the period of the return from exile and the rebuilding of the temple (Book 5).

The destruction of Jerusalem and the temple by the Babylonians in 587 BCE changed life forever for

1. For more on the Psalter's story, see J. Clinton McCann Jr., ed., *The Shape and Shaping of the Psalter*, JSOTSup 159 (Sheffield: JSOT Press, 1993), and Nancy L. deClaissé-Walford, *Introduction to the Psalms* (St. Louis: Chalice Press, 2004).

Homiletical Perspective

Psalm 146 names the God of Israel as "Lord." Many today hesitate to designate God as Lord, and there are perhaps good reasons to hesitate, but we owe it to the tradition to ponder just what kind of Lord Israel imagined.

This transcendent sovereign of Israel was both creator and judge, life-giver and justice-giver. The same God who "made heaven and earth, the sea, and all that is in them" also gives "justice for the oppressed . . . food to the hungry" (vv. 6–7). The sense of judgeship here is not one of fear and oppression, but of a welcomed Advocate who sets the prisoners free, defends orphans and widows, and passes judgment against those who abuse them, that is, "the wicked."

Contrast this with the lords of this world. When we put our faith in presidents and evangelists to bring about God's kingdom, we are doubly disappointed, as their administrations seem so often to sink into corruption and incompetence. As the psalmist says, in them there is no help, for they are mere mortals and their plans are as fragile as their bodies. So although God can certainly work through mortal leaders to bring forth the beloved community, we are called to remember that they are not worthy of our ultimate praise and trust.

Happy are those who put their trust in the eternal God who made heaven and earth. Once again we see

Psalm 146

Theological Perspective

Bible an immensely important source for the struggle for justice that has been part of our Western history and is so critically important today.

Alongside this strong support for freeing the oppressed, the Jewish Scriptures also have a great concern for conforming to the law. This is not necessarily in opposition to the liberation motif, because the Jewish law is profoundly influenced by the concern for justice for all. However, when God is depicted as concerned chiefly with our obedience, it can easily turn out that as the law becomes more complex, only those who are of higher social rank have a reasonable chance of living obedient lives. God's demand for righteousness can become a support for oppression rather than liberation. The contrast of the righteous and the wicked appears in this psalm as well, but it is subordinated to, and virtually equated with, the contract of the oppressed and the oppressors. Oppression is in itself wicked; in fact the psalmist seems to feel it is the epitome of wickedness.

The recitation of this psalm gives comfort to the victims; they feel that God is with them and seeks their fulfillment. The psalm assures them that this is no small thing, that the creator of heaven and earth is already feeding and healing and freeing them. There is no idea that God is coming to execute justice in the future. God is already, now and always, executing justice.

There is, of course, a problem with this message. In historical fact, the hungry often remain hungry; the blind remain blind; widows and orphans remain marginalized. How are they to relate their actual historical experience to this assurance of God's ever present support and action in their behalf? This has been a problem not only for ancient Israelites but for their heirs to this day. The Lord who made heaven and earth will reign forever; but in our day-to-day experience, the rule of oppressive mortals appears more evident than God's work against them. How are we to reconcile this profound contradiction?

There have been many ways of alleviating this tension. In Psalm 96 the problem was less acute, because the great works for the needy were not spelled out, and God was still coming to bring justice. However, in Psalm 146 the list of God's actions is impressive, and they are described as already happening. Perhaps the psalmist saw both the human action of oppressing and the divine action of liberation as occurring all the time. The psalmist's interest may have been to make sure that the oppressed did not identify God with their

Pastoral Perspective

it comes to our modern-day "princes"—our political leaders.

In Western democratic societies, someone is always running for office. The next presidential election seems to begin even before the previous one is completed. Candidates stand before us and tell of all that they will do for us. Our tendency is to look for these earthly "princes" (both women and men) to be our saviors. Psalm 146 provides a balancing corrective in reminding us of the limitations of earthly leaders and the danger of placing in them the kind of trust that should be reserved for God alone. This tendency to idolatry, particularly of the charismatic political leader, is very real. Still, others may feel that the words of Psalm 146 describe our present lack of leadership, particularly in our elected leaders.

The psalmist is aware of the very real hardships that continue to plague our human condition. The list of the needs that the LORD graciously responds to sounds amazingly contemporary: justice for the oppressed, food for the hungry, freedom for the falsely imprisoned, the lifting up of those who are "bowed down," love for those seeking to do what is right, protection for the stranger (or "alien," NIV), and support for the orphan and the widow. In the life of the United States, the questions concerning immigration will keep the issues of care for the alien at the top of the cultural dialogue for years to come. Those hearing this psalm will find that many of these words describe their own needs. When the Lord does meet those needs, the promise is that God's help will lead to happiness.

This beatitude found in verse 5 speaks of happiness for those who find their help in God. It raises other questions concerning the search for happiness in our world. Author Steve Salerno notes, "We are consumed by the pursuit of happiness."[2] Today, preaching a distorted gospel of prosperity and happiness continues to raise concerns for those seeking to be faithful to the message of Scripture. Yet how many of us who are parents have told our children, "All I want is for you to be happy"? Christian education scholar Rodger Nishioka comments that we have told this to our kids *and they have believed us*—that it is our job as parents to make our children happy. Nishioka goes on to say that he believes the job of parents is not to make our kids happy, but to help them find meaning in life.[3]

2. "The Happiness Myth," *Wall Street Journal*, Dec. 20, 2007, A17.
3. Roger Nishioka, comments to Shallowford Presbyterian Church staff, Atlanta, 2005.

the ancestors in the faith. King and court, symbols of nationhood, of being, were gone forever. The movement from lament to praise in the Psalter reflects the exigencies of life for the faithful who were attempting to find meaning in such tumultuous time. Only faith in the sovereignty of YHWH remained to unite the people and give them identity.

Book 5 of the Psalter celebrates YHWH's guidance and care for the postexilic community of faith in its new life situation. Its concluding doxological words begin with Psalm 146, an individual hymn of thanksgiving, in which a psalm singer praises YHWH (vv. 1–2), offers words of warning not to trust in earthly rulers (vv. 3–4), celebrates YHWH as creator and sustainer (vv. 5–9), and confirms YHWH's sovereignty for all time (v. 10).

In verse 1 the psalm singer urges the "soul" (*nephesh*), better translated "inmost being," to praise YHWH and continues in verse 2 with a statement that the psalmist will "praise" (*halal*) and "sing praises to" (*zamar*) YHWH for the duration of the psalmist's life. The words "praise" and "sing praises to" occur together in many hymns in the Psalter (see, e.g., Pss. 9, 33, 66, 71, 104, 105, and 135).

In verses 3–4, the psalm singer urges those listening to the song of praise not to trust in "princes" (*nedibim*), describing each prince as "a child of humanity" (*ben 'adam*) who will return to an "earthen state" (*'adamah*) when breath leaves them. The words of verses 3–4 echo Genesis 2, in which the first human (*'adam*) is formed by YHWH from the earth (*'adamah*), reminding humanity of the transitory nature of human existence in contrast with the sovereign God.

Many scholars cite connections between Psalm 146, the beginning of the end of the Psalter, and Psalms 1 and 2, the beginning of the beginning of the Psalter. Psalm 146:4 states that the plans of mortals will "perish" (*'abad*), the same word used to describe the fate of the plans of the wicked in Psalm 1:6 and rebellious rulers in Psalm 2:11. The word "happy" (*'ashre*) in 146:5 also occurs at the beginning of Psalm 1 and at the end of Psalm 2. *'Ashre* comes from a verbal root that means "go straight, advance, follow the track." English translations of the Psalter usually render the word as "happy" (NRSV) or "blessed" (NASB). The translation "blessed" brings to mind the Hebrew word *baruk*, which carries cultic/sacred connotations, while the translation "happy" does not convey the full depth of meaning of the Hebrew word. "Content," which connotes a sense of deep-

the God of creation and the God of history interwoven, the warp and woof of a single tapestry of life. This God is a nurse, a medic who "opens the eyes of the blind." This God is a social worker who "lifts up those who are bowed down," humiliated and oppressed. There is the sense of the therapeutic here, of a God who accompanies us on our journey, a companion with compassion. This God is also a political activist who sets the prisoners free and watches over the aliens in the land. All of these attributes of God demonstrate the steadfast love of YHWH, the Lord.

So Psalm 146 is a psalm of praise to the one who "keeps faith forever" (v. 6b). When it comes to faith, we usually put the emphasis on *our* need to keep faith: "keep the faith," "if you just had a little more faith," "do not lose faith." But our covenant tradition is based on a *mutual* faith—not only are we faithful to God, but God is also faithful to us, faithful to the promise that God made to us. God's faithfulness is the basis for this psalm's admonition that we should put our trust in God instead of princes, presidents, and priests who break their promises. So God is, indeed, worthy of our praise.

Our praise is the blossom of our gratitude. As recipients of one or more of God's attributes, such as executing justice for the oppressed or watching over the strangers, we give God thanks and sing God's praises. That is the meaning of the Hebrew word *halleluyah*—"Praise the Lord!" The psalmist has this kind of deep gratitude. He writes that he will "praise the Lord as long as I live; I will sing praises to my God all my life long" (v. 2).

We are called to lead lives of praise, lives of gratitude. We do experience moments of spontaneous praise and thanksgiving when some blessing or blessed event comes our way. However, to live a *life* of praise, day in and day out, is a spiritual practice that may require personal discipline and community support. Good things happen to us every day, even if it takes the eyes of faith to see them; and to consciously recognize them is the road to praise.

There are also times when it is hard to praise God. We need to acknowledge that there are also psalms of lament in the Bible, for lament is a part of life too. Often such psalms are songs of transformation that begin as lament and end as praise. Psalm 22 is one of those, the one that Jesus quoted on the cross (Mark 15:34). Remembering Jesus on the cross can remind us of God's faithful presence with us even in times of suffering. Submission, of course, is its own form of praise, in deed, with our whole lives.

Psalm 146

Theological Perspective

oppressors, but rather with every movement of creative response to that oppression. The point was not that oppression will end and a perfect world will replace it. The point was that the everlasting God, creator of heaven and earth, works in history for the liberation of the oppressed. Since human rulers come and go, and all die, God's everlasting work gives us assurance that our efforts and our hopes are not futile.

This way of understanding God and the world became more difficult as the exaltation of God's power intensified. In this psalm there is no denial that the princes of the world exercise real power. The point is simply that all that they do is ephemeral. God may not prevent their acts of oppression, but God works forever against them. On the other hand, there has been a tendency to think that glorifying God means accenting God's power. When that happens, it becomes more and more difficult to say that God is working against the dominant forces of society that nevertheless remain dominant.

Job is the classical expression of the results of this magnification of God's power. In Job, even Satan does God's will. Job and his friends all assume that God is the cause of Job's suffering. Job argues only against the assumption that he deserves his suffering. To him, God seems unjust. Indeed, anyone who identifies what happens in the world with what God wills to happen in the world is hard pressed to avoid this judgment of God's injustice.

In Psalm 146 God's greatness is certainly exalted, but God's action in the world is certainly not viewed as the cause of its injustice. God's role is a particular one, that of healing and liberation. There are many Christians today for whom this makes sense. I am one of them. Others prefer to declare that God calls all the shots and then to deal with the theoretical consequences. They find little support in this psalm.

JOHN B. COBB JR.

Pastoral Perspective

How does one find true happiness through help from God?

Perhaps this goes back to the choice between seeking help from earthly princes and seeking help from the eternal God of creation "who made heaven and earth." The deep happiness promised by God comes ultimately through the *actions* of God. Earthly princes and others may be agents of those divine actions, but there is a limit to what they can do. In seeking to find our needs met by God, we are also called to be agents of God's good action in our world. God uses us to work for justice, feed the hungry, bring sight to the blind (both physical and spiritual), love the righteous, and watch over strangers, orphans, and widows. Our praising God's help should ultimately lead to actions on our part in response to God's grace.

While Psalm 146 is placed here as Proper 5 in Ordinary Time, it is often found as an Advent reading. Given that context, one cannot help but hear the echoes of Isaiah's words of hope prophesying the child who is the "Prince of Peace." While the "princes" of this earth are mortal and limited in their ability to help, the Lord's faithfulness is forever. The birth of Christ brings us God in the flesh as the true "prince" who has come to establish God's reign on earth. Our search for a Prince of Peace leads us to the One who can bring God's peace—God's *shalom*—to our lives and to our world. This is a much needed word of hope that invites the hearer to place his or her trust in the One who can truly make a difference in the world. It is a word of hope that leads to a deeper happiness and peace, even in the face of difficulties. Eventually, it is a word that leads to where Psalm 146 both begins and ends—doxology, praising God for help that is so desperately needed.

C. GRAY NORSWORTHY

Exegetical Perspective

seated peace and feelings of settledness, may come closest to the root meaning of *'ashre*.

In Psalm 146, the "content" ones are those whose "help" (*'ezer*) is the God of Jacob. The word *'ezer* occurs in its noun form some sixty-five times in the Old Testament. In most occurrences, it refers to the "help" of God in a threatening situation. In Exodus 18:4, Moses says, "The God of my ancestor was my *'ezer* and delivered me from the sword of Pharaoh." In the Song of Moses in Deuteronomy 33:26, Moses says, "There is none like God, who rides through the heavens to your *'ezer*, majestic through the skies." In Psalm 33:20 we read, "Our soul waits for YHWH; YHWH is our *'ezer* and our shield." The word *'ezer* conveys the idea of a "help" that is a strong presence, an aid without which humankind would be unprotected and vulnerable to all sorts of unsettling situations.[2]

In verses 6–9, the psalmist describes how YHWH is the "helper" of the faithful, using a series of participial phrases—verbal forms that indicate YHWH's ongoing involvement in the life of the faithful. YHWH "executes justice," "gives food," "sets free," "opens eyes," "lifts up," "loves," "watches over," and "upholds." Many references to YHWH as "helper" to the faithful occur in Book 5 (see Pss. 107:33–42; 145:14–20; 147:2–6). YHWH "helps" the faithful, but verse 9b indicates a different fate for the wicked—their way will come to ruin, just as the way of the wicked in Psalm 1.

Verse 10 of Psalm 146 begins, "YHWH will reign forever," and ends with the same words with which the psalm began, "Hallelujah." The individual voice of Psalm 146 gives way in Psalm 147 to the community of the faithful and in Psalm 148 to all creation, culminating in Psalms 149 and 150 with all voices joined together to sing the final doxological words of the Psalter.

NANCY L. DECLAISSÉ-WALFORD

Homiletical Perspective

Even in times of the loss of a loved one, exercising our faith can turn our grieving into gratitude. We are transformed from the grieving demand, "I want more," to the grateful response, "Thank you, God, for the gift of this person in my life." That is one of the ways in which God opens blind eyes, sets captives free, and lifts up those who are bowed down.

This psalm is about more than personal piety. Embedded in Psalm 146 is a social conscience. There is a reason that the psalmist contrasts the lords of this world with the God of Jacob when it comes to "kingdom ethics." This is not pie-in-the-sky-by-and-by theology. The Lord of Israel is the divine image in which we have been created; so, implanted in our souls is the call to become the Beloved Community that executes justice for the oppressed and against their wicked oppressors, and gives food to the hungry, sets the prisoners free, upholds the widows and orphans, and watches out for the aliens in our land. For the psalmist, this is the work of righteousness, and the Lord loves the righteous.

A big part of our thanksgiving and praise is for YHWH's faithful promise of the already-not-yet reign of God as it appears in our lives. The sovereign who is both life-giver and justice-giver shows us signs and wonders in the already-in-process and coming completion of creation and the fulfillment of history.

DANIEL M. GESLIN

2. Note: The word translated "help" in the NRSV verse 3, in reference to mortal princes is not *'ezer*, but rather a word derived from the verbal root *yasha'*, meaning "deliver, save"—one of the words used to describe the "deliverers" whom God raised up in the book of Judges (see Judg. 3:9, 15).

Galatians 1:11-24

¹¹For I want you to know, brothers and sisters, that the gospel that was proclaimed by me is not of human origin; ¹²for I did not receive it from a human source, nor was I taught it, but I received it through a revelation of Jesus Christ.

¹³You have heard, no doubt, of my earlier life in Judaism. I was violently persecuting the church of God and was trying to destroy it. ¹⁴I advanced in Judaism beyond many among my people of the same age, for I was far more zealous for the traditions of my ancestors. ¹⁵But when God, who had set me apart before I was born and called me through his grace, was pleased ¹⁶to reveal his Son to me, so that I might proclaim him among the Gentiles, I did not confer with any human being, ¹⁷nor did I go up to Jerusalem to those who were already apostles before me, but I went away at once into Arabia, and afterwards I returned to Damascus.

¹⁸Then after three years I did go up to Jerusalem to visit Cephas and stayed with him fifteen days; ¹⁹but I did not see any other apostle except James the Lord's brother. ²⁰In what I am writing to you, before God, I do not lie! ²¹Then I went into the regions of Syria and Cilicia, ²²and I was still unknown by sight to the churches of Judea that are in Christ; ²³they only heard it said, "The one who formerly was persecuting us is now proclaiming the faith he once tried to destroy." ²⁴And they glorified God because of me.

Theological Perspective

In this passage Paul recounts his response to his conversion and call. He was transformed from a dedicated Jew, consumed with rage at the new teaching about Christ, into one of the gospel's most forceful evangelists. He insists this transformation came about not through any human preaching but through a direct revelation from Christ himself. He is explaining all of this to the Galatians to underscore his own authority to convey to them a true and accurate understanding of the gospel. Paul is at pains to explain not only that the revelation comes from Christ, but that upon receiving the revelation he made no effort to coordinate his work with the leaders of the fledgling Christian community. He is adamant about this: he met with no one, and when he did finally go to Jerusalem, he met only with Cephas and Jesus' brother: "In what I am writing to you, before God, I do not lie" (v. 20). It seems curious that he would be so vehement about his distance from the friends and family who knew and loved Jesus himself.

This letter is often read as Paul's movement away from Judaism to (Protestant) Christianity and, by implication, the supersession of Judaism by Christianity. We should notice, however, that his insistence on his independence from the Jerusalem leaders means that he is also moving away from

Pastoral Perspective

Exploring this text produces a number of fruitful connections with the pastoral concerns and challenges of congregations today.

The Priority of Grace. Paul addresses questions about the legitimacy of his apostolic authority by providing an autobiographical section. His initial emphasis on the divine revelation of the gospel *directly* to him (vv. 11–12), independent of any human source, may strike us as a bit egotistical, perhaps the misguided thinking of a spiritual Lone Ranger. Yet clearly something significant has to account for this persecutor of Jewish Christians making a 180-degree turn.

In verses 15 and 16 Paul describes how his conversion began "when God, who had set me apart before I was born and called me through his grace, was pleased to reveal his Son to me." Indeed, all conversion stories begin with God's decisive action. God always takes the initiative.

The direction often gets turned around in the church—not unlike the nationwide evangelistic campaign that was popular several decades ago, evidenced by Christians wearing buttons or displaying bumper stickers that announced, "I found it!"—as if Christians could reduce the mystery of the eternal God to the "it" they found! But even more

Exegetical Perspective

Apocalypse of Jesus Christ. Everything in verses 11–12 drives toward the final phrase: "a revelation of Jesus Christ," as it is translated by the NRSV. The section begins, "For I want you to know, brothers and sisters," which, here as often elsewhere in Paul, draws attention to what follows (the equivalent of "Listen up!"). Then the elaborate statement denying that Paul received the gospel from any human source points toward its genuine origin. Finally comes the climax: he declares that he received it through "a revelation of Jesus Christ." Is this translation accurate? It is almost surely influenced by Luke's dramatic stories of Paul's conversion in Acts 9, 22, and 26, but Paul offers no such account. The word "revelation" perhaps should be rendered as "apocalypse," which is both a literal rendering of the Greek and a more fitting term for the disruptive invasion of Paul's life sketched in the verses that follow.

A Look Back. In verses 13–14 Paul reminds the Galatian congregations of his "earlier life in Judaism." The implication is not that Paul was once a Jew but has now changed religions. His self-identification as a Jew persists (see Rom. 9–11 esp.). Instead, the word *Ioudaismos,* extremely rare in this period, signals that he was formerly engaged in a particularly devout and passionate form of loyalty to Jewish tradition. As

Homiletical Perspective

The apostle Paul was something of a Johnny Apple-seed of his day. Paul planted communities of the crucified and risen Christ all over Asia Minor in the fashion of the folkloric American planting his apple trees. Like Johnny, Paul then left the churches to flourish and bear fruit on their own. A little benign neglect never hurt anyone, right? Think again.

As last week's reading from Galatians revealed, drawn into the eddy of Paul's great flowing missionary work among the Gentiles of Galatia were other workers, the Missionaries.[1] These were Jewish Christians from Jerusalem who suspected that Paul was offering the adoptees into the faith a hedged and hobbled version of the Jewish Christian faith they presumably shared with Paul.

Nothing less than Paul's apostleship and the gospel he received are at stake in this seething communication to the churches of Galatia. Messenger and message are equally at risk, and though Paul would likely willingly sacrifice himself on the altar of "keeping the gospel of Jesus Christ pure," they are not easily separated, then or now. Preachers of this lection may get caught up in wondering to what extent their own person has

---

1. "Missionaries" is a convention based on scholarly conclusions, as noted by Richard B. Hays, "The Letter to the Galatians," in *New Interpreter's Bible,* vol. 11 (Nashville: Abingdon Press, 2000), 185.

Galatians 1:11–24

Theological Perspective

Christianity itself: its beliefs, authorities, forms of community, and beloved leaders, including Jesus' brother and one of his closest disciples. He experienced the peculiarity of his conversion to be a call, not only to Christ, but to a ministry to Gentiles. This ministry became the centerpiece of his understanding of the gospel. The teachings and practices of Jesus as remembered by his disciples, their understanding of his death, the forms of community they were devising were irrelevant to him. Neither the authority of the apostles nor that of Jesus' own teachings was significant to him. The only thing that really seemed to matter to him was that Jesus appeared to him and instructed him to take his message to non-Jews. He reconstructed "the gospel" so that it was amenable to this extension to communities that shared no Scripture, theology, or moral codes with Jesus and his followers. In the absence of these underpinnings, Paul made faith alone the entire content of Christianity. What exactly he meant by "faith" is not easy to decipher, even from reading through the whole corpus of his writings, but in this letter he emphasizes that it has to do with a liberation accomplished through the radically self-giving love of Christ. Faith replaces the (sinful) center of personhood with the living presence of Christ. This recentering qualifies the claims of all mediations, including leaders, Scriptures, and customs of Jews and Christians alike.

We should be disturbed by this for several reasons. This example of dogmatic, self-righteous, and intolerant attack on those with whom one disagrees has poisoned Christianity. The vehemence that Paul once directed against the Christian church in the name of (his understanding of) Judaism is now directed against the Jerusalem leaders in the name of (his understanding of) the gospel. Language of this sort can be taken to mean that variations of the "one true faith" (to which we or our community alone are privy) should be condemned and cursed. The imagined purity of doctrine justifies us in our natural hostility to those who disagree with us. Paul's strong condemnation of his opponents and utter confidence that he alone has possession of the true gospel has many imitators throughout history. Because of this, Christianity has often been oppressive and cruel. We should not be blind to this history as we try to understand Paul's words.

We might also be concerned about his insistence that his teaching comes from no person, that it is authorized by no church leader, and in fact exists in stubborn defiance of its leaders. This is not good

Pastoral Perspective

troublesome, the slogan diminished the divine initiative; it minimized the God who, in infinite love and mercy, comes looking for lost humankind in Jesus Christ. The line from the popular hymn "Amazing Grace" is instructive: "I once was lost, but now *am* found." Grace finds us.

By asserting minimal contact with the Jerusalem church and independence from the apostles, Paul is not setting himself apart as better than they; he is emphasizing the priority of grace. He is not saying, "Look at me, aren't I great?" but, "Look at how great the gospel is: it is the power of God to transform life!"

His detractors in Galatia may be suggesting that Paul received the gospel secondhand from the real apostles in Jerusalem, or that somehow in the process he misinterpreted the meaning of grace, but in verse 20 he swears he was not even influenced—much less commissioned—by them. His gospel is straight from the source, and he has never for a moment wavered from the divine revelation of radical grace.

Called for a Purpose. But divine revelation and the priority of grace to what end? Called for what purpose? So that Paul might experience personal peace, or assuage a nagging guilt complex, or be blessed with health and wealth? No. As Paul puts it in verse 16, he is called by Christ "*so that* I might proclaim him among the Gentiles" (v. 16).

Rick Warren's best-selling book *The Purpose Driven Life* opens with the simple assertion—"It's not about you"—but then proceeds to develop an intensely self-focused description of the life of faith, centered on the individual. Here in Galatians we see how the gospel exerts a centripetal force on Paul's life. It is *not* about him. The gospel propels him outside of himself and into the world for the gospel's sake.

Why is it that in his later years, Mr. Rogers, the kindly, cardigan-wearing kids' television show host, ultimately came to regret singing and saying to generations of American children, "You are special"? Because looking back he realized it was only half the story. He feared that, as children were being affirmed, they ended up feeling too good about themselves and ultimately neglected balancing their self-esteem with a radical humility and a deep regard for others.

It is not all about us. God's love is revealed in Jesus Christ to what end, for what purpose? To share God's grace in word and deed, especially with the last, the least, the lost.

However, it is not simply that the church has a mission in the world. Rather, the God of mission has a church in the world. It is not the church's mission.

Exegetical Perspective

verse 13b shows, that loyalty took the form of trying to destroy what he now recognizes as "the church of God." Paul himself never reports on his persecutorial activities (although see 1 Cor. 15:9), and it is possible that his harassment was more social and verbal than the physical violence depicted in Luke's later accounts (Acts 9, 22, 26). Whatever the shape of Paul's activity, he connects it with his own zeal for tradition, as is clear in verse 14. In an age that valued especially those things that were ancient, Paul's ardent desire to promote the "traditions of my ancestors" indicates that he was vigorously pursuing an honorable life. This slender memoir frustrates modern desires for biographical detail, yet its orientation around Paul's own pursuit of what he and his people regarded as right and proper comes through clearly.

God's Calling. The shift to verse 15 is stunning, as no explanation is offered, no account of an "event," no reflection on a change of mind or heart. Instead, the shift is from Paul's agency ("I was persecuting, trying," "I advanced," "I was zealous") to that of God. God is the subject of the long sentence that extends from verse 15 through verse 17, and Paul's "I" returns only in response to God's action. By affirming that God acted "before I was born"—or more literally, "from the womb of my mother"—Paul draws on imagery found in the accounts of prophetic calling in the Old Testament (see Jer. 1:5; Isa. 49:1–6). The second phrase, "called me through his grace," underscores this point. As in Romans 9:11, where Paul insists that God's choice of Jacob over Esau took place "before they had been born or had done anything good or bad," in his own life also Paul recognizes God's calling as exactly that: God's calling. Indeed, the disjuncture between verse 14 and verse 15 suggests that Paul was an eager volunteer, but his service was diametrically opposed to God's plan.

Verse 16 echoes the apocalyptic language of verse 12 in that God "revealed" or "apocalypsed" his Son to Paul so that "I might proclaim him among the Gentiles." As throughout the Bible, divine calling is not an end in itself, no merely private showing for Paul's own reflection and spiritual development. He is called with the very specific mission of proclaiming the gospel to Gentiles, and he might well have added here a repetition of 1 Corinthians 9:16 ("Woe to me if I do not proclaim the gospel!"). The remainder of verse 16 and verse 17 tumbles out in a rush, from the denial that he visited Jerusalem to the immediate journey into Arabia and then to Damascus. Although massive scholarly energy has

Homiletical Perspective

become mingled in their proclamation, their message. Must the preacher's own life necessarily be a validation of the message she or he preaches? One more thing to keep us awake at night.

It is lonely being a prophet. Experience has taught pastors this. One senses it was lonely being Paul. Every pastor can appreciate what is ahead for Paul as he seeks from afar to vindicate his apostleship and the gospel he had preached. It takes enormous time and energy to initially establish credibility and assert authority with any congregation. Strangers must be won over, suspicions allayed, common ground established, sympathies developed. Having spent his best evangelical energy bringing the new Galatian converts into the fold, Paul now faces the daunting task of having to do it *all over again.* Only now the people have been deliberately set against him, new suspicions sown, and new doubts raised. A sermon faithful to the strained dynamics of this text will not shy away from sensitively exploring the delicate interrelational ties between preacher/pastor and people and the matter of so-called pastoral authority in Paul's age and ours.

Paul lays out his curriculum vitae as an apostle, lest any had forgotten: called from the womb like the ancient prophets, a Pharisee's Pharisee in his earlier life, acclaimed for his gospel ministry in other regions of the Near East. Paul remains steady in his self-validating proclamation that he received his gospel directly from God with no intermediaries to muddy the message. It is clear that the Missionaries flatly denied Paul's claim, insinuating that his message was far more human than divine. Further, the Missionaries asserted that Paul had made an extended premissionary detour through Jerusalem and there received the "full" Jewish Christian version of the gospel only to later shear off the parts that were unpalatable to the non-Jewish Greeks.

The logic of the Missionaries is not hard to fathom. Who likes to place unpleasant and unfamiliar demands on church folk that one is working so hard to please? What preacher has not been tempted to preach the "hard parts" sotto voce, if not exclude them altogether? Ingratiating oneself with a new congregation is one of the ways we pastors "pay the rent." It is how we get established. Paul, the Missionaries argued, compromised the message in ways that may have been understandable, but were still unconscionable. It is possible they were aware of Paul's extravagant claim, made in other quarters, of being "all things to all people" (1 Cor. 9:22). Such claims make Paul vulnerable to the

Galatians 1:11-24

Theological Perspective

news to any religion that endures through time because of the authority of its institutions. Any lunatic can claim that Jesus has revealed himself to her or him. Even saintly and wise revelations can threaten ecclesial authority, and the church has been glad to sacrifice these to the greater good of stability. Much about Paul's thought became canonical in Christianity, but appeals to direct revelation are usually strenuously rejected.

If this letter is bad news for authoritarianism, it can be good news for those committed to the constant renewal of Christianity. It is good news for those outside systems of power who might see more clearly ways in which Christianity has cut off some of its own limbs in the name of tradition. It is good news for all those oppressed by the church: women, slaves, the poor. It is good news for all those lovers of Christ whose wisdom about the Divine is distorted or repressed by leaders of the church.

Stepping back from the heat of this controversy, it seems that Christianity absorbed more of James than of Paul. Though the Holiness Code and circumcision did not come to define Christianity, the rest of the Hebrew Scripture remains authoritative for Christians. The authority of the church and its leaders has also survived just fine, but Paul reminds us that, as important as tradition may be, it can never be adequate to the gracious and extravagant love God pours out on us. For Paul, corralling grace in a particular community or in relation to particular practices will always violate the gospel.

A student recently told me about trying to find a church in a new town. At one she was rejected because her father was Jewish, at another because her mother was Lutheran. Many churches make appropriate sexual practice (as defined by the Holiness Code) a condition for receiving the gospel. We seem to know a great deal about which sinners are precious to Christ. Paul is trying to convey to the Galatians, and perhaps to us, that Christ's revelation and Christ's love continually break through the bounds that religion sets on them. The church cannot be reminded of this often enough.

WENDY FARLEY

Pastoral Perspective

It is not only God's call; it is God's mission too, in which God's people are invited to participate.

Congregations might consider a service installing, or at least honoring, church officers in conjunction with this reading. Granted, none of us is an apostle, much less the apostle Paul; nevertheless God is still calling, and God's grace sets apart leaders to serve.

In addition, this text provides an opportunity to explore the use of "testimony" in the context of the worship service. While the emphasis in testimony or witness is often on the individual, and the message is mainly about what Jesus has done for *me*, it might be reappropriated to point to God and illuminate the instances where congregants have seen the transforming power of the gospel at work in the world.

Unity of the Church. Perhaps the exclusion of 2:1–14 is meant to spare us the gory details, but 2:1–14 not only continues to grapple with Paul's claim to apostolic authority and his relationship with Jerusalem; it also underscores what is at stake, namely, the unity of the church. The text clarifies that while Jerusalem apparently did not have problems with Paul ("they saw that I had been entrusted with the gospel for the uncircumcised" [2:7] and the "acknowledged pillars recognized the grace that had been given to me" [2:9]), he had problems with some of them because "they were not acting consistently with the truth of the gospel" (v. 14). They were changing their tune about salvation by grace through faith by requiring circumcision of Gentile converts. For Paul, this practice threatened a total corruption of the salvation by grace, insinuating that radical trust in Jesus alone was not enough. To reinstate the law as a means of salvation was fueled by racial bigotry, resulting in a segregated and severely compromised church.

Twenty centuries later the church continues to struggle with unity. When the church gathers on Sunday morning, it is still considered the most segregated hour of the week. One modern church-growth movement infamously sanctioned homogeneity, arguing that since birds of a cultural, social, or economic feather flock together, the church need not fight it.

Unity must not be mistaken for uniformity. Indeed there are differences within and between churches—different gifts, personalities, cultures and races, socioeconomic classes, ages, politics, and denominations—but there must be no divisions. The reconciling, unifying impulse of the one gospel remains.

HEIDI HUSTED ARMSTRONG

Exegetical Perspective

been expended in attempts to coordinate these details and those that follow with the accounts in Acts to produce a chronology of Paul's life, Paul's words serve that purpose rather poorly. What these statements do well is to confirm his assertion that he consulted with no human being, reinforcing his central statement: just as the gospel itself comes from God (1:1–4), its invasion of Paul's life could only have come from God.

The Proclaiming Persecutor. The final section of the lection (vv. 18–24) continues with a highly condensed report of Paul's later visit in Jerusalem with Cephas and James and then of his travel to Syria and Cilicia. Implicitly Paul affirms again here, even with an oath (v. 20), that his gospel does not come from these individuals. Indeed, the "churches in Judea" would not have recognized him had he arrived among them (v. 22). They did, however, know about him; they knew that the former persecutor had become the proclaimer (v. 23). This statement, taken together with verse 24, ably summarizes Paul's account of what has come to be called his "conversion." God made the persecutor into a proclaimer.

That God made the persecutor into a proclaimer serves—in part—to counter whispering campaigns that would demote Paul to a lesser rank and undermine his proclamation of the gospel. In the larger argument of Galatians, this account of God's doings, God's apocalypse that overtook Paul's life, serves as a paradigm of the gospel. In 3:27–29, Paul will insist that God has overtaken all of the categories into which human beings sort themselves, so that the only category that remains is "in Christ." In the final lines of the letter, he will claim that the whole world has been crucified, that there is in the gospel nothing less than "new creation" (6:15). While Galatians 1 may appear to show Paul playing defense for himself, in this larger perspective what comes into focus is that he is playing offense for God.

BEVERLY ROBERTS GAVENTA

Homiletical Perspective

charge of making the Jewish Christian gospel so plastic that it was no longer faithful to its Jewish roots. Paul counters the claims with a bit of chest-pounding. He reiterates his superb qualifications as a Jew's Jew—once a tormentor of Christians and superior to his peers in nearly every way. He even seems to be suggesting that those who revile him had once indirectly praised Paul and his reputation.

Paul's bold, almost boastful, claims of superiority and of his standing as the unique conduit for the gospel may be a bit of a stumbling block for those who are of this preacher's ilk. And Paul's überconfidence may remind moderate/progressive/liberal Christians of their more conservative kin who can often exude a nearly Pauline degree of confidence. Attempts to discuss differences of theology and biblical interpretation and authority can often result in conversation stoppers like: "Hey, you're not arguing with *me*, you're arguing with the *Word of God*." Sigh.

As we seek vindication of the gospel *we* have received, at times we preachers are in the position of needing to claim the freedom of which Paul will later speak in his letter (5:1ff.) to bring healing to some of Paul's other writings and other biblical texts that are famously used to limit the freedom of others. "God is still speaking!" is how one Protestant denomination describes the implications of this freedom in Christ.[2] We can only hope that if Paul is looking over our shoulders as we preach, he would affirm our desire and commitment to only deepen the freedom of which he wrote and preached.

As we work to enlighten and heal texts within and beyond Paul's own writing, it will sometimes be thought that we are superseding biblical authority. Charges of adapting the text to one's own needs, whims, and biases are as old as the biblical texts themselves and charges familiar to Paul. Such is a place where angels fear to tread: stepping into each and every pulpit and time of preaching and allowing the free and freeing good news of Christ to fill our proclamation in ways that are appropriate to each new day and each new challenge to freedom of and in Christ.

GREGORY H. LEDBETTER

2. "God is still speaking" is the slogan of the United Church of Christ, adapted from a quote by Gracie Allen: "Don't put a period where God puts a comma. . . . God still speaks."

Luke 7:11-17

¹¹Soon afterwards he went to a town called Nain, and his disciples and a large crowd went with him. ¹²As he approached the gate of the town, a man who had died was being carried out. He was his mother's only son, and she was a widow; and with her was a large crowd from the town. ¹³When the Lord saw her, he had compassion for her and said to her, "Do not weep." ¹⁴Then he came forward and touched the bier, and the bearers stood still. And he said, "Young man, I say to you, rise!" ¹⁵The dead man sat up and began to speak, and Jesus gave him to his mother. ¹⁶Fear seized all of them; and they glorified God, saying, "A great prophet has risen among us!" and "God has looked favorably on his people!" ¹⁷This word about him spread throughout Judea and all the surrounding country.

Theological Perspective

Earlier in Luke, Jesus preached the Sermon on the Plain, fulfilling his promise to "bring good news to the poor" (4:18; 6:17–49, esp. v. 20). In this story, Jesus raises the dead, performing wonders like the prophets of old (cf. 4:25–27; 9:19). Like the healing of the centurion's servant, the raising of the widow's son raises theological questions of *identity, character, and intent*—in relation to Jesus, and to God.

Luke paints Jesus' identity and intention in four dimensions. As with the previous story, Luke uses this narrative to certify Jesus' status as *a healer* and *a prophet through whom God is visiting the people* (v. 16). Jesus does not cast out demons, heal illnesses, or resuscitate the dead by the power of Beelzebul, but by the power of the Spirit of God (cf. 11:14–28; 1:35; 3:22; 4:1, 14, 18). Just as the healing of the centurion's slave resembles Elisha's healing of Naaman, Jesus' raising of the widow's son at Nain calls the reader's mind back to Elijah's raising of the widow's son at Zarephath (1 Kgs. 17:10, 17–24; cf. Luke 4:24–28; 7:39; 13:33; and 24:19).

The prophet of God is also *one filled with compassion for those who suffer.* When Jesus comes upon the widow as her son's bier leaves the city's gate, she is sobbing. She is surrounded by crowds, both from her funeral procession and from those following Jesus. Maybe she does not even see Jesus.

Pastoral Perspective

The Gospel miracles can make a life of faith very difficult for the average Christian. In tragic times we long for Jesus to show compassion and provide the grand miracle that will take away our despair. We cling to the vision that miracles should be like those in the New Testament, but we risk missing the smaller miracle moments in which God's compassion can enter into our upside-down world, touch our most pain-filled places, and restore our shattered hearts.

Imagine the scene. Jesus is walking toward the town gate, with his entourage only steps behind. Perhaps he can hear the weeping long before he can see the funeral procession. There is no mistaking the near-primal sound pouring out from a mother who has lost her child. It makes little difference that this child appears to be grown; the grief is deep. Perhaps it is this gut-wrenching wail of the widow whose only son has just died that rips into Jesus' heart, moving him to reach out with compassion. "Do not weep," he says. Unlike characters in other miracle stories, no one rushes to the front of the crowd asking for Jesus' help. Perhaps everyone thinks it is too late; after all, the young man is already dead. With a simple gesture Jesus reaches out, he touches the death bier, and life grabs hold of the body that lies upon it. "Rise up," he says to the young man.

Exegetical Perspective

This is the second panel in Luke's depiction of Jesus as God's eschatological prophet (v. 16) and should be read as a counterpart to the preceding story, which depicted Jesus' healing the centurion's servant becuse of the centurion's remarkable faith (7:1–10). In that story, Jesus had healed someone who was gravely ill; now the full extent of Jesus' power is displayed, for he not only heals but restores life to the dead. In the background of the initial story stood Elisha's healing of Naaman's leprosy. Here Elijah's revivification of the son of the widow from Zarephath is in view (1 Kgs. 17:20–24). Luke signals this by including the detail of Jesus' approach to the town gate (v. 12), which echoes Elijah's first meeting with the widow (cf. 1 Kgs. 17:10), and by the verbatim quotation of the Septuagint translation of 1 Kings 17:23 in verse 15 ("Jesus gave him to his mother"). Again, as in the previous story about the centurion and his servant, a contrast between Jesus and the Old Testament prophet is apparent. In that story Elisha was in view; here it is Elijah that serves as the archetype. In the Elijah story there is a contentious relationship between the widow and the prophet. She initially rebuffs his efforts and eventually blames him for the death of her son. In Luke, however, none of this obstinacy is evident. In fact, the widow is only seen by Jesus and never speaks to him directly. The

Homiletical Perspective

The strangest things happen at funerals. Family stories and the sharing of cherished memories generate both deep laughter and inconsolable tears. In this second story of God's graciousness from Luke 7, Jesus raises from death the son of a widow at Nain. When the heart of a mourner is split with grief, Jesus walks in through the gap.

As the story goes, Jesus was taking a road trip when this event took place. After healing the slave of a centurion at Capernaum, Jesus traveled on with his disciples and a large crowd to the town of Nain. The road was apparently crowded by a funeral procession as friends of the family held a widow's son aloft on his bier. As the grief-stricken procession passed nearby, we can imagine Jesus reaching out his hand in compassion for the mother.

"Jesus said to her, 'Do not weep.' Then he came forward and touched the bier, and the bearers stood still. And he said, 'Young man, I say to you, rise!'" (Luke 7:13–14). What followed was a deeply compassionate response to suffering both seen and hidden. We see the suffering of a woman at the loss of her son. What we do not see is the suffering of a widow who has lost everything. It is to this deeper suffering that Jesus speaks.

Once again Jesus crosses the line in his act of compassion. What appears to us to be empathetic

Luke 7:11-17

Theological Perspective

She does not ask for anything, but the text says that "the Lord saw her" (v. 13). Since she had already lost her husband, this son was her entire family, as well as her only means of economic support. She carries too the grief of any parent who buries a child. In this scene, Jesus takes the initiative, and his whole attention is on the woman. When he sees her, he feels "compassion" for her (*splanchnizomai*, v. 13), an intense inner emotion and sympathy that accompanies mercy. Luke uses this word in two later stories, when the Samaritan sees the stripped and beaten man (10:33), and when the prodigal father sees his lost son for the first time far down the road (15:20). This scene reveals Jesus' compassionate character and intent toward us. He meets our needs, even when we are too torn apart to ask for help.

For Luke, compassion, while entailing great emotional capacity, also leads to action. The Samaritan bandages the wounded man and brings him to an inn. The father runs toward his son and lifts him up. If compassion meant merely inner sympathy, Jesus' statement to the widow, "Do not weep," would hardly seem kind. Jesus, however, has not just empathy but the power to change fate. He is the prophet of God who is *filled with the divine power over life and death*. Jesus' word also has the power to raise the dead. As with the raising of Jairus's daughter (8:40–42, 49–56) and Peter's raising of Tabitha (Acts 9:36–43), this resuscitation displays the authority and power of the reign of God over death itself (cf. Luke 12:5). Jesus' sovereign power is greater than that of Peter. Peter must implore God to send power (Acts 9:40), but Jesus already possesses that power in himself. While Elijah, Elisha, and Peter need to employ intense physical contact, for Jesus it suffices to touch the bier. Above all, Luke shifts the transfer of divine, life-giving power from touch to the word of Jesus, his command to the son, "Be raised!" from the dead. While resurrection is of a different order—Jesus' bodily form is altered (cf. 1 Cor. 15:35–50)—the command points ahead to Jesus' resurrection and to Jesus as "the Author of life" (Acts 3:15), for his success is instantaneous and effortless.

Filled with the divine power of life, Jesus is not only a prophet or healer, but *the eschatological prophet*, the "stronger one" who is like Moses (3:16; 4:34; 5:32; 7:27; cf. Deut. 18:15, 18). Jesus, the healing Messiah, does not avoid even this difficult situation. He brings in the new order of God's reign, in which the dead are raised, the broken healed, and the poor blessed.[1] Thus

1. God's new order is contrasted with and greater than the old (cf. 7:26–28).

Pastoral Perspective

Then, we are simply told, "Jesus gave him to his mother." In this understated gesture the woman's shattered world is made whole again. Those who witness this moment are both stunned and somewhat afraid as the extraordinary nature of what has happened begins to sink in.

Who among us has not prayed for a miracle at some point in our lives? Who has not called out in challenge to all things faithful that a compassionate God would not make us suffer so? In these moments, miracles seem to be a sign that God is working to set things right in a world gone very wrong. Illness, death, financial ruin, chronic pain, divorce, depression, addiction, injured children, violence and abuse, mass trauma—the list is long of life circumstances that seem to dismantle our assumptions of the world as it should be.

Ronnie Janoff-Bulman, professor of psychology at the University of Massachusetts, proposes a frame for understanding traumatic experience, that is, for why we human creatures are so upended when tragedy strikes us. We live, she says, with certain core assumptions about the world, that is, that the world is benevolent (bad things will not happen) and meaningful (events of the world should make sense), and that the self is worthy (events in our world correlate to the good or bad that we bring into the world).[1] At first glance most of us might argue that we are certainly smart enough to know that the world is not fair and that sometimes tragedy follows no line of reasoning. Yet in that moment when our world comes crashing in around us, very often one of the first questions to rise from our lips is, how could this happen? Or why did this happen to me? What did I do to deserve this? These questions imply the very assumptions Janoff-Bulman suggests.

As people of faith, we go one step further, to ask where God is in the chaos that threatens us. Underlying Janoff-Bulman's assumptions are terrifying questions like, what would it mean if we no longer lived in a trustworthy world? What would it mean if events in our lives are random (without meaning)? If we assume a correlation between good behavior and good outcome, what would it mean if we have no control over the events of our lives? When all attempts to make right sense of the senseless prove futile, we turn to God to find meaning. Miracles are among the first signs to which

1. Ronnie Janoff-Bulman, *Shattered Assumptions: Towards a New Psychology of Trauma* (New York: The Free Press, 1992). The context of this theory, as the author intends it, is traumatic experience. I suggest that it can apply to a very broad understanding of traumatic and tragic human experience.

effect is to focus the story on Jesus' actions and the response of amazement and glorification that they inspire among the people who have observed his display of creative power (vv. 16–17).

The story also draws attention to the character of Jesus. He embodies the compassion and care that God desires of all God's servants. There are contrasts between this story and the story in 1 Kings. Unlike the Elijah story, in Luke's narrative the widow's son has died before Jesus arrives on the scene. Moreover, Jesus does not act because the widow has accosted him, as in 1 Kings, but because he feels compassion for the widow (v. 13). Jesus' compassion toward the woman reflects the grave nature of her loss. Already bereft of the security that her husband would have provided, the widow would now be completely dependent on her son for safety and sustenance. His death places her in peril, for she no longer has any fiscal or material support and is in danger of dying if her society does not respond with charity (Deut. 25:5–10; 26:12). Thus Jesus' response of compassion is more than fitting. The lives of both son and mother depend on his intervention.

Because of this, Jesus initiates actions that will restore her son to life and return her to a more secure place within society. Moreover, Jesus' actions are in and of themselves prophetic in nature. First, he acts on behalf of a widow, one of the socially and economically disadvantaged among Israel's people. In fact, Israel's prophets often refer to the peoples' treatment of widows as a mark of the nation's holiness (e.g., Isa. 1:17, 23; Jer. 7:6; Ezek. 22:7; Zech. 7:10). Jesus' actions demonstrate his right understanding of God's desire for mercy and social justice and thus his fulfilling of God's wishes for the compassionate care of all people. Second, in approaching the bier and touching it, Jesus makes himself ritually impure (see Num. 19:11, 16). In disregard for his own societal status, he acts on behalf of someone with little or no societal power.

In a final contrast to the 1 Kings story, although Elijah had to stretch himself over the dead son three times and cry to the Lord for help, Jesus simply touches the funeral bier and commands the young man to rise (v. 14). The young man responds as soon as he is addressed, sitting up and speaking—dramatic actions that clearly show that he has been reanimated because of Jesus' command. The immediate response shows the extent of Jesus' power. Like God he speaks life into existence, resuscitating the young man. Then he quite literally restores him to his mother: "Jesus gave him to his mother" (v. 15).

and generous would have been perceived as unrighteous behavior. For a male Jew, the body of the dead was considered unclean, and Jesus would have been forbidden to touch it. His response to an unprotected widow would have been equally suspect.

Widows held a tenuous position in Jesus' day. They were often linked with orphans as those without provision in Jewish society. Women lived under the protection of their father's household, and then of their husband's household. After the death of a husband, it was customary for the brother or other relative of the deceased to marry the widow. In cases where no male relative from the family of her husband was available, the widow moved to the margins of society and fell vulnerable to alienation and exclusion from the community and the simple daily provision of familial care. Further, the death of an only son would leave a widow without an heir and therefore unable to retain whatever means remained for her. Without an heir, all personal property reverted to the husband's family after his death.

Jesus' act of compassion demonstrated two things about the nature of God. First, Jesus served as a justice-making witness to the provision of God that is available to all. Jesus demonstrates once again God's regard for those at the margins. It is easy for us to forget the risks Jesus took to demonstrate the kingdom of God on earth. Notice that his compassion is extended to the mother who lived, not to the son who had died. Jesus was compassionate toward her for her sake. He transformed her mourning to joy, her desolation to hope.

Second, Jesus is willing to risk rebuke for exercising God's special mercy for the least among society. His mercy toward the widow is a foretaste of the compassion he felt toward his own mother from the cross. We read that "when Jesus saw his mother and the disciple whom he loved standing beside her, he said to his mother, 'Woman, here is your son.' Then he said to the disciple, 'Here is your mother.' And from that hour the disciple took her into his own home" (John 19:26–27).

We love Jesus for his compassion. He notices and responds to those at the fringes, who often live unseen. Most people would have stood respectfully by the side of the road as the funeral procession passed by, avoiding eye contact, perhaps murmuring quietly to one another or discussing the circumstances of the death. Jesus sees people as God sees them and responds to them as God responds to us.

At first we may not readily identify with the widow's circumstance. Women living in

Luke 7:11-17

Theological Perspective

Jesus is called "great" and "the Lord," and his work is God's personal action and will (7:13, 16).

As the eschatological prophet, Jesus reveals not only his own character and intentions toward humanity, but also God's. Besides the miracle, there are three amazing things about this story. First, for readers situated in a Hellenistic and Roman culture in which being moved by another was a sign of weakness, here (as in 10:33 and 15:20) that supposed "weakness" is associated with Jesus and, through him, with God. Compassion and mercy are the apex of God's character and of the new communal life in the Spirit (6:36).[2]

Further, while Jesus as savior is determined to forgive sins that break community (5:20–24), he is equally concerned with suffering. With Jairus's daughter and the Nain widow's son, Jesus acts to reverse the death of young people, deaths especially tragic. He does not ask either Jairus or the widow about their sins or those of their offspring. He simply has compassion for mortality's robbery of parents' children and the children's lost lives, and he acts to counter it. God's inbreaking salvation includes the redeeming of relations torn by suffering and mortality.

Finally, in contrast to the usual structure of such miracle stories, this one peculiarly describes a meeting between a parade of life (Jesus and his disciples) and a parade of death (the dead man, his mother, and the grieving crowd). What transpires reveals the reign of God in which the eschatological Spirit, indwelling Jesus and sent by God, transforms mortal existence into new life. "The dead are raised" (7:22).[3]

GREGORY ANDERSON LOVE

Pastoral Perspective

we look for proof that God's compassion will bring our world back into alignment.

Amazingly, like the widowed mother in our story, sometimes we actually get the grand miracle we pray for. The father or husband whose heart stops on the operating table is brought back from the clutches of death. The mother of two young children beats the odds and survives the cancer that all doctors said would kill her. More often than not, in spite of doing everything right and praying for every good thing, the sixteen-year-old who just got her license still dies when the car she is driving hits a tree. Where is God's compassion then?

We cannot stop ourselves from praying for even the most impossible of miracles, especially when it concerns the lives of those we love. We cling to a central message of the gospel: in Christ Jesus all things are possible. In reality our lives, like that of Jesus, are filled with messy unfinished edges, not the nice tidy ending that the widowed mother in our story experiences. We must come to recognize miracles that come in other less dazzling forms. Indeed, when we focus on only one vision of what is possible, we become blinded to the many moments in which God's compassion reaches into our lives to hear, touch, and stand in the chaos of life, helping us to find new meaning even in the greatest tragedy. Jesus can hear the cries hidden in the deepest crevices of our despair, just as he heard the heart of the grieving widow. He touches us in the place of our greatest pain, just as he reached into the place of death upon the funeral bier. Jesus steps into the chaos of our unpredictable, overturned, or shattered world to bring meaning from even the most desolate suffering.

M. JAN HOLTON

---

2. On invulnerability to being moved by others as a virtue in Greek and Roman culture, contrasted with the God illuminated by Jesus, see William Placher, *Narratives of a Vulnerable God* (Louisville, KY: Westminster John Knox Press, 1994), chap. 1; and Thomas Cahill, *Desire of the Everlasting Hills* (New York: Nan A. Talese/Doubleday, 1999).
3. While it is not Lukan, see Matt. 27:50–53.

Exegetical Perspective

The widow's son's "resurrection" is a mark that God's power is available to God's people through the person of Jesus. By providing this story with its allusions to the Elijah cycle, in both its agreements and divergences, Luke underscores that, in Jesus, God's actions are complete. Just as God has acted on behalf of Israel through the prophetic career of Elijah, so God now acts through Jesus (cf. Luke 4:24; 7:39; 9:8, 19; 24:19; and Acts 3:22 for other uses of the prophet typology). However, Jesus is not merely one among Israel's prophets, but the great prophet that God has sent to the people because of God's favor toward them (v. 16).

Taken together with the story of the centurion's servant, this episode anticipates John the Baptist's question in 7:20, "Are you the one who is to come, or are we to wait for another?" In response to John's messengers, Jesus recalls the words of Isaiah 61, which he had read in Nazareth (4:18–19). Now, after numerous instances of fulfillment, including the raising of the dead, Jesus has shown that he is, in fact, the anointed one for whom they were hoping. Thus with these stories Luke shows that John the Baptist and Jesus reprise God's prophetic actions. Those who recognize this know that John is more than a prophet; he is God's messenger sent to prepare Jesus' way (7:26–27). Jesus too is not simply the last in a line of God's messengers; he is the Son of Man, who, though rejected by the reigning religious, will be vindicated in the age to come (7:35).

STEVEN J. KRAFTCHICK

Homiletical Perspective

contemporary Western culture seldom experience the vulnerability of this widow who depended upon male protection to survive. Yet for many women throughout the world, similar mores remain. Whatever our social context, we can imagine the multilayered suffering triggered by this woman's loss.

While we may not have experienced the social and economic vulnerability of women in the first and second centuries, we do know the bereavement of a parent for a lost child. There is perhaps nothing this side of heaven more difficult to bear. At such a time, what we would not give to have the lost child restored to us. What we would not sacrifice to have Jesus walk into our grief and restore the dead to life.

Such compassion is almost too much to bear. Those who witnessed such an event during Jesus' ministry were seized with fear. They sensed divine presence and were undone by it. We watch detective television dramas about missing persons and pray over the faces of children on milk cartons, longing for that day and hour when our own broken lives will be restored.

When you preach this text, take a moment to help your congregation recall what they have lost and at what cost. Allow Jesus to extend compassion toward them as he extends mercy toward the widow. What is the good news Jesus brings when he reaches out to touch their grief? What is the act of compassion they are waiting to receive?

We live in the quiet gap between the sorrow that seems as if it will last a lifetime and God's promise of joy in the morning. God knows what it means to lose a son. Jesus raised up the son of the widow at Nain as God raised up Jesus from the cross, for our sake, reaching out his hand in compassion for us all.

VERLEE A. COPELAND

1 Kings 21:1-10 (11-14), 15-21a

¹Later the following events took place: Naboth the Jezreelite had a vineyard in Jezreel, beside the palace of King Ahab of Samaria. ²And Ahab said to Naboth, "Give me your vineyard, so that I may have it for a vegetable garden, because it is near my house; I will give you a better vineyard for it; or, if it seems good to you, I will give you its value in money." ³But Naboth said to Ahab, "The Lord forbid that I should give you my ancestral inheritance." ⁴Ahab went home resentful and sullen because of what Naboth the Jezreelite had said to him; for he had said, "I will not give you my ancestral inheritance." He lay down on his bed, turned away his face, and would not eat.

⁵His wife Jezebel came to him and said, "Why are you so depressed that you will not eat?" ⁶He said to her, "Because I spoke to Naboth the Jezreelite and said to him, 'Give me your vineyard for money; or else, if you prefer, I will give you another vineyard for it'; but he answered, 'I will not give you my vineyard.'" ⁷His wife Jezebel said to him, "Do you now govern Israel? Get up, eat some food, and be cheerful; I will give you the vineyard of Naboth the Jezreelite."

⁸So she wrote letters in Ahab's name and sealed them with his seal; she sent the letters to the elders and the nobles who lived with Naboth in his city. ⁹She wrote in the letters, "Proclaim a fast, and seat Naboth at the head of the assembly; ¹⁰seat two scoundrels opposite him, and have them bring a charge

Theological Perspective

It is an irony of the human condition that power weakens those who are most eager to exploit it. The powerful are vulnerable not only to those who would wrest power from them, but also to the corrosive force of their own greed. Instructive is the ancient Greek story of King Midas, who desires that everything he touch turn to gold. His greed robs him of the things that are essential for living. Food and drink turn to gold at his lips, and he loses his beloved daughter in the very act of embracing her. We learn from Midas that the joy and vitality of life are quickly extinguished by the stranglehold of greed on the imagination.

In a story from ancient Israel, King Ahab is made sick by his greed for a vineyard he cannot have. Our narrative highlights the toxic nature of Ahab's obsession: he takes to his bed and will not eat, so poisoned by his own covetousness that he would rather die than fail to acquire the object of his desire. The king has more than he needs—the seat of the northern kingdom is in Samaria, so the royal house here in Jezreel is only a secondary palace, after all— but those with untrammeled power become addicted to acquisition. The hapless vineyard owner, Naboth, simply wants to hold fast to his family's heritage. Here we may discern an implied critique of Ahab for threatening the old divinely ordained territory

Pastoral Perspective

Act 1 (vv. 1–10). The main characters in the first act of this "opera" text, as they enter the stage of biblical writing, are Naboth, good citizen, faithful tender of his vineyard; envious, weak Ahab; conniving Jezebel; a jury of upstanding citizens; and two scoundrels paid off to give false witnesses. The plot is set for injustice and tragedy. The jury sees the document stating that Naboth had cursed God and the king. The document bears the king's seal, falsified by Jezebel. The jury concludes it must be true. Naboth does not stand a chance. Guilty, they say. Penalty: death by stoning. Worse yet, his sons will also be killed; that is the law!

Intermission (vv. 11–16). We know by what we read in the background operatic text that indeed Naboth was stoned to death, a gory detail disturbing us to our core. We also learn that Ahab takes possession of Naboth's property, his envy satisfied. We can hardly wait for intermission to be over and the rest of the opera to play itself out. Evil cannot sing the final song, we think!

Act 2 (vv. 17–20). Enter Elijah, sent by God to condemn Ahab. While afraid of his old enemy's evil actions, Elijah obeys. The prophet tells Ahab God's message of condemnation. We in the audience know

against him, saying, 'You have cursed God and the king.' Then take him out, and stone him to death." [11]The men of his city, the elders and the nobles who lived in his city, did as Jezebel had sent word to them. Just as it was written in the letters that she had sent to them, [12]they proclaimed a fast and seated Naboth at the head of the assembly. [13]The two scoundrels came in and sat opposite him; and the scoundrels brought a charge against Naboth, in the presence of the people, saying, "Naboth cursed God and the king." So they took him outside the city, and stoned him to death. [14]Then they sent to Jezebel, saying, "Naboth has been stoned; he is dead."

[15]As soon as Jezebel heard that Naboth had been stoned and was dead, Jezebel said to Ahab, "Go, take possession of the vineyard of Naboth the Jezreelite, which he refused to give you for money; for Naboth is not alive, but dead." [16]As soon as Ahab heard that Naboth was dead, Ahab set out to go down to the vineyard of Naboth the Jezreelite, to take possession of it.

[17]Then the word of the LORD came to Elijah the Tishbite, saying: [18]Go down to meet King Ahab of Israel, who rules in Samaria; he is now in the vineyard of Naboth, where he has gone to take possession. [19]You shall say to him, "Thus says the LORD: Have you killed, and also taken possession?" You shall say to him, "Thus says the LORD: In the place where dogs licked up the blood of Naboth, dogs will also lick up your blood."

[20]Ahab said to Elijah, "Have you found me, O my enemy?" He answered, "I have found you. Because you have sold yourself to do what is evil in the sight of the LORD, [21]I will bring disaster on you."

Exegetical Perspective

The assessment in 1 Kings of Ahab, ruler of the northern kingdom of Israel, is that he did more evil than all the kings before him (1 Kgs. 16:30; 16:33). In chapters 17–19, Elijah the prophet opposed Ahab because of his support of the Canaanite god Baal. (See pp. 74–79 and 98–103 on texts from these chapters.) Here Elijah confronts Ahab about his complicity in the murder of Naboth in order to acquire his vineyard.

First Kings 21 contains the story of Ahab's acquisition of Naboth's vineyard (vv. 1–16) and Elijah's condemnation of Ahab (vv. 17–29). Today's lectionary reading puts verses 11–14 in parentheses as optional, and ends mid-sentence in verse 21a. More will be said about these lectionary choices in the following discussion.

The story of Naboth's vineyard is carefully crafted. The first scene (vv. 1–4) presents the initial inter-action between Ahab and Naboth. Verse 1 provides the setting, stating that Naboth had a vineyard in Jezreel, beside King Ahab's palace. In verse 2 Ahab asks Naboth to give him the vineyard, which Ahab wants to use as a "vegetable garden." There is no coercion apparent in Ahab's request. In fact, he offers to trade Naboth for a better vineyard, or to pay him the vineyard's value. However, there is a suggestion that Ahab's desire for the vineyard is at least

Homiletical Perspective

The sad story of the unwarranted execution of Naboth the Jezreelite gives the preacher an opportunity to ask some important questions about the death penalty and its place in a just society. In appeal after appeal, state and federal courts ponder the question whether certain forms of execution constitute cruel and unusual punishment. The questions raised by the case of Naboth go deeper than this. They force us to ask if the terms "death penalty" and "justice for all" are not, in fact, mutually exclusive terms.

At the very least, the use of the death penalty to eliminate Naboth to clear the way for King Ahab to take possession of Naboth's vineyard causes us to ask, can the death penalty be misused, can the death penalty be wrongly administered? Clearly the answer to these questions is yes.

We cannot prove the historicity of the story of Ahab and Naboth. However, history is full of stories like this. History is full of stories in which the powerful use the legal system to eliminate those they find to be inconvenient. Many of the inconvenient are jailed, harried, and harassed. Some lose their lives. William Brennan Jr., the late U.S. Supreme Court justice, once said, "Perhaps the bleakest fact of all is that the death penalty is imposed not only in a freakish and discriminatory manner, but also in

1 Kings 21:1-10 (11-14), 15-21a

allotments. Honoring the ancient tribal divisions of land is an express statute of God (see Num. 27:6–11; 36:9). The passionate earnestness of Naboth's response, "The LORD forbid that I should give you my ancestral inheritance" (v. 3), suggests that a great deal is at stake for the Jezreelite in protecting what belongs to him. The sulking king, by contrast, is shown to be both capricious and immature.

Like Midas, Ahab gains the object of his desire only at a tragic cost. His infamous wife Jezebel schemes to have two "scoundrels" bear false witness against Naboth. This flouts one of the Ten Commandments (Exod. 20:16, Deut. 5:20) and thus is not only a moral outrage but a grievous sin against the covenant of God with Israel. On the basis of the false accusation, poor Naboth is stoned to death, and Ahab seizes the vineyard by royal fiat. However, deeds done in darkness are always brought into the light of God's truth. The prophet Elijah pronounces God's judgment on the king's murderous greed. In the Deuteronomistic History, the prophetic word inevitably comes to fulfillment; Ahab cannot escape. Despite a cowardly effort to disguise himself on the battlefield, Ahab is mortally wounded by an archer's random arrow. He suffers for hours, propped up in his chariot, before succumbing (1 Kgs. 22:34–35); the awful delay dramatizes the futility of trying to cheat God's inexorable judgment. Jezebel too meets a gruesome end, and the dynasty of Ahab is destroyed in a river of blood (2 Kgs. 9–10).

The writers of the Deuteronomistic History know that royal power is easily corrupted into royal malfeasance. The books of Kings evaluate the reigns of kings of Israel and Judah according to whether the monarchs walk in idolatrous ways or remain true to the God of Israel; most often, the verdict is negative. Deuteronomy 17:14–20 places strict controls on kingly power in a concerted attempt to keep the king's mind fixed on God and his hand out of the royal coffers. The idealism of the Deuteronomistic view of kingship is never realized, however, according to its authors, except in the paradigmatic examples of the faithful kings Hezekiah and Josiah. So prophets in the royal court play a crucial role as the conscience of a monarchy that continually fails to live up to God's requirements for moral and spiritual leadership.

Early and late in Israel's traditions, the prophets proclaim a God who is outraged by the exploitation of the powerless. Israel is repeatedly exhorted to protect the resident alien, the widow, and the orphan. The holiness of God requires mercy toward the poor, as the Holiness Code (Lev. 17–26) makes

that somewhere God has said, "You shall not covet anything that belongs to your neighbor." God has also said, "Vengeance is mine." God's message is harsh, promising horrendous punishment for Ahab and for Jezebel, extensive to all males in their kingdom.

We cannot wait to see justice done, and for some kind of justice to be served for Naboth's wife and daughters, now left homeless and powerless without adult males around them. Perhaps the third act will bring on all this hoped-for justice.

Act 3 (v. 21a). Alas, today's opera leaves us hanging! There is no real ending to the story in its final act, other than a promise of future punishment, for the final words for the libretto today, the opera's text, are those uttered by God to Ahab, through Elijah: "I will bring disaster on you" (v. 21).

That is not an acceptable ending, we clamor! This cannot be the final word! This is not part of some Wagnerian cycle, one story continuing in another dramatic opera. We do not want to leave simply confirming what is said, that "Power corrupts and absolute power corrupts absolutely." We want more from God, we want justice. It is too bleak a night, we feel. We need the promise of a new day. In today's world, we in the audience suffer far too often because of evil perpetrated by people in power over us, in home, church, and the world. What kind of ending is this?

So we leave pleading with the psalm for today: "O LORD . . . listen to the sound of my cry. . . . in the morning I plead my case to you, and watch. For you are not a God who delights in wickedness; evil will not sojourn with you" (Ps. 5:1–4).

Opera Follow-up. As we leave the theater, we remember there is a commentary on the opera offered to those who wish to know more about it. Somewhat reluctantly we meet with others to find meaning in what we experienced.

We are pleased to see that the actor playing Elijah's part will address our concerns. The first thing we hear is that indeed the story continues in the next opera. We are assured that the author of the story is always faithful; as in other opera texts by the same author, at the end all will be well. Justice and love will be the final song.

Then the speaker addresses us as the character in the opera (the prophet/preacher):

I, Elijah, fearful of Ahab and Jezebel, was told by God to confront evil. I was to tell the king the words God instructed me to say. So I did, but I had questions about it all.

Exegetical Perspective

theologically problematic! The same Hebrew phrase, "vegetable garden," occurs in Deuteronomy 11:10 to describe Egypt in contrast to the promised land. The careful biblical reader might note that the suggestion of turning an Israelite's land into a vegetable garden would be an offense against both Naboth and God! Naboth's reply seems to confirm this. He refuses Ahab's request in the form of an oath: "The LORD forbid that I should give you my ancestral inheritance" (v. 3). Ahab then returns home and takes to his bed, sulking and depressed (v. 4).

The second scene (vv. 5–7) is a dialogue between Jezebel and Ahab. Jezebel asks Ahab why he is too depressed to eat (v. 5). He answers by repeating his conversation with Naboth (v. 6). Jezebel's response (v. 7) is threefold. First, she asks, "Do you now govern Israel?" This could be construed as a word of encouragement or as a sarcastic remark. Second, she tells Ahab to shake off his depression. Third, she says, "I will give you the vineyard of Naboth the Jezreelite" (cf. vv. 2 and 6—Ahab: "Give me your vineyard"; Naboth: "I will not give you my vineyard").

Scene three (vv. 8–14) describes Jezebel's plot against Naboth. She takes up Ahab's royal authority, writes letters using his name and seal, and sends them to the elders and nobles in Naboth's city (v. 8). Her "royal" instructions are that they proclaim a fast, seat Naboth in a place of honor, have two "scoundrels" bring a trumped-up charge against him, and then take him out and stone him to death (vv. 9–10). The charge against Naboth was, "You have cursed God and the king" (v. 10)—perhaps intended as a distortion of his oath refusing to give Ahab the vineyard (v. 3). Verses 11–13 describe the elders and nobles carrying out Jezebel's instructions to the letter. In verse 14, they send word to Jezebel that Naboth is dead. To omit verses 11–14 from the lectionary reading leaves hearers to assume that Jezebel's instructions were carried out. However, their inclusion in the biblical narrative dramatically emphasizes that Jezebel instigated and is responsible for Naboth's death.

The final scene (vv. 15–16) is another interaction between Jezebel and Ahab. The two verses are constructed in parallel fashion, which symbolically makes Ahab complicit with Jezebel in Naboth's murder. Both verses begin with the same phrase, "As soon as Jezebel/Ahab heard . . ." Jezebel's instructions to Ahab in verse 15, "Go, take possession of the vineyard of Naboth the Jezreelite," are echoed in Ahab's action in verse 16: "Ahab set out to go down to the vineyard of Naboth the Jezreelite, to take

Homiletical Perspective

some cases upon defendants who are actually innocent."[1] If even one person is executed without just cause, do we not need to step back from the practice and consider what we as a society are doing?

Often it is said that the Bible teaches an eye for an eye and a tooth for a tooth. It is argued that if someone takes a life, that person must pay with his or her own life. Yet, even if this were a perfect standard, we live in a decidedly imperfect world. Naboth's world was decidedly imperfect. Naboth took no one's life. Naboth took no one's eye. Naboth took no one's tooth. Naboth simply said that he could not bargain with King Ahab over that which was not his to bargain with, his field, his ancestral inheritance. Naboth inferred that the land was God's gift to his family and was therefore not his to sell, no matter how attractive the offer. Those blinded by fury are likely to claim they have been wronged when no wrong has been done. Those hungry for power and prestige are inclined to say they have been harmed when no harm has been done. How does the power of the state to execute fit in a world like this? Are there no more Ahabs? Are there no more Jezebels? Are there no more witnesses who will say anything for a price?

It is often said that the death penalty is the only way to rid society of those who would menace others. Perhaps the death penalty does mean that some "predators" die. Unfortunately, it can also mean that some die who pose no threat. Naboth was a good citizen. He listened to what the king had to say. He tried to live his faith. When a fast was called, he was present. He fulfilled his responsibilities. Was the world a better place because he was executed? Not in the least. His community lost an honest man. His faith lost a follower of God. His society lost someone who had his values straight. Does the death penalty make the world a better, safer, purer place? The evidence is at best inconclusive. If the case of Naboth is the only evidence we have to go on, we are forced to conclude that just the opposite is true.

Did the execution of Naboth bring any sense of closure or healing to those who saw him die? Often it is said that the administration of the death penalty brings such closure to the families of the crime victims. Because Naboth was victim and not perpetrator, it is difficult to argue this point from his story. Let it be noted, however, that Ahab, the one who was

---

1. Death Penalty Focus, *Myths and Facts about the Death Penalty* (San Francisco: Death Penalty Focus, 2008), http://www.deathpenalty.org/downloads/MythsBrochure2008Color.pdf.

1 Kings 21:1-10 (11-14), 15-21a

Theological Perspective

clear. The socially marginalized must be allowed to glean in fields and vineyards (Lev. 19:9–10); the deaf and the blind must be treated with equity (19:14); the elderly must be respected (19:32); Israelites must love the alien as themselves (19:34). The holy God is a God of mercy. Those who have been formed as God's holy people (Lev. 19:2; 1 Pet. 1:15–16) must themselves be merciful.

The Holy One stands against all systems that commodify and destroy the lives of human beings. Because God is merciful, empires founded on blood and exploitation are doomed. The story of Ahab's greed offers eloquent testimony to God's mandate that believers practice compassion and justice in their economic dealings. Consonant with this testimony are the Beatitudes of Jesus, the prophetic witness of liberation theology, and the robust cultural critique of postcolonialism. The evangelist Luke reminds us that the poor are blessed heirs of the kingdom of God (Luke 6:20). Matthew's testimony that the poor in spirit are blessed (Matt. 5:3) may be seen not just as a spiritualization of Luke's tradition but as an assertion that poverty of spirit, the utter opposite of acquisitiveness, is beloved of God.

Liberation theology preaches that the locus of God's saving work has always been the lives of the downtrodden. From Israel's deliverance from slavery in ancient Egypt to Central American peasants' struggles today for economic dignity, we see redemption afoot in God's grace to the poor. The Scripture insists that economic domination is an instrument of cultural oppression to be staunchly resisted. Only by dismantling the rhetoric and practices of empire can we honor our incarnate Lord in the faces of the vulnerable. On this, the voices of Scripture are unequivocal: the living God is known through solidarity with the weak and the powerless.

CAROLYN J. SHARP

Pastoral Perspective

Deep in my soul I remembered these things: in my trials, God always walked with me. After all is said and done, God has been there for me. This evil is not God's doing. These are evil actions perpetrated by corrupt power. In all of my life, I have not known evil to win out, no matter how long it seemed to dominate. I tell you, I have sung, "O rest in the LORD, wait patiently for God," many times in my life.[1]

Look, Israel is called "God's vineyard." This story is not only about evil's power or Naboth's property. God's people are God's vineyard, and even when such vineyard has been stomped, burned, robbed, and the night of despair seems long and unending, grace conquers evil power, and joy comes in the morning. That is what this story is about.

What can we see up to this point, without the next opera? One, that we are God's vineyard. We suffer all things such crops normally endure: droughts, floods, and calamities of all sorts. Yet we keep on hoping, not based on events currently engulfing us, but on what we have experienced from God in the past. Remember that God's justice will flourish. Remember the goodness of God in our own story. Good overcomes evil, mercy overcomes pain, and at the end, as with Jesus, life overcomes death. Remember that Grace, Jesus Christ, is the vine, and we are the branches. Wine of gladness will come. Life will come. So we rest in that hope and sing,

> This is my Father's world: Oh, let me never forget
> That though the wrong seems oft so strong,
> God is the Ruler yet.
> This is my Father's world: The battle is not done;
> Jesus who died shall be satisfied,
> And earth and heaven be one.[2]

And that is the *real* final song. We can go in peace.

GLÁUCIA VASCONCELOS WILKEY

1. A reference to the oratorio *Elijah* by Felix Mendelssohn (New York: G. Schirmer Publications, 1970).
2. Maltbie Davenport Babcock, 1901, in *The Presbyterian Hymnal* (Louisville, KY: Westminster/John Knox Press, 1990), 293.

Exegetical Perspective

possession of it" (cf. the instructions in Jezebel's letter, vv. 9–10, and the actions of the elders and nobles, vv. 11–13!).

The remainder of the lectionary reading (vv. 17–21a) contains Elijah's condemnation of Ahab. In verses 17–19, the word of YHWH comes to Elijah. He is instructed to meet Ahab in Naboth's vineyard (v. 18), and given instructions about what to say (v. 19). This word of YHWH to Ahab contains an indictment both for the murder of Naboth and for taking possession of his vineyard, and a judgment that dogs would lick up Ahab's blood in the same way and place as they did Naboth's (cf. the statement of Ahab's death in 1 Kgs. 22:38).

Verses 20–21a describe the subsequent meeting between Ahab and Elijah. Unlike Jezebel's words in verses 9–10 and verse 15, YHWH's words in verses 17–19 are not repeated here, either by the narrator or by Elijah. Instead, the indictment and judgment spoken by Elijah in verses 20–21a are framed in terms of the assessment of Ahab as "evil" (cf. 1 Kgs. 16:30): "Because you have sold yourself to do what is *evil* in the sight of the LORD, I [YHWH] will bring disaster [Heb.: "evil"] on you."

That parallel construction of indictment and judgment is probably one reason why the lectionary reading ends with verse 21a. However, the announcement of judgment continues in verses 21b–24 and includes not only Ahab, but also Jezebel and Ahab's descendants. This is followed by an editorial comment by the narrator on Ahab's evil nature (vv. 25–26). The chapter concludes with Ahab repenting after hearing the words of judgment (v. 27), and YHWH consequently deciding to postpone the "disaster" (Heb.: "evil") until the days of Ahab's son (vv. 28–29).

The lectionary reading focuses attention on the story of Naboth's vineyard. It becomes a cautionary tale about acts of oppression against those over whom any person or government has power. The news is full of situations around the world where that warning remains relevant today. The courageous, prophetic preacher may also need to ask whether we, as church or society, take the role of Ahab—as passively complicit in the evil perpetrated by the Jezebels of the world.

MARSHA M. WILFONG

Homiletical Perspective

supposed to benefit from the death of Naboth, is anything but satisfied. When Jezebel informed her husband that she had taken care of his problem for him, that the field he wanted was now his, he went to that field. What did he encounter there? Peace? Serenity? Satisfaction? Justice? Closure? He experienced none of these. Instead, he met his longtime nemesis Elijah, the prophet of God. "Ahab said to Elijah, 'Have you found me, O my enemy'? He [Elijah] answered, 'I have found you. . . . you have sold yourself to do what is evil in the sight of the LORD'" (I Kgs. 21:20). The death penalty offered no solace; instead, it brought further grief. Research by Death Penalty Focus, an anti–death penalty organization, shows that "many victims' families oppose the death penalty because it institutionalizes violence and creates more victims without addressing the root causes of violent crime."[2] It is hard to get to serenity by traveling the road of violence.

This passage closes with God saying to Ahab through Elijah, "You will reap what you have sown. You have brought disaster, you will suffer disaster." Is this a satisfactory ending? Do God's words make Naboth's family feel any better? Is there any honorable way to atone for what happened to Naboth? Is there any way to correct this miscarriage of justice? Even God's promises of justice ring a little hollow. Once a human life has been taken, there is a thundering finality that no words can remove. The story ends with Elijah and Ahab in the garden, pondering God's words, aware that something terrible has happened, aware that nothing can make things right. Is there some wisdom in this ancient tale for us?

H. JAMES HOPKINS

---

2. Ibid.

Psalm 5:1-8

¹Give ear to my words, O LORD;
   give heed to my sighing.
²Listen to the sound of my cry,
   my King and my God,
   for to you I pray.
³O LORD, in the morning you hear my voice;
   in the morning I plead my case to you, and watch.

⁴For you are not a God who delights in wickedness;
   evil will not sojourn with you.
⁵The boastful will not stand before your eyes;
   you hate all evildoers.

Theological Perspective

Basic to Israel's theology was the conviction that God is just and that, accordingly, in the world God rules, justice reigns. Yet people notice that matters are not so simple. In Psalm 5 the psalmist holds on to this conviction, but clearly his actual experience does not readily confirm it. His enemies, whom he regards as wicked, are unpunished. He himself is not secure.

The psalm is a plea to God to act as Israel's theology proclaims. It is a passionate promise to continue to act righteously, so that God's justice will vindicate the psalmist, but it expresses the perception that the actual situation does not fully accord with pious expectations.

The psalm expresses the situation of many believers through the centuries. Believers affirm God's power and justice. Much in daily experience confirms this conviction. On the whole, day by day, we are happier when we are loving and generous toward others than when we are hard hearted and withholding. Those who express their love to others in tangible ways often receive help from others when it is their time of need. Swindlers and cheats are often caught and punished. The virtuous are often honored. Those who work hard and are careful with their money generally do better than those who are lazy and spendthrift. In short, a rough justice

Pastoral Perspective

Pastors encounter those who are going through on a regular basis the kinds of struggles voiced in this psalm. The psalmist embodies the individual who cries out to God for help. The opening verses are filled with words such as "sighing" and "cry" as the psalmist begs the Lord to hear these words. For those struggling with how to give voice to their concerns in life, particularly for those who feel attacked by one's "enemies," these words can give voice and function as prayer to God. In fact, praying this psalm using the spiritual practices of *lectio divina* could be a wonderful way to engage God in one's struggle.

The language of the psalm is strong, portraying God as one who "hates all evildoers" and "abhors the bloodthirsty and deceitful." In addition, there is talk of "enemies." How does the faithful Christian view this in the context of other biblical passages? Jesus says that we are to *love our enemies* (Matt. 5:44). For the preacher and pastor, it will be necessary to speak truthfully about this genuine tension. Granted, Jesus' teaching to love one's enemies offers a reinterpretation of this earlier teaching, but this psalm still contributes insight to a complex and nuanced biblical perspective on how to view one's enemies.

According to the psalm, God hates evil. That which defaces creation and humankind, that which devalues what God created and called "good," is

⁶You destroy those who speak lies;
   the Lord abhors the bloodthirsty and deceitful.

⁷But I, through the abundance of your steadfast love,
   will enter your house,
I will bow down toward your holy temple
   in awe of you.
⁸Lead me, O Lord, in your righteousness
   because of my enemies;
   make your way straight before me.

Exegetical Perspective

Psalm 5 is classified as an individual psalm of lament. In it a lone voice pleads to God for deliverance from a particular situation of distress—perhaps a state of illness, perhaps oppression by others, perhaps some evil plotting against the psalmist. Its superscription (not included above) states that it is of David,[1] addressed to the choir director, to be sung according to a tune played on flutes. Individual psalms of lament typically consist of five elements that may occur in any place and in any order within the psalm: (1) an invocation, in which the psalmist calls on the name of God; (2) a complaint, in which the psalmist tells God what is wrong; (3) a petition, in which the psalmist tells God what the psalmist wants God to do; (4) words of trust, in which the psalmist outlines the reasons for trusting that God can and will answer the psalmist's petition; and (5) words of praise, in which the psalmist celebrates the goodness and sovereignty of God.[2]

Words of *invocation* abound in Psalm 5. Time after time, the psalmist invokes the presence of God. In verses 1–2, the psalm singer employs three distinct but common names for the sovereign—"O

1. For a full discussion of the meaning of "of David," see Nancy L. deClaissé-Walford, *The Book of Psalms: A Song from Ancient Israel* (St. Louis: Chalice Press, 2004), 32–35.
2. Ibid., 23–25.

Homiletical Perspective

This psalm raises the issue of prayer at the opening of the day, of what is popularly called "morning devotions." I was on an interfaith retreat once with a Native American man who went outside first thing each morning and bowed in respect to the four directions and what they represented to him spiritually. There is an element of that here, as the psalmist pleads his case to God in the morning and watches for an answer.

This psalm was written for a morning worship service, what we often call matins. Even though it was used in group worship, it is still a personal prayer. "Give ear to my words, give heed to my sighing" (v. 1), is similar to when we pray a personal petition in the prayers of the people on Sunday mornings and the congregation responds, "O Lord, hear our prayer." The address to "my King and my God" was a common address in ancient temple worship and reminds us that God is sovereign.

The speaker of the psalm is in trouble, perhaps legal trouble. His adversaries have brought a complaint against him. From the speaker's perspective, his rivals are bearing false witness against him. He needs to defend himself, and he wants God's help. Asking God to help us when we are in trouble is a common experience. Our initial prayer is often to ask God to take our side in a conflict, as Psalm 5

Psalm 5:1-8

Theological Perspective

operates widely in ordinary life. We have reason to affirm that the world is so ordered that righteousness is rewarded and sin is punished.

This justice is limited, however. There are times when the wicked prosper and show no signs of distress in doing so. All too often the righteous are oppressed. In the wider society, the forces of evil often seem triumphant. In the pages of history, sometimes eventually the scales are righted and the righteous are vindicated, but sometimes whole peoples are destroyed forever by the greed of others.

It is to the credit of the Hebrews that they did not conceal the limits of their official theology. In the preceding weeks we have seen that Psalm 96 expresses confidence in this theology by seeing that God is coming soon to bring the justice that is not now fully expressed. Psalm 146 is clear that while God is the creator of heaven and earth, there are powers in the creation that often work against the purposes of God.

Psalm 5 expresses a different spiritual attitude. Some call it "faith." This faith is holding firmly to official teachings even when the actual experience does not confirm them. One not only continues to believe these teachings are true, but one orders one's life according to them. One thereby intensifies the expectation that God will fulfill the expectations engendered by that teaching.

There is much that is attractive and admirable in those who hold fast to beliefs that are not evidently supported by the actual course of events, especially when this leads to courageous and generous actions. There are problems and dangers as well. Faith in this sense is beset by doubt. One senses this in Psalm 5. The serene confidence of Psalms 96 and 146 is missing. The psalmist is willing the destruction of his enemies, confident that God *should* bring that about, but not quite sure that this will happen. Faith in this sense can give way to rage when it is dramatically disappointed. It also leads to the depiction of Christians as believing what they are told to believe on authority, or even claiming to believe what in fact they do not believe.

This psalm reflects another danger in the official doctrine. Instead of understanding that good and evil are present in all of us, it may divide the world into those who are good and those who are evil. Typically then, we are the good ones, and the others are the wicked. The psalmist understands the good people to be those who worship God, and he assures God that he is and will continue to be a devoted worshiper. Since he is good, clearly those who oppose him are wicked.

Pastoral Perspective

always going to be something God "abhors." God's hatred is in response to the harm it does to those affected by evil—both the wronged and the wrongdoer. God's grace and mercy do not ignore the reality of evil and its effects. For the person who has faced genuine suffering at the hands of another, these words can provide comfort in knowing that God too is angry at the wrongdoing.

The "steadfast love" that creates the entryway for the psalmist to approach God's "house" and engage in worship is also at work in the world—seeking the restoration of those who are enemies of the good. Admittedly, "those who need restoration" describes all of us some of the time. While some have misused this text as a way to designate the enemies of God as those to be wiped out in the name of the Lord, the role of judge ultimately is reserved for God alone.

In his sermon "Loving Your Enemies," Martin Luther King Jr. asked a question that should be a part of any faithful reflection on this psalm: "How do we love our enemies?" King suggests that forgiveness, the recognition of the humanity of the evildoer, and the need to try to win over our "enemies" are all ways that may reflect the steadfast love that God has shown to us.[1] The movie *To End All Wars* provides a compelling look at how World War II prisoners of war try to live out their Christian faith at the hands of brutal guards who seem intent on destroying the humanity of the prisoners.[2]

Psalm 5:8 makes a request of God: "Lead me, O Lord, in your righteousness because of my enemies; make your way straight before me." The psalmist is asking for God to *make the way straight*—in other words, to make it clear how the psalmist can do righteousness in the presence of one's enemies. When we feel attacked by others, this is often accompanied by the feeling that our attackers are our "enemies." The situation may even feel like a crisis. In times of crisis there is a need for clarity—for the way to be made straight—so that one knows which way to go. In a crisis there is often little time for deliberation. (For example, if the house is on fire, it is no time for a conference on the best way to exit the building—you simply need to find the best way to get out and away from the danger.) Given this crisis, the psalmist's request is for clarity in order to do the right thing.

Yet doing what is right often seems to provoke the response of evil. Edwin Friedman has noted that

---

1. Martin Luther King Jr., *Strength to Love* (Philadelphia: Fortress Press, 1963), 50.
2. *To End All Wars*, 2004, 20th Century Fox.

YHWH," "my king," and "my God (*'elohim*)," a threefold repetition that is repeated by the psalmist's words of petition in the same verses (see below). Words of invocation appear again in verses 8, 10, and 12: "O YHWH," "O God (*'elohim*)," and "O YHWH."

The words of *complaint* come late in Psalm 5, not appearing until verse 9. Here the psalmist refers to the mouth, the heart (the equivalent of "the mind" in Hebrew thought), the throat, and the tongue. The source of oppression in Psalm 5 seems to be words, perhaps the hurtful and slanderous words of oppressors. In verses 4–6, the psalmist describes the oppressors as wicked, evil, boastful, evildoers, speakers of lies, bloodthirsty, and deceitful and affirms that God does not delight in such folk, will not tolerate them, and will destroy them.

The *petitions* of the psalmist to God are found in many verses of Psalm 5 (vv. 1–3; 8–11). The petitions in the first half of the psalm (vv. 1–8), however, have to do with how God should deal with the psalmist more than how God should deal with the psalmist's oppressors. In verses 1–2, the psalmist cries out to God to "give ear," "give heed," and "listen" (a threefold petition echoing the threefold invocation in the same verses).

Verse 1's "my words" comes from the verbal root "to say" and may better be translated as "my utterances," while the word translated "my sighing" comes from the verbal root "to muse over, to mutter." Thus we may picture the psalm singer being caught up in a verbal musing over God's involvement in the affairs of humanity and asking God to respond.

The psalmist's musing may be part of a night vigil at the temple or a sanctuary. Evidence from other biblical and ancient Near East texts indicates that worshipers facing some sort of threat (perhaps from oppressors, from illness, from the uncertainty of decision) would spend the night in prayer at a sanctuary (see, for example, 1 Kgs. 3:5; Ps. 3:5). In the morning, a priest would guide the worshiper in words of confidence in the guidance of God (Ps. 5:11–12). The psalm may also recount the journey of a psalmist who comes to the temple or sanctuary at the time of the morning sacrifice to present a plea before God. Whatever the psalmist's circumstance, verse 3 states that "in the morning" God hears the plea of the psalmist.

Verses 4–6 contain the words of *trust* of Psalm 5. God has provided in the past; God will provide in the future. The psalmist knows that God does not

does. We may even call our opponents names, like "evildoers." But as we stay in a state of prayer——or return to pray about the same concern again and again over time——we may hear an answer that is not what we expected. When we say, "Prayer changes things," we are usually thinking of external circumstances; but sometimes the thing that prayer changes is *us*. As we pray through a conflict, God may call us to change our position or our attitude. That is something for which we need to watch.

The psalmist characterizes his challengers as "evildoers," which he defines in the psalm as people who are "bloodthirsty and deceitful." Although, after careful discussion, most of us would agree that there is evil in the world, nowadays we tend to be cautious about using the words "evil" and "evildoers" cavalierly. To do so is to become boastful and arrogant, which is another way that the psalmist characterizes his rivals.

In my childhood, we had a fireplace in our family room. Each fall, my father would ask me to help him chop up a tree and make a woodpile for the winter. The year that I was ten, as I was piling wood, I complained about another student in my fourth-grade class whom I considered my enemy. I told my father about this boy's bad behaviors. My father pointed out situations in which I had done similar things and said, "Sometimes we judge most harshly people who, subconsciously, remind us of what we do not like about ourselves."

As most of us do, at least initially, as we pray for God's help when we are in conflict, the speaker in Psalm 5 has clearly already passed judgment against his foe, even though he is supposedly asking and watching for God's judgment. He tells God just whom the Holy One should hate, abhor, and destroy——namely, his rival. The psalmist takes absolutely no responsibility for his part in this conflict. He is pleading for vindication and divine retribution. We can recognize ourselves in such a prayer.

Those of us who follow Jesus Christ may hear an answer from God that we were not expecting. The author of Psalm 5 says of God, "You hate all evildoers. You destroy those who speak lies" (v. 5–6). Jesus taught,

> You have heard that it was said, "You shall love your neighbor and hate your enemy." But I say to you, Love your enemies and pray for those who persecute you, so that you may be children of your Father in heaven; for he makes his sun rise on the evil and on the good, and sends rain on the righteous and on the unrighteous. For if you love those

Psalm 5:1-8

Theological Perspective

This logic plays itself out on the world scene as well. We Americans, at least, divide the world into two groups, the good nations and the wicked ones. Since we know that we Americans are good, those who work with us on the international scene are also good. By definition, then, those who oppose our global polices are bad. Since we are on God's side, they are against God and deserve to be destroyed. This way of dividing the people with whom we have dealings (or the whole world) into two groups, "us" and "them," did not originate with the theology of divine judgment—it is deeply built into the human psyche everywhere—but the emphasis on rewards or punishments, support or destruction, can intensify and justify it. On the other hand, as Psalm 95 shows, the understanding that God is the creator of all can bring everyone into a common family not divided into the good and the wicked. The justice there anticipated is welcomed by all.

Doctrines matter. Indeed, they matter greatly; but at a certain level they do not determine their implications. The apparently identical doctrines of God as creator and judge can be so understood that they undergird a strong sense of common humanity and destiny under the sure hand of the one who is perfectly just. However, the same doctrines can intensify the human judgmentalism that justifies oneself and condemns one's enemies.

Paul saw the difference in terms of how we understand God's justice. Do we understand it as wrath or as love? He believed that Jesus revealed that God's justice is love. If we agree with Paul, we will abandon the expectation that God is on our side against our enemies. God is on the side of everyone. If we are on God's side, we will love our enemies, rather than calling on God to destroy them.

JOHN B. COBB JR.

Pastoral Perspective

when a leader becomes an agent for healthy change in any system—family, church, or nation—one should expect "sabotage" in response to the healthy change. As Friedman says, it "comes with the territory."[3]

The psalmist begins the prayer by calling out to God in the morning for help. This crying out may not prevent resistance from those who choose evil as a response to what is good. However, what one can hope for is to enter into God's "house" to worship and to be led by the God who can make the paths straight. This is the same God who, as Psalm 23 reminds us, prepares a table for us *in the presence of our enemies*. The Lord's leadership along the straight path can result in deeds of righteousness as our response to those who act as our enemies.

As the polarization of our world increases, voices such as the psalmist's will give rise to new visions that address evil and enemies in ways that are both cognizant of the complex reality of evil and faithful to the gospel's mandate to love our enemies. Ignoring the real threat of evil is inauthentic, but giving oneself over to retaliation, even in the name of the Lord, is less than what Christ calls us to do. The psalmist roots us in the genuine experience of one who is struggling to find divine help in facing the realities of life.

C. GRAY NORSWORTHY

---

3. Edwin Friedman, *A Failure of Nerve: The Problem with Leadership* (New York: Seabury Books, 1999), 11.

Exegetical Perspective

tolerate the wicked, evil, boastful, evildoers, liars, or deceivers. The knowledge may come from firsthand experiences of the psalmist, or it may come from the stories about God's workings in the lives of the ancestors in the faith. The God of the past and the present is a God of justice and provision.

The final element of a lament psalm, words of *praise*, is found in verse 7. Because of YHWH's steadfast love, the psalmist is able to enter the temple and bow down in awe-filled wonder.

In verse 8, the psalmist continues the petitions to God begun in verses 1–2 with requests that God "lead me" and "make your way straight before me." After gaining God's attention in the first verses of the psalm, the psalm singer now asks for guidance through the maze of oppressors confronting the psalmist on every side. The phrase at the end of verse 8 echoes the words of Isaiah the prophet, who admonishes his hearers in 40:3 to "make straight in the desert a highway for our God." The word "straight" comes from the Hebrew root *yashar*, which means "be straight, honest, firm, right." The God who created the world in which we live can surely provide straight and orderly paths out of the chaos of the world in which we live—oppressors and all.

Those who read Psalm 5 to its end in verse 12 will encounter additional words of trust, petition, invocation, complaint, and praise before the psalm's final words: "For you bless the righteous, O Lord; you cover them . . . with a shield." Psalm 5 depicts a psalm singer who comes into the presence of God, being battered by the words of oppressors, knowing that their words are not words of truth, and struggling to find a "straight" way (v. 8) in spite of oppressors.

Psalm 5's superscription identifies it as a psalm "of David." The books of Samuel tell us that David was constantly surrounded and oppressed—by Saul, by the Philistines, by his own children. His reliance upon God in times of trouble perhaps provided the inspiration for the words of this psalm.

NANCY L. DECLAISSÉ-WALFORD

Homiletical Perspective

who love you, what reward do you have? Do not even the tax collectors do the same? And if you greet only your brothers and sisters, what more are you doing than others? Do not even the Gentiles do the same? Be perfect, therefore, as your heavenly Father is perfect. (Matt. 5:43–48)

It may well take us a whole lot of prayer to arrive at the perfection that Jesus was talking about! Christ calls us to be so transformed in our nature that we treat with grace our enemies and anyone else whom we may think of as "evildoers." Could this even include undocumented immigrants, family planners, homosexuals, and people of different faith traditions than our own? Could human rights, like the rain, fall equally on everyone?

If we stay in a state of prayer long enough, and truly do keep watch for God's answer to our prayer, we may find that God is calling us to change our positions and attitudes. In verse 7, the writer of the psalm seems certain that God loves *him*. The theological question left unasked is if God loves his antagonists as well; but there is hope for the psalmist. He concludes in verse 8, "Lead me, O Lord, in your righteousness because of my enemies; make your way straight before me."

There is still hope that God will make straight and clear to the psalmist, and to us. "My thoughts are not your thoughts, nor are your ways my ways, says the Lord" (Isa. 55:8). God's righteousness is grace. Although the psalmist meant these words in the opposite way——that God's righteousness is damnation——perhaps, ironically, it is exactly "because of my enemies" that following God's righteousness of grace is what is needed. As Jesus wept for Jerusalem in Luke 19:42, the risen Christ still weeps for us and says, "If you, even you, had only recognized on this day the things that make for peace!"

DANIEL M. GESLIN

Galatians 2:15-21

¹⁵We ourselves are Jews by birth and not Gentile sinners; ¹⁶yet we know that a person is justified not by the works of the law but through faith in Jesus Christ. And we have come to believe in Christ Jesus, so that we might be justified by faith in Christ, and not by doing the works of the law, because no one will be justified by the works of the law. ¹⁷But if, in our effort to be justified in Christ, we ourselves have been found to be sinners, is Christ then a servant of sin? Certainly not! ¹⁸But if I build up again the very things that I once tore down, then I demonstrate that I am a transgressor. ¹⁹For through the law I died to the law, so that I might live to God. I have been crucified with Christ; ²⁰and it is no longer I who live, but it is Christ who lives in me. And the life I now live in the flesh I live by faith in the Son of God, who loved me and gave himself for me. ²¹I do not nullify the grace of God; for if justification comes through the law, then Christ died for nothing.

Theological Perspective

In some theological circles, Paul's Letter to the Galatians is understood to be polemic against "works righteousness" in favor of salvation through grace alone. The issue that Paul is addressing, however, is a little different. He is angry because he feels that Peter betrayed the agreement they had that allowed Jews and non-Jews to be equal partners in the early Christian community. If we think of a traditional practice as essential for faith, we exclude from our community lovers of Christ who practice differently than we do. This would have been catastrophic for Paul—and for all of us non-Jewish Christians. Paul and Peter, like Christians through the centuries, are struggling to live into the troubling reality of divine grace that has detached itself from tradition.

Paul implores the Galatians not to turn Christ into a new "religion." Religion itself was in a sense nullified by the cross. The perennially difficult truth of our condition is that neither our socially created divisions nor our religious commitments have any standing in the face of God's unbounded and ubiquitous love. Some early Christians retained Jewish practices, and others did not. Some communities focused on ecstasies and prophecy, others on service to the poor and sick. The leaders of the Jerusalem church agreed that the gospel could accommodate this variety. Paul could preach to Gentiles, Peter could preach to Jews.

Pastoral Perspective

We must not assume every Christian understands commonly used theological terms and concepts. Words like "redemption" and "sanctification," or, from this text, "justification" and "the presence of Christ in us," fly over the heads of some congregants and require thoughtful exploration.

Justification. Paul declares several times in this text that "a person is justified not by works of the law but through faith in Jesus Christ," and he thereby strikes a chord at the very heart of the gospel. Justification is what a computer's word-processing program does to the margins—straightening up the words so they are in right relationship to the page. This is what God does for sinners who are out of line. Messy human lives get straightened out, put in right relationship with God through Jesus Christ. The grace of Jesus Christ makes it happen *for all.* Jews are justified by grace. Gentiles are justified by grace. Christ alone has done what obedience to the law in general and circumcision in particular could never do: he has straightened out human beings with God and one another, resulting in solidarity, in a new community.

People are not justified by Jesus *and* the works of the law. While the underlying concern with circumcision will likely be a nonstarter for modern believers, it will be important to emphasize that

Exegetical Perspective

Made Right in Christ. Reading a Pauline letter is always a bit like eavesdropping on one end of a telephone conversation. In this text the hearing is complicated by the fact that Paul has been reporting to the Galatian congregations on his earlier confrontation with Peter in Antioch, when Peter (Cephas) withdrew from table fellowship with Gentiles, flip-flopping under pressure from "the circumcision faction" (v. 12). Verse 15 clearly comes from this heated exchange, since Paul speaks of "we ourselves" as "Jews by birth," and the Galatians are obviously Gentiles. The point he is arguing to Peter is the same point he wants to make to the Galatians (or to those Jews who have been offering the Galatians an alternate view of the gospel), making it hard to know where his reported speech ends and his current argument begins. As Jews (and not "Gentile sinners," the sarcastic language probably reflecting the attitudes of those gathered in Antioch), "we" know that God has justified or rectified "us" by means of Jesus Christ and not through the observance of the law, since the law is not able to bring about deliverance "from the present evil age" (1:4).

The NRSV reads "faith in Jesus Christ" in v. 16, but the notes explain that the Greek may be translated also as "the faith of Jesus Christ." Faith here can be a reference either to belief or trust in

Homiletical Perspective

Power struggles, exclusionary tactics, ecclesial face-offs, accusations of caving in to public opinion and hypocrisy. Sound familiar? These are all constants in public life and church life. In our own conflicted settings, we may fear for our sanity, but we should not ever presume that our congregations will not survive; conflict has been with us in the church since the beginning.

This text from Galatians reflects just such a conflict, between two giants of the early church no less: Paul and Peter. Apparently Paul is not the only one suffering from "people-pleaser syndrome." It is thin solace to us people-pleasers that both Paul *and* Peter now stand accused of wanting the good graces of others badly enough to soften the message. Paul declares that Peter has succumbed to ecclesial pressure and forsaken the heart of the gospel. Preachers and pastors know what it is like to run counter to the powers-that-be, only to feel the pressure to "rein it in."

Peter, Paul claims, lacks the courage of his convictions. Thrice-denying Peter has folded yet again. Some rock, this Peter. Paul's contempt is naked. Whatever else we wish Paul to teach us, it is not a short course on tact and diplomacy. For Paul the stakes were simply too high to *make nice* with Peter. It was not only the potential loss of the

Galatians 2:15-21

Theological Perspective

They did not have to produce identical communities, because the gospel did not depend on these things. This agreement was threatened when Peter waffled between his allegiance to Jewish tradition and allegiance to a new community devoted to Christ. For Paul, the gospel could survive plurality, but it could not survive the displacement of divine grace by binding customs and moral codes. Religious traditions give structure and meaning to our lives, but they also produce divisions in the human community among Catholics, Presbyterians, Greek Orthodox, evangelicals, liberals, Jews, Buddhists, and Muslims. Like Peter in his moment of indecision, we often feel more allegiance to our religious party than to the "Son of God, who loved me, and gave himself for me." But Paul's letter to Galatia is a reminder that being a Christian is not about allegiance to religious parties.

For Paul, faith recenters the mind, the heart, and the spirit so that one operates out of intimacy with Christ. Through this indwelling we participate in the ubiquitous love of God for ourselves and for all humanity. "I have been crucified with Christ; and it is no longer I who live, but it is Christ who lives in me" (vv. 19–20). Through death and resurrection Christ comes to dwell in the human heart and to produce a community based not on social distinctions but on love. This community should reflect our common human situation as recipients of grace and bearers of the Divine. The Divine dwells in Jews and Gentiles, slaves and free, men and women. This indwelling reveals the essential intimacy that exists between humanity and its creator, an intimacy that even we cannot neutralize, because it does not depend on us but on the graciousness of the living God. Faith allows the indwelling of Christ to become more transparent. Free from the logic of a social world built on the oppression of others, we are able to recognize others as bearers of the Divine. Faith is the site of unity, where God's desire for us and our own desire are woven together.

The divine compassion so urgently desires to display its love for humanity that God takes human form, walks among us, and shows us—in word and deed, in birth and death, and in victory over death— the intimacy and power of this love. Though Christians know this indwelling through the revelation of Christ, it can coexist with any religion, which is why Jews and Greeks alike could enter into Christian community. "Christ in us" requires nothing but faith that rests in the confidence that God is God. This was the stumbling block to the gospel in Galatia, and it remains the stumbling block

Pastoral Perspective

salvation is never a matter of Jesus *and something else:* not Jesus and certain cultural practices; not Jesus and a certain spiritual practice or theological perspective; not Jesus and a particular income level; not Jesus and a specific denominational brand; not Jesus and one political party; not Jesus and being good enough. Just Jesus. If anyone or anything else can be said to justify the sinner, the gospel is derailed, and, in the words of Paul's devastatingly abrupt conclusion, "Christ died for *nothing*" (v. 21).

Undoubtedly some congregants will take into account their deeply personal failures, their seemingly unforgivable sin, and struggle with such good news, wondering, "But did Christ die for this, too?" The church's answer must be an unequivocal, "No! Not for this, *too.* Christ died for this, period." No sin is an addendum to the cross. Not stubbornness or stupidity. Not addictions or depression. Not guilt or greed. God's grace is unconditional. That is why it is called *good* news!

What is often lost in the church is this very good news. It is as though the gospel is a valuable diamond on display, but the church focuses too much on the dark, velvet background of sin, the bad news. The sparkling gem of grace is diminished or missed altogether. Maybe this is why our churches are often seen as places of judgment and bad news, avoided by those who are troubled and struggling—the addict, the divorced person, the homeless. *Why would I want to go there? They would just make me feel worse.*

Of course, other options are available: the Hindu doctrine of karma; the Buddhist eightfold path; Islam's five pillars; the Jewish covenant; but none is quite so unconditional as the gospel of Jesus. Perhaps a fresh hearing of this text and experience of justification would compel congregations to become, in Lesslie Newbigin's description, the hermeneutic of the gospel, the interpretive key for "grace alone."

One way for the church to underscore the meaning of justification in a liturgical context would be to recover the Reformed practice of placing the Assurance of God's Grace *before* the Confession of Sin in the order of worship.

Continuing Presence of Christ. In what will likely be a jarring juxtaposition to modern ears, the vision of the faithful *life* offered by this text is *death.* Speaking on behalf of all Christians, Paul declares: "I have been crucified with Christ" (v. 19). This crucifixion is not simply a historic event that happened two thousand years ago on the outskirts of Jerusalem; it is an ongoing daily occurrence in the lives of

Jesus Christ or to Jesus Christ's own faithfulness. This tiny ambiguity (and similar ambiguities elsewhere in Paul) has in recent decades generated a scholarly version of the Thirty Years' War, with pitched battles over grammatical possibilities, relevant parallels, and theological implications. A cease-fire will require both sides to recognize that Paul's letters do affirm the importance of human faith, but that faith for Paul is always God's gift, never an act of human volition or intellect. It is a gift anchored in the death and resurrection of Jesus Christ.

Can Christ Serve Sin? Having eaten with Gentiles, and now having defended that action by arguing that human beings are made right ("justified") by "Christ's faith" and not by observing the Mosaic law, Paul comes up against the charge that he promotes sin. The outrageous question, "Is Christ a servant of sin?" shows in what stark terms Paul views the conflict. If Paul promotes sin by preaching that the gospel is granted to all without regard for the law, then Christ himself (or at least Paul's proclamation about Christ) is a servant of sin. What is at stake, especially for Paul himself, begins to come into view in verse 18: for Paul to insist on law observance for Gentiles, when he himself was ripped out of his own previous life with its aggressive zeal on behalf of the law (as in 1:13–14), would make him a transgressor.

Crucified with Christ. With verses 19–21, Paul's earlier comments about God's apocalypse in his own life (1:1–17) return in an acute form. As Paul understands, he actually did "die to the law" in order to "live to God" (v. 19). Paul cannot turn around and offer Gentile believers the option of taking on parts of the Mosaic law as a completion of the gospel, because he has "died" to his own earlier zealous actions on behalf of the law. Verses 19b–20 get to the heart of the matter, when Paul asserts that he has "been crucified with Christ" so that now Christ lives "in me."

What comes to expression in these familiar yet discomforting statements is the exclusive claim of the gospel Paul preaches. "Exclusive" has become a dangerous word in religious circles, as it should be when people make claims to know God's own disposition toward other people and other traditions. However, the exclusive claim Paul makes here is of a different order altogether, as he is acknowledging that the gospel is nothing less than God's takeover of his entire life. All that matters is Christ's life within and through him, which means

Galatian churches; it was the continuing erosion— and possibly the permanent denaturing and destruction—of the very gospel of Jesus Christ.

Many exegetes note that what may have been the issue for Peter, Barnabas, and others was the increasingly separatist energies of conservative Judaism, which was, interestingly, also exerting influence on Jewish *Christians.* While there were no explicit prohibitions against eating with Gentiles, observant Jews sought increasingly to eliminate any contact with non-Jews for the sake of the purity of their faith. Antioch, the place of Paul and Peter's confrontation, was a veritable mixing pot of people, cultures, and faiths. The tumbling of the old dividing walls of all kinds made utter sense to Paul, under the new freedom of Christ, but created a crisis for isolationist Jews and, as a result, Jewish Christians.

Paul was a *multiculturalist* far ahead of his time. Paul saw Jesus as the fulfillment of the long arc of God's love and God's inclusion, an arc bent toward making Gentiles full members of the family. The pressure from Jerusalem would seem to imply that Christian Gentiles would barely attain the status of stepchildren. For the factions that pressured Peter, only a full embrace of the laws and practices of Judaism would create a thin, admitting crack in the dividing wall.

Many who come out of nonchurched backgrounds into our congregations will find puzzling—if not outrageous—anything less than a full welcome of all who come. Intuitively almost, they seem to grasp the inclusionary energies of Jesus, whose life and ministry (and atoning death, Paul would add) annihilated any distinctions that once might have kept people segregated, for whatever reason. In his poem "Mending Wall," ostensibly about repairing breaches in New England stone walls, Robert Frost muses about the barriers humans erect in self-defeating attempts at protection and purity:

> Before I built a wall
> I'd ask to know what I was walling in or walling out,
> and to whom I was like to give offence.[1]

Like Paul, Frost seems to understand well the dangers of separation.

The old indictment that "the most segregated hour of the week is Sunday morning at 11:00" is an overly simplistic observation that fails to account for a host of complex realities. The unintended truth of

1. Robert Frost, "Mending Wall," *Robert Frost's Poems* (New York: Pocket Books. 1971), 95.

Galatians 2:15-21

Theological Perspective

for Christians today. For Paul, if Christ's gracious presence is demoted to an epiphenomenon of a new religious law, then the gospel itself is lost.

Paul speaks to the difficulty of sorting out what Christianity will be as it moves from its base among Jesus' Jewish followers out into the wide world. Notwithstanding his views on faith, Christianity did become a new religion and a new set of laws. Many Christians feel attached to the familiar beliefs, moral positions, liturgical customs, and songs of their community. In a pluralistic and changing world, it feels important to cling to these as if they were the gospel itself. These seem stable, reliable. They reflect our ordinary understandings of what allegiance to divine power should look like. Changing a hymnbook or rethinking an ethical position can make us feel as if "Christ died to no purpose." Paul reminds us that faith involves the perennial anguish of fidelity to a God that remains mysterious, even in God's most intimate revelations. He writes of the fragility of trust in unconditional love. He invites us to confidence in a cross that never ceases to disorient our minds.

Paul's depiction of the priority of faith gives us neither clarifying answers nor comforting practices. Instead, we are offered Christ himself. If we begin with faith, we can inhabit our traditions more lightly. We can enjoy the formation our particular community provides without insisting that it is the only way. Our faith can allow us to be nourished by tradition without assuming that those who practice differently have no knowledge of God. Faith gives us the confidence to honor our heritage, while recognizing the new things God is doing in other people's lives. Paul insists that our trust in this love is always justified.

In our own time, our conflicts with one another are as vehement as any in the early church. Paul's violent language might justify our intolerance, but his theology points to the freedom that is possible when we are crucified to the harsh logic of "our present evil age" and dwell instead in the ubiquitous love of Christ.

WENDY FARLEY

Pastoral Perspective

followers of Jesus. The form of the verb indicates that we not only are crucified but are being crucified continually. In contrast to a prevailing cultural fixation on self, we die to ourselves ("it is no longer I who live"), that Christ may live in us ("it is Christ who lives in me" [v. 20]). Crucifixion is not the end; it leads to new life in Christ. Christ is alive today in believers and in the body.

An awareness of this continuing spiritual presence of Christ may prove particularly fruitful for congregations implementing an increasingly business or corporate management model in their life together. The emphasis on developing vision statements and strategies, marketing programs and services, and determining healthy-church-index scores is often just busy work that decreases the church's understanding that it is a spiritual entity, called to be radically open to God at the core, and aware of what the living Christ is up to in the congregation's midst. It may be that what *we* want in our congregations, even the ministries we hold so dear, needs to be crucified afresh—because Christ is alive! The ongoing challenge is to pay attention to what the living Christ is up to.[1]

For individuals and congregations who struggle, there is hope; for if Christ is alive, out of death come new life and renewed purpose. This truth is underscored liturgically in the service of baptism, which acknowledges our death and new life in Christ. In baptism we are drowned, buried, and dead, and rise again to new life. Because this is Christ's work, by the presence of the Spirit, perhaps the water can be administered and the baptismal formula spoken *before* the person or parents speak their vows of commitment.

The Communion table also underscores the crucifixion of Christ and our crucifixion in him. In the modern world it is often about "what you have to bring to the table," but at the Lord's Table we bring nothing but our sin, and God does the work of spiritual renewal. Christ's continuing presence is made alive again in all who place their trust in him.

HEIDI HUSTED ARMSTRONG

---

1. See Andrew Purves, *The Crucifixion of Ministry: Surrendering Our Ambitions to the Service of Christ* (Downers Grove, IL: InterVarsity Press, 2007).

that the gospel is not an option or a lifestyle or a decision; it is the whole of life.

In light of this total claim by the gospel, verse 20b characterizes his life as "by faith in the Son of God, who loved me and gave himself for me." (Here the Greek again contains the same ambiguity found in 2:16, "faith in the son of God" vs. the "faith" or "faithfulness of the Son of God.") At several points Paul associates the death of Jesus Christ with love for humankind, whether that of Jesus himself or that of God, a notion found elsewhere in the New Testament as well. While recent investigation into the life of Jesus has made the quest for the "real" villains in the death of Jesus into a cottage industry, Paul's interpretation of the crucifixion is relentlessly theological. Jesus gave himself over in order to defeat the powers of sin and death, the powers of "the present evil age" (1:4).

At least by verse 20, the "I" who speaks is something larger than Paul himself, since Galatians is scarcely the antecedent of the latter-day spiritual memoir. Although the "I" is Paul's voice, his voice invites the Galatian congregations to join him in understanding that they too have been crucified with this loving Christ. In chapters 3–4, he will argue that the Spirit they have received means that they too "belong to Christ" (3:29).

Verse 21 concludes the passage with yet another statement of the conflict: rectification ("justification") comes through the death of Christ and not through the law. In the discussion that follows, Paul will construct an astonishingly bold critique of the law, reducing it to the status of a babysitter, whose goal is simply to ward off disaster (3:24). This critique is not against "legalism," but against any claim that threatens the gospel's exclusive claim. To paraphrase 6:15: neither the law nor the "unlaw" is anything—only God's new creation.

BEVERLY ROBERTS GAVENTA

the statement is that too many congregations live out their lives in functional isolation from the world around them. Congregational life, not unlike the all-consuming practices of Diaspora Judaism, can so thoroughly engage congregants with its own concerns that far too little time is spent at the tables of community need and pain. We are at risk of unintentionally keeping ourselves separate for the sake of creating exquisite, jewel-like, but ineffectual churches.

Paul takes leave for a time of the quicksand of conflict and steps back onto the terra firma of the gospel he has received, leaving his rebuke of Peter to present a dense nugget of gospel theology. Paul addresses these words to Jewish Christian readers of his letter, with whom he is most likely to be at odds. Here, as elsewhere, preachers will appreciate Paul's courage to address those with whom he disagrees. With an insider's tone, he describes the essential incompatibility between the old way and the new. It is not the old cultic traditions of observance of the law that can save, but simply faith in Jesus Christ, whose atoning death has demolished the old paths. Paul's example can lead us to use common ground that exists as a stepping-off point to forging new understandings. We might speak of the exclusionary practices of our own immediate ancestors before naming practices of radical inclusion that find support in Paul's example.

With zeal, Paul pushes the Jewish Christians to a point of either/or. "You cannot have things both ways!" he declares. We preach to listeners who are nourished by a culture that has made an art out of "having it both ways." Many wish, for example, for economic security and a kind of *benign affluence,* yet also claim to wish for economic justice that can be attained only by the secure and affluent becoming a bit less so—an ethic of "living simply that others may simply live." We want both. We would like the rising tide that lifts all boats to lift others without our having to give up anything. The truth is, there is not enough tide in the world to do that. We live in a world of limited resources. Something has to give. Paul's words condemn the Jewish Christians—and Peter—for only partly crossing the lines that divide, as well as the divided heart that is not yet ready to live fully in the dangerous freedom of Jesus Christ.

GREGORY H. LEDBETTER

Luke 7:36-8:3

³⁶One of the Pharisees asked Jesus to eat with him, and he went into the Pharisee's house and took his place at the table. ³⁷And a woman in the city, who was a sinner, having learned that he was eating in the Pharisee's house, brought an alabaster jar of ointment. ³⁸She stood behind him at his feet, weeping, and began to bathe his feet with her tears and to dry them with her hair. Then she continued kissing his feet and anointing them with the ointment. ³⁹Now when the Pharisee who had invited him saw it, he said to himself, "If this man were a prophet, he would have known who and what kind of woman this is who is touching him—that she is a sinner." ⁴⁰Jesus spoke up and said to him, "Simon, I have something to say to you." "Teacher," he replied, "speak." ⁴¹"A certain creditor had two debtors; one owed five hundred denarii, and the other fifty. ⁴²When they could not pay, he canceled the debts for both of them. Now which of them will love him more?" ⁴³Simon answered, "I suppose the one for whom he canceled the greater debt." And Jesus said to him, "You have judged rightly." ⁴⁴Then turning toward the woman, he said to Simon, "Do you see this

Theological Perspective

In the 2003 movie *Luther*, an early scene portrays Martin Luther wrestling with the character and intentions of God. "Have you ever dared to think that God is not just?" Luther asks his mentor, an elder monk. "He [*sic*] has us born tainted by sin, then He's angry with us all our lives for our faults, this righteous Judge who damns us, threatening us with the fires of hell!"

"Martin, what is it you seek?" the old monk asks.

"A merciful God! A God whom I can love. A God who loves me."

Luke's unique story brings Luther's question to the center: *What is the nature of God's righteousness?* The story also carries soteriological and christological questions. *How are we saved from sin and reconciled to God?* And *who is Jesus?* Is he a prophetic pretender, or the central figure through whom God inaugurates the hoped-for age of salvation? Luke interweaves the answers in his narrative.

At his dinner for Jesus, Simon is cautious, while the woman is expressive, giving Jesus the hospitality that Simon failed to give. While Simon gives Jesus no water for cleansing, she gives Jesus the water of her tears. While Simon gives Jesus no kiss of greeting, the woman continually kisses his feet. While he gives Jesus no oil for anointing, she extensively anoints his feet with ointment (vv. 44–46).

Pastoral Perspective

Shame is often an underlying factor in great social tragedies such as addiction and violence. Victims of public shame often become such objects of ridicule and shunning that they are dismissed, pushed to the margins of society where no one will miss them. Those who struggle with chronic shame can withdraw into themselves or lash out in rage. Those who struggle with shame cannot escape the label "unworthy." For them, and all of us, Jesus offers forgiveness and acceptance that lifts the heavy burden of shame, allows the forgiveness of self, and offers the freedom of authentic life lived in love and gratitude.

One can imagine the occasion. Jesus has arrived for a meal at the home of Simon, a Pharisee. It promises to be an evening of high hospitality. Though the invitation implies a cordial relationship between Jesus and Simon, the reader cannot but anticipate at least a hint of the tension that usually follows Jesus. Surely the air is thick with whispers from the crowds who have followed him as they peer through the entranceway, straining for a glimpse of the special guest.

In the midst of this mildly chaotic moment, a woman silently moves forward. Quite invisible to those present, she kneels behind Jesus. Like the woman with the hemorrhage (Luke 8:43–48), this

woman? I entered your house; you gave me no water for my feet, but she has bathed my feet with her tears and dried them with her hair. ⁴⁵You gave me no kiss, but from the time I came in she has not stopped kissing my feet. ⁴⁶You did not anoint my head with oil, but she has anointed my feet with ointment. ⁴⁷Therefore, I tell you, her sins, which were many, have been forgiven; hence she has shown great love. But the one to whom little is forgiven, loves little." ⁴⁸Then he said to her, "Your sins are forgiven." ⁴⁹But those who were at the table with him began to say among themselves, "Who is this who even forgives sins?" ⁵⁰And he said to the woman, "Your faith has saved you; go in peace."

⁸:¹Soon afterwards he went on through cities and villages, proclaiming and bringing the good news of the kingdom of God. The twelve were with him, ²as well as some women who had been cured of evil spirits and infirmities: Mary, called Magdalene, from whom seven demons had gone out, ³and Joanna, the wife of Herod's steward Chuza, and Susanna, and many others, who provided for them out of their resources.

Exegetical Perspective

The story in Luke 7:36–50 contrasts Simon's hospitality with the extraordinary behavior of an anonymous sinful woman. It highlights the nature of God's forgiveness and the necessity of a proper self-concept. Luke 8:1–3 serves as a transition from the stories concerning Jesus' identity as prophet to the further mission in Galilee.

In 7:18–35, which reveals the relationship between Jesus and John, Luke explains how those with little or no social status have accepted God's plan, but the religious elite have not (vv. 29–30). The section ends with Jesus' pronouncement that John was rejected by the religious authorities for being too ascetic, while he was rejected for being a "friend of tax collectors and sinners" (v. 34). Underlying both comments is the idea that social status often blinds us to our radical dependency on God for sustenance and mercy. Luke 7:36–50 picks up those contrasts.

The passage resembles the anointing stories found in Mark 14:3–9, Matthew 26:6–13, and John 12:1–8; however, the differences among them suggest more creative shaping by Luke than mere literary dependence. Luke's creativity is confirmed by his combining an example story (vv. 36–40), a parable (vv. 41–42), and a pronouncement (vv. 44–50) to demonstrate God's forgiveness and the loving actions that it creates.

Homiletical Perspective

Some people are addicted to Sudoku. The first thing in the morning, they flip through the paper for the daily puzzle, savoring the moment over a cup of French roast coffee. When asked why they are so passionate about these puzzles, they may tell you that they appreciate the regularity of pattern or the consistency of strategy. Whatever else happens in the day, they will later recall an early morning moment when everything fit together perfectly, just so.

Stories of God's graciousness through Jesus' ministry remind us much more of the hidden picture puzzles from children's magazines than the predictable patterns of newsprint Sudoku. In the Gospel according to Luke, we read a series of stories filled with hidden surprises.

The rich detail of Luke's storytelling helps us imagine the sight of the crowds, the dust of the road, the smells of the vendors as they approached a village. In the foreground are the disciples, ever listening, questioning, and responding to Rabbi Jesus. Jesus surprises us by reaching deep within each scene, responding to the hidden person we at first do not see.

Jesus responded earlier in this chapter to an outsider, a centurion, by healing his slave from a distance. At his next stop in this series of traveling stories, Jesus risked touching the ritually unclean coffin at a funeral to respond to a grieving widow by

Luke 7:36-8:3

Theological Perspective

We do not know the nature of the woman's sin. Perhaps by the phrase "a woman *in the city*" Luke means to imply her sin is prostitution. On the other hand, he could have said this directly if he intended this. What is clear is that her sin is a social one known by those in town. Furthermore, her behavior was so unusual, so against social convention—an anointing of the feet—that the early Christians remembered the event.[1]

For Simon, the righteousness of God means that God cannot endure sinners, and a follower of God gains salvation by upholding the purity code, with its separation of the elect from the sinners of the world (Lev. 5:2–3; 6:18, 27; 7:20; 22:4–9). Simon judges the woman to be a sinner and himself to be different from and above her in status. He thus distances himself from her. Simon also distances himself from Jesus, whom he quickly disregards as a prophet because he lets the unclean woman touch him (cf. Lev. 15:19–32). Jesus must not have been able to see the woman's heart, as any prophet should (v. 39; cf. John 4:19).

Jesus' response addresses the questions of the nature of righteousness, soteriology, and Christology. Countering Simon's contemptuous dismissal, Jesus demonstrates his *divinely given power and authority*. Jesus knows not only the woman's heart, but Simon's thoughts, proving by Simon's own criterion that Jesus is *a prophet*. However, Jesus also reveals himself as *the eschatological prophet*, the "stronger one" who shares YHWH's authority to forgive sins (vv. 48–50)[2] and YHWH's generous intention to heal life, restore relationships, and forgive the sinful (cf. 5:17–26).

Through his parable, Jesus further *counters Simon's misunderstanding of the divine righteousness*. Shockingly, the righteousness of God is the generous mercy of God (cf. 6:36), exemplified by the creditor who forgives the debts "by way of gift,"[3] by Jesus' attempt to persuade Simon toward a saving change in his perspective, and by Jesus' hospitable reception of the woman's gifts of love and gratitude for her own forgiven debt. Jesus contrasts the righteousness of God with the unrighteousness of human beings. Rooted in the sinful interior of the human heart,

---

1. In Israel, the head was anointed for kings, priests, and prophets. The body was anointed as an act of hospitality or daily care. An anointing of the feet only is an unheard-of act in antiquity (though cf. John 12:3). It may figure in the everyday care of a man by his wife or daughter, or in the lives of libertines, but it was a strange and startling public act.

2. As he earlier demonstrated his share in YHWH's divine power over life (7:1–10) and death (7:11–17), and later over chaos (8:25). Only God can forgive sins. No prophet, priest, or rabbi would dare to claim that prerogative.

3. *Charizomai*, v. 42; cf. also 7:21; Gal. 3:18. That a moneylender would forgive a debt simply because of an inability to pay is unusually kind.

Pastoral Perspective

woman risks dire consequences as she creeps forward to touch Jesus. Then something happens to this unnamed woman. Instead of shaking with fear and trepidation she begins to weep. Bending low, she tends to Jesus' dusty, dirty feet with her tears. She kisses them and then, clutching the costly oil, gently anoints them. The woman does not use a cloth or the hem of her skirt but, in an intimate gesture of deep love, unfolds her hair and dries the teacher's feet.

Like Jesus, she finds that her reputation has preceded her. Simon's knowledge of her sin implies that, whatever her wrongdoing, it carries with it a public shame. Her low, inward body gesture suggests that she has long been cast out from community gatherings. The shame that she carries has pushed her to the fringes of society and leaves her looking up at the world from a lowly place. Only when she touches Jesus does she become visible to Simon, causing him to mutter under his breath, "If Jesus were really a prophet, he would know about this woman." With his usual flair for seizing the teachable moment, Jesus offers a parable of forgiven debts to help Simon understand the depth of gratitude experienced when one's costly heavy burden is lifted. Jesus gently chastises Simon by pointing out that the woman he has judged so unworthy has offered the gifts of hospitality that Simon as host should have provided.

We turn our attention to the shame in this story. Both public shame, as experienced by the woman in this story, and personal chronic shame can have a devastating effect on their victims. Our culture is plagued by social tragedies—like addiction, domestic and sexualized violence, and eating disorders—that are permeated by shame. Shame itself is very complex. It can be a healthy, even helpful, internal gauge that alerts us when we have crossed a personal or social line of appropriateness. Most of us have felt that slight flush of the face and queasiness in our stomach as we remember some social blunder that caused us embarrassment. Sometimes we are shamed by making poor choices and failing others, especially the ones we love.

At another level, victims of adolescent schoolyard bullies can suffer so much harm that shameful moments become etched into the mind, to be relived for decades. Adult bullies can intimidate and ostracize in ways no less cruel than children. In its worst form, shame and humiliation can be used as tools of coercion and manipulation in acts of violence, abuse, and torture.

Chronic shame causes one to be overwhelmed by a sense of self-condemnation and unworthiness. It

Exegetical Perspective

A Pharisee (v. 36) by the name of Simon (v. 40) invites Jesus to a meal, which is interrupted by a woman widely known as a sinner (v. 37), though Luke does not name her sin. Some scholars surmise that she may have been a prostitute, but the story merely implies that her sin was grievous.

The woman planned to anoint Jesus' head with ointment. By indicating the flask was alabaster, Luke implies extravagance on her part, a feature central to Jesus' parable. The narrative provides no reason for her actions. Perhaps she had a previous encounter with Jesus or John and experienced their message of forgiveness.

She stands behind the reclining Jesus and so is nearer to his feet than his head. Overcome with emotion, she weeps. Again, we are not told why. She begins to wash Jesus' feet with her tears. Unloosing her hair, she dries his feet, kisses them, and anoints them with ointment. Jesus accepts her actions, but the Pharisee does not. Speaking to himself (cf. 12:17; 15:17; 16:3 for other internal conversations), Simon pronounces judgment on both Jesus and the woman. Simon concludes that Jesus cannot be a prophet, since he shows no knowledge that a sinner was touching him.

Ironically, precisely because Jesus does befriend a sinner, readers know that Jesus is the Son of Man and a prophet. Moreover, Jesus demonstrates the qualities of a prophet by knowing Simon's unspoken thoughts. Jesus challenges Simon's evaluation of him and the woman, using a parable about the forgiveness of two debtors. Both are unable to repay their debt; both are forgiven. However, one owes ten times as much as the other. The point? The depth of gratitude is proportional to one's recognized need for forgiveness. Simon understands this, as seen in his response to Jesus (v. 43). With this Simon utters a judgment on himself.

Jesus emphasizes this, contrasting the woman's actions and Simon's reception. Simon provided no water, no kiss, and no oil. The woman bathed Jesus with her tears, kissed his feet repeatedly, and used her costly ointment to anoint his feet. Nothing suggests that Simon acted incorrectly, but his actions are more about perfunctory etiquette than honoring Jesus. Jesus is a guest—just not a welcome one. The woman, however, acted with deep humility and graciousness, reflecting her gratitude. She transcended etiquette and expressed true hospitality.

Jesus explains this with his pronouncement about the woman's forgiven state (v. 47). The grammar is ambiguous and could be translated, "Because you have loved, your many sins are forgiven." However,

Homiletical Perspective

raising her son to life. The message is clear: the presence of God with us is good news for all people, for everybody—the powerful Roman soldier and his powerless slave, and the suffering widow and her restored son. Today we hear about God's graciousness toward the sinner who was considered unworthy to be in Jesus' presence. She becomes the forgiven one who is exalted for her faith.

Jesus casts an ever-widening net to catch the people of God. In so doing, he changes the rules of the game. The angel in the Lukan birth narrative proclaimed, "See—I am bringing you good news of great joy for all the people" (2:10). Jesus lives out that grand pronouncement through embodied good news for everybody. Jesus draws a circle around people previously standing at the margins, drawing them inside. For those previously at the margins of society, the new boundary lines are drawn by God in very pleasant places.

Not everybody responds positively to this change in the game. Imagine the living room of a Pharisee where Jesus comes to dine. The Pharisee rudely ignores common practices of hospitality, denying the road-weary Jesus a basin with which to wash or a towel to dry his feet. This is the host's way of saying, "It's great that you stopped by to see me. I'm sorry you won't be staying long."

Even though we affirm that the gospel is for everyone, at first we are surprised by whom Jesus chooses to draw in and lift up. As is so often the case in the Gospels, the truth sneaks up on us. We are then surprised by the discrepancy between what we think we know about the woman with the alabaster jar in today's story and what the story actually says.

Many people think of the woman who broke open the costly ointment as a prostitute. Nowhere in the passage is this suggested. Her love for Jesus and her sorrow for his coming trial become emblematic of her faith. Through her compassionate act of generosity in bathing his feet with her tears and drying them with her hair, she demonstrates abundant love. Her love for Jesus becomes the sign of God's extravagant love for us.

We want to hold her embarrassing love at a distance, but Jesus will have none of it. Jesus reveals who she is, in sharp contrast to our expectations. The word used to describe the woman comes from the Greek word *hamartōlos*, which means "sinner" or "sinful." Translated in this context, we imagine that "sinner" correlates with some moral failing or sexual sin. However, we see this word *hamartōlos* earlier in Luke describing none other than Peter.

Luke 7:36-8:3

Theological Perspective

unrighteousness is *contempt* for self, others, or God, and the resulting lack of graciousness and gratitude in relationships—traits exhibited by Simon, who is unaware of his own need for divine mercy.

If following the purity code or fulfilling the law does not save, *does love save, or at least prepare one for salvation?* Verse 47a has brought much exegetical debate since the Reformation, with traditional Catholics reading the Greek word "because" (*hoti*) as confirming the view that human love precedes and leads to divine forgiveness. The NRSV translates *hoti* evidentially ("hence" versus the KJV, RSV, NIV "for")—God's generous forgiveness precedes and is evidenced by the woman's great love—because this interpretation coheres with verse 47b and with the overall meaning of Jesus' parable. Luke, however, is highlighting *the interconnection between grace and gratitude*, not posing the question of who initiates faith, since, for him, both God and humans are actively involved in reconciliation. The centerpiece of the entire text is Jesus' proclamation that the creditor forgives the debt gratis, not because of anything done by the debtors. God's love and free forgiveness are central and prior for Luke, and realized through Jesus' cross, resurrection, and exaltation (cf. Acts 5:31; 13:38; 26:18). During his ministry, Jesus puts into effect this promised forgiveness of God by his performative speech-act (Luke 5:20; 7:48), inaugurating a reconciled relationship with God even before his passion.

Because it is *a relationship*, the new intimacy with God logically entails a human decision for a renewed connection with God, a decision enacted in repentance and baptism (cf. Acts 2:38). The capacity for love and gratitude is relationally connected to the ability to receive divine love, grace, and forgiveness, and the woman positively (as Simon negatively) reveals this interconnection. Similarly faith, as openness to grace, grasps the free forgiveness of debt and inbreaking reign of God, which are logically and chronologically prior (v. 50; cf. 5:20; 8:48; 17:19; 18:42; and Acts 15:11).

GREGORY ANDERSON LOVE

Pastoral Perspective

can take root in a child or an adult, with any event of rejection, failure, or helplessness. For those whose self-esteem is already tattered, it is not long before these failures make them feel as sinful and unclean as the woman in Luke's story. Eventually the constant fear of exposure will lead one to move through the world with a face perpetually cast downward in the ultimate physical shame response. Over time, if severe enough, shoulders will follow suit, slumping forward and causing the whole body to appear as though it is closing in on itself, shutting out the world in the process. Often drugs, alcohol, food, and other destructive behaviors are used to numb the intense feelings of low self-worth that pervade the life of one with chronic shame.

The last thing the woman in this story wishes to do is to find herself as the center of attention. Whatever draws her to Jesus must be stronger than what threatens to expose her. Even Simon's snide mutterings cannot deter her. Imagine the courage it takes to walk into the center of ridicule to express her love and gratitude for Jesus. Before Jesus has even said a word to her, the tears tell us that something has happened. She already knows the power of his love and acceptance. It is an overwhelming moment of gratitude and freedom.

Jesus says, "Your sins are forgiven. . . . go in peace" (vv. 48, 50). He is offering more than a forgiveness that merely wipes the slate clean. Jesus' forgiveness lifts the burden of shame, to give her value and worth in spite of how unworthy she feels. This kind of forgiveness allows us to release the moments in time when we feel like failures to ourselves, our families, or our God. For those with chronic shame, forgiveness can open the possibility that one is worth something. In fact, that one is worth quite a lot. This is freedom. Jesus reminds us that this freedom is the gift of a loving God. A heart that is bound by sin and shame withers and dies, but the love of a forgiving God lifts it to heights beyond our greatest dreams and causes it to sing in gratitude.

M. JAN HOLTON

this contradicts the parable and the story's logic. The NRSV is better ("her sins, which were many, have been forgiven; hence she has shown great love"), implying the woman's actions demonstrate she understands Jesus' forgiveness and benevolence. Because she deeply appreciates God's actions, Jesus grants public value to her, which then provides an occasion for further inquiry into Jesus' identity (cf. 9:20, 22, and 35, where Jesus' true identity is finally revealed).

Luke 8:1 recalls 4:43–44, where Jesus states that God has sent him to proclaim the good news of the kingdom. The reference to "the twelve" harks back to the calling of the apostles (6:12–16) and points forward to their upcoming mission (9:1–6). The reference to the women who accompany Jesus displays three important features. First, they are women "who had been cured of evil spirits and infirmities" (v. 2), underscoring the miraculous work Luke narrated in chapter 7 (7:1–10, 11–17, 20–23).

Second, they are women who "provided for them out of their resources" (v. 3). The word "provided" (*diakoneō*) typically refers to table service or provision of food in Luke/Acts (4:39; 10:40; 12:37; 17:8; 22:26–27; Acts 6:2); however, here it must also include the supply of the group's needs for its travels. The word that the NSRV translates as "resources," which can also be translated as "possessions" (*hyparchonta*), is important in Luke's Gospel. The use of one's possessions is an indication of the values one holds, including devotion to God (7:25, 12:13–21, 33–34; 14:33; 16:1; 19:8; see also the parables of the Prodigal Son, the Rich Man and Lazarus, and the Ten Pounds). Later in Luke the women demonstrate this devotion most profoundly by preparing Jesus' body for burial (23:49, 55–56).

Third, the women are named, in contrast to the anonymity of the woman who just served Jesus in the preceding story. Two of these women are also the first to report Jesus' resurrection: Mary Magdalene and Joanna (24:10). Joanna is further identified as the wife of Herod's steward, suggesting a higher social standing and providing a counterpoint to Herod's own perplexity at Jesus' identity (9:7–9). Traditional ancient Mediterranean gender roles are instantiated by the use of service language; however, this is mitigated by the fact that Jesus refers to himself as a "provider/server" in response to the disciples' rift over who will be greatest among them (22:26–27). Thus these women are exemplars of the communal humility that must exist among all Jesus' disciples.

STEVEN J. KRAFTCHICK

Jesus called his first disciple in Luke 5:8. "But when Simon Peter saw [the large catch of fish], he fell down at Jesus' knees, saying, 'Go away from me, Lord, for I am a sinful man.'" Simon Peter's sin is not named, nor is the sin of the woman with the alabaster jar. The focus of our questioning necessarily shifts from pondering what sins they may have committed, to how in their sinfulness they are willing to serve Jesus.

The woman with the alabaster jar joins the company of all of us who want to serve Jesus. Though broken and flawed like Peter, she becomes a means of grace for the glory of God. This gives us great hope that we too may be a part of God's continuing story.

Finally, the traveling stories end with a rarely preached lectionary text that demonstrates the work of Jesus through faithful women, proclaiming once again good news of the kingdom of God for all. The text tells us that the new insiders include both the twelve disciples and the women who travel with him and support him. As Peter, Andrew, and the others were previously named, now Mary, called Magdalene, Joanna, Susanna, and many others join them as followers of Jesus.

Jesus previously saved these followers from suffering. Mary was healed of seven demons, and the others were cured of evil spirits and infirmities. They became part of a growing cloud of witnesses to the kingdom of God, people like the faithful centurion, the healed slave, the restored widow, and the forgiven woman before them.

Here the author of Luke pulls out one more grand surprise. God's good news is made known once again through the witness of Jesus' radical inclusivity of all. God changes the rules in Jesus, which is good news of great joy indeed.

VERLEE A. COPELAND

1 Kings 19:1-4 (5-7), 8-15a

[1]Ahab told Jezebel all that Elijah had done, and how he had killed all the prophets with the sword. [2]Then Jezebel sent a messenger to Elijah, saying, "So may the gods do to me, and more also, if I do not make your life like the life of one of them by this time tomorrow." [3]Then he was afraid; he got up and fled for his life, and came to Beer-sheba, which belongs to Judah; he left his servant there.

[4]But he himself went a day's journey into the wilderness, and came and sat down under a solitary broom tree. He asked that he might die: "It is enough; now, O Lord, take away my life, for I am no better than my ancestors." [5]Then he lay down under the broom tree and fell asleep. Suddenly an angel touched him and said to him, "Get up and eat." [6]He looked, and there at his head was a cake baked on hot stones, and a jar of water. He ate and drank, and lay down again. [7]The angel of the Lord came a second time, touched him, and said, "Get up and eat, otherwise the journey will be too much for you." [8]He got up, and ate and drank; then he went in the strength of that food forty days and forty nights to Horeb the mount of God. [9]At that place he came to a cave, and spent the night there.

Then the word of the Lord came to him, saying, "What are you doing here, Elijah?" [10]He answered, "I have been very zealous for the Lord, the God of hosts;

Theological Perspective

"Message? God wasn't in the sound bites. God was in the silence bites."

So went one pastor's sermon on today's passage, which identified verses 11–13 as the theological heart of this text. When faced with congregants fully immersed in the trappings of contemporary North American culture, whether it be the flash and bang of Hollywood or the bluster endemic to cable political commentary, preaching the God who comes to Elijah in "a sound of sheer silence" (v. 12) can prove difficult to resist. In addition, such a sermon can almost write itself: "God's way of getting through to us is not through the sensational or the bombastic; God, instead, acts in our lives restrainedly and understatedly." "We need to take time out from the frenetic pace of our lives and embrace stillness and silence; through them God's word comes to us."

While there certainly are occasions for such sermons, biblical scholar Richard Nelson contends that 1 Kings 19:1–15a is not one of them. He bemoans the fact that this text is frequently used to inquire into the nature of revelation, which evinces, he believes, "a serious misreading of the narrative."[1]

Pastoral Perspective

"There is not much truth being told in this world. There never was. This has proven to be a major disappointment to some of us."[1] Hearing God's truth out of Elijah's lips was disappointing to King Ahab and Queen Jezebel. This third of five successive Elijah/Elisha stories relates Elijah's hiding from Ahab in the wilderness and receiving God's unexpected sustenance for his next ministry. As with many Ordinary Time texts, this is an invitation to experience God's unexpected encouragement for perseverance in the daily mazes of our lives, whether we are facing abundance, adversity, or dulling routine.

Humanity does a fine job of fooling itself about God's truthful intent for our daily maze-meandering lives. Anne Lamott puts it wittily:

> When I was a child, I thought grown-ups and teachers knew the truth. . . . It took years for me to discover that the first step in finding out the truth is to begin unlearning almost everything adults had taught me. . . . Their main pitch was that achievement equaled happiness, when all you had to do was study rock stars, or movie stars, or them, to see that they were mostly miserable. They were all running around in mazes like everyone else.[2]

1. Richard D. Nelson, *First and Second Kings* (Louisville, KY: John Knox Press, 1987), 123.

1. Anne Lamott, *Grace (Eventually): Thoughts on Faith* (New York: Riverhead Books, 2007), 1.
2. Ibid.

for the Israelites have forsaken your covenant, thrown down your altars, and killed your prophets with the sword. I alone am left, and they are seeking my life, to take it away."

[11]He said, "Go out and stand on the mountain before the LORD, for the LORD is about to pass by." Now there was a great wind, so strong that it was splitting mountains and breaking rocks in pieces before the LORD, but the LORD was not in the wind; and after the wind an earthquake, but the LORD was not in the earthquake; [12]and after the earthquake a fire, but the LORD was not in the fire; and after the fire a sound of sheer silence. [13]When Elijah heard it, he wrapped his face in his mantle and went out and stood at the entrance of the cave. Then there came a voice to him that said, "What are you doing here, Elijah?" [14]He answered, "I have been very zealous for the LORD, the God of hosts; for the Israelites have forsaken your covenant, thrown down your altars, and killed your prophets with the sword. I alone am left, and they are seeking my life, to take it away." [15]Then the LORD said to him, "Go, return on your way to the wilderness of Damascus"

Exegetical Perspective

The lectionary cuts this passage off too soon. The story in chapter 19 sets the stage for the downfall of Ahab's house and for the transfer of prophetic power from Elijah to Elisha. At the very least, verses 15b–17 must be included in the reading in order to explain who will complete the work Elijah has begun and to suggest how Jezebel and Ahab will be eliminated (through the agency of Hazael, Jehu and Elisha). Ideally, verse 19a would be included as well, since verses 9–19a form a rhetorical envelope beginning and ending with the word "there" (referring to "Horeb, the mount of God") and verses 16–19a form an envelope beginning and ending with "Elisha son of Shaphat."

Under David and Solomon, all of the tribes of Israel were organized into one united kingdom. After Solomon's death, however, the people of the ten northern tribes rebelled against the Davidic line of kings and set up their own kingdom, which they called Israel. Only the tribes of Judah and Benjamin remained loyal to the Davidic line of kings, who continued to rule over the southern kingdom, now called Judah. The northern kingdom of Israel, with its capital in Samaria, and the southern kingdom of Judah, with its capital in Jerusalem, coexisted (sometimes as enemies and sometimes as friends) for almost 200 years (until Israel fell to Assyria in

Homiletical Perspective

Verse 12 may be quite familiar to many who hear this passage: "and after the earthquake a fire, but the LORD was not in the fire; and after the fire a sound of sheer silence." Like many famous passages, this one challenges us to enable people to hear and think about it in a fresh way. Three themes that may offer fresh insights about the passage are Elijah as political dissenter, God's support of Elijah in the wilderness, and God's continuing call to Elijah.

Elijah the Political Dissenter. The probable redaction history of this passage sheds light on this theme. This and other stories about prophets may have been added to royal histories in the creation of the books of Kings. In other words, the story of Elijah may come from a nonroyal source and, by highlighting the faithful prophet, subvert the agenda of a court history. This passage may be the story of a dissenting voice, written by one who took issue with "official" histories.

The prophet Elijah will not adhere to the religious position of Queen Jezebel. He persecutes her false prophets (chap. 18), and she in turn threatens him with death. He flees to the wilderness because he is a political and religious dissenter. Elijah identifies himself as the only faithful prophet left among the Israelites.

1 Kings 19:1–4, (5–7), 8–15a

1 Kings 19:1-4 (5-7), 8-15a

Theological Perspective

According to Nelson, one should not make too much of the declaration that God was not in the wind, the earthquake, or the fire (vv. 11–12). The text's inclination to distinguish "the divine presence itself from its outward manifestations" follows, he argues, standard theological procedure as far as the Hebrew Bible is concerned.[2] Nelson further believes that there is no textual warrant to conclude that God is uniquely present in the "sound of sheer silence" that follows. Verse 12 makes no definitive determination concerning the nature of the relationship between God and the silence.

Nelson is no doubt reacting to commentators like John Gray, who concluded that the text's presentation of the "revelation of God in an intelligible communication rather than in the spectacular phenomena described marks an advance in man's conception of God as personally accessible and intelligible to man within the framework of human experience."[3] Gray's reading clearly reflects the general approach to revelation often taken by liberal theology, particularly its nineteenth-century Protestant version. When taken too far, however, this interpretive slant can lead to the very unbiblical notion that the conditions for God's revelation are things that can be anticipated ("God prefers to work in the stillness") or, worse, created by us ("Quiet your hearts, and *then* you will hear God").

While I am not as pessimistic as Nelson about the value of conducting explorations of the nature of revelation through verses 11–13 (surely there must be *something* special about the silence described in v. 12), his determination that this text is primarily about God's response to Elijah's loss of prophetic nerve should be taken to heart. The preacher who resists the temptation to talk tritely about the "God of silences" and invests his time and energy where Nelson recommends will, in the long run, be pleased with the sermon that results.

To this end, it is important that one recounts for the congregation the preceding events in chapter 18. There, on Mount Carmel, Elijah faces off against 450 prophets of the god Baal to determine which deity—YHWH or Baal—is the true God of Israel. YHWH, of course, triumphs where Baal fails, by consuming a designated sacrifice by fire. Elijah then leads those gathered in the slaying of Baal's prophets.

What is striking in chapter 18 is Elijah's confidence and resolve, which are nowhere to be

---

2. Ibid., 124.
3. John Gray, *I and II Kings: A Commentary* (Philadelphia: Westminster Press, 1976), 410–11.

Pastoral Perspective

Elijah escaped the maze by running into the wilderness. And there an angel fed him—twice! I know what a blessing it is to be fed. When my husband and I had our daughter, we received a steady stream of dinners in the first few weeks of her life. Until then, I had no concept of what a luxury it is to be fed a tasty variety of meals I did not have to plan, acquire, prepare, and clean up. I had not even realized just how much I needed to be fed—both spiritually and physically. Those in the pastoral profession are rewarded for being dogs at a whistlers' convention. Peeling ourselves away from the steady diet of adrenaline upon which first responders feed can feel as threatening as undergoing detoxification in a recovery center. Unfortunately, like any addiction, an adrenaline high gets us lost in our mazes and gets in the way of a relationship with God.

Congregants have barriers to their relationships with God too. One barrier might be a sense of inadequacy, as Elijah seems to be expressing in verse 4 when he compares himself to other great prophets. This story reminds us that although we may feel separated from God and are tempted to give up on both ourselves and our ministries, God is always providing for us. Why would God do otherwise? After all, God created each one of us uniquely for a purpose. We water the expensive plantings we put into our summer gardens and take interest in their flourishing. How much more does God want to provide for our blossoming!

Where is God when we feel needy? Elijah certainly expected to find God in the earth (quake), wind, and fire, but God was not there. Instead, God was in the sound of silence. Simon and Garfunkel had it right—we need to listen to those sounds of silence (e.g., the plight of the oppressed, the vacant faces of the homeless, the inarticulate cries of undernourished children), because in them God is encouraging us to persevere. Being stubborn people, we forget what Elijah learned: the presence of God is not always obvious. Our preconceptions of God's truth and ways in which God will communicate it get in our maze-minded way.

Children seem to grasp this truth much more readily. In the 2006 film *The Pursuit of Happyness,* a child is trying to tell his distracted father an old story while his father is trying to figure out where the two of them are going safely to spend the night: "A shipwrecked man prays to God to save him. A boat approaches, but the man tells it to go away because God will save him. The boat leaves. A second boat arrives, and the man sends it away, saying God

Exegetical Perspective

722/721 BCE). The stories of Elijah are interwoven with the political and religious history of the northern kingdom during the reign of King Ahab in the ninth century BCE.

First Kings 16:31–33 tells us that King Ahab had cemented an alliance with his Phoenician neighbors by marrying Jezebel, the daughter of the king of "the Sidonians," and by promoting the worship of their god, Baal, alongside the worship of YHWH in the kingdom of Israel. In chapters 17–18 Elijah appears suddenly on the scene to set up an overwhelmingly impressive demonstration of YHWH's superiority over Baal, culminating in the slaughter of all of the prophets of Baal (1 Kgs. 18). The story in chapter 19 begins with Jezebel swearing to get revenge on Elijah, who flees for his life, going first to the southern kingdom of Judah (v. 3), then into the wilderness, where he despairingly asks God to let him die (though he was not willing to let Jezebel kill him). Finally, he travels "forty days and forty nights" further into the wilderness, to "Horeb the mount of God" (v. 8).

Horeb is the name given in several biblical traditions to the mountain (more commonly called Sinai) where Moses and the people he led out of Egypt encountered and entered into a covenant with YHWH. Several details in the Elijah story encourage us to see a similarity between Elijah and Moses. Like Elijah (v. 4), Moses was sometimes frustrated enough to ask God to let him die (Num. 11:14–15). Elijah's journey of "forty days and forty nights" (v. 8) echoes the time Moses spent on the mountain (Exod. 24:18), and the cave on Horeb where YHWH "passes by" Elijah reminds us of the cleft in the rock where Moses stood while the glory of YHWH "passed by" (Exod. 33:22; 34:6). The tradition of connecting Elijah with Moses emerges again in the NT accounts of the transfiguration (Matt. 17:3, 4; Mark 9:4, 5; Luke 9:30, 33).

God does not seem particularly pleased to see Elijah there on Horeb. Both before and after YHWH passes by Elijah (vv. 9, 13), the Deity asks the prophet, "What are you doing here?" which may imply "Why aren't you back in Israel where you should be?" Both of Elijah's answers indicate that he overestimates his importance in the overall scheme of things. Elijah seems to see himself as YHWH's last hope (or at least as Israel's last hope) for eliminating idolatry among God's people. In 18:22 (as he challenges the wavering Israelites on Mount Carmel), as well as in 19:10 and 14, he says, "I alone am left [a prophet of the LORD]." His answer does not change, even after he has experienced the passing

Homiletical Perspective

We can interpret Elijah the dissenter both as an affirmation of prophetic dissent and as a challenging call to dissent. For church members who are disadvantaged socially and economically, Elijah the dissenter may be an affirming figure. His story here shows that God supports those who are marginalized or even persecuted. God supports the disenfranchised when they name and call attention to their situation. To be on the margin, to maintain dissenting views can be a positive experience, although not an easy one.

For church members who are affluent and socially or politically influential, Elijah the dissenter may represent a challenge. His willingness to offend the ruler and flee the center of power can be the opportunity to raise questions: At what price is your affluence? Are there situations in your lives right now that call for dissent—at the office, or a community meeting, or a church board meeting? Is there an unofficial story you should hear? Is there a voice you want to ignore, but that you still can recognize is a voice of prophetic dissent? Is God calling you to dissent?

We may be tempted to interpret Elijah's wilderness experience in primarily existential terms—the wilderness as a spiritual desert that any of us may experience. However, Elijah's foray into the wilderness is directly related to his activities as a political and religious dissenter. Dissenting may feel like a "desert experience" in relation to other people, but this story of Elijah suggests that it is also one in which God is present and through which God may equip people for work in the world.

God's Support in the Wilderness. A glib hearer might say that Elijah spends much of this passage whining. He is alternately self-righteous (the only faithful person in Israel) and full of self-pity (no better than his ancestors, ready to die). Elijah in this story is the kind of person to whom we might say, "Stop complaining and get over it; there are other people worse off than you."

The narrator tells us that God does not respond to Elijah this way, and God's action is our focus. After his first day in the wilderness, an angel ministers to Elijah and strengthens him for forty more days of wandering. When Elijah hides in the cave, God asks, "What are you doing here, Elijah?" (v. 13). There is no overt critique of Elijah's action or attitudes.

Different Christian traditions have different attitudes toward religious doubt and what counts as

1 Kings 19:1-4 (5-7), 8-15a

Theological Perspective

found in the text before us. He shows no hint of fear or doubt in his contest with Baal's prophets and is even so bold as to openly and sarcastically mock them in verse 27, despite being drastically outnumbered.

In chapter 19, however, YHWH's cocksure prophet comes unhinged. Afraid for his life after hearing of Jezebel's desire to eliminate him, Elijah flees to the wilderness and asks, four verses in, to die rather than face her wrath. Elijah, who earlier stood tall against 450 rivals, now desires to opt out of existence altogether. He later sequesters himself in a cave on Mount Horeb.

According to the mid-twentieth-century existentialists, the cold, hard fact of human existence is that we find ourselves adrift in an indifferent, even hostile, universe, shouldered with the added burden of having to summon the strength to continue on nonetheless. This is certainly how Elijah felt. "I alone am left," he says in verse 14, "and they are seeking my life, to take it away."

This text, however, shows Elijah to be in error here. As the apostle Paul recalls in Romans 11:1–6 (in arguing for the continued faithfulness of God to the original covenant with Israel), Elijah later learns that God has kept seven thousand free from that taint of Baal in Israel (1 Kgs. 19:18), which serves to highlight the unfounded and solipsistic nature of Elijah's despair ("I alone am left"). Huddled in his cave, convinced of his unique status as the last remaining person of faith, Elijah's primary temptation is to think that he has to go it alone, that it is all up to him. This illusion presents itself to us when our concepts of reality do not include the dynamic presence of God, which empowers us to trust in the resources of divine grace—which specializes in making the impossible possible.

That there is a future for him beyond the cave—and for Israel after Elijah—-is not rationally obvious to Elijah. Such insight can be received only as a gift from God (v. 15a), not inferred strictly on the basis of the immediate circumstances.

In other words, the catalyst for faith—which allows the understanding to surpass the limits set for it by reason—must originate somewhere other than the self or the situations in which we immediately find ourselves. It must originate instead in God, a monumental theological principle that can either help to illuminate, or be illuminated by this pericope.

TREVOR EPPEHIMER

Pastoral Perspective

will save him. The man dies of exposure. When he gets to heaven, he complains to God for not saving him when he prayed. God tells the man he sent two boats to save him but the man sent them away."[3] We must remain open to God's communication vehicles, rather than our preconceived expectations.

God often defies our expectations. When Elijah first responded to God's calling, he did not expect to have his life threatened by Queen Jezebel and then protected by an angel. Few of us would expect that. When my husband and I were pregnant, we discovered an entire publishing division was devoted to helping people overcome uncertainty. The original editors of *What to Expect When You're Expecting* have expanded their repertoire to include an overview of what to anticipate in each stage of a youngster's life. Wouldn't it be wonderful if we could have such a detailed overview of what to expect for each of life's major transitions? Just imagine the possibilities: What to expect when my high-schooler graduates; what to expect when my spouse and/or I retire; what to expect when I and my parents age.

We are a people who like to know what to expect; but when we stop expecting God in the seemingly obvious places, God exceeds our expectations. Helping our congregants reframe their maze-minded expectations and persevere is this text's call to action. Given that this lectionary reading falls in the summer, we can suggest this as the perfect time for slowing down sufficiently to hear God's sounds of silence. By alluding to the multiple ways Elijah receives provisions from God (ravens, a widow, an angel), we can also suggest looking at our past for hints as to how God will exceed our expectations in the present and future. Our understanding of God's truth for our lives will be more authentic for having escaped the false-expectation maze.

CARRIE N. MITCHELL

3. Author's transcription from film.

by of YHWH, indicating that he has not understood the message of the "sound of sheer silence" (v. 12).

The words translated "a sound of sheer silence" (*qol demamah daqqah*) can have more than one meaning (e.g., cf. KJV's "still small voice" and NIV's "gentle whisper"). *Qol* can mean either sound or voice, *demamah* can refer to a whisper, silence, or stillness (see Ps. 107:29), and *daqqah* can mean thin, small, fine, or sheer. According to verses 11–12, the symbols that were thought to indicate God's presence in Moses's time (i.e., wind, earthquake, fire; Exod. 19:16–19) are no longer indicative of God's presence in the world in Elijah's time. In contrast to the thundering presence of the storm god Baal, Israel's God is now present in "a sound of silence," as in the sound of the calm after a storm.

Both "a sound of sheer silence" in verse 12 and the tasks assigned to Elijah in versess 15–16 make the point that spectacular demonstrations of YHWH's power (such as the one Elijah staged on Mount Carmel) are not YHWH's only way of working in the world. God is also willing and able to work through historical and political processes (vv. 15b–16a) and with the help of prophets other than Elijah (v. 16b). Subsequent passages will say that Elijah tosses his mantle over Elisha (1 Kgs. 19:19–21), but does not in fact "anoint" him as God commands him to do, and that he leaves it up to Elisha to "anoint" Hazael, who will punish Israel for its sins (2 Kgs. 8:7–15), and Jehu, who will bring about the ignominious death of Jezebel (2 Kgs. 9:1–13, 30–37).

Expanding the lectionary passage to include verses 15b–19 allows the passage to make the point that, in spite of Elijah's apparent belief to the contrary, God works quietly behind the scenes through historical and political processes, as well as (if not better than) through spectacular miracles such as the one Elijah set up to happen on Mount Carmel.

KATHLEEN A. ROBERTSON FARMER

a true religious experience. This passage suggests that doubt may be appropriate in a believer's relationship with God. It also suggests that there is a variety of authentic encounters with God. An experience of God may be dramatic, ecstatic and overwhelming. But in this case, God is manifest not in the dramatic, but in "a sound of sheer silence."

God's Continuing Call. God speaks to Elijah three times. The first two times, God asks Elijah what he is doing in the cave. The third time God tells Elijah to go to Damascus and anoint a new king. In other words, God tells Elijah to go back to work. Elijah does not have to give up his frustration, but God will not let him give in to it.

The fact that God still calls Elijah, despite his frustration with the way of a prophet, can provide an affirming or challenging message. From this remote encounter between Elijah and God will come major events, for instance, the call of Elisha and the demise of Jezebel. God effects providence not only through singular, awe-inspiring events, like those described in chapter 18. God also effects providence over time through the interworkings of many called individuals. An affirming message is that God's call is not limited to a spectacular few. Everyone has significance in God's redeeming work. To paraphrase George Eliot, the greatest good may come from those who lead hidden lives and rest in unvisited tombs.

The message that everyone has a call can also be a challenge. It suggests that everyone is responsible for discerning what God may be calling them to do. The "sound of sheer silence" is not another way of talking about seeking peace and getting centered in the midst of life's pressures. In Elijah's case, it is the means by which God communicates the difficult call to ensure there is no idolatry among the Israelites.

To be sure, certain of life's pressures—for instance, to achieve a certain professional status or conform to certain expectations—may distract from God's call. Quiet time apart may be important for listening to God. Nonetheless, discerning God's call may bring other pressures, for instance, putting communal before personal good or taking an unpopular stand. This passage invites us to seek critical distance from our lives and listen carefully for God's voice, possibly to move beyond certain pressures and to embrace others.

HAYWOOD BARRINGER SPANGLER

Psalms 42 and 43

42:1As a deer longs for flowing streams,
  so my soul longs for you, O God.
2My soul thirsts for God,
  for the living God.
 When shall I come and behold
  the face of God?
3My tears have been my food
  day and night,
 while people say to me continually,
  "Where is your God?"

4These things I remember,
  as I pour out my soul:
 how I went with the throng,
  and led them in procession to the house of God,
 with glad shouts and songs of thanksgiving,
  a multitude keeping festival.
5Why are you cast down, O my soul,
  and why are you disquieted within me?
 Hope in God; for I shall again praise him,
  my help 6and my God.

 My soul is cast down within me;
  therefore I remember you
 from the land of Jordan and of Hermon,
  from Mount Mizar.
7Deep calls to deep
  at the thunder of your cataracts;
 all your waves and your billows
  have gone over me.
8By day the LORD commands his steadfast love,
  and at night his song is with me,
  a prayer to the God of my life.

9I say to God, my rock,
  "Why have you forgotten me?
 Why must I walk about mournfully
  because the enemy oppresses me?"
10As with a deadly wound in my body,
  my adversaries taunt me,
 while they say to me continually,
  "Where is your God?"

11Why are you cast down, O my soul,
  and why are you disquieted within me?
 Hope in God; for I shall again praise him,
  my help and my God.

43:1Vindicate me, O God, and defend my cause
        against an ungodly people;
    from those who are deceitful and unjust
        deliver me!
2For you are the God in whom I take refuge;
        why have you cast me off?
    Why must I walk about mournfully
        because of the oppression of the enemy?

3O send out your light and your truth;
        let them lead me;
    let them bring me to your holy hill
        and to your dwelling.
4Then I will go to the altar of God,
        to God my exceeding joy;
    and I will praise you with the harp,
        O God, my God.

5Why are you cast down, O my soul,
        and why are you disquieted within me?
    Hope in God; for I shall again praise him,
        my help and my God.

Psalms 42 and 43

Theological Perspective

Writers use analogies to evoke visceral responses to a particular concept, reality, or occurrence. In the first of the two psalms presented as a unit this Sunday, the psalmist uses the analogy of a deer's deep desire for channels of water to evoke the psalmist's longing for intimacy with God. The expression of such deep desire in both of the psalms assigned for today suggests that they were written sometime after the Babylonian exile, with two refrains of complaint and one refrain of petition.[1]

René Girard, anthropologist and literary critic, talks about human desire when we want something that another possesses as mimesis or imitation. People who oppress others often obsess over the lack of difference between themselves and those they deem "other." For example, all human blood is red, regardless of a person's ethnicity. To make ourselves feel superior to others with red blood, we have to create a reason for making them inferior. Thus the problem is not that people are so different, but that we mentally make them that way to justify our negative actions toward them.

Further, people tend to imitate or desire what the "other" possesses. We know and learn through mimetic desire, which happens when two or more people desire the same person, thing, place, or status. Mimetic desire involves imitation, in which the subject/disciple imitates the model/rival. When the model bans the disciple from obtaining the object of mutual desire, such desire leads to rivalry that gets resolved via a scapegoat.[2] For the crowd, the scapegoat becomes the perpetrator, which affords calm, moving the crowd from a violent catastrophe into peaceful harmony.[3]

In Psalm 42, the psalmist (disciple) has a deep desire for a relationship (object) with God (model). The depths of the desire appear to be languishing, for the psalmist's tears are like food, like bread—a daily source of sustenance, for the presence of God appears to be in absentia. Further, others ridicule the psalmist by asking where his or her God is (42:3). Such an affront echoes the account of Elijah and the prophets of Baal on Mount Carmel when Elijah taunts the Baal worshipers, challenging them to

Pastoral Perspective

The genius of the Psalms lies in the fact that they are both inspirational and instructive, both poetic and practical. They speak both to the heart and to the mind. To put it another way, the Psalms say the things we would like to say, if we had the wisdom, insight, and ability. Taken as a pair, Psalms 42 and 43 mirror a recurring Old Testament theme: the rational fear of being abandoned by God, accompanied by the heartfelt hunger and fervent hope that it not be so. The poet in the writer employs the graphic image of "thirst" to describe the human condition. What better image for spiritual destitution? Likewise, speaking to our rational side, the writer alludes to the taunts of the antagonists who challenge the psalmist's intellect with sarcastic reproaches such as, "Where is your God?" using the metaphor of tears as his only food day and night. Thus the author speaks of his spiritual life in terms of the most essential and elemental human needs—food and drink.

Aristotle, writing several centuries before Christ, came to the conclusion that the "thirst" of which the psalmist speaks is the thirst for "happiness." Contending that happiness is our most elemental and universal desire, the philosopher suggested that all human beings instinctively seek those things that make us happy—except, of course, those of us who find happiness in our misery. The problem, however, is that we are so often misdirected in our "thirst." Western culture bombards us constantly with enticing messages promising happiness through the satisfaction of our desires, or to use the biblical metaphor, "food that does not satisfy."

For Aristotle, however, happiness was not to be found in possessions, wealth, fame, or power. The primordial "thirst" of which the psalmist writes was, for Aristotle, the thirst for God, and the moral life lived in response to God's grace. Jesus must have had something similar in mind when he said, "I have said these things to you so that my joy may be in you, and that your joy may be complete" (John 15:11). The psalmist, either by personal experience or by inspiration, knows the source of the human thirst, yet knows as well the power of the tempter's taunt, "Where is your God?"

Biblical scholars tell us that these two psalms may be understood either as the individual expression of one who has experienced personal abandonment or as a liturgical device in which the psalm speaks "to the consciousness shaped by society and

---

1. J. Clinton McCann Jr., "The Book of Psalms," in *The New Interpreter's Bible*, vol. 4 (Nashville: Abingdon Press, 1996), 852.
2. René Girard, *The Girard Reader*, ed. James G. Williams (New York: Crossroad/Herder, 1996), 116. Also see my full treatment of this concept in *Misbegotten Anguish: A Theology and Ethics of Violence* (St. Louis: Chalice Press, 2001).
3. René Girard, *Things Hidden since the Foundation of the World*, trans. Stephen Bann and Michael Metteer (Stanford, CA: Stanford University Press, 1987), 291, 294–98, 305.

Exegetical Perspective

The laments and praises of Psalms 42–43 work because of their haunting imagery and sustained structures—the deer panting for flowing streams, tears as constant food, and the repeated "Why are you cast down, O my soul?" Typical of a complaint psalm, the grievance-juxtaposed-with-confidence pattern dominates. "God my exceeding joy!" trumps the doubly cried question "Where is your God?" as do the triple imperatives "Hope in God!" Together these psalms begin Book 2 of Psalms and introduce "Elohim" as the predominant divine address for adulation and complaint from here through Psalm 83. "YHWH" appears in our psalms only in 42:8, perhaps as a theological corrective, with climactic rhetorical effect. Connecting these psalms to the fuller Yahwistic Psalter, 42:8 is the central verse of the combined psalms reaffirming YHWH's covenant love amid complaints to Elohim about the "enemy."

Each psalm is self-sufficient enough to warrant their traditional division or suggest two recensions of a lament with expansions or abridgment (so, Psalms 14 and 53; 70 and 40:13–17; 108:1–5 and 57:7–11; 108:6–13 and 60:5–12). Uniquely adjacent, Psalms 42–43 invite treatment as one expression of hope (so the New English Bible). The two psalms hang together by the refrain in 42:5, 42:11, and 43:5 and lack of any superscription for Psalm 43. Verse 43:2 repeats 42:9 verbatim, apart from slight word changes that suggest progressive emphasis: "My rock" becomes "my refuge," "why have you forgotten me?" morphs into "why have you rejected me?" and "walk mournfully" Qal in 42:9, intensifies to Hitpael "walk *about* mournfully" in 43:2.

Structurally, these two psalms form three strophes (42:1–5, 42:6–11, and 43:1–5) of five, six, and five lines frequently with the five-beat *qinah*, the Hebrew lament meter. Synonymous parallelism, doublets, and key-word linkages develop theological wordplay. The longing soul (*nephesh*, more full-bodied than the *psyche* of psychology) pines for God, evocatively simulating a hind panting by water brooks in 42:1. The feminine verb *ta'arog* suggests audible anguish, with Joel 1:20, which rabbis and early commentators labeled as onomatopoetically akin to "braying." Parched agitation resonates in "my soul thirsts for God" (42:2).

Water imagery continues with "my tears" (42:3), "I pour out my soul" (42:4), and "deeps" and "cataracts," transliterated from the Septuagint (42:7), while Hebrew evokes sky-to-sea water conduits channeling the primordial deep (*tehom*) above and

Homiletical Perspective

Lament. Augustine's "Our souls are restless till they find their rest in you" might well trace its origin to the far more vivid psalmist's simile, "As a deer longs for flowing streams, so my soul longs for you, O God" (42:1). This sylvan image, reminiscent of the Song of Solomon, invites the reader/worshiper into an extended lyric that wanders through both psalms, alternating between extremes of questioning lament and complaint and confident hope and vindication. Three times, sounding like a *basso continuo* welling up from beneath, is the heartfelt refrain that begins with the self-questioning susurration, "Why are you cast down, O my soul, and why are you disquieted within me?" This gentle self-interrogation, without being fully answered, instead is countered by the encouraging exhortation to "Hope in God; for I shall again praise him, my help and my God."

Anne Lamott, the quirky and irreverent Marin County churchgoing memoirist, writes that her prayer characteristically oscillates between the two extremes of "Help me, help me, help me" and "Thank you, thank you, thank you."[1] In this extended lament, the psalmist shares fond memories of joining in the festal procession to the temple, while feeling overwhelmed by unspecified circumstances that are now preventing participation. The palpable sense of yearning is offered up to God as the sacrifice of a willing spirit that seeks to be restored to full fellowship in the company of worshipers. The present longing is only made more acute by a strong sense of exclusion in which "enemies" and "adversaries" are imagined who "oppress" and "taunt" the outcast faithful one with the ultimately discomfiting jibe, "Where is your God?"

The award-winning film *For the Bible Tells Me So* documents vividly the struggles of five families that continue to yearn while struggling for the full inclusion of their homosexual daughters and sons within religious communities that proclaim love while practicing exclusion. The fervent longing to be restored to the company of the faithful includes the anticipation of once again being able to join one's voice in a psalm of full-throated thanksgiving.

Faithful lament is not a wallowing in negativity. It is, recalling Luther's distinction between a "theology of the cross" and a "theology of glory," a matter of "calling a thing what it really is"—a frank and honest acknowledgment of the situation as it is

---

1. Anne Lamott, *Traveling Mercies: Some Thoughts on Faith* (New York: Random House, 1999), 82.

Psalms 42 and 43

Theological Perspective

produce evidence of their god. Here the Girardian triangle of disciple/model/object collapses, as both the relationship and God appear to be absent. Inquisitive people who ask about the psalmist's God scapegoat the psalmist (42:1–3).

With access to the temple apparently impossible, the psalmist responds by recalling the rituals that honor God with joy and praise. The reality of the absence of God weighs heavily on the psalmist, who wrestles soulfully with the disappointment of expectations and assumptions about what it means to be connected to God. The psalmist engages in reflection, hoping once more to be able to praise God (42:4–5).

Deep in despair, the psalmist reflects again on the impact of the perceived absence of God, remembering God's previous acts in history. Pressing the metaphor of water again ("deep calls to deep," 42:7), the psalmist speaks to ancient hurt and triumph in God that resonate with us in present time. When deep pain and chaos well up, the "stuff of life" can be overwhelming. We can lose not only intimacy with God but even the desire to be intimate, along with the power that unfolds when our mimetic desire is for relationship with God. Steeped in the memory of God's mercy, compassion, and love, the psalmist regains desire for relationship with God and does not remain in the abyss. Instead, by day or by night, amid despair or hope, the psalmist sings of God's steadfast love. The psalmist knows mimetic desire for God, prayerfully experiencing God (42:6–8).

Following the mix of complaint and confession, the mood changes as the psalmist affirms God as a stronghold and an anchor. Ambiguity remains, however, as the poet asks again: "Why have you forgotten me? Why must I walk about mournfully because the enemy oppresses me?" (42:9). When troubles assail us, we like the psalmist sometimes ask: "Where is God? Why are you down in the dumps, my soul, and why are you ill at ease?" (cf. 42:11a). Sometimes the mimetic triangle shifts, and God ceases to be our model of desire. Sometimes we feel estranged and lost.

Amid the dichotomy of divine strength and human suffering, the psalmist responds: "Hope in God; for I shall again praise him, my help and my God" (42:11b). So too we return to praise the God who is our model of desire; we become again the disciples for whom God is our rock, our help, and our hope.

The psalmist next offers a plea for vindication, a petition to God for justice in the imperative mood: "Vindicate me, O God, and defend my cause against

Pastoral Perspective

circumstances that do not support faith."[1] Either way, the ancient writer addresses our present time and condition. The echo of the unbeliever is everywhere heard in the land, and the temptation of social pressure can be overpowering, as the psalmist seems to know very well.

However, to those of every generation who are tempted, the psalmist enjoins the skeptic to "go to church," where one can join the throng "in procession to the house of God, with glad shouts and songs of thanksgiving, a multitude keeping festival" (42:4). The writer knows the power of the liturgy. Many of us are in church today because years ago we were expected (and sometimes required) to go. We would not on our own have chosen to go, and when we became older, we may even have stopped going altogether, but over time we came to acknowledge our thirst. Today there are men and women in church pews, pulpits, and theological seminaries who years ago were led reluctantly to the water by kind and caring parents and friends, only to discover that they liked it. This is the power of the liturgy. The danger for so many today is, as Simone Weil pointed out years ago, "not lest the soul should doubt whether there is any bread, but lest (by a lie) it should persuade itself that it is not hungry."[2]

Jay McInerney has written a parable of contemporary life about what happens to those who lose their sense of history. In his novel *Bright Lights, Big City*, a young man riding an uptown subway— trailing behind him the wreckage of a marriage, a career, and maybe a life—finds himself seated next to a Hasidic Jew reading Talmud. The man looks like something straight out of an ancient history book. Still, this modern-minded young man watches with fascination as this odd-looking stranger slowly moves his finger across the lines of the Hebrew, oblivious to the roaring sound and glaring lights of the modern subway. The young man reflects, "This man has a God and a history, a community. He believes he is one of God's chosen, whereas (he muses to himself) whereas, you feel like an integer in a random series of numbers. Still (he shakes his head) what a haircut."[3]

Can one not hear, over the rumble of the modern subway, an echo from the psalmist whispering, "Where is your God?"

1. James L. Mays, *Psalms*, Interpretation Series (Louisville, KY: John Knox Press, 1994), 175.
2. Simone Weil, *Waiting for God* (New York: Putman's Sons,1951), xxxi.
3. Jay McInerney, *Bright Lights, Big City* (New York: Random House, 1984), 56–57.

Exegetical Perspective

below the firmament, plus sealike "waves" and "billows" echoing Psalms 88:7 and 89:9 and Jonah 2. Despite three Golan area references in 42:7, where waterfalls seasonally "thunder," the psalmist metaphorically risks drowning in cosmically chaotic waters—not admiring nature! Antithetical subtleties link "thunder" (*qol*) with "glad shouts" (*qol*) (42:4), and the disparate locales—lonely upper Jordan primeval pandemonium vs. crowds happily swelling temple precincts. The repeated "disquietude" shares consonance (*hmh*) with "multitude" (*hamon*) mustering thanks in 42:5 and the calling of the deep (*tehom*) further binding these psalms lyrically.

The second stanza links 42:5's self-questioning with the declaration "my soul *is* cast down" (42:6), thereby setting up the interrogatives in 42:11 and 43:5 for a nuanced hearing. Notably, NRSV reattaches "my God" of 42:6 to the preceding verse anticipating the refrain "*and* my God" (42:11; 43:5). Yet the received Hebrew versification, "O my God" underscores the vocative dominating these psalms that climaxes in the direct, daring imperatives "Vindicate!" and "Send out!" (43:1, 3). Cohortative "I shall *surely* go" (43:4) evinces a double vocative promise "to praise you . . . O God, (O) my God." The first refrain (42:5) with its detachable "my God" syntactically implies losing faith and building self-doubt, while the second refrain (42:11) laments the "deadly pain" of adversarial taunts "where is your God?" (42:10), inciting an anguished plea for vindication (43:1). Consequently, the final soulful refrain (43:5) sounds defiantly triumphant according to the psalms' rhetoric.

Read closely, the paired "where is your God" (42:3, 10) suggests another key semantic contrast affecting translation and interpretation. The psalmist clearly fingers "adversaries [who] taunt me" (42:10), building on the collective "enemy" (42:9, mirrored in 43:2), with its "oppressive-squeezing" (root *l-kh-ts*, synony-mously akin to the parallel "my adversaries" [*ts-r-r*] "cramped, narrow, hard pressed"). However, in 42:3 the antecedent subject for "say to me continually" may simply be "my tears." No "enemies" or even "people" (NRSV) are mentioned here in the Hebrew text apart from "me" and the oft-recurring "my cast-down and disquieted soul." Perhaps, then, it reads "in *my* saying to myself, 'where is your God?'" So, the two psalms together move from an internalized grappling with faith to an external wrestling with faithlessness.

Twice the psalmist "remembers" (*zkr*). The second time, 42:6, the psalmist recollected God ("you") from afar "from the land of Jordan and of Hermon, from Mount Mizar." Earlier, 42:4, remembrance included

Homiletical Perspective

before a God who promises to vindicate and deliver the faithful. Mother Teresa of Calcutta's honest revelations about the "dark night of the soul" she endured during her days of greatest fame as a public saint are pointed to with glee by skeptics and atheists who are eager to discredit religious faith. As anyone who knows the Bible can attest, however, Jesus himself died with a cry of God-abandonment on his lips borrowed from the psalmist. The sense of God's absence, to be sure, remains troubling, and Jesus' "Why?" from the cross never fully is answered but, rather, is made nugatory in the resurrection.

Recently my congregation experienced a transforming grace note during worship. My announcement that our ninety-nine-year-old longtime member Alice, who was a fixture in the short pew in the front of the sanctuary, had died the previous week of a heart attack, elicited an antiphonal sigh from the assembled faithful. We were all looking forward to celebrating together her hundredth birthday! Her last time in worship she had sat in her usual front pew with her lovely eighteen-year-old great-granddaughter, newly arrived as a first-year student at nearby UCLA. Alice, a hardworking Swede born inside the Arctic Circle, had for years worked as a housekeeper for a well-to-do family in the tony Bel Air neighborhood of Los Angeles. She had told me during our morning Bible study that her great-granddaughter had never been baptized, and she was eager to worship with her in her much-loved church. It was a lovely sight to behold the two kneeling to receive Communion together. (I suffered no twinge of conscience for "bending the rules"!)

All this was memory as I read for the congregation a verse of the hymn of lament that serendipitously had been selected months earlier to be sung as our "sending" song. Not particularly fitting the appointed texts for the day, it was a new hymn for us set to the well-known tune "Finlandia," a hymn of lament that I found novel in its honest acknowledgment of the effects of aging on the faith community. Who knew it would provide just the words to articulate our grief at Alice's death?

As frailness grows, and youthful strengths diminish,
In weary arms which worked their earnest fill,
Your aging servants labor now to finish
Their earthly tasks, as fits your mercy's will.
We grieve their waning, yet rejoice, believing,
Your arms, unwearied, shall uphold us still.[2]

2. Mary Louise Bringle, "When Memory Fades," *Evangelical Lutheran Worship* (Minneapolis: Augsburg Fortress, 2006), #792.

Psalms 42 and 43

Theological Perspective

an ungodly people; from those who are deceitful and unjust deliver me!" (43:1). The psalmist assumes an attitude of intimacy, having direct discourse with God. The psalmist makes a case before God, asking for deliverance, for the psalmist does not want to be a scapegoat. This prayer is followed by a request for God's guidance (a reengagement of the mimetic triangle): "O send out your light and your truth; let them lead me; let them bring me to your holy hill and to your dwelling" (43:3).

Restored to the temple, the psalmist offers praise with much joy. At the end of Psalm 43, the psalmist reiterates the refrain used in 42:5 and 11: "Hope in God; for I shall again praise him, my help and my God." Those who repeat this refrain with the psalmist reaffirm that this God is our model and we are God's disciples. Our deep desire is relationship with our God.

CHERYL A. KIRK-DUGGAN

Pastoral Perspective

The metaphor of hunger and thirst is one of the most frequent images in all Scripture to emphasize the human need for God. The prophet Isaiah asked forthrightly, "Why do you spend your money for that which is not bread?" (Isa. 55:2). When Jesus encountered the woman at the well who asked him for a drink, he said, "Everyone who drinks of this water will be thirsty again, but those who drink of the water that I will give them will never be thirsty" (John 4:13). Still, no one has expressed the notion of our universal need for God more poignantly than the psalmist in the first of today's psalms: "As a deer longs for flowing streams, so my soul longs for you, O God. My soul thirsts for the living God" (42:1–2).

P. C. ENNISS

Exegetical Perspective

the textually difficult: "How (or when) I used to go in the *sakh*." Traditionally "throng," the root meaning of "closed-in" or "hedged-about," contrasts, in this positive use, the "cramped-squeezing" oppression elsewhere by the enemy and adversaries. The writer is among tight friends. A glad-shouting "throng" makes sense or, perhaps, "a shelter," following the Septuagint's "sacred booth." So, the dubious "I led them in procession" (*'eddaddem*) appearing in the Greek as "majesty" (Heb. *'adir*) may read: "I remember . . . I passed through the stately tabernacle into the house of God." Rather than leading others through sacral courtyards, the psalmist, in a crescendo of poetic doublets, asks that God's light and truth "lead and bring *me* to your holy mountain and dwelling-place"—out of the wilderness chaos into the city's comforting liturgics, like modern urbanites retreating into a peopled sanctuary, instead of escaping alone into nature worship, to remember better what we should believe.

Memory commands the soul to hope, literally, "wait," on God whom the psalmist again will praise (*'odeh*) in the final refrain as echoed penultimately (43:4) as "*'odeh* with the harp at the altar of God." The soul's persistent lament, "cast-down" (a rare root *sh-kh-kh*), makes a telling wordplay on its more positive etymological kin for "worship and bow down" (*sh-kh-h*). The threefold "hoping" and "praising" are not the familiar *tiqvah* and *hallelujah*. "Hope" (*ykhl*) implies "to stand waiting with endurance," while "praise" (*ydh*) connotes outward liturgical hand gesturing.

In sum, the semantics and structures coupling these psalms intone, invoke, and instill a hopeful refrain to praise boldly—still preachable and singable in congregations today—to quiet inward doubts and confront worldly pressures challenging faithfulness.

RICHARD D. BLAKE

Homiletical Perspective

Nicholas Wolterstorff's *Lament for a Son* is a poignant account of his struggle to come to terms with the death of his twenty-five-year-old son Eric in a climbing accident. In many ways it is a psalm of lament like Psalms 42 and 43, the honest wrestling of a faithful person with the experience of heartsick grief in which God's absence is deeply felt and yet a yearning for hope remains. As Wolterstorff has written: "Faith is a footbridge that you don't know will hold you up over the chasm until you're forced to walk out onto it. . . . Am I deluded in believing that in God the question shouted out by the wounds of the world has its answer? Am I deluded in believing that someday I will know the answer?" Still, he concludes, "I cannot dispel the sense of conducting my inspection in the presence of the Creating/Resurrecting One."[3]

JOHN ROLLEFSON

---

3. Nicholas Wolterstorff, *Lament for a Son* (Grand Rapids: Eerdmans, 1987), 76–77.

Galatians 3:23-29

²³Now before faith came, we were imprisoned and guarded under the law until faith would be revealed. ²⁴Therefore the law was our disciplinarian until Christ came, so that we might be justified by faith. ²⁵But now that faith has come, we are no longer subject to a disciplinarian, ²⁶for in Christ Jesus you are all children of God through faith. ²⁷As many of you as were baptized into Christ have clothed yourselves with Christ. ²⁸There is no longer Jew or Greek, there is no longer slave or free, there is no longer male and female; for all of you are one in Christ Jesus. ²⁹And if you belong to Christ, then you are Abraham's offspring, heirs according to the promise.

Theological Perspective

How much like a Jew does a Gentile need to be in order to be a Christian? This is an odd question to modern ears. The church has been so dominated by Gentiles since the late first century that the term "Gentile" itself has fallen out of our functional Christian lexicon. But in the middle of the first century, this was perhaps the most important moral question the church faced. Sex, money, and all the other concerns that dominate modern society's moral life were secondary.

It is the central moral question for the early church because it is a deeply theological question. God made promises to Abraham and Abraham's heirs. Gentiles are not natural heirs. So how do God's promises apply? If the promises apply to Gentiles, God seemingly treats Israel in an arbitrary way. If they apply to Jews, then how does the crucified Jesus matter to Jews? The dilemma seems clear. On the one hand, the new church could worship a God who is willing to break promises— but that will take them away from their claim that Jesus is Emmanuel, God with us. On the other hand, they can pursue a vision of the continuing faithfulness of God's promises to Abraham—which seemingly excludes Gentiles and makes the new gospel of the crucified Lord irrelevant to Jews. Pursuing either road would delegitimize the church's

Pastoral Perspective

The mood in the fellowship hall of the Episcopal church in the midsized northern Georgia town was tense and electric. Just weeks after the announcement of the ordination of a gay Episcopal bishop in New Hampshire, such "town hall" meetings were taking place in selected host churches across the diocese. I was serving a small mountain parish nearby, and tensions were high there as well. I was keen to attend the meeting, to take a reading of the spirit of those in attendance. The bishop would be there to speak to the issues that faced our churches, and the responses promised to be deep, wide, and intensely expressed. This promise was fulfilled. Emotions were indeed intense, and the anxiety in the room was palpable. I look back on that meeting now with a sense of wonder that we were able even to agree to disagree, much less achieve some measure of reconciliation with one another.

As an observer on the margins of the room, I understood clearly that many were angry, others were sad, and still others were scared. Some experienced all of these emotions at once. This mélange of feelings created a crucible within which real dialogue would prove difficult, if not impossible. At one point during the conversation when emotions threatened to spiral out of control, a colleague stood and quoted Galatians 3:23–29. He then asked us to consider what was most

Exegetical Perspective

Standing on the premise that God raised Jesus from the dead (1:1), Paul insists that the new age of faithfulness has dawned in the life, death, and resurrection of Jesus. God's law may have guided the people of faith through the age preceding the Christ's arrival, but it is now only through faith in the risen crucified Christ that one becomes rightly related to God (3:26) and to other persons (3:28) in the manner God intended from the time of Abraham (3:29).[1]

Children of God by Tutelage (vv. 23–25). For Paul, the new eschatological era has begun with the crucifixion and resurrection of Jesus the Messiah. Paul's temporal perspective is clear. There is a time before the law that begins with Abraham (Adam) and continues to Moses (3:17). There is a time of the law's jurisdiction that spans from Moses to Jesus (3:24). Finally, there is a time after the law, the time of the Messiah's immediate rule (3:25). Paul's temporal view forms the background for his striking pronouncement that the children of God "were held under the law, kept under restraint for the destined

Homiletical Perspective

Our denomination was having yet another of its wrangles over sexuality. I was tired of it, weary of the luxury of being a fully franchised heterosexual (although a woman in ministry, with which some take issue). "Enough," I said. "I am sick of this. Let's all get on with feeding the poor and taking the good news to the world." I felt clear eyed and holy as I spoke.

Thanks be to God for wise friends. One of mine turned to look at me. "Carol," he said, "this is a struggle for the soul of the church. Go home and read Galatians."

I did. He was right.

The battle cry of Galatians 3:28 is the high point of Paul's letter. Here is the vision that drives Paul, along with his frustration at its denial by those he has brought to Christ. He cannot keep this glorious word to himself, and neither should we. May Paul's prodding burst us out of our closets of complacency; may the Spirit energetically "out" us as saved by grace, jubilantly filled with Christ, new creations from the inside out.

The late Roy Pearson, at one time president of Andover Newton Theological School, cited a painting entitled "The Monarch Comforts His Soldiers." In it, the king is "encouraging" his troops forward with the point of his sword at their backs. One meaning of "comfort" is "making strong." One

1. For Paul's central theological commitments in Galatians, see Robert A. Bryant, *The Risen Crucified Christ in Galatians* (Atlanta: Society of Biblical Literature, 2001), 143–235.

Galatians 3:23-29

Theological Perspective

witness that in its corporate life it reveals the unified body of Christ.

Because these are important questions, Paul does not simply respond to the agitators in Galatia by reminding his audience that the church's leadership in Jerusalem had approved his ministry and his message. Instead, he treats the occasion as an opportunity to deal with these substantive questions.

Context suggests that the agitators' answer to the questions sounded something like this: "The law complements the gospel. Let Gentiles keep those parts of the law that are clearly a part of the Abrahamic covenant—namely, circumcision (and perhaps those parts of the law described in Acts 15:20)—as a way of confirming their place in the covenant. Doing this will not only clarify their place but will also connect the new church to a Rome-approved faith, and we are better off if we don't attract Roman attention."

Paul rejects this answer. What the agitators see as a theologically reasonable and politically advantageous compromise, Paul sees as a danger. To keep one part of the law only opens the door to requiring that Gentiles keep the whole law, and that will undermine the foundational gospel claim that human righteousness is the result of divine action, not human obedience. The Galatians must rethink both their theology and their politics.

Rethinking their theology will mean seeing that there *had been* an appropriate purpose for the law—namely, to train Israel in its preparation for the Messiah—but with the coming of the crucified Lord, that purpose was no longer needed. Faith made the law's training unnecessary. To extend Paul's metaphor of the law as *paidagōgos,* those who are "in Christ Jesus" have graduated from the law's training. Paradoxically, we reach maturity in our failure to be able to stand on our own.

However, if none of us can stand on our own, then the basic politicoreligious distinctions between the obedient and the disobedient, the mature and the immature, the accepted and the rejected break down. Thus the Galatians must rethink their politics as well. This will mean seeing each other as clothed in Christ so that even basic human distinctions of race, class, and gender break down.

In a church that celebrates equality in the face of social stratification and unity in the midst of individual distinctiveness, Galatians 3:28 holds an especially beloved place. As such, the question is not whether this text is useful; if anything, it has become a cipher of usefulness. The question is whether it can surprise us. It can. Repeatedly.

Pastoral Perspective

important about our common faith, in light of our baptismal covenant to "respect the dignity of every human being."[1] The invocation of this passage from Galatians, in the context of our common baptismal covenant, seemed to have a powerful impact on the tenor of the conversation. The anxiety in the room lessened as courtesy and respectful reciprocity, previously at risk, increased.

I have thought often about this pivotal moment, now several years past. As a family therapist and pastoral counselor—who also serves a particular parish—I have tried to understand from various vantage points what happened that day. Both theological exegesis and human-science perspectives have proved helpful in answering my question.

In the "family narrative" of the people of Israel invoked in Galatians 3:23–29, Paul understood the "law" as serving a kind of parenting, disciplinary role until such time as the children of Israel became grown-ups—in short, until they became fully functioning adults. In the complex social and cultural milieu of Paul's time, one might even imagine a slave who served as a babysitter or, to use a Western image, an au pair. This raises the question of how we understand adulthood, both developmentally and theologically. What might it mean to become an adult in relation to Christ—to use Paul's language—to become a grown-up child of God? Further, how might this understanding coincide with human sciences understandings of the developmental achievement of adulthood? Moreover, might these two understandings critique and enhance one another in dialogue?

Paul seems to suggest that in the time between the exodus and the coming of Christ, the people of Israel needed a caretaker to shepherd their developmental process to adulthood. One might view this period as one of adolescence—and a rather protracted and challenging one at that. With the coming of Christ, however, as Paul understands it, the people of Israel need to come into their own as adults. The outward and visible sign of this was (and remains for us) *faithfulness,* also translated as "trustworthiness" and "reliability." Just as the Messiah was faithful—a template or role model for the mature Israelite—so might the people answer by going and doing likewise.

Indeed, the term "children of God" hearkens back to the exodus story and is evocative of an adolescent

---

1. In the service of Holy Baptism in the Episcopal Church, the celebrant asks those assembled, "Will you strive for justice and peace among all people, and respect the dignity of every human being?" (*Book of Common Prayer* [New York: Church Publishing Corp., 1979], 305).

Exegetical Perspective

faithfulness to be revealed" (*eis tēn mellousan pistin apokalyphthēnai*, 3:23, my trans.).[2]

Using the language of "apocalypse" (cf. 1:12–16), Paul asserts that God has revealed in Jesus the faithfulness that God desires. Indeed, prior to our text, Paul has argued that the "seed" (*sperma*) of Abraham (3:16) is Jesus the faithful one, through whom the promise is now given to all who believe in him (3:22).[3] Now he adds that Jesus is God's promised one through whom God's measure of faithfulness is shown and by whom God's pledged inheritance comes. Even more, Jesus reveals God's way of being a faithful human—one who trusts God completely, even on a cross (cf. 2:16; 3:13–14, 22, 25a).

What, then, shall one make of Paul's curious critique of the law? According to Paul, God gave the law "because of transgressions" (3:19). The law exposed selfishness and self-righteousness—sin and idolatry of every sort. It uncovered rebelliousness against God's will. The law did not have the power, however, to make people holy. It was not a remedy for sin; its work was diagnostic. It could be obeyed, but it did not seal within hearts a love for God and neighbor (cf. Isa. 54:13; Jer. 24:6–7; 31:31–34; 32:38–41). Thus Paul says that the law served as a tutor (*paidagōgos*), a gift from God to guide the people of Israel until they came of age to receive their full inheritance when Christ came. The law was given to prepare Israel for Christ's coming (Gal. 3:23).

Christ has now come, accomplishing for humanity what it could not do on its own—save itself from sin. The true heirs of Abraham, then, are not those who keep the law but those who follow Christ, the "seed" of Abraham. Moreover, Paul insists that the promise of God to Abraham and Abraham's trust in God preceded the law and are, therefore, better than trust in the law (3:15–18). If one belongs to Christ, then, one must be a "seed" of Abraham (3:29) whose life and relationships will be governed by the Lord's own eschatological Spirit, which is available in this new era to Gentiles and Jews alike (4:1–7). All of God's children may now relate to God directly through the Spirit of his Son rather than through the tutor called "law." God has ended the law's work as a tutor, because the age of faith has now come (3:13–14, 24–25; 4:2–6).

Homiletical Perspective

function of the Holy Spirit is to prod us into battle for lived-out grace. The preacher may well ask, "Are we willing to stake our mission and church membership policies on Galatians, especially 3:28?"

Answering yes to this question drives hard against our stubborn self-centeredness. It is difficult for most American congregations to grapple with the truth that the gospel does not begin with us. When choosing churches, we have too long sought the reassurance of similarity rather than the evidence of the Spirit's presence. The most profound differences between people known to Paul, like the differences between people known to us, are nothing compared to the power of Christ to reconcile all things—Christ who has with God made one body out of an infinitely varied tapestry of believers.

Where is the church that lives out this vision? Where is the denomination that has not compromised its soul with a complacent disregard of this energetic word: "for all of you are one in Christ Jesus"? In a book called *What's Wrong with the World*, G. K. Chesterton wrote, "The Christian ideal has not been tried and found wanting; it has been found difficult and left untried."[1] When will we try it? When will the church proclaim its life-giving truth to the world, rather than cannibalize itself by targeting its own members, weakening its own witness from within?

The chief obstacle remains our stubborn tendency toward self-centeredness. Earlier in this letter, Paul's words ring out: "I have been crucified with Christ; and it is no longer I who live, but it is Christ who lives in me" (2:19b–20a). An Alcoholics Anonymous group that is part of our church quotes a pastor whose name is long forgotten: "It's not necessary that you believe in God. What's necessary is that you know that you're not God." Paul wrote to another congregation easing away from the gospel's diamond-hard truth: "From now on, therefore, we regard no one from a human point of view. . . . if anyone is in Christ, there is a new creation: everything old has passed away; see, everything has become new!" (2 Cor. 5:16–17).

Twenty-first-century Christians—every one of us at some time or another—balk at this. We peer through our rosy lens of "We shall overcome *someday*." Meanwhile, preachers are called both to declare and embody the radical notion of the kingdom of God coming among us *today*. That calls

2. While this prepositional phrase may be interpreted as temporal (e.g., NRSV), I take it to be purposive (cf. Rom. 8:18; *pros tēn mellousan doxan apokalyphthēnai*).

3. See Richard B. Hays, *Faith of Jesus Christ* (Chico, CA: Scholars Press, 1982), 157–67.

1. G. K. Chesterton, *What's Wrong with the World* (New York: Dover Publications, 2007), 23.

Galatians 3:23-29

Theological Perspective

The first surprise—at least for those of us in the Western world—comes in recognizing that the rejection of basic human distinctions is not equivalent to the shearing away of all group-identifiers, leaving only the individual awaiting Christly apparel. One does not become a Christian and then join the church; one joins the church in becoming Christian. Baptism is not the project of shedding all our group-identifiers until we stand naked and can be clothed in Christ; it is discovering that being a member of the family of God is our true group-identifier. All too often, we moderns forget this in our preoccupation with the individual, whether at the liturgical level of personal confession, the cultural level of expressive individualism, or the political level of inalienable human rights.

The second surprise follows from the first. It is that being clothed alike in Christ does not mean that distinctions disappear. Paul's change in conjunctions ("Jew or Greek, . . . slave or free, . . . male and female"), written, perhaps, both to counter gnostic claims about the abolition of sexuality and to reaffirm the church's claim on Genesis 1:27, suggests that the distinctions persist but lack determinate bearing for the faith. (Paul could hardly write a letter arguing against other members of the church unless he could recognize both that there are differences—and hence disagreements—and that those he disagree with are also members of the church.) We heirs of Abraham regularly forget this and determine the structures of the church according to the old distinctions, whether those structures have to do with gender roles, class advantages, or race relations.

This at least hints—perhaps *only* hints—at a third surprise: to be clothed in Christ—and thereby shaped neither by individual categories nor by old distinctions—may mean that relations in the church might best be understood as mirroring relations in the Trinity. Three distinct persons are nevertheless one God. Many distinct Christians are nevertheless one church. While Galatians lacks a doctrine of the Trinity, it may still allow for the echoes of Trinitarian relations in the church—even if those relations are fully realized only at the eschaton, when all Abraham's heirs come fully into their inheritance.

MARK DOUGLAS

Pastoral Perspective

tribe, moving through the wilderness toward adulthood and the *freedom* that obtains, along with the responsibility and trust that connote such a developmental passage. Liberation from bondage in Egypt, viewed in this way as a process of healthy self-differentiation, was embodied in the form of Jesus, whose own process of self-differentiation was individual *and* communal—seen both in his coming into his own as the Messiah and in the spirit of baptism writ large for all.

For Paul, those who are in Christ Jesus are now seen no longer as sojourners on the journey out of childhood and adolescence but, rather, as adult members of the family of Abraham. Differences of gender, race, ethnicity, and class still exist but are now radically transcended by one's status as a trustworthy, faithful, reliable grown-up *in Christ*. Clear parameters of relationship among oneself, God, and others are thus established, and the bondage of childhood—the need for a "disciplinarian" or caretaker in this sense—has ended.

For churches now divided along theological, ethnic, or cultural lines, these passages are a powerful summons to the unity of the church as an adult, "grown-up" response to divisions. Indeed, one might say that being an adult person of God calls upon us to behave as if we are free, trustworthy, responsible, faithfully self-differentiated *people of God*, for whom the need of a disciplinarian parent is long past.

I believe something along these lines happened in that parish hall. Perhaps the collegial summons from Galatians called upon each of us to ask whether we would behave as grown-ups or continue to bicker like adolescents still in the bondage of a hoped-for freedom not yet obtained. I hope that some of those gathered saw the promise of healthy relations one with another requiring *both* boundaries and flexibility, and relationship amid difference. Paul's words provide the occasion for asking the pastoral theological question whether it was more important to be right or to be in a healthy, well-boundaried relationship to the body of Christ, amid difference.

J. WILLIAM HARKINS

Exegetical Perspective

Children of God by Trust (vv. 26–29). God's Christ, who revealed faithfulness on the cross, is also the one with whom God's people now have intimate fellowship. By faith in Jesus Christ, one becomes a child of God (3:26). Believers are baptized into Christ and have put on Christ (2:16–21; 3:27). They belong to Christ (3:29). For Paul, the true offspring of God are the faithful in Christ who trust in the living crucified Christ Jesus and exercise that trust in the way that they live (5:16–25). Faithfulness is now the basis upon which God's blessing is given and received.

In Christ, a new people is formed. God's act of grace through Jesus has broken through the barriers of race, social position, and gender—partitions that ordinarily foster inequality and injustice among individuals and communities. Indeed, because believers participate in the life of the risen crucified Christ, they no longer recognize even the most polar class divisions of Jew and Greek, slave and free, male and female (3:7–8, 9, 18, 21–22, 24, 26–29). Social distinctions are obliterated in Christ. They do not mar relations between those who are in Christ or impede a believer's relation with God. By trust alone, believers of any culture and class are free to be "one in Christ Jesus" (3:28)—one with God and each other. They are united as they participate together in his life.

Paul's essential point here is that God has done a new thing in Christ Jesus. The blessing of Abraham has now come through the Jews to the Gentiles by means of the seed of Abraham—Jesus—just as God promised (Gen. 12:1–3). The family of Abraham, which was once divided (Gen. 16:1–16; 21:1–34), is now united by faith in the risen crucified Christ. Moreover, God is now supplying the Spirit of his Son to all who believe (Gal. 3:2, 5, 14; 4:6) so that they may all do the works of Christ (cf. 5:6). This means, of course, that one's life and relationships cannot go on as before. In Christ, God has created a new family that will exhibit a new kind of fellowship where all of God's children are at home.

ROBERT A. BRYANT

Homiletical Perspective

us to an astounding diversity beyond our own preference, inclination, or design: "We don't play the major role. If we did, we'd probably go around bragging that we'd done the whole thing! . . . God does both the making and the saving" (Eph. 2:8–9, *The Message*).

In the midst of complex immigration controversies, "There is neither native born nor illegal immigrant." In a society dramatically divided by income, "There is neither monied nor working class nor poor." In a society polarized by race, "There ares neither people of color nor people of no color." In the season of elections, "There is neither Republican nor Democrat nor Independent . . ." And, to repeat Paul's own words: "There is neither male nor female." For you all are one in Christ!

Paul says that Christ alone matters: Christ our unity, Christ our focus, Christ the line of energy along which relationships run, Christ the beginning and the end, Christ the cause for which we live, Christ from which nothing can take us, not even death—especially not death.

A Christmas letter from friends reports on their son attending a seminary whose intellectual and community practices make me cringe. My proud heart stumbles on Galatians 3:23–29. Is the student not also clothed with Christ? Undoubtedly he is. Then he and I and all the rest of the roiling infuriating delightful mob of those crying, "Jesus is Lord," are all one in Christ Jesus.

"Paul manages to offend virtually everyone" in this passage, writes Beverly Roberts Gaventa.[2] The offense that Jesus Christ would have us absorb becomes the amazing grace that will set us free.

> Grace alone which God supplies
> . . . .
> We will go forth in grace alone.[3]

CAROL E. HOLTZ-MARTIN

---

2. Charles B. Cousar, Beverly Gaventa, J. Clinton McCann, James D. Newsome, eds., *Texts for Preaching: A Lectionary Commentary Based on the NRSV—Year C* (Louisville, KY: Westminster John Knox Press, 1994), 396–98.
3. Words and music by Scott Wesley Brown, Jeff Nelson, "Grace Alone," © 1998 Maranatha! Music.

Luke 8:26-39

²⁶Then they arrived at the country of the Gerasenes, which is opposite Galilee. ²⁷As he stepped out on land, a man of the city who had demons met him. For a long time he had worn no clothes, and he did not live in a house but in the tombs. ²⁸When he saw Jesus, he fell down before him and shouted at the top of his voice, "What have you to do with me, Jesus, Son of the Most High God? I beg you, do not torment me"— ²⁹for Jesus had commanded the unclean spirit to come out of the man. (For many times it had seized him; he was kept under guard and bound with chains and shackles, but he would break the bonds and be driven by the demon into the wilds.) ³⁰Jesus then asked him, "What is your name?" He said, "Legion"; for many demons had entered him. ³¹They begged him not to order them to go back into the abyss.

³²Now there on the hillside a large herd of swine was feeding; and the demons begged Jesus to let them enter these. So he gave them permission.

Theological Perspective

When Jesus steps out of the boat "opposite Galilee," he steps into a life-and-death drama. A Gerasene man runs to meet him. He is in every way "unclean." Driven by a legion of demonic forces, the man is scarcely human anymore. He lives in the tombs among the dead. He is naked, unpredictable, violent, and alone. He is also a Gentile; thus the phrase "opposite Galilee" refers to much more than geography. It also suggests many ways in which Jesus intentionally "steps out" to confront what is "opposite" life. This is a christological narrative demonstrating that no one is beyond the reach of Christ's redeeming, healing love.

As the only Lukan account in which Jesus deliberately goes to Gentile territory, this boundary-crossing story foreshadows the time when Jesus' disciples will be sent to be witnesses "in Jerusalem, in all Judea and Samaria, and to the ends of the earth" (Acts 1:8). They too will go to outsiders who suffer from every kind of evil. They will be sent in the power of Jesus, whose salvation is for the world. The grace of God reaches beyond every barrier that sin has built.

While in the previous story Jesus has authority to command wind and wave, now the Son of the Most High has power over demons. Although his judgment of the demons may not yet be complete,

Pastoral Perspective

The awesome power of God can be difficult to comprehend, especially in the context of ordinary daily life, yet that power, while beyond our human frame of reference, has the capacity to transform lives. In Luke 8:26–39, the demons feared it, the possessed man was saved by it, and the neighbors did not know what to make of it, when Jesus demonstrated that God has absolute dominion over evil and an unparalleled compassion for those who seem lost.

The first one to greet Jesus as he arrived in the land of the Gerasenes was a man who was in great torment. His need is well documented in the initial verses of this pericope. He was considered possessed by demons, so worn out and distressed that he wore no clothes and lived among the tombs, an outcast in his community, so feared that he was often bound by shackles and kept under guard. At first glance, this situation is a classic encounter between good and evil: the power of God vs. the grasp of the demons. Over the years, interpreters have been tempted to explain the demonic condition in contemporary terms, proving either that demons do indeed exist or that the man had a psychiatric condition better understood in our modern context. A resolution to this classic conundrum is not essential to understanding the depth of this man's distress, nor should it distract from the larger themes of this passage.

³³Then the demons came out of the man and entered the swine, and the herd rushed down the steep bank into the lake and was drowned.

³⁴When the swineherds saw what had happened, they ran off and told it in the city and in the country. ³⁵Then people came out to see what had happened, and when they came to Jesus, they found the man from whom the demons had gone sitting at the feet of Jesus, clothed and in his right mind. And they were afraid. ³⁶Those who had seen it told them how the one who had been possessed by demons had been healed. ³⁷Then all the people of the surrounding country of the Gerasenes asked Jesus to leave them; for they were seized with great fear. So he got into the boat and returned. ³⁸The man from whom the demons had gone begged that he might be with him; but Jesus sent him away, saying, ³⁹"Return to your home, and declare how much God has done for you." So he went away, proclaiming throughout the city how much Jesus had done for him.

Exegetical Perspective

As the gospel in miniature, miracle stories contain a plot through which the evangelists portray Jesus' power to rescue lives from misery. Luke's account of the Gerasene demoniac contains all of the familiar elements of this plot: (a) the diagnosis of the malady and cry of misery, (b) Jesus' healing response, and (c) the restoration of the tormented one to wholeness and the amazement of the crowds. It also has the familiar elements of exorcisms: the demons' recognition of the exorcist and the rebuke of the demon (vv. 28, 30–31). However, unlike an earlier account in Luke (4:33–37), this is no simple exorcism. In no other instance does Jesus encounter a legion of demons possessing one person, and nowhere else do the evangelists offer such dramatic proof of the exorcism as in the drowning of the swine.

The narrative movement of Luke's Gospel indicates the focus of this story. From the opening lines, the Gospel has announced that Jesus reverses the fortunes of those of low estate (1:48, 52). The "good news to the poor," which Jesus announces in his inaugural speech (4:18), becomes a reality in the healings and exorcisms that follow (4:33–44; 5:12–16). When John the Baptist sends messengers asking if Jesus is "the one who is to come," Jesus points to the signs of the kingdom in his ministry: "The blind receive their sight, the lame walk, lepers

Homiletical Perspective

The eighth chapter of Luke's Gospel contains a whirlwind of Jesus' teaching, preaching, and miracle working. The miracles themselves point to the authority of the one who proclaims God's coming kingdom, revealing Jesus' power over nature (22–25), demonic forces (26–39), illness (40–48), and even death (49–56). The same density of material in the eighth chapter as a whole is also represented in this story. The preacher has at her or his disposal ample material for multiple sermons. Taking them up in the order they appear in the narrative, I will touch on three possible preaching trajectories, each linked by a concern for identity.

The first touches on Jesus' healing as effecting, among other things, a restoration of individual identity. While we live in a world that is largely skeptical of demon possession and exorcism, little is gained either trying to equate the demoniac's condition with mental illness or apologizing for the worldview of the Gospel writer. The story is not only—perhaps not even primarily—about physical healing (although it is, indeed, in part about healing), but about the restoration of one man's identity. The demoniac's response to Jesus is one of the more heartbreaking verses in Scripture. Asked for his name, the man replies that he has none; or, more accurately, he says that his name is "Legion," that is, "a

Luke 8:26-39

Theological Perspective

Jesus liberates and heals the man. Salvation is holistic, bringing life to body, mind, spirit, and relationships. In a final demonstration of healing love, Jesus sends the nameless man home, where he becomes the first missionary to the Gentiles.

There are ambiguities in this story, unanswered questions that have always troubled interpreters of this text. Why did Jesus negotiate with the demons and allow them to go into the pigs? Why did Jesus allow the pigs to be destroyed? Was this violence necessary?

From one perspective, the story raises questions of theodicy and eschatology but does not fully answer them. Until the final judgment, God exercises a measure of judgment and containment of evil, yet evil still has the power to wreak havoc, and living things still suffer consequences. That is, this text demonstrates a partially realized eschatology: the kingdom of God has arrived in Jesus who has power over nature, demons, and illness, but the final judgment of the demons must wait for the future. In this perspective the story does not attempt to explain unanswerable questions but reflects the ambiguity of outcomes when faithful disciples live holy lives.

Seen from another perspective, the story emphasizes Jesus' complete authority to judge and exorcise the demons. According to ancient Middle Eastern demonology, evil spirits cannot survive in water (see, e.g., Luke 11:24, where Jesus describes demons inhabiting "waterless regions"). When Jesus gives the demons permission to enter the herd of swine, the demons plunge to their own destruction along with the pigs. The removal of a legion of evil spirits is worth the unfortunate loss of the animals.

Traditional interpretation treats the swine typologically, so that they emphasize the uncleanness of the narrative setting. Because their destruction is unimportant to Jesus, for whom pigs are unclean, it should not trouble readers very much. This explanation is unsatisfying, because to the people whose living depends on the pigs, their loss is catastrophic. The swineherds are understandably afraid and, despite the miraculous healing, want Jesus to leave. From this standpoint, the story demonstrates that the coming of the gospel brings upheaval and sets in motion forces that will disrupt economic and social arrangements. The good news will not seem good to everyone. Sometimes disciples will need to "shake the dust off their feet," because their message will not be welcome (Luke 9:5; 10:11).

Amid these ambiguities, this story reveals much about the love of God. We do not know how the

Pastoral Perspective

The cause of the man's affliction is undefined, but there is no doubt regarding its intensity. His life is essentially out of his control. When Jesus asks, "What is your name?" he replies, "Legion," indicating that the influences upon him were many. So it is for many of us, even among those who call Jesus Lord. The thought that we are in control of our lives, or even that we allow God to be in control, is often debunked by the realities around us. Vocational concerns, financial pressures, broken relationships, and even the day-to-day details of life itself vie for our attention and eat away at both time and resources, distracting from the most important priority, being in relationship with God. In the first book of his *Institutes*, John Calvin warns us to be aware of such distractions and always to keep in mind "that we have to wage war against an infinite number of enemies, lest, despising their fewness, we should be too remiss to give battle, or thinking that we are sometimes afforded some respite, we should yield to idleness."[1] Being aware of the barriers that stand between us and the fullness of life with God is essential if we are to receive the transforming power God offers.

Note that the unclean spirit within the man is the first to recognize the deity of Jesus and the ultimate futility in resisting. The primary question is not, "who are you?" but rather, "what are you going to do with me?" Simply recognizing the presence of God is not the same as committing oneself to that presence. The demons' concern was for self-preservation—even if it meant entering into an unclean herd of swine. Ironically, the sanctuary of safety that the demons selected turned into the means of their destruction, as the newly inhabited pigs rushed headlong into the lake and drowned. Meanwhile, the man sat gathering his senses, finally safe at the feet of Jesus.

When we encounter the presence of God in the confusion of our lives, we are faced with a similar problem. While accepting the healing and salvation of Christ may seem logical from a point of view of faith, our human instincts sometimes drive us in different directions. Just as the man in this story seems to have no will of his own but is led to and fro by the demons within, we often resist change and flee to the familiar, living a life that makes no sense from a perspective of faith. Only when the man fell before Jesus did he find any kind of hope. We find peace and transformation at the feet of our Savior, not in a shelter of a life directed by other influences.

---

1. John Calvin, *Institutes of the Christian Religion*, ed. John T. McNeill, trans. Ford Lewis Battles (Philadelphia: Westminster Press, 1960), 1.14.14.

are cleansed, . . . and the poor have good news brought to them" (7:22). When the opposition misinterprets the exorcisms, he responds, "If it is by the finger of God that I cast out demons, then the kingdom of God has come to you" (11:20). Inasmuch as ancient people regarded all illness as the result of the power of evil, Luke makes no distinction between healings and exorcisms. In the battle with evil powers, Jesus foreshadows his ultimate triumph over evil, as indicated in his response to the disciples' report of exorcisms, "I watched Satan fall from heaven like a flash of lightning" (10:18). Thus the encounter with the Gerasene demoniac is one of numerous examples of the battle with evil powers that accompanies Jesus' proclamation of the kingdom.

While the passage shares many elements with the account of this exorcism in the other Synoptics (Matt. 8:28–34; Mark 5:1–20), the distinctive features of Luke provide the focus. The locale suggests the initial clue. The manuscript tradition reflects the confusion of the copyists over the precise location in all three Synoptic accounts (cf. Matt. 8:28; Mark 5:1). The NRSV follows the best evidence in locating the scene in Luke's account in the "country of the Gerasenes, which is opposite Galilee" in Gentile territory. Thus Luke has anticipated the larger narrative of the Gentile mission that he develops in Acts. The miserable man whom Jesus encounters is not one among many who cry out for healing; rather, he is the ultimate outcast. As a foreigner in a land where the raising of pigs is basic to the local diet and economy, he is an outsider to the people of God, and his home in the tombs is a perpetual source of uncleanness. As a demoniac with a particularly severe malady, he is homeless even among his own people.

Although a conversation with a demon is not uncommon in exorcism stories (see Luke 4:34–35), the extended conversation in 8:29–31 and the other Synoptic accounts is without parallel. It probably reflects the ancient belief that demons that are exorcized actually look for a place to rest "in waterless regions," as Jesus suggests in a subsequent conversation (11:24). In this instance, the demons fear the abyss, the "watery deep" of Jewish cosmology and the final prison of Satan (Rev. 20:3), but prefer to enter the swine, the worthless creatures in Jewish thought. The dramatic visual demonstration of the exorcism in the stampede of the pigs into the lake (Luke 8:32–33) is Luke's vivid demonstration of the victory of Jesus over demonic powers.

multitude." Oppressed by too many demons to count, he has lost himself in the cacophony of their voices and has ceased being a self, an individual, a person. Hence he spends his days raving alone in the wilderness, a danger to himself and others, separated from his community and even himself.

How many of our hearers are similarly overwhelmed by the voices raging at them from inside and out, denigrating their identity and driving them to places of extreme loneliness or despair? While we dare not blithely banish their demons and expect them to be healed, we can restore to them their name, their birthright as children of God. It is said that when Martin Luther felt oppressed by the devil, he would take courage by shouting, "I am baptized!" In this way he grounded his confidence of salvation in God's external, objective act of drawing him into the Christian family through the water and word of baptism. Similarly, the names and claims that the voices of this world may shout at us do not have the last word. We can declare that God claims us once, again, and always as God's own beloved children. In this way we may announce God's promise, restoring to our hearers the name and identity given them by God.

A second element of this story worth exploring is more troubling: while Jesus has power over the demons, he does not exercise similar authority over the people. They are, surprisingly, not overjoyed at Jesus' healing; rather, they are afraid and ask him to leave. He who has conquered wind and storm to come to them and heal one of their own seems powerless to command even their respect. What is it, we may wonder with our hearers, that causes such deep fear? While there are a number of possibilities, I suspect it is the way in which Jesus' presence and power disrupts the social order. While they were unable either to cure or to contain the demon-possessed man, the villagers at least were accustomed to him. He knew his place and they knew theirs—or, more accurately, they knew his place, out in the wilds. Perhaps understandably, they are alarmed when the former demoniac comes once again among them, even though he has been cured, because the social order to which they have become accustomed is utterly upset.

Odd as it may sound, we often prefer the devil we know to the freedom we do not. Congregations too can take a false sense of security from the dysfunctions they have learned to cope with, and they fear what change—even change for health—may bring. Communal identity is in this sense more

Luke 8:26-39

Theological Perspective

Gerasene man fell into his pitiful state, but he is not unlike homeless people today, who wander the urban wastelands of bridge abutments and alleys. Many of them are mentally ill, unable to live a normal life with a job, family, home, or basic necessities. Homeless people are at much greater risk of being victimized by assault, rape, and murder, the demonic legions that plague our streets. The homeless are "unclean" and unwelcome in most communities, inhabiting situations from which few are able to return to ordinary life. Every city has its Gerasenes. The Gerasenes are our neighbors. (For the question of neighbor identity, see the story of the Good Samaritan, Luke 10:25–37.)

Just as Jesus went to the Gerasene, his followers today are called to step out of the boat on the "opposite" side. The mission of Jesus' followers is to take the healing and liberating love of God to broken and desolate regions, to those whose lives are bound by demonic forces they cannot control. Indeed the missional language of exorcism and healing has been a notable feature of baptismal vows since antiquity. Baptismal candidates and confirmands promise, among other things, to resist Satan and the spiritual forces of wickedness in whatever ways they present themselves. To be baptized is to commit to going to the opposite side with Jesus.

We also find in the eucharistic liturgy the commission to go to the opposite side with the good news of salvation. From ancient times, Christians have understood that to share in the Table of the Lord is to take into themselves the very power and mission of Christ. To participate in Communion is to say yes to God's missional call.

When the great fourteenth-century theologian Julian of Norwich saw the redemption of Christ juxtaposed against the devil's destructive power, she "laughed greatly," for she saw that in the end the "fiend" would not prevail.[1] Every wound and sorrow inflicted by wickedness would, in Christ, become a source of honor and glory as it was healed. Julian's vision is borne out in this christological narrative of salvation. All the former wounds of the Gerasene demoniac become catalysts of redemption as the healed man goes among his people to tell them what Jesus has done.

ELAINE A. HEATH

Pastoral Perspective

Rather than recognizing and celebrating the God-given good fortune of their neighbor, the people of the surrounding countryside were struck with fear. How ironic that the demons accepted the authority of God in Jesus so much quicker than the Gerasenes! That they should fear the Son of God more than the unclean spirits that had harassed this man so intensely is a demonstration of the emotion that sometimes accompanies an encounter with the holy (see, e.g., Luke 1:12; 1:30; 1:65; and 2:9). Indeed there is some truth to the observation that we sometimes prefer the troubles we know to changes we do not know. There in front of them was the evidence of God's power, a gift given for their benefit. The demons that had plagued this man for so long were gone, not simply driven away, but destroyed. As for the man, his life was visibly changed; he was no longer a victim, but a victor, transformed and given a new chance at life by this one that the demons had called the "Son of the Most High God." Yet the people of the area asked Jesus to leave, willingly forfeiting any opportunity to further benefit from this amazing power that he brought into their midst. This reminds us of his previous encounter in Nazareth in Luke 4:28–30.

"Return to your home, and declare how much God has done for you" (v. 39). With those words, Jesus sent the man who was healed back to his own city, to serve as witness to all regarding what had transpired. On a personal level, he had been the recipient of life-changing grace, but as a rehabilitated member of the Gerasene community, and as one who had encountered the power of God intimately, he had an important story to tell.

RICHARD J. SHAFFER JR.

---

1. Julian of Norwich, *Showings*, trans. and with an introduction by Edmund College and James Walsh (New York: Paulist Press, 1978), 201–2.

Exegetical Perspective

The extended narrative of the results of the exorcism (8:34–39) brings together the Lukan themes and places the focus of the story in sharp relief. Luke has given a vivid demonstration that Jesus brings "good news to the poor" (4:18) as he collapses the larger narrative into this story. The transformation of the young man epitomizes the theme of reversal, for the one who was once naked and possessed (8:27) is now "clothed and in his right mind" (8:35). The observers report that this once-miserable creature has been healed (8:36). This story is not merely a healing, however, for the words "heal" and "save" are the same in Greek. Jesus has come, according to Luke, "to seek out and to save the lost" (19:10), and this man is one of the many of those "lost" who discover wholeness in Jesus. Luke's readers would see in this man an example of many who come to Jesus to be saved (Acts 4:9, 12; 11:14). One who has been excluded from the people of God because of his uncleanness is now welcome and cleansed.

This story also suggests that the salvation of some creates hostility in others. The scene of swineherds who beg Jesus to leave their country anticipates a later scene in Acts in which the exorcism of a slave girl deprives her owners of their source of income (Acts 16:16–24). In numerous instances, the Christian mission had a financial impact on communities, creating hostility among those whose financial world was shaken by the impact of the gospel.

Although the scene of the once-miserable man now "clothed and in his right mind" would have been an appropriate end to the story, Luke's special interest is evident in the epilogue, which is not contained in Matthew. Whereas in Matthew's account, the healed man immediately disappears from the narrative, in Luke's version he asks if he can be "with Jesus," apparently hoping to join in the itinerant mission. Jesus' response, "Return to your home, and declare how much God has done for you," reflects Luke's understanding that, while some disciples accompany Jesus in his itinerant life, others share his ministry at home (10:38–42). The one who was once homeless now has a home. The one who has experienced the power of the kingdom announces the kingdom to others.

JAMES W. THOMPSON

Homiletical Perspective

difficult to change than individual identity. Indeed, if Luke's depiction of Jesus' ministry is any indication, effecting change among a fearful community can be even more difficult than stilling storms or casting out demons.

The third element worth examining is the curious response Jesus offers to the man now cured from his possession. Restored to his right mind, the cured man begs to follow Jesus. Little wonder! Here in his native land he has been, literally, no one. What reason is there for him to remain? Yet while Jesus regularly invites persons, "Follow me," this time he commands this man to stay and "declare how much God has done for you." This may offer a clue for dealing with the dilemma we noted above. Jesus may actually be bequeathing the responsibility and the authority to effect communal change to those in the community who have felt Jesus' presence and power. Perhaps what these people need is not a demonstration of Jesus' power but the living testimony of the one who has been healed and restored. If the man were to leave, how easy it would be for his neighbors to revert to the status quo. With him constantly among them, renewed in mind, body, spirit, they must reckon with God's determined action for health and life.

Similarly, while there may be times when we are called to journey to unfamiliar parts in response to God's call, at other times following Jesus may mean staying where we are, bearing witness to the mighty acts of God we have experienced firsthand in our own lives. Communal restoration may be in this way inextricably linked to individual healing, as one lost self leads others to discover anew their own identities and possibilities.

Whichever direction the preacher ultimately chooses, she or he should point with candor to both the very real challenges and the abundant possibilities that arise when Jesus comes among us to call us to ourselves by calling us to himself.

DAVID J. LOSE

2 Kings 2:1-2, 6-14

[1]Now when the LORD was about to take Elijah up to heaven by a whirlwind, Elijah and Elisha were on their way from Gilgal. [2]Elijah said to Elisha, "Stay here; for the LORD has sent me as far as Bethel." But Elisha said, "As the LORD lives, and as you yourself live, I will not leave you." So they went down to Bethel. . . .

[6]Then Elijah said to him, "Stay here; for the LORD has sent me to the Jordan." But he said, "As the LORD lives, and as you yourself live, I will not leave you." So the two of them went on. [7]Fifty men of the company of prophets also went, and stood at some distance from them, as they both were standing by the Jordan. [8]Then Elijah took his mantle and rolled it up, and struck the water; the water was parted to the one side and to the other, until the two of them crossed on dry ground.

[9]When they had crossed, Elijah said to Elisha, "Tell me what I may do for you, before I am taken from you." Elisha said, "Please let me inherit a double share of

Theological Perspective

Whenever texts with apocalyptic elements find their way into the lectionary, it forces the preacher to ask him or herself an important question: In an age that is growing scientifically and technologically more sophisticated by the minute, should we still expect reasonable persons to take seriously biblical apocalyptic accounts involving chariots and horses of fire and persons being dramatically taken up into heaven?

For the hardened fundamentalist and the old-school liberal, the question is an elementary one, and the answer arrives quickly. For the former, to refuse to accept the literal truth of such an account is to undermine the credibility and subsequent authority of the Bible, which must be upheld at all costs. For the latter, to give serious consideration to such things is to gamble recklessly with the most important gauge of Christianity's vitality: cultural and intellectual relevancy.

For one who rejects fundamentalism as a clumsy reaction to the historical-critical method of biblical interpretation, and yet is wary at the same time of old-school theological liberalism, because of its tendency to grovel before the canons of modern rationality, 2 Kings 2:11 prompts one to take some serious theological inventory: What role should the theology implicit in biblical apocalyptic accounts play in the way one thinks about the Christian faith

Pastoral Perspective

When we think of a favorite mentor, we often ask ourselves: how has he or she nurtured us in our callings? This fourth Elijah/Elisha story in the lectionary cycle narrates the passing of the prophetic mantle from Elijah to Elisha, thus providing a tutorial for our discipleship endeavors. Several stages can be perceived in the process: inviting, developing, testing, parting, grieving, and confirming.

Inviting. Following God's command (1 Kgs. 19:16), Elijah sought Elisha while the latter was plowing and cloaked him with his mantle. Although Elisha initially asked to kiss his parents goodbye, he ultimately sacrificed his oxen, thereby sealing his break with old ways of being (1 Kgs. 19:19–21). Elisha's request to bid farewell to his parents is akin to most of our initial reactions when we are called out of our daily routines and into new situations.

Our daughter was recently diagnosed with autism. Among the many ways this stretches our family has been her reaction to any change. Her initial reaction is always "No." However, once she has had the chance to process the proposal, she will often accept it. Helping her to be unafraid of these constant invitations to change and open to new expressions of discipleship remains our biggest growth opportunity.

your spirit." ¹⁰He responded, "You have asked a hard thing; yet, if you see me as I am being taken from you, it will be granted you; if not, it will not." ¹¹As they continued walking and talking, a chariot of fire and horses of fire separated the two of them, and Elijah ascended in a whirlwind into heaven. ¹²Elisha kept watching and crying out, "Father, father! The chariots of Israel and its horsemen!" But when he could no longer see him, he grasped his own clothes and tore them in two pieces.

¹³He picked up the mantle of Elijah that had fallen from him, and went back and stood on the bank of the Jordan. ¹⁴He took the mantle of Elijah that had fallen from him, and struck the water, saying, "Where is the LORD, the God of Elijah?" When he had struck the water, the water was parted to the one side and to the other, and Elisha went over.

Exegetical Perspective

Although four chapters intervene, this story is the logical sequel to 1 Kings 19, where YHWH told Elijah to "anoint Elisha . . . as prophet in your place" (v. 16). The intervening chapters tell us about further atrocities committed by Ahab and Jezebel (1 Kgs. 20–21), how Ahab died as a result of a battle with an unnamed king of Aram (1 Kgs. 22:29–40), and how Ahaziah son of Ahab died after ruling only two years in Israel (1 Kgs. 22:51–53).

In 1 Kings 19 we were told that Elijah simply "threw his mantle over" Elisha as he passed by him, in a reluctant and only partial response to YHWH's command. At that time, Elisha simply followed Elijah and became his "servant," not his successor (1 Kgs. 19:21). Now it seems that Elijah's reluctance to give up his position to Elisha continues. Elijah repeatedly urges Elisha to stay behind (vv. 2, 4, 6), but Elisha responds each time using a traditional oath formula to swear that he will not leave his mentor alone.

In 1 Kings 18–19 Elijah had referred to himself as the only prophet of YHWH left alive, but this story speaks of one "company of prophets" in Bethel (2 Kgs. 2:3) and another in Jericho. More than fifty of the Jericho prophets (vv. 5, 7) follow Elijah and Elisha down to the Jordan. The literal sense of the Hebrew says they are "sons of the prophets," but Amos 7:14 makes it clear that this idiom refers to

Homiletical Perspective

While an omniscient narrator tells us in the opening verse what is this story's climax—the whirlwind's taking Elijah—the story also conveys a sense of suspense. The suspense enters in verse 10, when Elisha asks Elijah for double Elijah's share of the spirit and Elijah responds, "If you see me as I am taken from you, it will be granted; if not, it will not." Although the narrator tells us that Elisha cries out, "Father! Father!" as Elijah ascends to heaven, the suspense is not completely resolved until verse 14, when the narrator tells us, "When he [Elisha] had struck the water [with the mantle left behind by Elijah], the water parted to the one side and to the other." Only when we learn that Elisha, like Elijah, can part the Jordan, do we know Elisha has received the spirit.

Elijah's ascension may be what draws our attention first. Other than the brief mention of Enoch in Genesis 5:24, Elijah is the only OT figure who ascends bodily. Even Moses dies, buried in an unknown tomb. For Christians, Elijah's ascension clearly connects to NT themes about Christ (some believe Jesus is Elijah returned, some believe Jesus calls on Elijah from the cross, Christ ascends to heaven). However, the suspense the narrator builds in relation to Elisha's call suggests two themes with rich possibilities for preaching: (1) God's immanence and transcendence and (2) Elisha's discernment.

2 Kings 2:1-2, 6-14

Theological Perspective

at present? Is it relevant only for biblical literalists and premillenialists, or does it have something important to say to mainline theological liberals and moderates as well?

If the preacher finds the courage to move an apocalyptically charged verse out of the margins and into the interpretive center, while simultaneously and successfully navigating a hermeneutical path between fundamentalism and old-school liberalism, he or she perhaps will find that the resulting sermon not only uniquely challenges the congregation, but also stretches his or her personal theology in unexpected and creative directions.

Such an approach breaks from the usual mainline practice in the pulpit of steering clear of verses like 2 Kgs. 2:11, due perhaps to the fact that the preacher is unsure how to handle them. It seems a bit odd, however, for a congregation to hear a dramatic account of a man being taken up into heaven, accompanied by horses and a chariot of fire, and not hear another word about it for the remainder of the service. Once 2 Kings 2:1–2, 6–14 is read in the context of worship, verse 11 will become, for those with ears to hear, the elephant standing in the middle of the sanctuary. I would challenge the preacher not to run from it, but to address it head-on. It could even be used to illuminate the text as a whole.

It is not easy to preach a text with imagery that stands in contrast to the way most congregants experience the world to work. The theological significance of verse 11 is directly related to the larger struggle that stands at the center of not only 1 and 2 Kings but also the Hebrew Bible as a whole: the struggle between YHWH and Pharaoh. (It is no accident, for instance, that the apocalyptic events described in v. 11 are bookended by reenactments of the flight from Egypt in vv. 8 and 14.)

In the Hebrew Bible, Pharaoh does not meet his end in the book of Exodus, but he later haunts Israel in the form of its own kings who, intoxicated and blinded by political power, forget that the God under whose authority they serve not only despises tyrants, but also is inclined to intervene against them if they lead the people to apostasy or oppress the most vulnerable among them. The return of Pharaoh in the guise of such kings is, of course, a situation with which readers of 1 and 2 Kings are quite familiar; like their predecessor in Egypt, these monarchs are constantly and anxiously at work keeping the existing political structures from which they profit in good working "order." YHWH, on the other hand, is the transcendent one who not only demands

Pastoral Perspective

Developing. Although Scripture makes no mention of Elisha between his calling and today's text, Elijah is busy pronouncing God's judgment upon Kings Ahab and Ahaziah. Since Elisha is serving Elijah, he is getting great on-the-job training! The early church knew the importance of on-the-job training. Immediately following Pentecost, the apostles welcomed 3,000 new converts who "devoted themselves to the apostles' teaching and fellowship, to the breaking of bread and the prayers" (Acts 2:42).

Those four elements form the basis for Logos, a midweek ministry founded in 1965, which develops new disciples through Bible study, recreation, common meals, and worship skills.[1] An ever-growing team of joyously dedicated disciples has perpetuated this high-yielding ministry in our congregation for almost fifteen years. I believe this time-intensive ministry is an excellent example of Dietrich Bonhoeffer's insistence upon costly grace for the development of disciples. Bonhoeffer writes,

> Cheap grace is the mortal enemy of our church. Our struggle today is for costly grace. Cheap grace is grace . . . without costs. Cheap grace is grace without discipleship, grace without the cross, grace without the living incarnate Jesus Christ. . . . Costly grace is the gospel which must be sought again and again, the gift which has to be asked for, the door at which one has to knock. It is costly, because it calls to discipleship; it is grace, because it calls us to follow Jesus Christ. It is costly because it costs people their lives; it is grace because it thereby makes them live.[2]

Testing. Elijah encouraged Elisha to stay behind three times, and each time Elisha insisted upon following. This parallels Peter's threefold denial of Christ in his passion, and the resurrected Christ's thrice asking Peter if he loved him (John 18:15–18, 25–27; 21:15–19). It is human nature to test the limits of love. Our own children test us to make certain we love them no matter how distinctively they are behaving. Elijah's example shows us that God calls us to keep loving God's children of all ages, even when we doubt their commitment or do not like their behavior.

Parting. Elisha's shock at the chariots of fire that separate him from Elijah reminds us that even anticipated separations are painful for those left behind. A beloved member of our congregation, Ted

1. www.logosministries.com
2. Dietrich Bonhoeffer, *Discipleship* (Minneapolis: Fortress Press, 2001), 43–45.

professional prophets (those who make a living as prophets). The fifty prophets from Jericho stand at a distance (v. 7), perhaps because in the previous chapter two sets of fifty soldiers and their captains were said to have been consumed by fire called down on them by Elijah.

When Elisha asks for a double share of Elijah's spirit (v. 9), he is not asking for twice the power of Elijah, but for twice what any other "son" might get. The "double portion" is the share of inheritance given to a firstborn son (Deut. 21:17). Elisha wants to be seen as Elijah's rightful heir. Elijah makes it clear that the handing on of the prophetic spirit is not under his control (v. 10).

Elijah's mantle is the symbol, not the source, of his power. In Hebrew, as in English, "mantle" (*adderet*) has a double meaning, referring both to a loose, sleeveless garment (such as cloak or a robe) and to a symbol of authority. On Horeb, when Elijah heard the "sound of sheer silence," he wrapped his face in his "mantle" (1 Kgs. 19:13). Later on, he "threw" it over Elisha (19:19), as Elisha was plowing in a field. In this passage, Elijah rolls his mantle up and uses it like a rod to strike the water of the Jordan (v. 8), reminding us of the time when Moses used his staff (a symbol of his authority from God) to strike the Nile and turn it into blood (Exod. 7:20). When Elisha picks up Elijah's fallen "mantle," he is claiming this symbol of prophetic authority as his own. In a practical sense, he also is replacing his own garment, which he has torn as a sign of mourning (v. 12). The prophetic succession is pictured as a human (not a divine) endeavor. While God may have endorsed and supported it, the transfer of power takes place without a direct encounter between Elisha and YHWH.

The parting of the waters of the Jordan "until the two of them crossed on dry ground" (v. 8) should remind us of other significant water-based miracles in Israel's history (the parting of the Red Sea in Exod. 14 and the parting of the Jordan in Josh. 3). When Elijah and Elisha crossed the Jordan near Jericho, they entered the territory of Moab, where Moses died. Elijah is "taken" here in Moab, reminding us again (as in 1 Kgs. 19) that Elijah and Moses are comparable figures. When Elisha subsequently parts the waters for himself (v. 14), it becomes apparent that Elisha was to Elijah as Joshua was to Moses (see Num. 27:18–23 and Josh. 3:7–16). The general acceptance of Elisha as Elijah's replacement (vv. 15 ff.) is underscored in a later passage when Elisha's lament in verse 12 is repeated by King Joash as Elisha is dying (2 Kgs. 13:14).

God's Immanence and Transcendence. The miraculous occurrences in this story—the parting of the Jordan and Elijah's ascension—call our attention to God's sovereign power. God participates in—indeed orders—creation, but is also wholly distinct from it. The images of the chariot and horses of fire and whirlwind, which appear unannounced in the middle of a conversation in today's text, invite us to reflect on the implications of God's transcendence. Twentieth-century Swiss theologian Karl Barth emphasized God's transcendence in his writing, critiquing human philosophies and institutions. The images in this passage provide an opportunity to challenge members of the church with questions about the role of Christianity and the church in criticizing and transforming culture. The images of God as majestic and sovereign also provide an opportunity to identify and explore the difference between anthropocentric and theocentric perspectives, or the difference between being self-centered and God-centered. In what ways do churchgoers conflate what *is* with what we can discern about God's will? In what ways do churchgoers confuse what they want with what God calls them to do?

This passage's images and references to God's sovereign power can also offer a reassuring message. This message is captured in the words of the African American spiritual, from about 1862, by Wallis Willis, "Swing Low, Sweet Chariot." Willis wrote, "Swing low, sweet chariot, / coming for to carry me home. I looked over Jordan, and what did I see, / Coming for to carry me home? / A band of angels coming after me, / Coming for to carry me home." Here, the chariot represents deliverance (although it may also represent a challenge to the institution of slavery). That God is sovereign can be a message of hope to those who are marginalized.

This message of hope is also one of empowerment. The means by which Elijah ascends to heaven are also the means by which Elisha receives the spirit. If the chariot and whirlwind represent divine support and deliverance, they also represent God's empowerment of believers for ministry in the world. God is transcendent and also immanent in history, through God's engagement with faithful people.

Elisha's Discernment. Suspense develops in this story because we do not know until the very end whether or not Elisha will receive the spirit Elijah has received. Elisha himself does not know, until he parts the Jordan with Elijah's mantle. We can almost hear Elisha ask himself, "Will I see Elijah ascend? Will I be

2 Kings 2:1-2, 6-14

Theological Perspective

obedience at Pharaoh's expense, but also fuels insurgencies against his repressive and corrupt political reigns.

Israel's main challenge is remaining faithful to YHWH in a world in which Pharaoh appears to have all the power. Israel's continual temptation is to buy into Pharaoh's view of reality and operate, as the pragmatists advise, as if immanent power were everything and transcendent power nothing. The unique call of the prophet, in this context, is to open the nation's eyes to the illusory nature of Pharaoh's power and the ultimate reality of YHWH's. In order to do so, however, the prophet must be equipped with the penetrating vision that is required to perceive YHWH's supreme power and authority through Pharaoh's thick smoke screen.

It is no coincidence, then, that the authenticating test for Elisha, who wishes to take the mantle of the great prophet Elijah, concerns vision. In response to Elisha's request for a "double share" of Elijah's spirit, or the right to succeed him, Elijah states, "[I]f you see me as I am being taken from you, it will be granted you; if not, it will not" (v. 10).

What follows next, of course, is the apocalyptically charged verse 11, in which chariots and horses of fire arrive as Elijah ascends to heaven in a whirlwind. Elisha excitedly cries out, "The chariots of Israel and its horsemen!" (v. 12) in order to confirm that he has, in fact, seen Elijah being taken up. He has the requisite vision to perceive the reality of YHWH's activity in the midst of a world held under the illegal and illusory jurisdiction of Pharaoh and his heirs. This, finally, is what marks him Elijah's rightful successor.

The question that can be posed from pulpits today is whether the church can see the world clearly at present, as Elisha could, or whether it finds itself lost in, and blinded by, the smoke screens of the Pharaohs among us. The key to the church seeing clearly may be for it to learn to see apocalyptically, which has more to do with vision and discernment in the present, Elisha demonstrates, than with literalism as regards the biblical past and future.

TREVOR EPPEHIMER

Pastoral Perspective

Pollock, also known as Christ's Globetrotter for the ninety-one building projects he completed in twelve countries during his lifetime, died at age ninety-five with his work boots on. Among Ted's best aphorisms is the assurance, "God's work done God's way never lacks for funds." Ted always said he was ready for God's chariot whenever it would take him. He meant it, not just because he knew his Bible well, but because he knew he had faithfully raised his seven children to walk in Christ's footsteps and had mentored countless others in their own transformational missions.

Grieving. Knowing Elijah would be taken from him did not minimize Elisha's grief; rather, it made his own ministry more poignant. Composer Giacomo Puccini wrote a number of famous operas. In 1922 he was suddenly stricken by cancer while working on his last opera, *Turandot,* which many now consider his best. Puccini said to his students, "If I don't finish *Turandot,* I want you to finish it for me." Shortly afterward he died. Puccini's students studied the opera carefully and soon completed it. In 1926 the world premiere of *Turandot* was performed in Milan with Puccini's favorite student, Arturo Toscanini, directing.

Everything went beautifully until the opera reached the point where Puccini had been forced to put down his pen. Tears ran down Toscanini's face. He stopped the music, turned to the audience, and cried out, "Thus far the Master wrote, but he died." A vast silence filled the opera house. Toscanini smiled through his tears and exclaimed, "But his disciples finished his work." When *Turandot* ended, the audience broke into thunderous applause.[3]

Perpetuated ministries are richer for the connectedness they bring the body of Christ.

Confirming. Elijah knew Elisha would be his successor but left that revelation to God (1 Kgs. 19:16). Although Elisha asked to inherit a double share of Elijah's spirit, Elijah did not promise it to him; rather, he called Elisha to vigilance upon his departure so that God's will might be revealed directly. When Elisha did see Elijah's dramatic departure, picked up his passed-on mantle, struck the water, and crossed over, he was confirmed in his new role. Whom are we nurturing? How are we nurturing them? Part of our own personal spiritual discipline must be the discipleship of others who might assume our mantles, as Elisha assumed Elijah's.

CARRIE N. MITCHELL

---

3. http://home.twcny.rr.com/lyndale/Pentecost%205C.htm, accessed August 30, 2007.

Exegetical Perspective

The whirlwind (*se'arah*) is sometimes associated with theophanies (as in Job 38:1; 40:6), but here (as in 1 Kgs. 19) God does not appear in the whirlwind. In verses 1 and 11 the wind is merely the means by which Elijah is "taken." To be "taken" meant to avoid the grave, to enter directly into the presence of God. Like Enoch, who simply "was not" because God "took" him (Gen. 5:24), Elijah was "taken" into heaven directly. The speakers in Psalms 49 and 73 use the same word for taken (*laqach*), translated by NRSV as "receive," to verbalize their hope to share the same fate (Pss. 49:15, Eng.; 49:16, Heb.; 73:24). Elijah's avoidance of an ordinary death sets the stage for the later traditional expectation that he would return to call Israel to repentance "before the great and terrible day of the LORD comes" (Mal. 4:5; see Matt. 17:10–12; Mark 9:11–13: Luke 9:18–20) and helps explain why Elijah appears alongside Moses at the transfiguration of Jesus (Matt. 17:3; Mark 9:4; Luke 9:30).

While Elisha claims his inheritance and is recognized as Elijah's successor (v. 15), subsequent passages show Elisha operating in a style that is quite different from his mentor's. Unlike the solitary figure of Elijah, Elisha works closely with several prophetic "companies." His miracles are quite secular, most often done for the benefit of the "sons of the prophets" and their families, and usually have no moral or religious implications (though the healing of Naaman may be an exception). Elisha finishes the work assigned to Elijah in 1 Kings 19:15–17 ("anointing" Hazael as king of Aram and Jehu as king of Israel). As he skillfully manipulates political and historical events, Elisha serves the purposes of the God who works behind the scenes of human history, in the "sound of sheer silence" (1 Kgs. 19:12).

KATHLEEN A. ROBERTSON FARMER

Homiletical Perspective

able to part the Jordan as Elijah did? Will the Lord grant me the spirit?"

The suspense Elisha must feel, and which the story generates in us, parallels our actual experiences. Our lives are full of suspense: "Will the cancer treatment work? Will the marriage counseling work? Will the new community center be able to provide for the neighborhood? Will my child make it through high school? Will I be downsized out of a job?"

Given that we all, to some degree, participate in experiences like Elisha's, we can look at his actions in this story as a model for our own encounters with the unknown. Three times Elijah directs Elisha not to continue with him. Three times Elisha says, "I will not leave you" (vv. 2, 4, 6). Then Elisha states that he wants a double portion, meaning the primary heir's share of Elijah's God-given gifts. In 1 Kings 19:16, the Lord instructs Elijah to anoint Elisha as his successor. Yet, as verse 10 indicates, Elisha has no guarantee that God will give him the same gifts that Elijah received. Elisha pursues his call, with no guarantee that God will respond. Elisha follows what he understands to be God's will, although he does not know clearly what God's will for him is. Elisha must discern God's will by participating in events. He must watch the chariot and the whirlwind. He must pick up the mantle. He must attempt to part the Jordan. Elisha confirms his call through his actions.

Elisha suggests for us that faithfulness may be expressed by a commitment to discerning God's will. Faithfulness may be expressed by embracing the suspense or ambiguity that is part of life, and asking, "What is God calling me to do in this situation?" Elisha also suggests that we may have to discern God's will through action. This challenges us to develop and maintain a God-centered perspective— a perspective implied by Elisha's persistence in following Elijah and pursuing the prospect of God's empowerment. Sometimes we may prefer security and certainty to God's empowering us for a risky calling. In seeking security and certainty, we may ignore or confuse our own desires and conventions with God's direction. Elisha's experience invites us to seek critical distance from our own interests, to grapple with uncertainty, and to strive to forward God's purposes in the choices we make.

HAYWOOD BARRINGER SPANGLER

Psalm 77:1-2, 11-20

¹I cry aloud to God,
  aloud to God, that he may hear me.
²In the day of my trouble I seek the Lord;
  in the night my hand is stretched out without wearying;
  my soul refuses to be comforted.
. . . .
¹¹I will call to mind the deeds of the Lᴏʀᴅ;
  I will remember your wonders of old.
¹²I will meditate on all your work,
  and muse on your mighty deeds.
¹³Your way, O God, is holy.
  What god is so great as our God?
¹⁴You are the God who works wonders;
  you have displayed your might among the peoples.
¹⁵With your strong arm you redeemed your people,
  the descendants of Jacob and Joseph.   *Selah*

Theological Perspective

Sounds are ripples of communication within the universe. Most sentient beings, the waters, and various meteorological expressions (from rain to earthquakes) make sounds. Awareness of sound requires a capacity to hear. The philosopher asks: *When a tree falls in a forest without a hearer, has there been a sound?*

When the psalmist cries out, there is an expectation that God is present, cares, and hears. Crying audibly signals a sense of agency on the part of a self who has a relationship with God. The psalmist does not languish because the cries fall on deaf ears, as Macbeth languished after his wife's death, lamenting, "It is a tale told by an idiot, full of sound and fury, signifying nothing" (Act 5, Scene 5). Rather, the psalmist has an underlying certainty that this lament matters to God.

In responsorial angst, one is vulnerable before God, in pain, seeking the Lord. Paradoxically, divine presence is not enough to quiet the weary, troubled soul who refuses comfort. Discomfort is so great; one may experience a huge void amid freedom, choice, and anxiety.

When left inconsolable, one could self-medicate and possibly fill such a cavern with compulsive use of alcohol, drugs, sex, overspending, gambling, food, and/or work. With online poker, home shoppers

Pastoral Perspective

Inconsolable despair, utter hopelessness, ultimate resignation, total abandonment: these words convey the mood of Psalm 77. Most of us have days when we feel down and depressed, anxious or afraid, but that is not the mood of this writer. The mood of this writer is despair unto death. One can only imagine the mind and mood of a suicide, moments before pulling the trigger or swallowing the pills.

"My soul refuses to be comforted," cries the psalmist (v. 2). All that comforted in the past is no longer available. The sense of God's benevolent presence, once so powerfully felt, has vanished. The psalmist has entered the valley of the shadow of death. The writer has sunk so deeply into depression that he is incapable of imagining that there is any help. The psalm makes no plea, no petition for God's intervention, as might have been the case in the past.

Although the psalm is written in the first person, it is not clear whether it is uttered as an individual lament or as a corporate wail reflecting the mood of the nation. Either way, the emotion expressed is hopelessness.

So what does the psalmist do? He does what we all tend to do in times of deep despair. The psalmist retreats into memory, focusing on better times when life appeared full and meaningful, when God seemed

¹⁶When the waters saw you, O God,
    when the waters saw you, they were afraid;
    the very deep trembled.
¹⁷The clouds poured out water;
    the skies thundered;
    your arrows flashed on every side.
¹⁸The crash of your thunder was in the whirlwind;
    your lightnings lit up the world;
    the earth trembled and shook.
¹⁹Your way was through the sea,
    your path, through the mighty waters;
    yet your footprints were unseen.
²⁰You led your people like a flock
    by the hand of Moses and Aaron.

Exegetical Perspective

Psalm 77 restructures conventional phrasings of distress and praise to create a new hopeful song—a muted lament turning hymnic to affirm God's past power and providence as a still-viable hope for the morrow. The psalm is clearly crafted from several intertextually paraphrased sources. Indicative of this blending, a full range of names for God appears: *Elohim, El, Adonay, Elyon,* and *Yah,* plus second- and third-person-singular pronouns speaking to and about God. The final composition offers its own shape with the placement of three *selah*s, otherwise untranslatable. They form four strophes, at first alternating between anguished, prayerful reflection (with Pss. 86:7 and 142:3) and a pledge to recollect God's past redemptive deeds. "Remembering" (*zkr*) anchors both prayer and pledge. The third *selah*, verse 15, frames a hymn of theophanic storm imagery echoing the exodus and, possibly, creation after Habakkuk 3 and Psalms 18, 97, and 114. Psalm 77 is a thesaurus of importunate verbs—crying, seeking, meditating, musing, moaning—yet pointedly lacks words of outright lamentation. "Grief" is as sad as this song "of Asaph" sinks in some soul-felt night of vexed meditation "according to Jeduthun" (in superscription, not included above) that "the right hand of the Most High has changed," in the central verse 10.

Unlike other psalms in the Asaph collection sung "according to" tune names, "Lilies," "the Gittith,"

Homiletical Perspective

Remembrance. If lament is one faithful response to grief in the felt absence of a comforting God, remembrance of God's past presence, musing and meditating upon God's wondrous deeds of old, provides another possible antidote. Wandering through a side street of Germany's Kulturstadt Weimar one bright Saturday afternoon in the midst of my sabbatical, I looked up to see written on the side of a building the words "*Die Welt ist voll alltäglicher Wunder.*" Immediately I decided that this saying (attributed to no less than Martin Luther himself) just had to be the epigrammatic theme of my journey, all the more amazing for having been serendipitously encountered not in a book or a lecture but as (decorous) graffiti. Yes, indeed, I nodded in agreement (and go on nodding), "The world is full of everyday wonder!" The trouble is that we too often lack eyes to see, and that is where remembrance comes in. It is in retrospect that God's wondrous ways are recognized.

The sufferer of Psalm 77 is evidently an insomniac, one kept awake (as the omitted verses of our reading go on to tell in excruciating detail) by the gnawing suspicion that God's promises and steadfast love may have ceased forever. As he confesses in verse 10, in highly original lament language, "It is my grief that the right hand of the

Psalm 77:1-2, 11-20

Theological Perspective

networks, access to credit cards, alcohol sold in grocery stores, and designer drugs made from cough medicine, finding a fix becomes easy. The psalmist refuses to hide, pretend, or avoid pain. The trauma of discontent is visceral. The psalmist experiences unspeakable distress, while assuming God usually answers and comforts those who seek God. Even this memory is painful, a lament, for no comfort is forthcoming: only moaning, unceasing prayer, and meditation amid sounds that signify nothing (vv. 1–2).

Later (vv. 11–20), moments of introspection shift to a ritual of divine remembrance. The psalmist recalls God's previous works and wonders. The poet thinks about what God has done. The recollection becomes a meditation in which the psalmist listens for the sounds of God, in lieu of speaking to God. Adoration and recognition of God's holiness emerge in this sacred space, through personal testimony. Bishop Thomas L. Hoyt Jr. says that testimony is shared practice, where one speaks her or his truth to the community about what they have seen, heard, and experienced for the edification of all. When one testifies, others must be present to receive and evaluate the shared communication. Testimony or witness occurs to encourage others and affirms what God has done.[1]

The psalmist testifies to God's greatness and uniqueness. God's salvific acts redeem descendants of those liberated in ancient Israel, imitating the exodus experience. Central to biblical testimony, which anchors the transition in the text, is the import of communal memory, necessary for codifying transcendent moments where one moves from deep pain to communal and personal hope. The hymn within this psalm recites and reveals the God who is really real and always the marker of truth amid paradox and contradiction. The psalm gives us permission to pronounce personal fears and doubts, aware that faith can coexist with doubt, as we recall God's faithfulness.

With new boldness and certainty, the psalmist evokes the movement of creation, using water imagery. Drought, tsunamis, hurricanes, and floods have made us more conscious of the impact, movement, and power of natural waters.

Such profound, primordial movement found in Scripture and nature emerges eloquently in the arts, especially in music. Joseph Haydn's *The Creation* is an oratorio, a large sacred musical work for soloists,

Pastoral Perspective

real and present. Only, instead of bringing resuscitated hope, his reflection provokes even newer questions, resentment, and deeper doubt. He begins to entertain the unbearable thought that God has changed: "Will the Lord spurn forever, and never again be favorable? Has his steadfast love ceased forever? Are his promises at an end for all time? Has God forgotten to be gracious?" (vv. 7–9a).

As he wallows in despair, the psalmist names the source of his greatest fear: "It is my grief that the right hand of the Most High has changed" (v. 10). When the Scriptures use the phrase "the right hand of God," they are speaking metaphorically of God's power to deliver and redeem. The question that torments the psalmist's mind is the question every doubter knows only too well: "Have I been wrong about God all along?"

Having emotionally hit "rock bottom," the psalmist does what at first seems strange, though it is not that unusual for those who have experienced severe doubt. The writer begins to "doubt his doubts." Even the style of the writing changes; the writer begins to address God directly, instead of focusing on his own woe. As James Mays puts it in his commentary on the Psalms, "The very shift in style gives the effect of presence."[1]

Not unlike the prodigal son of Scripture or the homeless derelict of contemporary times, the psalmist remembers "home." He engages in a nostalgic journey backward as he reflects once again, even more desperately, on the past when God was a redemptive presence ("I will remember your wonders of old. I will meditate on all your work, and muse on your mighty deeds," vv. 11b–12). Again it is not clear—nor does it really matter—whether the revived conversation with God is personal or on behalf of the nation. What matters is that trust in God is beginning to emerge once again, and the catalyst for the revelation is memory.

In 1987, fifty years after the infamous *Kristallnacht*, when rioting mobs roamed the streets of German cities destroying Jewish homes and places of business as a prelude to the Holocaust, Elie Wiesel addressed the German Reichstag. "We remember Auschwitz and all that it symbolizes because we believe that in spite of the past and its horrors, the world is worthy of salvation; and salvation, like redemption, can be found only in memory."[2]

---

1. Thomas L. Hoyt Jr., "Testimony," in *Practicing Our Faith: A Way of Life for a Searching People*, ed. Dorothy Bass (San Francisco: Jossey-Bass, 1998), 91–94.

1. James Luther Mays, *Psalms*, Interpretation Series (Louisville, KY; John Knox Press, 1994), 252.
2. Elie Wiesel, *From the Kingdom of Memory: Reminiscences* (New York: Summit, 1990), 201.

Exegetical Perspective

Psalm 77 refers to "Jeduthun," a personal name regularly connected with Asaph in Nehemiah and Chronicles. This fact, along with its deep memory reviving exodus motifs, suggests a postexilic setting. Psalm 39, however, connects Jeduthun with David in a poem of bitter accusations against YHWH more pessimistic and singularly composed than Psalm 77's multilayered and temperately redacted text that eventually offers hope via remembrance.

The dubious KJV reading of a running "sore" unceasing in the night, verse 2, comes from a combination of the unusual root word *ngr* (literally, "to flow" or "gush"), rendered "stretched out" (NRSV), and taking "my hand" to imply the flesh having been struck, as in Job 23:2. Alternately, when compared with the near verbatim and more logical phrase in Lamentations 3:49—"my eyes flow without ceasing, without respite"—Psalm 77:2 abridges the agony and substitutes "my hand" for "my eyes" to soften further our psalm's lamentation in favor of an ambiguous gesture of imprecation—an oft-extended hand.

Through the first *selah* (v. 3), the psalmist soliloquizes about God in a cry for comfort. "Aloud [literally, "my voice"] to God, I cry aloud (my voice) to God, that [God] may hear me" (v. 1). The anxious tone uses stairlike syntax with synthetic triplet parallelisms stepping up the tension. "My soul" neatly parallels "my spirit," verses 2 and 3, as "faints" succinctly captures "refuses to be comforted." Slight variations in word choice and syntax ("my soul is weary" // "[he/it] searches my soul") rescue the poetics from wooden predictability. The near verbatim recast of verse 3 in verse 6 binds strophes 1 and 2, as does the frequency of cohortative verb forms ("I shall *surely* cry out," v. 1; "moan" and "meditate," vv. 3, 6; and "muse," v. 12, along with "surely remember" [*zkr*]).

Omitted in the lectionary, strophes 2–3 (vv. 4–15) join wide-eyed worrying to hard questions. Nuanced uses of "I remember" (*zkr*), strategically placed in verses 3, 6, and 11 (three times with emphatic cohortative), further underscore this psalm's motif of hushed distress resolved through remembrance to offer hope. NRSV varies *zkr*'s meaning as "think of," "commune," and "call to mind" as well as "I remember." Under the influence of the Septuagint's "reasoning [with one's heart in the night]," "commune" in verse 6 derives from the cryptic Hebrew "I shall surely remember *my music*." The recollection of hymnic "days of old" is exactly how hope crescendos in the final strophes, and the lectionary's focus reaffirms God's creative power and evokes God's works of glory as of old.

Homiletical Perspective

Most High has *changed*" (emphasis mine). The terrifyingly real fear is not that God is unable to intervene to save as in Israel's past, but that God's saving intention may have altered, as articulated in the caustic query, "Has God forgotten to be gracious?" (v. 9a)

Robert Davidson has suggested that what is undermining the psalmist's "spiritual sanity is the yawning gap between the tradition of faith in which he has been nurtured and the grim present which seems to call into question every statement in the traditional credo. For him it is the character of God that is at stake." The psalmist's anxiety is that "God is no longer the God in whom he had been brought up to trust." God is not the answer but is part of the problem.[1]

If God's constancy is under question, the strategy of recalling God's saving wonders of old is moot. Yet this is just what the psalmist resorts to in liturgical-sounding language extolling his wonder-working God. It is as if the cadences of praise themselves are designed to soothe his anxiety until in verse 20 he bursts into song in the words of a hymn that, Davidson claims, "likely reflects ancient Canaanite poetic style" in its borrowing of mythological language that portrays "the conflict between the gods of order and creation and the forces of chaos."[2]

Is it, perhaps, that the remembrance of *Heilsgeschichte* alone offers inadequate assurance, unless it is accompanied by the ever-present evidence of a natural theology that is translucent if not transparent to God's creativity and power? Yet the hymn ends on a note that leads back to YHWH's will to save, evident in the unseen "footprints" of the "way. . . through the sea" in which Israel was led "like a flock" by "the hand of Moses and Aaron" (vv. 19–20). One cannot help but hear echoes of the comforting shepherd imagery of the Twenty-third Psalm, as well as other Scriptures like Ezekiel 34 and John 10.

My mother asked me, her pastor son, to visit her old friend Jessie, who was dying of kidney failure in a nearby hospital. Jessie was also the mother of my old boyhood friend, Gary, and so I told my mother I would be happy to visit her. She was evidently glad to see me, but the tall, robust farm woman I knew as a boy had become an emaciated ghost of her old self. I innocently asked Jessie how she was doing, and immediately out poured a stream of complaints and laments and descriptions of the maladies from which

1. Robert Davidson, *The Vitality of Worship: A Commentary on the Book of Psalms* (Grand Rapids: Eerdmans, 1998), 250, 248.
2. Ibid., 250.

Psalm 77:1-2, 11-20

Theological Perspective

chorus, and orchestra, with a libretto that weaves together materials from Genesis and Psalms, along with John Milton's *Paradise Lost*. U.S. composer Randall Thompson wrote in 1940, amid warfare in Europe, a plaintive, inspiring, introspective a cappella choral work that uses only the one word "Alleluia" for the entire piece, and concludes with "A-men." For Thompson, this work echoes that God gives and God takes away,[2] reminiscent of this psalm that asks where God is, when you suffer so. To sing this work is to know a sense of Rudolph Otto's *mysterium tremendum*; it is ethereal and haunting, inspiring and awful, echoing a cosmic birth, of quiet waters being troubled. The unaccompanied voices swell in incredible harmony that quietly and powerfully exudes the holy. The resulting passionate intensity reflects holiness, praise, and worship.

'How Great Thou Art," a great hymn of the church by Stuart K. Hine, also reflects God's great wonders and works. This song extols the marvels and miracles of God in nature and creation, in Jesus Christ, and in the eschatological joy one experiences when Christ returns to be with us—all cast in song and celebration, extolling the greatness of God. Like the psalm, this hymn signals the import of worship and the centrality of God. We are to be in relationship and to remember divine works and wonders, amid mystery, holiness, and eschatological hope.

From the African American literary tradition, James Weldon Johnson expresses similar sentiments in his song-poem "Creation," from his seven-movement work *God's Trombones*.[3] "Creation" generates a parallel passion and deep appreciation for creation as it focuses on divine architectural design and emotional connectivity. The poem conveys divine loneliness as desire or catalyst for God's acts, framed by word painting of divine ontological reality, set anthropomorphically as God smiles and pronounces divine work as good.

Whether in Scripture, oratorio, hymn, or poem, the creation event told in Genesis and signified in the Psalms is a powerful literary and artistic resource. The opportunity to rehearse and remember creation in Psalm 77 engages liturgical witness, the balm of memory and salvific hope, and a spirituality of liberation—freedom from angst and the abyss.

CHERYL A. KIRK-DUGGAN

Pastoral Perspective

Miroslav Volf, himself a victim of persecution in the former Yugoslavia, now professor of systematic theology at Yale Divinity School, has written a powerful book on the importance of memory as a source of redemption, healing, and hope. Volf, however, is not glib or naive in his assertion that salvation comes through memory. Like Wiesel, he knows that memory can also lead to destruction and death. Revenge, retaliation, resentment are all dependent upon memory. In the Deep South, it is not uncommon to see a bumper sticker exhibiting the Confederate battle flag and the words "Forget Hell!" Not all memory is redemptive.

Thus it becomes imperative that one remember "truthfully," which is always difficult because we have so much invested in "our side" of the story. In fact, no memory can ever be absolutely truthful or entirely trustworthy. Nonetheless, the effort must be made to remember truthfully, and then to interpret the meaning of the memory in a wider context not previously considered. Healing comes when one remembers truthfully, remembers therapeutically (or "interpretatively"), and learns from the past.

This is precisely the way the writer of Psalm 77 finds deliverance from his despair. His own recent experience has not worked. Only as he begins to place his particular memories in a larger moral framework than his own, calling on the communal memory of the faith community, is his hope restored.

Because the psalm takes the form of a hymn or a liturgical recitation, rather than a more formal prayer petition, the case may be made that it reinforces the power of liturgy in our own worship services. Through our hymns and other elements of worship, we call to mind our collective memory of God's saving activities across the centuries. As every preacher knows, a Sunday worship service in which the sermon has been a little thin can be saved by the recitation of the creed and the singing of the hymns. While tradition can become demonic, it can also save people from the tyranny of the present.

P. C. ENNISS

---

2. http://en.wikipedia.org/wiki/Alleluia_%28Thompson%29
3. http://www.poetry-archive.com/j/the creation.html; "Creation" is in *The Book of American Negro Poetry*, ed. James Weldon Johnson (New York: Harcourt, Brace & Co., 1922).

Exegetical Perspective

Strophe 3 (vv. 10–15) shows three poetic couplets of five declarations and one rhetorical question recollecting the exodus "wonders" made known to God's people. The effect is a singsong statement of faith that engenders optimism by countering the tension of the earlier three couplets of grievances, all interrogatives, in verses 7–9. So, "What god is so great?" (v. 13) rhetorically answers strophe 2's anxious questioning "Has God forgotten?" (v. 9).

Following the final *selah,* verse 15, strophe 4 summarizes God's imminent puissance gleaned from a cache of storm imagery such as Psalms 18:7–15 and 97:4. The hymnic meter here returns to stairlike poetics building intensity. The repeated catchwords "tremble," "thunder" (*qol* = "voice") contrast the muted voice of the psalmist earlier, and "the waters," both as rain and as sea, further recasts the exodus motif. Counterpointing strophe 1's three-step structured anxiety at God's apparent absence, the tension here in strophe 4's triplets presumes a holy terror at the divine presence. The anthropomorphism of "the waters" who "see and fear" (v. 16) faintly echoes the apostrophe to the sea and the Jordan in Psalm 114. Mention of "the deeps trembling" (v. 16) hints at a mythic struggle between God and the "deep" at creation. Passage "through the sea" suggests the wonders at the Reed Sea, although the unusual term *shebil,* parallel to "way," denotes elsewhere (Jer. 18:15) ancient well-worn tracks. Alternate versions suggest the plural reading "Your paths through many waters," which again may hark back to multiple victories over primordial chaotic waters—crossing the Reed Sea and the Jordan—seen as new acts of creation, and offer the hope that God will act again.

The nonpoetic tagline, verse 20, returns the reader to the exodus allusion in strophe 3, marrying it with the final strophe's theophany to answer the psalmist's earlier distress—an answer meant to comfort a postexilic Israel, coupling hope with memory. Led by "the hand of Moses and Aaron" semantically connects with the "strong arm" of verse 15 and counters the central grief in verse 10, which accuses God of a negligent "right hand," and the imploring prayerful "hand" gesturing of verse 2.

Psalm 77 is fit for those occasions when an uplifting hymn, not always recollected in tranquility, can assuage a congregation in doubt-filled, anguished times by "surely remembering" the foundations of our hope-filled faith—creation and redemption.

RICHARD D. BLAKE

Homiletical Perspective

she was suffering. It was as if my simple question had unplugged a drain clogged with an accumulation of junk that needed to be emptied.

I listened patiently to my mother's dying friend, experiencing the truth of the old saying that "confession is good for the soul." Then I read a psalm, had prayer with her, and shared the bread and wine of Communion. As I was getting ready to go, Jessie looked up from her bed, from which we both knew she would not be returning home, smiled through her parched lips, and said (as I remember), "Thanks, John, for coming to see me and for listening to me. You know, my own pastors drive all the way into the city here to see me, and they think it's their job to cheer me up. But you were willing just to listen to me—and that is what I really needed."

I nodded my head and have kept nodding my head over the years at the truth of Jessie's deathbed observation. In our human extremity of illness or grief, anger or disappointment, what we need is not cheering up, but someone we trust, to lend an ear to our lament. What makes the Psalms so vital for so many over so many generations is the permission-giving example they have provided in encouraging the faithful to say whatever is on one's heart in the presence of God, even when one is not all that certain that God is listening (see Mark 15:34, e.g.). Further, the Psalms demonstrate for us that we do not have to clean up our act or our language before daring to bare our souls to God. As the oldie-but-goodie hymn sings it, "What a privilege to carry ev'rything to God in prayer."

> Are we weak and heavy-laden, cumbered with a load
> of care?
> Precious Savior, still our refuge—take it to the Lord
> in prayer.
> Do your friends despise, forsake you? Take it to the
> Lord in prayer.
> In his arms he'll take and shield you; you will find a
> solace there.[3]

JOHN ROLLEFSON

3. Joseph Scriven, "What a Friend We Have in Jesus," *Evangelical Lutheran Worship* (Minneapolis: Augsburg Fortress, 2006), #742.

Galatians 5:1, 13-25

¹For freedom Christ has set us free. Stand firm, therefore, and do not submit again to a yoke of slavery. . . .

¹³For you were called to freedom, brothers and sisters; only do not use your freedom as an opportunity for self-indulgence, but through love become slaves to one another. ¹⁴For the whole law is summed up in a single commandment, "You shall love your neighbor as yourself." ¹⁵If, however, you bite and devour one another, take care that you are not consumed by one another.

¹⁶Live by the Spirit, I say, and do not gratify the desires of the flesh. ¹⁷For what the flesh desires is opposed to the Spirit, and what the Spirit desires is opposed to the flesh; for these are opposed to each other, to prevent you from doing what you want. ¹⁸But if you are led by the Spirit, you are not subject to the law. ¹⁹Now the works of the flesh are obvious: fornication, impurity, licentiousness, ²⁰idolatry, sorcery, enmities, strife, jealousy, anger, quarrels, dissensions, factions, ²¹envy, drunkenness, carousing, and things like these. I am warning you, as I warned you before: those who do such things will not inherit the kingdom of God.

²²By contrast, the fruit of the Spirit is love, joy, peace, patience, kindness, generosity, faithfulness, ²³gentleness, and self-control. There is no law against such things. ²⁴And those who belong to Christ Jesus have crucified the flesh with its passions and desires. ²⁵If we live by the Spirit, let us also be guided by the Spirit.

Theological Perspective

"For freedom Christ has set us free." It is a wonderful sentence, conveying in a few short words not only a gospel claim—that Christ has set us free—but a missional cause: that our lives and actions are to reveal that freedom. What does such freedom look like? After all, Paul is soon issuing imperatives and suggesting that those who are free should make themselves slaves to one another. Apparently, Christian freedom does not look like living an unencumbered life.

The idea that freedom means the absence of encumbrances may be popular but it does not hold weight. Freedom is not the absence of entanglements; entanglements are the means by which freedom becomes meaningful. Who is freer: the confirmed bachelor or the husband and father discovering the range of emotions, values, and possibilities made possible through those relationships? Who will be freer: people in a society that votes for leaders who shape the laws that govern them or people in a society in which people have stopped voting? Who is freer: the woman who chooses to take ordination vows that bind her to the church or the one for whom ordination is not an option? Freedom is not separation from relationships; it is a feature of relationships that becomes especially apparent as a result of our relationships with Jesus Christ.

Pastoral Perspective

A dear friend and colleague recently died after a courageous, yearlong battle with leukemia. A priest for more than forty years, he came to the cathedral where we were both associates in a part-time capacity. His "retirement" afforded him the ability to focus on those areas of ministry he most deeply loved: contemplative prayer, spiritual formation, and liturgy. He was a wise and gentle mentor to those of us who were younger in "priest years," and a gift in so many ways to the parish. After numerous hospitalizations, second and third opinions, two extensive rounds of chemotherapy, and a joyful but short-lived remission, the cancer returned with a new vigor and intensity. In consultation with his family, my colleague made the decision to cease all but palliative care, and to die on his own life-giving terms.

In one of our last conversations he said, "I have had so much love."

"Yes," I replied, "there are so many who love you and are grateful for you."

"That may be," he replied, "but what I mean is that there are so many whom I have loved. I have so much gratitude for the love God has enabled me to give away." We were quiet for a few minutes. Then he said, "Having made the decision not to continue with treatment has freed me to focus on quality of life rather than longevity. It has given me the

Exegetical Perspective

Paul asserted earlier in Galatians that the old age and new age of Jewish apocalypticism are not entirely separate (4:4–9). Consequently, both evil and righteousness are possible during this time between the ages. People were in bondage to sin before God sent the Christ and Christ's Spirit (4:8). Presently, however, God is revealing Christ (1:1, 4, 12, 16), the Spirit (3:2, 14; 4:6), and faithfulness (3:23) so that God may be known intimately (4:9) and that God's people may exhibit self-sacrificing service in the manner of Jesus Christ (4:9–19). God's children, then, may now relate to God as true daughters and sons (4:7) and live righteously as God desires (2:16, 20–21; 5:5–6, 22–25), even if it is still possible for them to sin (4:9) and use others for selfish advantage (4:17). In this in-between age of the Spirit, Christians may exhibit attributes of Christ (5:16, 22–25). This is the temporal framework for Paul's discussion of the Christian life (5:13–6:10).

In today's text, Paul focuses on the practice of Christian freedom (5:13–25), taking up the theme that he struck so forcefully in 5:1. He has been developing this topic throughout the letter, however, by pointing to his own freedom (1:1, 10) and that of fellow believers (2:4; 3:28) and arguing that Jesus' followers are the true children of the "free" woman Sarah (4:22–23) and belong to the free realm of

Homiletical Perspective

Weather projections threatened a winter storm. We had prepared for a big Sunday, but as I answered the parsonage phone, I gained an impression that many were eager for me to cancel worship. As in the past, I counseled my folk to make their own decisions about their safety. I would be leading worship.

Worship has become optional. Too many of us think we should not be inconvenienced (allowing extra time, dressing differently, walking a bit further from the car) and we certainly do not think we should take risks (not for a gathering that we can join next week, unless something more urgent or more pleasurable arises). I ponder the pastoral failings that have led to congregants viewing worship as more social occasion than lifeline. Do we come to worship seeking too little? Or is littleness what we find?

Several times in my life I have worshiped in faith communities whose spiritual and emotional wellness seemed organically bound up in the worship event's effective ability to connect them with God's living Word. I sensed that what happened in those sanctuaries brought people essential encouragement and sustenance for another week. The power of those events was astonishing. For the first time, each time, I awakened to my own need for an authentic church.

In today's text Paul makes impossible requests of us: to eschew "fornication, impurity, licentiousness,

Galatians 5:1, 13-25

Theological Perspective

This brings a new question: What kind of relationships follow from (and create the possibilities for) Christian freedom? Paul's brief answer is that Christian relationships ought to be shaped by neighbor love. His longer answer contrasts desires of the flesh and fruit of the Spirit.

The shorter answer is not surprising. Neighbor love was emphasized by the law (Lev. 19:18) and reiterated by Jesus (Matt. 22:39). It is interesting that Paul does not turn to the cross to describe neighbor love. *Agapē* is not self-sacrifice. If anything, Paul's vision of neighbor love recognizes that people not only do but ought to value themselves: you would not want someone else to "bite and devour" you, so do not do so to them. In the face of a tradition that has sometimes pushed Christians (and especially those Christians whose freedoms have been limited or denied because of cultural and political inequalities) to think of neighbor love as self-sacrifice, Paul's emphasis on equality ("become slaves to one another," v. 13) and reciprocity ("if . . . you bite and devour one another," v. 15) highlights the significance of the "as yourself" that sits at the back end of the Golden Rule.[1]

Paul's longer answer involves a contrast between "the desires of the flesh" (v. 16) and "the fruit of the Spirit" (v. 22). Rather than an extended excursus on those terms' meanings, though, he provides us with lists of each. As a result, commentators have sometimes struggled to discern what the two terms mean. The absence of extended excursus does not leave us entirely lost, however, as the lists shape the way we understand the terms. As such, the church theologian will want to explore the lists (vv. 19–21, 22–23) in at least as much detail as she explores the terms.

Toward that end, bear several points in mind. First, we ought to resist any too-simple opposition between the material and the spiritual. The works of the flesh include both material desires (e.g., fornication, drunkenness) and spiritual ones (e.g., idolatry, sorcery); the fruit of the Spirit enriches not only our spiritual lives but our relationships with the stuff of the world. The opposition is centered in ethics, not ontology; as such, this dualism does not go all the way down. In contemporary cultures—whether secular materialist or religiously spiritualist—that all too often draw a bright line between material and spiritual realms, such Manichean flights of fancy should be resisted.

1. The most important analysis of the meaning(s) of neighbor love is still probably Gene Outka, *Agape: An Ethical Analysis* (New Haven: Yale University Press, 1972).

Pastoral Perspective

freedom to see in a new way how much love there has been, is now, and will be. Love is meant to be given away. That is what the incarnation is all about." We sat together in silence, in the early spring sun, on his back deck, with the goldfinches and nuthatches feasting at his birdfeeder. A few days later, he was gone.

One of the truths my colleague helped me see was that bondage takes many forms, and we must be courageous in naming them. Moreover, freedom from bondage requires the wisdom and courage to ask in what context we understand our freedom, theologically and pastorally, and to what end that freedom shall be used. In my pastoral work I see many forms of bondage: political, economic, religious, psychological, and spiritual. In the process of liberation from bondage, one must pass through a liminal, transitional phase within which one asks what one is being freed up to do. In other words, freedom from the constraints of bondage must be freedom for a *particular* purpose.

For my colleague, the liberation from the vicissitudes of his increasingly desperate medical treatment allowed him to appreciate in a new way the deeper, richer dimensions of the many forms of love that sustained him throughout his life. He was able to rest easy and without anxiety in the secure knowledge of resurrection, and to practice that resurrection in the form of *gratitude* for the love he had given away—a practice to which he could now turn his full attention.

In these verses from Galatians, Paul is saying unequivocally that freedom is *for love.* For Paul, the harsh debates and infighting among the young Christians in Galatia were outward and visible signs of an ongoing enslavement. In a dilemma similar to that of my colleague, they had discovered occasions for bondage in the very context designed to be life giving for them. The Galatians were allowing debates over circumcision to be given precedence over the law of loving one's neighbor as oneself. Focus on the flesh in the form of circumcision paradoxically prevented appropriate "re-ligion" (from the Latin *ligare,* meaning "to bind together"). Letting go of the "law" required liberation from considerations of the "flesh"—in this case from matters of circumcision, and in the case of my colleague, from medical care that paradoxically would limit his quality of life. In both cases the task was that of turning attention to the power of the Spirit to direct their decisions, relationships, and, indeed, their core identity as human beings and children of God.

Exegetical Perspective

God's Jerusalem above (4:24–26). In short, he has already made the case that life in Christ (2:20) brings freedom from bondage to the law or to any pagan practice (4:5, 8–10), and this forms the basis for his frequent use of the imperative now (5:13–6:10). The authentic Christian life is lived without fear (2:12) in the freedom that Christ brings.

Freedom Defined (vv. 13–15). Christian freedom is not unrestrained permission to do whatever one pleases. Paul reminds the Galatian Christians that God called them to freedom, but he adds, "Do not use your freedom as an opportunity for the flesh" (or "for self-indulgence," 5:13b). He does not use the term "flesh" (*sarx*) derogatorily, as though human bodies are inherently evil. Rather, "flesh" is often Paul's shorthand for self-centered living as opposed to God-centered living. Thus the counterpoint to life in the "flesh" is a life of loving service for the benefit of others (v. 13c); it is "faith working through love" (v. 6). Love is the way that freedom in Christ expresses itself (v. 13d). Indeed, freedom in Christ makes radical loving service possible, which fulfills the will of God for human relationships (v. 14).

Freedom to love and serve in the manner of Jesus is God's intention for humankind. Freedom is a gift from God given through faith. Like all good gifts, though, it can be misused and even cause harm (v. 15). Paul knows that people can misuse their freedom to dominate others. Conversely, people who love and serve can be taken advantage of and abused. Paul thus moves to distinguish between self-centered living in the realm of the "flesh" and God-centered living in the dominion of the Spirit.

Walking by the Spirit (vv. 16–25). Paul warns against the "works of the flesh," which are reflected in a host of self-centered practices (vv. 19–21). Freedom may be misused. Paul exhorts the Galatians to rely instead on the Spirit's power for experiencing true freedom. Love, joy, peace, patience, gentleness, and self-control are but some chief examples of the Spirit's fruit that are actualized in and among believers (vv. 22–23). To bring this point home, Paul appeals to the risen crucified Christ as the basis for understanding the meanings and the relationships of servanthood, freedom, love, and the Spirit.

For Paul, the relation between the risen Jesus who lives as the crucified one and the believer's life and behavior is apparent. Paul writes, "Those who belong to Christ Jesus have crucified the flesh with its passions and desires" (v. 24). Following Jesus, they

Homiletical Perspective

idolatry, sorcery, enmities, strife, jealousy, anger, quarrels, dissensions, factions, envy, drunkenness, carousing, and things like these" (vv. 19–21). This will not happen naturally, nor will it happen apart from the Holy Spirit's chosen vehicle, the church. The flesh—that is, the unaided, disconnected human spirit—will wring its metaphorical hands and fill its spiritual void with some form of the above list of terribles. If we cannot depend upon the love of God, we will darn well find another form of dependency.

The first six months I lived overseas after college were awash in loneliness; late each weekday afternoon I would buy a paperback mystery and read it to make endurable the solitary evening. Over the weekends a clump of U.S. teachers would meet and critique the culture that functioned so differently from our own. Sunday nights the homesickness sharpened as I found my way back to the flat I shared, with a mattress on the floor and increasingly unrealistic memories of home.

Finally, it was make-or-break time. I would cut the ties that bound me to my discontent and try my host country on its own terms. With little enthusiasm, I stayed in town to visit a church near my workplace. The second time I showed up, the head usher remembered me, his kindness startling tears into my eyes. The third time I did not duck out during the final hymn and gained an invitation to a home for Sunday dinner. The effect of that loving, laughing, singing congregation's connection to Jesus Christ would come to permeate every aspect of my life. It was a wondrous thing to stumble into the hands of the living God.

I was fortunate in being away from all that had been familiar to me, so that the lines of my life's finitude became hardened and clear. Then I could realize my need for God, the aching Augustine-named void that clamors to be filled. I had tried to fill it with escape literature, running complaints, and quasi-friendship. None of these make Paul's list of evils, but they were my own excellent ways of avoiding God. I had not of my own making the slightest inclination to "not use your freedom as an opportunity for self-indulgence, but through love become slaves to one another. For the whole law is summed up in a single commandment, 'You shall love your neighbor as yourself'" (vv. 13–14).

How does the preacher awaken people in the pews to the truth that our temptations may be less spectacular than those on Paul's list, but no less deadly? "I am warning you, as I warned you before:

Galatians 5:1, 13-25

Theological Perspective

Second, Paul's problem with the flesh is not that it desires but that its desires are disordered; it wants the wrong things or wants good things in the wrong way—usually too much or too little. Wanting sexual intimacy, it pursues fornication; wanting contact with the Divine, it pursues idols; wanting joy, it carouses. Connecting this point to Paul's emphasis on freedom suggests that disordered desires enslave us to our passions and destroy community. To Paul's readers, that claim would be obvious—as he points out in verse 19. Indeed, the list Paul provides is similar to any number of lists floating around the Greco-Roman world at the time. For example, both Plato and Aristotle compose similar lists. For Paul, however, the appropriate response to disordered desire is neither the rejection of desire nor surrender to it. Instead, it is to desire properly, which is made possible by the work of the Spirit, which also desires. In contemporary cultures that manifest themselves in the stoic refusal to desire or the libertine refusal to have those desires reshaped, the patient practices of having our desires remade takes time and Spirit.

This connects to a third point: this fruit is more than just the benefit that accrues from being guided by the Spirit in ways that allow us freely to love our neighbors. It is the virtues that, with God, we inculcate in order to pursue such benefits. The Spirit shapes us through them to be the particular kind of people to whom this fruit tastes sweet. As such, there is both an eschatological character to these fruits—a way that desiring them and shaping our desires through them finds completion only when we are made whole—and also an ethical recognition that our vision of the world and our actions in it interact with each other. It is not that we discern what God has done on our behalf and then love our neighbors in response. Rather, discerning what God has done in Christ and what Christ has done for us shapes the way we love our neighbors, and loving our neighbors helps us see what God has done. In contemporary cultures that pursue utopian ends regardless of the means by which they are reached, or disallow idiomatic visions of the good from being expressed in public in order to emphasize fair procedures, the eschatological ripening of these fruits reveals both the nature of the Spirit's actions and the ends for which we are being remade by that Spirit.

MARK DOUGLAS

Pastoral Perspective

In these passages we find Paul emphasizing the work of the Holy Spirit in the renewal of membership in community—that *binding together* of the Messiah's faithful people—and the new life that results. This is, for Paul, the source of the fruit of the Spirit such as love, joy, peacefulness, generosity, and so on. They are taken up by the Spirit and into the community of the body of Christ.

I do not mean to suggest that my colleague's decision to end the aggressive medical treatment was easily reached. It was not. He did not reach it in isolation or without disagreement, debate, and at times agonizing discussion with friends, colleagues, and family. It was a discussion that took place in community and with intentionality. Likewise, I do not believe that the fruit of the Spirit to which Paul asks that we attend rules out disagreement and conflict. Indeed, pastorally understood, conflict is part and parcel of intimacy and the risking of oneself in community. When we enter that place of codiscerned vulnerability, however, generosity, patience, kindness, and faithfulness can provide "palliative care" amid the inevitable disagreements that ensue. Such qualities are excellent companions on the journey, when we risk intimacy with others in community.

Among the gifts my colleague gave us was that he was fully alive when he died. Just as clinging to life beyond the point at which it ceases to be "life-giving" is a form of enslavement, so is practicing our faith with a zeal which gives rise to anger, malice, divisiveness, and other ills to which the flesh is heir. To be sure, persons ought to be rightly suspicious when they are called only to joy. This need not blind us to the life-giving possibilities available to us even in those places where our embodiment as human beings allows both for conflict and for the presence and guidance of the Spirit, in love.

J. WILLIAM HARKINS

Exegetical Perspective

have died to the narcissistic powers of the flesh and are no longer under its spell (3:1). Instead, believers live under the rule of the Spirit. They exercise self-control and put the needs of others ahead of their own needs. Indeed, even as Jesus exchanged places with sinful humanity, taking upon himself the curse it deserved (1:4; 3:13), in order that humanity might receive God's blessing (2:20; 3:14), so also Jesus' followers are free and empowered to serve others in the same loving and self-sacrificing ways. There is no power for this ethic apart from the power that God gives in the Spirit. Through Christ's crucifixion, the Spirit of the risen one is now available to the children of the promise, who have been transferred by faith into the realm of God's rule (3:14; 4:4–7). By faith, Jesus' followers are enabled to practice divine faithfulness, which is love—a primary gift of the Spirit and a characteristic of everyone who calls Jesus Lord (5:6, 13–14, 22).

Walking by the Spirit is not an option for Christians. Either one is governed by the controlling power of the "flesh" (v. 17) and will exhibit unrighteousness (vv. 19–21), or one is under the controlling power of the Spirit (v. 18) and will display God's own righteousness in the world (vv. 22–23). This is why Paul is so adamant that the Galatians "walk by the Spirit" (vv. 16, 25), "live by the Spirit" (v. 25a), and "be led by the Spirit" (vv. 16, 18, 25b). The faithful Christian life is a matter of active participation.

Of course, it is noteworthy that Paul uses the active form of the verb "to crucify" (*estaurōsan*) in verse 24, which is to be distinguished from Paul's earlier use of the verb in a passive form in 2:19 (*synestaurōmai*). Earlier, Paul asserted that faithfulness begins when a believer dies to every other controlling power but lives for God in Christ Jesus. Here in verse 24, Paul indicates that believers are responsible for their own participation in actively crucifying the "flesh" with its self-interested passions and desires. This process of dying is possible through fellowship with Jesus the crucified. As believers participate in the ongoing work of putting to death those powers pitted against God's will for their lives, they become empowered with new life and live increasingly in the realm of the Spirit—exercising freedom responsibly, until they inherit the kingdom of God.

ROBERT A. BRYANT

Homiletical Perspective

those who do such things will not inherit the kingdom of God" (v. 21).

One commentator has said that Paul is reminding us that Christ's perfect freedom engages us in a call. That call carries obligation to neighbor as well as to God, to invest ourselves in the community of faith, to put up with the sandpaper of fellow congregants' wearisome ways against the rough edges of our own unholiness. That call impels us to prepare our hearts for worship, so that we must be fed or know sharp hunger; to exist in community with such openness and generosity that our neighbor's well-being is part and parcel to our own.

Some years ago a member of our congregation carelessly hurt the feelings of another. I do not recall the details, but remember witnessing the planting of seeds of a rift. The next Sunday I found the one who had given offense waiting anxiously on the front steps of the church, his choir robe billowing in the morning breeze. I noticed and wondered. When the one offended showed up, he held out his arms to her with words of apology. She forgave him with a brief, warm hug. They remain friends to this day.

I remember the incident because of the readiness, promptness, and sweet humility with which peace was made. I remember it because of its rarity. I remember it because Christians are charged with giving and receiving such forgiveness. "For you were called to freedom, brothers and sisters; only do not use your freedom as an opportunity for self-indulgence, but through love become slaves to one another. For the whole law is summed up in a single commandment, 'You shall love your neighbor as yourself'" (vv. 13–14). What must happen is as simple as Paul's clarion call to forget everything but Christ.

Our freedom in Christ is not evidenced by results but by our character. As one commentator has said, it is shown not by what we do but by the fruit we bear: "love, joy, peace, patience, kindness, generosity, faithfulness, gentleness, and self-control. There is no law against such things" (vv. 22–23).

Preacher, make it so.

CAROL E. HOLTZ-MARTIN

Luke 9:51-62

⁵¹When the days drew near for him to be taken up, he set his face to go to Jerusalem. ⁵²And he sent messengers ahead of him. On their way they entered a village of the Samaritans to make ready for him; ⁵³but they did not receive him, because his face was set toward Jerusalem. ⁵⁴When his disciples James and John saw it, they said, "Lord, do you want us to command fire to come down from heaven and consume them?" ⁵⁵But he turned and rebuked them. ⁵⁶Then they went on to another village.

⁵⁷As they were going along the road, someone said to him, "I will follow you wherever you go." ⁵⁸And Jesus said to him, "Foxes have holes, and birds of the air have nests; but the Son of Man has nowhere to lay his head." ⁵⁹To another he said, "Follow me." But he said, "Lord, first let me go and bury my father." ⁶⁰But Jesus said to him, "Let the dead bury their own dead; but as for you, go and proclaim the kingdom of God." ⁶¹Another said, "I will follow you, Lord; but let me first say farewell to those at my home." ⁶²Jesus said to him, "No one who puts a hand to the plow and looks back is fit for the kingdom of God."

Theological Perspective

The journey through Galilee is now finished, and Jesus "set[s] his face to go to Jerusalem." He is resolute, single minded, and prophetic in the manner of Moses and Elijah, with whom he has conversed in 9:28–36. Yet Jesus is more than a prophet. He is the Messiah. In this text Jesus begins in earnest to prepare his disciples for what lies ahead. The tone is sober. Jesus has already begun to warn the disciples that he will be betrayed and put to death (9:21–22, 44). Partnership with Jesus in his mission will require rugged commitment. The disciples must learn how to respond to rejection and persecution. To be a Christ-follower is to walk the way of Jesus regardless of the outcome.

The narrative begins with a reference to Jesus' future ascension: "When the day drew near for him to be taken up" (v. 51). The disciples are being readied for their ultimate mission following Pentecost. Luke's central, soteriological theme continues in this passage, with the disciples going into a Samaritan village to prepare the way for Jesus. Samaritans are outsiders to the Jewish community, with much enmity between the two groups, but Jesus plans a mission into a Samaritan village. His authority to forgive and heal extends to all people, including the racially and religiously "mixed" Samaritans. To their credit, the disciples go to the

Pastoral Perspective

Faith can be expressed and experienced in a variety of ways, but there comes a time in each one's journey when it is necessary clearly and unequivocally to declare the depth of that commitment. God's place in our lives is neither a matter of convenience nor something that can be taken for granted or assumed. Unlike other human endeavors, our commitment to God is a heartfelt matter, rather than the result of a logical decision-making process. When choosing to turn with Jesus "to go to Jerusalem," factors such as love and grace play a far greater role than criteria such as length of association or depth of knowledge. Adopting a life of discipleship cannot be a part-time or momentary commitment. It is a life-changing shift in direction and priorities, in which our human needs and wants become subservient to the call of our Lord.

There is a tendency to resist. The journey Jesus walked was a difficult one, eventually ending in the cross. In an era of numerous choices and instant gratification, that kind of commitment is difficult to wrap our minds around. Luke 9:51 marks a significant transition in Jesus' life and ministry. Jesus had been teaching about the sacrifice that would eventually be required of him; now his realization that "the days drew near for him to be taken up" caused him to change direction, heading toward Jerusalem and the death he would meet there.

Exegetical Perspective

Although all three Synoptic Gospels portray a Galilean ministry of Jesus, followed by his entry into Judea and Jerusalem (cf. Matt. 19:1–2; Mark 10:1), Luke heightens the drama of this journey, placing approximately one-third of his Gospel within a travel narrative (Luke 9:51–19:28). That Luke's interests are more theological than geographical is suggested by the fact that he offers repeated reminders that Jesus is on his way to Jerusalem (13:22, 33–34; 17:11; 18:31; 19:11, 28), although he provides no geographical markers to indicate progress on the journey.

Luke introduces the travel narrative in 9:51 in language calling attention to the decisive turning point in the story. The critical moment is suggested in the words "When the days were fulfilled for him to be taken up" (the NRSV "when the days drew near" does not fully capture Luke's intent). The language of fulfillment corresponds to Luke's emphasis on the Christ event as the middle of time (cf. 1:1; 4:21; Acts 1:2). Luke has pointed to this time earlier in the narrative, recalling that Moses and Elijah discussed Jesus' "exodus" (NRSV "departure"), which was soon to take place in Jerusalem (Luke 9:31). In this instance Jesus will be "taken up" in Jerusalem. Although "taken up" can be a reference to the ascension (Acts 1:2, 11, 22), Luke probably refers to all of the events that will take place in Jerusalem,

Homiletical Perspective

At the turning point of C. S. Lewis's beloved *The Lion, the Witch, and the Wardrobe*, several significant characters encourage each other with reports that Aslan, the great lion and true ruler of oppressed Narnia, has reappeared to fight the evil witch. Their words of encouragement to each other are as potent as they are succinct: "Aslan is on the move."

In today's reading from the Gospel of Luke, something similar is happening as these verses, which open the second half of Luke's account of Jesus' ministry, herald Jesus' journey to Jerusalem and the cross. Having preached, taught, and worked miracles, Jesus suddenly hears like a silent clarion the call to turn toward Jerusalem, and the rest of Luke's narrative depicts his steadfast journey there. In short, Jesus is on the move.

While Jesus' face may be set to Jerusalem, he does not take the most direct path. In fact, there is almost no discernible logic to the collection of stories and incidents Luke relates, and there is no easy way to identify the route Jesus followed. Luke's concern, it turns out, is primarily neither narrative nor geographical, but theological: the stories Luke shares reveal the character of Jesus and, in turn, the Father who sent him and the mission Jesus has been sent to accomplish.

The two scenes grouped together in today's lection offer insight into Jesus' call. Both occur

Luke 9:51-62

Theological Perspective

Samaritans with Jesus' message. They are willing to reach out as Jesus does, beyond familiar boundaries.

Their generosity is short lived. When they are turned away by the Samaritans, the disciples respond with anger. James and John want to incinerate the village, just as Elijah called down fire from heaven against the prophets of Baal. This request earns a sharp rebuke from Jesus and leads into a series of potent conversations on the cost of discipleship.

Temptations around the use of power will face the disciples in the future, and indeed will always face the church. The disciples have already been told that when they are rejected, they are simply to shake the dust from their feet and announce that the kingdom of God has come near (Luke 9:5, repeated in 10:11 with the sending of the seventy). In the story of Samaritan rejection, it is clear that retaliation of any kind is not an option for disciples. The use of violence to enforce Christian faith is counter to the spirit of Christ. While a rejection of the gospel brings eschatological consequences, judgment belongs to God alone.

Linked to Jesus' refusal to abuse power is his detachment from material possessions, an attitude he expects in his followers. The discipline is jarring and subversive. "Foxes have holes and birds have nests," Jesus says to a potential disciple, but "the Son of Man has nowhere to lay his head" (v. 58). God incarnate is essentially homeless, apart from the hospitality of others. What does this mean for his followers? How should it affect their relationship with material possessions? What about their careers and families? The call to discipleship is a call to open hands, a practice the saints and mystics call "detachment." No one can cling to possessions and faithfully follow Christ.

The austere demands of this text have inspired Christian monasticism from antiquity, especially in what Catholics name the evangelical virtues of poverty, chastity, and obedience. Although at times interpretations of this text have led to extreme asceticism and gnostic dualism in regard to body and spirit, it is unlikely that Jesus practiced or promoted extreme asceticism. His opponents, after all, caricature Jesus as a "drunkard and glutton" (7:34), which, though an exaggeration, reveals a fully embodied Savior. A more probable meaning is that Jesus is relativizing every aspect of human life to the central importance of the *missio Dei*. Even the most basic elements of life—food and shelter—are secondary.

Though Jesus' ethos of *kenōsis* (self-emptying) has been distorted at times into a disembodied

Pastoral Perspective

In our own lives we also face significant times of transition. Early in our faith development, we are often focused on learning more about Scripture, the church, and what it means to be a child of God. We revel in the knowledge that we are loved fully and completely by a wonderful, caring Savior. We share together in the marvelous fellowship that is the body of Christ. We feel renewed, nurtured, and marvelously fulfilled. As our faith grows and matures, our life in Christ slowly merges with our life in the world. We come to realize that living by the Way is more than just a private endeavor, no matter how meaningful. In order to have true meaning and integrity, it must be our identity; we must recognize and live it in every part of our being. No matter what our gifts or imperfections, the mature Christian must willingly walk alongside Jesus, even if that journey compels us to make difficult choices that a more secular existence might otherwise avoid.

Resistance can take many forms. Jesus' new direction met with considerable opposition, sometimes hostile, often puzzled. Many of those who were sent to prepare the way were opposed rather than received. Although they clearly misunderstood the reason for his journey to Jerusalem, the people of Samaria were defiant, seeing him only in relation to his pilgrimage to the Holy City. Because he was not welcomed, his disciples James and John were indignant, suggesting that punishment be brought to bear from heaven. Jesus does not choose to punish those who are reluctant to support him, even today. Instead, we are reminded again and again that ours is a Savior of love, who is not about punishing all who resist or compelling everyone to get in line or face the consequences, but one who invites those who believe to walk the journey with him.

Not all are ready to take that path. The second half of this pericope (vv. 57–62) is composed of a series of encounters in which the sincerity and depth of faith of several potential followers are put to the test. On the surface, each response seems reasonable and appropriate. When we look at these encounters in the context of Luke 9:51, it is apparent that following Jesus is seen as only one among a number of priorities, with each person putting something ahead of his or her desire to follow the Lord.

The first scenario (vv. 57–58) finds an exuberant fan along the way proclaiming, "I will follow you wherever you go." Not an unreasonable statement, perhaps it has crept into our prayers from time to time. In fact, most Christians would probably agree that following Jesus is primary to their basic faith

including the death, resurrection, and ascension. Jerusalem is, therefore, the place of Jesus' destiny. To "set his face" is a prophetic act suggesting stern resolution, recalling the setting of Ezekiel's face against Israel to prophesy (Ezek. 6:2; 13:17; 14:8). As Jesus indicates later in the travel narrative, Jerusalem is the place where prophets die (Luke 13:34).

Jesus' journey to his death provides the context for the stories of discipleship that follow in 9:51–62. On this journey, as in the Galilean ministry, disciples follow Jesus (cf. 5:11), share in his ministry (9:1–5), and take up his cross (9:23). In contrast to Matthew and Mark, which portray a journey through Perea on his way (Matt. 19:1; Mark 10:1), Luke depicts a journey through Samaria, the direct route to Jerusalem. To travel through Samaria is a major challenge, since Jews and Samaritans do not associate with each other (John 4:9), because of hostilities that are centuries old. Josephus records continuing acts of violence against Jewish pilgrims passing through Samaria on their way to Jerusalem (*Jewish War* 2.232). Nevertheless, Jesus involves the disciples in a mission to the despised Samaritans, anticipating the subsequent mission of disciples to spread the gospel beyond Judea and into Samaria (Acts 8:4–25). The disciples soon learn the risks of such a mission, for unlike others who had welcomed Jesus (Luke 7:36; 9:1–5; cf. 10:38–42), the Samaritans did not receive Jesus because his face was set for Jerusalem.

In their request to call down fire from heaven on the inhospitable Samaritans, the disciples have apparently forgotten Jesus' earlier instruction to respond to rejection by "shaking the dust" from their feet (9:5) before going on to the next village. They desire to imitate Elijah, who called down fire from heaven to consume the messengers of the king (2 Kgs. 1:10). By rebuking the disciples and moving on to the next village, Jesus again teaches the disciples to respond to the inevitable rejection, not with violence, but by the continuation of the mission in new venues.

In the brief narratives of the would-be disciples, Luke indicates further dimensions of discipleship as Jesus continues "along the road" to his destiny. Luke shares the first two stories (9:57–60) with Matthew (8:19–22) and adds the third (9:61–62) from his own special material. Although the Lukan Jesus has already said that those who follow him must take up the cross daily (9:23), the first would-be disciple makes an enthusiastic offer to follow wherever he goes. Unlike the other would-be followers, he places no conditions on his discipleship. The encounter with the Samaritans has been a vivid reminder that

almost immediately after Jesus was transfigured on the mountaintop and attended by Moses and Elijah in the sight of his most trusted disciples. The first scene depicts Jesus' rejection by a Samaritan village and the righteous anger of James and John, expressed by their request to call down fire from heaven to consume the villages. While these two disciples may seem rather overzealous to us, we should note that Elijah twice called down fire to consume opponents, and it may be that, having just seen Jesus in the company of this prophet, James and John have this example in mind. Jesus refuses. Only verses earlier he had told his followers to receive hospitality where it is offered and, if it was refused, to shake the dust off their sandals and move on. Vengeance, violence, is not part of Jesus' vision.

Curiously, Luke gives no reason why the Samaritans would not receive Jesus. Whether he is rejected because he will not stay to perform miracles in this village, or because he defies their communal sense of what a messiah should be, or even because he is traveling to the disputed center of Judaism matters little to the evangelist. Luke does, however, link the Samaritans' reaction to Jesus' setting his face for Jerusalem. What is central, apparently, is not the Samaritans' rejection but, rather, Jesus' single-mindedness of purpose.

This focus provides a link to the next vignette. At first glance, it is difficult to tell why the requests of Jesus' followers evoke such harsh rebuke from him. After all, bidding farewell to family and honoring one's parents by burying them hardly seem extreme. A contrast with Elijah—who allowed Elisha to mark an ending to his life with his family before joining the prophet—is likely intentional. The point, however, is not that Jesus demands more than Elijah but, rather, that Jesus' road is more compelling. He cannot and will not be drawn away from his purpose and destiny. Jesus recognizes that the journey to Jerusalem and the cross that waits there brook no compromise. To eschew violence, to embrace suffering for the sake of another, to refuse comfort, privilege, status for the sake of fidelity to God's vision and mission are, to say the least, countercultural; perhaps they even run contrary to the natural human instincts for preservation, safety, and comfort. In this regard, we might detect something of a truth-in-advertising element to Jesus' rebuke of his would-be followers. Those who would embrace Jesus and his mission must be under no illusions of what it will mean for them.

At this point, then, perhaps the most significant question facing the preacher is to determine whether

Luke 9:51-62

Theological Perspective

spirituality, it is a teaching that is strikingly counter to materialistic culture today. This text raises many questions for the contemporary church. In what ways do Jesus' words about his own homelessness critique ecclesiology? What might it mean for the gathered people of God to practice this kind of *kenōsis* in regard to material possessions and place? How can Christians provide responsibly for family and community without selling out to a consumeristic culture?

Commitment to discipleship leads to a testing of loyalties on every front. At times the demands of the gospel will violate familial and cultural norms. "Let the dead bury the dead," Jesus says to a potential disciple who places lengthy funerary customs ahead of the call to mission (9:60). Jesus' shocking words about the father's funeral seem harsh and unloving, even though he may be referring to the placement of the deceased father's bones in an ossuary box long after the father's death. His point is that when other loyalties to family, community, and tradition claim first place, disciples will compromise the call on their lives.

The Orthodox doctrine of *theōsis* and Western doctrines of sanctification refer to the transformation of the disciple through the indwelling Holy Spirit. In this text the disciple is called to live in union with Christ in Christ's life and mission, in the power of the Spirit. That is, disciples are called to a sanctified life, "setting their faces toward Jerusalem," utterly abandoning themselves to the love and purposes of God. Like farmers preparing the field for planting, disciples must look ahead to the future, keeping in mind the future harvest. They must put their hand to the plow and not look back. Apostolic power to preach, teach, and heal will be given to them, yet they will also experience rejection and persecution. The journey to Jerusalem, beginning with the Samaritan village, will show them how to travel the apostolic way in the spirit of Christ.

ELAINE A. HEATH

Pastoral Perspective

and beliefs. The big question is, What does that mean? Is it simply a matter of listening and learning, or is there a deeper commitment involved?

Rather than replying with a simple, "Come along," Jesus cuts to the chase by responding, "Foxes have holes, and birds of the air have nests; but the Son of Man has nowhere to lay his head." Those who choose to follow in his path may find that they have no place to call home, either physically or culturally. In the first case, while serving in Jesus' name may take place right outside your front door, it is unreasonable to expect that a call to service will always be limited to a particular locale. In the second case, Christian values and service are not always politically correct or culturally popular. Following in the Way may put a believer at odds with the secular world, a condition that should never hinder our resolve. Our path is identified by the things we treasure, the priorities we set, and the way we treat others. See Luke 12:34.

This point is emphasized in the second scenario (vv. 59–60), where Jesus issues the simple invitation, "Follow me." In this case the prospective follower responds with a request to go and bury his father first. Contrast this to the disciples' response in Luke 5:11. Exegetically, there is a clear implication that there are more significant priorities to attend to before one is free to follow. In the third scenario (vv. 61–62), those priorities take the form of family needs and obligations. What initially seems a reasonable request is actually another obstacle to living out one's call. These excuses represent a request to go in a different direction. What Jesus offers is the opportunity to follow on a journey of faith.

The Christian journey does not demand that we reject our responsibilities to family and vocation but, rather, encourages us to see those needs in the light of our faith and through the lens of our deepening commitment to Christ.

RICHARD J. SHAFFER JR.

Exegetical Perspective

"the Son of Man has no place to lay his head," for they have denied him the hospitality on which he depends. Therefore those who follow Jesus can expect the same destiny. While Luke portrays some who serve Jesus in their own villages (8:39; cf. 8:1–3) and provide hospitality (10:38–42), he speaks of the special demands on those who follow Jesus on this critical mission.

Whereas the first would-be disciple volunteers to follow Jesus, Jesus summons the second one, "Follow me." In view of the Torah's commandment, "Honor your father and your mother" (Exod. 20:12), and Jewish traditions regarding the responsibility to provide for their burial (Tob. 4:3–4), the man's request that he be allowed to bury his father is reasonable. Interpreters who debate whether the man's father was already dead probably miss the point of the dialogue, for Luke's primary concern is that the man placed conditions on his willingness to follow Jesus. Jesus' response, "Let the dead bury their own dead," indicates that the man did not recognize the urgency of the moment, for the demands of discipleship supersede the normal obligations of the Torah. Like the people in the parable later in Luke's narrative (14:16–24) who continued the normal activities of buying land and marrying without seeing the urgency of the moment, this man did not recognize that the call of Jesus takes precedence over "father and mother and children and brothers and sisters" (14:26).

The third would-be disciple volunteers to follow Jesus (vv. 61–62), but also makes a reasonable request. His response recalls Elijah's call to Elisha to become a disciple (1 Kgs. 19:19–20) and Elisha's request that he be permitted to kiss his father and mother good-bye. Whereas Elijah granted the request, Jesus says, "No one who puts a hand to the plow and looks back is fit for the kingdom of God," alluding to the fact that Elisha was plowing (1 Kgs. 19:19) when Elijah called him. To "look back" is to place the demands of the family above the call of discipleship. To have the aptitude (NRSV "be fit") to share Jesus' work of proclaiming the kingdom is to accept demands that are more stringent than those of Elijah. Jesus' disciples share in both his rejection (vv. 51–56) and his destiny (vv. 57–62).

JAMES W. THOMPSON

Homiletical Perspective

this passage is primarily about discipleship. That would be easier to do if the disciples fared better in Luke's treatment, but they do not comprehend the multiple predictions of Jesus' fate that he offers. They quarrel about greatness immediately after his foretelling of the cross. They fall asleep in his hour of need. They betray and desert him and consider the initial testimony of his resurrection "an idle tale."

For this reason, I think the larger narrative trajectory of Luke's Gospel would suggest a different emphasis: Jesus' commitment to embrace the cross for the sake of the world. The heart of these passages is neither the road of discipleship nor Jesus' heroic courage in facing the cross. Rather, it is a single-mindedness of purpose that is prompted by God's profound love for humanity and all the world. At the beginning of his account, Luke traces Jesus' lineage back to Adam, offering a link not merely to David or to Abraham but to all humanity. By the end of his account in Acts, Luke has extended the trajectory of the gospel from Jerusalem to Rome and thereby the whole world. Jesus' concern, according to Luke, is universal. Similarly, it is rooted in forgiveness. After all, it is only in Luke that Jesus on the cross forgives those who have crucified him.

This emphasis on God's all-encompassing love is highlighted in these passages by the rejection of violence against the Samaritans: it is not simply contrary to Jesus' vision but incompatible with his very identity and mission. Similarly, those who would embrace and be embraced by the radical love of God made known in Jesus and his cross must necessarily see that this love is contrary to all human conceptions of love. Everything—friendship, familial connections, piety, discipleship—looks different when viewed through the lens of God's sacrificial love. The preacher who emphasizes this love may be surprised at the reactions such a sermon provokes. After all, there are people in our world, and even parts of ourselves, that we may not believe deserve such consideration. Whatever the reaction, the preacher who treads this homiletic road will be in good company.

DAVID J. LOSE

2 Kings 5:1-14

¹Naaman, commander of the army of the king of Aram, was a great man and in high favor with his master, because by him the LORD had given victory to Aram. The man, though a mighty warrior, suffered from leprosy. ²Now the Arameans on one of their raids had taken a young girl captive from the land of Israel, and she served Naaman's wife. ³She said to her mistress, "If only my lord were with the prophet who is in Samaria! He would cure him of his leprosy." ⁴So Naaman went in and told his lord just what the girl from the land of Israel had said. ⁵And the king of Aram said, "Go then, and I will send along a letter to the king of Israel."

He went, taking with him ten talents of silver, six thousand shekels of gold, and ten sets of garments. ⁶He brought the letter to the king of Israel, which read, "When this letter reaches you, know that I have sent to you my servant Naaman, that you may cure him of his leprosy." ⁷When the king of Israel read the letter, he tore his clothes and said, "Am I God, to give death or life, that this man sends word to me to cure a man of his leprosy? Just look and see how he is trying to pick a quarrel with me."

Theological Perspective

Second Kings 5:1–14 contains a number of rich theological avenues for preacher and congregation to explore. First, there is the wonderful contrast between the inability of bumbling kings to communicate effectively (vv. 4–7) and the power of God to restore Naaman to health completely (v. 14). Secondly, in verse 7, the king of Israel rhetorically asks, "Am I God, to give death or life?" which could fuel powerful sermons on, among other things, a broken health-care system that plays God with people's lives or a government's decision to send soldiers to fight a war of choice rather than necessity.

On another front, a slave girl—the ancient world's consummate nonperson—delivers the good news to Naaman that there is relief for his suffering (vv. 2–3). This is yet another biblical instance of those to whom society attributes little intrinsic value serving as effective heralds of the power and presence of God.

In addition, there is the text's clear witness, by way of Naaman, an Aramean, that the providence and healing reach of Israel's God is not limited to the people of the covenant. Israel is elected, this suggests, not to the exclusion of the rest of creation, but in order to provide a concrete witness to God for its benefit and on its behalf, a principle magnanimously exemplified by the Israelite slave girl.

Pastoral Perspective

Kaboom! Our congregants probably are thinking more about Fourth of July fireworks than they are about God's continuing providence in our personal and collective lives. The latter is what we witness in this final text from the lectionary's Elijah/Elisha cycle: Elisha providentially heals the Aramean Naaman.

Surprisingly, Elisha plays an indirect part in this drama. The supporting actors are the king of Israel and the Aramean general, Naaman, both of whom misconceive how God acts. The main actor, God, demonstrates God's continuing providence for individuals and nations and foreshadows the establishment of baptism as one of two visible signs pointing to God's invisible truth.

The king of Israel was disturbed enough by Naaman's petition to adopt the mourning action of tearing his clothes. Rather than seeing an opportunity for God to act through the request, he saw a trap set by the Aramean king. Elisha's offstage action helped the king see God's providential direction.

The king of Israel made what psychologists call a fundamental attribution error. He overestimated the internal and underestimated the external factors when trying to understand the behaviors of the Aramean king. His error is common. Think of the times we have been driving and the person in front of us executes an unexpected move. Our first reaction is to call the

8But when Elisha the man of God heard that the king of Israel had torn his clothes, he sent a message to the king. "Why have you torn your clothes? Let him come to me, that he may learn that there is a prophet in Israel." 9So Naaman came with his horses and chariots, and halted at the entrance of Elisha's house. 10Elisha sent a messenger to him, saying, "Go, wash in the Jordan seven times, and your flesh shall be restored and you shall be clean." 11But Naaman became angry and went away, saying, "I thought that for me he would surely come out, and stand and call on the name of the LORD his God, and would wave his hand over the spot, and cure the leprosy! 12Are not Abana and Pharpar, the rivers of Damascus, better than all the waters of Israel? Could I not wash in them, and be clean?" He turned and went away in a rage. 13But his servants approached and said to him, "Father, if the prophet had commanded you to do something difficult, would you not have done it? How much more, when all he said to you was, 'Wash, and be clean'?" 14So he went down and immersed himself seven times in the Jordan, according to the word of the man of God; his flesh was restored like the flesh of a young boy, and he was clean.

Exegetical Perspective

Following the traditional paragraphing of the Hebrew and English texts, the lectionary cuts this passage off at verse 14. On the one hand, dividing the text this way acknowledges that the words at the end of verse 15 ("please accept a present from your servant") introduce the next story about Gehazi's greed and are not essential to Naaman's story. But if the passage runs verses 1–14, then Naaman's healing seems to be only one more miracle among the many attributed to Elisha in chapters 2–6, and Naaman becomes simply one more witness to the power Elisha has inherited from Elijah. Only Naaman's status as a prominent foreigner distinguishes him from the other beneficiaries of Elisha's miracles. Cutting the pericope off at verse 14 focuses our attention on the miracle itself, rather than what happens because of the miracle (i.e., the conversion of Naaman).

On the other hand, including verse 15 in the reading of the story allows the listener to conclude that prophetic miracles have a purpose beyond themselves: the miracle convinces Naaman that "there is no God in all the earth except in Israel" (v. 15). Elisha had assumed that the healing of Naaman would reinforce his own status as a prophet (v. 8). But verse 15 tells us that God accomplished through the agency of the prophet even more than the prophet had in fact intended. With the

Homiletical Perspective

This story is characterized by irony. The people who should be in the know, such as the king of Israel, appear clueless, while the marginalized, such as the Israelite servant girl, perceive accurately what God is doing. The central figure, Naaman, who seeks healing, almost cheats himself of his healing because of his arrogance. This irony invites us to reflect on two ideas: both the knowledge of God and the truth of our circumstances may come from unexpected sources, and God's providence is complex and does not always match our assumptions. Elisha's response to Naaman also invites us to consider the ways we respond to people currently outside the church, who seek a place in the Christian community.

Unexpected Sources of Knowledge. The irony that people with little power or wealth perceive God's work, when the powerful may not, recurs in the OT and NT. In this story, a captive Israelite girl proposes a solution to the general Naaman's problem. The king of Israel is perplexed by Naaman's problem, and Elisha, apparently not at the royal court, offers to help both the king and the general. The general's servants show him the weakness of his own reasoning, coaxing him to take the treatment Elisha recommends. In other words, the officials of Aram, the king of Israel, and the general do not perceive

2 Kings 5:1-14

Theological Perspective

What makes the slave girl's witness effective is that she knows about Elisha and the reliability of the God in whose name he prophesies. She is one of God's chosen people and a participant in God's bold and risk-laden social project: entering into an intimate, historical relationship with a specific people who live in a particular part of the world and who see, as all human beings do, through unique cultural lenses forged by traditions and past experiences.

One of the longest-standing debates in the history of Christian theology concerns general revelation, the witness to God that is "out there" for those with minds that reason and eyes that see. Psalm 19:1, for instance, states that "the heavens are telling the glory of God; and the firmament proclaims his handiwork," which suggests that significant things about God can be known in and through the created order. Echoing this, Paul, in Romans 1:20, writes that God's "eternal power and divine nature, invisible though they are, have been understood and seen through the things he has made."

Most Christian theologians do not dispute that there is a general witness available to all. The debate turns, rather, on whether this witness leads human beings to the kind of knowledge of God that they need most and, further, what the relationship of this witness is to special revelation, God's self-disclosure in and through concrete historical and cultural channels. Historically, the three main positions taken in this debate are that (1) general revelation is a useful preparation for special revelation; (2) special revelation, in a fallen world, can stand only in contradiction to the ways in which sinful humanity receives and mishandles general revelation; and (3) special revelation is, at best, a parochial reflection and, at worst, a harmful distorter of general revelation, which is superior to it.

While 2 Kings 5:1–14 does little to give either of the first two positions any leverage over the other, it does stand in contradiction to the third position, which received considerable attention during the Enlightenment and enjoys support among those who now champion Enlightenment views on religion. According to this view, the persistence of historical, culturally concrete religion stands as an unhelpful obstacle to the unification of humanity, which can best be achieved by adherence to culture-transcending, universal standards of reason and morality. If Jews, Muslims, and Christians, for instance, would only jettison the "tribal" moorings of their respective theologies, progress could be made in peaceful coexistence and cooperation.

Pastoral Perspective

person names and attribute an internal character flaw to the person. More often than not, there is an external factor (such as an obstacle in the road) causing the unexpected maneuver. God is the external factor acting in relation to the Aramean king, but the king of Israel cannot perceive this until Elisha reveals it.

Naaman misconceives God's actions through Elisha on both a personal and a nationalistic level. When Elisha sends only a messenger to Naaman with instructions for how he can be healed, Naaman rails at the perceived insult. Naaman then takes umbrage at Elisha's choice of river in which he should wash, claiming that the rivers of his own nation are superior. On both levels, Naaman's pride prevents his perceiving God's providential acts conveyed by Elisha, Elisha's messenger, and Naaman's own servants.

Naaman pridefully expects his wealth and power to obtain his cure. When that fails, he expects a theophany from God in order to heal him. On both counts, Naaman misconceives God's providential actions. One way to understand providence is to see it as "God's preserving creation, cooperating with all creatures and guiding or governing all things toward the accomplishment of God's purposes."[1] God does not create some people who are immune from tragedy (as invincible teenagers would like to believe). Similarly, God does not leave us bereft of support when tragedy does strike; rather, God employs ordinary people to act in extraordinary ways.

In the biblical era, many believed that those with physical disabilities or suffering from debilitating circumstances were in their situation as a result of God's judgment upon their sinfulness or that of their parents. Jesus clarifies God's rejection of that misconception in his encounter with a blind man in John's Gospel (John 9:3, "Neither this man nor his parents sinned; he was born blind so that God's works might be revealed in him"). Jesus reframes tragedy as an opportunity for revealing God's providence. Elisha reframes the king's clothes-rending lament as both an opportunity for showing God's providential care for all people and as an evangelical witness to Naaman for faith in YHWH, regardless of his nationality.

A recent poll by the Barna Group showed that 9 percent of the adult American population identifies itself as having no faith.[2] That figure represents 20 million of the nation's 220 million adults. More

---

1. Donald K. McKim, *Presbyterian Questions, Presbyterian Answers: Exploring Christian Faith* (Louisville, KY: Geneva Press, 2003), 25.
2. The Barna Group, Ventura, CA, June 17, 2007, http://www.barna.org. This research group specializes in faith issues.

Exegetical Perspective

traditional division of the text (vv. 1–14) it seems that Naaman's obedience leads to his healing. With the inclusion of verse 15, it becomes clear that Naaman's healing (his experience of grace) leads to his confession of faith. Thus theological presuppositions play a part in deciding where the story that begins in verse 1 should end.

Naaman is introduced to us as an Aramean whose prominence derives from the role he has already (unwittingly) played in the working out of YHWH's will through political and historical processes. Naaman was in "high favor" with the king of Aram "because by him the LORD had given victory to Aram" (v. 1). While neither the king of Aram nor the king of Israel is named in this story, the literary setting implies that the victory mentioned here refers to the battle that led to Ahab's death (1 Kgs. 22:29–38). In Elijah's time, God had promised to wipe out Ahab's line (1 Kgs. 21:17–24), but that has not yet happened. In this literary setting, it appears that the king of Israel mentioned in verses 5–7 is Jehoram, son of Ahab, who reigned for twelve years after his brother Ahaziah's death (2 Kgs. 3:1).

King Jehoram is justifiably upset when the Aramean general who was responsible for his father's death pays him a visit and delivers a "letter" (*sepher*) containing what seems to be an impossible demand from the king of Aram (v. 6). The king of Israel "tore his clothes" (v. 7) as a sign of his distress (Gen. 37:34; 2 Kgs. 11:14). His exclamation, "Am I God, to give death or life?" (v. 7) echoes the vocabulary of Deuteronomy 32:39. Thus Jehoram seems piously aware that healing can come only from God. Unlike the captive Israelite girl, he is not aware of (or is not willing to acknowledge) the presence of a prophet in Israel who can bring about such healing. Thus he thinks the king of Aram is engaged in a political maneuver, trying to find a pretext for another war (v. 7).

While servants (or slaves) play a key role in the story, their reasons for doing so are not specified. With the narrative economy typical of biblical stories, we are not told what motivates the unnamed captive Israelite girl to draw Naaman's attention to the healing powers of "the prophet who is in Samaria." And when Naaman is enraged by Elisha's directions to wash away his leprosy in the waters of the Jordan, we are not told what motivates his servants to persuade him to give this embarrassingly simple cure a try (v. 13). If their honorific use of "father" rather than the more usual "master" or "lord" indicates more than mere polite respect (2 Kgs. 2:12; 1 Sam. 24:11), this is not spelled out in the text.

Homiletical Perspective

where and how God is at work. The captive girl, the servants, and the itinerant prophet do perceive where and how the Lord is moving.

This irony may provide hope to contemporary churchgoers who are disempowered and marginalized. Alternately, it may sound tough hearted to churchgoers who enjoy affluence and influence. The story makes clear that material disadvantages are not spiritual disadvantages. God calls people regardless of circumstance. God can empower the disenfranchised to find their own voices in the midst of their circumstances and to work for greater justice. Conversely, the passage implies that material advantages may hinder a believer's perceptions of God. It invites those with power to identify, pay attention to, and learn from those who are marginalized.

Whatever sociological context we are in, we may create and act on stereotypes about those who are different from ourselves. We all tend to turn one who differs from us into an "other" who is somehow problematic and should therefore be ignored or dismissed. Every one of us is probably someone else's "other." The irony that wisdom and insight come from unexpected sources invites us all to strive to curb this tendency. This story encourages us to recognize that any person may have important insights and be an instrument of God's saving work.

Complexity of God's Love and Purposes. Naaman states preconceptions about the way his healing should take place. He expects at least a little special attention from the prophet. Elisha's directions do not match these preconceptions. We might expect God somehow to punish Naaman for his pride, at least by withholding healing, but, ironically, God heals Naaman, who is Syrian and not Israelite and who is skeptical of Elisha's God. The irony of Naaman's healing offers the opportunity for careful thought about the ways we understand God's involvement in our lives and the lives of those around us.

Like Naaman, we sometimes assume that our expectations are the measure of God's ability to work in creation. We want God to do something for us, in the particular way we want it done, on a schedule we devise. I once heard a member of a healing prayer group remark, "*Our* group gets results," implying that the group's expectations of healing were the measure of God's ability, much as Naaman judges the efficacy of Elisha's God through his preconceptions about the way in which his healing should occur. The irony of Naaman's healing discourages our tendency to look for God's work in terms of our own desires or expectations.

2 Kings 5:1-14

Theological Perspective

Our text suggests just the opposite. Reaching out a healing hand to a member of a different race, culture, or religion does not require that one check one's traditions at the door in the interest of meeting that person on "neutral ground." The slave girl is able to help Naaman by drawing on the resources her religion and culture provide, not by jettisoning them. Were she to put those things aside and approach Naaman as a blank slate, a girl from nowhere, Naaman would not have found relief from his leprosy. In like manner, Elisha calls Naaman to immerse himself not in the domestic Syrian waters he prefers (v. 12), but in what, to him, are the foreign waters of the Jordan, a river that is, up to this point, usually spoken of in terms of its ability to separate Israel from its neighbors (Num. 34:12).

In this story, healing happens because of three main factors. First, the slave girl is strong enough to embrace and make use of the traditions of her nation while enslaved in a foreign land in which she is a cultural and religious outsider. Second, Naaman demonstrates similar courage in his willingness to seek help from a theology and a culture that are both strange to him, a willingness that is concretely expressed by his voluntary immersion in the waters of the Jordan (v. 14), the site of important events in the history of God's dealings with Israel (e.g., Josh. 3:1–17).

The third and most important factor in all of this is God. The slave girl, Elisha, and the river Jordan are set apart, not because they are intrinsically unique, but because God elects to work through them, in all their particularity, for the good of Naaman. God does not operate here by way of the impersonal vacuousness of above-the-fray generalities but chooses, rather, to meet humanity where we really live—in time and space, and in history and culture.

God works in this text through what is not only culturally specific but also foreign and strange. This should say something to contemporary persons, congregations, and societies now struggling with racial, cultural, and religious differences. It should also function as a wake-up call for us who always seem to be caught looking for the God of the Bible in the same old places—or in no place at all.

TREVOR EPPEHIMER

Pastoral Perspective

significantly, the percentage of adults claiming no faith is increasing with each successive generation. Why is it so hard for a significant percentage of Americans to believe in God? Maybe it is because all human beings, like Naaman, can misunderstand God's providence.

William Sloane Coffin sheds some light on why some people do not have faith in God. He says, "If we misconceive of God as Father Protector, as one, so to speak, in charge of all the uncontrolled contingences along the way, then each disappointment reduces what may confidently be affirmed about God. And this is how most people lose their faith." He goes on to say, "There is nothing anti-intellectual about the leap of faith, for faith is not believing without proof but trusting without reservation."[3] Naaman was afraid to trust.

If we mistakenly think God is controlling our lives rather than preserving, cooperating, and guiding us, the first hint of difficulty in our lives shatters our ability to "trust without reservation." With a more robust understanding of God's gracious providence, we are better able to discern how to make the most of God's providential actions in our lives, regardless of what external pressures we encounter.

Today's social, economic, and political pressures leave us little reason to "trust without reservation." When faced with similar pressures, the founders of the United States elected to "form a more perfect union, establish Justice . . . and establish this Constitution for the United States of America." God's answer to the pressures we face in every era is to graciously gift the church with the sacraments to establish and nurture faith. Both baptism and Communion are visible signs pointing to God's invisible grace. Sacraments can reinforce this more robust understanding of God's providence and help all of us avoid the king's error of attribution and Naaman's prideful misconceptions.

When Naaman was able to "trust without reservation," to accept the simple instructions "Wash and be clean," he was healed (v. 14). His cleaning foreshadowed Jesus' baptizing us with water through the power of the Holy Spirit. When we share in baptism and Communion, we both remind ourselves of God's providence, reinforce our ability to "trust without reservation," and share that trust with those who are touched by each one of us—maybe at the Fourth of July fireworks!

CARRIE N. MITCHELL

3. William Sloane Coffin, *Credo* (Louisville, KY: Westminster John Knox Press, 2004), 8 and 16.

Exegetical Perspective

However, the narrator does give us an unusually detailed look into Naaman's thoughts (vv. 11–12). Naaman tells us that he has several reasons for becoming angry (v. 11). His pride is wounded by the low-key, if not outright rude, reception he receives from Elisha. The prophet does not even come to meet with him directly, but sends a messenger. Naaman clearly had preconceptions about how the miracle would be performed (v. 11) and feels somewhat insulted that the prophet did not make a big production out of calling on YHWH (vv. 10, 11). The Hebrew word meaning "big" (*gadol*) is translated "great" in verse 1 and "difficult" in verse 13. Thus Naaman is said to be "a big man" (*'ish gadol*), and he expected his cure to be a "big deal" (*dabar gadol*). Ironically, when he follows the advice of the little girl (*na'arah qetanna*) who had been taken captive by the Arameans on one of their raids into Israel (vv. 2–3), his diseased flesh becomes like the flesh of a little boy (*na'ar qaton*).

When Naaman's flesh was returned (*wayyashob*) to normal (NRSV "restored," v. 14) he himself "returned" (*wayyashob*) to "the man of God" and made his confession of faith (v. 15). It is his experience of salvation that brings about his faith, not the other way around!

Jesus uses the healing of Naaman as a model for his own ministry among non-Israelites (Luke 4:27). When Jesus publicly accepts his call (Luke 4:18–19), the citizens of Nazareth expect him to carry it out among his own people. They are angry when he tells them he intends to exert himself on behalf of foreigners, as his predecessors Elijah and Elisha had done. Jesus, like Elisha, intends to heal outsiders, even those considered enemies of Israel, to make clear that the grace of God is extended to those who do nothing to qualify for salvation.

KATHLEEN A. ROBERTSON FARMER

Homiletical Perspective

Naaman's healing does not occur as he expects, but as God chooses.

Like Naaman, we also may make our expectations the measure of God's work, when we assume that God is exclusively on our side regarding all sorts of relationships—interpersonal, international, between ourselves and the natural world. The irony of Naaman's healing also discourages this tendency of ours. His healing shows God as nonvindictive, including different groups of people in divine purposes.

Approaching the Unchurched. This story suggests the breadth and complexity of God's love, not only through the irony of Naaman's healing, but also in the way Elisha engages Naaman. Elisha indicates that our understanding of the complexity of God's purposes bears both on the ways we conceive of ourselves and others in relation to God, and the ways we actually respond to those who seek God.

Elisha only appears twice in this story. He sends word to the king of Israel, and he dispatches his servant to give instructions to Naaman. If this were a movie, Elisha would have little more than a walk-on part. However, Elisha's presence in the story is greater than his actual appearance.

Elisha's response to Naaman represents a way those who are churched may respond to those who are unchurched. Naaman is not part of the elect of Israel. He is a conqueror of part of Israel. He does not profess faith in the Lord. Yet Elisha offers to heal him. Naaman is healed, even with his doubt, even without professing Elisha's God as the one true God (v. 15).

Similarly, we who are churched may reach out to the unchurched without first requiring of them what we consider an appropriate confession. This story moves us to welcome strangers without insisting that they first embrace all the theological and ecclesiastical beliefs of our particular tradition. By deemphasizing up-front commitments, this passage also implicitly cautions against our pushing seekers too quickly to become committed members—to be in church every Sunday, tithing, teaching Sunday school, serving on a committee or board. Naaman's experience suggests that we should enable people to experience God's love and power and that ironically this experience may bring forth their confession of faith (v. 15).

HAYWOOD BARRINGER SPANGLER

Psalm 30

¹I will extol you, O Lord, for you have drawn me up,
  and did not let my foes rejoice over me.
²O Lord my God, I cried to you for help,
  and you have healed me.
³O Lord, you brought up my soul from Sheol,
  restored me to life from among those gone down to the Pit.

⁴Sing praises to the Lord, O you his faithful ones,
  and give thanks to his holy name.
⁵For his anger is but for a moment;
  his favor is for a lifetime.
Weeping may linger for the night,
  but joy comes with the morning.

⁶As for me, I said in my prosperity,
  "I shall never be moved."
⁷By your favor, O Lord,
  you had established me as a strong mountain;

Theological Perspective

During the Pentecost season of fiery anointing and inspiration, Psalm 30 resonates with phenomenal encouragement, illuminating difficult realities, ambiguities, and uncertainties of our lives. Set as prayer (vv. 1–3), this praise psalm notes that God does not let our enemies overcome us. When we cry out for healing, God succors us; God offers relief and help for us during bad times and good, for the God of Sarah, Hagar, Rachel, and Leah promised never, ever to forsake them or us. God provided the psalmist deliverance from terrors of horrific disease. This same God brings us from destitution or depression, sickness or misery; heals and restores us; cures us and makes us whole again. While we have heard God's love for us preached, what do we do with all the suffering in our midst?

Suffering that occurs amid natural disasters, illness, and human-directed violence does not indicate God's absence. God is good news, regardless of what happens. Being human, we need reminders about God's faithfulness, given destructive tsunamis, hurricanes, droughts, and floods. We need to know that the millions suffering debilitating diseases, from Alzheimer's to HIV/AIDS to cancers, and the thousands of people who experience organ failure, waiting for transplant operations that may never come, are not being punished by a wrathful divinity

Pastoral Perspective

Has there ever lived a soul so hardened, a heart so cold, or a mind so thoughtless as never to have felt the urge to say, "Thanks"? Such a one may not have addressed the God most of us know, may only have addressed some "unknown god," another person, or simply "luck." Nevertheless, is there a human being so utterly void of the primordial instinct toward gratitude that he or she has never felt the urge to say, "Thanks"?

Years ago, while I was serving a small new church struggling to establish itself in the community, the congregation did their generous best, and still the salary was meager. Our small family was by no means poor, but money was tight. With a new baby on the way and our first house to furnish, finances were a struggle. Consequently, it came as a welcome surprise to us when one day there arrived in the mail a dirty, rumpled five-dollar bill. It arrived in a plain envelope, hand addressed, with no return address and no note, but there it was: an old five-dollar bill.

A month later the same thing happened. Again, there was no return address, no note—just a single dirty five-dollar bill. The pattern continued for more than a year, and with each monthly mystery gift my wife and I searched our brains for some clue to the identity of our benefactor. At Christmas, we meticulously compared the handwriting on the

you hid your face;
    I was dismayed.

8To you, O Lord, I cried,
    and to the Lord I made supplication:
9"What profit is there in my death,
    if I go down to the Pit?
Will the dust praise you?
    Will it tell of your faithfulness?
10Hear, O Lord, and be gracious to me!
    O Lord, be my helper!"

11You have turned my mourning into dancing;
    you have taken off my sackcloth
    and clothed me with joy,
12so that my soul may praise you and not be silent.
    O Lord my God, I will give thanks to you forever.

Exegetical Perspective

Psalm 30's variegated poetics develop through subtle word links between four strophes extolling and thanking YHWH for life-saving rescue. The psalmist, after suffering deathlike separation from God and unashamedly contending with heaven, celebrates a marvelous recovery and then summons others to praise also, confident that YHWH will hear and help again.

While unreliable for dating, the superscription ("A Song at the dedication of the temple. Of David," not printed above) suggests a 187 BCE reapplication. The mention of "a *mizmor*—a song of the *hanukkah* of the house belonging to David" has ambiguities that determine how we read the psalm. What exactly belongs to David? By the Maccabean restoration, neither temple nor any psalms could rightly be "David's," except in retrospective metaphors of faith. Consequently, the psalmic voice closely identifies with this latter-day turbulent history and reconsecrated temple, mixing verses drawn from Israel's store of personal and national thanksgiving songs, such as Hezekiah's political, philosophical, and private amalgam of lament and thanksgiving, Isaiah 38:9–20, as well as Psalm 90's quotable expressions of faith.

Strophe 1 (vv. 1–4). Verses 1–3 invoke YHWH three times, the first instance preceded by the organizing purpose of the psalm ("I will uplift you[r name]"),

Homiletical Perspective

Thanksgiving. This is self-evidently a song of thanksgiving in which, as Walter Brueggemann has observed, "the speaker is now on the other side of a lament or complaint." And so the psalm concerns "a rescue, intervention, or inversion of a quite concrete situation of distress which is still fresh in the mind of the speaker."[1] The psalmist does not bother to give us the details of his plight but begins by praising YHWH for an act of deliverance variously described in the past tense as "you have drawn me up, and did not let my foes rejoice over me" (v. 1), "you have healed me" (v. 2b), "you brought up my soul from Sheol" and "restored me to life" (v. 3). Not content to praise God by himself, the psalmist enlists other "faithful ones" in singing thanks to the "holy name" of God his deliverer (v. 4).

Thanksgiving, as G. K. Chesterton has memorably suggested in his little book on Francis of Assisi, is a matter of celebrating one's dependence upon God. "Dependence" literally means "a hanging from." For Chesterton, Francis following his conversion came to see the world, as it were, upside down. It is as if, in one of his strange dreams, Francis saw the city of Assisi, with its massive foundations and walls and

1. Walter Brueggemann, *The Message of the Psalms* (Minneapolis: Augsburg, 1984), 125–26.

Psalm 30

Theological Perspective

for their sins or their parents' sins. Even when we accept the fact that natural disaster and illness occur, it is difficult to think of the millions of unnecessary deaths and the destruction that occur annually because of human choice: homicides, suicides, deaths due to drunk driving, hate crimes, rapes and sexual abuse, domestic violence, civil and global wars.

Theologically, questions about why suffering occurs come under the heading of theodicy (Gk. *theos* [God] and *dikē* [justice]). If God is all-good and all-powerful, why does evil continue to exist? Two Christian thinkers who treat this question are Augustine, who presents the free-will argument (God gives humanity free will; hence bad things happen because fallible human beings make wrong choices), and Irenaeus, who presents the soul-making argument (the spiritual and moral development of immature creatures occurs, amid divinely appointed good and evil, toward God's perfection and good purpose). Such philosophy often seems to fall short when we are hurting. Given the amount of global illness and disease, anxiety from global economic devastation, and the need for divine bailouts, some question God's grace and capacity to heal.

Healing does not necessarily mean cure from illness. Healing can occur when a person comes to accept her or his impending death or incurable malady, aware that God remains steadfast. Further, suffering is not an eternal reality. New life unfolds as experiential joy comes in the morning. Morning can indicate the next day, or next moment: instances of realized joy. That we suffer does not mean God forsakes or abandons us. We can experience joy following the "mourning in the morning," signaling our God-given lives are gifts (vv. 4–5).[1]

One historic minister of the gospel whose compelling faith reckoned with the profound nature of this psalm was Peter Marshall (1902–49), pastor of the New York Avenue Presbyterian Church in Washington, D.C., and chaplain of the U.S. Senate. Marshall loved God and God's people mightily. He moved his congregation's music ministry from a staid, proper vocal quartet to a flourishing choir. He gave newlyweds privacy in the church when the husband was about to be shipped off to war. When there was no room inside, people would stand outside in the rain to hear Marshall preach. He

Pastoral Perspective

anonymous envelopes to the handwriting on our Christmas cards, without any success. Until this day, I do not know who sent those five-dollar bills. While we were deeply grateful, it became exasperating not to know whom to thank.

The writer of Psalm 30 has no such problem. The psalmist knows his benefactor and names God with confidence ("I extol you, LORD"). Moreover, he identifies the reason for his gratitude: he has been healed from what appears to have been a deathly illness. Thus with uninhibited exuberance and thanksgiving he credits God for turning his mourning into dancing.

Many may recognize the same feeling upon hearing the words "cancer free," "the child is going to be all right," or "the fever is gone." Some people, however, do not connect the dots to God and prefer more secular sayings, such as "we beat the odds" or "thank our lucky stars." The psalmist, on the other hand, is confident that his deliverance is due to God's loving grace and connects his praise directly to his prayers for deliverance. The writer knows from experience the feeling of having been abandoned by God. He knows the agony of what he calls God's "anger." Nonetheless, his faith prompts him to cry out, "O Lord, help me."

It is risky theology to connect healing directly to answered prayer. There is too much evidence of times when conscientious prayer "did not work." There are too many hucksters offering healing for a mail-in contribution. Nevertheless, the psalm does offer a style of prayer and praise that reflects life's reality.

In his commentary on this psalm, James Mays writes, "The Psalm shows how prayer and praise can together become a rubric for holding the experiences of life in relation to God."[1] The psalmist admits to times when he felt God was hidden ("you hid your face," v. 7), suggesting previous experiences when his prayers may have gone unanswered. Nevertheless, even in his darkest moments of doubt and despair, he keeps a residual sense of God's prevailing providence that prompts him to plead, "Hear, O LORD, and be gracious to me! O LORD, be my helper!" (v. 10). With healing comes the writer's renewed trust in God's providence, through good times and bad, the result being that "Now he sees his life as a vocation of thanksgiving to the Lord."[2]

Novelist Ray Bradbury paints a contemporary literary portrait of this psalm in his short story

1. Walter Brueggemann, *The Message of the Psalms*, Augsburg Old Testament Studies; A Theological Commentary (Minneapolis: Augsburg, 1984), 126–27; J. Clinton McCann Jr., "The Book of Psalms," in *The New Interpreter's Bible*, vol. 4 (Nashville: Abingdon Press, 1996), 797.

1. James L. Mays, *Psalms*, Interpretation series (Louisville, KY: John Knox Press, 1994), 142.
2. Ibid.

which corresponds with the last words of the final strophe ("I will praise you"). Midway through the psalm an inverse scenario counters, "Will dust praise you?" (v. 9). Another negated inversion, verse 1, keys on a second motif, "joy"; God does/did not allow enemies to "joy (rejoice) over me," which shares root *smkh* in verse 11: "clothed with joy." While thematically akin, "joy [of] the morning," verse 5, is rooted in *rnh*—an exclamatory shout of glee. Memorable poetics build on such synonyms and their placement.

Strophe 1 propounds weighty existential reasons for gladness: "you have drawn me up [like water from a well]," "you healed me" after "I cried-for-saving." Analogous to being "drawn up" comes "you brought up . . . my soul" from Sheol and "restored-me-to-life," either "from among those who are gone down" or (the Hebrew is ambiguous) "from *my* going down" to the Pit, again neatly paralleling being healed in the prior verse as well as echoing the first half of verse 3. But, can individual resurrection be so factually literal for the psalmist, or is it metaphorically national for Israel? Indeed, it sings the very fate of the former temple once destroyed and brought to dust, yet now rebuilt. This *mizmor*-song "belongs to" the rededicated house.

Verse 4 stands apart. A priestly voice summons worshipers to sing to YHWH in an even trimeter couplet that breaks with the dominant 4 + 2 and 4 + 3 metrical rhythms of accented words in the paired Hebrew phrases of strophe 1. This liturgical interlude prepares for strophe 2's initial change of address about God and underscores the primary intent of the psalm—worshipfully to give thanks—binding the first and last strophes. As duplicated exactly in Psalm 97:11, the "holy *name*" (*zeker*), verse 4, means much more than the rubric YHWH. Psalm 6:5, reminiscent of Psalm 30:9's lament, signifies *zeker* as "your remembrance" and suggests a memorial, pillar, or monument, appropriate to a summons to sing sacred commemorations within a sanctuary.

Strophe 2 (vv. 5–7). Verse 5's leading "For," like verse 12's "So," persuades the congregation to offer thanks. The uneven 3 + 2 and 5 + 4 accent patterns return with verses 5–7. Statements with quick ripostes declare profound theological issues and summary converse consequences. Echoing Isaiah 54:7, God's anger is but "for a-brief-moment" in a tightly turned antithetical phrase of assurance about a lifetime of favor. Its parallel imagery of "lodging for the evening" personifies weeping as a pilgrim petitioner spending the night in temple courtyards. The terse contrast lacks a verb, usually supplied (NRSV) as "comes."

high towers, inverted so that they seemed to be hanging precariously from the sky. Chesterton imagines of Francis:

> He might see and love every tile on the steep roofs or every bird on the battlements; but he would see them all in a new and divine light of eternal danger and dependence. Instead of being merely proud of his strong city because it could not be moved, he would be thankful to God for not dropping the whole cosmos like a vast crystal to be shattered into falling stars.[2]

An attitude of gratitude, thanksgiving for the invisible but durable thread of God's dependable grace, comes to mark the faithful community's response to God.

Verse 5 begins with honest acknowledgment that God's wrath can also be experienced by the faithful, but insists that, put in perspective, it seems but a moment of anger compared to a lifetime of divine favor. In one of the most memorable lines in all of the Psalms, its couplet echoes in purest poetry, "Weeping may linger for the night, but joy comes with the morning" (v. 5b). In retrospect, whatever negativity our psalmist suffered now seems fleeting. Then, catching himself, he immediately goes on to accuse himself of an overweening self-satisfaction, a full-of-himselfness, that reminds one of the boast of the rich farmer of Jesus' parable (Luke 12:16–21). The soaring sense of individual self-sufficiency and independence "in my prosperity" that the psalmist confesses leads him to the presumptuous thought: "I shall never be moved" (v. 6). God, he claims, led him to this point of delusionary self-assurance, but he accuses God of leaving the scene of the crime—resulting in something more, I suspect, than the mere "dismay" the NRSV weakly translates as his reaction to God's disappearance (v. 7).

Next comes a classic example of the faithful follower walking the very thin line of taunting God with the sarcastic jibe that in effect is a baiting of God: "What profit is there in my death, if I go down to the Pit? Will the dust praise you? Will it tell of your faithfulness?" (v. 9). Not long ago a learned retired professor friend asked me one of those showstoppingly simple-sounding questions that is still bothering me: "Why does God need our praise, anyway?" In his query I heard him implying that it seemed somewhat primitive and anthropomorphic of the God of the Bible to be so preoccupied with

2. G. K. Chesterton, *St. Francis of Assisi* (Garden City, NY: Doubleday, 1928), 74–75.

Psalm 30

Theological Perspective

understood the need to have an intimate relationship with God, one of daily worship and praise. Marshall lived the spirit of Psalm 30, believing we must praise the God of this psalm with deep gratitude, in covenant faith.

While the dead sleep and cannot praise, our living purpose is to praise God: the only focus of our confessional adoration. Confession indicates commitment, an unapologetic willingness for ultimate intimacy with God. For Marshall, this God (in twenty-first-century vernacular) is not a wimp, a wuss, or a flake. This God gets angry that people suffer, are overwhelmed, and experience disorientation.

After this joyous orientation is established and becomes an old frame of existence, where joy and shouting God's praises is normative, disorientation occurs again when God seems absent. God hides God's face: the presence, the intimacy is blocked, hidden, secretive.[2] When we feel God is missing in action, we lament and pray, often bewildered. We want to know where God is. Steeped in a faith, we plead for divine help and grace to help us. We experience the cycle of life, related to God, from well-being to death to new life.

The prayer of the psalmist concludes with celebration and a reiteration that God does turn our sadness into dancing, our pain to joy, as we no longer wear the garments of penitence. The joy is so unspeakable that we cannot be quiet. We must give thanks to God forever. When we stop to express daily our adoration, gratitude, and appreciation to God, neither nagging vicissitudes nor catastrophic events can keep us from the joy of the Lord.

CHERYL A. KIRK-DUGGAN

Pastoral Perspective

"Getting Through Sunday Somehow." The scene takes place in an Irish pub on a bleak Sunday afternoon. A disheveled old man, with too many emptied glasses in front of him, stares into the mirror over the bar and mourns for anyone who might hear, "What have I done for a single mortal soul this day? Nothing. . . . The older I get the less I do for people. . . . It's an awesome responsibility when the world runs to hand you things. For instance; sunsets. . . . That's a gift, ain't it?"

A fellow inebriate a few stools away agrees obligingly, "It is." Encouraged, the old man now more loudly says, "Well who do you thank for sunsets?" The newfound friend answers reluctantly, "Not me," which only encourages the old man to further oration.

"Then ain't you horribly guilty yourself? Don't the burden make you hunchback, all the lovely things you got from life and no penny down?" The other says, "I never thought," to which the old man is quick to respond, "Think man! . . . Act, man, before you're the walking dead."[3]

Theologian Karl Barth is reported to have declared that there is only one sin, suggesting that the single sin from which every lesser sin emanates is the sin of ingratitude—the failure to comprehend the theological truth that human life in all its beauty, abundance, and possibility is a gift. No one has recognized the undergirding truth beneath Barth's statement better than the psalmist: "O LORD my God, I will give thanks to you forever."

P. C. ENNISS

---

2. In her recently published letters, Mother Teresa notes that she was not aware of God in the last fifty years of her life. See Mother Teresa to the Rev. Michael Van Der Peet, September 1979 in *Time*, Aug. 23, 2007, David Van Biema. See Mother Teresa and Brian Kolodiejchuk, *Mother Teresa: Come Be My Light* (New York: Doubleday, 2007).

3. Ray Bradbury, "Getting Through Sunday Somehow," in *I Sing The Body Electric!* (New York: Harper & Row, 1946), 298–99.

Exegetical Perspective

Literally, "a shout-of-joy *belongs to* the morning." Joy connotes crying aloud in praise or proclamation at daybreak, counterpointing any nocturnal anguish. Typical of laments, the psalm clouds over until "joy" returns in the final strophe.

Verses 6–7 recollect the cause for weeping that sets up strophe 3's bitter argument with YHWH, momentarily diminishing the salvific successes of strophe 2. First-person-singular pronouns and possessives redound, verse 6, to emphasize "*my* prosperity"—not necessarily a careless indolence but the very "security" Psalm 122:7 prays for Jerusalem. To be "unmoved" suggests a mountain not tottering (Isa. 54:10; Pss. 46:2; 125:1) or a kingdom (Ps. 46:7). So verse 7 depicts the favored situation (of a lifetime, v. 5) that literally "caused my mountain to stand as a strength." Again, Jerusalem's temple mount must be metaphorically considered, especially in light of God's once "hiding-face"—contrasting the Levitical benediction, Numbers 6:24–26, and mirroring Ezekiel 39:26's exact term for exile—requiring, then, a restoration of the temple on "a very high mountain" (Ezek. 40:2). "I was dismayed" understates the crisis; "terrified" better fits the context, as with Job 23:16 and Exodus 15:15.

Strophe 3 (vv. 8–10). These verses implore YHWH for help. "What profit is my death [literally, "in my blood"] or my going down to the Pit [*shakhat*]," countering strophe 1's "brought up from Sheol" after going down into a pit (*bor*). "Will dust praise you?"—as much the ruined nation, the dust of its toppled temple and abandoned blood sacrifices, as any individual's slaughter and grave.

Strophe 4 (vv. 11–12). These verses return to the joy and thanksgiving of verse 5, with a similar pattern of delight displacing distress. Mourning becomes dancing, sackcloth metaphorically transmutes into joy, neatly summarizing Jeremiah's vision of Zion restored (Jer. 31) and confirming verse 1: YHWH did not allow Israel's enemies to "joy" over its demise. "Praise" is not sung by "my soul" exactly but by a "glory" (see v. 12 NRSV note) that "will not be silent." Despite the parallel with the first person in the second clause of verse 12, "*I* will thank you," this "glory" speaks more to YHWH's holy presence seen by Ezekiel returning to the temple and filling it, along with God's people summoned there to intone thanks.

The on-again, off-again hope in these poetics may still preach patience for a congregation, under deadening personal and societal circumstances, to pray boldly for revitalization.

RICHARD D. BLAKE

Homiletical Perspective

being praised and thanked, like someone lacking in self-esteem.

My provisional answer was that Israel's prophets (particularly Amos, Hosea, Jeremiah, Isaiah) were always careful to point to the need for "right worship" that emphasized doing justice rather than cultic sacrifice. This is the kind of praise sought by YHWH—a praise that reflected Israel's covenant loyalty not in slavish obeisance but in righteous behavior. The question nags, however, and I suspect a more satisfying answer to the question of why God needs the dust's praise goes back to YHWH's desire for relationship, suggested in the creation stories of Genesis 1 and 2 and the creation of humankind in the divine image.

The bottom line is sheer doxology. As Brueggemann rightly points out, the purpose of the psalm is to keep alive the memory of the prerescue situation, so that the occasion of God's transforming deliverance remains a power for living and a passion for praise. The language is again beautifully active, evocative emotionally, and therefore truly memorable: "You have turned my mourning into dancing; you have taken off my sackcloth and clothed me with joy" (v. 11). God turns out to be not only the object of the faithful one's praise, but also the subject who makes such thanksgiving possible.

Consider singing in response to this psalm the lively contemporary hymn set to an English folk tune, "Come, Join the Dance of Trinity." Picking up on the Greek word *perichōrēsis*, meaning literally "to dance around," a term used by early theologians to convey the idea of the Trinity's mutual interrelationship, the hymn invitingly bids us to join our bodies in praise of the triune God who has "made room within their dance" for the likes of us. The hymn concludes:

> Let voices rise and interweave, by love and hope set free,
> To shape in song this joy, this life: the dance of Trinity.[3]

JOHN ROLLEFSON

3. Richard Leach, "Come, Join the Dance of Trinity," in *Evangelical Lutheran Worship* (Minneapolis: Augsburg Fortress, 2006), #412.

Galatians 6:(1-6) 7-16

¹My friends, if anyone is detected in a transgression, you who have received the Spirit should restore such a one in a spirit of gentleness. Take care that you yourselves are not tempted. ²Bear one another's burdens, and in this way you will fulfill the law of Christ. ³For if those who are nothing think they are something, they deceive themselves. ⁴All must test their own work; then that work, rather than their neighbor's work, will become a cause for pride. ⁵For all must carry their own loads.

⁶Those who are taught the word must share in all good things with their teacher. ⁷Do not be deceived; God is not mocked, for you reap whatever you sow. ⁸If you sow to your own flesh, you will reap corruption from the flesh; but if you sow to the Spirit, you will reap eternal life from the Spirit. ⁹So let us not grow weary in doing what is right, for we will reap at harvest time, if we do not

Theological Perspective

The concluding chapter of Galatians is an odd chapter. On the one hand, it is a summary of the arguments Paul has made in the first five chapters of the book; the relations between circumcision and law, Spirit and flesh, and individual responsibility and corporate concern are all encapsulated in it.

On the other hand, every aspect of the summary introduces a new paradox. Having argued against the threats that come with the corruptions of the flesh (5:16–21), Paul nonetheless writes a profoundly carnal chapter. Having strongly argued against circumcision (5:2–12), Paul concludes that neither circumcision nor uncircumcision is anything (6:15). Having argued for the priority of God's gift of freedom-shaped grace (5:1), Paul writes that we will reap whatever we sow (6:7). Having argued that the Spirit provides the clearest testimony to the truth of his words (1:10–12), he points to the marks on his own body as evidence to that truth (4:12–14). Having suggested that his adversaries should just go castrate themselves (5:12), he argues that those who are detected in a transgression should be restored in a spirit of gentleness (6:1).

What is a church theologian to make of it? Or, to ask that question differently, what are we to make of the fact that the parts that feel new in the chapter also introduce paradoxes? How are we to think about paradoxes in Scripture?

Pastoral Perspective

The discerning preacher will find much from which to choose in these passages, born as they were in the context of a Galatian church in crisis. Under stress, any family system—churches included—may resort to infighting and engage in behavior based on difference, including the relegation of those who are different to the status of the "other." Such crises can and often do result in emphases not on theological virtues and practices, but rather on divisions more reflective of the society at large—rigid interpretations of law, rather than expressions of faith informed by the pastoral virtue and spirit of compassion. In these passages, Paul is attempting to call the church he helped establish "in Christ" back from the abyss of divisions created by decidedly un-Christian issues and practices. These verses are filled with both caveats about life in community and suggestions as to pastoral praxis—in this case, the practice of the art and discipline of living in Christian community.

In the small mountain Episcopal parish I served for a number of years, we developed and taught a course on lay pastoral care, designed to equip laypersons with theory and skills in pastoral care and to empower them to use these skills in community—both in the church and beyond. We began carefully with the theological summons of our baptismal covenant, in which we promise to "seek and serve

give up. [10]So then, whenever we have an opportunity, let us work for the good of all, and especially for those of the family of faith.

[11]See what large letters I make when I am writing in my own hand! [12]It is those who want to make a good showing in the flesh that try to compel you to be circumcised—only that they may not be persecuted for the cross of Christ. [13]Even the circumcised do not themselves obey the law, but they want you to be circumcised so that they may boast about your flesh. [14]May I never boast of anything except the cross of our Lord Jesus Christ, by which the world has been crucified to me, and I to the world. [15]For neither circumcision nor uncircumcision is anything; but a new creation is everything! [16]As for those who will follow this rule—peace be upon them, and mercy, and upon the Israel of God.

Exegetical Perspective

The climactic conclusion of Paul's address to the Galatians is homiletically rich. Here Paul draws together all the major themes that he introduced at the beginning of his letter-speech and developed toward this very end.[1] With these final words, Paul epitomizes the Christian life as bearing one another's burdens—doing good to all people—and he highlights how the faithful become such new creations and constitute the new Israel of God.

Fulfilling the Law of Christ (vv. 1–6). Continuing the line of argument that he struck forcefully in 5:13, Paul adds here that freedom in Christ brings responsibility for the welfare of others. In Christ, believers become keepers of their brothers and sisters. The authentic Christian life humbly devotes itself to the benefit of others, sharing and receiving whatever is helpful. In this way, believers fulfill the "law of Christ," which may refer to the messianic law of the eschatological age, the Mosaic law redefined, the love commandment, and self-sacrificing service in the manner of Jesus Christ.

Of course, Christians are not entirely free from sin. Although sin may have lost its complete control

1. For an analysis of Paul's chief thematic developments in Galatians, see Robert A. Bryant, *The Risen Crucified Christ in Galatians* (Atlanta: Society of Biblical Literature, 2001).

Homiletical Perspective

Paul's final words to the worrisome community in Galatia pulse on the page. One imagines the apostle pacing, dictating as his scribe scribbles ("See what large letters I make when I am writing in my own hand!" v. 11). Paul excoriates the circumcision party, who have slapped down the Galatians' assurance. False teachers told gullible Galatians that one comes to Jesus only by way of obedience to Moses's law. The pastoral patience of verses 1–6 gives way to warning: "God is not mocked" (v. 7a). Step back, beloved coinheritors of Christ's grace. Turn around and free-fall into the freedom of God's marvelous truth.

We face the Galatian dilemma every day, setting litmus tests in the way of those who would drink at the well of grace. The preacher must assist the congregation to ponder the relation between freedom and obedience. Today, what millstones do we tie around the necks of God's children?

The stones are as varied as our faith communities. Election seasons find pastors preaching one Christian way to vote. Raising one's hands in prayer may take one beyond the pale for those who confine their praying to closets. Human sexuality brings out the grace-guarders' energy.

Do we say, "Your experience must mirror mine"? Or "You must be born again"? Or "You must give away all that you possess"?

Galatians 6:(1-6) 7-16

Theological Perspective

There are several possible answers to that question, each of which carries a degree of legitimacy within it, but none of which feels complete. The first answer is to reaffirm the "dominant position" taken on such paradoxes within the bulk of the letter and to resolve the difficulties raised by contrasting positions by contextualizing them. Taking this approach, a theologian would remind hearers that Paul's claim in verse 7 that "God is not mocked, for you reap whatever you sow" is not a rejection of the claim that Christians are justified by grace made possible through the crucified Jesus, but a recognition that actions have natural implications that follow from them. Those who pursue the flesh simply will have more trouble discerning the prodding of the Spirit. Again, she would remember that, precisely because circumcision cannot have implications for Gentiles who wish to enter the church, they should not be asked to undergo it.

This first approach reminds us that Scripture functions as a normative authority in our lives, but it is precisely Scripture's diversity and complexity that makes such normativity meaningful. In a complicated world, we need both the trustworthiness of Scripture's central witness and the ambiguity of the full text. Otherwise, we may manipulate it and turn it into a simple answer book—which would, in the face of the world's complexity, make it quite literally otherworldly.

This approach, however, does not clarify how to discern between majority and minority positions. Different Christians find the "core" of the good news in different places. As a result, such an approach throws Christians back into the very dilemma that they were attempting to avoid: adjudicating between texts in order to resolve the paradoxical. More importantly, it suggests that complexity should be governed and paradoxes can be resolved, if we just think hard enough about them. It treats faith as a cognitive matter and cognition as a means of escaping the dilemmas of finitude.

A second approach is to encourage Christians to "live in the paradox": to treat the presence of apparently incommensurable statements as an opportunity to affirm that faith is greater than understanding, that truth is never straightforward, and that God can mysteriously hold together what would otherwise be divided. We are justified by faith through grace alone, but free will matters. We are not bound by the law, but should fulfill the law. We should "work for the good of all," and "especially for those of the family of faith" (6:10). The new creation has come, and yet we wait for it.

Pastoral Perspective

Christ in all persons, loving your neighbor as yourself . . . strive for justice and peace among all people, and respect the dignity of every human being."[1]

In the beginning, enthusiasm for the class was palpable and inspiring. Together we began to imagine the possibilities for the harvest that might follow our seasons of learning about grief counseling, visitation in hospitals, continuous care facilities, and care for the chronically ill— possibilities like elder care, a "casserole patrol" as a form of crisis ministry, lay eucharistic visitation, and other forms of pastoral care. By summer, we proposed to the vestry the parameters of a new ministry of lay pastoral care. This was subsequently approved. New life in community suddenly existed where none had previously been, in the service of "bearing one another's burdens," to use Paul's language. We were delighted.

Soon, however, problems began to emerge. Some became worried about best practices and methodology, others about who among them had the best and most appropriate gifts and graces for particular forms of ministry and why. Opinions about overlapping forms of care and responsibility began to overtake the implementation of the very practice we were seeking to engage. Some began to justify their qualifications for particular tasks, emphasizing their spiritual gifts. Even the clergy staff began to disagree about what the laity should and should not be "allowed" to do. In some instances, these debates took on a personal tone. Feelings were hurt. Persons were becoming preoccupied with the letter of the "law," rather than the spirit of compassionate life in community we sought to embody. Our communal efforts at bearing one another's burdens were becoming a burden to us all.

In these verses from Galatians Paul assiduously avoids being critical of individuals in the church, even as he offers practical instructions on life in community—indeed, life in *Christian* community, based not on the law of Moses but on the spirit of the Messiah. In the midst of the crisis of the young church in Galatia, Paul encourages self-giving in faithful service, gratitude, and humility, rather than arrogance, hubris, and emphasis on differences based on spiritual gifts and graces. For Paul, life in community should be governed by faithful stewardship of *all* resources, a stewardship marked by "sowing to the Spirit" (v. 8), rather than the flesh. Of course, in

---

1. *The Book of Common Prayer* (New York: Church Publishing Corp., 1979), 305.

over believers, it is still possible for the faithful to transgress God's will by living according to the flesh (5:16, 18; 6:1). When this occurs, the whole community of faith, in a spirit of gentleness, is responsible for guiding the transgressor back into the path of faithfulness. Those who offer correction and instruction, though, are especially vulnerable to the perverting power of pride and must proceed in utter humility.

Living Responsibly (vv. 7–10). As much as Paul wants the Galatians to live in the freedom that Christ gives, he also wants them to understand that God, who makes this new life possible, also judges. All will be held accountable for their actions and reactions. Thus Christians cannot presume upon the mercy of God. Indeed, they are still under God's judgment in the present—"you reap whatever you sow" (v. 7; cf. Rom. 1:18–32). Salvation is by faith, not works, but actions are not inconsequential. Believers and nonbelievers "sow" their actions throughout their lives—for good or bad—and reap either "corruption" or "eternal life" (v. 8). Complacency in serving others is not a Christian virtue.

Living under the Spirit's direction and power causes individuals to do what is right in the present eschatological age (v. 9). When the day of judgment comes, those who have persevered in doing the work of Christ will enter the kingdom of God. Paul believes that the eschatological age of the Spirit is at hand. Twice in two verses (vv. 9–10) he uses the word *kairos*, which means "appropriate time" and a "decisive point in time," to describe the present time. Now is the opportune time for Jesus' followers to *do* what is right for the welfare of others (v. 9); now is the fitting moment for *accomplishing* works of love (v. 10; see also Rom. 13:11). Foretastes of life eternal are accessible, and the day is coming when the hope of righteousness will be fulfilled for those who walk by the Spirit, loving their neighbors as themselves.

Being the New Israel (vv. 11–16). With the full establishment of God's kingdom in sight, Paul directs his hearers' attention once more to the risen crucified Christ and their current situation. Writing in his own hand now, using large letters like a parent writing for a child (v. 11),[2] Paul clarifies the difference between himself and his opponents: they are more concerned with the outward appearances of faithfulness, typified by law observance and

Or "You must be heterosexual"?

Or "You must vote Republican/Democrat"?

Or "You must believe everything you hear on Fox News, and nothing you hear on NPR"?

Or vice versa?

I once was told earnestly that Christians should never listen to opera. It is tempting to make our experience of God's truth *the* experience of God's truth. It is the most human—in Paul's terms, the most "fleshly"—tendency in the world. A. J. Conyers notes: "All religion, and every practice of religion, and in fact all of human life is in danger of being marshaled into the service of the human ego."[1]

It is easy for the Galatians to fall away from the gracious nature of the gospel; it is easy for us. Next time God's Spirit teaches you a painful lesson—and She will—remember that Peter, apostle extraordinaire, is also brought to his knees. Paul takes on Peter's impetuous flexibility: in the presence of pentecostals Peter speaks in tongues; in mainline churches he listens to organ music with reverence. Peter eats freely—until the Jews come to town. Then he eschews the Gentile way. Paul challenges him, saying, "Peter, you are a Jew, but you live like a Gentile. So how can you force Gentiles to live like Jews?" (2:14b CEB).

Despite direction from the divine dream factory—his stunning vision at Joppa (Acts 10:9–16)—Peter is not comfortable making others *uncomfortable*. How often do we preachers try just to blend in? Paul scolds Peter, telling him to stop being a hypocrite: circumcision, schmircumcision, you know perfectly well it no longer matters: "*a new creation is everything!*" (6:15b; emphasis added). How shall we test ourselves against Paul's teaching? Two dimensions emerge:

1. *The true gospel produces a church in which unity exists with remarkable diversity.* In this congregation do we largely look alike, dress alike, think alike, speak alike, spend alike, and vote alike? Paul teaches that the gospel will produce congregations in which unity exists with amazing diversity. Timothy was circumcised (Acts 16:3) because some Jews were aware that Timothy's father was a Greek; in Galatians, however, Paul heatedly and repeatedly insists that circumcision is not required of Titus, also a Greek, nor of any Gentiles who follow Christ. Paul models radical freedom. Can we follow his lead?

Dr. Daniel Chetti, American Baptist Church/USA missionary to Beirut, tells of Muslims who have

---

2. Ibid., 226.

1. A. J. Conyers, *The Loss of Transcendence and Its Effect on Modern Life* (South Bend, IN: St. Augustine's Press, 1999), 131.

Galatians 6:(1-6) 7-16

Theological Perspective

This approach recognizes both human limitation and God's power. Rather than making faith a matter of intellectual assent, it connects it to trust. Those who live in paradox rest in the belief that there is wisdom deeper than understanding. Unlike the first approach, this stance does not express the same desire to relieve the tensions of the paradoxical (and thereby close off possibilities for further reflection) by imposing order on them.

Refusing to submit to the desire to relieve tensions is not the same as resisting the temptations of premature closure, though. Treating paradoxes as beyond human understanding effectively forecloses the very project of seeking understanding that structures faith: *fides quaerens intellectum*. This approach is quiescent rather than questioning; it submits rather than struggles; it accepts the present at the cost of a desire for the future. If the life of faith involves growth and change, then "living in the paradox" is, ironically, not very lively—and not especially driven by the eschatological vision that "new creation is everything!"

The third approach takes up the project of attempting to learn from paradoxes, partly by attempting to learn from the first two approaches. With the first approach, it recognizes the cognitive component of growth in faith. With the second, it recognizes that cognition will not settle paradoxes and that growth in faith must therefore include trust. Yet unlike both, it refuses to end prematurely the projects of pursuing individual sanctification and corporate welfare. It recognizes that after the cross of Jesus Christ, the world has been crucified to us and we to the world (and so the kingdom has come) but that we still carry the marks of those crucifixions on our (old) bodies (and so the new creation is still to come). As it is empowered by the Spirit, this third approach treats paradoxes not only as the products of faith, but as occasions for hope and opportunities for love. Galatians 6 may be a summary, but it is not a conclusion. Instead, its effect is to drive readers back into its first five chapters, seeking the fresh insights that are possible only because we have already read it through and in the process learned from it.[1]

MARK DOUGLAS

Pastoral Perspective

this case Paul was speaking to those for whom circumcision had become the most important outward and visible sign of membership in community. This can be extended, however, to all those emphases to which the flesh is heir, including our human tendency to engage in sowing hubris, pride, spiritual arrogance, division, and other "nettlesome" forms of behavior whose harvest of nettles is its own reward.

Late in the summer following the formation of the lay pastoral care ministry, one of the founding members was unexpectedly stricken ill. En route to London on a plane high over the Atlantic, she had a life-threatening heart attack; she was resuscitated and kept alive by CPR until the plane returned to New York. She was stabilized in hospital there and eventually returned to a lengthy convalescence at home in the mountains. Somehow, this crisis in the community provided the occasion for the original vision of the lay pastoral care ministry to emerge and coalesce around her care. The various committees sprang into action without rancor or emphasis on who should do what or why. Gifts and abilities seemed to sort themselves and come to life. Tasks were delegated and carried out with enthusiasm and faithfulness. A spirit of grace prevailed.

To use the language of Paul (and the benefit of hindsight), I now recognize this experience as one of resurrection—of "new creation." Indeed, this is the theme at the heart of the *pastoral* message of Galatians. With the new, Spirit-given life of the Messiah, the old world has fallen away—has died on the cross—and the new creation has been born. The "law" has been replaced by new life in the Spirit, neither dependent on nor enslaved by rigid interpretations of "best practices." The congregation's experience with the lay pastoral care ministry—a ministry thriving to this day—called us back to our baptismal covenant. We were reminded that compassion is a practical pastoral virtue that transcends law and invokes grace in action, joy in the spirit. It respects the dignity of all human beings. In this spirit, bearing one another's burdens with grace is not burdensome slavery but freedom in Christ.

J. WILLIAM HARKINS

---

1. This essay owes much of its wisdom to Charles T. Mathewes, "The Liberation of Questioning in Augustine's *Confessions*," *Journal of the American Academy of Religion* 70, no. 3 (Sept. 2002): 539–60.

Exegetical Perspective

circumcision, than with doing the work of the crucified Christ (5:6, 14; 6:2, 10), which will always draw opposition from the powerful, privileged, prejudiced, and protected. Faithfulness in Christ cannot be improved through observance of the law or any part of it (2:15–21; 3:10–14, 21–29). So Paul admonishes the Galatian Christians to reject the way of those who "want to make a good showing in the flesh" *(thelousin euprosōpēsai en sarki*, v. 12). The way of prestige and self-promotion over others (v. 13) is diametrically opposed to the way of the cross, which is Paul's way and the way of everyone who follows Jesus (1:4, 10; 2:1–7, 11–21; 3:1–5; 4:8–20; 5:10–11). Paul's opponents are unwilling to risk persecution for carrying out the law of Christ. Paul, on the other hand, glories only in the risen crucified Jesus Christ.

The dividing line between Paul and the agitators of the Galatian churches is the cross of Christ (5:11b; Phil. 3:18). The cross reveals the faithfulness of Christ and what God has done to rescue sinners (1:4). Circumcision epitomizes human trust in the law for salvation. Paul trusts only in the grace of God in Christ; such radical trust is insufficient for the agitators. Thus Paul declares emphatically that his only basis for boasting is "the cross of our Lord Jesus Christ" (v. 14), which lies at the heart of the gospel (3:1, 13; 4:4–5; 1 Cor. 1:17–23; 2:1–2). God's decisive victory over evil occurred with Jesus' self-offering upon the cross and his resurrection from the dead. Faith in the crucified Christ breaks sin's perverting power and reveals God's transforming love. Paul knows this firsthand (1:1, 11–16; 2:15–21), and the Galatians know it too (3:1–5).

Paul also calls attention to two other crucifixions—his and the world's (v. 14). He means that he has died to the corrupting influence of a world in rebellion against God; its values and influences no longer drive him. All that counts is "new creation" living (v. 15). Certainly, new creation language is apocalyptic (cf. Isa. 42:9; 43:18–19; 65:17; 66:22; Rom. 5:17–21). For Paul, God has overturned the verdict of the law (3:13) and inaugurated the new age with the resurrection of Jesus from the dead (1:1–4). Yet the future kingdom's realities are present now through trust in the New Creation Jesus Christ crucified whom God raised from the dead and whose New Creation Spirit transforms lives and relationships. This is the new "Israel of God" (v. 16), through which God is blessing all the families of the earth (Gen. 12:3).

ROBERT A. BRYANT

Homiletical Perspective

come to love Jesus Christ. The All-Saints International Congregation in Beirut, Lebanon, welcomes such to the Communion table whether or not they have been baptized, since baptism for a Muslim can lead to disinheritance, being shunned by family, or even death. Shall the table be open? The community prayed for a word from God and the word came: "This is My table. It is not yours; it does not belong to any denomination's doctrine; it is Mine."[2] The true gospel produces a church in which unity exists with remarkable diversity.

2. The true gospel produces a church of miraculous unity. The Amish community in Nickel Mines, Pennsylvania, is legendary for its response to the horrific slaughter of five young girls and severe wounding of five more. The community's actions reflect with brilliant clarity who and whose they are as dedicated followers of Jesus Christ. In following their example, shall we first give up our cars, disconnect electricity, and make our clothes plain? Must one adopt a set of behaviors in order to stay within the faith? "No!" cries Paul. Instead, bear fruit! "If you sow to your own flesh, you will reap corruption from the flesh; but if you sow to the Spirit, you will reap eternal life from the Spirit" (v. 8).

What did the Amish community of Nickel Mines sow to the Spirit? They sowed radical forgiveness. They took seriously the work of Jesus Christ on humanity's behalf, forgiving the shooter, reaching out to his family with food that same day, and later with a share of the cash that poured in from Americans who sorrowed with them. They were and are a light to the church. "So let us not grow weary in doing what is right, for we will reap at harvest time, if we do not give up" (v. 9). The true gospel produces a church of miraculous unity.

So do not be bewitched.
Do not listen to those who would gild the gospel.
Do know Christ, and the power of the resurrection.

"For neither circumcision nor uncircumcision is anything; but a new creation is everything! As for those who will follow this rule—peace be upon them" (vv. 15–16).

CAROL E. HOLTZ-MARTIN

2. Daniel Chetti (guest speaker, ABC/USA World Mission Conference, United Church, Canandaigua, New York, October 8, 2007).

Luke 10:1-11, 16-20

¹After this the Lord appointed seventy others and sent them on ahead of him in pairs to every town and place where he himself intended to go. ²He said to them, "The harvest is plentiful, but the laborers are few; therefore ask the Lord of the harvest to send out laborers into his harvest. ³Go on your way. See, I am sending you out like lambs into the midst of wolves. ⁴Carry no purse, no bag, no sandals; and greet no one on the road. ⁵Whatever house you enter, first say, 'Peace to this house!' ⁶And if anyone is there who shares in peace, your peace will rest on that person; but if not, it will return to you. ⁷Remain in the same house, eating and drinking whatever they provide, for the laborer deserves to be paid. Do not move about from house to house. ⁸Whenever you enter a town and its people welcome you, eat what is set before you; ⁹cure the sick who are there, and say to them, 'The kingdom of God has come near to

Theological Perspective

Just what does it mean to take the good news to the world? What is the appropriate exercise of apostolic authority? How should Christians respond when their mission is greeted with indifference or hostility? For a contemporary church that has come to think of Matthew 28:18–20 as the only evangelistic commission, this text offers a strikingly different perspective.

Whereas Jesus sent the Twelve out in mission in chapter 9, now he sends seventy (or seventy-two, as the LXX reads). The number seventy implies all of humanity, as Genesis 10 provides a list of all the nations of the world, numbering seventy. Here again the Lukan soteriological theme is repeated: salvation is for all of humanity.

The apostles are to go ahead of Jesus into the towns to prepare the way for him. There is a sense of urgency, with Jesus asking the disciples to pray for more laborers for the harvest, because it is plentiful and the laborers are few (vv. 2–3). The mission is holistic—preaching, teaching, and healing—and the apostles have the same authority for these ministries that Jesus himself has. The gospel of peace will take the seventy into direct conflict with Satan, whose power falls before the divine mission (10:17–20). Even so, they are to go peaceably, with the message that the kingdom of God is near. They are to be like "lambs among wolves."

Pastoral Perspective

The essence of the Christian message extends far beyond any particular time or space. Neither is it limited by the one who shares it or the venue in which it is heard. The life-changing power of the gospel may be expressed in a wide variety of languages, an infinite number of places, by many different types of teachers (or preachers); and yet at the center is the hope offered to every one of us in the name of Jesus Christ.

After Jesus set his face toward Jerusalem (Luke 9:51), the time that was available for him to share his message was limited. He sent special messengers (9:52) as a means of extending the reach of his teaching and to prepare the ground for his arrival, and then appointed seventy others to go out in pairs to prepare the people to receive him (10:1). Initially he sent them out to visit "every town and place where he himself intended to go," saying, "The harvest is plentiful, but the laborers are few" (v. 2). When they returned, they rejoiced at the reception they received, saying, "Lord, in your name even the demons submit to us!" (v. 17).

Today we rejoice that the authority of his name is still the powerful means by which our lives are transformed. The seventy messengers may have long since died, but God continues to call new evangelists, teachers, and preachers to extend the message of the

you.' ¹⁰But whenever you enter a town and they do not welcome you, go out into its streets and say, ¹¹'Even the dust of your town that clings to our feet, we wipe off in protest against you. Yet know this: the kingdom of God has come near.'...

¹⁶"Whoever listens to you listens to me, and whoever rejects you rejects me, and whoever rejects me rejects the one who sent me."

¹⁷The seventy returned with joy, saying, "Lord, in your name even the demons submit to us!" ¹⁸He said to them, "I watched Satan fall from heaven like a flash of lightning. ¹⁹See, I have given you authority to tread on snakes and scorpions, and over all the power of the enemy; and nothing will hurt you. ²⁰Nevertheless, do not rejoice at this, that the spirits submit to you, but rejoice that your names are written in heaven."

Exegetical Perspective

Although the Synoptic Gospels agree that Jesus sent the Twelve in pairs to extend his ministry of word and deed (Matt. 10:1–42; Mark 6:6–11; Luke 9:1–5), only Luke records an additional mission by the seventy(-two). Luke's first mission occurs during Jesus' Galilean ministry and is apparently directed toward Israel. The mission by the seventy(-two) occurs during Luke's travel narrative as Jesus journeys through Samaria toward Jerusalem (9:51–56). By incorporating the material that he shares with Matthew's mission to Israel into the instructions for the expanded mission, Luke has shifted the focus. While the manuscript tradition is equally divided over the precise number of the disciples (seventy or seventy-two), no one disputes that the number has a symbolic significance, reflecting the author's normal practice of reporting stories with echoes from the OT. Interpreters have observed either an allusion to the seventy elders in Israel (Exod. 24:1; Num. 11:16) or the table of nations in Genesis 10:2–31. Despite this uncertainty, the mission of the seventy(-two) indicates the expanded scope of the mission, foreshadowing the time when the larger circle of disciples will bring the message of the kingdom "to the ends of the earth" (Acts 1:8). Whereas the Matthean parallel instructs disciples not to go to Samaria (Matt. 10:5),

Homiletical Perspective

In this passage we witness the further development of our Lord's ministry that, if attended to carefully, has great implications for the life and ministry of our own communities of faith. It is appropriate that it falls in the middle of Pentecost, the season emphasizing the growth of the church (hence the color green), as this lection is concerned very much with mission.

Straightaway there are several intriguing questions: Who are these seventy, and from where did they come? Is it possible that some are those would-be followers of the previous chapter? Is Luke trying to downplay the significance of the Twelve by increasing so greatly the number of those Jesus commissions? (In Luke's account the Twelve have never been Jesus' only followers; earlier he describes the significant role a number of women play in supporting Jesus.)

Wherever one comes out on these questions (and no definitive consensus exists among scholars), it is important to note the clear development and expansion of Jesus' mission throughout Luke's Gospel. For most of the early chapters in the narrative, Jesus has been the main actor. He has preached, taught, and performed miracles throughout the land. More recently, he has authorized some of his followers to do the same, first authorizing the Twelve, then sending

Luke 10:1-11, 16-20

Theological Perspective

Having apostolic authority in this text means having the power to cure the sick, exorcise demons, bestow peace, and announce the kingdom of God (9:2–3). It also means having the courage and freedom to go forth in vulnerability and intentional poverty, to travel lightly, and to depend on the hospitality of others. It means a nonviolent response to rejection at the hands of others. All of these actions are done to prepare others to receive Jesus. When the apostles see the power of God manifested in their ministry, they are not to rejoice over their apostolic role, but rather because their names are written in heaven. Everything about the apostolic mission, in other words, subverts the systems of power and privilege in the world.

The peace the apostles are to offer is more than a greeting or demeanor. Peace is representative of the kingdom of God, the salvation that is *shalom*. Ironically, this peace is conflictive, because it arouses the hostility of demonic powers. At times the apostles will seem to be walking among "snakes and scorpions" (v. 19), because of the violent reaction against the gospel. They are given the power to resist these forces, shaking the dust from their feet in response. Those who resist the message will face eschatological consequences, but judgment belongs to God and not the apostles (vv. 12–15).

In the history of interpretation the "harvest" (v. 2) has sometimes been designated as all of Israel, drawing especially from Isaiah 27:12. At other times it has been understood to be all who will be saved. Today the harvest terminology is problematic for some people because it seems to dehumanize people with an "us" and "them" differentiation. Using the language of "harvest" can seem to imply passivity on the part of those who have yet to experience the gospel. What exactly does it mean to be "harvested"? This text can also be problematic for interreligious dialogue in a religiously pluralistic context. Is it appropriate to speak of "harvesting" anyone? While these questions are important, if the mission is carried out as Jesus commands, with its eschewal of worldly power, status, and wealth, the harvest metaphor hardly carries connotations of exploitation and superiority. "Harvesting" instead implies coming to full maturity and being gathered into the reign of God.

The tradition of mendicant orders is rooted in this and a few other texts. While the laborer deserves room and board (the hospitality of those among whom he or she serves), nothing more is to be expected or received. Apostles are to take "no purse," meaning, nothing in which to accumulate wealth.

Pastoral Perspective

gospel. Even now, the nature of the messenger is not the essential factor, for even ordinary Christians who are living out their lives of faith are empowered to share the word of God and to encourage others to believe and follow. The church must be aware that the message, not the messenger, is the focus of our existence. Our world is bigger, we are two thousand years removed from Jesus' walk on earth, and our use of technology for communication is widespread; yet the power to encourage others to hear, change heart, and submit is still in the name of the one we call Lord.

The instructions Jesus gave to his seventy messengers were remarkably specific and left little doubt that their task could prove difficult. Saying that he was "sending [them] out like lambs into the midst of wolves" (v. 3), he encouraged them to take only what they were wearing and to carry nothing with them. There was to be no distraction from the main intent of their visit. They were to stay in one house and eat what was provided. Hospitality was to be accepted, and a blessing offered in return. Their work was to offer peace, cure the sick, and share the news that the kingdom of God was near. Their focus was to be on the gifts that came from God, not on the personalities of the messengers who brought them.

The message that these servants of God brought to the people of the towns and villages was essential and immediate. They preached that the kingdom of God was important to all, both those who received them and those who did not. With the power to transform lives, the kingdom would be realized soon in the presence of Jesus Christ, who both traveled the countryside and commissioned those who spoke in his name. They were vitally concerned with the imminence of that message. This was not a time to delay, but a time for decision. As Jesus drew nearer to Jerusalem, the prospect of the cross (see 9:22) would magnify that message.

For many believers, the immediacy of the kingdom dims with the passage of time. We are essentially very practical people, living in our own context or setting, changing as the situation dictates, yet living within parameters that we can see, touch, and feel. The coming of the kingdom demands a change in our perspective. Whether that means living in the presence of Christ today or living with him in the hereafter, we must begin to see the challenges of life through a lens provided by God, rather than a perspective built by human endeavor. Time, however, numbs us. The passing of each year leads us, chronologically, away from the promise of the coming kingdom, and dims our sense of expectation.

Exegetical Perspective

Luke depicts a mission "to every city and place" Jesus was about to visit (10:1) during the journey through Samaria. While Luke portrays this mission as an event of the past, he probably expects his community to recognize many of the realities of the continuing mission of his own time.

The images that frame the narrative indicate the urgency of the mission within an apocalyptic framework. The metaphor of the harvest, which Luke shares with Matthew's "limited commission" (Matt. 9:37–38), is a familiar apocalyptic image (Matt. 13:39; John 4:35) for the end, when "the one who sat on the cloud [swings] his sickle over the earth, and the earth [is] reaped" (Rev. 14:16) in order to gather the faithful people of God. Similarly, the image of Satan falling "like lightning from heaven" (Luke 10:18) is an apocalyptic theme for the ultimate defeat of evil (Rev. 12:9; 20:2, 7–10). The motif of the names written in heaven (Luke 10:20) corresponds to the portrayal in Revelation of those whose faithful endurance is ultimately vindicated (Rev. 3:5; 13:8).

The apocalyptic framework indicates the urgency of the expanded mission and the place of the disciples in a cosmic drama. Whereas Jesus indicated earlier that the disciples share in fishing for people (Luke 5:10), he now announces to a wider circle that they are participating in the ultimate harvest that separates the faithful from the unfaithful in the coming of the kingdom. The mission of the seventy (-two), like that of the Twelve, is to extend the work of Jesus, who proclaimed "good news to the poor" (4:18) and displayed the arrival of the kingdom through his healings and exorcisms (cf. 11:20). Thus Jesus commissions the disciples to continue his own work of healing the sick and proclaiming that "the kingdom of God is at hand" (10:9, 11).

The plentiful harvest calls for a large work force to reap the crops before they spoil. The disciples can respond by praying for more workers and joining in the missionary effort (10:2). They share not only in the mission of Jesus, but also in its deprivation, dangers, and risks. The disciples share in the vulnerability of the one who had no place to lay his head (9:58) and depended on the hospitality of others (9:51–56). The image of sheep in the midst of wolves (10:3) suggests that persecution accompanies the mission (cf. John 10:12). Although the wolf and the lamb will feed together in the ultimate messianic kingdom (Isa. 11:6; 65:25), the lambs fear the wolves in the present. The command not to take a bag, purse, or sandals and not to greet anyone on the way

Homiletical Perspective

others ahead of him. At this point in the narrative, Jesus commissions seventy followers to take his message to all those places he himself expects to go, authorizing them in very much the same way he authorized the Twelve earlier. This continual expansion of those drawn into Jesus' mission anticipates Luke's second volume, the Acts of the Apostles, and the transferal of responsibility for mission from Jesus to those who receive the Holy Spirit at Pentecost and beyond. Jesus does not do everything for his disciples, then or now. Rather, he does what they cannot do, so as to empower them to accomplish the mission he has set before them.

While I would caution against looking for a blueprint for ministry in the details of Jesus' instructions, four aspects are worthy of attention, any of which could contribute a promising theme for a sermon. First, Jesus promises that the harvest is abundant. He sees abundance where others might see scarcity. This is decidedly not because he is an optimist but, rather, because of his faith in "the Lord of the harvest" (v. 2). Jesus does not commission the seventy to prepare a harvest; that remains God's responsibility. Rather, Jesus commissions his disciples (1) to gather the harvest in and (2) to pray that other laborers will join them in this important work. While our contexts for ministry may have changed from that of the seventy, Jesus' commission to his followers remains essentially the same. God is responsible for the growth of our communities. We are called to be open to this growth; to plan, organize, and work in a way that anticipates, rather than impedes, such growth; and to pray for and invite others to join us in gathering the harvest God has prepared.

Second, inescapable vulnerability is implicit in the mission to which Jesus calls his disciples. The seventy will be going into a hostile world, yet Jesus does not arm them for battle; rather, they will go out like lambs. Similarly, they are to bless those homes that receive them; and even if they are rejected, they are not instructed to offer curses (recall Jesus' rebuke of James and John in the previous chapter for wishing to call down fire upon those who refused to receive Jesus). God's peace, Jesus declares, will rest naturally upon households that value and cultivate peace, but will return from those that do not.

While Jesus declares that the laborers deserve pay, he also instructs them to rely on the hospitality of those who receive them. They are not to carry with them the provisions they will need; nor are they to move about the town cultivating a network of

Luke 10:1-11, 16-20

Theological Perspective

This aspect of the apostolic mission is perhaps the most subversive in contemporary, consumeristic culture. What would it look like for the church to embrace an ethos of intentional poverty?

Jesus commands the apostles to eat what is set before them, words that will find new depths of meaning in Acts 10 when Peter experiences the vision of the sheet. Even the "normal" expectations of religious dietary law are to be set aside for the sake of the gospel. Apostolic commissioning means detachment from many traditions and cultural norms, in order to be peaceable to those among whom the apostles are sent. All aspects of life are subsumed to the central task of the mission. This is one of the reasons that the gospel of peace is conflictive.

The role of hospitality in the mission cannot be overstated. The hospitality of the seventy is shown in their mission of peace, in which they eschew all forms of exploitation, self-centeredness, and personal gain. Their single purpose is to prepare others to encounter Jesus. This is done peacefully, through grateful presence and conversation. The apostles must be relational and respectful in order to be invited into others' homes, where they might share the gospel of the kingdom of God. Theirs is a vulnerable position, for they cannot force receptivity or hospitality on the part of others. The apostles must be willing to go without food, shelter, or welcome for the sake of the gospel.

The hospitality of those to whom the apostles are sent is an openness to hear and respond to the gospel. If the apostles are truly representative of Jesus, they can expect a positive response from many, for the harvest is plentiful and ready, Jesus says. What is lacking is laborers who are prepared to go forth in the apostolic spirit described in this text.

ELAINE A. HEATH

Pastoral Perspective

A renewed sense of vitality comes to this passage through a similar change in perspective. Rather than exegeting Luke only as those who are awaiting the promises of the coming kingdom, what happens if we see ourselves following in the footsteps of the messengers appointed to bring to the world news of the kingdom? As Christians, we are blessed to benefit from both perspectives, living as those who teach the reality of the resurrection, while continuing to share our expectation of the fulfillment of its promise.

As messengers, we have a powerful calling. The Lord appoints us to go out into the world ahead of him. We are not to find on our own a way to live in Jesus' footsteps; instead, we are given specific instructions to share the good news with vitality and anticipation. No longer is the burden of persuasion on us, for we are not the focus. Now, very clearly the focus of our message is on the coming of Christ and our call to live each day in his name. Our authority is not in our status, possessions, or abilities; but, like those first messengers, we are to encourage everyone to follow and submit in the name of our Lord. That power is already attested by the seventy who "returned with joy, saying, 'Lord, in your name even the demons submit to us!'" (v. 17). As present-day messengers, that joy is ours as well, for we have been appointed by Christ to share the good news of the coming of the kingdom. We rejoice, not in the power of our accomplishments, but in the knowledge that our "names are written in heaven" (v. 20) by the one whose name is the most powerful of all.

RICHARD J. SHAFFER JR.

Exegetical Perspective

(10:4) suggests the urgency of the moment, when there is no time to exchange pleasantries along the road as the disciples share the itinerant life with Jesus. The absence of the minimal necessities for travel indicates their total reliance on God and the hospitality of others.

The parallel instruction for the disciples' entry into houses (vv. 5–7) and cities (vv. 8–12) is a further indication of both the urgency of the moment and the mixed response that the missionaries will receive. As they receive hospitality in homes, the urgency of the moment demands that they accept both the food and the lodging (v. 7). Similarly, in the cities they should be content with the food that is set before them (v. 8). The twofold reference to the foods may suggest that, in the expanded mission to the nations, the coming of the kingdom takes priority over food laws.

The mixed response to the disciples' mission anticipates the ultimate separation that accompanies the harvest. In the houses, they will encounter some who are children of peace (lit., "sons of peace," NRSV "shares in peace") and some who are not (v. 6). Similarly, in the cities they will encounter those who welcome them (v. 8) and those who do not (v. 10). This portrayal may reflect the experience of the church in Luke's own time.

The mixed response to the disciples' mission corresponds to the sifting that accompanies the harvest, for the mixed result of their mission has ultimate consequences. On the one hand, those who reject the message of the kingdom will at the harvest receive a fate worse than that of Sodom and Gomorrah (v. 12). On the other hand, the disciples' mission results in victory. When they report that even demonic powers are subject to the name of Jesus, Jesus exclaims, "I watched Satan fall from heaven like a flash of lightning" (vv. 17–18), for he recognizes in their triumph the anticipation of the ultimate victory of the kingdom. The names of those who participate in the risks and deprivations of the mission "are written in heaven," for they belong to the company of those who are gathered at the harvest.

JAMES W. THOMPSON

Homiletical Perspective

supporters. Rather, they are to remain with a single household, willing to receive what they are offered and remain dependent on the support of those to whom they are ministering. Because most persons in our congregations are more accustomed to giving aid than receiving it, it will be easy to miss the vulnerable dependence Jesus commands from his disciples.

Third, the successes of the seventy have far greater significance than they perceive. While their accomplishments are, at one level, no more than echoes of Jesus' earlier work, Jesus declares that they portend the downfall of Satan and the inauguration of a new age. There is more happening here than meets the eye, as the net effect of the disciples' acts of fidelity far exceeds what is apparent. Similarly, to this day, wherever we attend faithfully to our Lord's mission and accomplish acts of mercy in Jesus' name, the kingdom of God is being announced, the reign of evil is being challenged, and the promise of God's consummation is being made.

Fourth, and perhaps most importantly, Jesus declares that there is something even more significant than the triumphs of the seventy: "I have given you authority . . . over all the power of the enemy; and nothing will hurt you. Nevertheless, do not rejoice at this, that the spirits submit to you, but rejoice that your names are written in heaven" (vv. 19–20). What matters more than the earthly and spiritual successes of Jesus' followers is the eternal relationship with God they enjoy through him. This relationship is theirs by grace, for they are simultaneously recipients of, and heralds to, the grace and mercy of God embodied in Christ. As they journey to Jerusalem and see the depths to which God's grace extends, they will be called to witness to what they have seen, confident that, regardless of the visible outcomes of their ministry, their place in God's kingdom is secure.

DAVID J. LOSE

Amos 7:7-17

⁷This is what he showed me: the Lord was standing beside a wall built with a plumb line, with a plumb line in his hand. ⁸And the LORD said to me, "Amos, what do you see?" And I said, "A plumb line." Then the Lord said,

"See, I am setting a plumb line
    in the midst of my people Israel;
    I will never again pass them by;
⁹ the high places of Isaac shall be made desolate,
    and the sanctuaries of Israel shall be laid waste,
    and I will rise against the house of Jeroboam with the sword."

¹⁰Then Amaziah, the priest of Bethel, sent to King Jeroboam of Israel, saying, "Amos has conspired against you in the very center of the house of Israel; the land is not able to bear all his words. ¹¹For thus Amos has said,

'Jeroboam shall die by the sword,
    and Israel must go into exile
    away from his land.'"

Theological Perspective

With the image of a plumb line measuring a faulty wall, Amos conjures a pithy metaphor for complacent Israel's predicament. In a time of relative peace and prosperity, the plumb line illustrates a fatal flaw in the community's structure; it has come out of "true" with itself. The plumb line represents a congruity between the uprightness of God's law and the harmony of just social relations. It also implies the unavoidability of Israel's death, for faulty construction must be torn down.

Amos makes religious audiences uneasy still today, for his message seems to shake the certainty that sin will not frustrate the divine covenant, that God's promises will always overcome even the judgments we deserve. It is a standard homiletic comfort that God accepts our shoddy workmanship and somehow makes something beautiful of it anyway. Even the prophets who denounce infidelity and injustice with fearful consequences usually hold out God's readiness to welcome back the repentant. Amos, however, is uncompromising; God's patience has come to an end. "Israel shall surely go into exile away from its land" (v. 17)—and what is Israel apart from the land of relationship with God? The people of Israel will surely be killed and shattered. God has turned finally away from this people.

Pastoral Perspective

Our text is a story of divine judgment upon a powerful politician by a prophet of God. The greatest pastoral challenge of preaching this text is that we live in an age that considers itself immune from the judgments of anybody, including those of a righteous God. Despite our judgmental willingness, even eagerness, to have two million Americans incarcerated, we are squeamish about God's judgment. One of the projects of the European Enlightenment and its aftermath was to create a world in which we were immune from any external judgment other than that "which seems personally right to me." Kant, the intellectual father of the modern world, sought a humanity in which individuals freely applied judgments to themselves that were based upon reasonable criteria derived exclusively from themselves.

"Who are you to judge me?" is the Kantian legacy. In a recent nationwide poll, young adults, asked why they avoided the church, complained, "The church is too judgmental."

So our challenges with this text from Amos are mostly pastoral rather than exegetical. We preachers have got our hands full in proclaiming a story about a God who does not hesitate to enlist a theological amateur like Amos in the task of holding accountable a powerful political priest like Amaziah.

¹²And Amaziah said to Amos, "O seer, go, flee away to the land of Judah, earn your bread there, and prophesy there; ¹³but never again prophesy at Bethel, for it is the king's sanctuary, and it is a temple of the kingdom."

¹⁴Then Amos answered Amaziah, "I am no prophet, nor a prophet's son; but I am a herdsman, and a dresser of sycamore trees, ¹⁵and the LORD took me from following the flock, and the LORD said to me, 'Go, prophesy to my people Israel.'

¹⁶ "Now therefore hear the word of the LORD.
You say, 'Do not prophesy against Israel,
and do not preach against the house of Isaac.'
¹⁷ Therefore thus says the LORD:
'Your wife shall become a prostitute in the city,
and your sons and your daughters shall fall by the sword,
and your land shall be parceled out by line;
you yourself shall die in an unclean land,
and Israel shall surely go into exile away from its land.'"

Exegetical Perspective

Prophecy is the gifted ability to see what other people cannot or will not see. Prophets focus primarily on the moral and spiritual condition of a nation; they do not simply predict future events, but warn of consequences to injustice.

The lections for today and next Sunday include two of the five visions of Amos that report the prophet's experience of perceiving God's word (cf. Isa. 6; Jer. 1:11–19; Ezek. 1:1–3:11). Four of the visions begin with "what God showed me," literally "made me see"; prophetic vision is revelation. Since there is a progression in the visions, we need to look at the first two briefly.

The visions in chapters 7–9 are like nightmares—terrifying images of the destruction that looms over the northern kingdom of Israel. In the first vision, God is fashioning a devastating invasion of locusts. In the second, a heat wave leads to catastrophic drought. For us, locust plagues and drought are simply natural disasters; within the biblical covenant tradition, however, such disasters are divine curses attributable to the people's moral failure (Deut. 28:22–24, 38, 42). For Amos, the primary failure is social injustice (see essay on 8:1–12 for next Sunday, pp. 244–49).

Amos poses the covenant theology succinctly in 3:2: "You only have I known of all the families of the earth; therefore I will punish you for all your

Homiletical Perspective

It is a misnomer simply to refer to the book of Amos as being among the "minor" prophets. Anyone who has been given a message directly from the Almighty and then has the task of delivering these often cutting words of justice and truth to God's people, especially those in authority, can never be classified as having a role that is of lesser importance. Evidence of this can be found in the several themes that present themselves in this particular passage: a measure of judgment and guidance, the fear of the religious status quo, and the credibility of the prophet.

A Measure of Judgment and Guidance. Verses 7–9 contain one of the more memorable and vivid images in the book of Amos. A plumb line is a very simple yet necessary tool—a weight affixed to the end of a string —utilized in the construction of a wall. Reliant upon gravity, it gives the builder a true measure of that which is straight, and its usage is crucial if the structure is to be strong and enduring. Some cringe at the mere thought of judgment from God. They ask, "How could a loving God make judgments against a covenant people?" It is, however, exactly this loving nature of God that allows such an exacting measure of judgment.

The Fear of the Religious Status Quo. It is impossible to read the passage without noticing the posture

Amos 7:7-17

Theological Perspective

Because it seems difficult to preach confidence in God's grace after this kind of message, the church has often read the doom of Amos as a stern moral lesson to observe social justice, rather than a theological account of its relationship with God. In a book rich with imagery of hypocrisy and injustice, perhaps the condemnation intensely expresses God's outrage at a people that would "buy the poor for silver and the needy for a pair of sandals" (8:6). Perhaps the prophet wants to convict their hearts, to make them see that, because they have systematically crushed the poor and ignored the needy, they indeed deserve to see their sons and daughters fall by the sword (v. 17). Perhaps the rhetoric of condemnation intends therapy for hardened hearts, and so the solace of the usual prophetic pattern remains implicit: if only they turn in repentance, God will welcome them back.

Surely there is something to that kind of moral reading. Amos decries systemic exploitation of the powerless and commonplace humiliation of the lowly. He sees the role of public religion in masking the injustice and rages against the way official worship effectively justifies social sin.

Reducing Amos to social exhortation makes the text too easy, for Amos seems to anticipate a new kind of prophetic theology. Amos is willing to announce that, through social sin, covenant with God can come to an end, that a land gained by promise may yet be lost in exile. Those confident in their election may yet be rejected. The reformer John Calvin saw in Amos testimony to the enduring justice of God's saving will, and therefore counsel for the church not perversely to let its faith insulate its heart from God's will. God's faithfulness to the relationship means precisely that God remains just and therefore ready to judge sin. Later, in the twentieth century, theologian Karl Barth suggested that Amos shows a paradox of salvation: God's condemnation of Israel is part of its election. Barth argues that we should interpret Amos's Israel through the election of Jesus Christ as the rejected one.[1]

In other words, Amos forces his audience to decide how God's grace meets stubborn injustice. For Amos, God's way of covenanting with a people of faith wholly corrupted by social sin may involve death and sacrifice. What does it mean to say to a community claiming divine favor, and yet living on the backs of the poor, that God's redeeming justice is

Pastoral Perspective

Amaziah has ingratiated himself with the royal court through his duties at the sanctuary at Bethel. There is a long history of the so-called court preacher, who has the ability to speak pleasing words to powerful people, soothing their consciences and telling them what they want to hear.

This cozy arrangement between a religious professional and powerful politicians might have gone on forever, had it not been for the intrusive word of God that came to a farmer named Amos, enlisting him as a prophetic speaker of the truth. Now Amaziah will be told some unpleasant truth, his comfortable world will be disrupted, and he will be made to face the facts. God does not look at things the way that Amaziah looks at things.

In our day we tend to think of judgment in an exclusively negative way. A judging God is what we got over when we discovered a loving, gracious God. You have no doubt heard the old chestnut, "The Old Testament is a collection of laws and judgment; the New Testament is a collection of love and grace."

This is not only a grossly unfair characterization of the Hebrew Scriptures, but also a mischaracterization of biblical views of judgment. In the Bible, the judgments of God are part of the graciousness of God. A biblical judge is someone who not only makes judgments about the rectitude of behavior, but also actively seeks to work justice, to set things right. We affirm in the Apostles' Creed that one day the Lord "*shall come* to judge the quick and the dead." In the end, as at the beginning, we do not come to Jesus; he comes to us. The God who comes to us as seeking shepherd and searching woman (Luke 15) comes to us this time as loving judge, to set things right between us and God.

In modern life, most of us just want to be left alone, left to our own devices to live our lives as we please, immune from judgments upon our lives that are not exclusively self-derived; but the God of Israel and the church will not leave us alone. God comes to us, sometimes through the words of a prophet like Amos, loving us enough to tell us the truth about ourselves.

Reformed theologian Emil Brunner speaks of God's judgments upon us as God's "resistance."[1] Against the pressure of our sin, God applies a counterpressure. God's resistance to our evil tends to be considered by us, in our evil, as wrathful injustice, but considered as a mechanism of our redemption, it

---

1. John Calvin, *Calvin's Commentaries*, vol. 14, lect. 67. Karl Barth, *Church Dogmatics* II/2 (Edinburgh: T. & T. Clark, 1957), 392–409.

1. Emil Brunner, *The Christian Doctrine of Creation and Redemption* (Philadelphia: Westminster Press, 1949),118.

iniquities." Election as God's special people ("my people," 7:15) entails a special moral responsibility; it does *not* entail invulnerability to divine judgment.

The visions move from what *might* be to what *will* be. Initially, Amos intercedes and God cancels the locusts and the drought. But with the third vision, Amos no longer intercedes; in the fourth, God restricts him to silent stupefaction; and in the last, Amos does not speak at all. The progression demonstrates that Amos is not a merciless preacher of doom who relishes Israel's punishment, but a defender whose defendant is willfully beyond redemption. Previous passages demonstrate Israel's culpability and refusal to repent in the face of punishments, including locusts and drought (4:6–11).

Visions three and four (7:7–9; 8:1–3) present a different structure. God asks Amos what he sees, Amos identifies an object, and God then interprets the significance of the object (with a pun in 8:2); God refuses ever again to forgive, then describes the coming disaster. It is as if we are witnessing the moment of inspiration in which the prophet realizes the *significance* of what he sees. At first, he, like everyone else, sees only a construction worker with a plumb line (cf. below) or a basket of summer fruit; but with God's interpretive word, Amos sees a society's moral crookedness and *the end*.

Today's lection juxtaposes two quite different literary units (vision and biography), but both focus on the religious and political institutions of Israel—king and dynasty, priest and temple. This religiopolitical connection may be why the biographical anecdote (vv. 10–17) appears in between visions three (7:7–9) and four (8:1–3).

The vivid image of a plumb line measuring the "crookedness" of Israel is homiletically rich. Unfortunately, recent investigation suggests that "plumb line" is an incorrect translation of an obscure word that means "tin." But "tin" does not render an easily recognizable meaning either. There is no consensus on the translation. The preacher might want to acknowledge the problem but continue to use "plumb line," which is not inconsistent with the rest of the vision. Indeed, it is possible that the prophet *is* the plumb line, providing another reason why the confrontation with Amaziah follows.[1]

The meaning of verse 9 is unambiguous: the religious shrines and the royal house will be destroyed ("house" can be both building and

taken by Amaziah, identified as the priest of Bethel. As royal priest, he thought it necessary to send a word of warning directly to King Jeroboam. Amaziah was obviously concerned that Amos's words threatened the king's authority, but perhaps there was more at stake. Amaziah himself was also threatened, because Amos's prophecy spoke with greater power than his own words and actions did. This untrained "seer" hit a particular nerve—saying things that should and could have come from Amaziah's own mouth, if he had not been so interested in protecting his own sense of self-worth. Whatever the reason for Amaziah's response, it is quite clear that he and Amos are serving different masters.

This passage calls to mind a chapter in American history that can be termed both heartwrenching and inspiring. The struggle for civil rights in the United States was marked by some of the vilest actions that human beings were able to inflict upon one another. It was also characterized by expressions of courage that continue to touch the soul of a nation. Prophetic voices of justice sought to move the nation beyond the less-than-adequate place it had been, even to the point of challenging the rather embarrassing efforts of some clergy who were either comfortable with the status quo or fearful of where radical (but necessary) change might lead.

Today's passage from Amos calls to mind the "Letter from Birmingham Jail" of the Rev. Dr. Martin Luther King Jr. Just as Amaziah, the priest at Bethel, was "concerned" about the welfare of the citizens of Israel, a group of eight leading Caucasian clergymen (Protestant, Roman Catholic, and Jewish) was "concerned" about Dr. King's presence in Birmingham in 1963. Likening himself to prophets of Amos's era, King wrote, "I am in Birmingham because injustice is here. Just as the eighth-century prophets left their little villages (such as Tekoa) and carried their 'thus saith the Lord' far beyond the boundaries of their hometowns . . . I too am compelled to carry the gospel of freedom beyond my particular hometown."[1]

Churches—members and especially leaders—must beware of the temptation of becoming seduced by the status quo. Every prophet must struggle with the temptations of comfort and power along with the shadow of fear. Just as the children of Israel feared leaving the land of captivity and then longed for a return to a life of servitude, we too can find it

1. The entire text of the "Letter from Birmingham Jail" can be found in Martin Luther King Jr., *Why We Can't Wait* (New York: Harper & Row, 1964), 77–100.

1. H. G. M. Williamson, "The Prophet and the Plumb-Line," in *In Quest of the Past*, ed. A. S. Van Der Woude (New York: Brill, 1990), p. 116 and n. 69.

Amos 7:7-17

Theological Perspective

on offer? Can that mean anything else than a summons to a kind of death?

Recall that one of Martin Luther King's trademark lines came from Amos. In speeches and sermons over his life from Montgomery to Memphis, King would clinch the power of an oration by proclaiming, "Let justice roll down like waters, and righteousness like an everflowing stream" (5:24). King would consistently name his anticipation of beloved community with words from a prophet condemning a people to death.

Notice, however, whom the text vindicates. For Amos, Israel's coming judgment vindicates the God of the crushed poor and the ignored needy. It vindicates a promised land in which people tend their own soil within a living economy in which there is no longer fear of violence or hunger (see 9:13–15). God's judgment vindicates the nearness of justice in a world where it seems far off, the inevitability of justice in a nation of violent systems and hardened hearts.

As King came to see American racism rooted in a political economy indifferent to the poor and committed to warmongering abroad, he too began to anticipate that God's offer of justice to a people wholly corrupted by social sin must come as a word of judgment and require a kind of death. Indeed, King's faith in the God who remains just made such judgment certain. For the faith of the prophet from the underside, God's sure judgment tells of the unavoidability of justice, of the final intolerance of God for a moral economy of exploitation and misery.[2]

For King, that meant the political community of America and the faith community of the church had to die and be born again. God accepts our shoddy constructions, yes, but not with what Dietrich Bonhoeffer would call "cheap grace." Amos's text points us in a different direction from that of Bonhoeffer's call to individual discipleship, but the concept is similar: grace is free, but not without cost. God's grace and God's love of justice cannot be separated. When God calls a community suffocated by its own injustice and entrapped by violence, he bids it come and die.[3]

WILLIS JENKINS

Pastoral Perspective

is love. This God is not only righteous but also loving—loving us enough never to leave us to our own devices.

Much of contemporary Christian theology in North America, when it attempts to be gracious, sentimentally portrays us as hapless victims. Thus we would-be victims are offered therapy rather than judgment and healing. Orthodox Christian theology depicts us, despite any injustices we may have suffered along life's way, as perpetrators who, deserving God's wrath, receive God's mercy. Sometimes God's mercy has a way of feeling like God's judgment.

Troubled by the denial and blaming that I found in my own church in a time of decline and diminishing returns on evangelistic efforts, I consulted an organizational consultant, who said something like this. "Every troubled organization is full of fear. In such a situation, leaders have the responsibility to face the fear and to tell the truth, to say, 'You are in denial because you are fearful that you don't have the resources to face the truth about your condition and do something about it.' A leader must put an organization in pain that it has been avoiding at all costs. The leader tells the truth out of faith that the organization already has the needed resources to face facts."

I believe that he was talking about judgment.

One concluding observation: Amos pleads that he is not a prophet or even a close relative of a prophet (v. 14). He is a common farmer. This sort of pleading by the prophet is typical of biblical prophets. Who wants to stand up to the lackey of the king and speak words of judgment that are sure to provoke the king's wrath? Despite Amos's pleading, the divine voice simply commands, "Go!" The prophet speaks words of judgment, not out of some personal conviction, but rather from a divine, external summons: Go!

It is an unenviable assignment to be summoned by God to speak truth to power; but any preacher worth her salt is commissioned for such an assignment. Perhaps we preachers ought to share with our congregations some of our trepidation and reservations at being enlisted by God to speak the truth, to make judgments, and to risk rejection. This prophetic vocation is our supreme moment as preachers and as congregations.

WILLIAM H. WILLIMON

2, Listen especially to King's later sermons in *A Call to Conscience*, ed. Clayborne Carson and Kris Shepard (Time Warner Audiobooks, 2004).

3. Paraphrasing from Dietrich Bonhoeffer, *The Cost of Discipleship* (London: SCM Press, 1959), 43–60.

Exegetical Perspective

dynasty). Piety without justice is hypocrisy (cf. 5:4–5, 21–24); power without justice is autocracy.

The fusion of sanctuary and palace in verse 9 leads into the biographical account of Amos's confrontation with the priest of Bethel, Amaziah.[2] Bethel is something like northern Israel's "national cathedral." The collusion of religious and political institutions is blatant when Amaziah says to Amos, "[Bethel] is the king's sanctuary." One would have thought it was God's. Amaziah's anxious criticism of Amos's message as treasonous "conspiracy" is not without historical warrant (cf. 2 Kgs. 9:1–3, 14; 10:9); it is also a pithy expression of the vulnerability of power to the pen: "the land is not able to bear all his words" (v. 10; cf. 1 Kgs. 18:17–18).

Amaziah scorns Amos as a "seer" who earns his living as a crystal ball gazer (cf. 1 Sam. 9:5–10:16). Amos replies that he is not, in fact, a professional prophet or a member of a prophetic guild, but that God has called him out of his ordinary life to prophesy. His authority comes not from an office but from divine revelation and commission. He then denounces Amaziah and adds him to the accursed (cf. v. 17 and Deut. 28:30, 32, 36). Exile—usually removing the ruling class to the land of the conqueror—was an established policy of imperial intimidation. Within a generation, Amos's warning proved true (2 Kings 17).

The combination of prophetic vision and religiopolitical confrontation is a classic example of "speaking truth to power." Genuine prophets really are the plumb lines who determine the degree to which a society is "upright" in terms of social justice (the priestly tradition could function this way also, Amaziah notwithstanding; cf. Ps. 15). Perhaps the full weight of Amos's radical prophecy can be appreciated only if we consider how treasonous it would sound to say "God curse America." If we cannot say that, dare we say, "God bless America"? Note again Amos 3:2.[3]

The burden of prophecy is the divine commission to announce God's curse when necessary, a task that is inherently subversive and risky. Sometimes those who speak unbearable words (v. 10) must bear the "cost of discipleship" (Bonhoeffer).

THOMAS W. MANN

Homiletical Perspective

difficult to move into an unknown future. This void can be filled only by the power of faith.

The Credibility of the Prophet. In every age the question has been asked, "By what authority do you speak?" Every generation is concerned about whether its leaders have the appropriate credentials to fulfill their responsibilities. We like to know that our physicians have the proper degrees and necessary training to care for our bodies. The same can be said for our teachers, pharmacists, and lawyers. We are pleased to know that the pilots of our airplanes have the hours of training necessary to transport us safely.

Another way of addressing this same issue in the religious community is to make the simple request, "Tell me the nature of your 'call.'" Laced throughout this passage is the subject of credibility. Amaziah, the priest of Bethel, challenges the authority of the prophet Amos. In his words to King Jeroboam he asserts, "Amos has conspired against you in the very center of the house of Israel" (v. 10). Amaziah mocks Amos directly, as he dismisses him and his message by saying, "O seer, go, flee away to the land of Judah, earn your bread there, and prophesy there; but never again prophecy at Bethel" (vv. 12–13a). Amos counters by saying, "I am no prophet, nor a prophet's son" (v. 14a). He asserts that he is (only) a shepherd and a dresser of sycamore trees. He does not point to his "degrees" or his station in life to justify his call as a prophet. He merely notes the source of the calling: "The LORD took me from following the flock, and the LORD said to me, 'Go, prophesy to my people Israel'" (v. 15).

Where we went to school, where we were raised, and who our parents happen to be do not ultimately tell the whole story about us. What *does* matter is whether or not our calls originate with God. A prophet's credibility is confirmed when the essence of that which is prophesied comes to fruition and the people are moved to faith.

JOHN E. WHITE

---

2. See Shalom Spiegel, "The Message of Torah: Amos Versus Amaziah," in *The Life of Torah*, ed. Jacob Neusner (Belmont, CA: Wadsworth, 1974), for a satirical application to the civil rights era.

3. See the paraphrases quoted by Daniel Carroll, *Amos* (Louisville, KY: Westminster John Knox Press, 2002), 55–57.

Psalm 82

¹God has taken his place in the divine council;
  in the midst of the gods he holds judgment:
²"How long will you judge unjustly
  and show partiality to the wicked?   *Selah*
³Give justice to the weak and the orphan;
  maintain the right of the lowly and the destitute.
⁴Rescue the weak and the needy;
  deliver them from the hand of the wicked."

⁵They have neither knowledge nor understanding,
  they walk around in darkness;
  all the foundations of the earth are shaken.

⁶I say, "You are gods,
  children of the Most High, all of you;
⁷nevertheless, you shall die like mortals,
  and fall like any prince."

⁸Rise up, O God, judge the earth;
  for all the nations belong to you!

Theological Perspective

The Failure of the Divine Council. Today's psalm is unusual in important respects; indeed, it has been characterized as "in some ways unique" by a commentator of some generations ago.[1] Two theological themes offer themselves to the preacher, linked by the use Jesus makes of a quotation from this psalm, reported in John's Gospel (10:31–38).

The first is the significance of the image of the divine council for a deeper understanding of the *development of Israel's doctrine of God.* The radical affirmation of Israel's one God to the exclusion of all others (notably in the First Commandment, and in the *Sh'ma Yisrael,* "Hear, O Israel: The LORD is our God, the LORD alone," Deut. 6:4) most congregations will know. Less familiar, and likely not well understood, will be the traces of Israel's struggle with the polytheism that was more characteristic of the cultures of the ancient Near East.

We may trace a line, from the Priestly account of creation in Genesis (1:26: "Let *us* make humankind in *our* image") through prophetic visions reported in 1 Kings (22:19: "I saw the LORD sitting on his throne, with all the host of heaven standing beside him") and Isaiah (6:8: "Whom shall I send, and who will go

1. George S. Gunn, *God in the Psalms* (Edinburgh: Saint Andrew Press, 1956), 96.

Pastoral Perspective

Prophetic words concerning justice pour out from the prophets and from the psalmist. "Let justice roll down like waters," proclaims Amos 5:24. "Give justice to the weak and the orphan," commands Psalm 82:3.

In the U.S. legal world, lower courts make judgments. If we believe their decision demonstrates partiality rather than justice, we may take the case all the way to the Supreme Court. We accept that route because we know—from home, work, congregation, community, and nation—that appeals are made to the highest-ranking individual or body.

Some families see this when the oldest child becomes "the boss." In other households, ultimate power lodges with both parents, or with a particular parent. Classic images of justice coming from the highest-ranking person in the home were burned into the consciousness of many of us in the 1950s by a television world in which the Cleavers showed domestic "perfection." Justice was meted out when Mr. Cleaver came home. Later depictions of family justice came with the *Brady Bunch* and *7th Heaven,* as families worked together to make positive decisions. The comedic side of family life emerged in the 1970s with the dysfunctional Archie Bunker in *All in the Family,* George Jefferson on *The Jeffersons,* and the Bundy family on *Married with Children.*

Exegetical Perspective

Mythology is often just below the surface of OT thought. Here it bubbles to the top in plain view. This psalm opens a window on an assembly in the heavenly realm. The key question for interpreting the psalm is not locating the exact ancient Near Eastern sources of mythology the author used, but what purpose the author makes of the mythology for the sake of the reader.

The psalm begins abruptly. A meeting of divine beings is already in progress as the psalm opens. The psalmist does not divulge when the assembly took place or whether the assembled beings had any notion that they were in for such a fiery judgment scene. Although the NRSV meekly has God "take his place" in the assembly, the Hebrew indicates that God stands to deliver the rebuke. The usual position for judgment is sitting, as on a throne (see Dan. 7:9–10). Does God's stance indicate an intensity of feeling or a claim of authority?

Who exactly are the "gods" attending the meeting? Ancient Near Eastern literature is replete with divine pantheons and contests among divine beings. The OT writers have a love-hate relationship with this notion of a heaven full of divine beings. The prophets thunder against idolatry and syncretism, yet heavenly beings appear throughout the OT in early and late texts. The overall trajectory

Homiletical Perspective

This psalm, like others by Asaph,[1] displays his passion for justice and his clear-eyed vision of God as one who speaks and acts powerfully on behalf of God's people. In moving from text to sermon, the questions surrounding the assembly of gods could easily derail a message, and it will be important to address the issue without dwelling on it. As interpreters of the word today, we may understand these "gods" to refer to the local deities of the surrounding nations, to those nations' tyrannical human rulers, or even perhaps to the leaders and wealthy people of Israel (all children of the Most High).

Others interpret them along the lines of the principalities and powers discussed in Ephesians (Eph. 6:12), as systemic forces bent on evil and destruction. However ambiguous their identity, their actions are not. Their deeds are deeply displeasing to the judge of this assembly. These powerful figures have been summoned and called to account for behavior that greatly displeases God. For similar scenes, see Job 1:6–12, Psalms 29, 58, 75, and 1 Kings 22:19–23. After the "gods" are indicted (vv. 2–4), the case is summarized and the verdict is announced (vv. 5–7).

---

1. Asaph was a musician hired by David and then Solomon (1 Chr. 6:39; 2 Chr. 5:12). Psalms 50 and 73–83 are attributed to Asaph. Reference to Asaph is in the superscript, not included in this volume.

Psalm 82

Theological Perspective

for *us*?") to Job (1:6: "One day the heavenly beings came to present themselves before the LORD, and Satan also came among them"), in which God is conversing with a divine council, a gathering of other deities whom God addresses, if not as equals, at least as cohabitants of the heavenly realm. In other places we catch glimpses of discord, even struggle, among other inhabitants of the heavenly realms (Dan. 10:13, 20, 21).

Israel's polytheism and its movement toward the affirmation of a single God have been explored in the scholarly literature for more than a hundred years. For our theological work today, the hint of a well-populated divine realm in this morning's psalm offers important avenues of reflection.

First, it makes plain how humans throughout history—down to the present day—have encountered difficulty in imagining or speaking of a single, unitary divinity. Our study of the history of religions teaches us of a broad movement from polytheism toward the unity of the Divine in many traditions; but this is a movement that spans centuries, even millennia. The idea of a divine realm comprising a number of distinct and active personalities seems never too far from the human imagination. We may adduce a number of reasons for this.

—Our own imaginations are so essentially limited that the breadth of God's imagination and creative activity is simply beyond our capacity to speak of meaningfully. The absolute otherness of God is something we rebel against in a variety of ways—and this is one of them. We reflexively seek to make God more accessible, more like us, by bringing God "down to size" and rendering the Divine into a variety of emanations.

—Human societies are characterized by constant competition, even conflict, among the powerful, who strive to control a greater share of power and authority among themselves; we have difficulty imagining that the same is not true in the realm of the Divine.

—We ourselves are so broken and divided, trapped in the ceaseless conflict between our wayward will and what we know to be the path of virtue, that we cannot conceive of a God not somehow similarly divided and troubled.

The thrust of these observations is to suggest a theological anthropology that lies at the heart of our encounters with polytheism. In plain words, our ideas of God will always be limited by our human capacity for understanding the Divine, and our

Pastoral Perspective

Viewers laughed as children, the maid, or the doormat wife stepped in to overrule the authority of the father on these shows.

Looking beyond family life, the appeal for justice in the work world may occur when a midlevel boss unfairly promotes someone who offers a bribe. The plea for justice may come from those not promoted and go beyond the midlevel to the top boss. When positions of prestige or public leadership in a congregation are handed out according to the amount someone donated to the capital campaign, the plea for justice may go to the church board, elders, or a judicatory team. From a community perspective, the era of political kickbacks may not reside only in history books. Today an ethics committee or staff in the mayor's office may be called in to rule for justice.

On a national level, in the United States "the number of registered lobbyists in Washington has more than doubled since 2000, to more than 34,750, while the amount lobbyists charge their new clients has increased by as much as 100 percent."[1] Why? Because many who govern the land (congressional members and staff) are willing to be courted by those who seek special attention, favors, and decisions. K Street in Washington, where many lobbyists have offices, has become a home for those seeking to influence the decision makers. Even with a plethora of laws, the potential for earmarks showing "partiality to the wicked" increases with thousands of lobbyists.

In Psalm 82, the cry is for God, the supreme judge (chief justice), to step into the divine council and take action. Why? Because the council, a gathering of the gods of all the nations, is the place where the universe is governed. This governing council has made unjust decisions, favoring the wicked. Those decisions resulted in oppression against the weak, the needy, the orphan, and the destitute (vv. 3–4).

Who are the weak, the needy, the orphan, and the destitute in your community? Are there waiting lists for Section VIII housing? Are there people living on the streets or in their cars, after losing their homes in foreclosure? Are the uninsured charged more for health treatment at the hospital, while those with insurance pay less? What happens to the families of soldiers suffering from post-traumatic stress disorder or brain injury? What happens when the soldier is discharged and there is no VA hospital for miles?

1. http://www.washingtonpost.com/wp-dyn/content/article/2005/06/21/AR2005062101632.html (June 25, 2005, *Washington Post*, A01).

Exegetical Perspective

of the OT is toward monotheism, but the authors make use of mythology and polytheistic motifs with some frequency. The beings in Psalm 82 seem to have administrative duties on earth, but the psalmist does not go so far as to state that each being has a country or people under its authority.

The accusation against the gods is that they have perverted justice. They have acted unjustly and have shown "partiality" (literally, "lifted up the faces" in approval) toward the wicked. Even though justice is a theme often associated with the prophets, the idea runs throughout the OT. At a basic level, justice is simple fairness. All people should receive their due in the legal system. All people should have access to goods and services. All people should be given an opportunity to thrive and flourish. Those who are vulnerable and defenseless should receive adequate attention and protection. The rich and powerful should not receive preferential treatment. These "gods" have had the responsibility to uphold and enforce this system of justice. They have failed in their responsibility. God judges their failure.

The psalm reveals the source of God's wrath. God looks with special solicitude on the weak, the orphan, the poor, and the needy. God is especially incensed at the exploitation of the weak at the hands of the strong. Although scholars dispute who walks in darkness in verse 5—the "gods" who are being judged, or the poor and needy—the verse seems to continue the thought of verses 3–4, where the vulnerable are the subjects. Walking in darkness, not seeing a way out of their predicament, is a part of the plight of the vulnerable. They lack the knowledge and the means to help themselves. Powerful human beings and especially powerful gods should help them.

The consequence of the failure of the "gods" is that the whole creation suffers a kind of instability. The "foundations of the earth" are literally the pillars that hold up the dry land of creation. Those pillars shake at the injustices allowed and perpetrated by the gods. The image seems to be an earthquake—an attention-getting event to say the least. Injustice shakes the creation to its very core. One thinks of the Lord saying to Cain that Abel's blood "is crying out to me from the ground" (Gen. 4:10). The creation—even dirt—responds to injustice. This threat to creation justifies God's fierce anger at the gods who have neglected the poor and needy.

This meeting of the gods has resembled a court scene all along. The prophets portray God holding people accountable in scenes resembling courts. Micah depicts a court scene in which the mountains

Homiletical Perspective

Though divine councils and earth's rumbling foundations can seem just obscure and problematic enough to send a preacher packing for the Gospel lesson, this text holds great potential for preaching. Its striking opening scene brings in all the tension of a courtroom drama, but one carried out at a cosmic level; it deals with issues that are immensely more important than those haggled over in a TV episode of *Law and Order*. There is a good reason why such shows are so popular today. They tap into a longing to see justice done, to see right triumph over wrong, and truth uncovered beneath deceit.

As preachers we can strive to portray this cosmic courtroom scene so that it resonates with that innate longing within our listeners. We can draw on current events around the globe and in our community, describing in vivid and compassionate terms the ways that the weak and the needy are being deprived of justice and kindness. Often, in the face of such blatant evil as child prostitution rings or oppressive migrant labor practices, it seems that wicked people and systems loom large, tower over the poor, and hold them in an inexorable grip. In the face of that, we become immobilized and fail to act. In this psalm we see the reality that God will one day call oppressors to account in ways that will make them shrink down to size, cower in fear, and stumble blindly.

The psalmist's vivid personification of evil displays a reality that listeners in our congregations know intuitively from their struggles against evil, whether within themselves, in broken relationships, or on a more systemic level in society. They know that evil is pervasive and tenacious; it is both personally embodied and institutionally perpetuated. Those who choose to be agents of evil on earth forfeit their vision; they are portrayed here as lacking awareness and insight. In the grip of blindness they stumble and stumble even further as the ground beneath them begins to shake. The lack of social justice has caused the fabric holding their society together to unravel; that instability is felt at the very core foundations of the earth.

Numerous movies (such as *All the King's Men* and *A Man for All Seasons*) illustrate how easily those in power can be corrupted, and preaching this psalm may involve a challenge to those with wealth and power in our pews. Of course, all of us are prone to cutting corners in small ways at work or on our taxes. The bigger issue here is not the absence of justice, but the failure actively to *pursue* justice. As we follow God's line of questioning, we see God's passion for the poor and the weak. First, God

Psalm 82

Theological Perspective

encounter with polytheistic ideas—including those we may find in Scripture—is simply one expression of that limitation.

A second theological avenue opened by reflection on this psalm has to do not with the polytheism we observe as students of religion, but rather *the polytheism we create in our own cultural context*. Our utter fascination with celebrity and the thrall in which we are bound by consumerist contrivances point to our continuing tendency to set up our own gods and pay them homage, to sacrifice to their honor and glory with our pocketbooks and our personhood.

Jesus, accused of blasphemy in John's Gospel (John 10:31–38), quotes verse 6 of this psalm in confounding the charge. Pointing directly to the presence of other "gods" in the Scriptures by which he is being condemned, Jesus argues that if God can refer to lesser deities as "gods," then one sent by God is surely entitled to be so called. Central to his argument is an awareness of the ease with which human societies—especially religious communities—confuse their own preferences with the authority of God.

Today's psalm lays waste to lesser deities and the human tendency to accord them a status approaching the place of our life with God. It makes painfully clear that God's justice will never be the chief purpose of the gods we create from our human obsessions. Our judgments will always be imperfect; we will always mistake the popular or powerful for the deserving. Those in whom we invest our respect and admiration will always fall short of the standard of God's justice. "They have neither knowledge nor understanding, they walk around in darkness" (v. 5). Consider the dramatic contrast between the red-carpet images of the demigods of our day, bathed in the adulation of a thousand blinding strobe lights, and this harsh estimate of the fumbling and stumbling of any gods we set up in the worlds of entertainment, sports, politics, business—even, let it be said, in the church.

In the end, as the psalm reminds us, even the gods that we set up and give homage prove to be mortal and passing. Simply put, there are no equals to God—no matter how fervent our worship or how extravagant our sacrifices to those whom we would count as worthy of ourselves.

MARK D. W. EDINGTON

Pastoral Perspective

Standard appeals for justice might go to community trustees, to churches with food pantries, to nonprofit clinics, to the Veterans Administration. But what happens when their response is like that of the divine council in Psalm 82?

Then the appeal goes out for true justice, to the God who will judge the earth. The psalm asks God to intervene and rule in a way that rescues the weak and the needy. What happens today to individuals or congregations oppressed and standing on the downside of a justice issue?

Here it is important to clarify the ways we understand God working. God engages in the quest for justice more often through the actions of individuals or groups than through direct intervention. Reading this psalm can strengthen our conviction that God can use each of us. We then act in accordance with what we believe God expects.

When we are among "the weak and the orphan . . . the lowly and the destitute," our appeal is to those who demonstrate true justice. We call those in authority to right action, appealing to their desire to give justice to those in need. When our place is among those called to rescue the weak and maintain the right of the lowly, we do well to align ourselves and our actions with the God of justice. We distance ourselves from those who "have neither knowledge nor understanding" (v. 5), for the other side of the psalmist's appeal to God is what happens to the divine council.

What judgment is rendered on the trustees, the congregations, the hospitals, the VA? What does the psalmist understand God will do to the judgment makers who have ignored or abused their roles? What becomes of those who "walk around in darkness" (v. 5)?

Verse 6 speaks in God's voice: "You are gods, children of the Most High, all of you." Not only here, but also in 1 Kings 22:19–23 and in Jeremiah 23:18–22, God comes into the midst of the council and is acknowledged as the top boss, the chief justice, the God among gods. The gods of the council, clearly of less authority, face God's judgment. The psalmist understands God's role and quotes the decision against the council. Their status is reduced. These gods will no longer live forever, but will "die like mortals" (v. 7). Only the true God remains, and this God will bring justice to life. To this God belong all the nations of the earth.

LINDA MCKIERNAN-ALLEN

Exegetical Perspective

and hills are the jury (Mic. 6:1–8). In Psalm 82, God hears no evidence. As is typical of prophetic court scenes, God is both prosecutor and judge. The "gods" are not permitted to speak or defend themselves. God knows the evidence and pronounces a death sentence. Verses 6–7 imply that gods cannot die—or at least think they cannot. Nevertheless, God has the power and authority to do away with them. In contrast to Near Eastern myths, the scene is not a struggle or a great battle. God is sovereign. God has given the "gods" the authority they have. God can take that authority away and even end their existence. Justice is that important.

The psalm makes skillful use of mythology, the idea that events in the heavenly realm affect life on earth, and vice versa. Scholars can argue whether the psalm is early or late, based on its use of mythology. The important question for contemporary readers is how the psalmist uses the mythology. What effect does it have on the reader? The psalm obviously draws upon the prophetic demand for justice. In that sense the psalmist is like Amos, roaring against the mistreatment of the poor and defenseless (see, e.g., Amos 2:6–8). In terms of literary artistry, the psalmist is like the prophet Nathan. Nathan confronted David indirectly about his sins (2 Sam. 12). By enabling the reader to "overhear" the court case against the "gods," the psalmist confronts the reader with the sins of injustice. Indirectly, the psalmist proclaims that people are judged for injustice, that God cares passionately about the poor and defenseless, and that the creation itself recoils at the suffering of the powerless. Nathan said to David, "You are the man!" (2 Sam. 12:7); the psalmist says to the reader, "You are the gods!" The last line of the psalm implores God to act, but also warns the reader that God may just respond!

CHARLES L. AARON

Homiletical Perspective

charges the powerful with their wrongdoing in failing to secure justice, and then God exhorts them actively to advocate for the destitute. They are called to risk their own security as they roll up their sleeves to rescue and deliver orphans right out of the hands of their enemies.

The story of Paul Rusesabagina's courage during the massacre in Rwanda in 1994 (made popular in the movie *Hotel Rwanda*) would make a powerful example of rescuing the weak and needy from the hand of the wicked. It would be good to balance that heroic story with a local, everyday story of someone in our own community who has labored on behalf of the weak. If there are social workers, public defenders, or others engaged actively on behalf of the disenfranchised in our congregations, a phone interview about how they fight systems of evil, what they find most discouraging, and where they find sources of hope, would give texture to the sermon. A testimony from someone in the congregation who has bravely taken a stand on behalf of the powerless would be highly effective as well.

Many of our listeners long to see justice done on earth, and to be agents of justice. They long to embody God's justice with fierce, bold acts of love toward those in need. They may desire this more than we know, because their lives may not display this desire: They too often find themselves caught up in the mundane details of life, as do we in pastoral leadership. This psalm is primarily an indictment of the powerful, but it is also a call to all of us to use whatever power we have to work on behalf of the needy. Such work flows out of an accurate vision that God is the owner of all the nations (v. 8). This confession of truth situates us rightly before God and before creation, not as owners, but as stewards commissioned to care for the environment and the earth's inhabitants. We are all prone to blindness, and we too can forget our mortality (v. 6) when we get a taste of power. This psalm calls us to look to God for vision, and to depend on God with humility as we go about seeking justice.

LISA LAMB

Colossians 1:1-14

¹Paul, an apostle of Christ Jesus by the will of God, and Timothy our brother,
²To the saints and faithful brothers and sisters in Christ in Colossae:
Grace to you and peace from God our Father.
³In our prayers for you we always thank God, the Father of our Lord Jesus Christ, ⁴for we have heard of your faith in Christ Jesus and of the love that you have for all the saints, ⁵because of the hope laid up for you in heaven. You have heard of this hope before in the word of the truth, the gospel ⁶that has come to you. Just as it is bearing fruit and growing in the whole world, so it has been bearing fruit among yourselves from the day you heard it and truly comprehended the grace of God. ⁷This you learned from Epaphras, our beloved fellow servant. He is a faithful minister of Christ on your behalf, ⁸and he has made known to us your love in the Spirit.

Theological Perspective

Colossians 1:1–14 provides a theological lens for its proclamation by sketching a christological vision of ecclesiology in the hues of specific issues faced by the Colossian church. In doing so, the text points us toward a homiletic that draws upon profound theological reflection on the union of a church's context with systematic reflection on the person of God.

The first chapter of Colossians pivots around a christological hymn in verses 15–20. Colossians 1:1–14 weaves the church into this image of Christ by naming their participation in the gospel of Christ described in the hymn. After a brief salutation, Paul offers thanks for the Colossian church, which is rooted in the hope produced by the word of truth brought to them by Epaphras (v. 7). He structures this thanksgiving to reinforce his contention that the Colossians can rest assured of their redemption in Christ, because the fruits of their church parallel those of faithful churches throughout the world. In asserting his thanks in this manner, Paul lays out a distinct ecclesiological vision. Faithful churches grow in the knowledge of Christ they have received. This growth is evident in the tangible fruits of faith, hope, and love present in the community.

Paul's claims regarding the relationship between good works and faith may not be as starkly rendered

Pastoral Perspective

Church historian Justo González is both a friend and neighbor. In addition to being a scholar, he is a United Methodist pastor and is married to my retired colleague Catherine González, a church history scholar in her own right and a Presbyterian pastor. In one of our many conversations, he explained the difference between United Methodists and Presbyterians in this way. Several years ago, when he was about to go into the hospital for surgery, his United Methodist friends consistently told him, "Justo, I am praying for you." His Presbyterian friends consistently told him, "Justo, I am thinking about you." "That's the difference," he says with a twinkle in his eyes. "United Methodists will pray for you while Presbyterians will think about you." If one follows González's tongue-in-cheek contrasting of these two church traditions, then the passage that opens the letter to the saints and faithful brothers and sisters in Christ in Colossae is more United Methodist than Presbyterian.

Following the first two verses of greeting, which closely resemble other letters from the apostle Paul, the first information the writer shares with the church is that prayers of thanksgiving are being offered for them because of their faith in Jesus Christ and their love for all the believers. What good news!

9For this reason, since the day we heard it, we have not ceased praying for you and asking that you may be filled with the knowledge of God's will in all spiritual wisdom and understanding, 10so that you may lead lives worthy of the Lord, fully pleasing to him, as you bear fruit in every good work and as you grow in the knowledge of God. 11May you be made strong with all the strength that comes from his glorious power, and may you be prepared to endure everything with patience, while joyfully 12giving thanks to the Father, who has enabled you to share in the inheritance of the saints in the light. 13He has rescued us from the power of darkness and transferred us into the kingdom of his beloved Son, 14in whom we have redemption, the forgiveness of sins.

Exegetical Perspective

This gem of a letter, purporting to be written by Paul and Timothy to a church founded by Paul's fellow worker Epaphras, reassures its recipients that in Jesus Christ they have all that they need for the spiritual life. The theological riches of Colossians have tended to be obscured in Pauline scholarship by a focus on two probably insoluble problems: its authorship and its implied opponents. We leave the question of authorship open, but for simplicity we refer to the author as "Paul." With regard to the second issue, apparently some other teachers are telling the Colossians that they fall short in spiritual matters and are judging them in regard to eating habits, religious rituals, ascetic practices, and visions or the lack thereof (2:16–23).

For our purposes, it is not important to discuss possible sources of such teaching, but it is crucial to attend to the wealth of the text in front of us. Here we find a universal, cosmic, and sovereign depiction of Christ as the one who holds together and graciously reconciles all things. In typically Pauline fashion, the letter emphasizes first the overflowing abundance and sufficiency of God's grace in Jesus Christ, and then the outflow of that grace in "love, which binds everything together in perfect harmony" (3:14).

Today's lesson comprises a long, carefully structured greeting, including thanksgiving and

Homiletical Perspective

The opening portion of letters of the classical age displays a standard protocol of greeting in which the writer offers thanks for the recipient. However, the images and ideas of this Colossian prayer of thanksgiving seem to tumble upon each other much like individual items seen through the door of a working clothes dryer. The issue of this greeting for the preacher, then, is not a struggle to "find something to preach on," but rather the challenge to shape a sermon plot with a sense of sequence and direction out of this tumble of imagery and ideas. Lacking a narrative form, preachers will search in vain for a story to plot our sermon for us. What is a preacher to do?

The opening greeting includes images and concepts of opposition and progression. The former have been used to great advantage by structuralist interpreters, especially in their analyses of narrative biblical texts. In the latter instance (ideas and images that embody progression or sequence), those of us called to preach are always on the lookout for mobility in the text that can translate into mobility and intention in the sermon. Once we have identified the core oppositions and progressions that lurk in the text, we are better poised to shape a homiletical plot that moves the listeners toward "the kingdom of [God's] beloved Son" (v. 13b).

Colossians 1:1-14

Theological Perspective

as they are in the epistle of James,[1] but they are just as forceful. Colossians was written, at least in part, to combat a variety of teachings that ran counter to the Pauline gospel and were causing division within the Colossian church. Paul rebukes false doctrines present in Colossae that range from "self-abasement" (*tapeinophrosynē*, 2:18) and legalism to the worship of angels and false mysticism. In his rebuttal of these counterfeit teachings, he does not merely offer proper doctrine. He authenticates his assertions regarding the proper understanding of Christ on the basis of the fruit born in Colossae: "From the day you heard [the gospel] and truly comprehended the grace of God" (1:6).

For Paul, false teaching threatened the redemption of the church and its communal life. He believed that a faithful gospel not only pointed to the proper beliefs and practices of the church, but also fostered a confidence in the truth and efficacy of God's self-revelation. In Colossians 1:3–7 Paul gives thanks for the Colossian saints in Christ. This proclamation of thanksgiving intertwines the central Pauline triad of faith, love, and hope in heaven and on earth. The earthly fruit of the community of faith reflects that which is set aside for it in heaven (v. 5). This fosters an image of the gospel of Jesus Christ as good news that engenders hope through faith rooted in God's love and redemptive activity.

Pauline theology rests on an unwavering commitment to the fidelity and the efficacy of God's continuing self-revelation. Knowledge of this activity is not merely disembodied truth; it is transforma-tional. As such, it has profound ethical implications. To be rescued from the "power of darkness" and moved to the kingdom of the beloved Son is to be transferred from the hopelessness of ignorance toward becoming a community made alive in the truth of the Word. Paul's assertion is that hope in Jesus Christ produces the fruits of the Christian life that are the product of Christ's love. Through their union with the crucified and risen Christ, the Colossians participate in a hope for salvation that entails a form of living visible in Christian communities anywhere the gospel is faithfully proclaimed.

The primary sin of false teachings is that they undermine this hope. They foster a rejection of the fullness of Christ's love by returning people to a realm of ignorant practices and beliefs. This separates them from the truth of God's salvation in

Pastoral Perspective

More than simply thinking about them, the apostle is praying for them. In this way, the apostle is connected to the believers in Colossae and everywhere else.

In the early church, the ancient monks understood this connection. They believed that a life of prayer manifested itself in a relationship with others and that prayer, as dialogue and union with God, had the effect of holding the world together. It is little wonder, then, that prayer features so prominently in Paul's letters to the early Christian communities. Prayer not only draws these fledgling communities closer to God; it is also what holds these fragile groups together.

So why are so many Christians reluctant to pray? For some, the reluctance is a result of experiencing persons who use prayer as an attempt to portray themselves as "holier than thou." After all, Jesus himself warned against the hypocrites who prayed in public to bring attention to themselves. Others may be afraid of imposing their own spiritual practices on friends and family members who may not believe as they do. Some view prayer as a quaint and outdated display of personal piety that more "mature" Christians have outgrown.

In *The Way of the Heart: Desert Spirituality and Contemporary Ministry*,[1] theologian Henri Nouwen says that one problem with prayer is that many Christians view it largely as an intellectual exercise—an "activity of the mind" that reduces prayer to simply speaking with God or thinking about God. This is a problem, Nouwen writes, because viewing prayer as thinking about God makes God into an object that needs to be scrutinized or analyzed. Successful prayer, then, is understood as prayer that leads to new intellectual discoveries about God.

Nouwen is quick to affirm that certainly the intellect plays an important role in the practice of prayer, but he worries that focusing only on the mind in prayer reflects a modernist notion that everything can be reduced to reason and subjected to rational control. Nouwen prefers to look at prayer as an activity of the heart and encourages us to reclaim the Jewish understanding of heart as the source of all physical, emotional, intellectual, moral, and volitional energies. From the heart arise unknowable impulses, as well as conscious feelings, moods, and wishes. The heart includes reason and is also the center of perception and understanding as

---

1. "Do you want to be shown, you senseless person, that faith apart from works is barren?" (Jas. 2:20.)

1. Henri J. M. Nouwen, *The Way of the Heart* (San Francisco: Harper & Row, 1981), 71.

prayer for the Colossians and concluding with a vigorous affirmation of their redemption. That redemption is both cosmic in scope and personal in application. Such a combination of cosmic and personal dimensions is thematic for this letter, which asserts the saving power and lordship of Christ in every corner of the universe and of human society (see, e.g., 1:6, 15–23; 2:15; 3:1–4).

When we consider that the author was in prison (4:10, 18), this affirmation of Christ's sovereign liberation takes on a special poignancy and power. Over against the forces that bind us, Paul proclaims that we have been "rescued from the power of darkness" and transferred to the kingdom of God's beloved Son (1:13). The word translated here "rescued" is the same word used in the Greek version of the Old Testament to depict God's deliverance of Israel from slavery in Egypt (Exod. 12:27; 14:30). Here the language of liberation echoes God's deliverance of Israel.

As we read through this text, four further themes catch our attention. First, immediately we learn that the source of the Colossians' love and faith is "the hope laid up for you in heaven" (1:5). In 1:12 we learn that the content of this hope is "the inheritance of the saints in the light." "Hope" links the present Christian walk (1:10, 22–23) with a heavenly existence already established by God. In 1:27, "Christ in you, the hope of glory" grounds this expectation in the present action of the indwelling Christ. Most emphatically, 1:11–12a displays the connection between the hope of glory and hopeful endurance: "May you be empowered with all power according to the might of his glory, for all endurance and patience with joy giving thanks to the Father" (my trans.). We cannot generate such joyful hope by ourselves or from ourselves, but Christ working within us can and does create and sustain hope, which in turn gives us courage to love.

Second, we encounter a close relationship between the actions of the Colossians themselves and the action of the gospel in both the world and the Colossian congregation. In 1:6, *the gospel* is "bearing fruit and growing" throughout the whole world, including among the Colossians themselves. In 1:10, Paul prays that *his hearers* themselves will "bear fruit in every good work" and "grow in the knowledge of God." That is, God's universal reconciliation of the cosmos through Christ becomes visible and embodied in the daily life of the church as it is animated by the word of the gospel.

Third, the close link between "good works" and the "knowledge of God" ensures that we will not

Oppositions
—*Light versus darkness.* This is perhaps the basic opposition (found explicitly in v. 13). The church in Colossae is being rescued from the power of darkness that abounds in that place through the power of God in Christ Jesus.
—*Fruitfulness in ministry vs. lives not worthy of the Lord.* This image of fruit-bearing appears in two locations within the pericope—in verses 6 and 10. In both instances, there is implied an opposite condition, an absence of fruitfulness.
—*Empowerment by God vs. conformity to the authority of darkness.* Here, the former is emphatic in the text. What the writer intercedes for is a church "empowered with all power." Lacking such empowerment, Christ's people may not be able to stand against the darkness.

Progressions
—*Saints on their way to fruitfulness.* The notions of a holy people and a missional people are linked in this text. (Oddly, some within the contemporary North American church tend to see the two in opposition.)
—*Saints in Colossae becoming aware of their place within all the "saints in light" (v. 12).* The saints in Colossae could so focus on their own holiness in the Spirit that they overlooked the "saints in light" ecumenically and eternally. Therefore, the writer prays for the spiritual gifts necessary for this community of saints to identify itself within the entire *ecclesia*.
—*Bearing fruit leading to growth.* Commentators have noticed this seemingly backward agricultural progression. After all, do not plants need to grow before they bear fruit? Since the writer of the epistle uses this sequence in two locations, something is at stake here other than agrarian misinformation!

These progressions or sequences, along with the oppositions in the text, lend themselves to a homiletical plot that trades on these dynamics. Although other approaches offer ways to shape a sermon that are mobile and sequential, and lead to some clear intention or outcome, the sermonic "loop" developed by Eugene Lowry is perhaps the best at handling these oppositions and progressions. Here, a narrative sermon plot invites the congregation from an initial *conflict* to complication by way of some probing analysis. Then a *sudden shift* occurs that is born of the gospel, which then leads to a final *unfolding* that was unimaginable prior to the

Colossians 1:1-14

Theological Perspective

Christ. Paul is keenly aware of the intimate relationship between knowledge and practice. His own comprehension of the grace of God enables him to "toil and struggle with all the energy that [Christ] powerfully inspires within me" (v. 29). Confidence in the hope of the gospel is a crucial gift of God given through faith. False teachings undermine that confidence both directly and by dividing the community between those who follow the gospel and those committed to alternative visions of God. This results in a diminished faith in the gospel and hinders the church from continually experiencing and propagating the fruit that flows from Christ's love.

Paul is calling the Colossians to continue to clothe themselves "with the new self, which is being renewed in knowledge according to the image of its creator" (3:10). His admonition makes a claim upon the church to take care that the wisdom that it imparts to its people is a faithful gospel. They are to proclaim a word of God that produces the fruits of endurance, patience, and joy both within the community and in its engagement with the world. Paul's warning is not rooted in a somber image of creation, but rather a joyous faith in the sovereignty of God. It is an ecclesiology rooted in the victory in Jesus Christ. He paints his picture of the church in Colossae in the bright hues of prayers of thanksgiving. As Lewis Donelson notes: "The spirit of thanksgiving to God for God's acts of salvation which pervades the letter . . . connects to the theological theme of hope."[2]

For Paul, prayers of thanksgiving are the proper foundation for the church because its life rests in the certainty of Christ's salvific work. Communicating this certainty fosters a hope that produces effervescent acts of Christ's love in the world. It is a task whose claim on our own communities requires us to examine both the content of the gospel we preach and the fruit it produces. The theology of Colossians 1:1–14 calls for gratitude for the ways in which our church reflects the beloved community, and offers prophetic motivation for us to move further toward the embodiment of Paul's vision.

MATTHEW FLEMMING

Pastoral Perspective

well as the will. In this way, prayer does not limit our relationship with God to interesting words, right thoughts, interesting conversations with God, or pious emotions. By its very nature, prayer changes us and draws us closer to God.

This understanding of prayer helps us read verse 9 with new eyes when the writer tells the believers that "we have not ceased praying for you." If one understands prayer as only an intellectual exercise, for Paul and Timothy to pray without ceasing conjures up visions of a marathon prayer session where each must take turns sleeping and eating so as never to stop speaking to God. If one, however, understands prayer as an exercise of the heart that involves all of life, then to pray without ceasing is to understand that prayer continues within one's self when one is talking with God or with others, participating in a meeting, doing yard work, or even sleeping. Prayer of the heart is the active presence of God's Spirit at work in one's life. This is likely what the apostle means when he tells the believers that he and Timothy have not ceased praying for them. This gives new understanding to Paul's admonition in 1 Thessalonians 5:17 to pray without ceasing.

The apostle and Timothy are connected to the believers in Colossae through their prayers of petition and thanksgiving and through the evidence of the believers' faithfulness in bearing fruit and in their growth in the knowledge of God. This is no glib or superficial connection, like what sometimes occurs when well-meaning persons say, "I am praying for you" or "I am thinking about you." Rather, this is a connection of the heart—of one's whole being joined with another—through the Holy Spirit. Sadly, the phrase "I am praying for you" can often mean nothing more than a well-intended expression of concern. When we understand prayer as located in the heart, then all who have entered into our lives, and even those who are beyond our knowing, are brought into God's presence at the center of our being. According to Nouwen, this is a mystery for which words are inadequate, yet it is the very nature of God that in some wondrous way we are redeemed, strengthened, and joined together with the whole church.

RODGER Y. NISHIOKA

2. Lewis Donelson, *Colossians, Ephesians, 1 and 2 Timothy, and Titus* (Louisville, KY: Westminster John Knox Press, 1996), 17.

confuse claims of esoteric wisdom with the true knowledge of God, which always issues in practical love of one's neighbor. Indeed, throughout this letter Paul repeatedly employs words relating to perception and cognition. The gospel is "the word of truth" (1:5–6), in which the Colossians have "heard" and "truly comprehended" God's grace. Paul prays for their "knowledge of God's will in all spiritual wisdom and understanding" (1:9), that they may "grow in the knowledge of God" (1:10). The connection between knowledge and love recurs in 2:2–4 and is developed extensively in 3:1–17, where the "things that are above, where Christ is, seated at the right hand of God" (3:1) have a distinctly ethical expression here "below," through "compassion, kindness, humility, meekness, and patience" (3:12). Such "knowledge" contrasts with claims of "philosophy" and "visions" that lead to arrogant judgment rather than humble service (2:8, 16–23). Although the situations are different, there is a parallel here with Paul's instruction to the Corinthians about the use of spiritual gifts to build up the church, rather than to pass judgment on one another (1 Cor. 12–14).

Fourth, in 1:13–14 two different pictures of salvation combine. The first is that of liberation from the powers of darkness and transfer to the kingdom of the Son. Such language evokes apocalyptic images of suprahuman powers holding humanity captive. The dominant motif here is the liberation of helpless creatures, not the forgiveness of guilty sinners who are responsible for their choices. The second image, in 1:14, is precisely the latter: "in [Christ] we have redemption, the forgiveness of sins." Romans 3:23–25 also speaks of "redemption" in terms of the expiation of sins. Scholars have tended to separate these two models of salvation in Paul's letters, noting particularly that Paul speaks very rarely of forgiveness, but here in Colossians there is no tension between the two: all humanity is both enslaved and in need of forgiveness, simul-taneously under the power of sin and guilty of sins. This theme will receive more elaboration in the commentary on Colossians 2:6–19 on pages 280–85.

SUSAN GROVE EASTMAN

"torque" that turned the sensed outcome from bad news to good news. We draw on our structural analysis in order to shape the material in Colossians 1:1–14 into such a narrative plot:

1. *Conflict.* We open the sermon with a quandary. The epistle seems to get it wrong about how churches thrive and grow. Pastors these days are sent or called to "grow a church," and techniques abound that counsel best methods for achieving the goal. (Image: a "toolbox" offered for sale on the Internet to get a church to grow.) Oddly, the writer to the Colossians has it backward. First, this apostle insists, we bear fruit. Then we grow! There is no mention of technique, of "toolboxes" for church growth.

2. *Complication.* Then things became even more baffling. The writer first calls us to be a holy people, to live lives befitting the gospel. Does this writer not know that some of us like to divide the church? After all, the disciplines of the Spirit that lead to holiness are not known for their relevance. If we are only about good causes in the world, then we may become invisible, lost in its darkness. (A pastor who listened to the inaugural sermon of a new bishop observed that it would have been a good speech by the chief executive of the United Way—all about service, with no reference to Jesus Christ!)

3. *Sudden Shift.* Through God's own doing in Jesus Christ, we have been "rescued" from the power of darkness and "transferred" into the kingdom of God's beloved Son. It is all grace. When we set out with a "toolbox" of some sort to grow or even to achieve holiness, we slip back into darkness. (Image: The icon of the *anastasis.* The risen Christ emerges from the tomb and raises old Adam and Eve from their graves. Here are the firstfruits of the resurrection. We are raised from darkness!)

4. *Unfolding.* Now look at signs of amazing growth. (The preacher will want to celebrate some examples in the life of the parish.) See, too, how the old wall between holiness and mission falls away. Finally, we discover that, through the grace of God in Jesus Christ, we have been "trans-ferred" into the kingdom and given a share of the inheritance of all the saints of light. (Image: The vision we sing in the last verse of "For All the Saints," concluding with "Alleluia!")

RICHARD L. ESLINGER

Luke 10:25-37

25 Just then a lawyer stood up to test Jesus. "Teacher," he said, "what must I do to inherit eternal life?" 26 He said to him, "What is written in the law? What do you read there?" 27 He answered, "You shall love the Lord your God with all your heart, and with all your soul, and with all your strength, and with all your mind; and your neighbor as yourself." 28 And he said to him, "You have given the right answer; do this, and you will live."

29 But wanting to justify himself, he asked Jesus, "And who is my neighbor?" 30 Jesus replied, "A man was going down from Jerusalem to Jericho, and fell into the hands of robbers, who stripped him, beat him, and went away, leaving him half dead. 31 Now by chance a priest was going down that road; and when he saw him, he passed by on the other side. 32 So likewise a Levite, when he came to the place and saw him, passed by on the other side. 33 But a Samaritan while traveling came near him; and when he saw him, he was moved with pity. 34 He went to him and bandaged his wounds, having poured oil and wine on them. Then he put him on his own animal, brought him to an inn, and took care of him. 35 The next day he took out two denarii, gave them to the innkeeper, and said, 'Take care of him; and when I come back, I will repay you whatever more you spend.' 36 Which of these three, do you think, was a neighbor to the man who fell into the hands of the robbers?" 37 He said, "The one who showed him mercy." Jesus said to him, "Go and do likewise."

Theological Perspective

Anyone asked to state the *essence* of Christianity (and in a religiously pluralistic society Christians are asked to do that, both implicitly and explicitly, every day) would not err too greatly by pointing to this parable of Jesus. Fortunately, human intuition has sensed this with considerable regularity. The story of "The Good Samaritan" is probably Jesus' most familiar parable.

Unfortunately, such familiarity—as the saying goes—can also breed a certain contempt; for there is a tendency to reduce the parable to simplistic terms that appeal only to shallow minds: "Be nice like the Samaritan, not nasty like the clergy!" True goodness and obedience to the spirit of the divine imperative in this parable are not so easily managed. We are not told what reflective background the Samaritan brought to his act of mercy, but if we have any depth of experience and self-knowledge, we know that such behavior is neither automatic nor unthinking.

The unfortunate one in the ditch represents as much of a nuisance to the Samaritan as to the two "religious." Every truly moral act presupposes an astonishing store of meditation-upon-experience that is "theological," whether it is called that or not. The seeming simplicity of this and other parables of Jesus should not be the occasion for denigrating the complexity of Paul's theology of "Jesus Christ and him crucified" (1 Cor. 1:23), as liberal theology

Pastoral Perspective

In his posthumously published book on the Decalogue, Paul Lehmann rings the changes on the relationship of the gospel to the law. Lehmann says, in so many words, that when we understand the law as gospel, we present our obedience to the law as behavioral proof of faith. Then to justify ourselves, our increasingly refined understanding of the law's demands places human opinions and tradition on a par with revelation. The law is the means we have been given to arrive at the ends of God. When we seek to live as if the gospel were law, we set off down a road not knowing where we are going. We travel by grace as radically vulnerable disciples, sent (as the disciples in Luke had just been sent) to respond to the human in the other along the way. The other calls forth "the obedience of faith in a world made and redeemed for being human in."[1]

The lawyer who stands up to test Jesus likely understands the law as gospel. He is, after all, a lawyer! In response to the lawyer's question about eternal life, Jesus presciently cuts to the chase: "What is written in the law? What do you read there?" Likely believing his life to be behavioral proof of the obedience of faith, he quotes the law. Still he cannot

1. Paul Lehmann, *The Decalogue and a Human Future* (Grand Rapids: Eerdmans, 1995), 18.

Exegetical Perspective

When wrenched from its narrative context, as has happened in the history of its reception, Jesus' parable of the Good Samaritan often gets reduced to something like a medieval morality play. As Luke presents the parable, however, nestled between verses 25–29 and verses 36–37, it does much more than endorse compassion, generosity, and etiquette for travelers. It demands that its hearers embrace opportunities to practice love for others in powerful ways and perhaps to learn from surprising sources how to do that.

Luke refers to Jesus' interlocutor as a "lawyer" (*nomikos*), a term synonymous with "scribe," an expert in interpretation of the Mosaic Law. Consistent with an earlier characterization of lawyers (7:30), the narrative highlights the man's insincerity and thereby infuses the scene with a sense of conflict. The lawyer aims to "test" *(ekpeirazō)* Jesus, openly challenging the authority and insight of the uncredentialed Galilean. Jesus parries, and it appears the two men find common ground in Deuteronomy 6:5 and Leviticus 19:18, until a follow-up question, "Who is my neighbor?" extends the confrontation by asking Jesus to interpret the scope of the latter text. Because this question stems from the lawyer's desire "to justify [*dikaioō*] himself," it attempts to limit who rightly qualifies as his neighbor, to confine the

Homiletical Perspective

When a parable becomes a cliché, can it still function in the life of the community? A "Good Samaritan" is commonly recognized as anyone who comes to the aid of another. But is this really what Jesus was getting at? Was he only offering a variation on "Be helpful when you come across people in trouble"? Was he just giving us a parable to make us feel guilty when we ignore a homeless person?

I do not want to exclude offering help to those depending on the kindness of strangers, but this parable goes beyond that. It not only lays down a big challenge but makes an even bigger offering of gospel or good news. This is a story for people who recognize that they are on a journey—not just a journey from womb to tomb, but from birth to rebirth, from partial life to abundant life. The gospel proclaims what God pours into the hearts of all those who journey in a dangerous world.

In the framing story, Jesus is on his way to Jerusalem: "When the days drew near for him to be taken up, he set his face to go to Jerusalem" (9:51). Jesus is on the way to his death, when he meets a lawyer, who wants to know how to move toward life: "What must I do to inherit eternal life?" Some hear hostility in his words, but others say this "testing" is part of rabbinic dialogue. Perhaps he speaks for all

Luke 10:25-37

Theological Perspective

habitually has done. To move an individual from the condition of "natural" self-preoccupation to one of profound concern for others, the whole gospel—with the cross at its center—is required.

At the same time, "the learned" are apt to make the connection between action and reflection, ethics and theology, too complicated. The church fathers loved allegory to the point of finding every detail of this parable hiddenly "meaningful" (the journeying victim is Christ; the innkeeper is the church; the two coins are the sacraments, etc.). Contemporary preachers, armed with a little psychology, can cause the message of Jesus in this parabolic gem to appear so complex that their hearers are left in the end with the impression every compassionate act requires such a burden of self-analysis and contemplation that the act itself would likely never occur!

Do not mistake it: the "message" here is stunningly simple—though it is not simplistic. Even the scheming "lawyer" (the German, more accurately, reads *Schrift-gelehrter*—scholar of the Scriptures), bent on self-justification, grasped that at once. Who was the neighbor? Unable on account of his religious exclusivity to answer straightforwardly, "The Samaritan," he replied, "The one who showed him kindness" (v. 37 NEB).

While we may fault him for failing to acknowledge that the real neighbor was a despised foreigner, a believer in a rival creed, we should find it remarkable that this "expert in the law" breaks through all the wordiness of religious legality by naming *kindness* as the true mark of "the neighbor." That puts the matter in terms wonderfully appropriate today, for it is precisely "kindness" that is so conspicuously absent from the life of our world—a world driven by competition, greed, and individualism, but also (let us note) a world whose most ethically minded often seem apt to be more concerned for rights than for forgiveness, for justice than for mercy, for equality than for compassion.

The late Kurt Vonnegut, that crypto-evangelist, grasped the essence of Christianity when he was asked by a young American from Pittsburgh, "'Please tell me it will all be okay"—which is perhaps the contemporary American equivalent of asking for eternal life. "Welcome to Earth, young man," Vonnegut said. "It's hot in the summer and cold in the winter. It's round and wet and crowded. At the outside, Joe, you've got about a hundred years here. There's only one rule that I know of: Goddamn it, Joe, you've got to be *kind*."[1]

Pastoral Perspective

leave well enough alone. For when Jesus tells him to love God with everything in him, and to love his neighbor as himself, he can obey only if he knows exactly what the law commands.

There is, of course, a bit of the lawyer in us and in those whom we serve. To caricature us all, the many for whom the law is the gospel seek refuge in rules, glorify boundaries, enumerate norms, and codify discipleship. Here the significant question is often a question that asks after definition and therefore desires to set a limit: precisely whom am I to love as myself? When law is gospel, I am the actor, and my actions ultimately must be justified by my understanding of and obedience to the law humanly defined.

To answer a question that seeks definition and limit, even with the most expansive and inclusive words language can dare, is to affirm the law as gospel. It is to allow the questioner the continued illusion of control. It is to reinforce the presupposition that the life of discipleship is a life marked by knowing the good from evil, rather than a life meant and purposed to know only God and God's mercy.[2]

The story Jesus tells the lawyer—the story we attempt to tell one way or another from the pulpit, in the hospital room, around the meeting table, before an open grave—is the story that casts us and those we serve not as actors but as those acted upon by a love whose limitless goodness we cannot fathom. It is also a story that spells the end of the world ordered by our increasingly narrow definition of the neighbor, the neighbor defined by the law as gospel. The story Jesus tells is the story of the gospel as law.

If we are to tell this same story in the communities we are called to serve, we will lead our people down that dangerous road from Jerusalem to Jericho. Perhaps those who travel this road believe that obedience is the behavioral proof of faith, where an increasingly refined understanding of the law's demands has placed human opinion and tradition on a par with revelation. Beaten and stripped of control, we are left helpless and half dead by the side of the road. The keepers of the tradition, the tradition by which we have justified ourselves, simply pass us by. Somehow their definition of the good does not compel them to love us as they love themselves. Rather, another character traveling the same road we were traveling—an unlikely character for whom the gospel apparently is law—comes near, sees, and is moved with pity. Our human condition

---

1. Kurt Vonnegut, *A Man without a Country* (New York: Seven Stories Press, 2005), 107.

2. Dietrich Bonhoeffer, *Ethics* (New York: Simon & Schuster, 1995).

Exegetical Perspective

collection of people whom he must love. This strategy of self-vindication contrasts him with those in 7:29 who rightly justify (*dikaioō*) God; they, unlike him, generously affirm God's purposes and reflect God's righteousness. With a parable and his concluding words Jesus reorients the assumptions behind the lawyer's contrived question, prodding him to expand his understanding of what it means to be a neighbor and to love a neighbor.

The injured man in the parable is a Jew, as suggested by the wider narrative context and the setting in which his attack occurs. Jesus does not explain why the priest and Levite—highly esteemed Jewish religious figures associated with the Jerusalem temple—neglect to assist one of their own people. The parable treats their staying across the road from a fellow Jew in need as a shocking event. Nothing indicates that they think the victim is dead or that they fear contracting contamination from a corpse; even if the man were dead, such purity concerns would be insignificant compared to the weightier need to arrange for the burial of an exposed body. The point is that two people who presumably represent the identity and piety of the victim do not express any concern toward him and remain unwilling to assume the risks that come with pausing in a dangerous place. The two act in identical ways: each arrives, sees the man, and passes by on the other side. Nothing can excuse their refusal to reach out.

The Samaritan's introduction jolts the audience. "Samaritan" is the first word of the Greek sentence that begins with verse 33. He appears out of place on a Judean road. To most Jews in Jesus' world, this character represents an enemy, the other. The historical roots of the Samaritan-Jew conflicts remain unclear, although 2 Kings 17:24–41 attributes them to the forced migration of foreign peoples into what had been the northern kingdom, after the Assyrians' conquest (eighth century BCE). During Jesus' time, Samaritans and Jews claimed to worship the God of the ancient Hebrews, but each group had its own Scriptures, temple, and religious practices. Elsewhere (9:53) Luke reaffirms the deeply strained relationships between these peoples, when Samaritans turn Jesus away because "his face was set toward Jerusalem," toward the centerpiece of most Jews' religious world. Differing ethnic identities and longstanding cultural antipathy give every reason to assume that the Samaritan in the parable and the wounded traveler will have nothing to do with each other.

Homiletical Perspective

of us who want to attain "eternal life," a deeper intimacy with God, even now.

Jesus responds, "What does the law say?" The man fittingly quotes the Torah (Deut. 6:5 and Lev. 19:18): "You shall love the Lord your God with all your heart, and with all your soul, and with all your strength, and with all your mind; and your neighbor as yourself" (10:27). Jesus commends him: "You have given the right answer; do this, and you will live" (v. 28). Then, the lawyer comes back with the question that evokes the parable: "And who is my neighbor?" (v. 29).

So we get a story of another journey. A man is going down from Jerusalem to Jericho, from David's city of peace, perched high on a hill, twenty miles through the wilderness, to Jericho, located at the edge of the Dead Sea. It is a dangerous road, not one to travel alone. He is attacked by robbers, stripped of everything, brutally beaten, and left for dead. First a priest passes by, then a Levite. Both see him, both cross the road to avoid him. Jesus' listeners understand why: the man appears dead, and if either priest or Levite were to touch someone dead, they would make themselves ritually unclean. These men know the law, like the lawyer questioning Jesus. It calls them to maintain purity for worship. Besides, this could be a trap. So they go to the other side of the road, picking up their pace.

Along comes a Samaritan. The Jews held Samaritans in contempt, seeing them as unfaithful to the law of Moses and to the temple worship in Jerusalem. The contempt was mutual. Luke records an occasion where Jesus himself experienced it: a Samaritan town refused to receive him on the way to Jerusalem. James and John wanted Jesus to call down fire from heaven, but Jesus rebuked them (9:51–56.)

In Jesus' parable, the Samaritan does not pass by. He draws close, "moved by compassion," moved by the spirit of God poured into his heart to cross over to where the man lies. Seeing the man is alive, he pours oil to cleanse the wound and wine to dull the pain; he picks him up, takes him to an inn, and promises to return to resolve whatever is owed. This Samaritan has already received eternal life. He is living it then and there.

A year or two ago I read about a twelve-year-old Palestinian boy, Ahmad Khatib, who had been shot and killed by Israeli soldiers during street fighting near his house in Jenin, the West Bank. The boy had been holding a toy gun. He was taken to an Israeli hospital, where he died after two days. His parents made the decision to allow his organs to be

Luke 10:25-37

Theological Perspective

What Vonnegut did not say (though one suspects he knew it well enough) is that human kindness, when it is real, is only our poor response to the kindness of the One who made us and who tries to keep us human,

> For the love of God is broader
> Than the measure of the mind;
> And the heart of the Eternal
> Is most wonderfully kind.[2]

The *great* lesson of this parable—for Christians today—can be glimpsed only if the biblical ethic of kindness is put together, as it is in the parable, with the recognition that such behavior frequently emanates from unexpected sources, and in doing so calls *us* up short. For the parable to achieve its full shock value in *our* context, a preacher ought to try substituting for the word "Samaritan" (which means little or nothing to our contemporaries) words such as "Muslim," "Sikh," "Buddhist," "Jew," or even, in some communities one can think of, "Catholic."

Until it is grasped that at the level of *true* morality—that is, where basic attitudes and acts are concerned, where "the fruits" by which we are "known" (Matt. 7:16) become conspicuous—genuine goodness and moral authenticity cannot be restricted to any one people or creed and do not depend upon having learned the "right" theoretical answers! Without in the least denigrating theology or doctrine, Christians ought to recognize (as did the Reformers with their much-underused concept of "common grace") that there is in the human spirit a certain "impulse to kindness" that may or may not be the consequence of this or that creed, moral code, or faith tradition.

What would it mean for interfaith dialogue if such recognition were shared, at least as a beginning, by all participants? What if, in every interfaith encounter, our residual human capacity for compassion were prodded by a transcendent Voice whispering in our would-be-believer's ears, "For God's sake, Christian, be kind!"

DOUGLAS JOHN HALL

Pastoral Perspective

has called forth "the obedience of faith in a world made and redeemed for being human in," as Lehmann put it. This is not just anyone who comes near, sees, and is moved with pity. As Amy-Jill Levine insists,

> We should think of ourselves as the person in the ditch and then ask, "Is there anyone, from any group, about whom we'd rather die than acknowledge, 'She offered help' or 'He showed compassion'?" More, is there any group whose members might rather die than help us? If so, then we know how to find the modern equivalent for the Samaritan. To recognize the shock and possibility of the parable in practical, political and pastoral terms, we might translate its first-century geographical and religious concerns into our modern idiom.[3]

Levine proceeds to be more specific than the lawyer ever imagined when he asked his question of Jesus. Who is the one who proved neighbor? Who is the one who loved God with heart, mind, soul, and strength, and so loved the neighbor as the self? For Levine, as a Jew, it is a member of Hamas who showed mercy. In a lecture on the same parable before an audience who had experienced the horrors of September 11 firsthand, she suggested the one who proved neighbor was a member of Al-Qaeda.

Suddenly this familiar parable, often used to encourage good Christians to aid a traveler whose car has broken down on a dark and stormy night (later litigation be damned), has become a parable that flies in the face of the law as gospel. When the lawyer at the end of the story realizes he, and not Jesus, is the one who is being put to the test, he manages to say that the one who has proved neighbor is the one who showed mercy. He cannot bring himself to say the word "Samaritan." Sometimes that nameless admission is redemption enough, this side of the grave.

CYNTHIA A. JARVIS

---

2. Stanza 6, "Souls of men, why will ye scatter," by Frederick William Faber (1814–63). The adjective "kind" and its derivatives appear four times in this hymn.

3. Amy-Jill Levine, *The Misunderstood Jew* (San Francisco: Harper Collins, 2006), 148–49.

Exegetical Perspective

The Samaritan's compassion stands in diametric opposition to the unconcern of the priest and the Levite. The Samaritan treats the man not as an enemy but as one dear to him, as shown in the multifaceted care he provides. His exemplary deeds, born from compassion, demonstrate the lengths to which love goes. Authentic love does not discriminate; it creates neighborly relationships, because by its nature it meets the needs of others.

Jesus does not return to the lawyer's original question and ask him to identify who in the parable he should consider to be *his* neighbor. When Jesus asks the lawyer to name which character "was a neighbor to the man who fell into the hands of the robbers" (v. 36), he reorients their conversation away from the lawyer's question about limiting one's responsibility. The lawyer wants to define who deserves his love, but Jesus' parable suggests that love seeks out neighbors to receive compassion and care, even when established boundaries or prejudices conspire against it.

Jesus' question in verse 36 also forces the lawyer to admit which character demonstrates what it means to act in a neighborly way. His refusal to utter "the Samaritan" as his answer underscores the parable's deep offense. A Samaritan is the exemplar. The lawyer is pushed to learn about genuine love from the deeds of one whom he regards as his enemy. To be committed to love of neighbor involves a willingness to see an enemy as a benefactor, one who can offer instruction about true compassion and righteousness.

Sermons on this text should avoid moralizing that stops short with only banal appeals to celebrate or welcome strangers. Preachers must bring to light the parable's scandalous edge, emphasizing its capacity to drive hearers to identify, humanize, and embrace the most unlikely candidates for their own neighborly relationships. Biblical scholar Amy-Jill Levine suggests an avenue into experiencing the scandal: "To hear this parable in contemporary terms, we should think of ourselves as the person in the ditch, and then ask, 'Is there anyone, from any group, about whom we'd rather die than acknowledge, "She offered help" or "He showed compassion"?' More, is there any group whose members might rather die than help us? If so, then we know how to find the modern equivalent for the Samaritan."[1]

MATTHEW L. SKINNER

Homiletical Perspective

harvested for transplant to Israelis. Six people received his heart, lungs, and kidneys, including a two-month-old infant. His mother, Abla, said, "My son has died. Maybe he can give life to others." These parents made their own journey into the compassion of God and were living eternal life.

If you check several translations of the lawyer's response to Jesus at the beginning, some put a comma before "and your neighbor as yourself," while others place a semicolon there (v. 27)—a small difference, it would seem, but perhaps not. In Margaret Edson's magnificent play *Wit*, there is a conversation about the use of punctuation in John Donne's Holy Sonnet Six. Evelyn, a teacher, rebukes Vivian, a student, for using an edition marked by "hysterical punctuation" in the final two lines, especially the use of a semicolon where a simple comma would do. Evelyn histrionically recites the last two lines, noting aloud its punctuation: "And Death—*capital D*—shall be no more—*semicolon!* Death—*capital D*—*comma*—thou shalt die—*exclamation point!*" She then urges another version: "And death shall be no more, *comma*, death, thou shalt die." The simple comma, she suggests, conveys that "nothing but a breath—a comma—separates life from life everlasting."[1] A simple comma suffices. I think the same applies here. A simple comma will do. To love God is to love neighbor is to love God. This ongoing flow of love allows eternal life to begin even now, as the parable confirms.

The parable of the Good Samaritan is a story for travelers on the road, a scriptural GPS, routing us in the only direction God desires—the way of love and compassion for others. This is more than a parable about a helpful stranger; it is about the transforming power of God at work in those who travel the dangerous roads in our world, moving us into the fullness of life, eternal life, here and now.

JAMES A. WALLACE, C.SS.R.

---

1. Amy-Jill Levine, *The Misunderstood Jew: The Church and the Scandal of the Jewish Jesus* (San Francisco: HarperSanFrancisco, 2006), 148–49.

1. Margaret Edson, *Wit* (New York: Faber & Faber, 1999), 14–15.

Amos 8:1-12

¹This is what the Lord God showed me—a basket of summer fruit. ²He said, "Amos, what do you see?" And I said, "A basket of summer fruit." Then the Lord said to me,

"The end has come upon my people Israel;
 I will never again pass them by.
³The songs of the temple shall become wailings in that day,"

says the Lord God;

"the dead bodies shall be many,
 cast out in every place. Be silent!"

⁴Hear this, you that trample on the needy,
 and bring to ruin the poor of the land,
⁵saying, "When will the new moon be over
 so that we may sell grain;
and the sabbath,
 so that we may offer wheat for sale?
We will make the ephah small and the shekel great,
 and practice deceit with false balances,
⁶buying the poor for silver
 and the needy for a pair of sandals,
 and selling the sweepings of the wheat."

Theological Perspective

In this compact text, dense with stomach-turning images of judgment, Amos proves the evocative, creative character of prophetic witness. The summons to justice may be simple—love God and love your neighbors, especially the poor—but, in a systemically unjust world, that call must overcome hardened hearts and social evils ingenious in their escapes from simple, suffering truths. Sometimes God's call to justice can come plainspoken, or in a wordless embrace. In worlds of pervasive corruption, however, the prophet cannot simply announce the path of justice, but must craft a message that both illustrates and overcomes the way that sin has deadened a people to the words of life. Amos's rhetoric aims to over-whelm, to suffocate, to cut off every avenue of religious escape. By doing so, it depicts how social evil has overwhelmed a people, suffocating them with distorted religious practices and exploitative political institutions that over time have cut off the possibility of hearing about God's justice.

The text begins with a Hebrew pun that jarringly connects the summer's fruit to looming demise and ends with a desperate people suffering a famine of God's words. Both associations work to produce dissonance in symbols of religious solace. Once an innocent blessing, the land's ripe produce now portends doom. Hitherto an everlasting comfort,

Pastoral Perspective

We in the United States have just had our celebration of Independence Day. July Fourth is the day when we celebrate the gift of our country's freedom, our national independence. Amos has a different sort of word to the nation, a word of *dependence* upon the judgments of a righteous God. When we celebrate our nation, we tend toward self-congratulation. We think of ourselves as good, free, and righteous, but God's judgments may be different from our judgments. According to Amos, to be a person of faith is to be dependent upon and tethered to the righteous judgments of God.

Part of Israel's greatness was that the people saw themselves as accountable to something higher and more substantive than their own opinions. In today's text, however, the prophet Amos has some threatening, troublesome words for Israel. The Lord of Israel holds up a plumb line (7:7) against Israel. When he does, the nation is found deeply wanting.

From time to time one hears someone lament the "moral decay in America." Usually the lament con-cerns a perceived decline in personal relationships, sexual behavior, and family values. In contrast, note that Amos voices divine concern about those areas of morality that are related to economics (8:4–6). He is especially concerned about the treatment of the poor. Furthermore, Amos voices divine judgment against a

⁷The LORD has sworn by the pride of Jacob:
Surely I will never forget any of their deeds.
⁸Shall not the land tremble on this account,
and everyone mourn who lives in it,
and all of it rise like the Nile,
and be tossed about and sink again, like the Nile of Egypt?

⁹On that day, says the Lord GOD,
I will make the sun go down at noon,
and darken the earth in broad daylight.
¹⁰I will turn your feasts into mourning,
and all your songs into lamentation;
I will bring sackcloth on all loins,
and baldness on every head;
I will make it like the mourning for an only son,
and the end of it like a bitter day.

¹¹The time is surely coming, says the Lord GOD,
when I will send a famine on the land;
not a famine of bread, or a thirst for water,
but of hearing the words of the LORD.
¹²They shall wander from sea to sea,
and from north to east;
they shall run to and fro, seeking the word of the LORD,
but they shall not find it.

Exegetical Perspective

The vision that begins Amos 8 established the warning "THE END IS NEAR" that appears in innumerable cartoons, but there is nothing comic in Amos's prediction. This vision is the fourth of five (see exegesis for last Sunday, pp. 221–25) that conclude with God's relentless judgment against the northern realm of Israel in the early eighth century BCE. The "end" will be national destruction and exile (7:17; 9:4), from which none shall escape (9:1). Following the vision there are an indictment (8:4–8) and a series of judgment oracles (vv. 9–10, 11–12, 13–14), each beginning with a temporal reference that echoes the eschatological tone.

God shows Amos an ordinary object and employs a pun that signifies the threat (Shalom Paul coins an artful paraphrase with "summer fruit," "summary hour").[1] God will no longer spare Israel from the consequences of injustice (contrast 7:1–6; cf. 7:8). As a result, the royal court (cf. 2 Chr. 35:25) will resound with funeral hymns instead of praise songs (cf. "mourning," vv. 8, 10; 5:1, 16–17). Unburied corpses of the guilty will litter the streets—an unspeakable massacre ("'be silent,'" v. 3).

The severity of the punishment fits the severity of the crime (vv. 4–8; 2:6–7; 5:11). Israelites "trample

1. Shalom Paul, *Amos* (Minneapolis: Fortress Press, 1991), 253.

Homiletical Perspective

It is incredibly painful to be openly criticized. This is only compounded when you hear that your actions are responsible for the demise of a once-proud nation. In the case at hand, insult is added to injury as the message comes from a sheepherder, a commoner named Amos who claims to be God's spokesperson. We should never lose sight, however, of the truth that it was the injustice imposed upon the people by their political and religious leaders that led to their demise.

The Significance of the Fruit. An obscure movie from the 1970s titled *Robin and Marian* stars Sean Connery and Audrey Hepburn as the aging legendary figures of Robin Hood and Maid Marian. Prior to the tragic conclusion of the film, the director takes great care to display a bowl of fruit on the table in their room. Once their fate has been sealed, the camera scans over to the fruit to reveal that the fruit has become overly ripe—rotting and well past its prime.

Amos 8 begins with the prophet being shown a basket of fruit, but not just any fruit. It is a basket of "summer fruit" (v. 1). The time of the harvest has come and gone for the people of Israel. Could the wording of verse 3 possibly be more graphic? "'The songs of the temple shall become wailings in that

Amos 8:1-12

Theological Perspective

God's covenant words are no longer there, even for those seeking them. In abundance, there is word of famine, and in famine, word of nothing but God's abandonment. In the paragraphs between, the earth darkens, worship songs become wailing, the land heaves like the flooding Nile, feasts turn to desolate mourning, and dead bodies are strewn about. The intensifying images of doom can seem excessive, even vitriolic, but Amos's hyperbole is not the mere dismissible ecstasy of outrage. Its excessiveness responds to the inescapability of a sinful political economy.

In other words, Amos's rhetoric demonstrates the theological stakes at issue through its moral inventiveness. His creative hyperbole illustrates how life within an unjust social ecology can make it nearly impossible to hear God's words. His almost unthinkable images dramatize an almost unthinkable situation: a world in which God's words cannot be heard. Amos shows that prophetic witness must not only outstrip society's capacities to discredit the words of justice; effective prophetic witness must in effect create the conditions for its own hearing by convincingly narrating the corruption at the heart of its own discrediting. The prophet's task requires rhetorical strategy with audacity proportionate to the injustice it opposes. His words must silence society's discrediting religious noise and political spin long enough for people to hear simple words of justice.

In this dense series of condemnations, Amos's vision names and takes away the things in which a corrupt society seeks refuge from justice—a ripe harvest, its identity as a people, the stability of earth, religious worship, the rhythms of the sun, and even covenantal assurance that God can be sought out when the consequences of social wrong loom on the horizon. These are all good things, indeed gifts from God; but the prophet must show that they all serve God's justice. Disconnected from the patterns of neighborly justice, these good things no longer speak of the people's blessing but of their sure collapse. The task of the prophet is to reestablish the intrinsic relation of all God's good things with justice, and the certainty that injustice will bring catastrophe.

By connecting each good thing to judgment, Amos silences its function as a legitimating symbol for a violent economy. Just after Amos makes the ripe fruit basket stand for God's judgment, he announces that the Lord demands silence—not an accounting of their blessings, not pleas for forgiveness of God's chosen people, not repentance from the promised-land community, not even lamentations from the

Pastoral Perspective

specific class of persons. He singles out the merchants who cannot wait for the religious holiday to end so they can get back to fleecing the poor with their high prices for grain.

God threatens fierce, dire consequences against an economically unrighteous society, promising dark days ahead (vv. 8–10). This prophet does not take injustice against the poor lightly. He tells his greatly contented society—made up of people who think they are secure in their prosperity and wealth—that they will disintegrate into dark, disruptive chaos. God is not nice to those who glibly transgress the righteous laws of God.

We in the United States have just enjoyed a couple of decades of prosperity, but it has not been a prosperity that has been enjoyed by all. An unfair tax code has literally enabled the rich to get richer and the poor to become poorer. It has been a tough couple of decades, not only for the poor but also for the middle class, who have seen their gains in salary and benefits fall away as many of them slipped below the income level that made them middle class.

The United States fought the most expensive war ever in Iraq and borrowed money from our grandchildren to pay for it. Improvements to the nation's infrastructure were neglected during the same period of time. Unwilling to raise taxes in order to pay for the war, our nation accumulated massive debt. Our politics appears to benefit those who have economic clout in our society. The poor, the overtaxed, and the economically burdened have no advocate—no one, that is, except a righteous God and the prophets who serve that God.

What would Amos preach to us? I have a friend who teaches theology at Oxford University. He opens his theology class by asking the students, "With what is theology concerned?" The students typically answer, "God," or "Religion," or "Spiritual things." He corrects their misapprehension, "No, *Christian* theology is concerned with everything!" There are presumably religions that are concerned exclusively with personal, private happiness, with individual morality, but neither Judaism nor Christianity is one of those religions. In Judaism and Christianity, God not only creates the world but continues to interact with it and to take care of everything in it. This God makes no distinction between "religious" concerns and "secular, nonreligious concerns." This God is concerned with everything.

Today's text from Amos gives preachers a grand pastoral opportunity to remind our people that worship of the God of Israel and of the church is not

on the needy, and exterminate the poor of the land" (v. 4, my trans.). "Terminate" and "Sabbath" (v. 5) have the same Hebrew root, suggesting the ironic hypocrisy of Israel's religious observances (5:21–24). Unscrupulous merchants can hardly wait for the Sabbath to end, when they can resume cheating the needy by shortchanging them (e.g., selling a twelve-ounce pint) or overcharging them (e.g., using an eighteen-ounce pound weight; cf. Deut. 25:13–16). Even a small overcharge (the price of a pair of flip-flops) could result in destruction, for wealthy people ruthlessly exploit the socioeconomic system in which people who cannot afford to pay debts must sell themselves or a child into indentured service (Exod. 21:1–11; widows and orphans were particularly vulnerable—see 2 Kgs. 4:1–7 for a poignant example). The practice is legal, but is it moral? Amos castigates a culture that turns the pairing of law and justice into an oxymoron.

God's punishment is as certain as Israel's pride (v. 7; cf. 6:8). The catastrophe will be like an earthquake or like the annual flooding and receding of the Nile. The cosmic and personal dimensions expand in verses 9–10. As in the African American spiritual—itself an echo of the cry for justice[2]—the sun will "refuse to shine." The reversal of religious festivals to funerals, praise songs to dirges (v. 3), deepens into the worst grief imaginable—the loss of an only child (v. 10c).

Amos has already referred to famine and thirst, both past and future (4:6–8; 7:1–6). Now he warns of a greater deprivation—an absence of God's words (vv. 11–12), a spiritual yearning that is deeper than the need for food and water (Deut. 8:3). People will search "from sea to sea," "seeking the word of the LORD, but they shall not find it." In Deuteronomy, God's word is not in heaven or beyond the sea, but "very near to you; . . . in your mouth and in your heart for you to observe" (30:11–14). Israel has refused to do this word, primarily because it has dissociated seeking God from seeking justice (5:4–7). Now it is too late (cf. 9:2–4). God will abandon them. It will be like an endless "dark night of the soul," as if Israel can recite only those psalms of lament that speak of the silence and absence of God, with no hope of God's response: "My soul thirsts for God, for the living God. When shall I come and behold the face of God?" (Ps. 42:2; cf. Pss. 63:1; 143:6). Amos's answer is, "Never again."

2. See James Cone, *The Spirituals and the Blues* (New York: Seabury, 1972), 102–7; Donald G. Mathews, *Religion in the Old South* (Chicago: University of Chicago, 1977), 217–22, 231–36.

day,' says the Lord GOD; 'the dead bodies shall be many, cast out in every place. Be silent!'"

A Word of Warning to Those Who Dare to Abuse the Poor. The words of Jesus are abundantly clear: "It is easier for a camel to go through the eye of a needle than for someone who is rich to enter the kingdom of God" (Mark 10:25). This statement makes those of us who live comfortable lives in comfortable homes very uncomfortable. Jesus' claim that those who exercise political, religious, and social power are responsible for the welfare of the whole people has its roots in statements made nearly 800 years earlier.

Verse 4 of our text begins with words that are beyond equivocation, "Hear this, you that trample on the needy, and bring to ruin the poor of the land." The implication is that the leaders of Amos's time had clearly abused their power in order to benefit themselves, while the poor in the community were ignored. The greed of the powerful was so complete that they could not wait until the Sabbath was over so that they could resume the business of "ripping off" those with few choices and even fewer resources. The ephah represented a unit of measure; the shekel was the standard unit of weight in ancient Israel. To make the "ephah small and the shekel great" (v. 5) meant that customers would receive less than they had paid for. Rich merchants would accumulate more and more unjust wealth. The author of the text goes as far as to say that the powerful are trading the poor as mere chattel ("buying the poor for silver and the needy for a pair of sandals," v. 6). They sell the sweepings of the wheat—a combination of the chaff, dirt from the floor, and perhaps a few grains of wheat.

Their sin reminds this writer of contemporary political leaders who may forget their mandate to serve the people, choosing instead to serve themselves and their friends by voting to approve bills that are more for their personal gain than for the common good. Pastors who encourage their congregants to give in order to increase their own salaries, but ignore the larger ministry of the church, are guilty of the same crime. Let us not forget business leaders who have accumulated their wealth on the backs of underpaid laborers.

The Pride of Jacob. Pride goes before the fall. As the full text of Proverbs 16:18 reads, "Pride goes before destruction, and a haughty spirit before a fall." Pride can make people think that they are above reproof and that judgment will never come their way for any

Amos 8:1-12

Theological Perspective

spiritually yearning. The prophet's words silence all those symbols of grace in order to name what they have masked: the needy trampled and the poor oppressed. What does God care for loud worship, the prophet has asked earlier (5:21–23). A dishonest, exploitative economy corrupts the land and makes the people indifferent to their neighbors. Amos clinches the picture of indifference with reference to those "buying the poor for silver and the needy for a pair of sandals" (8:6).

For Amos, it is not just the hearts of those particularly callous slavers that frustrate justice; it is that God's justice can scarcely be imagined in a world where such things happen in normal course. Thus the prophet's creative task: to make of the everyday world a sufficient outrage that the words of justice can be heard. That is a task of both rhetorical creativity and faithful courage. Augustine, who was otherwise not a regular admirer of Old Testament prose, marveled at the inspired power of Amos to fulfill the task.[1] Modern prophets like Mahatma Gandhi and Martin Luther King realized that their world required a kind of social rhetoric, a creativity that dramatized the inevitable conflict of social sin and social justice on the streets.

Amos therefore leaves today's reader with a theological question that is equally a creative problem: What does prophetic witness require today in order to get the poor on the political agenda of an indifferent governing class? How does one say in a complex market society that the way to God's heart is with the uninsured, the homeless, the excluded? How does one dramatize the stomach-turning wrongs of a promethean sense of progress wholly bent against the land and its helpless creatures? It will not do flatly to moralize the oppressed or simply to denounce an unjust system. The prophet must find ways to silence languages of a people's gods and goods long enough to let the words of justice be heard. To do so, she must evocatively depict the wrongness of a society in which people, land, and God have come apart, in order that a world built on injustice can see its unavoidable destruction, it surely coming collapse.

WILLIS JENKINS

Pastoral Perspective

limited to Sunday. Worship continues in what we do at the office on Monday and continues throughout the week. This God does not want just our "heart" or our "soul." This God wants all of us.

This is not a Sunday when we forsake our "pastoral" concerns and allow ourselves to be more "prophetic." For Amos, this is a false dichotomy. Amos represents and speaks for a God who loves Israel enough to call Israel to account. Israel lives under the judgments of a God who loves Israel, who wants this people to be a "light to the nations," to show forth to the world what a people can do when they are owned by, accountable to, and called by a true and living God.

Amos does not shrink from naming names, from citing specific instances of injustice and inequality. If the preacher is squeamish about making such "political" or "economic" statements in a sermon, then the preacher ought to cite Amos as the preacher's model. If the congregation squirms under such close prophetic scrutiny—if they think that the preacher has lapsed into mixing religion with politics and spirituality with economics—then the preacher ought to remind the complainers of the precedent set by Amos and the requirements for worshiping the true and living God! There is no shortage of names that can be named today. There is no dearth of specific instances of injustice and inequality that can be cited, at least for the preacher who is willing to call Amos as his or her witness.

One way you can tell the difference between a true and living God and a dead and fake god is that a false god will never tell you anything that will make you angry and uncomfortable!

WILLIAM H. WILLIMON

---

1. Augustine, cited in *Ancient Christian Commentary on Scripture*, vol. 14, ed. Alberto Ferreiro (Downers Grove, IL: InterVarsity Press, 2003), 83.

Exegetical Perspective

The lectionary omits verses 13–14, perhaps because of the obscurity of verse 14, but the catchword "thirst" connects with verse 11. Various translations are possible, referring either to illicit forms of the worship of God or to oaths sworn in the name of other gods. In either case, the beautiful people have put their trust in an ugly theology. The "beautiful" are no doubt members of the society's elite, those who feast on lamb and veal and drink wine from bowls, but have no concern for the decadence of their lifestyle, much less the plight of the poor (6:4–7). Soon the tables will be turned, and they "shall faint for thirst" (cf. Lk. 1:53).

Amos was an "outside agitator" from Judah—a southerner who spoke to a northern audience in a time of national security and material affluence, the latter enjoyed by the few at the expense of the many. His words may be as difficult for us to bear as they were for Israel and its political ruler (7:10–13). There is a shocking brutality to the images of divine judgment and punishment: drought and famine, the savage violence of warfare, the ignominy of defeat and exile. Although there are glimmers of hope that Israel will repent and avoid judgment (5:4–7), their past behavior makes that extremely unlikely (4:6–12), conveying an unrelenting sense of doom.

We may not want to draw a cause-and-effect connection between social injustice and military defeat, just as we are uncomfortable with the image of God wielding or at least commissioning the sword of war (7:9; 9:1), but Amos's condemnation of the wealthy and powerful might be more welcome if we could see it from the perspective of the "trampled"—the poor and needy who are nickeled and dimed into subjection.[3]

THOMAS W. MANN

Homiletical Perspective

of their actions. Many a reputedly great empire (e.g., Rome, Egypt, Great Britain, and, dare we say, the United States of America) has also been a victim of its own pride. The "pride of Jacob" (v. 7), also found in Amos 6:8, apparently refers to the arrogance of the nation of Israel, which once thought that it was above harm.

A Reversal of Expectations. The prophet Amos, called as God's true spokesperson, comes up from Judah to sound a different tune. The deeds of the people of Israel (particularly their leaders) will not be forgotten (v. 7). The destruction will be complete, as the whole land shall "tremble" and all of its residents will "mourn" (v. 8). Things will not transpire "on that day" in a way that befits the expectations of the powerful; instead, it will be as if the Lord will make "the sun go down at noon, and darken the earth in broad daylight" (v. 9). Feasts will be turned from occasions of celebration into a time of mourning. Songs will not bring messages of praise and joy, but of lamentation (v. 10). Mourning will be severe, "like the mourning for an only son (v. 10).

The Loss of Something More Necessary Than Bread and Water. "You never quite miss something (or someone) until it is gone," the old saying goes. Amos's prophecy is not intended for the poor, the needy; his words are for those who seemingly have it all. Scarcity of bread or water, as bad as that might be, is not of concern to them, nor are they concerned that they might hunger or thirst for the words of the Lord. Still, "the time is surely be coming, says the Lord GOD," when a "famine" of God's words will come upon the people. The time will come when they travel throughout the world as they know it—from "sea to sea, and from north to east"—running frantically "to and fro, seeking the word of the LORD, but they shall not find it" (v. 12).

JOHN E. WHITE

---

3. Barbara Ehrenreich assumes such a perspective in her book *Nickel and Dimed: On (Not) Getting By in America* (New York: Metropolitan Books, 2001). In her work as a waitress, "The worst [patrons], for some reason, are the Visible Christians—like the ten-person table, all jolly and sanctified after Sunday night service, who run me mercilessly and then leave me $1 on a $92 bill" (p. 36).

Psalm 52

¹Why do you boast, O mighty one,
    of mischief done against the godly?
    All day long ²you are plotting destruction.
    Your tongue is like a sharp razor,
    you worker of treachery.
³You love evil more than good,
    and lying more than speaking the truth.   Selah
⁴You love all words that devour,
    O deceitful tongue.

⁵But God will break you down forever;
    he will snatch and tear you from your tent;
    he will uproot you from the land of the living.   Selah
⁶The righteous will see, and fear,
    and will laugh at the evildoer, saying,

Theological Perspective

Confrontation with the Powerful Proud. Today's psalm addresses a difficulty many faithful people have in reconciling their own theological understanding with the world as they experience it—the fact that the powerful often seem to act in ways at variance with virtue. The answer offered may not be greatly comforting, but something about it is genuinely human and authentic to the experience of the psalmist and his community.

From a theological perspective, the psalm is not an indictment of power per se, but a specific critique of the ways in which the powerful exploit their authority and position to act in ways inconsistent with God's purposes. In the world of the Psalms, *all* power held by human authorities is a gift—and a responsibility—from God, a gift that can as easily be withdrawn. There is no guarantee, however, that the responsibility will be honored and carried out in accordance with God's purposes. Indeed, the view of kingship held in the Psalms is not uniform or harmonious. Writing half a century ago, George Gunn noted two understandings of kingship in the historical accounts of Israel's consolidation—one championing the Davidic kingship and the other evoking fear that this accession to the will of the people would threaten

Pastoral Perspective

It is hard to imagine a text that draws a clearer distinction between the mighty and the righteous. The language is direct, pointed, and judgmental. Readers easily ascertain which side of this distinction is preferable. Verses 1–4 define the "mighty one" who boasts, lies, and loves evil. Verses 6–7 identify "the righteous" who claim true security in God's love.

In this psalm, the cruel, deceptive actions of the mighty one are directed against all that is good. Of course, those in the faith community will likely delight in the divine response to that mighty one, described graphically by the psalmist in verse 5: "God will break you . . . snatch . . . you . . . uproot you." After that comes the promise that the "righteous will see . . . and will laugh at the evildoer" (v. 6).

Stories abound of scams against people of faith. People looking for security have found roofers who grab a fat down payment and then disappear with leaks still destroying a sanctuary; prayer partners who promise healing only to disappoint; appeals for mission support only to find the outreach limited to a dishonest fast-talker; promises of Holy Land tours that evaporate after seed money is sent.

In such situations, it is understandable that those victimized would want to see God punish the mighty one. The hurting ones would easily delight, laughing

⁷"See the one who would not take
   refuge in God,
but trusted in abundant riches,
   and sought refuge in wealth!"

⁸But I am like a green olive tree
   in the house of God.
I trust in the steadfast love of God
   forever and ever.
⁹I will thank you forever,
   because of what you have done.
In the presence of the faithful
   I will proclaim your name, for it is good.

Exegetical Perspective

A speed bump in the form of a translation tangle prevents too quick a rush into this passionate psalm. The first line of the psalm itself (following the super-scription) is clear enough. The psalmist is in attack mode, with a demanding question ("Why do you boast?") and a sarcastic epithet ("O mighty one"). What exactly does he say after the first line? Does he continue the accusation against the "mighty one," as the NRSV assumes? Does he contrast the boastful arrogance of the accused with God's faithfulness, as some other translations suggest (see, e.g., the Jewish Publication Society translation, the Tanakh)?

What is it that lasts all day long? Is it the plots of the accused, or God's faithful love? The advantage of the JPS rendering is that it follows more closely the wording of the Hebrew text as it stands. The advantage of the NRSV decision is that it makes the first stanza more consistent. The affirmation of God's steadfast love (JPS) seems to interrupt the flow of thought in the first few verses, which pile up the sins committed by the accused. Because the NRSV translation requires too many changes, perhaps the best decision is to opt for the JPS.

If one decides to stick with the Hebrew text, what sense does the translation make? Is the psalmist accusing the opponent of failing to comprehend the

Homiletical Perspective

Part of the homiletical intrigue of this psalm is that it does not directly address God until the last verse. Rather, according to the superscription, in this psalm David confronts an enemy, Doeg (Saul's chief shepherd), first spelling out the wrongs he has done and the heart from which his deceitful acts flow, and then laying bare the destruction awaiting him. Preachers will want to sketch in quick, vivid strokes the dramatic story of how Doeg, in a desperate bid for Saul's approval, tattled on David to the king and then, at Saul's request, brutally murdered eighty-five priests, as well as women, children, and animals (1 Sam. 22:8–19).

The incident reveals Doeg to be a conniving political climber with no moral compass, willing to go to any lengths to please Saul and improve his own standing. David does not mince words in his appraisal of Doeg's character, which is revealed by boastful and deceitful words and malicious actions. It appears that Doeg will emerge unscathed, not brought to account for his evil. David needs to look with the farsighted vision of faith, trusting in God's power.

A key question to ask as we lead our congregations into this psalm is, how does it serve David to utter the words of this psalm? What are the psychological and spiritual benefits to be gained

Psalm 52

Theological Perspective

Israel's unique relationship with YHWH as its only king.[1]

The "mighty one" (v. 1), then, we may regard as a putative leader, one who wields authority. It is immaterial whether the language was intended to speak of a specific leader in Israel's history (as the superscription at the beginning of the psalm, not included above, seems to imply); the moral question in play is not about whether authority is inherently evil, but whether an individual who has come into authority over others does or does not exercise that power in accordance with God's expectations.

The tripartite structure of the poetry of the psalm—the bill of particulars constituting an indictment of the "mighty one," the herald of God's coming punishment, and the psalmist's own role within the drama—might be seen as exemplifying in microcosm Walter Brueggemann's hermeneutical contention that the whole of the Bible's witness can be seen as "*the costly reality of human hurt* and *the promised alternative of evangelical hope.*"[2] The mighty one's failings are failings precisely because of the human hurt associated with the exercise of leadership: those who are faithful and powerless are subjected to troubles ranging from mischief to destruction; they are humiliated and made the object of derision. Instead of helping those under authority flourish more fully into God's desire for them—the true calling of one in whom YHWH vests authority—the mighty one is constraining them, frustrating their hopes, denying their personhood.

Against the reality of hurt is arrayed the hope of God's justice. It is significant that a specific expression of this punishment will be that God "will snatch and tear you from your tent" (v. 5b), that is, God will remove from the mighty one both the authority vested and the attendant privileges of power. The justice coming will be, appropriately, the experience of what the mighty one inflicted on the powerless: humiliation and derision ("The righteous . . .will laugh at the evildoer," v. 6). Having failed to aid the broken and despairing, the mighty one will face being broken down, removed from the very source of life—the covenant community of Israel ("the land of the living," v. 5).

Pastoral Perspective

at the uprooted ones now suffering as a consequence of their actions.

However, the world as we know it is not so clearly demarcated. "Mischief makers," "sharp-tongued workers," and those who lie when the truth is too painful might describe any number of people. Individual members of congregations have been known to function in self-serving and destructive ways, as well as whole faith communities. Trusting in abundant riches (v. 7) appears to be a national identity marker in twenty-first-century America.

Where does one safely put trust? What is true security? Does it come from accumulating the most money, the most "stuff," or the most influence and power? Our answers may indicate the fascination many have with the "rich and famous" of North American society. Attention, media frenzy, and big payments for inside information make life challenging for many highly paid athletes, entertainment stars, and people at the top of business.

Dangers abound in faith circles as well. Some television evangelists have become laughingstocks when their empires collapse. Some pastors, in large or small congregations, have destroyed their ministries by loving evil more than good. When these individuals lie, boast, and practice deceit, their stories become headline news.

Others, both within and outside faith communities, live in a cultural ethos that promotes commerce as our means of security. Buying things demonstrates our identity as "mighty." Bumper stickers declare, "The one who dies with the most toys wins." In the face of the terrorist attacks of 9/11, the U.S. president counseled the country to go shopping.

In the twenty-first century, Americans face a rising rate of bankruptcy, home foreclosures, credit card debt, and living beyond our means. We are saving at a negative rate, spending more than we are making. This may be due, in part, to our being bombarded by advertisements. Consider these figures as one demonstration of the problem: the average child sees 20,000 thirty-second TV commercials in a year. By age sixty-five, the average American sees 2 million TV commercials![1]

The push to consume is not limited to advertisements. In 2008, the U.S. government sought an economic stimulus. Rather than reducing taxes, subsidizing health-care costs, or finding ways to support the housing market, the U.S. government

---

1. George S. Gunn, *God in the Psalms* (Edinburgh: Saint Andrew Press, 1956), 71–72.

2. Walter Brueggemann, "Bodied Faith and the Body Politic," in *Old Testament Theology: Essays on Structure, Theme, and Text*, ed. Patrick D. Miller (Minneapolis: Fortress Press, 1992), 70; emphasis in original. See esp. Brueggemann's argument that "voices of hurt and hope predominate in the Psalms," 84–86.

1. http://www.csun.edu/science/health/docs/tv&health.html.

Exegetical Perspective

marvelous dependability of God's steadfast love? Is the psalmist trying to shame the accused by contrasting his treachery with God's love? The debate will continue, and each preacher will have to decide.

Identifying the form of the passage is another disputed point among interpreters. The psalm obviously contains elements of different kinds of poems. Scholars have identified traces of prophetic accusation, lament, and wisdom. The goal of the psalmist is likely not to create a pure form, but to accomplish as much as possible. Drawing upon different genres enables the psalmist to cover more ground. The psalmist wants to condemn abusive injustice, give vent to frustration, and extol the wisdom of trusting God. Integrating rhetoric from three traditions, the psalm accomplishes more than any one genre could.

Verses 1–4 constitute the first section of the poem. This section bears the most similarity to prophetic accusation. Isaiah 22:15–19 is often cited as an example of the same form as this part of the psalm. Although the author of the superscription, not printed in this volume, is sure that the psalm is about Doeg (see 1 Sam. 21–22), the psalm itself gives no indication of the object of the accusation or what exactly the accused did. The reader can infer that the accused has acted treacherously, spoken maliciously, and abused wealth. The accusations against the psalmist's opponent are hyperbole. Although the exaggerated language of the psalm gives us no reliable historical information, it drives home the seriousness of the sins of the accused.

The next section, verses 5–7, continues the form of prophetic accusation. The emphasis shifts to the punishment to be meted out both by God and by the community of the righteous. The predicted death sentence imposed by God will be exacerbated by the derision of the righteous. Has the accused oppressed the righteous, so that their derision is a catharsis?

Wisdom themes emerge in verses 8–9. This part of the psalm resembles Psalm 1, which compares the wise to a tree planted by streams of water. The psalmist believes that trust in and gratitude toward God provide more stability and long-term hope of reward than do riches and power.

Although the psalmist was likely directly hurt by the actions of the accused, the psalm does not truly bear the marks of lament. The psalmist is more angry and defiant than given to lamentation. Nevertheless, commentators have noticed that the ending of the psalm sounds like the ending of an

Homiletical Perspective

from putting these feelings into words, rather than simply cursing his enemy under his breath or keeping his concerns to himself? In what sense can verbalizing our gripes with our enemies (even in an imagined monologue like this one) become a *prelude to prayer*? Too often, our complaining about ill-treatment or slander from another does not end in the serene confession of trust and thanksgiving that we see here (vv. 8–9). So the pattern of David's complaint forms a model for us in our quest to bring all of life into God's presence. The pattern provides the shape of a sermon as well.

David begins with a question. He is incredulous as to Doeg's motivation for behaving and speaking as he has. How often we too, when we have been wronged by others, find ourselves stunned, unable to comprehend the motives or rationale for their words and actions. Not only has Doeg behaved appallingly, but he is boasting about it! He not only commits evil deeds, but he revels in plotting more of them. Perversely, he enjoys watching the destructive power his tongue and sword can wield. David names Doeg's sin with clarity and boldness.

He does not stop there. In verse 5, David looks out into the future, using what he knows of God's character as judge of evil and defender of the weak, and foretells Doeg's demise. At the end of a series of violent verbs detailing God's actions (break, snatch, tear, uproot), David introduces the metaphor of the tree, hinting at it with the warning that Doeg will be *uprooted* and carted off to the scrap heap. This nicely foreshadows the contrasting metaphor of the well-rooted tree.

After warning of God's forceful action against Doeg in the future, David foretells, with a much more benign trio of verbs, a more positive future for the righteous (v. 6). With no need to take vengeance in their hands, they will simply *see, fear,* and *laugh.* The action of fearing balances and precludes potentially vindictive excesses of merely seeing and laughing. The righteous do not see and mock; they see and humbly fear. For the stain that permeates Doeg's heart has tainted them as well, and the sight of his destruction serves to hold up a mirror to their (and our) own tendencies toward grasping for power or selling out to gain approval. Chastened by a healthy fear of God and of their own human frailty, they then can laugh. Laughter implies freedom and peace. In the midst of heightened vision and sober fear, the righteous are confident of the goodness of the path they have chosen. The laughter described here is not derisive laughter, but the laughter of the

Psalm 52

Theological Perspective

The power of the theological teaching in this text lies not in its apparent sanction for vengeance, but instead in its *insistence on distinguishing between God's justice and ours.* This may be explored in a number of ways.

God is the righteous judge. The Christian must live in response to our Lord's requirement of forbearance (Luke 6:37–38), even under conditions of extreme provocation (Matt. 5:38–39). We may not forget that God *is* the righteous judge. Our temptation is always to put ourselves in God's place and to mete out the judgment we believe God should exercise over the unjust "mighty ones." The discipline we are called to live by as followers of Christ is to understand that the systems of justice we construct in human communities are limited by our own fallibility. God's justice is not constrained by such limitations, and God's judgment—difficult though this idea is for contemporary Christians—is absolute.

Human leadership is always fallible. The fate of the mighty one reminds us that, while leadership takes many forms in our lives, human leadership must *always* involve humility. Authority over other humans, no matter what form it takes or the degree to which one holds it, inevitably carries with it a moral hazard arising from our own fallenness. It is easy enough to regard this teaching as applying only to those in positions of recognized leadership; but simply to live as members of a powerful and wealthy society is to share in a position of privileged leadership in a world where the vast majority of humans have nothing like the economic or political advantages we take for granted.

We wait in faith and hope. Christians, as people living by faith pointed toward the coming of God's kingdom, must confront and not deny the costly reality of human hurt. Our call to be people who live pointed toward a horizon of evangelical hope does not give us license to neglect or ignore the very real pain inflicted on many by fallible and arrogant human "mighty ones." Our place is to be those who perceive that injustice, whether far away or next door; who insist that it be named and acknowledged; and whose hope in the justice of God spurs us to redress those failings through prayerful discernment and purposeful action.

MARK D. W. EDINGTON

Pastoral Perspective

sent a check to every taxpayer, along with the encouragement to spend. Is it any wonder many believe security comes in buying more stuff? Shopping is now identified as the prime pleasure of teenage girls,[2] and purchasing something is seen as an expected part of every shopping trip. Shopping is encouraged to keep the economy moving.

The search for security may also be the natural result of possessing influence and power. Secret Service personnel protect our "most powerful" people. Security companies continue to grow in order to provide protection for American troops and construction personnel in Iraq. Americans working in many countries around the globe find it necessary to be driven in bulletproof cars, taken directly to plane doors, and surrounded by electric fences in their homes because they are ripe targets for kidnapping.

Those seeking security by false means are subject to ridicule, writes the psalmist (vv. 6–7). True security does not come by way of money, stuff, or power. True security does not come in outdoing others, through deceit, or in the company of evil and falsehood. Rather, true security comes in trusting "the steadfast love of God" (v. 8b).

Those who trust God are "like a green olive tree" (v. 8). Olive trees do not easily disappear. They do not grow for a season and then die. They are long lived, and have been known to survive years of neglect and drought. Their root shoots provide regeneration. The righteous one, rooted into the house of God, provides a true contrast to the mighty one who is uprooted by God from the land of the living (v. 5).

Rather than trusting in money, stuff, or power, the righteous will trust in the steadfast love of God, who has acted faithfully. If that is how God wants faithful people to live, how do we do it?

According to the psalmist, righteous people live not for themselves but ground their lives in gratitude, worship, and faith-full actions, thus distinguishing themselves from those who "go for the gusto." Communities that practice thanksgiving, offering, and outreach are like healthy olive trees.

LINDA MCKIERNAN-ALLEN

---

2. Percentage of American teenage girls who report store hopping as favorite activity: 93 percent (Lawrence Shames, *The Hunger for More* [New York: Times Books, 1989], 147).

individual lament psalm. Lament psalms typically end in affirmation of God's goodness (see Ps. 13:5–6). The lamentation provides the catharsis that allows faith room to grow. The catharsis for this psalmist is venting his anger at the accused.

What does the psalm accomplish with this fusion of rhetorical styles? The psalmist models one who is oppressed by the powerful. Instead of lamenting his situation, the psalmist demonstrates the prophetic courage to denounce his oppressor. The usual woes of lamentation are replaced in the psalm with bold accusation. The poet stands up to the oppressor, denounces the oppressor, even mocks the oppressor with defiant sarcasm ("mighty one" in the first verse is a taunt). The psalmist shows the serenity of wisdom, not from the standpoint of one who is comfortable, having time and leisure to reflect on God's teachings, but from the standpoint of one who has been vulnerable to the abuse of the rich and powerful. Nevertheless, the psalmist trusts in God, who champions his cause.

The psalm gives the preacher the opportunity to speak to the persistent low self-esteem of the oppressed and the poor. The "victim" in the psalm stands "in the face" of the oppressor, confident in God's judgment of oppression. The hyperbole in the accusations of the psalmist might reinforce self-righteousness (do people really "love" evil and love to lie?), but they give permission for anger at oppression. The anger of the poem transforms serenity from passivity to genuine trust. When the psalmist seeks refuge in God, it is not an act of cowardice, but of faith.

One weakness of the psalm is its lack of reflection on the motivation behind evil. The psalmist assumes that the opponent is evil simply for the sake of being evil. The psalm does not explore the neediness, fear, anxiety, and insecurity behind evil and oppression. Certainly God judges evil and oppression, but does not judgment hope for transformation?

CHARLES L. AARON

wise woman of Proverbs 31:25 who "laughs at the time to come."

In contrast to Doeg's shallow boasting, verse 8 shows David boasting in what God has done for him. He describes his life with the rich image of a hardy, evergreen olive tree, not out in a field somewhere but in the house of God. The image carries some of the irony of Psalm 23:5, with its feast spread out in the midst of enemies. David envisions himself as spiritually rooted in the presence of God and safe in that place, though physically he is in the wilderness, embattled on every side. He has staked his future on God's promises, and now waits for the promised kingship with a deep sense of hopeful trust. His words here pulsate with glad contentment. We sense that he feels God's renewing energy flowing through him, like light as it nourishes leaves, or like water as it sustains roots. This tree is content and at rest, but it is not idle; it is producing fruit prolifically. Like the olive tree, David stands in the midst of the community of believers, confessing and proclaiming the goodness of God.

In preaching this passage, not many in our hearing will identify with Doeg, whose crimes were so shockingly excessive, but we all share tendencies toward compromise in the pursuit of success or the approval of a supervisor. We may subtly twist the truth to portray ourselves in a more favorable light, at times even damaging the reputations of colleagues in the process. More likely, the challenge listeners will relate to is that of responding with grace and faith to ill-treatment or difficult circumstances that leave them feeling embattled. David is a model of honesty and of turning to God with confident peace. His vision of God allows him to see that God is his only source of strength, protection, and ultimate fruitfulness. More than once he likens his life to that of a tree (cf. Ps. 1), one that sinks down deep roots as it waits for sunlight and water from the creator and sustainer of life and in the process provides fruit that renews and enriches the lives of others.

LISA LAMB

Colossians 1:15‑28

[15]He is the image of the invisible God, the firstborn of all creation; [16]for in him all things in heaven and on earth were created, things visible and invisible, whether thrones or dominions or rulers or powers—all things have been created through him and for him. [17]He himself is before all things, and in him all things hold together. [18]He is the head of the body, the church; he is the beginning, the firstborn from the dead, so that he might come to have first place in everything. [19]For in him all the fullness of God was pleased to dwell, [20]and through him God was pleased to reconcile to himself all things, whether on earth or in heaven, by making peace through the blood of his cross.

[21]And you who were once estranged and hostile in mind, doing evil deeds, [22]he has now reconciled in his fleshly body through death, so as to present you holy and blameless and irreproachable before him—[23]provided that you

Theological Perspective

Colossians 1:15–20 is commonly understood as a christological hymn that predated the Letter to the Colossians as a hymn or liturgical text. Within Colossians, it serves as the primary exposition of the person of Jesus Christ and his relationship to the church. Given that Paul draws a strong connection between knowledge and morality, the hymn is the basis of both his cosmic and ethical assertions. Paul contends that the church at Colossae can hold fast to the gospel because its claims of reconciliation with God are rooted in Christ's sovereignty over all of time and creation.

The content and structure of Colossians indicate the influence of Stoicism and Jewish Wisdom literature. Both sources assert that the universe was ordered by the benevolence of God, who creates through a divine intermediary such as Wisdom or the law. Since humanity was also created in this manner, people possess within themselves the capacity to sense and locate the "divine order." By adhering to the moral shape of the "divine order," people can live in accordance with God's intentions for creation. The Christ hymn develops its cosmic understanding of the person of Jesus in this fashion.[1]

1. This passage was the source of enormous controversy in the Trinitarian debates that led to the ecumenical councils at Nicaea (325 CE) and the first council at Constantinople (381 CE). Arian Christians drew upon the hymn's

Pastoral Perspective

Jesus Christ is the firstborn of all creation. He is truly unique. There is no other like him. Both in his relationship to God and in his being as God's revelation and redeemer of the whole world, he is stamped with a finality and completeness that knows no compromise. He is both the subject of creation, meaning that all things have been created through him and for him, and the cosmic reconciler, through whom God restores harmony between God and all of the creation. Thus begins the magnificent Christ hymn that forms the foundation for this letter. Lest anyone misunderstand, this community is marked as "Christian" because of its belief in these essential claims about Jesus Christ. It is a bold reminder of our purpose. The church is the body of Jesus Christ, and it is Christ whom we proclaim.

One would think this is clear, but it is not that simple. Theologian Brian McLaren writes in his book *A Generous Orthodoxy*[1] about his own confusion and growth in understanding this Jesus Christ whom we are called to proclaim. He describes the "seven Jesuses I have known." McLaren begins with his upbringing as a child when he first met Jesus, whom he calls the "Conservative Protestant

1. Brian D. McLaren, *A Generous Orthodoxy* (Grand Rapids: Youth Specialties, 2004).

continue securely established and steadfast in the faith, without shifting from the hope promised by the gospel that you heard, which has been proclaimed to every creature under heaven. I, Paul, became a servant of this gospel. [24]I am now rejoicing in my sufferings for your sake, and in my flesh I am completing what is lacking in Christ's afflictions for the sake of his body, that is, the church. [25]I became its servant according to God's commission that was given to me for you, to make the word of God fully known, [26]the mystery that has been hidden throughout the ages and generations but has now been revealed to his saints. [27]To them God chose to make known how great among the Gentiles are the riches of the glory of this mystery, which is Christ in you, the hope of glory. [28]It is he whom we proclaim, warning everyone and teaching everyone in all wisdom, so that we may present everyone mature in Christ.

Exegetical Perspective

Today's epistle lesson divides into three sections: a "hymn" in praise of Christ (vv. 15–20), the application of Christ's action directly to the Gentile Christians in Colossae (vv. 21–23), and Paul's reflections on his ministry to the Gentiles (vv. 24–28). As throughout the letter, however, Christ, the Colossians, and Paul himself are closely related.

The poetic structure of 1:15–20 suggests that the passage belongs to an early Christian hymn or liturgy. It divides into two stanzas (vv. 15–16 and vv. 18b–20), bracketing the central affirmation that Christ is "before all things," the one in whom "all things hold together," and the "head of the body, the church." In the Greek text, verses 15 and 18b are parallel: "who is the image of the invisible God, the firstborn of all creation" and "who is the beginning, the firstborn from the dead" (my trans.). The central affirmation of Christ's priority in creation and in the church is also structured by two parallel phrases in Greek: "and he is before all things" (1:17a); "and he is the head of the body, the church" (1:18a) (my translation). Thus Christ has preeminence in both creation and redemption, as the agent and goal of the first creation, holding it all together, and as the agent and goal of the new creation, brought about by his reconciling death on the cross. The all-inclusive character of these claims is conveyed through the

Homiletical Perspective

There is wide consensus among scholars that the heart of this passage—verses 15–20—is hymnic in literary form and structure. Moreover, most agree that this hymn proclaims the highest Christology in the New Testament. Controversies, however, concern issues of provenance and purpose. Is this hymnic section derived from the liturgical life of the church at Colossae, or was it written by the author of the epistle or someone close to that source? There is evidence for both conclusions, but not clear and compelling enough that either position has come to sweep away the other. For the purposes of our proclamation of this text, may we simply agree that we have a remarkable hymn before us, one that sings of a lofty, cosmic Christology? With this agreement in mind, the preacher will need to turn with attentiveness to the christological content of this hymn and an analysis of what the hymn sings against.

The high Christology of the hymn begins with the claim that Jesus "is the image (*eikōn*) of the invisible God, the firstborn of all creation" (v. 15). Implied here are several core and radical claims: (1) Jesus is the sole person to have this status after the Adamic fall; (2) the humanity of the earthly Jesus is inextricably united with the preexistent and cosmic Christ; (3) both the economy of redemption

Colossians 1:15-28

Theological Perspective

The hymn begins with the claim that Christ is the "image" (*eikōn*) of God (v. 15). "Image" is used in a technical fashion to draw a distinction between God, Christ, and creation. However, as the fullness of God rests in Christ, "image" also denotes a manifestation of God's power and being that casts Christ's creative and redemptive activities as the unequivocal work of God. Verses 16 and 17 establish Christ's sovereignty over all creation. Not only is everything created in Christ (v. 16), but everything in the created order is "held together" (*synistēmi*) in him. Thus, all powers—be they earthly, demonic, or angelic—live each moment within the lordship of Christ.

This claim reinforces Paul's assertion in Colossians 2:18–19 of the foolishness of worshiping any being other than Christ. Creation can only receive nourishment through Christ, who sustains all of existence. In presenting creation in this fashion, the Christ hymn shifts the conception of the structure of the universe in Stoic and Jewish Wisdom literature from an independent, divine law to Jesus Christ, a person who *is* the law.

Verses 18–20 are of enormous importance to Christian ecclesiology. The hymn parallels the language of Ephesians (1:22) in drawing upon the vision of Christ as the "head" (*kepalē*) of the church. In both epistles, the headship of Christ is grounded in his redeeming activity. This intimately connects the mission of the church with salvation in Jesus Christ. Just as he is "the firstborn of all creation" (v. 15), Christ is also "the firstborn from the dead" (v. 18). Thus, the person in whom all things were created and are sustained is the one who rose from the dead. The hymn has already established that all things are structured and held together in Christ. Therefore, Jesus possesses the power to facilitate the stark transformation of the created order that occurs in resurrection. The "blood of his cross" (v. 20) facilitated a reconciliation between God and creation that was fully within Christ's capability.

Having established the basis for certainty in the gospel through the Christ hymn, Paul calls upon the Colossians to remain steadfast in the truth they received. In verse 22 he asserts that reconciliation to God in Christ will enable the church to present itself as "holy and blameless and irreproachable" before

---

assertion that Christ was the "firstborn of all creation" (v. 15) to support their contention that Christ was a created being. The finest concise rebuttal of the Arian exegesis of Colossians remains that of John Calvin in his commentary on Colossians. See *Calvin's New Testament Commentaries: Galatians, Ephesians, Philippians and Colossians*, trans. T. H. L. Parker, ed. David W. Torrance and Thomas F. Torrance (Grand Rapids: Eerdmans, 1996), 308–9.

Pastoral Perspective

Jesus." This Jesus was "born to die," he writes. The focal point was Jesus' innocent death on the cross for McLaren's sins.

Over time, McLaren struggled with this view of Jesus because it seemed an individualistic, legalistic view with personal but no global import. As a young adult, McLaren next met the "Pentecostal/ Charismatic Jesus." This Jesus was present, personal, and dramatically involved in everyday life through the Holy Spirit, but nagging questions about God's concern for the whole world, for history, and for creation frustrated McLaren. This led him to the "Roman Catholic Jesus." McLaren loved the way this Jesus helped him focus on the Eucharist and the connection to ancient tradition that was beyond his present experience, but the exclusivism of the church in this view troubled him.

For a time, he worshiped the "Eastern Orthodox Jesus," which emphasized the Trinity, affirmed mystery, and still engaged the world. This led him to the "Liberal Protestant Jesus," with a focus on social justice that grew from personal experience of faith in Christ. From there he ventured to the "Anabaptist Jesus," with its historic focus on peace and nonviolence, and from there to the "Liberation Theology Jesus," who confronted injustice in the whole of society and stood in solidarity with the poor and oppressed.

In this way, McLaren illustrates the complexity of proclaiming Christ. While he does not argue that one of these interpretations is the true Jesus, he does remind us that the purpose of the church is to proclaim Jesus Christ, whoever that church understands Christ to be. That, too, can be complex, given our human need for certitude against the solipsistic claim that all belief is relative and therefore subject to our individual whims or conceptions of the truth.

Professor David Ng, much like the apostle Paul and Brian McLaren, sought to remind the church of its central purpose when he wrote *Youth in the Community of Disciples*.[2] Concerned that the church had become distracted from its essential identity as the body of Jesus Christ and its central task of proclaiming Christ, he wrote that the purpose of the church is not to be a place of entertainment where persons, and especially young people, come to be spectators while worship leaders and Bible teachers "put on a show," using whatever gimmicks and

---

2. David Ng, *Youth in the Community of Disciples* (Valley Forge, PA: Judson Press, 1984).

repeated references to "all," "all things," and "everything," which occur eight times in the hymn. Furthermore, the repetition of "in heaven and on earth" (v. 16) and "on earth or in heaven" (v. 20) underscores the cosmic scope of both creation and redemption in Christ.

Christ thus is preeminent in all things, the basis for every other claim in the letter. The hymn's cosmic language ensures that Christ is superior to any lesser religious claims concerning "thrones or dominions or rulers or powers" (1:16; 2:8–9, 15) to which the Colossians might be subject (2:18, 20). We do not know precisely what this language denoted for Paul, but it seems to refer to spiritual forces that transcend human individuals or institutions. These forces have an ambiguous position in the letter: they are part of creation (1:16) over which Christ rules (2:10), yet they also are part of the power of darkness from which we have been rescued (1:13) and over which Christ triumphed on the cross (2:15). Created, hostile, disarmed, and reconciled—this is the ultimate story of the powers. At present their reconciliation is not complete, insofar as the Colossians needed to be "rescued" from them, and still need to be warned against their pernicious effects. While we may not completely identify the "powers," we can have a clear idea of their impact on human behavior: they are linked with repressive, exclusionary rules and judgments that threaten the Colossians' confidence in Christ (2:16–23). We also can be clear about their ultimate reconciliation and submission to Christ.

Furthermore, the global scope of the hymn's depiction of the church displays a Christian identity that transcends all ethnic and cultural claims or practices. The metaphor of the church as "the body" in 1:18 and 2:19 echoes 1 Corinthians 12:12–27 and Romans 12:4–5 and anticipates Ephesians 1:23; 4:15–16. Most notable in Colossians, however, is the church's universal embrace of "every creature under heaven" (1:23) and "everyone" (1:28) in a renewal that includes "Greek and Jew, circumcised and uncircumcised, barbarian, Scythian, slave and free" (3:11). This expansion of the baptismal formula found in Galatians 3:28 and 1 Corinthians 12:13 emphasizes that in the body of Christ we belong to a worldwide community that trumps all divisions based on ethnicity, gender, social class, or nationality. This community is not grounded in a general notion of human "oneness," because such a triumph over ancient and powerful divisions is not humanly possible. Rather, as is true of creation and particularly of the church, in Christ *alone* "all things hold together" (1:17).

and ecclesial life together derive from the cosmic Christ who is the head of the church (v. 18).

This catalog of things that have stood in opposition to God provides the preacher with the tension and even chaos necessary for a sermon to be born out of the hymn. The text sings of such earthly and cosmic entities as "thrones," "dominions," "rulers," and "powers" (v. 16) and proclaims that they are part of the creation (not coeternal with Christ) with purpose endowed by their creator. However, they are fallen and have the capacity for evil and enslavement. The church will need now to make the life-and-death decision of whether to give itself over to these powers—thereby becoming itself enslaved by them—or to claim Christ as its sole head and thereby become numbered among the "saints in the light"(1:12). Homiletically, we will adopt the "moves and structures" method of David Buttrick for the purposes of shaping the sermon.

Moves and Structures: The Cosmic Christ. Move 1: We are not surprised that "thrones" are included among those things that can be in opposition to God's purposes. Their intent was good. After all, they were created by Christ. Yet we know all about thrones—the trappings of power that go with them and those who occupy them. So much good they can do, and yet so much harm they have done. Whether those who sit on these thrones are called president or prime minister or just major, there is always a temptation for those who call themselves Christians. We are tempted to cozy up to those on the throne in order to give us prestige, security, or some power of our own. (The preacher now turns to the challenge of naming these thrones for the listeners. An example listing may function best here rather than an extended story illustration. Draw from the congregation's world, which is vast and hugely formed by the culture's media.)

Move 2: There are other powers that can enslave. They can bore down within a person and reach out to capture others nearby. Just think of how an addiction works. It is a "social disease," with deeply personal effects and widely ranging devastation. Even entire societies can become addicted, enslaved. The outcome is always the same unless there is redemption: these powers lead to death. (The concretion here could be a brief narrative that illustrates the deadly effects of the power of addiction.)

Move 3: One other temptation confronts the church when we try to make Christian faith "believable"—whether in a world like that of the

Colossians 1:15-28

Theological Perspective

God as long as they remain steadfast in what they were taught. Paul's counsel is rooted in the close relationship between gospel and ethics in Colossians. If the Colossians understand the knowledge they have received, they will live according to the hope in Jesus Christ that it reveals.

In verses 24–28 he asserts that the love shared within the Christian community includes bearing affliction for the sake of the gospel. Paul uses himself as an example of this suffering. While the Christ hymn indicates that God has "reconcile[d] to himself all things" through the blood of Jesus Christ, Paul identifies the activity of the church as completing this mission in Christ for the entire world. This pushes the church beyond its doors and embraces the suffering that Christians experience in proclaiming the gospel as the fruit of the faith, hope, and love of their community. The struggle itself is not an individuated experience. Instead, it is the completion of the very suffering of Christ through which redemption occurred.

This view of the nature of God's salvific activity in Jesus Christ is enormously empowering to the church. Given that the source of the gospel communicated to Colossae by Epaphras was Christ's self-revelation to Paul (Gal. 1:12, 15–16), the knowledge of God possessed by the church is sufficient for salvation. Thus, the legalism, self-abasement, and worship of lower beings (2:16–18) creeping into the church at Colossae is unnecessary. Just as Paul united the faithful work of churches throughout the world with the activity of God in heaven, his vision of the church binds the entire narrative of redemption within the body of Christ. Given that Christ is the very structure of creation, to live in accordance with his gospel is to follow the grain of the universe. Thus, living in harmony with the gospel produces good works that bear witness to the divine order of all things in heaven and on earth.

MATTHEW FLEMMING

Pastoral Perspective

novelties they can pull out of their bag of tricks so that everyone has fun. The church is not some theological theme park where frantic leaders, fearful of ever boring or frustrating their customers, employ an ever-escalating array of techniques.

Ng also wrote that the purpose of the church is *not maintenance*—to be a safe place, a refuge for its members—until Christ comes again. This vision of the church as perpetual purgatory requires nothing of its members except that they wait and not stir things up, lest they become more anxiety ridden than they already are. The key purpose of this kind of church is to keep the status quo. Abhorrent of disruption, change, or even growth, the church focuses on itself by keeping its members comfortable without challenges. Keeping its members in this continuous holding pattern, the church simply tries to survive.

Furthermore, Ng wrote, the purpose of the church is *not fellowship* where the entire energy of the congregation is focused on its social relationships, so that each person feels as if he or she belongs. Certainly, he argues, fellowship is an important dimension of the church, but it is not the church's central purpose. Fellowship-focused churches act as little more than social organizations that exist for their own members, rather than for the worship of God as the body of Christ. With a tendency to be insular—and more often than not exclusive—the congregation whose primary purpose is fellowship tends toward a more therapeutic focus; the emphasis is one's comfort within the larger group, rather than whether one is living one's life faithfully.

Finally, Ng also wrote that the purpose of the church is *not protection*, where the community, terrified of the world beyond its walls, invests all its energies in constructing a safe place where its members can dutifully worship, study, and enact their sacred rituals. These congregations ultimately forbid any interaction with outsiders until the strangers have been duly tested and assimilated. For Ng, the real purpose of the church is clear—to be the community of disciples of Jesus Christ and as such, to proclaim Christ. We do not proclaim entertainment or fun or fellowship or maintenance or protection. The apostle Paul would agree with Ng. The church of Jesus Christ does not exist for us. We exist for one reason: to proclaim Christ the firstborn of all creation!

RODGER Y. NISHIOKA

Exegetical Perspective

Three aspects of the church's identity require further comment. First, while it is internationally inclusive, it is also vigorously centered on Christ as the one and only Lord, not only of the community of faith, but of all humanity. This universal embrace is not about an indifferent tolerance of different religions, but about Christ's sovereign rule: "Christ is all, and in all!" (3:11). Philippians 2:10–11 carries the same sense. At the same time, the global acclamation of Christ is entirely God's doing, and not dependent on any human confession of faith.

Second, perhaps the most radical character of the church's universal embrace is to be seen in the inclusion of God's enemies, of whom the Colossians themselves are exhibit A. Picking up the theme of redemption from 1:13–14, Paul addresses them directly in 1:21: "You who were once estranged and hostile in mind, doing evil deeds," you also and particularly, even you, Christ has reconciled. The Colossians are not exceptional in their former status as enemies of God; they are representative of all humanity in need of reconciliation and redemption. Even in their particular identity as Gentile believers, they are signs of the mystery of God's reclamation of the whole world (1:27–28; see Eph. 3:1–10).

Finally, the three occurrences of "body" in today's passage point to the intimate union among Christ, the church, and Paul. Christ is "the head of the body, the church" (1:18); Christ has reconciled the Colossians "in his fleshly body through death" (1:22, literally "in the body of his flesh"); Paul himself "completes" (literally "fills up") in his own "flesh" what is lacking in Christ's afflictions for the sake of Christ's body, the church (1:24). It is not that Christ's death is insufficient, but rather that physical affliction accompanies Paul's mission of presenting "everyone mature [literally "complete"] in Christ" (1:28; see also Gal. 4:19). Because he belongs to the body, when Paul suffers, Christ suffers, just as when the whole church suffers, Christ suffers. Here is mutually participatory language, in which the church's bodily existence now carries forward the reconciliation accomplished by Christ's crucifixion and resurrection on behalf of the whole creation.

SUSAN GROVE EASTMAN

Homiletical Perspective

Colossians or in our own. The tactic is familiar and chronic: when faced with a pluralistic world with all kinds of gods and causes, just ratchet down your Christology to make Jesus fit in. Diminish your Jesus until he will not disturb or upset anyone. Good thinking—until we learn that the world's powers now have us where they want us: harmless and tamed. (The imagery here is important. How does the church "downsize" Jesus Christ in the name of apologetics? One Sunday school curriculum, for example, had a chapter designed to get students to "appreciate Jesus.")

Move 4: But what if Jesus Christ is the image of God? Imagine—all things created through him, all things fulfilled in him, creator of all that is, both seen and unseen. Consider all these powers—these "thrones" and "dominions." If Christ is the "firstborn of all creation," then these powers were created by him and through the cross have been "dethroned." They can no longer enslave. What if everything holds together in the One who is the image of God? (Perhaps this is the place to depict the icon of Christ the Pantocrator. The haloed Christ looks at the viewer with a solemn, loving stare. His right hand is extended to teach, and in his left hand he holds the Holy Scriptures.)

Move 5: This cosmic Christ does not just "reign on high, in heavens above." He is the head of the church. We are all one within the church, for we all have one head of the body. While the powers and thrones may have different names, there is only one name, Jesus Christ, for the One who is our head. So sing the song, not just in our worship, but in our working and serving and playing in the world. Sing of the firstborn of creation. (There are numerous ways in which to image this move. One approach would be to image the mission outreaches of the parish as ways to sing the song. In this final move, we will need to invite the assembly to imagine ways in which they are little icons of the One who is the image of God.)

RICHARD L. ESLINGER

Luke 10:38-42

³⁸Now as they went on their way, he entered a certain village, where a woman named Martha welcomed him into her home. ³⁹She had a sister named Mary, who sat at the Lord's feet and listened to what he was saying. ⁴⁰But Martha was distracted by her many tasks; so she came to him and asked, "Lord, do you not care that my sister has left me to do all the work by myself? Tell her then to help me." ⁴¹But the Lord answered her, "Martha, Martha, you are worried and distracted by many things; ⁴²there is need of only one thing. Mary has chosen the better part, which will not be taken away from her."

Theological Perspective

As I write, I am conscious of the latest edition of a journal I respect, casually but perhaps not accidentally placed on the left side of my desk. Its theme is mission, and the attractive cover features a bon mot attributed to Francis of Assisi: "Preach the Gospel at all times—if necessary use words."

My eye moves from this wonderfully provocative sentence to the Gospel text in front of me, the familiar episode of Jesus with two friends, Mary and Martha, sisters of Lazarus. I am caught by the juxtaposition of the phrase "if necessary use words" and Jesus' approval of Mary, who had done "the one thing needful" (KJV) when she sat listening to Jesus' *words*.

One understands well enough that Christians today should be wary of words. Our world is full of words: the words of political leaders that are meant to persuade us of the rectitude of their policies (and are sometimes downright lies!); the words of German academics in the 1930s, who like most of the intellectuals in the Third Reich, found it convenient to be neutral with respect to Hitler's race policies (when they were not openly supportive); the words of the advertisers and hucksters of countless products, most of which we do not need. If we are to be honest, we should also include the words of the televangelists, clergy, church courts, and theologians; for we are certainly not immune from the diseases of rationali-

Pastoral Perspective

Mary apparently was eager to be a disciple, sitting as she did at Jesus' feet, spellbound by his words. There is no telling how long she had been rapt when Martha reached the limit of her selfless tolerance and interrupted to ask if Jesus cared about the injustice his presence had caused. Save for Martha's outburst, one imagines the same scene in countless houses as the seventy set out to proclaim the gospel. Some must have gathered to hear what the disciples had to say while others busied themselves with table service. So it goes in most households, including the household of faith. Some are destined to live out their discipleship in the details of the common life: preparing meals, counting money, caring for the homebound, organizing outreach to the poor. Others are disciples in service to the word: study and prayer, worship and preaching, evangelism and teaching.

Both are necessary, as Luke soon will acknowledge in the book of Acts (Acts 6:1–6), but in these two scenes, Luke privileges the latter. "There is need of only one thing. Mary has chosen the better part," says Jesus (vv. 41–42). What does this imply about the ordering of our lives toward sanctification and service within the church today? More to the point of Luke's story, how are we to show hospitality when the kingdom of God comes near?

Exegetical Perspective

This story attracts interest because it is one of a limited number of biblical texts that offer an obvious sanction for a liberating understanding of women's participation in all facets of Christian discipleship. A woman sits and learns at Jesus' feet—possibly in the process transgressing cultural expectations—and Jesus approves, implying that all dimensions of sharing in his ministry are open to women and men alike. Some interpretations proceed, however, as if the text's celebration of Mary's activity demands denigration of Martha's. Such readings have rightly encountered opposition from (among others) John Calvin, who criticizes those who claim this passage to assert the superiority of the contemplative life over active service, and from contemporary feminist exegesis that rejects the implication that Martha fails by embracing the roles her society assigns her (diligent service), while her sister succeeds by acting like a man (learning).[1] Close attention to the text illuminates some of the issues cited by these exegetes and avoids simplistic assumptions that yield misdirected interpretations.

Little can be said about the two sisters, for this Lukan passage marks the only place either appears in

1. See the brief overview of these issues and concerns in Loveday Alexander, "Sisters in Adversity: Retelling Martha's Story," in *Women in the Biblical Tradition*, ed. George J. Brooke (Lewiston, NY: Edwin Mellen, 1992), 167–75.

Homiletical Perspective

When Jesus decided to drop in on Martha and her sister Mary, Martha's first impulse was to get something going in the kitchen. In doing this, she was being faithful to the tradition of hospitality begun long ago when Father Abraham welcomed three guests to his tent (Gen. 18:1–10). Just as Abraham turned to Sarah to assist with the duties of hospitality, Martha expected Mary to do the same. Martha's expectations did not include Mary's plopping down on the rug at Jesus' feet and leaving all the work for her.

That, however, is exactly what her sister did. Mary was in no hurry to come into the kitchen. While Martha was flipping through the cookbooks, boiling the water, chopping up the vegetables, and setting the table for three, Mary settled down at the feet of their friend and guest, attentive to what he was saying. In fact, by sitting at Jesus' feet, Mary had taken the posture of a disciple. Who could blame Martha for banging a few pots and putting the plates on the table with a sturdy thump?

Perhaps Jesus heard the bustling around back there and, after a while, even the muttering. Martha was not one who kept her feelings under a tight lid. Since Jesus was pretty sharp at gauging what was going on in people's hearts, he knew what the muttering was all about, long before Martha's

Luke 10:38-42

Theological Perspective

zation, self-promotion, and sheer rhetoric! Words, in our wordy, hypercommunicative society, have become unprecedentedly cheap. The silence that is needed for words to have meaning is noticeably lacking both in those who speak and in those who hear.

Yet God, in the tradition of Jerusalem, is a speaking God—*Deus loquens*—and the creature God makes "in God's image," the human creature God calls to covenant partnership, is a speaking animal. Luther thought that the designation *Homo loquens* was a much better and more biblical way of defining the human than the classical and Renaissance concept *Homo sapiens*. Unlike the God of Genesis, we cannot actually *create* by fiat; our words cannot achieve by themselves what is needed; but our calling to a priestly role within the sphere of creation requires us not only to comprehend, in some degree, *God's* Word, but also to find for ourselves the words that are needed, under the conditions of history, to communicate God's Word to all the others whom we represent. How shall they hear without a preacher?

Despite our appropriate wariness—indeed, our weariness—of words, then, Christians are still called both to listen to Jesus' words and to work very hard at finding "the right words" to communicate God's Word for the here and now. The theologian or preacher or teacher of church school who gives up on words must ask himself or herself whether this is out of modesty in the face of the great mystery of *God's* Word or because of certain personal limitations—perhaps even sheer laziness!

The struggle between word and deed, the speaker and the doer, the contemplative and the activist, will no doubt be with us until the end of time; and the complaint of the one about the other will undoubtedly recur in the future as frequently as it has in the past. Who does not sympathize with Martha, reduced to the drudgery of service while her sister enjoys the excitement of "theological discussion" with Jesus? Mary could legitimately complain of Martha, too—as Jesus does on *this* occasion—for immersing herself in activity without sufficiently considering the rationale and end of all her care-filled work.

Undoubtedly in the close friendship of Jesus with this family there were *other* occasions when Martha was praised for her caring deeds and Mary gently chided for her ease and chatter. Different occasions call for different emphases. Moreover, *either* posture, assumed to the point of preoccupation or ideology, courts very serious problems. Activism without contemplation ends in aimless "doing" that usually aggravates existing difficulties. In its "Justice, Peace,

Pastoral Perspective

If Joel Green is correct when he writes that "Jesus' encounter with Martha and Mary clarified the nature of the welcome he seeks not only for himself but also for his messengers—that is, for all who participate in the drawing near of God's dominion"[1]—then a community that is hospitable to Christ is a community marked by the attention the community gives to God's word. A church that has been led to be "worried and distracted by many things" (v. 41) inevitably will be a community that dwells in the shallows of frantic potlucks, anxious stewardship campaigns, and events designed simply to perpetuate the institution. Decisions will be made in meetings without a hint of God's reign. Food and drink will appear at table without Christ being recognized in the breaking of bread. Social issues may be addressed, but the gospel is missed in acts that partake of politics as usual.

This often leads a congregation to get downright ornery. Night after night, members leave home to crank out the church and return as clueless and empty as they were when they walked out the door. Endless meetings breed resentment in otherwise pleasant Christians because the church's business is being done without any word of the God whom they thought they had agreed to serve. Martha comes to mind. If we miss the one needful thing (v. 42), if we do not give singular attention to the address of God in season and out, then we should not be surprised when the nominating committee turns up at our study door with an empty slate.

On the other hand, when a congregation is led to position itself at Christ's feet—reading Scripture together and asking after its meaning, listening to substantive sermons and wrestling like Jacob for God's blessing, studying and nurturing a faith that seeks understanding—then even the details of the common life begin to resound with good news. Luke's casual setting for this story is a home—a reminder that every pastoral call is potentially an occasion to listen for God's word or to participate in the drawing near of God's dominion. Some of the more profound moments in ministry begin when we join a dinner party where an off-the-cuff question provides the opening for a conversation about life's meaning and purpose; or we enter a hospital room where another's physical vulnerability leads to a confession concerning a crisis of faith; or we arrive late to a meeting and manage to turn a mundane discussion toward the mystery of life together.

1. Joel Green, *The Gospel of Luke*, New International Commentary on the New Testament (Grand Rapids: Eerdmans, 1997), 433.

Exegetical Perspective

the Synoptic Gospels. In John 11:1–12:8, Jesus raises Lazarus of Bethany from the dead and interacts with him and his sisters, Martha and Mary, but neither Luke nor John reveals a clear awareness of the events depicted by the other. The sisters' importance for Luke resides in their evident devotion to Jesus, seen in Martha's hospitality, Mary's interest in his teaching, and Martha's calling him "Lord."

In preparing a meal (see below), Martha fulfills her socially mandated role. Mary, in assuming the role of a student at the feet of a teacher (see Acts 22:3), challenges culturally proscribed boundaries. According to a literal rendering of verse 39, "she sat listening to his word." Other Lukan texts likewise commend listening to the word of God or Jesus' words (5:1; 6:47; 8:11–15, 21; 11:28). So it is not entirely surprising that Jesus speaks supportively about Mary, who seems to have taken the initiative herself to sit with Jesus, as a sign of her devotion to him. Mary is scarcely the first woman of her time to become a pupil of a male religious figure, but her sister's comment indicates that she is expected to perform other tasks in this particular occasion.

The scene pivots midway through verse 40, when Martha makes her comment. In complaining that her sister has left her alone to serve as host, she breaches her hospitality. Instead of addressing Mary, she puts her guest on the spot. Her frustration— certainly not her desire to offer hospitality through service—is the problem that Jesus addresses in verses 41–42.

The Gospel of Luke applauds those who provide service to Jesus, indicated by the verb *diakoneō* (4:39; 8:3; 10:40). Often this term, along with the noun *diakonia,* in Luke–Acts refers to food preparations and table service, as it appears to do in this passage. However, in Luke's writings and outside the NT, it can also indicate service and ministry more broadly. Jesus refers to himself as "one who serves" in 22:26–27 (cf. 12:37). He therefore cannot criticize Martha because she chooses to offer diligent service in the "many tasks" (*pollē diakonia,* v. 40) that need to be done to provide for her guest(s) and household. Such tasks are themselves manifestations of discipleship. Her problem lies, in this instance, in succumbing to distraction while performing them. The verb rendered "distracted" *(perispaomai)* in verse 40 refers to drawing away or diverting something. Criticizing Mary (and, subtly, Jesus) for leaving her alone, Martha insinuates value judgments upon the different activities the sisters choose to perform. This reveals that her practices of hospitality are eclipsing

Homiletical Perspective

frustration exploded into words, but he waited until Martha spoke. "Lord," Martha began, "don't you care . . ."—showing that Mary wasn't the only one under scrutiny—"don't *you* care," she repeated, and then the gaze fell on sister Mary, "that my sister has left me *by myself* to do the serving?"

As a matter of fact, Jesus did not care. I like to think he smiled when he said, "Martha, dear friend, you are worried and distracted by many things." This is an important moment to notice in the story. He is not going after Busy Martha, but Worried and Distracted Martha. He is speaking to his dear friend Martha, who has worked herself into a state of anxious distraction over the meal she wanted to have for him. She has focused her frustration not only on her sister but now also on her friend and guest, and lost sight of the one she significantly calls "Lord." Jesus is gently calling her to refocus. Hospitality is not primarily about the food; more important is the focus.

For years this story was interpreted to prioritize the contemplative life over the active life. The "better" life was the life of prayer and contemplation; the "quiet" life was seen as "more perfect" than the active. More recently, other challenging interpretations of this story have been offered. Some suggest that this narrative reflects an effort within the early community to remove women from the active sphere of service in the church. This interpretation leaves us with a story that mirrors that same tendency among some Christian churches today to restrict the role of women in ministry, especially in leadership positions. Here we have Luke weighing in on the side of restriction, calling Martha from service/ministry to join Mary in choosing the "better part" (v. 42), a more passive posture, sitting serenely before the Lord, listening in rapt attention. This interpretation sadly contends that Luke's Gospel is not a gospel-for-women, but one for keeping women in their place, subservient to men. Mary's "better part" is sitting passively at the feet of her Lord, while Jesus reprimands Martha for being caught up in anxiety and worry, even though she is serving him.

However, this story can be read differently. It does not necessarily affirm the contemplative over the active life, and it should not be used to deny women their gifts and calls to ministry. Theologian John Shea observes that, while in English we hear that Mary has chosen "the better part," in Greek the word is translated as "good." Mary has chosen the "good" part, meaning she has chosen "the connection to God who is good, the ground and energy of effective

Luke 10:38-42

Theological Perspective

and Integrity of Creation" process, the World Council of Churches named the "great instabilities" that form the three-pronged crisis of our epoch. Too many of the activistic "answers" to the crisis exacerbate the situations they are intended to "fix" because the *questions* involved in the situation (especially the complex interrelatedness of the three "instabilities") have not been profoundly wrestled with. On the other hand, only the unthinking could fail to recognize the myriad ways in which thought—including very serious biblical, theological, and other scholarship— regularly serves the duplicitous purposes of those who, their rhetoric notwithstanding, simply do not wish to "get involved."

The problematic implicit in this juxtaposition of thought and act, word and deed, necessitates a perennial vigilance on the part of serious Christians. What is needed is the sensitivity to recognize when it is Martha, and when it is Mary, who ought to be reminded of the dangers implicit in her posture. New occasions teach new duties. Persons and churches characterized by unending wordiness, whether that means allegedly high academic scholarship or "evangelical" loquaciousness, need to hear Jesus' words to the *Schriftgelehrter*—the alleged Bible-expert!—of the previous pericope (Luke 10:25–37): "Go and *do* . . ."

If, on the other hand, I have perhaps overemphasized the dangers of a "doing" that has not first listened and tried to find words to express what it has heard, that is because it seems to me clear enough that most liberal and moderate Protestants in the North American context need most to hear Jesus' commendation of Mary, who did "the one thing needful." On the occasion at hand, she did not immerse herself in activity but in the necessary business of listening to Jesus' words.

DOUGLAS JOHN HALL

Pastoral Perspective

Still, there is this matter of the necessary work into which some are thrown when God's dominion draws near. Luke not only presumed people would be in the kitchen preparing food and drink for the seventy on a mission; he also acknowledged the need for a standing office composed of "seven men of good standing, full of the Spirit and of wisdom" (Acts 6:3) who would be given the task of waiting on tables. What, then, should the church make of Jesus' rebuke of Martha, for whom the devil apparently was in the details? "The nature of hospitality for which Jesus seeks," writes Green, "is realized in attending to one's guest, yet Martha's speech is centered on 'me' talk (3 times). Though she refers to Jesus as 'Lord' she is concerned to engage his assistance in her plans, not to learn from him."[2] When anxiety in well-doing becomes the measure of our hospitality, then the church has forgotten the One whom it has been gathered to serve. When Christ is proclaimed as instrumental to the church's program, then the community has ceased to attend to the Word that first called it into being.

You and I are in the service (*diakonia*) of Christ as, by his grace, we forget ourselves. Such acts of service, said Karl Barth, are "usually done in concealment, so that by their very nature no great glory can attach to them, and they can be undertaken and executed only as pure, selfless and unassuming service which might well be hampered or even totally spoiled by even occasional attempts at domination."[3] Humility is the only conceivable posture when in word and sacrament the kingdom of God draws near. In this regard, only one comes to mind. No doubt when dinner was finally served that night at Martha and Mary's home, the guest was revealed, in the breaking of bread, to be their hospitable, humble, hidden host.

CYNTHIA A. JARVIS

2. Ibid., 437.
3. Karl Barth, *Church Dogmatics* IV/3 Second Half (Edinburgh: T. & T. Clark, 1962), 891.

Exegetical Perspective

their purpose. Hospitality that is "anxious and troubled" (v. 41, my trans.) loses its focus, which is Jesus, who is Lord and guest.[2]

British biblical scholar Loveday Alexander catalogs several ways in which this text has been misread.[3] One concerns interpreters' tendency to polarize Martha and Mary, forcing readers to put the sisters' actions in opposition to each other. Another involves characterizing Martha and Mary, along with their deeds, as one-dimensional, as if the story were an allegory wherein each woman represents a paradigm. A third tendency is to assume that the passage is primarily about women and their roles, as if gender takes center stage.

Preachers and teachers should guard against these assumptions, for the text cannot support them. First, neither the narrator nor Jesus sets Martha's and Mary's *activities* in opposition. When Jesus praises Mary's having chosen "the better part" (v. 42), he refers to her singular focus on Jesus himself. "There should be only one thing" (v. 42, my trans.): this does not mean one form of devotion, but one object of devotion. To be genuine, acts of discipleship—whether contemplative, active, or anything else—need to maintain such a focus. Martha's problem is that her service strays from attending to its rightful object of devotion, the Lord Jesus.

Second, nothing about the passage suggests that the activities these women pursue represent types of lifestyles, or that Jesus' final statement lays down a general rule that always values particular expressions of discipleship over others. Indeed, to use this story to justify claims that certain kinds of devotion to Jesus supersede others is to fall into the same trap of self-affirmation that ensnares and draws away Martha.

Third, that Martha and Mary are women makes the story especially interesting, to be sure, and Jesus' approval of Mary does add legitimacy to the observation that among Jesus' followers the ways of Christian discipleship were open to men and women. This does not mean the passage is primarily a story about women's behavior, and Jesus' gentle criticism of Martha's distraction hardly springs from uniquely female struggles.

MATTHEW L. SKINNER

Homiletical Perspective

action."[1] He sees the story not as reinforcing a Martha-Mary dichotomy but calling for a recognition that God is both inside and outside, sustaining us while summoning us to work and, through our service, to bring about a world of justice, mercy, and peace. It is not an either/or message but a both/and message.

A few years ago, Tom Friedman had a column on the op-ed page of the *New York Times* called "The Taxi Driver."[2] He told of being driven by cab from Charles de Gaulle Airport to Paris. During the one-hour trip, he and the driver had done six things: the driver had driven the cab, talked on his cell phone, and watched a video (which was a little nerve-racking!), whereas he had been riding, working on a column on his laptop, and listening to his iPod. "There was only one thing we never did: talk to each other." Friedman went on to quote Linda Stone, a technologist, who had written that the disease of the Internet age is "continuous partial attention." Perhaps it is not only the disease of the Internet age; perhaps it has always been with us, and just the causes of our inattention have altered.

Is it possible that this story of two sisters offers us an ongoing plea from the Lord to focus on him, to give him some "prime time," some continuous *full* attention, just as we do for our close friends? At least, this is what we do, if we want to keep them as close friends. This same Lord calls us to focus on him when we gather on Sunday, to move from our place of being "worried and distracted by many things" to one where we are in touch with the one thing needed, the good part that will not be taken away. There we will connect with the source that brings both peace and energy to all our undertakings.

JAMES A. WALLACE, C.SS.R.

---

2. Later, in Luke 12:22–26, Jesus cautions against worrying (using *merimnaō*, the same verb I translate above as being "anxious").

3. She makes her points, which include more than the three related here, in "Sisters in Adversity," 177–85.

1. John Shea, *The Spiritual Wisdom of the Gospels for Christian Preachers and Teachers: The Relentless Widow, Year C* (Collegeville. MN: Liturgical Press, 2006), 203.

2. Thomas Friedman, "The Taxi Driver," *New York Times*, Nov. 1, 2006, http://select.nytimes.com/2006/11/01/opinion/01friedman.html?_r=1&scp=1&sq=%22The%20Taxi%20Driver%22&st=cse.

Hosea 1:2-10

²When the LORD first spoke through Hosea, the LORD said to Hosea, "Go, take for yourself a wife of whoredom and have children of whoredom, for the land commits great whoredom by forsaking the LORD." ³So he went and took Gomer daughter of Diblaim, and she conceived and bore him a son.

⁴And the LORD said to him, "Name him Jezreel; for in a little while I will punish the house of Jehu for the blood of Jezreel, and I will put an end to the kingdom of the house of Israel. ⁵On that day I will break the bow of Israel in the valley of Jezreel."

⁶She conceived again and bore a daughter. Then the LORD said to him, "Name her Lo-ruhamah, for I will no longer have pity on the house of Israel or forgive them. ⁷But I will have pity on the house of Judah, and I will save them by the LORD their God; I will not save them by bow, or by sword, or by war, or by horses, or by horsemen."

⁸When she had weaned Lo-ruhamah, she conceived and bore a son. ⁹Then the LORD said, "Name him Lo-ammi, for you are not my people and I am not your God."

¹⁰Yet the number of the people of Israel shall be like the sand of the sea, which can be neither measured nor numbered; and in the place where it was said to them, "You are not my people," it shall be said to them, "Children of the living God."

Theological Perspective

Hosea's metaphors of marriage and infidelity describe the covenantal intimacy of people, land, and God with unprecedented emotional charge. "The land commits great whoredom" (v. 2), and the Lord reels, like a shamed and cheated husband caught between anger and brokenhearted forgiveness. Hosea's inventive use of marital tropes carries two significant theological propositions: (1) God experiences love's suffering, and (2) how the people dwell within creation matters for how they dwell with God.

Both are fertile, controversial propositions, but rarely does the church follow those theological lines into the text, because Hosea draws attention beyond the written word. Hosea makes himself into a living symbol of the word he bears from God. He finds a new way to create prophetic disturbance: by marrying a "wife of whoredom" and having "children of whoredom," Hosea makes his family into a parable of broken covenant, embodying the tawdriness of the community's unfaithfulness and the depth of the Lord's dishonor.

This visceral prophetic commission fascinates and confounds interpreters. That God's word would involve actual union with Gomer has been a scandal to many different readers—for quite different reasons. Some commentators have recoiled from Hosea's apparently immoral commission and the association

Pastoral Perspective

There was a time when one heard people say, "Although I am not an active member of any church, I still consider myself to be very religious." At some point even generic "religious" became too specific for comfort. Now one hears people say, "Even though I am not really a religious person, I do consider myself very *spiritual*." This is the great faith of our time— faith as a vague feeling of something or other, out there, or within, something that gives us a sort of warm feeling about some indescribable, indefinable, something. Call it spirituality lite.

This is the result of a project begun at the birth of modernity. In order to get the modern world going, we found it necessary to render God into Aristotle's unmoved mover. We could not stand an interventionist, engaged, and involved God who intruded into our closed, law-abiding natural world. So we made God into an abstraction, a concept, a detached cosmic bureaucrat, just following the rules. William James noted that the notion of "God" is easier for enlightened, modern people to handle if we conceive of God as conducting a wholesale rather than a retail business. God at some remove from the world is less threatening to our desire to run the world as we damn well please.

Well, this Sunday the prophet Hosea introduces us to a very different sort of God. Hosea intrudes

Exegetical Perspective

Hosea prophesied in northern Israel about 750–740 BCE, a tumultuous period involving political intrigue and violence, both domestic and international. Religious syncretism allowed other deities to compete with YHWH for Israel's allegiance. For Hosea, politics and religion shared a common fault—they involved "affairs" in which Israel exhibited infidelity.

God tells Hosea to take "a wife of whoredom" and have children by her. Through chapter 3 the prophet's family life and Israel's life before God are inseparably linked. His broken marriage reflects Israel's broken relationship to God: "for the land commits great whoredom by forsaking the LORD" (v. 2).

Before we attend to the metaphor of whoredom, we consider the three children and their names, each chosen by God (cf. Isa. 7:3, 14; 8:1–4). Jezreel ("God sows") connotes fertility (see below) but here is identified with the place where the king Jehu committed atrocities, including two regicides, twenty beheadings, and one massacre (2 Kgs. 9–10). Hosea apparently condemns Jehu for the extent of the bloodshed and for the reversion of his dynastic successors to the Baal worship and idolatry that Jehu was anointed to eradicate (Hos. 7:3–7; 8:4–6).

Lo-ruhamah deepens God's judgment, abandoning the very quality of mercy or compassion

Homiletical Perspective

An Unreasonable Command? A first reading of the first chapter of Hosea evokes dismay. Why would a loving and caring God command a faithful servant to marry a whore? There is simply no way to add a sugary-sweet glaze to this particular introduction. Hosea was commanded to marry a prostitute, one who sold herself for money or for trade, who was in every sense unfaithful.

It may be easy to criticize a person who has been in this walk of life, but we must understand that the reasons for being relegated to this station can be many and quite complicated. Gomer could have been led to this life by an incredibly dysfunctional family system, perhaps even one with sexual abuse. Maybe she ran away from the semblance of a home at a very early age and discovered the only possible way to make ends meet. Thousands of young people across the globe are sold into the slavery of prostitution every year, even in the twenty-first century. Drug habits have led others to become prostitutes. There are also economic realities in which very few unskilled labor positions exist, and even fewer for women than for men. Sociologists can provide us with a much more complete description and understanding of the phenomenon of prostitution, but its intricacies cannot be ignored.

We are not told why or how Gomer, Hosea's eventual wife, became a whore. Perhaps she was one

Hosea 1:2-10

Theological Perspective

of God's will with sensuality. So a line of Christian commentary has suggested that Hosea does not actually unite with a whore, but narrates an imaginative allegory that expresses a spiritual relationship with God. On this reading, Gomer might prefigure the prostitute who anoints the feet of Jesus, a loose woman serving as a symbol of God's grace redeeming human cupidity.

Others see the scandal of Gomer in the troubling gender assumptions of both Hosea and his later interpreters. Literal or allegorical, Hosea's struggle with "a wife of whoredom" relies on assumptions about male honor in a patriarchal society, where autonomous female sexuality is a threat and female unfaithfulness can jeopardize a community's dignity. Hosea's shaming technique relies on this patriarchal hermeneutic; his symbolic marriage clearly puts Israel in the place of the unfaithful female, and he can count on his audience burning with the indignity. The allegorical Christian interpretation only transfers the androcentrism into a Hellenistic register, correlating the whore's sexuality with the unruly human will.

We cannot overlook, then, how Hosea's gender position inflects his portrayal of God as he invites his audience to identify with the emotional register of a dishonored husband. Precisely because Hosea's patriarchal perspective on marital infidelity shapes his understanding of God's response to a sinful community, we can imagine alternative ways of reading. What if the prophet had been a woman? How would that change the portrayal of Israel's ruptured covenant? What shames and violences of marriage would she use to invite her audience to identify with God's experience?

Whatever we decide about Gomer and the figure of the whore, however, notice that we occupy her place in this prophetic narrative. She is the person of the people before God, the typological figure of humanity. Now consider Gomer's mute passivity in all this. We know nothing about who she was or how she interpreted this experience. That has in part to do with the patriarchal context, but also offers a clue that human experience is not the emotional center here; God's experience is.

Therein lies a greater theological scandal, sometimes overlooked in our fascination with whoredom. Hosea's marital drama models the emotional life of the Lord's experience with Israel, in sorrow, anger, and longing. In this text, the names of Hosea's three children seem to stand for God's shamed remembering, burned anger, and resigned abandonment. In the final verse, God's heart turns to restore his lover, as the

Pastoral Perspective

with a pushy, challenging, perhaps even offensive metaphor for our relationship to God: we stand before God as an adulterous spouse stands before a long-suffering, loving, faithful spouse. What we might prefer to call "doubt" or "a spiritual quest for possible religious alternatives," the book of Hosea indelicately names "harlotry." Even though you don't know what the word means, it just sounds bad! Although we might like to keep our conversations with God cool, calm, and polite, in today's first lesson the emotional temperature is turned up; there is heated, passionate, anguished name-calling, shouts and cries, and angry pleading. Can we worship this much of a God?

In numerous places in the Old Testament, YHWH is called a "jealous God." Sorry, if you prefer your gods to be exalted, distant, balanced, cool, and calm. YHWH is passionately committed to Israel. All that this God is has been invested in this people and their well-being. YHWH has delivered Israel, taken sides, given Israel a good and bounteous land, invested heavily in this people. Much is at stake in Israel's life before God. Israel's religious wandering is therefore rather offensively labeled as adultery, prostitution, and harlotry. Conversation between Israel and YHWH quickly becomes heated, acrimonious, and fierce because YHWH is so completely committed to Israel that YHWH takes Israel personally.

Any law enforcement officer will tell you that she would rather walk in on a bank robbery than a marital argument in a bedroom. We call crimes committed in the name of love "crimes of passion." If it is true that YHWH is a jealous sort of God—possessive, fiercely attached to us, determined to retain a relationship with us, passionately committed to us—then we can expect the "spiritual life" to be that way too.

Our challenge as modern people, trained that the best way to think about things is through detached, objective, dispassionate analysis, is not to allow the repulsive quality of the prophetic metaphor to repel us (God commands the prophet Hosea to marry a prostitute?). Rather, we are to allow this shocking image to lead us into a fresh understanding of the nature of the God of Israel and the church. The infidelity of Gomer to Hosea pushes us toward engagement, embodiment with matters that we would be more comfortable keeping safely "spiritual," abstract, cool, and detached. The biblical text this Sunday will not allow us to do that.

Within Hosea's challenging parabolic metaphor is good news. What is God like? Jesus responded with

Exegetical Perspective

(NRSV "pity") that Israel cherished (we can read v. 7 as a continuation of the syntax of v. 6, condemning Judah also ["*nor* will I have pity . . . or save them *from* . . ."]).[1] In covenant traditions God is "merciful and gracious, slow to anger, and abounding in steadfast love and faithfulness," (Ps. 103:8; Exod. 34:6). Similarly, God has compassion on Israel just as parents have compassion on their children (Ps. 103:13)—indeed, the word for "mercy" or "compassion" (*rachamim*) derives from the root *rechem*, which means "womb," suggesting maternal emotion. But *God's* "steadfast love and faithfulness" depends on *Israel's* steadfast love and faithfulness, in that it benefits those who *keep* covenant and remember to do God's commandments (Ps. 103:18). The tension between God's love and justice, grace and law, is, of course, a fundamental theological problem; *here* the child No-Mercy signals that the tension is broken in favor of justice (but see below).

With Not-My-People, God disowns Israel. The covenant relationship—expressed most succinctly in the expression "my people" (*'ammi*)—is completely broken. The name *lo-'ammi* constitutes abandonment of God's former identity as Israel's redeemer and covenant sovereign (Exod. 3:7; 6:7; 19:5–6), established in the exodus and reiterated with figures like Saul (1 Sam. 9:16) and David (2 Sam. 7:7–8).

The lectionary ends with v. 10, but our reading should continue through 2:1, where the names probably are references to the people as a whole. The view here replaces the prophecy of doom with hope, signified by the name changes. Despite the time of tribulation, there will be another time of restoration, in which northern and southern realms will be united again under one "head." Like Hosea in his broken marriage, God will revive the relationship with Israel.

The metaphor of whoredom is a powerful expression of Israel's infidelity; it is also fraught with hermeneutical dangers involving our conception of God and the implications for human behavior, particularly the treatment of wives by husbands.

In addition to prostitution, Hosea also accuses Israel of adultery (5:7; 7:4). The two are different, of course, in that prostitution involves sex for material reward. Although prostitution carries a deeper stigma, both are injurious to the relationship of husband and wife. Hosea can use the terms in parallel (2:2; 4:13–14). Accordingly, "promiscuity" would be preferable to "whoredom" in verse 2.

Homiletical Perspective

of the sacred prostitutes of the "cult" religion of Baal.[1] While this assertion need not be definite for the argument to have force, it does give insight into the biblical author's frame of mind. In Hosea's time, one of the most grievous of sins was to syncretize one's religion. That the relationship between Hosea and his wife was symbolic becomes clear in the second verse: "The LORD said to Hosea, 'Go, take for yourself a wife of whoredom and have children of whoredom, for the land commits great whoredom by forsaking the LORD.'" The whoredom or harlotry of Hosea's wife stands for so much more than sexual infidelity. It includes ways in which business practices were carried forth, the manner in which political decisions were made, and, of course, the belief (or lack of same) of the people in YHWH, the Lord God of Israel.

There is an ageless message that rings true from the prophet Hosea: God is always faithful, while human beings rarely are. Elizabeth Achtemeier states the same truth in a slightly different voice, "God promises to do what human beings ought to do but cannot."[2]

What Kind of Family Is This? There is a certain logic behind the naming of a child. Sometimes parents seek to honor a member of the family who has achieved greatness. Sometimes one is named simply after the mother or the father. Sometimes a famous name from history is drawn into the naming of a newborn child. What makes the naming of Hosea and Gomer's children so unique is that the names YHWH gives them present such negative images.

The first son, probably born within the first year of the marriage, was named Jezreel, which literally means "God sows" or "God plants" (v. 4). The Lord obviously wanted to recall the site where Jehu massacred the worshipers of Baal, the kings of both Judah and Israel, and the evil Jezebel, as God (through the prophet Elisha) had directed him to do (2 Kgs. 9–10). So why does the Lord now want to use the child's name as a sign that the house of Jehu must come to an end?

The answer appears to be that Jehu's line (personified in the reign of Jeroboam II) has become as corrupt as that of Ahab and Jezebel. The significance of this name, Jezreel, is that the army of Israel will suffer a military defeat at this site, and the name of Hosea's first child signals the loss of the kingship:

---

1. Francis Andersen and David Freedman, *Hosea*, Anchor Bible 24 (Garden City, NY: Doubleday, 1980), 189.

1. James Luther Mays, *Hosea* (Philadelphia: Westminster Press, 1969), 26.
2. Elizabeth Achtemeier, *Minor Prophets I* (Peabody, MA: Hendrickson Publishers, 1996), 3.

Hosea 1:2-10

Theological Perspective

lectionary text concludes in hope that abandonment will turn to renewed embrace. In six verses, then, we have a brief of the lover's psyche. If its sexuality vexes Hellenistic sensibilities, the text's depiction of God's romantic suffering totally confounds it. Here the impassible God suffers because of a particular love—and God's word for humanity arrives from within that suffering.

How will humans respond? Hosea's modeling of God's experience invites the people into a matching kind of love, a devotion profoundly of the heart. The experience of Gomer, our experience, will then find its voice and come alive within God's experience, but we must take care lest this interpretation also stray toward disembodied allegory. Hosea's understanding of the covenant takes place not only in the interior landscape, but in the practices of dwelling with actual soil.

The opening is specific: it is because of "the land's" infidelity that the Lord calls Hosea. While commentators often take "land" as shorthand for "all the residents," throughout the book Hosea connects Israel's infidelity to the whole creation community, sometimes in lines reminiscent of our own times ("even the fish of the sea are perishing," 4:3). In restoration, God makes Israel a new covenant with the community of creation (2:18), and with it the land's fertility is restored, as God "sows" Israel back into the land (2:22–23). Israel's trespass thus involves the whole community of creation and seems to lie in improper practices of inhabitation. The sexual tropes suggest the specific problem may have been participation in fertility cults. If so, then, as scholar Walter Brueggemann observes, Hosea is about the mistaken notion that nature's economy runs separately from God's economy.[1]

The infidelity at issue then is not just a disorder of the heart or of social justice; it involves a rupture of faith from the land, as if the Lord of Israel were not also the God of creation. For our time of environmental crises, recovering this land theology in Hosea may be particularly important. Contemporary theologian Ilaitia Tuwere draws on Hosea to describe the theological character of the Fijian church's dwelling with its bounded place and its resistance to economies of alienation.[2] Hosea may be a prophet for a church that must proclaim anew how God's people are wedded to creation, in a marriage of nature and grace.

WILLIS JENKINS

Pastoral Perspective

stories about a shepherd who relentlessly searches until the one lost sheep is found, the woman who seeks until she finds her one lost coin, the father who waits until the lost son comes home (Luke 15). God is like that. God is determined to retain that which belongs to God.

This is good news in a religious culture that often becomes confused into thinking that our relationship to God is dependent upon us. We come to church to think, to believe, to feel, to behave in the right ways, so that God will love us. Religion is the assignment that you are given by God in order for you to keep close to God. No. Hosea—through vivid, striking, even offensive metaphor—reveals the heart of a God who passionately loves, forgives, seeks, finds, waits, pleads, and saves. Time and again this God forgives. Relentlessly this God does not just sit back waiting for us to come to our senses and return to relationship. This God is the long-suffering spouse who is willing to be in pain for the sake of us. This God hounds us until we turn, return, repent, relinquish, and come back.

Today's text from Hosea is more than a little shocking. It is a scandal. To compare our relationship with God to a messed-up marriage in which a sexually promiscuous, repeatedly unfaithful spouse is repeatedly forgiven, taken back, excused, and loved is a scandalous idea, not often thought in polite, proper religious circles. It is not very "spiritual."

Thus Paul says that a God who loves so much that God is willing to be crucified for the unfaithful beloved is a *skandalon* to the world (1 Cor. 1:23; Gal. 5:11). Yet to those of us who are being saved, this scandal is our salvation. Only a passionate, unseemly God who is willing to risk scandal could possibly save a bunch of adulterers like us.

Thanks be to God.

WILLIAM H. WILLIMON

---

1. Walter Brueggemann, *The Land: Place as Gift, Promise, and Challenge in Biblical Faith*, 2nd ed. (Minneapolis: Fortress Press, 2002), 97–99.
2. Ilaitia Sevati Tuwere, *Vanua: Towards a Fijian Theology of Place* (Suvi: Institute of Pacific Studies, 2002).

Exegetical Perspective

The metaphor of promiscuity functions on two levels, both covenantal. Israel's relationship to God is formalized politically by a covenant in which God is the suzerain and Israel the vassal. The relationship can also be familial, a marital covenant with God the husband and Israel the wife, with the respective genders determined by Israel's predominantly male model of God (cf. Jer. 31:31–32). To further mix metaphors, Hosea also talks about the relationship between God and Israel as parent/child (cf. Jer. 3:19–20).

Thus, in Hosea, Israel is guilty of infidelity on three levels: sovereign/servant, husband/wife, parent/child. God is an offended ruler, a cuckold, and a wounded parent. Fundamentally, all involve unrequited love. While this may be obvious in the familial models, it is also true for the political, where the central commandment is "to love the LORD your God with all your heart" (Deut. 6:5). Here the primary meaning of love is allegiance, fidelity, and faithfulness.

Israel's "lovers" are other gods, especially the Canaanite Baal, but also foreign powers, like Assyria or Egypt. Israel has prostituted herself with Baal, and the "pay" (2:12) is fertility—"they give me my bread and my water, my wool and my flax, my oil and my drink" (2:5). But YHWH provides these (2:8; cf. Deut. 8). (Recent study discounts the influence of alleged "fertility cults" in Hosea's critique.)[2] Israel seeks security by flirting with international powers (8:9), but YHWH provides their security.

The promiscuity metaphors assume a model of God that is male, jealous, angry, vengeful, and arguably abusive (see 2:3–14). If we forget that this *is* a metaphor, and therefore not literally true, then "a husband's physical abuse of his wife comes to be as justified as God's retribution against Israel."[3] That said, the metaphors of prostitution and adultery can be a means to focus on ways in which we are willing to "sell our souls" for a god who is no more than an idol (8:4–6). From whom do "all blessings flow"? What are the "principalities and powers" that claim our allegiance (see Epistle lection, Col. 2:15)? What would it take for us to "prostitute" ourselves?

THOMAS W. MANN

Homiletical Perspective

"On that day I will break the bow of Israel in the valley of Jezreel" (v. 5).

The second child, a daughter, is given the name Lo-ruhamah, which means "not loved" or better still "not pitied"(v. 6). Any child given this name, especially a daughter, would be an embarrassment for the parents and for the nation. On a larger scale, the name suggests that YHWH will no longer forgive a people who have been unfaithful for far too long.

After the second child has been weaned, a third child, a son, is born. The Lord gives him the name Lo-ammi, which means "not my people" (v. 9). There is a negative progression in the naming of the children, culminating in Lo-ammi, or rejection. "You are not my people" and "I (YHWH) am not your God." As Mays asserts, "this does not mean that Yahweh is done with Israel."[3] However, it does mean that the relationship has changed significantly.

A Promise of Restoration. Just when it appears that the situation cannot get any worse, there is a note of reprieve. Even though it is quite apparent that God has grown weary of a people who have turned their backs on him, word comes that they will not be forgotten after all. "Yet the number of the people of Israel shall be like the sand of the sea, which can be neither measured nor numbered" (v. 10). Even though the people have previously been told otherwise, an everlastingly faithful God relents of the anger shown in verse 6 by saying that Israel is no longer "not my people." Instead, now you shall again be called, "Children of the living God" (v. 10). What a sign of hope in the face of utter despair!

JOHN E. WHITE

---

2. Elaine Goodfriend, "Prostitution (OT)," in *Anchor Bible Dictionary*, ed. David Freedman (New York: Doubleday, 1992), 5:505–10; and Karel Van Der Toorn, "Prostitution (Cultic)," ibid., 510–13; Gale A. Yee, "Hosea," in *Women's Bible Commentary*, ed. Carol Newsom and Sharon Ringe (Louisville, KY: Westminster John Knox Press, 1992), 208–9.
3. Yee, "Hosea," 212.

3. Mays, *Hosea*, 30.

Psalm 85

> ¹LORD, you were favorable to your land;
>   you restored the fortunes of Jacob.
> ²You forgave the iniquity of your people;
>   you pardoned all their sin.   *Selah*
> ³You withdrew all your wrath;
>   you turned from your hot anger.
>
> ⁴Restore us again, O God of our salvation,
>   and put away your indignation toward us.
> ⁵Will you be angry with us forever?
>   Will you prolong your anger to all generations?
> ⁶Will you not revive us again,
>   so that your people may rejoice in you?
> ⁷Show us your steadfast love, O LORD,
>   and grant us your salvation.

Theological Perspective

The Faithful in a Wayward Nation. This week's psalm speaks so clearly in the collective that it cannot but invite reflection on the relationship between the faithful and the broader society—more pointedly, the nation.

Exegetical reflections on this psalm situate it at a troubled moment in Israel's history, when past glories were being remembered fondly in the midst of difficulty and disaster for the nation of Israel. Theologically the text sets before us *questions of God's providence and care* for the nation. It demands that we consider carefully the position of the individual believer, and the community of the faithful, when the "nation" is not coterminous with the believing community, and it invites reflection on how, and whether, the faithful should pray for the interests of the state.

Does God Care for Us? The experience of the psalm-singing people is that of feeling God's favor has been removed from them. Once they were great, favored, prosperous, a nation unto themselves; now they are scattered, powerless, evicted from their home, even wondering whether they will be able to preserve the essentials of their identity as a people.

Our own situation in the United States could not possibly be more different. We write, think, and

Pastoral Perspective

For a community facing difficult times, Psalm 85 speaks a word of encouragement and confidence in God. As a prayer, this psalm incorporates clear memory of God's past actions, a plea for this moment, and a confident statement of what the future will hold. Psalm 85 challenges listeners truly to hear God's word of peace, which attunes not only the believers but the land itself to God's goodness.

Clearly, the people who first heard this psalm were invited to remember the actions of God. God had already responded by restoring the fortunes of Jacob, forgiving and pardoning the people, and turning away from anger. In confidence, then, the psalmist makes a poetic plea for restoration in the present moment. Historically, this psalm may have been a response to the challenges of the postexilic era.

Twenty-first-century Christians are able to look back in history to affirm God's actions over the last three millennia. Reflecting on biblical stories, we remember the Hebrew people coming out of bondage; the development of holy history through the prophets; the life, death, and resurrection of Jesus; and the reality of the early church. Building on what we know from the past, we look to the situation in which we are living today.

This text seeks to inspire and assure believers. Just as God was active in the past, God's positive actions

⁸Let me hear what God the Lᴏʀᴅ will speak,
   for he will speak peace to his people,
   to his faithful, to those who turn to him in their hearts.
⁹Surely his salvation is at hand for those who fear him,
   that his glory may dwell in our land.

¹⁰Steadfast love and faithfulness will meet;
   righteousness and peace will kiss each other.
¹¹Faithfulness will spring up from the ground,
   and righteousness will look down from the sky.
¹²The Lᴏʀᴅ will give what is good,
   and our land will yield its increase.
¹³Righteousness will go before him,
   and will make a path for his steps.

Exegetical Perspective

How does one bridge the gulf between what one deeply believes to be true about God and the messy circumstances of real life? How does a situation of suffering affect our beliefs about and relationship to God? With serious reflection and honest emotion, the psalmist explores these questions, arriving at a stance of faith in God and brilliant images and insights about God's character.

The lack of precision in the Hebrew verbal system has led translators to suggest some intriguing possibilities for verses 1–3. Although the verses are in perfect tense, indicating completed action, some translators have assumed that the psalmist was looking to the future in this part of the poem. In this understanding, God will show favor to the poet and the community (see the translation by the Jewish Publication Society). If this rendering is correct, the whole psalm anticipates God's favor. The NRSV is most likely correct that the psalmist is reflecting on YHWH's past actions, even seeking to remind YHWH of this past favor. YHWH's past favor was comprehensive. YHWH acted in ways that changed the physical and material circumstances of the people ("restored the fortunes of Jacob"), and the spiritual relationship with the people ("forgave," "pardoned," and "withdrew . . . wrath"). The form of this section of the psalm is a prayer, intended to

Homiletical Perspective

The psalmist comes to God on behalf of his people with empty hands and a rich memory. The poet gives voice to a communal lament and speaks a hope-filled longing that the people will receive from God those blessings that God has graciously given them in the past. In preaching this text, a challenge we face is that communal lament is not practiced today. It would be useful to consider with our listeners what has replaced it (ranting on blogs, griping over coffee at work, and individual numb despair) and what forms it could fruitfully take today. How can the psalmist's pattern of prayer inform our prayers for our society and for the world? How does reflection on this psalm give permission for us to express our anguish at the injustice in our world, places in which we perceive the absence or even anger of God? How does it widen the scope of what we may envision and dream for ourselves, our communities, and our world? How can the themes and postures before God found here inform and give shape to our own lamentation and intercession? We will consider the psalmist's pattern of looking back with gratitude (vv. 1–3), naming current reality with truth and longing (vv. 4–7), and speaking boldly to others the words of hope that we will hear as we go to God in prayer (vv. 8–13).

The psalmist begins by recounting the outpouring of favor from God that resulted in a past event of

Psalm 85

Theological Perspective

preach in the most prosperous nation in the history of nations. All other nations must take account of ours. Our fears for our own security do not realistically extend to the possibility of being put out of our homes by a foreign invader. We are at the zenith of our power.

That is exactly the problem. A theological critique of our circumstances views our sense of foreboding as symptomatic of our true state—soul sickness. Perhaps God's favor has been removed from us too. Once we were admired and extolled by nations everywhere as a people dedicated to good, to human dignity, to freedom. Now we have difficulty believing this about ourselves, while the world often sees us as menacing, willful, and arrogant. We lose faith that our institutions will provide justice, that our work will provide prosperity, that our schools will provide opportunity.

What meaning does "God's favor" have in the present day? If baptism is "an appeal to God for a good conscience" (1 Pet. 3:21), then it may be *the prayerful discernment of the community of the baptized* that remains our only means of correcting the position and course of the nation's affairs vis-à-vis God's will for us. Our prayers "are the means by which the disciples become partakers in the heavenly treasure for which they pray."[1]

That community of disciples is responsible for considering, critically and faithfully, how it would actually look for God's will to be done on earth as it is in heaven, rather than simply ascribing God's favor to whatever it has seized upon as advantageous to its own preferences. "In the end the whole world must bow before that will, worshipping and giving thanks in joy and tribulation."[2] Yes, God cares for us—but God cares for those who seek to live in accordance with God's will, far more than for any one nation.

Community and Nation. For the psalmist, "people," "nation," and "land" were all different ways of expressing the same idea. Ancient Israel was a rooted theocracy, a nation characterized by the ideals of uniformity of belief, custom, and ritual; consolidation of power under the Davidic king; and a divine mandate to occupy a specific extent of land.

The faithful of our own day and place live under vastly different circumstances. Our faith does not

Pastoral Perspective

need to continue in our present situation. In some congregations, you may still hear the plea for restoration ringing out in this old chorus:

> Revive us again—fill each heart with Thy love,
> May each soul be rekindled with fire from above.[1]

Revival allows God's people to rejoice in God. The gift of God's steadfast love comes as God's anger is set aside. Restoration allows the community to move into or return to a sense of peace. Faith communities rejoice as we experience true renewal.

What of those faith communities that are not revived? Some are weary, diminished in number, facing economic challenges, and unsure about how to continue. Others may believe God is angry with them because of their self-protective and bland lives. Still other congregations fear any change, but wonder at the apathy and lack of joy evident when they gather.

Psalm 85 addresses that possibility in verse 8a. What would it mean for us today to hear God speak peace to God's own people? Especially in a politically charged time, such language or action might open amazing ministry opportunities. Here are three suggestions:

—If you live in a community with warring factions (e.g., opposing gangs or political parties, loggers and "tree-huggers," immigrants and border-protectionists, militarists and pacifists), arrange a public dialogue that gives each group the chance to express their point of view. Have a moderator ask questions (planned ahead, or written by audience members and edited to be read by the moderator). Give each side equal time to respond. Invite participants to reflect on what it would take to hear God speaking peace to the people gathered. Read Psalm 85:8–13 as a part of opening the time, and repeat verse 8 as the closing moment of reflection or prayer.

—Arrange an education forum time to hear from Christian Peacemaking Teams (CPT) in person or through media.[2] Moving from that presentation, invite your faith community to reflect on the ways they hear God speaking "peace" in the face of the conflicts described by the CPT speaker/s. What would it take for your community to actively participate with CPT?

---

1. Dietrich Bonhoeffer, *The Cost of Discipleship*, trans. R. H. Fuller (New York: Macmillan, 1963), 185. NB: this is taken from Bonhoeffer's line-by-line consideration of the Lord's Prayer and its significance for the spiritual formation of the community of faith; here, the focus is on "Thy will be done on earth as it is in heaven."
2. Ibid.

1. William P. Mackay, in *African American Heritage Hymnal* (Chicago: GIA Publications, 2001), #569.
2. For more information on Christian Peacemaker Teams (CPT), see http://www.cpt.org/.

move YHWH to action. Perhaps the psalmist seeks to bolster his own faith at the same time.

In verse 4 the poet changes to petition. Something in the circumstances of the people has changed. The fortunes that once had been restored have again dissipated. The divine wrath that had been withdrawn has returned in full force. The most common suggestion about the historical background of the psalm is the aftermath of the return from exile. The return from Babylonian captivity was seen during that period as both a restoration of fortune and forgiveness of sin (see Isa. 40:2). The initial joy of the return morphed into lament as conditions failed to live up to expectations (Isa. 63:15–64:7). This psalm echoes the sentiment of the prophet (Third Isaiah) that God must act again for the people. The psalm addresses YHWH as "God of our salvation." This title refers both to God's concrete actions on behalf of the people and to salvation as forgiveness and restored relationship.

God's character is an important subject for this psalm. The poet takes seriously God's wrath. The psalmist assumes that the circumstances of the people derive from God's anger. The psalmist remains confident that steadfast love is also part of God's character. The psalm itself does not explore the dynamic between God's anger and God's steadfast love. Does God's anger arise spontaneously? The psalmist does not offer a confession to appease God. The pleading tone in these verses seems intended to affect God's disposition. God can choose to put away wrath and show steadfast love.

At verse 8 the poet shifts from exhorting God to a kind of self-exhortation. In the midst of the difficult circumstances of the people, the psalmist commits to listen for God's word. No longer speaking to God, the poet speaks to the self about God. The poet is confident that God will change the circumstances of the people again ("salvation" in v. 9) and manifest the divine presence with the people ("glory"). Although the form and tone of the psalm are not primarily confessional, the psalmist does not want the people to give up on God and turn to folly (see the NRSV v. 8 footnote). The poet wants the people to continue to fear God, even in this downturn in their situation.

In the last four verses, 10–13, the poet's language soars to beautiful heights. Here we find both the most profound theology of the psalm and the most exquisite expression. The poet who has exhorted God to show steadfast love once again now confidently declares that steadfast love and faithfulness will meet.

redemption. It involved three components: restoration of land and fortune, forgiveness, and a cessation of God's wrath. This psalm is written from a point in history well beyond that initially celebrative and hopeful time. Since then, the people have been hammered with losses and disappointments. Their land is not producing, struggles abound, and the word on the street is that God is absent.

The psalmist surveys the current landscape and laments on behalf of his community, concluding that they need a renewal of God's work in the current struggle. Like bread left unwrapped on a counter for several days, the people's hearts have grown stale and dry; they are muddling through their days with little sense of the fresh joy of God animating their lives. The psalmist perceives that God is indignant and angry with them. Homiletically, the wrath of God is a difficult theme, historically either used to bludgeon listeners into obedience or avoided altogether. Here it would be worth considering what tended to make God angry in the Hebrew Scriptures: injustice, apathy toward the poor, and idolatry. The psalmist's plea for God to remove God's anger is a plea for God to restore social justice and righteousness in society and to renew hearts to singular devotion to God.

The next movement the psalmist makes is to seek the voice of God, in wording reminiscent of Moses's seeking God in an oracle (Num. 9:8). The psalmist describes a setting crowded with competing voices, clamoring for attention and claiming authority to interpret the present crisis. So the psalmist insists, "Let me hear what God the LORD will speak" (v. 8). Here is a posture of solitude and silence before God, a still point in which God's voice may be discerned. Our world is crowded with experts offering quick solutions to all that ails us, personally or globally. These voices pander to our fears and anxieties, and seldom yield peace. To pursue and discern the voice of God amid the racket of distracting noises is a disciplined choice. "Let me hear . . ." is a homiletical hinge for this text. It was crucial that the psalmist made a quiet space within which to hear the promise of God.

The word of God to God's people is *peace*. We have all experienced those moments when the words of another or the words of Scripture were able to "speak peace" to us in the midst of a crisis and its emotional turmoil or despair. Here God speaks peace to those who turn, or lean forward in their hearts toward God. This turning involves a paradoxical mix of passion and surrender. The movement is a disciplined turning away from all other potential sources of peace and salvation, and a

Psalm 85

Theological Perspective

constitute a set of organizing ideals for our political structures. Instead, those structures regard all religious beliefs with strict neutrality. We have no special claim to particular influence in shaping the nation's objectives, no special privilege to chart the course of its policy, no special mandate over the land in which we live. On the contrary, we are called to live harmoniously with those of many faiths and those of no faith in a richly blessed land to which virtually none of us have any claim, either from providence or history.

What then is our place to be? Do we pray for God's favor to come only upon us, the community of the baptized? Have we any right to offer our prayers for the welfare of a secular nation that may not wish to have them? Conversely, is it arrogant of us not to do so? At a deeper level, do we have any business holding in prayer *any* specific interests or objectives that might be regarded as political, and hence the prerogative of the state? Should the neutrality of the state as regards religion carry with it an insistence on strict neutrality of the church as regards the state, as such writers as Robert Audi have argued?[3]

Congregations often have a conflicted relationship with patriotism, and with good reason. As Christians, we owe primary allegiance elsewhere. Lending the support of our prayer to any national aspiration cheapens our relationship with God for undeserving ends. Our prayer life is intended to bring us into line with God's will. How we then act in our role as citizens is a matter for a prayer-informed conscience. It is less clear that the ecclesiastical structures of the community of the faithful should concern themselves with state issues. The psalm contends that other concerns lie closer to the heart of the church—discerning and following the call of God.

MARK D. W. EDINGTON

Pastoral Perspective

—Invite people interested in worship and liturgical movement to use Psalm 85 as the basis for a worship service. Allow time for the team to plan worship for a particular Sunday. Choose carefully how to present the concept of God's speaking peace. A planning group might read through the text together, take time to reflect on it silently, read through it again, and then brainstorm possible ways to center worship on this psalm. Plan ahead, giving your congregation notice about what to expect, and make it possible to have conversation following worship if you anticipate emotional responses.

Perhaps a skit could suggest ways God speaks peace in the present moment. You could write a litany for peace as if it were coming from Israelis and Palestinians, from Iraqi and American soldiers, from Katrina-weary victims still fighting to reclaim their homes. Perhaps you could invite someone engaged in ministries with the poor in your community to preach, especially focusing on ways you can respond to the needs of those yearning for revival.

Psalm 85 is directed to people, but also to "the land" in verses 1, 9, and 11–12. All these verses explicitly connect the land to God's action. In a season when many are focusing on ecojustice and the pressures of climate change, Psalm 85 certainly can help us focus attention on God's intention for the land. In what ways can faith communities pay attention so that God's "glory may dwell in our land" (v. 9)? How can we encourage and support faithfulness to spring up from the ground (v. 11)?

Since the assigned date for this text is in July, could your faith community meet outdoors as you reflect on it? Changing the normal location for class or for worship opens new awareness. If you are in a setting where the land has been completely covered by paving and buildings, what would it take to create a pocket garden or a roof garden? If you have open land, consider planting late summer or fall flowers, or vegetables. Could several people come together to plan, plant, and care for a community garden?

Focus on your participation in God's provision of "what is good" (v. 12a). Past, present, and future together allow "the land [to] yield its increase" (v. 12b) and all to hear God's word of peace.

LINDA MCKIERNAN-ALLEN

---

3. Robert Audi, *Religious Commitment and Secular Reason* (Cambridge, UK: Cambridge University Press, 2000), esp. part I. NB: Audi's acknowledgment of certain conditions under which this expectation of neutrality could be suspended: "under conditions of tyranny, freedom and democracy might be restorable only if churches *do* support candidates for (public) office" (43, emphasis in original).

Exegetical Perspective

Perhaps because of the poet's circumstances, he thinks the two have been estranged. God's wrath has stood between God's unmerited grace and favor (steadfast love) and God's reliability (faithfulness). God is not at heart a God of wrath. Not only will God's steadfast love return, but it will be a faithful love, so that the people will not have to worry about another capricious turn toward anger. The poet's most startling insight comes in the second half of verse 10. Restored relationships ("righteousness") and wholeness ("peace") will kiss. The people have felt estranged from God (in v. 6 the people are unable to rejoice). Righteousness will be the answer to that estrangement. The circumstances of the people have fallen apart (the need for restoration in v. 4). God's peace, understood as wholeness and stability, will address those circumstances. That these two attributes of God will "kiss" couches the new action of God in terms of affection, even romance.

Two of God's attributes (faithfulness and righteousness) that have seemed to be in short supply will surround the people, rising up from the ground and coming down from the sky. The image of faithfulness springing up from the ground recalls plant life in springtime, signifying renewal. Righteousness will look down from the sky, evoking protection and concern. Both righteousness and faithfulness will come in abundance.

The coming changed circumstances of the people are affirmed in verse 12. The people will experience not only a restored sense of God's presence, but prosperity and fulfillment. The final image in verse 13 is of righteousness as a kind of plow that will clear away all of the things that have hindered the feeling of God's presence.

The psalm gives the preacher the opportunity to explore how contemporary people understand God's wrath. We do not want to affirm that every bad circumstance or bit of bad luck reflects God's anger ("What did I do to deserve this?"). Nevertheless, circumstances may make us feel estranged from God. The poem surrounds the language of God's wrath with affirmations of God's steadfast love, faithfulness, and peace. God has shown those attributes before the present circumstances, lamented in the psalm, and the poet is confident that God will display them again, in abundance.

CHARLES L. AARON

Homiletical Perspective

hopeful and eager turning toward the true source of deliverance and *shalom*.

While the psalm involves pleading for God to act, the final verses make clear that we are not pleading because God is unwilling to act. God is not standing far off, coolly debating whether to come to the aid of the people. Rather, God's salvation is near! As God's people turn, God enthusiastically pours out blessings. Verses 10–13 animate several virtues or divine attributes, portraying them first as royal courtiers or long-lost friends greeting each other with a kiss, then as sunlight or rain coming from the sky, to be met by plants and trees springing up from the ground. The fecundity of the scene is reminiscent of the scene in the Disney movie *Fantasia*, where new life springs forth with dazzling vitality upon the earth, after a devastating fire that has left the land grey and bleak.

As we look out at our nation, we sense the same spiritual dryness and lethargy that the psalmist perceived. As our listeners look inward, many will find that they too have faced losses and disappointments. They feel barrenness in vocational, spiritual, or relational spheres, and we preachers may as well. As a nation, as church bodies, and as individuals, we stand in need of renewal. The realism of this psalm gives us permission to come before God with honest and bold lament; yet the final verses show us that sorrow need not be the end of the story. It calls us to lift our eyes to see the energizing, revitalizing work of God. The vivid image of the fertile field yielding what is good gives us a vision that can enlarge the scope of that for which we dare to pray today. We come before God in need of restoration. Let us hear what God wants to speak to us: words of peace, words of salvation, words that call us to turn, and turn again, to God.

LISA LAMB

Colossians 2:6-15 (16-19)

⁶As you therefore have received Christ Jesus the Lord, continue to live your lives in him, ⁷rooted and built up in him and established in the faith, just as you were taught, abounding in thanksgiving.

⁸See to it that no one takes you captive through philosophy and empty deceit, according to human tradition, according to the elemental spirits of the universe, and not according to Christ. ⁹For in him the whole fullness of deity dwells bodily, ¹⁰and you have come to fullness in him, who is the head of every ruler and authority. ¹¹In him also you were circumcised with a spiritual circumcision, by putting off the body of the flesh in the circumcision of Christ; ¹²when you were buried with him in baptism, you were also raised with him through faith in the power of God, who raised him from the dead. ¹³And when you were dead in trespasses and the uncircumcision of your flesh, God made

Theological Perspective

The theology of Colossians exhibits the strong influence of Stoicism and Jewish Wisdom literature in its conception of the universe. Both sources conceived of creation as organized on the basis of a divine intermediary such as Wisdom or the law. Thus, the blessed life is one that follows the moral structure of this mediator. People who are able to follow this "divine order" receive blessings from the universe that are born of living in harmony with creation. Paul identifies the intermediary as Jesus Christ (Col. 2:6–8). In doing so, he dramatically alters Stoic cosmology by asserting that the foundation of the universe is not *something*, but *someone* the Colossians have received (*paralambanō*).

The Christ hymn in Colossians 1:15–20 defines the person of Christ in grand, universal terms. Even the radical notion that the mediator had a human body in which he reconciled all things with God is tied to the cosmic narrative. On its own, this understanding of Christ could be viewed as something outside the realm of the church at Colossae, a cosmic vision of a being who blazed a trail to salvation for the Colossians. However, Paul's description of the relationship of Christ to the church in chapter 2 proscribes an understanding of Christ as an outside force to be copied in word and deed. Given that the community of faith lies within

Pastoral Perspective

Human beings are created to be meaning makers. Arguably, this quest for meaning is what separates us from the rest of the created order. It is what marks us as *imago Dei*, created in the image of God. When we confront an event in our lives, whether it is joyous or tragic, momentous or mundane, we wonder what it all means. Why do we do this? We do it because the search for meaning shapes our sense of identity. How we make meaning of our lives shapes our understanding of who we are and why we exist.

Developmental theorists argue that this shaping of individual identity is a crucial task that begins as children use the word "mine" to claim a toy for themselves or insist to their parents and caregivers that "I can do it myself!" For most of us, this shaping of an individual identity takes on new importance during our adolescent years, when concerns about independence and freedom become paramount. All developmental theorists agree that this task of shaping an individual identity never ceases; it continues for the rest of our lives.

As we grow in our individual identities, we begin to understand that who we are is shaped in large part by those around us—by the communities to which we belong. Despite the American concept of the rugged individualist or the myth of the "self-made" man or woman, we eventually come to realize

you alive together with him, when he forgave us all our trespasses, ¹⁴erasing the record that stood against us with its legal demands. He set this aside, nailing it to the cross. ¹⁵He disarmed the rulers and authorities and made a public example of them, triumphing over them in it.

¹⁶Therefore do not let anyone condemn you in matters of food and drink or of observing festivals, new moons, or sabbaths. ¹⁷These are only a shadow of what is to come, but the substance belongs to Christ. ¹⁸Do not let anyone disqualify you, insisting on self-abasement and worship of angels, dwelling on visions, puffed up without cause by a human way of thinking, ¹⁹and not holding fast to the head, from whom the whole body, nourished and held together by its ligaments and sinews, grows with a growth that is from God.

Exegetical Perspective

In this extremely dense and significant lesson we come to the heart of the gospel—God's gracious deliverance of humanity through the death and resurrection of Christ, and our sharing in that deliverance through union with Christ in baptism. The logic of this passage, as of Colossians as a whole, is that of an interchange of experience: because Christ shares fully the human condition, we share Christ's destiny.

The structure of 2:6–19 is parallel to that of 1:12–23: introduction (vv. 6–8); a hymn in praise of Christ (vv. 9–15); and application of the hymn to the Colossians themselves (vv. 16–19, although this section could be extended through v. 23). In typically Pauline style, the imperatives of the introduction and application bracket and draw their rationale and nourishment from the central heart of the passage, the work of God in Christ. Indeed, "the faith" in which the Colossians are to be established (v. 7) is faith that has as its source and object "the working of God" (v. 12, my trans.).

Paul begins with words of encouragement: "As you therefore have received Christ Jesus the Lord, continue to live your lives in him" (v. 6). Elsewhere we hear of "receiving" the gospel (1 Cor. 15:3; Gal. 1:9, 12; Phil. 4:9; 1 Thess. 2:13; 4:1); here it is clear that the content of the gospel is not simply a set of

Homiletical Perspective

The entire witness of today's pericope is marshaled against some "deceitful philosophy" that threatens the faith of the Colossian church. Although the specifics of this conviction remain vague, it seems to hold some sin as unforgiven and unforgivable. In response, the writer of the epistle once again focuses the attention of the reader or listener on the cosmic Christ. In Christ, "the whole fullness of deity dwells bodily, and you have come to fullness in him" (2:9–10a). Now the one in whom such fullness dwells is head not only of the church (1:18) but also of "every ruler and authority" (2:10b).

In Christ's death on the cross, all fullness of deity became his and the powers that enslave have been emptied of their potency. Moreover, the old contract —that we would of our own strength live godly lives—has been nailed to the cross. It was "a statement that was true in the sense that [believers] were guilty of real trespasses but also a statement no longer valid because God had determined to forgive them."[1]

The faithful participate in this mystery of redemption by way of their baptism. They are buried with Christ as they descend into the waters and are raised with him by the same power of God that raised Jesus from the dead. Hence, Chrysostom announces,

1. David M. Hay, *Colossians* (Nashville: Abingdon Press. 2000), 99.

Colossians 2:6-15 (16-19)

Theological Perspective

Jesus, the church that embodies the gospel is the body of Christ. The structure of the universe is within the church.

Understanding this reality is a cause for thanksgiving, because the victory over death has already been won (1:22). The ethical implication of this conception of Jesus is significant. Paul's theology casts the ethical form of the Christian life as the product of the church's gratitude for what Christ has accomplished. It is a theological ethics of victory, rather than an attempt to mimic behavior that will put the church in harmony with the universe. Paul has reversed the predominant sacred model of working from a philosophical insight or ritual practice *toward* God to one that views revelation as gift *from* God.

This is the basis of Paul's denouncement of "empty deceit" in Colossians 2:8. The dominant philosophical schools such as Stoicism and Platonism held that knowledge was something to be unlocked within the individual. Paul's theology asserts that knowledge of God can only come from God. Therefore, the insights of philosophy are merely "human tradition." He believes the "elemental spirits of the universe" (*stoicheia tou kosmou*) are the demonic principalities and powers of this world. Just as Paul unites God's work on heaven and on earth,[1] he also casts the activities of "things visible and invisible"—whether they are false teachings or "thrones or dominions or rulers or powers" (1:16)—as forces united in opposition to the church of Jesus Christ.

A fundamental theme in Colossians is Paul's reassurance that these powers cannot defeat the church because Christ has already defeated them. Thus the "elemental spirits" (2:8) are seeking to turn the church away from the life in Christ that they have already received. Paul reminds the Colossians again in 2:9–10 that in Christ "the whole fullness of deity dwells bodily, and you have come to fullness in him, who is the head of every ruler and authority." Given the cosmic power of Christ, the church at Colossae need not fear anything.

Paul then turns his attention to those who would require circumcision for Gentiles to join the church. As in his argument against false teachings and hostile powers, he asserts that circumcision is unnecessary, because Christ has already set the church aside as God's own. As Daniel Harrington states, this "spiritual circumcision" (*peritomē acheiropoiētō*) in Christ "removes that aspect of the human person

Pastoral Perspective

that these are concepts or myths that do not represent reality. No one can survive as an individual. There is no such thing as a self-made man or woman. Eventually, we must come to understand that our individual identity is part of a larger shared identity.

The task of shaping a shared identity is the hard work facing the believers in Colossae. Struggling with outside influences to which they once adhered, these believers are trying to develop the common, shared identity without which no community can exist. Indeed, a shared identity is one of the essential elements that define a community. Simply living in proximity to one another or sharing a common language is not enough. The believers in Colossae, like the other new Christian communities throughout Asia Minor, were working to form their identity in the midst of a culture that was sometimes indifferent and at other times competitive and even combative. What message, then, would help this community further develop and strengthen its shared identity? The writer to the Colossians decided on a message of memory, because collective memory is an essential component of a community's shared identity.

Today's passage is an invitation from Paul and Timothy to the community in Colossae to remember where they came from and to live faithfully out of that powerful source of remembering. Remember, they write, that you are rooted in Christ and built up in him. Remember you are established in the faith. Remember what you were taught. This is a poignant and powerful call to shared identity through the practice of collective remembering.

All communities are made up of memories. Theologian Frederick Buechner writes in *A Room Called Remember* that there is no escaping some memories, even if we want to avoid them. Every person we have encountered, every place we have visited, every event we have experienced—all these are instilled in our memory and come rushing back to us, even if we wish to suppress them.

"In one sense," he writes, "the past is dead and gone, never to be repeated, over and done with, but in another sense, it is of course not done with at all or at least not done with us."[1] These kinds of memories, Buechner explains, are part of us, even part of our shared identity, whether we like it or not. They seem to have some power or control over us. Beautiful or terrible, they are part of every

---

1. See Col. 1:5 as well as the Christ hymn in 1:15–20.

1. Frederick Buechner, *A Room Called Remember* (San Francisco: Harper & Row, 1984), 4.

ideas, a doctrine, or a teaching, but the living Lord. To receive the gospel is to receive a royal visitor who takes up residence and rules in our lives. The verb translated "live" is literally, "walk," which was a common idiom for a way of life. The logic of this sentence corresponds to that of Galatians 3:2–3: faced with converts who are hearing from other sources that their spiritual "walk" is lacking in some way, Paul takes them back to the beginning of their life in Christ.

It is only after such a reminder that Paul issues warnings against other preachers who threaten their faith, in 2:8, 16–19. In verse 8 he warns, "See to it that no one takes you captive through philosophy and empty deceit." He then expands on the nature of such "philosophy": it is based on human tradition and on the "elemental spirits of the universe," rather than on Christ. It is "empty," which has the sense of "futile," because it comes not from Christ but from lesser sources. "Tradition" is usually an honored word in religious institutions, but here it has the sense of merely human injunctions that lack divine authority (see v. 22) and put unnecessary burdens on God's children. Jesus speaks similarly in Mark 7:8–13. The word translated "elemental spirits" is more difficult to understand. It means, at minimum, the basic elements that make up the physical world, but those elements were sometimes personified as spiritual entities. Apparently, in Colossae human regulations concerning ascetic practices were linked to these elements (2:20–23; cf. Gal. 4:9).

Over against all such regulations, Paul grounds his readers in Christ, beginning his exhortation with the image of being "rooted" in Christ (v. 7) and ending it with the image of a body nourished by the head and growing "with a growth that is from God" (v. 19; see 1:6, 10). The intervening verses string together a series of remarkable images of Christ in relationship to humanity. Virtually identified with God, Christ is the one in whom "the fullness of deity dwells bodily," but also in Christ, the Colossians themselves have "come to fullness" (vv. 9–10). This language of fullness runs throughout these chapters (1:9, 19), and carries the sense of God's rule throughout creation (see Jer. 23:24; Wis. 1:7). By speaking of Christ's fullness and the Colossians' fullness in one breath, then of Christ's authority over every ruler and authority, Paul gives his readers the strongest possible grounds for resisting human condemnation or disqualification (vv. 16, 18).

Subsequently, we hear a complex exposition of baptism in relationship to circumcision and to

nothing is more blessed than this burial, whereat all are rejoicing, both Angels, and men, and the Lord of Angels. At this burial, no need is there of vestments, nor of coffin, nor of anything else of that kind. Would you see the symbol of this? I will show you a pool wherein the one was buried, the other raised; in the Red Sea the Egyptians were sunk beneath it, but the Israelites went up from out of it; in the same act he buries the one, generates the other.[2]

The deceitful philosophy is a lie. All believers are baptized into Christ, have died with him, and are raised with him. The indicting contract of their obligation—which they defaulted—is nailed to the cross, laid aside by God.

Homiletical Plot: Dying and Rising. A sermon based on this analysis of the Colossians text could be plotted as follows:

Move 1: There is a "deceitful philosophy" abroad in the church, one that weakens the body of Christ. It says that some sins are not forgivable, that some theologies and church parties remain in sin. This philosophy assumes that Christ's work of redemption is limited by human beliefs and actions. In almost every parish, there are those who give every evidence of being among the faithful. Others do not know that they really do not believe they are worthy enough to be among the saints of the light. Maybe it was a sin that remains in the past, seemingly unforgiven. Some may have learned from some preacher in the past that they were too guilty for Christ to save. It is a deceitful philosophy, no matter what its origin. (The concretion here could be a brief illustration. A young woman tells her pastor she is "bad." After a brief conversation, the pastor realizes that the parishioner is a beautiful child of God raised by parents who needed a scapegoat in order to make themselves feel valued.)

Move 2: This deceitful philosophy even infects entire churches and denominations. "We are the good ones," thinks one group, "and those people are evil." The "good ones" then base their actions on this stereotype. Of course, there is the chasm that runs through most former mainline denominations, a dividing line of hostility between liberals and evangelicals. Some on each side adopt the deceitful philosophy and indict the other as unforgivable sinners. (We might image this move by putting

---

2. Chrysostom, *Homily 7 on Colossians.* http://www.newadvent.org/fathers/230307.htm (accessed January 16, 2009)

Colossians 2:6-15 (16-19)

Theological Perspective

(carnal body) that is opposed and hostile to God."[2] Paul then carries his argument into a sacramental theology by equating circumcision with baptism. This comparison is meant to demonstrate once again the sufficiency of church's salvation in Christ. He does not simply argue that the Colossians *will* rise from the dead; he asserts that, in their baptism, they *have* risen from the dead (2:12).

Paul's conception of salvation as a partnership between the church and God is readily apparent in his description of what occurs in baptism. God has reconciled all things to himself (1:20). In Christ, the community of faith is raised with Christ through faith. Thus baptism is the first act in which a Christian participates in the salvation of the world. In this redemption the order of existence is overturned. Even the law itself was nailed to the cross in Christ's death and resurrection (2:14). Such power makes Christ's sovereignty over the rulers and authorities of the world inevitable. Paul does not merely claim that Christ defeated the powers of this world; he asserts that Christ humiliated them by making a public example of the feebleness of their power. Their apparent victory in nailing Christ to the cross was the means of their unmasking as insignificant forces in comparison to the living God.

Following Colossians 2:15, Paul pivots to the delivery of warnings, admonitions, and the prescription of household codes. The credibility of his declarations is rooted in the glory of the living God he describes as the head to the church's body. For Paul, the Christian's task is not to ascend to God; rather, it is to live in gratitude for the resurrection that has already occurred in Christ. Paul is not merely replacing one form of legalism with another. Rather, he casts ethics as a reflection of what the church has become, a community of the resurrected, rather than as activities engaged in order to achieve salvation. This marks the ethical mandates of his opponents as vacuous and unnecessary. In light of Paul's description of the cosmic Christ, all heresy is *empty* deceit.

MATTHEW FLEMMING

Pastoral Perspective

community's memory. Buechner reminds us that most congregational memories, at least in the form of congregational biographies, are very carefully constructed and usually intentionally leave out the unpleasant events. Nevertheless, no matter how carefully we try to suppress them, these memories still live on, if only in whispered gossip or as wounds that have not been given the opportunity to heal.

These are not the kinds of memories that Paul and Timothy are invoking for the believers in Colossae. They are calling on the community to active remembering, a much more deliberate and willing corporate act. They are calling on the community to remember as an act of worship that forms their theological core.

Remember, they tell the community, that in your baptism you put off the body of flesh and were raised with Christ through faith in the power of God. Remember that God forgave all your trespasses and triumphed over the rulers and authorities of the day. The kinds of memories that Paul and Timothy are calling on the community to remember are the memories that shape their shared identity and give them a sense of resilience, power, and purpose. These are not the kinds of memories cited by Frederick Buechner, which seem to have control over us. Rather, these are the kinds of collective memories that we invoke when we sing "Amazing Grace, How Sweet the Sound" or "The Church's One Foundation."

In the rich tradition of the great African American spirituals, these memories remind us both who we are and how we have survived. We need to claim these memories as a community, because our individual memories can be faulty; left on our own, we are prone to self-centeredness and self-pity. Memory in shared identity lifts us as a community, defines us with a sense of purpose, and draws us closer to God. By shared memory we grow as a body, and our strength is renewed, as Paul and Timothy write, by the power that comes from God. When a community is in struggle, it is best to use the gift of intentional corporate memory to rekindle and strengthen the shared identity that will sustain it now and in the future.

RODGER Y. NISHIOKA

---

2. Daniel Harrington, *Paul's Prison Letters: Spiritual Commentaries on Paul's Letters to Philemon, the Philippians, and the Colossians* (Hyde Park, NY: New City Press, 1997), 108.

Exegetical Perspective

Christ's death and resurrection (vv. 11–12). "Spiritual circumcision" (literally "a circumcision made without hands") is a metaphor for union with Christ through baptism and for its effect, which is the removal of "the body of the flesh" (v. 11). This may be a reference to circumcision as an excision of the flesh and therefore of fleshly desire. It also may suggest the ancient practice of removing garments before baptism, symbolizing the removal of the "old self," and putting on new clothes after baptism, symbolizing the "new self" (3:9–10).

As in 1:13–14, in 2:13–15 the language of forgiveness is combined with that of deliverance from hostile powers. Here two powerful metaphors depict the forgiveness and the deliverance accomplished by Christ. First, in verses 13–14, forgiveness comes not by Christ's death satisfying a demand of divine justice, but by God (or Christ—the subject of the verb is unclear) "erasing the record that stood against us with its legal demands." The verb translated "erasing" has the sense of "wipe clean, leave no trace," while the "record" denotes a list of IOUs, of unpaid debts. In the ancient world, such a list might be posted on a pillar for all to see, but here it is nailed to the cross and thereby rendered null and void.

Second, the same verb used to describe disrobing for baptism (2:11; 3:9) here describes the effect of the cross and resurrection on the rulers and authorities (see 2:10, where Christ is "head" over these same powers). In the NRSV it is translated "disarmed," which presents the image of God's vanquished enemies, disarmed and perhaps stripped in humiliation, being led as captives in a triumphal procession. Alternatively, in the context of 2:11 and 3:9, the imagery may come from the baptismal liturgy: as the baptizand strips off the "body of flesh" that belongs to the old creation, so Christ stripped off the powers that rule in this sphere, even as he hung naked on the cross. If so, the paradox is extreme. Exposing and humiliating the crucified one, the "rulers and authorities" themselves are exposed and vanquished.

SUSAN GROVE EASTMAN

Homiletical Perspective

listeners in a position to overhear these parties talking about the others. "Goofy liberals," sneers one group; the other lumps all evangelical members of the body as "crazy fundamentalists.")

Move 3: What if this philosophy is one of deceit? What if God has nailed all our violated contracts to the cross, setting them and our sins aside? If Christ is the head of the whole body of believers, that changes everything. The one body takes priority over the cliques and parties we devise for ourselves. We now can lay aside the divisions within our soul. (The move can be imaged at an ecclesial level by depicting a foot-washing service we inadvertently find ourselves attending. We are in the midst of "those people," the others. Yet, when the time comes, we find ourselves helpless, having our feet washed by those "goofy" or "crazy" people. Then we turn and wash the feet of someone who must be goofy or crazy too. We leave changed at a soul-deep level.)

Move 4: Now truth comes clear. All of us have died with Christ in our baptism. The old Egyptians within us lie dead in the sea. But we Israelites now come up out of the water freed from bondage to sin and death, forgiven, and healed. We have died and are buried. We are raised out of the waters of our saving "through faith in the power of God." The deceitful philosophy lies floating down there in the sea among the Egyptian dead, descending with our sins. It is buried there. Through the grace of God, we are raised with Christ to new life and life together in the body. Christ is our head, for us all. Death shall have no dominion. (The preacher could now depict the interior of the ancient baptistery in Florence, Italy. The interior dome features a huge mosaic of the cosmic Christ, "his wounds still visible above." Surrounding the Pantocrator are countless coffins of the dead, who are now being raised to new and everlasting life. They ascend from their coffins to join all the saints of the light. The mosaic looks down on the baptistery and its font; it is painted above those going down into the waters of their saving, painted in blues and reds and glorious golds.)

RICHARD L. ESLINGER

Luke 11:1-13

[1]He was praying in a certain place, and after he had finished, one of his disciples said to him, "Lord, teach us to pray, as John taught his disciples." [2]He said to them, "When you pray, say:
Father, hallowed be your name.
Your kingdom come.
[3] Give us each day our daily bread.
[4] And forgive us our sins,
for we ourselves forgive everyone indebted to us.
And do not bring us to the time of trial."
[5]And he said to them, "Suppose one of you has a friend, and you go to him at midnight and say to him, 'Friend, lend me three loaves of bread; [6]for a friend of mine has arrived, and I have nothing to set before him.' [7]And he answers from

Theological Perspective

The Westminster divines insisted that "the chief end of man [sic] is to glorify God and enjoy him [sic] forever." While this is no doubt profoundly true, it has too seldom been heard profoundly. Like other affirmations of divine sovereignty and human duty, this classical definition of the proper goal of humankind is regularly translated forthwith into the imperative mood: you are doing what you ought to do, as a human being, only when your whole being is focused on God, and this means—to be concrete—when you forget yourself! Thus the "good news" of God's radiant glory (doxa), the source of humankind's joie de vivre, is translated into yet another commandment that none can obey with anything like depth or sincerity. Gospel once more becomes law—the besetting sin of religion.

When this "law" is applied to the practice of prayer, it means that our prayers are legitimate only when they become mental marathons of self-abnegation and immersion in the ineffable Divine—an accomplishment that, for most of us ordinary mortals, is a little like an insomniac telling himself to get to sleep. We are burdened by centuries of exhortation and technique concerning "right" prayer. As a result, one darkly suspects, only a small percentage of avowed Christians actually *pray* very often, or, if we do sometimes pray, we tend to judge

Pastoral Perspective

"If God is not," wrote George Buttrick, "and the life of man poor, solitary, nasty, brutish and short, prayer is the veriest self-deceit. If God is, yet is known only as vague rumor and dark coercion, prayer is whimpering folly: it were nobler to die. But if God is in some deep and eternal sense like Jesus, friendship with Him is our first concern, worthiest art, best resource, and sublimest joy."[1] "Lord, teach us to pray," say the disciples to Jesus. Ministers hear the same request, season in and season out. What can we learn in Luke of this conversation, for which *we* were made, no less than the flock we have been given to tend?

After offering the disciples a template for prayer that has become the prayer written for two millennia on the human heart, Jesus begins with a story that begs Buttrick's first point. If God is not, then is prayer no more than the veriest self-deceit? Sometimes this appears to be the case when at midnight both preacher and parishioner beseech the silence for help to no avail. If God is not, we think, how pathetic to bow our heads, bend our knees, and cry our grief, our needs, our sorrows to the empty air around us or the ego within us: the veriest self-deceit.

Human doubt concerning prayer may honestly be a matter of intellectual debate, but more often than

1. George Buttrick, *Prayer* (Nashville: Abingdon Press, 1942), 15.

within, 'Do not bother me; the door has already been locked, and my children are with me in bed; I cannot get up and give you anything.' ⁸I tell you, even though he will not get up and give him anything because he is his friend, at least because of his persistence he will get up and give him whatever he needs.

⁹"So I say to you, Ask, and it will be given you; search, and you will find; knock, and the door will be opened for you. ¹⁰For everyone who asks receives, and everyone who searches finds, and for everyone who knocks, the door will be opened. ¹¹Is there anyone among you who, if your child asks for a fish, will give a snake instead of a fish? ¹²Or if the child asks for an egg, will give a scorpion? ¹³If you then, who are evil, know how to give good gifts to your children, how much more will the heavenly Father give the Holy Spirit to those who ask him!"

Exegetical Perspective

Weaving together material from different sources, Luke depicts Jesus teaching his followers about prayer and encouraging them of God's reliability.[1] The Third Gospel's attention to Jesus' praying is notable (3:21; 5:16; 6:12; 9:18, 28–29; see also 18:1; 21:36), and prayer distinguishes the communities of faith in Acts (1:14; 2:42; 12:12; 13:3; 20:36). According to Luke 11, through prayer believers participate in God's commitment to bring forth God's reign.

The Lord's Prayer (vv. 1–4). The differences between Matthew's and Luke's versions of Jesus' prayer likely stem from various ways the prayer evolved through the earliest churches' worship. In both versions the prayer offers corporate petitions, consistently speaking in the first-person plural. The prayer's format and subject matter closely resemble other ancient Jewish prayers. Its vocabulary and emphases align with Luke's theological perspective. For example, referring to God as Father was a familiar practice for Jews in Jesus' world; yet, in the context of the narrative, the prayer's opening word also recalls previous statements about the Son revealing the Father (10:21–22).

1. Verses 2–4 resemble Matt. 6:9–13; vv. 5–8 are uniquely Lukan; vv. 9–13 are very similar to Matt. 7:7–11.

Homiletical Perspective

How do you pray? Who taught you to pray? What do you pray for? When I reflect on my childhood, I remember that my family prayed. My mother would say her prayers daily from a small book, crammed with special prayer cards collected over the years. She would refer to "the good Lord who knows best." My "second father" (I never liked the word "stepfather") worked from a truck checking gas meters for the Baltimore Gas and Electric Company and would often eat his lunch sitting in a back pew in church, talking to "the Man upstairs"—a phrase no longer in sync with our times, but for him it signaled a respectful yet familiar relationship. Both my parents and grandparents taught me to pray, more through example than specific words. From them I learned God was good, someone to be turned to on a daily basis.

In Catholic school I learned four reasons to pray: to praise God, to thank God, to ask God's pardon, and to ask God for what I needed, or even wanted—provided prayer ended with "however, not my will but yours be done," like Jesus at Gethsemane. Later, while becoming a member of the Redemptorists, a Roman Catholic religious order, I was taught mental prayer, to meditate and contemplate. The founder of my religious order, Alphonsus Liguori, wrote a spiritual classic called *Prayer, the Great Means of Salvation*, in which he emphasized the necessity of

Luke 11:1-13

Theological Perspective

our efforts deeply flawed. Our spontaneous, some-times desperate cries for help seem—by the criteria of the experts on the subject—pathetically lacking in praise, thanksgiving, intercession, and the other components requisite to truly *God-centered* prayer.

That is why the prayer Jesus taught his disciples is so wonderfully refreshing, and perhaps why over the centuries it has remained the one prayer that even lapsed Christians remember. It does not require of us that we become anything we are not already. It is a deeply *human* kind of prayer. It is a prayer for human beings, that is, for creatures *in need*.

To be sure, the exemplary prayer of Jesus begins in a manner of which the Westminster theologians could approve, namely, with the "glorification" of God: it acknowledges straightaway the *transcendence* of God ("in heaven"), the *otherness* of God ("hallowed be your name"), the *sovereignty* of God ("Your kingdom come"). Even here, though, it assumes an unmistakably human orientation: the transcendent One is "our Father"; God's holiness is God's presence to us as One whom we may name; God's reign (kingdom), however it may extend beyond our ken, is intended also to this planet—earth! There is no interest here in "God-as-he-is-in-himself," "God alone," or "God up there and out there" (as Bishop John A. T. Robinson put it).[1]

This is strictly in keeping with the biblical conception of the matter from beginning to end. The Judeo-Christian picture of the divine is of One who is *with us*, just as we humans are never separable from God—however persistently we may attempt it! The ontology of the tradition of Jerusalem is a relational ontology, in which none, whether creature or Creator, exists in isolation from the others. Biblical *theology*, therefore, is not just about "God"; it is about God-in-relationship-with-us—as Karl Barth put it in a true if awkward sort of term, "theo-anthropology." So even in its address and salutation, our Lord's model prayer includes the one who prays.

After this briefest of salutation, the prayer moves to the human condition with what must seem, to the properly theocentric, unseemly haste. How direct, how ungenteel, how almost rude it seems! "Give us. . . . Forgive us. . . . Lead us. . . . Deliver us." Not only does the prayer rush from glorification to petition in a manner very different from the usual patterns of human behavior where favors are being sought; it shuns all indirect rhetoric to the point of

Pastoral Perspective

not, such doubt concerning God's real presence issues from despair, from an experience of life as poor, solitary, nasty, brutish, and short. Therefore Jesus begins his instruction by acknowledging the silence with which all who pray have been met. The lesson is straightforward: sometimes human persistence in prayer is where we must begin, God's silence not-withstanding! He tells of the person who goes to a friend at midnight, a friend who is initially unrespon-sive, suggesting by analogy that sometimes only *because* of human persistence will God eventually wake up, come down, and answer the door on which we have been knocking. Prayer, says Jesus in so many words, arouses the slumbering God!

What immediately follows Jesus' first lesson in prayer is the command to pray: "Ask . . . search . . . knock." Now and again, this is the only good counsel a minister can give a congregant who has lost the thread of the conversation for which she was made: "*Just do it!*" Other times a petitioner needs to be told he is already praying. When the only word possible for one in extremis is "Help!" then the pastor would do well to direct that single word Godward. The communication that is prayer, when that prayer is more than a sigh too deep for words, is human anguish or fear or longing or gratitude entering language.

Buttrick asks of our teacher a deeper question: what if this God to whom we pray indeed *is*, but has *chosen* to remain unknown to us. What if God is like a stern parent whose presence is unmistakably real but whose intentions are hidden and whose actions appear arbitrary? Then we are left to beg for mercy with no assurance that the one to whom we beg has the least bit of sympathy for our plight: prayer as whimpering folly. Here Jesus turns our imagination toward the known response of a parent to a child's request. For many in the world, the turn is a dangerous one! Parents have been known to give offspring a snake instead of fish, a scorpion instead of the requested egg. Jesus' point is that even in the best-case scenario, even when a parent meets a child's deepest desire, that parent is not worthy to be compared with the one made known to us in Jesus, the one he has just invited us to call Father.

Finally Buttrick concedes that "if God is in some deep and eternal sense like Jesus, friendship with Him is our first concern, worthiest art, best resource, and sublimest joy." If God is and has chosen to be known by us in the one who is teaching us to pray, then prayer becomes a conversation with one who is our friend. "Suppose one of you has a friend," says Jesus.

---

1. John A. T. Robinson, *Honest to God* (Louisville, KY: Westminster John Knox Press, 2002), 13.

Exegetical Perspective

Five short sentences constitute the prayer. The first two are similar, in that each makes a confession—God has indeed shown God's name (self) to be holy, and in Jesus, God's reign has come near (10:9, 11)—while also yearning for a more complete realization: that all people would come to honor the name of the Lord, and that God would establish the fullness of God's reign. Both sentences, then, ask for about the same thing.

The prayer's next three sentences address three essential needs. The word in verse 3 usually translated "daily" (*epiousios*) is problematic. It does not appear in Greek literature prior to Matthew and Luke; based on its etymology, it could mean "daily," "tomorrow's," or "necessary." The eschatological tenor of the prayer's first two sentences may suggest that Jesus speaks of "tomorrow's" bread, in longing for the messianic banquet, yet the clear mention of "each day" and the present-tense imperative "give" in verse 3 indicate a request for the necessary *sustenance* that people require daily.

The next need is *forgiveness.* The prayer asks the Father for release from "our sins." God's forgiveness serves as stimulus for us to recognize our need to forgive those indebted to us.[2] With a present-tense verb Jesus acknowledges that forgiving others is a never-ending process; but the aorist imperative at the beginning of the sentence expects definitive forgiveness from God.

The final sentence appeals for *preservation.* "The time of trial" (*peirasmos*) is not "temptation," as enticement to do evil; Jesus asks for protection from circumstances that test or imperil faith, especially through the threat of persecution (see Luke 8:13; 22:28; Acts 20:19).

The Friend at Midnight (vv. 5–8). The NRSV's rendering of this paragraph's ambiguous syntax makes it difficult to see that verses 5–7 mean to describe an unlikely scenario. These verses relate what in Greek is a single question along the lines of "Could this happen to any of you?" The question anticipates a negative answer: none of Jesus' hearers would expect to have a friend say what is said in verse 7. A friend who refuses to help in such a situation would violate conventions of hospitality and incur shame. Jesus' point is that *even* if the sacred obligations of friendship and hospitality cannot compel a friend to respond (an absurd proposition!), still a friend will

2. By using the phrase "everyone who sins against us," the NIV obscures the shift in v. 4a from sin before God to indebtedness among people.

Homiletical Perspective

prayer, writing that those who pray are certainly saved. More recent voices that influenced my attitude toward prayer are Thomas Merton, who spoke of prayer as the communion of our freedom with God's ultimate freedom, and Anne Lamott, who wrote that she has two basic prayers: "Thank you, thank you," and "Help me, help me, help me."

We all have our own prayer history, but today's Gospel takes us back to the beginning of praying *with* and *in* Jesus Christ. Our Gospel today is more than a recounting of a pious moment in the life of Jesus, more than a story of how we got the Our Father, more than a lesson from Jesus the teacher. Jesus taught his disciples *how* to pray and *for what* to pray. Prayer was an integral part of his life. Luke's Gospel points out that Jesus "would withdraw to deserted places to pray" (5:16) and at other times "he went out to the mountain to pray; and he spent the night in prayer to God" (6:12; also 9:18). Jesus prayed before he chose his apostles (6:13–16) and when he fed the five thousand (9:16); he prayed the night before he died (22:39–44) and from the cross itself (23:34, 46). Prayer was part of his life, even unto death.

So, when Jesus responded to the request of his followers that he teach them how to pray, what he taught them became important—and has remained important—for the life of the church. He gave them —and us—words to address God, words to praise God, and, only then, words to petition God. Jesus begins, "When you pray, say: 'Father, hallowed be thy name; your kingdom come.'" We are to approach God as "Father," as "Abba," one we relate to intimately. Much has been written about this one word, inviting us to think of God as one who looks upon us as family, to whom we are as dear as if we were God's very own children. In a world where existence was so fragile—a condition that has not changed but only increased today—Jesus' prayer reminds us that there is one who has power over all and who is near to us. The two phrases that follow call on God to be God: "Hallowed be your name" and "Your kingdom come." They implore God to truly take charge of life, our lives, to bring justice and peace to our world, something only God can bring about.

The remaining petitions concern three basic needs: food ("Give us each day our daily bread"), forgiveness ("And forgive us our sins, for we forgive everyone indebted to us") and fidelity ("And do not bring us to the time of trial"). These petitions name what is essential for the life of our individual bodies, the life of our communal body—be it society, the

Luke 11:1-13

Theological Perspective

pushiness! Pious convention has conditioned most of us to repeat this prayer so quietly and reverentially that we fail to recognize how we are risking an aggressiveness incommensurate with bourgeois manners. There is no "Please," none of the softening, pious (and often wheedling) interjections that often mark what is called "spontaneous" prayer—"Oh dear Father," "blessed Lord," "sweet Jesus," and so on—just "Give us, forgive us, lead us, deliver us"!

Does this not seem rather . . . forward, brazen? Is it not a pretty drastic application of Jesus' warning (in Matt. 6:5f.) to avoid unnecessary wordiness and the kind of dissemblance practiced by the "hypocrites" and "heathen," who "think that they will be heard because of their many words" (Matt. 6:7)? No, because the whole assumption of this prayer is that it is uttered out of a condition of real *necessity*. The one who prays thus is driven by great need—there is neither the inclination nor the time for dissemblance or pretence. The object of prayer, Christianly understood, is not so much to lose oneself in the contemplation of the Divine as to find oneself—to become, so far as possible, who one *is*.

One is (1) dependent—ergo "Give us"; (2) guilty—ergo "Forgive us"; (3) lost and vulnerable—ergo "Lead us," "Deliver us." Because the One to whom we pray is not ordinarily "glorious" (like the gods we create in our own image!) but glorious in loving, we are able sometimes through our most honest acts of prayer to find that our very weakness is the occasion for encounter with the Source of new strength.

The verses following Jesus' model prayer (vv. 5–13) serve only to reinforce the point the prayer itself has made: prayer is not a meek, contrived, and merely "religious" act; it is the act of human beings who know how hard it is to be human. Real prayer cannot be faked. Its only prerequisites are sufficient self-knowledge to recognize the depths of our need, and enough humility to ask for help. "Ask (Really ask! Keep on asking!) and it will be given you"—*and is being given you already in the asking*!

DOUGLAS JOHN HALL

Pastoral Perspective

He is that friend for those who enter into this holy conversation. In him we know to whom we are talking when we bow our heads and close our eyes. In him we have been addressed and included in the conversation for which we were made. The silence that had led us to experience our lives as poor, solitary, nasty, brutish, and short has been broken by the Word, who is, in flesh, the answer to our every prayer.

Each instruction Jesus gives the disciples invites them to enter into a relationship. That relationship involves a conversation, and the conversation begins with a word. God has first spoken the one Word to us in Jesus Christ; now we need only muster the good sense to speak back. If by God's grace we do, we will find ourselves (literally) in conversation with a friend who knows our every weakness because he himself has cried out in anguish and been met with silence. How else but in conversation with him, through the words of Scripture and the witness of his church, could we trust that God is a God who will come after us when we are lost, dine with us when we are cast out by all others, welcome us home after we have wasted our lives, and who will keep us from falling too far? How else but as God's Spirit (ours for the asking) intercedes between these words that bear witness to God and our poor, solitary, nasty, brutish, and short lives without him, how else will we find ourselves accompanied along the way?

If God is in some deep and eternal sense like Jesus, we can talk: through thick or thin, come hell or high water, no holds barred, because nothing—neither death nor life nor angels nor principalities nor powers nor things present nor things to come nor height nor depth nor any other creature—will be able to silence the Word that answers our prayers in his flesh.

CYNTHIA A. JARVIS

Exegetical Perspective

finally supply bread because of the desperate "persistence" of the one asking. As the subsequent verses make clearer, Jesus' illustration characterizes God as eager to give assistance; God, even more than a friend, is obliged and committed to respond to those in need. At the same time, people should pray with a persistence so determined that it borders on presumptuousness (cf. 18:1–8).

Ask, Seek, Knock (vv. 9–13). God gives what is necessary and beneficial, not whatever we desire. The wider context sets the establishing of God's reign as the primary focus of believers' prayers. Just as Jesus later (12:29–31) says to "strive" (*zēteō*) for that reign, so people are to ask and "search" (*zēteō*, v. 9) for it. A lesser-to-greater logic, signaled by "how much more" in verse 13, pervades these verses. If even broken parents care for their children, how much greater must be God's capacity to provide that which truly nourishes. Perhaps the supreme expression of this is God's gift of the Holy Spirit, which represents God's pledge to bring the new age of salvation to fulfillment (see Acts 2:1–36). The gift of the Spirit demonstrates God's commitment to answering the Lord's Prayer and declares God's intention to do so through those who receive the Spirit.[3]

Conclusion. Fathers, in any era, parent in very different ways. The appearance of this relational term at the outset of Jesus' prayer does not by itself characterize God as a nurturing and compassionate Parent. The whole of this passage, which describes God's care and fidelity, provides an essential sketch of who the Father is. Detached from the sketch of a reliable God who gives the Holy Spirit, verses 1–4 might be taken as wishful thinking, lofty expectations spoken to a deity who too often seems silent. Detached from Jesus' prayer, verses 5–13 might seem to offer empty promises, blithely suggesting that God dispenses favors and blessings like a vending machine. Christians should not pray to get whatever they want. They should pray for God to bring the fullness of God's reign to fruition. These verses affirm God's commitment to accomplishing this, and those who pray as Jesus taught should expect that God intends to use them as a means toward doing so.

MATTHEW L. SKINNER

Homiletical Perspective

church, or the world—and the life of our ongoing relationship with God. These are the gifts of the kingdom, which will not be refused, because they flow from our being united with the very being of God, who sustains, forgives, and is faithful to us.

Jesus ends this prayer session with a parable and some advice urging persistence. John Pilch suggests that a better translation of persistence, given the culture of Jesus' world, would be "shamelessness."[1] In a world where hospitality was highly prized, the continuous and shameless knocking would broadcast to the world the shameless behavior of a friend who stays in bed rather than answer hospitality's urgent need. So, keep on asking, searching, knocking—be equally shameless in your prayer so that "God will not risk having his clients expose divine shamelessness for refusing to take care of them as a good father or patron would." Here God is presented as sleepy friend who needs to be shaken awake by a shameless friend. Luke goes on to say that God's way of giving exceeds that of human friends, gifting all who ask with the Holy Spirit.

Today's Gospel invites us to reflect on the story of our prayer life and where it has taken us. We owe a debt of gratitude to those who put us on the path to prayer as an essential part of our life. So we continue to ask, Lord, teach us to pray. Teach us truly to pray the words given by your Son, calling on God as our parent and protector. We can take comfort from the fact that, even when we do not know how to pray as we ought, the Holy Spirit helps us in our weakness with sighs too deep for words (Rom. 8:26–27). For our part, we continue to teach those entrusted to us to pray as Jesus taught us, confident that our prayer will find favor with our God.

JAMES A. WALLACE, C.SS.R.

---

3. Verse 13 marks the first time in Luke's Gospel that Jesus promises the Holy Spirit to people (cf. 3:16). This promise anticipates much of the book of Acts (see also Luke 24:49), connecting the experiences of the church with Jesus' ministry of God's reign.

1. John J. Pilch, *The Cultural World of Jesus, Sunday by Sunday, Cycle C* (Collegeville, MN: Liturgical Press, 1977), 116–17.

Hosea 11:1-11

¹When Israel was a child, I loved him,
and out of Egypt I called my son.
²The more I called them,
the more they went from me;
they kept sacrificing to the Baals,
and offering incense to idols.

³Yet it was I who taught Ephraim to walk,
I took them up in my arms;
but they did not know that I healed them.
⁴I led them with cords of human kindness,
with bands of love.
I was to them like those
who lift infants to their cheeks.
I bent down to them and fed them.

⁵They shall return to the land of Egypt,
and Assyria shall be their king,
because they have refused to return to me.

Theological Perspective

The prophet Hosea speaks compellingly to the situation of the northern kingdom in the final days before it falls to Assyria, interpreting God's relation with God's people through the lens of his own life experience. He sees poignant parallels between Israel's faithlessness and that of his unfaithful wife, Gomer. In the present text, Israel's waywardness is likened to that of a wayward son. Hosea's prophetic critique of social, political, and religious disintegration in the face of Assyria's imperialistic aggression is insistent. In his view, the turning to political alliances with Syria and Egypt and the turning to idols ("the Baals") demonstrate that God's reliability and God's claims have been forgotten, and the covenant relationship has been broken. There are consequences looming on the horizon in the form of the collapse of the northern kingdom and Assyria's triumph.

Although the text is very context specific, it speaks powerfully beyond its time and place to people of God in every time and place. From a theological perspective, there are issues and themes arising that have broad application.

The theological question "What is God like?" is illumined in the text. The tender care of God for the people of God is portrayed as that of a parent with beloved children: teaching them to walk, bending

Pastoral Perspective

At the core, this is one of the oldest stories there is. It first gets told in Genesis. It gets told in a thousand different ways throughout the pages of the Bible. God loves us, entirely. God creates us, delivers us, and tends us. The more God pursues, the more we turn away. It is the story of our shame. It is the story of God's grace. We know how it ends—God does not give up. Our knowledge of the ending may dull our hearing to the retelling of grace that once amazed. Hosea does not tell; he shows. What he shows are portraits of a love whose beginnings we cannot remember and whose end echoes with the roar of transforming power. He walks us down the long hall of our communal memory and points to the pictures hanging on its walls.

Here are snapshots of tender, perfect moments. A mother bends over her baby's crib, lifts his chubby body to her face, smells his sweet baby breath, presses her lips to his belly. His dark thick hair, his fat thigh rolls, his pink bow lips—she loves every inch of him, and entirely. Her love flows not simply because he is beautiful (although he is), but because he is hers; she made him. This mother's whole being leans toward this baby, whom she adores, and she pledges everything she has to his nurture and care. She would do everything for this child. She would give up everything for this child, and she has.

⁶The sword rages in their cities,
  it consumes their oracle-priests,
  and devours because of their schemes.
⁷My people are bent on turning away from me.
  To the Most High they call,
  but he does not raise them up at all.

⁸How can I give you up, Ephraim?
  How can I hand you over, O Israel?
  How can I make you like Admah?
  How can I treat you like Zeboiim?
  My heart recoils within me;
  my compassion grows warm and tender.
⁹I will not execute my fierce anger;
  I will not again destroy Ephraim;
  for I am God and no mortal,
  the Holy One in your midst,
  and I will not come in wrath.

¹⁰They shall go after the LORD,
  who roars like a lion;
  when he roars,
  his children shall come trembling from the west.
¹¹They shall come trembling like birds from Egypt,
  and like doves from the land of Assyria;
  and I will return them to their homes, says the LORD.

Exegetical Perspective

Hosea 11 conveys one of Scripture's most poignant portrayals of YHWH, Israel's God. The chapter sketches God's relationship with Israel from its onset in Egypt to the audience's own disastrous age and on into the future, when YHWH will return the Israelites to their homes. One of a series of speeches begun in Hosea 4:1, the unit contains four main sections (vv. 1–4, 5–7, 8–9, and 10–11). With the exception of verse 10, God speaks in the first person.

Our passage showcases Hosea's literary artistry and immense theological insight; it also bears the imprint of later Judean compilers who affirmed that the import of Hosea's prophecies did not end after Assyria destroyed Israel's northern kingdom in 721 BCE and who (re)interpreted and supplemented Hosea's speeches in light of their understanding of YHWH's will and purpose for Judah. Riddled with linguistic problems, the book of Hosea is the most difficult portion of the Hebrew Bible to reconstruct.

Hosea uses a rich array of metaphors to illumine the covenant uniting YHWH and Israel. Janet M. Soskice defines "metaphor" as "that figure of speech whereby we speak about one thing in terms . . . suggestive of another."[1] Metaphors enable us to

1. Janet Martin Soskice, *Metaphor and Religious Language* (Oxford: Clarendon, 1985), 15.

Homiletical Perspective

Entrance into the text's opening imagery will not be difficult for most listeners. One need not have been a parent to possess vivid memories of young children with those who care for them. Who has not seen wobbly toddlers cheered by beaming adults? Or a child held to a mother's cheek? Or a parent shouting, "Come back here!" to a kid who keeps right on running?

God has such memories, says the text. God remembers young Israel, little Ephraim—recalls bending to feed him, teaching him to walk, leading him, holding him, calling out his name. The child, of course, has no such memories. Who of us recalls our first steps or the faces of those who held our hands at the time? Those who nurtured us hold recollections, like photographs, of who we once were and of how the early days predicted—or did not predict— the people we have since become.

God's parenting memories are pained. Ephraim, an early runaway, is running still, in a mad return to enslavement. The once-liberated nation has invested its freedom in bad religion, bad politics, bad social arrangements. Their mothering, fathering Liberator is affronted, heartsick, angry. As bloodshed overtakes them, worse outcomes await them; and God is in the consequences.

God is also turning through the photo album of Ephraim's childhood, but the eyes do not focus

Hosea 11:1-11

Theological Perspective

down to them, lifting them up as infants to the divine cheek, feeding, healing, leading (vv. 3–4). Theological themes of divine accommodation, incarnation, self-emptying (*kenōsis*), and making room (*zimzum*, discussed later) for the other resonate with this picture of God as one who *bends down and lifts up*.

John Calvin speaks of divine "accommodation" in terms of God's self-revelation. The radical difference between God and human beings makes a certain accommodation on God's part necessary to communicate with us at all. With respect to Scripture, Calvin comments, "As nurses commonly do with infants, God is wont in a measure to 'lisp' in speaking to us."[1] God lovingly accommodates to our capacities.

The wonder of the Word made flesh (John 1) in the incarnation is also called to mind by this image. Barth speaks of incarnation as a movement, originating in the divine freedom of love, of divine "condescension" or "humiliation" (a bending down) that reveals the reconciling reality of "God with us."[2] The ancient Christian hymn in Philippians 2:5–11 similarly gives account of divine self-emptying in which one who "was in the form of God . . . emptied himself," taking on "the form of a slave."

In the Jewish kabbalistic notion of *zimzum*, in the act of creation, the God who is "all in all" makes room for an "other" to be. This requires a kind of contraction or concentration or withdrawal into Godself. In a sense, God creates a space within Godself, for another to be and to become. This seems an important conceptual parallel to the notions in Christian theology of divine accommodation, self-emptying, and incarnation.

All these theological themes point toward a vision of God as one who "bends down and lifts up" like the loving parent in this text from Hosea. This is what God is like. As the passage proceeds with this portrayal of God, the reader is all the more astonished that the people of God should turn away from such a one to lesser gods. They seek other alliances and go after idols of their own construction. A second key feature of the passage theologically is the implicit critique of divided loyalties and the problem of idolatry.

Idolatry is not having images and icons and works of art and concepts that may (or may not) *point* us toward the God, but mistaking these pointers for

1. John Calvin, *Institutes of the Christian Religion*, ed. John T. McNeill, trans. Ford Lewis Battles (Philadelphia: Westminster Press, 1954), 1.13.1.
2. Karl Barth, *Church Dogmatics*, IV/1, ed. G. W. Bromiley and T. F. Torrance (Edinburgh: T. & T. Clark, 1936–1962), 177.

Pastoral Perspective

We take another step down the hall, to gaze at another picture. The mother is teaching her toddler to walk. The picture shows a scene frozen in time, but we can piece together what happens before and after it. "That's it, you've got it, come to Mama," she coos. He waddles forward, face turned up toward hers, eyes shining with the thrill of his power and with an adoration that mirrors hers. He falls, he cries, she scoops him up in her arms. She wipes away the tears and tends the little hurts. He will not remember this, but she will.

Hosea walks us down the hall, showing us portraits of things we cannot remember. God is that mother, Hosea reminds us; we were that baby, that toddler. We do not remember, but God does. This text uses language of the heart, but its images go for the gut. There are more pictures to see, but we might rather turn our eyes: pictures of how we ran when God called; pictures of the tantrums we threw, the promises we broke, the wreckage we created; pictures of our violence, our hatred, our self-loathing. We are the children who were loved from the start; we are the children who turned away. God stood on the porch calling after us as we sped away; we broke God's heart.

Hosea's gorgeous images carry certain risks and challenges for the preacher. They are so vivid and compelling that almost anyone can readily see and understand. For some, though, the images may kick up old and difficult grief. How does the pastor preach this text (or read it in worship, for that matter) in a room with a father whose child no longer speaks to him or a mother whose child has died? Anyone who has lost a child—through death, addiction, alienation, or other formidable separation—will hear in these words their own unbearable grief. Others, who have cut off a relationship with a parent, may hear their own guilt or anguish. The pastor will want to handle this text with a sensitivity toward such grief—or even toward the possibility of such a grief, since we do not always know the hardest truths about people's familial relationships.

Another pastoral challenge in this text is the issue of gender. For the preacher anxious to present feminine images of God to the congregation, this text may seem ideal. The text itself offers almost no gender pronouns, since the words are framed as God's own. The images of parental love could easily be assigned to either gender and, in the eyes of some, may seem a more natural fit with feminine imagery. Using feminine pronouns, though, can run the risk of continuing the sexist association of nurture and

describe *less-understood* entities in language "suggestive of" *better-known* entities. In chapters 1–3, for example, Hosea illumines God's covenant with Israel by means of a marriage metaphor that depicts Israel (and its capital city, Samaria) as an unfaithful wife who abandons YHWH, her husband, to pursue Baal, a male storm and fertility deity worshiped by Canaan's native inhabitants (see, e.g., Hos. 2:8, 13, 16, 17).

Hosea 11:1–4. In chapter 11, Hosea casts God as the loving father of an adopted boy, Israel: "When Israel was a child, I loved him; and out of Egypt I called my son" (v. 1). The parent/child metaphor is particularly apt, because it invites Hosea's audience to view the covenant joining God to Israel as not only intimate, intensely emotional, and resilient, but also filled with promise and anticipation, as father and son grow *into* a relationship they create together. "Egypt" appears also in 11:5, 11. In 11:1, it evokes Israel's exodus from Egyptian slavery.

Tragically, Israel reacts to his father's summons as youngsters often do: the more YHWH calls, the more they go away. Two parallel lines describe the ongoing rebellion: they "kept sacrificing" to the Baalim; they kept "offering incense to idols" (v. 2), thereby violating the covenant's most basic requirements—exclusive loyalty and steadfast obedience.

In verse 3, YHWH expresses the bewilderment of parents whose children do not acknowledge their tender care. Hosea's metaphor appears more maternal than paternal, since Israelite mothers most often helped toddlers take their first steps, took them up in their arms, and healed them. The initial lines of verse 4 continue the father/son metaphor: God has led Israel gently with cords of human kindness/bands of love. The NRSV translation, "I was to them like those who lift infants to their cheeks," requires a change in the standardized Hebrew text from *'ol* ("yoke") to *'ul* ("infant"). With minor emendation, this same line can be translated, "I lifted the yoke from their neck/ and bent down to feed them" (NIV).

Hosea 11:5–7. God announces rebellious Israel's punishment: they will return to Egypt, and Assyria will rule over them. A destroying and consuming sword will whirl in their cities, because the Israelites refuse to return to their God. Scholars seeking a historical context for Hosea's speech point to the reign of Hoshea, Israel's last king, who sought Egyptian assistance after withholding tribute from his Assyrian overlord about 724 BCE (see 2 Kgs. 17:3–4). While the text of verse 7 is difficult, it

where we might expect. They are looking less at the child than at the one who feeds, coaches, and calls the child: *I loved, I called, I taught, I took them in my arms, I healed, I led with cords of kindness, I bent down, I fed.* These lines can be heard as something much more than a litany of reproach by an aggrieved parent. They can be heard as a parent's recollection of herself, a return to the memory of her heart's deepest commitments to the child. These are the parent's truest verbs. In a way, what the text discloses is nothing less than God remembering God.

So God asks the pained question: "How can I give you up? How can I hand you over?" God has stopped speaking *of* Ephraim and speaks (at least rhetorically) *to* him. Ephraim does not likely hear it, having raced elsewhere. No matter. This is less about Ephraim than it is about the commitments and pathos of God. "*How can I . . . ?*" In times of catastrophe, we have always asked, "How can God allow it?" Here a curtain is pulled back to disclose *God* asking—four times— "How can I allow it?" Even God must struggle with the theodicy question. There is something almost violent in the struggle. "*My heart recoils within me*" (v. 8). It is as if what has been happening to Ephraim is now happening within God.

The outcome is compassion. The reason for it is simply, firmly stated: "*I am God and no mortal.*" While the present roils with betrayals and their consequences, God is remembering. What God remembers most of all is this: "*I am . . . the Holy One in your midst*" (v. 9).

To be the Holy One in this crisis is to liberate. God, like a lion, roars freedom for captives. The roar fills the earth: animals prick up their ears and bolt, human conversation ceases, faces lift, weapons are lowered, doors swing open. In the beginning, God created the heavens and the earth with speech; in this historical moment, God liberates with a roar. A new exodus is to occur, but its character and tone will be different. In the first, the Holy One was the Parent, calling by name and teaching to walk. This time the Holy One is the Lion, freeing a failed people with regal ferocity.

They will make their return with trembling. They had been like children running into traffic; they will come home shaken. Will it be their brush with death that makes them tremble, or will it be their new knowledge of wildness and danger in the Holy One's compassion? In any case, it is promised that God in devastating anguish and resolve will bring the guilty home, and such returns are cause for trembling.

Preachers of this text should guard against sentimentalizing. The God imagined here is not the

Hosea 11:1-11

Theological Perspective

God. In the normal anxiety that attends finite and fragile human existence, it is natural to seek to secure ourselves, and idolatry arises in that self-seeking and self-securing activity. We invest ourselves in intermediate goods (e.g., national security, personal well-being) but are disappointed because these things inevitably fail. Whenever we take something out of its rightful place in our lives and raise it to the status of the ultimate, we break the harmony of life. Whatever mundane good we make ultimate is thereby overburdened and destroyed in our very act of raising it to ultimacy. It cannot fulfill a God-shaped job description and loses its quality as a gift of grace when it becomes the central focus of our lives. Only God is ultimate, only God can secure us and secure us, finally, against the need to be secured.

God is our source and our end, the ground of our being and our heart's true home. When we turn away from the source of our being and integrity, we fall into a kind of disintegrated nothingness. No longer oriented toward God, we are *dis*-oriented. Wandering from our true home, we are lost. Idolatry, among other things, is a pattern of self-destruction. The divine response in this text is not unlike that of most loving parents who are never more angry with their children than when they do self-destructive things. God's anger has a distinctive character, beyond typical human manifestations. "I am God and no mortal, the Holy One in your midst" (v. 9). Anger does not lash out or cause God to turn away from God's people. Instead, God's "compassion grows warm and tender" (v. 8). God's wrath is the fire of God's love, ordered toward restoration, not destruction.

The passage ends with a hopeful word. Waywardness and its consequences do not have the last word. God's intentions are still redemption, restoration, and return. The ones who have turned away, become disoriented, and wandered from home are not left to their own devices. They are called home, and like lion cubs responding to the summons of the parent lion, like doves with their homing instinct, they will return (vv. 10–11). The wayward children are still beloved children of a God who bends down and lifts up.

ANNA CASE-WINTERS

Pastoral Perspective

parenting with the female gender. Using masculine pronouns runs the risk of perpetuating lopsided and sexist understandings of God as male. It is possible to use no pronouns at all, and simply to refer to God as Parent; however, "Parent" sounds cold and impersonal compared to the more intimate "Mother" or "Father" and may therefore evoke a mood out of keeping with this text and its message. Some pastors resort to grammatical gymnastics to avoid any of these problems; the result can be ideologically pure but verbally cluttered and clunky. For the pastor concerned about issues of language and gender when it comes to speaking of the Divine, there are no clean options. Whatever choice the pastor makes about gender and language, the subject of the sermon is not the gender of God. The direct, personal questions from God in this text must not be compromised; these words cut, and they ought to.

For the first six verses, God speaks *about* the painful rejection of the children, culminating in the sad pronouncement, "My people are bent on turning away from me" (v. 7). Now God turns to speak *to* those children: "How can I give you up . . . ? How can I hand you over?" (v. 8). The consequences of our rejection and betrayal would rightfully be our destruction; God's compassion will not allow it: "For I am God and no mortal, the Holy One in your midst, and I will not come in wrath" (v. 9). Our failings will not be the final word; our obliteration will not be the last picture on the wall.

This is not the story of the "prodigal" son who, having struggled with his own bad choices, finally turns and comes home. This is the story of a prodigal God who—in anguish, heartbreak, and the fiercest love—comes seeking out the children who have strayed. The last picture will be this one: God, like a lion, roars; the children come trembling home.

STACEY SIMPSON DUKE

Exegetical Perspective

suggests that YHWH will not respond to Israel's pious but insincere attempts to solicit divine aid.

Hosea 11:8–9. These two crucial verses invite their audience into the interior life of YHWH. Although Israel has rejected God's love (vv. 1–5) and its punishment has begun (vv. 6–7), the prospect of utterly destroying Israel leads YHWH to struggle between wrath and love.[2] Some scholars assert that God's four questions in verse 8a are rhetorical questions—that is, God asks them in order to elicit from Hosea's audience answers that God already knows. (Admah and Zeboiim, like Sodom and Gomorrah, were cities famous for their complete and permanent destruction; see, e.g., Gen. 10:19; Deut. 29:22–23.) But J. Gerald Janzen counters that YHWH's questions are real, not rhetorical. God's inner struggle concerning Israel's future is overcome only when God undergoes a change of heart, in which wrath and love unite in God's impassioned ("warm and tender") decision not to destroy Israel (v. 9b; note that "no"/"not" appears four times in v. 9). In Janzen's words, "The change which takes place in Yahweh is 'wholehearted.' All the components of the divine life—including, specifically, both the divine wrath and the divine love—grow fervently together in a new purpose to which the divine life becomes resolved."[3] God's ability to bring about this transformation within God's own self distinguishes YHWH from human beings ("for I am God and no mortal"), who, confronted by an internal emotional stalemate, must too often decide between one emotion or another—a decision that results in the loss of "part of one's own concrete self." The word "holy," which appears only here in the book of Hosea, characterizes the God who has resolved, "I will not come in wrath."

Hosea 11:10–11. History tells us that the Assyrians defeated the northern kingdom of Israel, annexed its territory, destroyed its capital city, Samaria, and exiled much of its population in 721 BCE. Yet 11:10–11 look beyond that catastrophe, and Hosea's own lifetime, to a future when YHWH will roar "like a lion," summoning "his" trembling children (note the return of the father/son[s] metaphor) from the west, from Egypt, and from the land of Assyria and restoring them to their homes. The closing formula, "says the LORD," signals the end of this prophetic speech.

KATHERYN PFISTERER DARR

Homiletical Perspective

adoring, enthralled parent of recent invention, anxiously accommodating the ever-so-special child. We should not be plucking at heartstrings as we tell of God's parental care or grief or final restoration of the child. There is real tenderness and pathos in the metaphor, but it is not saccharine. Its focus is not even on the child but on the Parent's labored choice to act as holy deliverer. Grace for this child is expressed in a roar.

The sermon's shape might unfold along the same lines and in the same sequence as does the text. The opening image—God as nurturing, frustrated, and grieving parent—is so accessible and so riveting that the text essentially begins as God had done with Ephraim: calling our names and leading us by the hand. We are led through an unsettling landscape of betrayal, catastrophe, and the misery of God. In the end we arrive at the promise of a fearsome deliverance and a restored but altered community. The text is framed with liberations, one past and one future, both accomplished by God's calling forth, gentle or fierce. The center of gravity in the text, and surely in the preaching of it, is the anguish of God. It begins as anguish over Ephraim's infidelity and devastation, but it quickly deepens to an agonizing travail within God. God is suffering a contradiction, is impaled on it; and the liberating roar is wrung from a kind of wound.

The sound of it can still be heard. Some thought they heard it at Golgotha and again on the third day. It roars now over all that is ruined and over those who have done the ruining. To hear it and be lifted and turned and led by the sound of it toward home is to have more than enough reason to tremble with awe.

PAUL SIMPSON DUKE

---

2. See J. Gerald Janzen, "Metaphor and Reality in Hosea 11," *Semeia* 24 (1982): 7–44.
3. Ibid., 30–31.

Psalm 107:1-9, 43

¹O give thanks to the LORD, for he is good;
    for his steadfast love endures forever.
²Let the redeemed of the LORD say so,
    those he redeemed from trouble
³and gathered in from the lands,
    from the east and from the west,
    from the north and from the south.

⁴Some wandered in desert wastes,
    finding no way to an inhabited town;
⁵hungry and thirsty,
    their soul fainted within them.

Theological Perspective

Sometimes gratitude overwhelms us. We experience moments individually and collectively when thankfulness in inescapable. A certain life event—the birth of a child, a wedding or graduation, a baptism or anniversary—can lend itself to unabashed gratitude. Sometimes at worship one finds a sense of thankfulness that is unanticipated and surprising, and we turn to God in celebration and appreciation. Suddenly, before we know it, the confession of the psalmist becomes our own affirmation: "O give thanks to the LORD, for he is good; for his steadfast love endures forever" (v. 1).

We know there are reasons to be hesitant. We recognize that life is fragile and can get out of hand at a moment's notice. We know there are inequities in life that should temper praise, forcing us to resist glib gratitude. In fact, the realities of the world, evident at any moment on any cable news network, can drive us toward cynicism more readily than thanks. Nevertheless something—the moment, an event, or a place—wells up within and we let it out. Everyone, including the psalmist, has experienced such moments. Indeed, the Psalms run the gamut from profound celebration of God's goodness to abject depression that God has turned away from creation and may never return.

In this classic psalm the gratitude is palpable, and it gives way to wonder and celebration, but not

Pastoral Perspective

Psalm 107 opens with a characteristic biblical affirmation about God: God is good. This goodness shows itself in love that is "steadfast" toward us. It *endures*, and it endures *forever*. Human perversity tempts God to renege on it, but God never does. There is always a loophole, a stay of execution, a new covenant. So the psalmist, mindful of this reliable pattern, sings confidently from the start, "God is good! God's love endures forever" (v. 1).

Some pastors fret that emphasis on love glosses over sin and judgment, underplaying the necessity of repentance. Others' experience suggests that most Christians are hardly in danger of ignoring these things. If they are in peril, it is because they cannot get out from under them. Their God withholds love until they measure up. It ebbs and flows in proportion to good behavior, orthodoxy, church attendance, or some other "work."

This distortion of divine love twists human love too, and leads to a lifetime of striving for approval. Of course, as Luther discovered, striving is useless. The precious insight of the Reformers—who loved the Psalms—is that God's favor is not the result of repentance, nor a reward for obedience. It is the permanent gift that makes judgment bearable, repentance likely, and obedience possible. As pastor Ray Stedman writes, "The thing that finally gets to

⁶Then they cried to the Lᴏʀᴅ in their trouble,
and he delivered them from their distress;
⁷he led them by a straight way,
until they reached an inhabited town.
⁸Let them thank the Lᴏʀᴅ for his steadfast love,
for his wonderful works to humankind.
⁹For he satisfies the thirsty,
and the hungry he fills with good things.
. . . .
⁴³Let those who are wise give heed to these things,
and consider the steadfast love of the Lᴏʀᴅ.

Exegetical Perspective

Psalm 107 is typically classified as a psalm of thanks-giving, although it is difficult to assign a precise classification, because it also contains elements of hymns (the LXX restores a "hallelujah!" to v. 1, as in 106:1) and Wisdom psalms (e.g., v. 43). In the traditional division of the Psalter, it is the first psalm of Book 5. Some commentators, however, have suggested that it more properly belongs at the end of Book 4, noting that its focus on Israel's history fits with the themes of Psalms 103–106 and that verses 2–3 may represent a response to 106:47, which implores YHWH to gather in the people from among the nations.

In its canonical form in the Hebrew Bible, Psalm 107 is a song of thanksgiving to YHWH for deliverance from a variety of difficult situations. After the introduction (vv. 1–3), it is clearly divided into two main sections: a liturgy (vv. 4–32) and a hymn (vv. 33–42). Some scholars have suggested that this may result from a combination of two previously independent psalms. Whether or not this is the case, the progression from liturgy to hymn makes sense in a cultic setting, which may be indicated by the mention of thanksgiving sacrifices in verse 22. If verse 3 is read to reflect the gathering in of the people during a pilgrimage festival, the cultic function may be specified further: this is a

Homiletical Perspective

Since the Psalms were written, not so much to tell a story or to pass on information, but for actual use by congregations and individuals, the primary question for anyone encountering them is, "How can *I* sing this song?" The task of any preacher of the Psalms is always, at least in part, to help the congregation answer that question. For many parishioners and congregations, the truth and beauty of the first verse of Psalm 107 will be so clear that the preacher's task will be a relatively easy one: these ones will have walked in the door singing this song, and the preacher will simply seek to build on and enhance that experience.

The very next verse, on the other hand, presents what will be a challenge for many. Those who have been redeemed from trouble say, or should say, that God is good. This is echoed several times throughout the psalm: *some* (but not all) cried to YHWH in their trouble and were delivered/saved/brought out from distress. The preacher needs to ask herself, How many in the congregation class themselves among those whom God has *not* delivered/saved/brought out from distress? Who has recently suffered the death of a loved one? Who is living with depression or with terminal illness? Who has not yet been gathered in from exile? Who feels as though she is still wandering in the desert? For whom and how many would

Psalm 107:1-9, 43

Theological Perspective

without memory. As often happens in the psalms, gratitude is tinged with irony, a painful recollection of days when praise came less readily, or when the divine presence was experienced even in difficulty. Memory gives context to immediate and profound praise, deepening the moment. Those who have known "trouble" may celebrate God's provident deliverance (v. 2).

At times, gratitude is shaped by place, sacred or profane. Robert C. Dentan suggests that "This psalm was perhaps sung by groups of pilgrims who came to Jerusalem to celebrate one of the festivals, offering thanks for escape from various dangers."[1] Today similar praise may burst forth from those who continue the pilgrimage tradition, confronting distinct but parallel vicissitudes of travel to Jerusalem, Mecca, Rome, Canterbury, or Angkor Wat. Others may return to places where God's presence was previously clear and find renewal amid struggles and distress.

Context leads the ancient singer to recall those who "wandered in desert wastes" (v. 4), what the KJV calls "wilderness." In Hebrew this wilderness is the *erets midbar*, itself an image fraught with meaning and mystery. As Leslie J. Hoppe notes, there are multiple ways to understand the *midbar*. It may refer to a place where sheep are taken to graze, but is a location "not suitable for permanent residence" since shepherd and flock must move on when the "resources of a particular area are depleted."[2] The dangers of the desert/wilderness are also significant, especially for "town-based" individuals who do not know how to survive in such inhospitable environs. Likewise, it is a reminder of where the people of God—Israel, in this case—have been in their colorful and complicated history. The desert is simply a rite of passage, experienced by the early Hebrews and from which they have been delivered. They endured in the wilderness testing, and that in itself is ground for thanksgiving.

Dangerous as it is, for some people the "desert wastes" may be a place of solitude and even safety. Hoppe comments that the people who lived far from civilization in the desert at Qumran, from the second century BCE to its destruction in 68 CE, "did not choose to live in the Judean desert out of any ascetical motivation. They went there to be safe from the attacks of 'the wicked priest' and 'the sons of

Pastoral Perspective

us, breaks the back of our rebellion, and sets us free from our emotional hang-ups is the unqualified love of God that never lets us go."[1] Pastors who affirm this truth in season and out are routinely drenched in people's tears as this graceful message unblocks reservoirs of relief and amazement. Far from feeling let off the moral hook by it, people who finally believe it often become eager, committed disciples.

God's goodness is a "straight way" in the "desert wastes" where we are lost, the hubbub of an "inhabited town" at the pathway's end, the gripping joy of knowing that we will again have human company in the land of the living (vv. 4, 7). For the psalmist, there is nothing theoretical about God's goodness. It attends to particular circumstances and bends to real need. God's goodness *does us good*. We need God to do us good. After all, as M. Scott Peck famously put it, "Life is difficult."[2]

The verses of Psalm 107 selected for this week focus particularly on the hardship of desert wandering, an allusion to Israel's wilderness years, or perhaps to the Babylonian exile, from which God delivered the people when they cried out (v. 6). Wandering people sometimes do not know how lost they are. When they notice, they are often so far gone that no help seems possible. Afflicted by the restlessness typical of the affluent West, they wander from marriage to marriage, diet to diet, spiritual path to spiritual path, drug of choice to drug of choice. For the aimless soul, frantic with appetites, nothing can satisfy except the grounding, orienting love of God. The good news of Psalm 107 is that it is never too late. A way out can be had for a cry.

Crying out is not mere desperation, however. It is an act of worship: "I cannot do this, but *you* can!" When people say that they do not know how to pray, one can demystify the subject by suggesting that "Help!" is prayer par excellence. It is adoration that acknowledges our reliance on God's providence and welcomes God's decision to be *for us*. In the instant it takes to say it, we get our bearings. "Help!" places us in right relationship with the only one for whom all things are possible. Its repetition also schools us in the expectant trust necessary to undergird a daring life of gospel witness.

The psalm also addresses people who must enter a wilderness not of their own making—the approaching death of a spouse, the silent maze of

---

1. *The New Oxford Annotated Bible*, ed. Bruce M. Metzger and Roland E. Murphy (New York: Oxford University Press, 1991), 768.
2. Leslie J. Hoppe, *A Guide to the Lands of the Bible* (Collegeville, MN: Liturgical Press, 1999), 131.

1. Ray C. Stedman, "A Song of Restoration" (Discovery Publishing: Peninsula Bible Church, October 5, 1969), http://raystedman.com/.
2. M. Scott Peck, *The Road Less Traveled: A New Psychology of Love, Traditional Values and Spiritual Growth* (New York: Simon & Schuster, 1998), 15.

Exegetical Perspective

communal song of thanksgiving before thanksgiving offerings during a pilgrimage festival at the temple in Jerusalem.

Both the liturgy and the hymn are connected by a focus on God's *hesed*, an important Hebrew concept translated by the NRSV as "steadfast love," but perhaps better rendered as "faithfulness" or "loyalty." Throughout the Hebrew Bible, *hesed* is often used to describe God's nature and character, particularly with regard to God's relationship with the people of Israel, often in a covenantal sense. This divine attribute of *hesed* frames the entire psalm (vv. 1 and 43) and is highlighted by one of the key refrains of the liturgy (vv. 8, 15, 21, 31). The underlying theology of the psalm is that YHWH's loyalty to the people and fidelity to the covenant provoke the instances of divine deliverance celebrated in both the liturgy and the hymn.

The liturgy (vv. 4–32) can be further divided into four stanzas: verses 4–9, 10–16, 17–22, and 23–32. The liturgical and poetic nature of these stanzas is exemplified by the highly structured and repetitive pattern they follow. Each stanza begins by describing a scenario of difficulty or distress (vv. 4–5, 10–12, 17–18, and 23–27), followed by two refrains: cries to YHWH and subsequent deliverance (vv. 6, 13, 19, and 28) and an exhortation to give thanks to YHWH in response (vv. 8, 15, 21, and 31). The repetition of these identical phrases punctuates the liturgy and perhaps indicates the responsive parts of priest and congregation in the temple.

Most commentators follow the translation of the NRSV and understand the second refrain (v. 8 and passim) primarily as an exhortation to give thanks to YHWH. Dahood reads this differently and translates as follows: "Let these confess to Yahweh his mercy, and his wonders to the children of men." In this reading, "his mercy" and "his wonders" are read chiastically and the exhortation is both to give thanks to God and to provide a witness to the nations of God's care for Israel, giving the refrain a sense of universal proclamation not found in the NRSV.[1]

The lectionary reading includes only the introduction to the psalm (vv. 1–3), the first stanza (vv. 4–9), and the concluding exhortation of the hymn (v. 43), which, as we have already seen, helps frame the entire psalm as a celebration of God's *hesed*. Since most commentators agree that the scenarios of the four stanzas are meant to be representative of a broad

1. Mitchell Dahood, *Psalms III: 101–150*, Anchor Bible 17A (Garden City, NY: Doubleday, 1970), 78, 82–83.

Homiletical Perspective

singing this song feel like a lie? For how many is the question of theodicy not just academic? How might the church help them in learning to sing Psalm 107?

A preacher might make at least two interpretive moves to help these ones learn to sing this song. The first is the rational, let's-think-this-through-logically, head-centered move. It goes something like this: none of us deserves to be rescued from terrible situations, but through God's goodness, some of us do get rescued. It is not much, perhaps, but some is better than none, the argument goes. Depending on your theology, you might explain the existence of the terrible things we face in a number of different ways: original sin, Satan, or "bad-things-happen-to-good-people" come to mind. Preachers who choose this move will be faced with the task of convincing a congregation that an all-powerful Creator who chooses to save some, but not all, is a God worth singing about.

The second interpretive move appeals more to the heart and depends more upon people's lived experience. It concedes that—with a collection of songs designed to give voice to the often-irrational reactions of human souls—spending too much time looking for rational explanations and precise cause-and-effect relationships misses the point. Basically, it encourages the congregation not to worry too much about exactly *why* we give thanks to God for near misses, but to just do it and see if it fits. "Remember the time you were waiting for test results at the hospital and they came back negative? Wasn't the first response of your heart to say, 'Thank God!'?" "Remember when your kid almost got hit by a car but didn't?" To be mundane: "Remember the time you thought you were going to miss your plane, but you sprinted up to the gate to find the flight had been delayed and you were in plenty of time? Were not the first words in your mind, 'Thank you, God!'? Did it not feel right, regardless of exactly why you thought you were doing it?" The preacher who puts the congregation in touch with experiences such as these will help them to experience the Psalms, not as treatises that need to make sense, but as prayers that need to be sung.

The good news—for both those who can, and those who cannot, easily give thanks to God for salvation in their lives—is that ultimately Psalm 107 is not so much about what happened in the past as it is about what we have to look forward to in the future. If in the past God was good, full of loving-kindness, gathering the exiles from afar, and guiding the people through the desert, then those who are

Psalm 107:1-9, 43

Theological Perspective

darkness' who ruled Jerusalem." For them it was a place of "transition and preparation."[3] At best, therefore, life in the desert is temporary, and getting through the *midbar* is an occasion to praise the one who brought the pilgrims and the exiles safely through it.

In reentering these texts, contemporary readers might cautiously consider the spirituality of those for whom life or at least certain life moments may seem like "desert wastes" more personal and psychological than geographic. Life can become a wilderness from which persons try to escape, even as they look for the presence of God amid pain and struggle. For these pilgrims, we can hope that the grateful confession of the psalmist may eventually become possible. The sometimes-absent God is revealed when "they cried to the LORD in their trouble" and were delivered from their distress (v. 6). Indeed, the imagery is profound, as the psalmist insists that the pilgrims were led in a "straight way, until they reached an inhabited town" (v. 7). The idea of the "straight path" or "right way" is a consistent theme in many of the psalms (e.g., 16:11; 25:4; 27:11; 139:3).

The psalmist does not hesitate to reflect on the multifaceted impact of physical deprivation, noting that these wanderers were "hungry and thirsty," a condition that affected the entire person, physical and spiritual. Indeed, the writer spiritualizes freely as to the benefits of God's "straight way." In the end, it is God who "satisfies the thirsty" and fills the hungry "with good things" (v. 9). The worshiping community sings out its gratitude for the God who may fulfill their external and internal needs.

Gratitude is essential to spiritual experience, calling persons to look beyond themselves to the one whose "steadfast love endures forever" (vv. 1, 43), but there are dangers. Glib gratitude may trivialize the struggles of those who at particular moments in their lives have no energy for thankfulness. Some gratitude may be a long time coming and should not be rushed. An easy thankfulness may blind us to the difficulties and inequities present in the world and the church. At its best, gratitude may slip in on us when we see life in unexpected ways at unanticipated moments, when the goodness of God appears in places we thought it could never be found.

BILL J. LEONARD

Pastoral Perspective

Alzheimer's, a partner's abandonment, a child's shipping out to war, a sudden depression, a public failure or humiliation. The psalm's assertion of God's reliability in such circumstances may serve the apprehensive Christian as a preemptive strike on crippling fear and inoculation against the fainting of the soul (v. 5).

The psalm's grateful affirmation of God's love is also widely doubted. "Life itself," writes Robin Myers, "passes daily judgment on the idea that [a loving God is in control], that good deeds and righteous living exempt us from mindless tragedy, or that the meek will inherit anything other than a crushing debt and a dead planet."[3] So the singer reminds us that if the worst has happened to us and, by God's grace, we have lived to tell about it, it is our duty to speak. "Let them say so," says verse 2. Let them testify!

Testimony is telling the truth, and it is a practice of resistance to evil. According to verse 42, unfortunately omitted from the lectionary text, speaking up is the way the righteous compel the wicked to pipe down. Truthful speech about God's steadfastness counters the lie that God does not care or does not even exist. Evil's invitation to despair is drowned out by the joyous sound of God's praise in human thanksgiving.

Pastors know that suffering destroys faith as often as it strengthens it. A community of grateful testimony can make the difference. A parishioner in trouble is blessed to be part of a wise, discerning people (v. 43) that knows how to tell the story of God's abiding love in its own words, from its own experience. When one person's internal compass gyrates wildly, the church's compass remains true: "God is good; God's steadfast love endures forever." The congregation that learns to "say so" (v. 2) as the refrain of endless instances of grace can be the saving hand of God for people in difficulty—which is to say, just about everybody, sooner or later.

J. MARY LUTI

---

3. Ibid., 132.

3. Robin Myers, "In Praise of the First Coming," *The Christian Century*, November 15, 2000, 1183.

Exegetical Perspective

range of experience and are not necessarily tied to particular people or situations, this lectionary truncation does not distort or otherwise alter the meaning of the psalm as a whole.

There is disagreement among scholars regarding the contextual reference and historical location of this psalm, particularly the verses of this lectionary reading. The question is whether the scenarios described refer to the exodus from Egypt or the restoration after the Babylonian exile. Arguing for the latter, many scholars understand this psalm to come from a postexilic context. This is supported by the portrayal in Second Isaiah of the exile and restoration as a new exodus (e.g., Isa. 43:14–21). It has also been suggested that verses 2–3 are postexilic additions influenced by the language of Isaiah 62:12 ("the redeemed of YHWH") and Isaiah 43:5–6 (gathering in from the four cardinal directions). Numerous commentators suggest that this psalm might represent an answer to the plea of Psalm 106:47, which also seems to reflect the hopes of an exiled people.

Other scholars have maintained that this psalm could just as plausibly refer to the exodus from Egypt and therefore come from an earlier, preexilic context. In support of this understanding, it can be argued that the new exodus motif in Second Isaiah is not original to the prophet and was instead derived from older cultic traditions such as this psalm. Further, it has been noted that redemption language (from the Hebrew root *g'l*) is also used to describe YHWH's salvation of Israel from Egyptian bondage, not just with respect to the Babylonian exile (e.g., Exod. 6:6, 15:13; Pss. 74:2; 77:15; 78:35).

In the end, it is not necessary to choose one context over the other. It seems entirely plausible that an older song about the exodus would be appropriated by an exilic or postexilic people and adapted to fit their new situation. The theological message of this psalm works equally well in either context: God is active as redeemer in the history of Israel as well as in the lives of individuals. Further, the adaptation of an exodus tradition for a postexilic context, whether in this psalm or in Second Isaiah or in both, opens up possibilities for contemporary hearers of this song to adapt it to their particular contexts and situations as well.

JOHN W. VEST

Homiletical Perspective

wise know that God will be, and do, the same in the future.

A sense of exile from home, of being lost and alone, is a near-universal part of the human experience. People find themselves wandering in the desert wastes of postmodern capitalist societies, in small towns from which they could not escape, in unhealthy relationships, in confusing situations, in addictions or dark nights of the soul. The list is, unfortunately, endless. On the other hand, God's love is also endless, and the news that God's intent, God's promise, is to guide us from the waste to the pleasant places in the future, even as God did in the past, is good news indeed.

From that piece of the gospel, it is a small leap to our own calls to act like God in a hurting world. The evening news affords plenty of examples with which the social-justice-oriented preacher can work. There is the exile that gay, lesbian, bisexual, and transgender people face from much of the church. There is the exile of the poor, the "hungry and thirsty" from, well, everything (here note the ways v. 9 speaks to Jesus' Beatitudes and Mary's Magnificat). There is the plight of refugees of conflicts across the globe, who long to hear of God gathering them back together. There is the exile of thousands of Mexicans who each year head out into the trackless desert waste fleeing economic injustice at home and calling out for guidance in the desert and hope in the United States. Finally, in coming years, as deserts take over more and more arable land throughout the world, and if the threatening global water shortage progresses, the promise of God coming to save lost ones in the desert will take on new poignancy and immediacy for everyone, not just the exiles.

As congregations full of people who practice giving gratitude to God for their salvation head out to do God's work in these and similar situations, the song they sing will be something very like Psalm 107.

QUINN G. CALDWELL

Colossians 3:1-11

[1]So if you have been raised with Christ, seek the things that are above, where Christ is, seated at the right hand of God. [2]Set your minds on things that are above, not on things that are on earth, [3]for you have died, and your life is hidden with Christ in God. [4]When Christ who is your life is revealed, then you also will be revealed with him in glory.

[5]Put to death, therefore, whatever in you is earthly: fornication, impurity, passion, evil desire, and greed (which is idolatry). [6]On account of these the wrath of God is coming on those who are disobedient. [7]These are the ways you also once followed, when you were living that life. [8]But now you must get rid of all such things—anger, wrath, malice, slander, and abusive language from your mouth. [9]Do not lie to one another, seeing that you have stripped off the old self with its practices [10]and have clothed yourselves with the new self, which is being renewed in knowledge according to the image of its creator. [11]In that renewal there is no longer Greek and Jew, circumcised and uncircumcised, barbarian, Scythian, slave and free; but Christ is all and in all!

Theological Perspective

Reminding his readers of their baptism, the writer invokes two striking images conveyed by this initiatory rite. First, baptism is a dying and rising with Christ, death to an old way of life and resurrection into a new way. Second, baptism breaks the cosmic power of sin by incorporating the initiate into the church, "hidden with Christ in God" (v. 3). The church is not the kingdom of God, but it does anticipate in its communal life the eschatological fulfillment of all things. Protestant Christians have emphasized the judicial model of salvation, Luther's "justification by faith," and neglected the participationist model, in which sin, a cosmic power that enslaves human beings, is overcome, not through an atoning sacrifice, but through incorporation into a new reality, the body of Christ. The participationist model does not signify a different kind of salvation but represents another attempt by New Testament writers, especially Paul in Romans, to conceptualize the salvation that has been accomplished by Christ. This model, less vulnerable to individualistic distortions, is linked closely to a new way of life that anticipates God's ultimate future, when the kingdom will come in all of its glory. The transformation is gradual (note the present character of the perfect tense in v. 10), but baptized Christians are expected to live by new

Pastoral Perspective

The Letter to the Colossians was written in part to help keep members of the early church loyal to the gospel of Jesus Christ. Many early Christians, unsure of the future, were attracted to a variety of false teachings. Some claimed that individuals could gain special knowledge of future salvation. Others argued about the physical and spiritual state of Jesus. Others disagreed about who could be part of the early church. As Jesus did not return within a few years of his resurrection and ascension, there was increasing uneasiness about the future.

Our church members today face a similar uneasiness. It has been many centuries, and Christ has not returned. Warnings of terrorism and economic downturn make members uneasy. People in our pews are unsure about what the future holds in their personal and professional lives. They look to those proclaiming the gospel for some good news about the future and for some insight into where they might look to find direction.

Colossians 3 provides some direction. It helps us realize that part of our future is hidden from us by God. According to Colossians 3, our new life is "hidden with Christ in God." The verb tenses in the Greek indicate what our life experience confirms, that the new life that God has accomplished for us in the past and will make clear in the future has not

Exegetical Perspective

The eleven verses of the epistle reading fall into two distinct parts. Verses 1–4 are a transition section of the letter that holds together the first major portion of the letter (1:9–2:23), which is doctrinal teaching, with the second part of the letter (3:5–4:6), which is more practical admonition. In turn, verses 5–11 form the opening segment of the hortatory portion of the letter, emphasizing the necessity of being done with inappropriate pre-Christian patterns of life and embracing a truly Christlike manner of living.

The opening major section of the body of the letter (1:9–2:23) teaches that God, through God's beloved Son Christ Jesus, brought about a reconciliation between God and humanity that brings believing humanity to live in faith in a new relationship to God. The transitional verses, 3:1–4, build on that teaching by referring to the Christians as having been "raised with Christ." Christ himself is "above . . . seated at the right hand of God" (v. 1). Thus the Christians are admonished to live as if they too are already in heaven, since effectively they are, because they have been raised with Christ. Verse 2 is a straightforward exhortation to "do this . . . not that." On the one hand, the Christians are to focus on or think about those things that are characteristic of God ("above" = heaven, the abode of God and Christ); on the other hand, the Christians are told to

Homiletical Perspective

In the lectionary calendar, it is midsummer, but chapter 3 of the Letter to the Colossians strikes the tone of New Year's resolutions. The call to turn over a new leaf and live a new life in Christ is consistent throughout the passage: a time for ending bad habits and beginning again as a new self. Of course, the secular mandate to change our ways usually does not address the depths of the lists proposed by the letter writer here: "fornication, impurity, passion, evil desire, and greed (which is idolatry)" (v. 5) and "anger, wrath, malice, slander, and abusive language" (v. 8). The harsh specificity of these lists is balanced in tone in the passage by the language and invitation to seek something higher, by implication something greater and more fulfilling.

One particular stumbling block for congregations is the apparent stridency of this call to transformation, for it moves well beyond the normal cultural language of change into language of life and death. Hearing that "you have died, and your life is hidden with Christ in God" (v. 3) and that for these reasons you should "put to death, therefore, whatever in you is earthly" (v. 5) takes the conversation into a much more extreme place, and depending on the issues of the day, Western Christians in the twenty-first century do not always experience the faith journey acutely or intensely. Circumspectly considering the

Colossians 3:1-11

Theological Perspective

standards encapsulated in the catalogs of vices and virtues that follow.

It is easy to read the catalogs of vices and virtues in Colossians 3:1–11 and elsewhere as quaintly moralistic, unnecessarily restrictive codes that miss the big questions of love, compassion, peace, and social justice. Serious moral reflection in light of contemporary experience reveals how shortsighted that is. For example, greed (v. 5) is frequently condemned but rarely analyzed. Our forebears, on the other hand, including Ambrose, Augustine, Thomas, Luther, and Calvin, had much to say about greed. Greed is not simply a craving for money, material goods, and honors; it is the inordinate desire for precisely those goods that the culture has determined bestow status and privilege on their owner. Greed is, therefore, idolatry, as the writer says, because greed deceives one into overvaluing finite goods, thinking that this house, this car, or this promotion can satisfy the soul's deepest longings. Greed is yet more insidious, often disguising itself as prudent planning for the future, like the rich fool in Jesus' parable (Luke 12:13–21). Greed destroys community and spawns other vices: oppression, exploitation, and self-deception.[1] As Jesus repeatedly warns his followers, "You cannot serve God and wealth" (Matt. 6:24; Luke 16:13).

Perhaps nothing garners unanimous applause among Christians more than an exhortation not to lie (v. 9), but truth telling can be very difficult, especially if it means being open to painful truths about ourselves or about matters that really cost us something. Reinhold Niebuhr reminds us that much of our ignorance is not simple ignorance; it is often willed ignorance, the refusal to face the truth that stares us in the face.[2] For example: Are we honest in our study of Scripture, truthfully and responsibly seeking its wisdom; or do we use Scripture to confirm our preconceived notions about what is true or false, good or evil? What would it mean to be honest about the role of our Christian forebears in blessing military conquest in the New World, in justifying slavery, in supporting vicious pogroms against Jews? What does it mean to be honest about living conditions in Third-World nations, many of which are causally related to our comfortable affluence? Do we really want to know the truth about global warming and the Iraq War? For Christians who have been baptized into the body of

Pastoral Perspective

totally been revealed to us in the present. That can be frustrating when we are trying to figure out what comes next in our lives, but at least pastorally this realization removes some of the pressure from us to have all the answers now.

While God guides and sustains us, how God's providence and our actions interact is one of life's mysteries of faith. It is comforting to read that the problem with our lack of clarity is not with us. It is not our inability to figure out God's plan that keeps us unsure about the future. The Pauline author in Colossians explains that God has hidden part of the future from us. We have to rely on God in faith. We have to wait. We have to be patient.

Waiting can bring out the worst in us. Waiting in line at the bank or restaurant can make us frustrated. Waiting at a red light in our car can make us competitive. Waiting for answers from a costumer-service agent on the phone can make us angry. When we have to wait, our worst behaviors can emerge. The Pauline author in Colossians argues to early Christians that they should relinquish their previous, unholy behaviors and act holy for the sake of the new relationship they have been given in Christ. "Set your minds on things above" (v. 2), the author writes, imploring the church to act their best and let go of the impure behaviors. That is hard to consistently do in the world of distractions. The Greek verb for "set" in Colossians emphasizes the need for constant focus on doing right.

Distraction and impatience are problems in our churches today. If we are not careful, that lack of certainty of the details of God's ultimate plan can become an excuse not to follow the part of God that we *do* know. Whatever it is that we experience that keeps our actions chained to our base selves must be challenged by the part of our souls that is looking for Christ. If we are patient about finding Christ, Christ will find us.

There is a strong pastoral concern in Colossians 3 about the unity of the church as well. Our lesson ends with the words "Christ is all and in all." The early church needed a reminder to look toward the Christ in each of us. Many early Christians found it harder to see their spiritual connections than to see their differences. The early church faced differences between Jew and Gentile, barbarian and Scythian, slave and free. Differences like those were very important when a person's primary allegiance was to region, ethnicity, or economic status—not as much when a person's primary allegiance was to Christ.

---

1. See William Schweiker, "Reconsidering Greed," in *Having: Property and Possession in Religious and Social Life*, ed. William Schweiker and Charles Mathewes (Grand Rapids: Eerdmans, 2004), 249–71.
2. Reinhold Niebuhr, *The Nature and Destiny of Man*, vol. 1, *Human Nature* (New York: Charles Scribner's Sons, 1941), 194–98.

avoid those places and things (and persons?) that are contrary to God and God's will and purposes ("earth" = where Christ is not and where fellowship with Christ is precluded).

Verse 3 returns to the perspective of Colossians 2:12, where the Christians are told/reminded that they were buried with Christ in baptism; here they are told/reminded that they are dead ("you have died") with Christ, perhaps most obviously to the allure of that which is of the "earth." The old life that the Christians once lived is now defeated through the life-giving death (1:20) of Christ on the cross as Christians too experience a spiritual death to the power of evil (1:21–22). Essentially, the Christians' past can no longer determine their present and future.

The phrase "your life is hidden with Christ in God" in verse 3 uses language ("hidden") that is most often associated with apocalyptic perspectives. Both Colossians 1:25–27 and 2:2–3 employ this language of "hiddenness" in order to make the same point that is emphasized here, namely, that God's hidden mystery (of reconciliation) is related to and realized in Christ, in whom Christians now have a new life and relationship to one another as well as to God.

Here in verse 4 one encounters the only explicit reference in this letter to the future revelation or coming of Christ. This note of "future eschatology" should temper any temptation of the reader/interpreter to conclude that the eschatology of Colossians is exclusively a thoroughly "realized eschatology." Colossians does portray that the Christians not only died (2:20) with Christ, but that they are even raised (3:1) with Christ. Nevertheless, this mention of Christ's future revelation clarifies that God's work in reconciliation is not complete. The new life in Christ has yet to find its ultimate manifestation. The good news promised in this verse is that when Christ is revealed the Christians will share in his glory (triumph over evil).

Verse 5 opens the more explicitly hortatory section of the letter (3:5–4:6), admonishing the readers to bring to an end ("put to death") the aspects of their lives that are contrary to God's will ("whatever in you is earthly"). The appeal is a call to complete devotion that envisions the elimination of ungodliness. Verse 5 names five behaviors and attitudes that are labeled "idolatry": "fornication, impurity, passion, evil desire, and greed." This list—and the one that follows in verse 8—is not meant to be exhaustive, but illustrative. All five items named here had sexual connotations in antiquity. Moreover, the actions and attitudes named can be and

mind-set and milieu of congregants and culture will inform the preacher's use of life-and-death speech.

Another issue for the preacher is how to address the text without getting tangled up in unhelpful dualisms: things above vs. things earthly, dead and hidden vs. alive and revealed, old self vs. new self. While some comparisons are helpful, and in this particular reading necessary, oversimplifying good and evil, black and white does a disservice to the congregation and to the biblical text. These can be openings to explore what "things above" we are called to seek and to set our minds upon, and also creative opportunities for reimagining "that renewal [in which] there is no longer Greek and Jew, circumcised and uncircumcised, barbarian, Scythian, slave and free; but Christ is all and in all" (v. 11) for the particular locale and time. Still, the caution remains to avoid precious dichotomies.

While the chapter does present a coherent message about what a new life in Christ is about and what it is not about, the flow of the pericope is at the same time remarkably dynamic. The chapter opens with almost lyrical language about the raised life and all that is above: the location of Christ and the appropriate placement of our attention and focus (vv. 1–3). It continues with more poetry about revelation and glory (v. 4). Almost abruptly, then, instruction and didactic teaching follow, and the reader is brought both metaphorically and literally down to earth (v. 5). Several verses of condemnation of various and sundry behaviors follow (vv. 6–9). The wording then begins to soar again with imagery of the clothing of new self, mirroring the image of the Creator (v. 10), and the passage concludes with a typically Pauline formulation of classes of people whose distinctions have now vanished (v. 11). Rhetorically, it is intriguing that in a lectionary segment with attention to things above and things earthly, the reader or listener is taken on a parallel virtual roller-coaster ride, ascending and descending emotionally throughout the passage.

Also worthy of note from a rhetorical perspective is the letter writer's seemingly linguistic reversal in presentation about the new life in Christ. Twice the reader or listener is offered lists of actions and manners that are no longer acceptable, deeds that should be put to death. These things are *revealed,* while aspects of the new self and the new life remain obscure, even *hidden.* No lists of new habits, new ways of living, new virtues are included in this portion of the letter. The preacher then must decide what liberties to take in unveiling just what a life

Colossians 3:1-11

Theological Perspective

Christ, who is the truth (John 1:17), truth telling ought to be not an occasional act of honest speaking, but a way of life that is free to see reality, including one's own reality, for what it is.

Further, the new reality embraced by the church breaks down the ethnic and class divisions that distribute status and privilege in the larger society. Even barbarians and Scythians are to be included (v. 11)! The breaking down of barriers that separate people remains a daunting challenge for the church, complicated both by different creeds and worship styles and by sharp, even hostile, differences on economic and social issues.

Most troubling in verse 11 is the conspicuous absence of "no longer male and female," the concluding phrase of the familiar triptych in Galatians 3:28. Is this a careless oversight? Perhaps, but not likely! There is substantial evidence that Paul's churches attempted to break the power of patriarchy in the early congregations, but in the second and third generations, which likely included among their writings Colossians and 1 Timothy, patriarchy reasserted itself and established a norm that has distorted male-female relationships for the last 2,000 years. Most of us are appalled to read the misogynist statements of our theological saints, such as the comment by Clement of Alexandria (ca. 150–215), "Every woman should be filled with shame by the thought that she is a woman." Patriarchy becomes most visible today in debates over the ordination of women, but it also infects our sexual attitudes and practices and aggravates the sexual abuses cataloged in verse 5. Patriarchy has often combined with racism in North American culture to objectify black women as simply dark bodies existing for the sexual pleasure of white men. This legacy of patriarchy and racism has a long reach and makes it very difficult for the church to confront effectively the predatory sex that bedevils our culture. This legacy also makes it difficult for even the most well-meaning of partners to move toward a truly human sexual relationship based upon equality, consent, mutual vulnerability, and mutual giving.[3]

Yes, even the writers of Scripture have blind spots. Then, of course, so do we. How long before the Christian church inserts a fourth panel in Galatians 3:28: "No longer gay and straight"?

JOHN C. SHELLEY

Pastoral Perspective

We face divisions today along ethnic, social, racial, gender, economic, political, military, familial, and geographic lines. Fortunately for us, the God who hides is still the God who guides us to the Christ inside us. "Christ is all and in all": that is a broad statement the Pauline writer makes. It makes all the difference. If Christ is in all of us, than we all are guided at some level by the same Spirit, larger than us. If Christ is in all of us, then our older way of relating can be superseded by our new way of trusting. If Christ is in all of us, then we are all searching for God's revealed direction together.

The Pauline author of Colossians writes with care for the early church, suggesting that we recognize the commonality among all believers. All who have experienced the grace of God have the Holy Spirit guiding them. We may not know exactly what the future looks like in our lives, but we know who holds the future.

Our faith in Jesus Christ unites all believers. The author of Colossians was concerned that people were not being faithful to the gospel. The author's solution was for us to recognize that God is near to us. The gospel of Christ is not far away in a time that will never come, in a land far away, or in the minds of a few know-it-alls. Christ is in the hearts of the people in our church pews. Their actions can be holy because God can make them so. We should not think God is so distant that it does not matter how we act. Our actions should flow from our gratitude for God's gift in Jesus Christ. That fact can create loyalty to the gospel and reassurance for our people.

DAVID E. GRAY

---

3. See Miguel De La Torre, *A Lily among the Thorns: Imagining a New Christian Sexuality* (San Francisco: John Wiley & Sons, 2007).

sometimes are the objects of false worship—false gods that isolate the humans embodying such standards from God.

Verse 6 sounds again the apocalyptic eschatological note already heard in verse 4. Here, however, one hears of the negative side of God's intervention, the judgment of the "earthly" or idolatrous realities that lure humans away from an appropriate relationship to God. In turn, verse 7 simply states that those to whom these admonitions are made have previously been involved in such inappropriate, ungodly living.

Verse 8 names five additional attitudes and actions (actually vices) in a list that many interpreters judge to be typically Jewish (as is the case with v. 5 as well). The list focuses on personal relations in the church. The direction to "get rid of" these things is a statement in metaphorical terms that suggest that one should take off these vices and put them away like a garment. In kind, verses 9–10 extend the concern with Christian community, telling the readers not to lie to one another and telling them why they are not to do this and why and how they can comply with the admonition: they have "stripped off the old self" and "clothed [themselves] with the new self"—a statement that extends the metaphorical perspective introduced in verse 8. These ethical exhortations conclude with a phrase ("which is being renewed in knowledge according to the image of its creator") that makes clear that new life as a Christian is not merely a matter of putting away vices and picking up virtues. Rather in Christ (who is the image of the creator) the Christian comes to know life and to live life differently. This is a renewal of the whole self, in conjunction with God and by God, not merely an improvement of some of life's parts.

Verse 11 makes a statement similar to the famous declaration of Galatians 3:28. Here, however, the declaration of God's overcoming of human differences is expanded. The point is this: in God's new world that is created in Christ, all such differences become unimportant, even irrelevant.

MARION L. SOARDS

"hidden with Christ in God" (v. 3) looks like to contemporary listeners.

The preacher then has many avenues to choose when constructing the sermon. Always, the epistles offer a chance to explore the travelogue of the early Christian founders, and given that lectionary followers find themselves in the middle of summer, with travelers arriving and leaving their pews weekly, this is one moment when that vehicle might work particularly well. Also, noting the timing of the lesson, the preacher could consider the Shakespearean model of a midsummer dream, and the opening lines attract a creative revisioning of what things we might seek "that are above" (v. 1). This is not to demean the opening by comparing it to a dream, but to elevate the exploration to a right-brain perspective of just what is our ideal life, unconstrained by daily expectations, demands, and schedules. Simply looking at the verbs offered in the selection inspires some new thinking in this vein: seek, set your minds, reveal, put to death, get rid of, clothe, renew.

Reconsidering the two lists of vices and opening them up for examination and investigation need not be daunting, and presents an occasion for speaking to the reality of many congregants' home and work lives. Similarly, holding up the concluding list of "Pauline types" and breathing new life into some of these examples of renewed relationships opens up possibilities for tangible connections with parishioners' lives. Just what are the clothes of the new self?

Finally, "sett[ing] your minds on things that are above, not on things that are on earth" (v. 2) appears both as the launch into instruction, but also as difficult gospel teaching in light of "do not worry about your life" (Matt. 6:25), and may be one of the most important challenges and callings Christians are given.

KATHERINE M. BUSH

Luke 12:13-21

¹³Someone in the crowd said to him, "Teacher, tell my brother to divide the family inheritance with me." ¹⁴But he said to him, "Friend, who set me to be a judge or arbitrator over you?" ¹⁵And he said to them, "Take care! Be on your guard against all kinds of greed; for one's life does not consist in the abundance of possessions." ¹⁶Then he told them a parable: "The land of a rich man produced abundantly. ¹⁷And he thought to himself, 'What should I do, for I have no place to store my crops?' ¹⁸Then he said, 'I will do this: I will pull down my barns and build larger ones, and there I will store all my grain and my goods. ¹⁹And I will say to my soul, Soul, you have ample goods laid up for many years; relax, eat, drink, be merry.' ²⁰But God said to him, 'You fool! This very night your life is being demanded of you. And the things you have prepared, whose will they be?' ²¹So it is with those who store up treasures for themselves but are not rich toward God."

Theological Perspective

The centerpiece of this passage is the parable of the rich fool, a person who is more concerned with storing excess riches than with striving for God's realm. Framed on either side by Jesus' teaching, the parable paints a vivid image of the dangers of wealth for its own sake. Those who have possessions in abundance risk the sin of greed: "enough" is never enough, "more" is only to be hoarded, and "I, me, and mine" matter more than anybody else. Greed is a problem primarily because its focus on the self keeps people from being "rich toward God" and rich toward others. The human propensity toward greed stands in striking contrast to God's providential care for rich and poor alike, as well as to the Lukan theme of appropriate stewardship of one's possessions.

His barns already bursting to overflowing, a rich man harvests a bumper crop with no place to store it. Desiring to keep this bounty for himself, and not being one to concern himself with the problem of waste, he plans to tear down the old barns, construct larger ones, store up his crops, and then sit back and enjoy the excess. This farmer stands as a negative example for the followers of Jesus: if you want to know how *not* to live as a disciple, just be like this person.

Those who read and hear the parable might ask, what is so wrong with storing the overrun of crops?

Pastoral Perspective

The power of today's Gospel lesson can sneak up on a congregation like the critics who stalk Jesus at the close of Luke 11. Midsummer is often a time for family vacations and leisurely coffee hours. It is tempting to assume that the imperative of the Christian life can be relaxed a little bit while people settle into the welcome routines of rest, recreation, and travel. For those who stay put, however, the Gospel text this week sizzles and spits like a backyard grill. That includes the visiting pastor or the seminarian who innocently agrees to preach on this lively text while the called pastor is away on vacation.

Today the word calls the congregation to a deeper spirituality and trust in God. While a sermon on deepening one's relationship with God may seem like easy fare, fit for a hot-weather weekend, the invitation to a renewed relationship with God comes only after Jesus exposes our human greed and anxiety about money and then employs a parable to singe away any illusion that the godly life is synonymous with the American ideals of prosperity and success.

Where do money issues intersect the life of the congregation? Just about everywhere. The family feud, set before Jesus for him to resolve in Luke 12:13–14, can be found in almost any parish. Beyond matters of inheritance, money serves as a kind of

Exegetical Perspective

From Luke's theological perspective, riches (i.e., having wealth, possessions, and elite economic status) are not neutral. They are inherently negative. People become rich by exploiting the poor. People use riches to enhance their own status (14:7–14) and lavishly to enjoy their own positions in life (16:19–31). Mary first revealed God's negative attitude toward the rich and lofty (1:51–53). Jesus also shares such a negative attitude (6:20–26). This text recalls and expands on these perspectives by depicting the life-threatening nature of riches.

In this context, Jesus is teaching his disciples amid a crowd of thousands (12:1) when an unnamed individual interrupts Jesus with a demand of his own (v. 13). He asks Jesus to tell his brother to divide an inheritance with him. According to Judaic inheritance practices, an older brother would receive two-thirds of an estate while the younger would receive one-third (see Deut. 21:16–17). This brother (presumably the younger, less powerful brother needing outside arbitration) wants Jesus to help him possess his rightful possessions.

Jesus' question in response indicates that Jesus' role is not mediator of familial inheritance disputes (v. 14). Instead, Jesus issues an emphatic warning to the crowd to be on guard against insatiable greediness, because the meaning and value of one's life is

Homiletical Perspective

"You fool!" This is strong language—usually reserved for hurling as an invective against adversaries with whom all hope of reasoned discourse has broken down. These words of Jesus as told by Luke sound even more dismissive. Suggesting no alternative to the rich man's "best practice" business strategy, God abruptly utters the put-down, along with an edict: "Your soul has been bankrupted by your balance sheet; foreclosure is imminent. You're dead!"

Unlike Luke's stories about a Good Samaritan, a Lost Sheep, and a Prodigal Son (but alarmingly akin to those about the Rich Man and Lazarus, the Ten Pounds, and the Wicked Tenants), this parable contains no last-minute rescue engendering a "happily ever after," and no maneuvering room for home-stretch corrections of wrong turns taken. Luke's Jesus seems to have an "attitude" about those with abundant resources!

So do some preachers. Many are the sermons on this text that boil down to, "You can't take it with you, so be generous with your assets—especially to the church." Is this the intended thrust of the saying that concludes the story ("So it is with those who store up treasures for themselves but are not rich toward God," v. 21)? What does it mean to be "rich toward God"? The story leads us to a cliff edge—and leaves us there.

Luke 12:13-21

Theological Perspective

Frugal-minded folk have long stashed excess food and supplies in silos, pantries, and basement shelves; they have saved for rainy days, squirreled away funds for retirement, and even secreted dollar bills under mattresses. Is not this a prudent hedge against future economic uncertainty? After all, this is precisely what the young Joseph advises Pharaoh after interpreting a dream to mean seven years of plenty and seven years of famine (Gen. 41:17–36): store up the excess in the fat years so that there will be enough for everybody in the lean ones. Further, does not this man deserve to "eat, drink, and be merry" in celebration of his extreme good fortune? Any number of feasts and parties throughout the Bible give ample evidence for the practice of celebrating the harvest or rejoicing at signs of good fortune.

To be sure, saving for future material needs is one component of proper stewardship of God's bounty. Appropriate concern for the future is balanced, however, with the injunction to give glory to God and to care for one's neighbor, to provide for the poor and the marginalized, for those without access to the world's wealth or even to basic needs of survival. We should note that the man in the parable demonstrates neither of these twin aspects of stewardship—return to God and care for neighbor— mainly because he has become so focused on himself that he has forgotten both the God who caused the earth's bounty and the neighbor without access to that bounty. We might note, as well, how the pronouns "I," "me," and "my" dominate the story, whether in English translation or in the Greek text. Here there is concern only for himself, not for his neighbors, for those who have no land to produce their own crops, for the alien, the widow, and the orphan at the margins of society (e.g., Exod. 22:21–22), for any whose lives are at risk due to their limited access to resources. Throughout Luke's Gospel, as well as in the development of the church over the centuries, the act of giving to the poor remains a central element of the sanctified life. The man in the parable is so self-centered, however, that he cannot see beyond what he considers to be "his" harvest, "his" barns, and "his own" life.

At least two additional issues are at stake. First is the reminder that God is the author of life and death, as well as the creator of a land that produces food for its inhabitants. In theological terms, it is divine providence that has made possible the excess crops. The parable's protagonist, however, ignores the hand of God in his good fortune and focuses only on the benefit accruing to himself. Nowhere

Pastoral Perspective

thermostat for issues of anxiety and control in the congregation itself.

As the work of Edwin Friedman[1] and Peter Steinke[2] on family systems illustrates, money matters often reveal the true heart of a church organization, as well as of our individual households. Money is always about more than money. Our spending, our saving, and our general attitude toward material wealth are all invested with emotions and memories. A capacity to trust in God can deepen only as other matters lessen their grip in our lives. Today's Gospel text sets that reality before the congregation in the starkest terms.

For those who preach, this text offers a healthy inventory for assessing one's own readiness to be "rich toward God" in a culture in which the social status of clergy is in decline. Before challenging the congregation about its collective values and financial commitments, it is a good pastoral discipline to examine one's own relationship toward money and public esteem.

When it comes to money and worldly treasures, what values do you as a preacher carry forward from your childhood? Does a commitment to a life "rich toward God" (Luke 12:21) continue to provide you with a sense of deep and abiding joy, or have other worries and financial pressures begun to erode your confidence in the grace of the Christian life? Are you able to speak directly and frankly with other leaders in the congregation about money, savings, and financial stewardship, or are there underlying tensions whenever the budget, your compensation, or your spending habits are under discussion?

Jesus' candor in this passage may sound surprising, if not shocking, to those worshipers who come to church expecting nothing to change in their lives. Summer offers a rare opportunity for reflecting on the intersection of faith and money. That both preacher and people may be feeling the pinch of a changing national economy allows issues of money, prosperity, and life goals to be discussed in a more natural way. Free from the urgency that often sur- rounds a fall stewardship campaign, midsummer worship is a fine time for examining congregational practices in a less anxious and more reflective way.

The preacher who plans ahead for the congregation to hear this week's Gospel lesson can

1. Edwin H. Friedman, *Generation to Generation* (New York: Guilford Press, 1985) provides a comprehensive overview of family-systems thinking.
2. Peter L. Steinke, *Healthy Congregations: A Systems Approach* (Herndon, VA: Alban Institute, 2006) and *Congregational Leadership in Anxious Times: Being Calm and Courageous No Matter What* (Herndon, VA: Alban Institute, 2006) illustrate how the dynamics of family systems are at play in congregations.

Exegetical Perspective

not established through accumulating abundant possessions (v. 15). In the economic realities of the first-century world, insatiable greediness also had communal implications. If one person became richer and richer, it meant others conversely would become poorer and poorer, because economics was a zero-sum game. One's life was always intertwined with the lives of others as well as with God.

To illustrate his claims in verse 15, Jesus presents a parable concerning a rich man's dilemma. A few points should be noted regarding the parable's opening in verse 16. First, the fact that the person is described as being rich casts him in a negative theological light, given what has been said about the rich in 1:52–53 and 6:20–24. Second, this rich man is not a simple farmer with a small plot of land. Rather, he controls much of the agricultural produce over an entire region or district.[1] Third, in the prevailing theological perspective of the day, this rare bumper crop would have been regarded as a generous blessing from God.

Instead of a blessing, however, the rich man initially regards his plentiful harvest as a dilemma, since he has nowhere to store his crops (v. 17). His concern over inadequate storage space shows that he has no intention of either selling or sharing his crops at this point in time. He is seeking a long-term solution, which he discloses in verse 18. He will tear down his current storage facilities and build even bigger ones. In and of itself, this is not automatically a negative action. Actually, there is a very positive scriptural precedent for gathering in bountiful harvest and saving it for the future. This is exactly what Joseph instructed Pharaoh to do (Gen. 41:32–36).[2]

This particular rich man, however, is no Joseph, who wisely discerned the times and acted appropriately for the benefit of those in need. Rather his focus is solely inward, as he tells his inner self to relax, eat, drink, and be merry, because he has many good things stored up for many years to come. His solution to his dilemma of abundance also has communal implications. In future times of scarcity he will become even richer, as others will be dependent upon him and the prices he sets for food.[3]

There is a significant irony in his instructions to himself at the end of verse 19. "Relax, eat, drink, and be merry," echoes Isaiah 22:13, which also adds the

1. Bernard Scott, *Hear Then the Parable. A Commentary on the Parables of Jesus* (Minneapolis: Fortress Press, 1989), 132.
2. Ibid., 134.
3. Joel Green, *The Gospel of Luke*, New International Commentary on the New Testament (Grand Rapids: Eerdmans, 1997), 491.

Homiletical Perspective

Perhaps we should have expected it. Not only has Jesus just declined to take up a case of distributive justice ("Friend, who set me to be a judge or arbitrator over you?" v. 14); in the immediately following pericope, he seems to disallow resource management altogether ("Do not worry about your life, what you will eat, or about your body, what you will wear," v. 22). How realistic is such a Franciscan ideal—even for Franciscans? Is there no place in God's economy for building bigger barns?

Money *matters* to Luke's Jesus—that is undeniable (although certain preachers, particularly in affluent parishes, sometimes dance around it), yet more is involved here than how much one manages to make or bank. The issue is not so much investments and dividends as it is *distractions*.

In the Lukan Gospel lectionary reading two weeks ago, Jesus is receiving hospitality from Mary and Martha (the latter apparently doing the heavy lifting with respect to the logistics). Martha complains that Mary is not doing her fair share (an interesting permutation on the situation that provokes *this* parable—someone who asks Jesus to take sides in a dispute regarding fair shares of a family inheritance). Jesus tells Martha she is "distracted by many things." In the press of immediate perceptions, Martha has lost perspective. In her multitasking, Martha has missed out on her one critically important, vocation-centering obligation.

Both the man focused on the inheritance he *does not* yet have (but wants to gain) and the rich man focused on resources he *does* have (but wants to enlarge) are afflicted by a variation on Martha's problem—essentially "the other side of the same coin." The disgruntled brother and the enterprising rich man are not distracted by *many* things, as Martha is. Rather, both are distracted by their respective fixations on *one* thing: the additional resources each might somehow garner ("If only my brother would divvy up!" "If only my barns were bigger!").

When Jesus counsels "not to worry" about food and clothes (as next he does), he is not necessarily urging a radically Franciscan lifestyle; he is addressing the pervasive human disposition to grub for and grasp after what almost always distracts our focus from what can be acquired only through God's gracious gift ("Do not be afraid, little flock; it is your Father's good pleasure to give you the kingdom," 12:32).

The issue (for Martha, the discontented brother, the rich man, and us) is *careful discernment regarding various dimensions of value*. Such discernment is

Luke 12:13-21

Theological Perspective

does he offer thanksgiving to God for the abundance of his land.

Second, the man seems to have forgotten that all created life is bounded by death, a reality that comes to bear whatever the quantity of one's possessions. In the end, and sooner rather than later, death will separate him from his overflowing barns. "You cannot take it with you," so the popular saying goes; alternatively, we might say, "there are no storage facilities in heaven." Despite barns filled to the brim, the man's days are numbered, a fact he seems to forget as he congratulates himself for his fine lot in life.

With all this excess at the center of his life, the man plunges into the trap of idolatry, an idolatry that is often idolized by our culture. The nearly constant message of today's media is that life does, indeed, consist in the abundance of possessions. We are encouraged to spend more, have more, and use more; to supersize and maximize; to bank on the appearance of wealth as a sign of the good life. Insofar as the culture cultivates a propensity to buy things we do not need, it champions a way of life that this parable characterizes as folly.

The parable might sound a different note in a different context. If one lives in utter poverty, without access even to the basic necessities of life, the promise of wealth is not cast aside lightly. However, the parable calls on all, rich and poor alike, to reflect carefully about what we want and why we want it. Are our desires and standards for what is enough driven by a determination to store up treasures for our own pleasure, or by our understanding of God's blessings and our true purpose in life? Will we measure our lives by the standards of the media, seducing us to want more and more, or by the call of the gospel to be rich toward God?

AUDREY WEST

Pastoral Perspective

create a context for honest conversations about personal money management, financial values, and life goals. Might the sermon prepare the way for workshops during the education hour on money matters for kids, young adults, empty nesters, and retirees? The congregation might take time to prepare for a series of estate-planning consultations or to delve into the economics that drive the cost of the local housing market and consumer goods. Where there is a capacity to see money as part—not the center—of the Christian life, congregations can broker useful knowledge and discussion that bring fiscal realism together with gospel faith.

Midsummer also offers an engaging time to talk about the congregation's investment in mission. For what does the congregation toil and save? Does the history of money matters in the congregation itself suggest areas for further reflection? What were the money values of the founding generation? Is giving driven by mission, or is mission limited by giving?

Imagine gathering an intergenerational group and setting a single question before teams of three or four: *What does it mean for us to be a people who are "rich toward God"?* Linking the sermon to such a discussion suggests that Jesus' conversation with the disciples in this lesson is as pertinent to the communal reality of the church as it is to the individuals hearing today's lesson.

When all is said and done, Luke 12:13–21 invites preacher and congregation alike to place their trust in something more durable than the volatile fluctuations of a global economy. Instead of banking on more and larger storage barns, God invites all into the eternal economy of Christ's grace and mercy. That is good news in every season of the year.

PATRICIA J. LULL

reason for such unbounded celebration: "For tomorrow we die." This man is so totally self-absorbed that as he does not take others into account; neither does he take his own mortality or God into account. God, however, takes him into account (v. 20). The contrast between the rich man's self-perception and God's perception is quite stark. The rich man thinks he has it made in the shade for years to come, but God judges him a fool, because his own self will be demanded that very night. He has made elaborate preparations to guarantee himself a comfortable, self-indulgent future but has not prepared for his own impending mortality. God's question in verse 20b is left hanging in the air because the man considered no one beyond himself. In many ways he has now experienced exactly what Jesus asked his disciples to consider in 9:25: "What does it profit them if they gain the whole world, but lose or forfeit themselves?"

Jesus' conclusion (v. 21) rounds out his words on insatiable greed in verse 15. Here is the final, fatal outcome for one whose life was the abundance of their possessions. Here is the fate of one who stockpiled for himself and was not rich toward God. While this text does not tells us what being rich toward God entails, both prior and subsequent Lukan texts provide clear insights. Being rich toward God entails using one's resources for the benefit of one's neighbor in need, as the Samaritan did (10:25–37). Being rich toward God includes intentionally listening to Jesus' word, as Mary did (10:38–42). Being rich toward God consists of prayerfully trusting that God will provide for the needs of life (11:1–13; 12:22–31). Being rich toward God involves selling possessions and giving alms as a means of establishing a lasting treasure in heaven (12:32–34).

The man in the parable and people who emulate his pattern of life are fools for leading isolated, self-absorbed lives, because everything they have given themselves ends with death. Life is not had by the possessions one has. Life and possessions are a gift of God to be used to advance God's agenda of care and compassion, precisely for those who lack resources to provide for themselves.

RICHARD P. CARLSON

especially challenging when money is at stake. It can be even more difficult when the presenting problem involves a "fair" distribution of capital and labor. Perceptions regarding both are often immediate and intense. Perspective is essential in discernment—and often hard to come by.

"You fool!" This is not a phrase recommended for "trying at home." Luke's Jesus does not employ it here because he has a "Son of God" exemption from rules that otherwise apply. The phrase, in this context, is not an invective; rather, it is vividly descriptive of the actual situation. Distractions occlude clear discernment and lead to choices and commitments that are often tragically foolish. No one sets out to make stupid decisions! When information relevant to decision making is merely overlooked or inaccurately assessed, ensuing misperception is relatively easy to correct. Checked and prompted, we can look again and adjust accordingly ("Now I see!"). If we have an inveterate predisposition to distraction, however (either too many things, or one big thing), it is hard to put things in perspective. Frames of reference are not easily dislodged. The parable's shock therapy of sharp warning is an intervention of last resort.

This way of reading the Rich Fool parable provides a way of understanding the other three named earlier. The parables of the Rich Man and Lazarus, the Ten Pounds, and the Wicked Tenants all involve characters whose tragic, foolish actions devolve from the misuse of resources. More deeply, they too are about distraction and discernment. The purple-clad rich man is so distracted by his banquets that he cannot see Lazarus. The talent-burying servant is obsessed by the vision of a tyrant master. The tenants are so caught up in keeping it all that they murder the owner's "beloved son" so that "the inheritance may be [theirs]." (Similar reads can be given to the parable of the Great Banquet and, in a curious way, the parable of the Dishonest Manager—who comes, not to see different things, but to see things differently.)

That brings us back to what Luke invites today's preacher to wrestle with: what *does* it mean to be "rich toward God"? This is a question of discernment well worth asking.

DAVID J. SCHLAFER

Isaiah 1:1, 10-20

¹The vision of Isaiah son of Amoz, which he saw concerning Judah and
Jerusalem in the days of Uzziah, Jotham, Ahaz, and Hezekiah, kings of Judah....

¹⁰Hear the word of the LORD,
  you rulers of Sodom!
Listen to the teaching of our God,
  you people of Gomorrah!
¹¹What to me is the multitude of your sacrifices?
  says the LORD;
I have had enough of burnt offerings of rams
  and the fat of fed beasts;
I do not delight in the blood of bulls,
  or of lambs, or of goats.

¹²When you come to appear before me,
  who asked this from your hand?
  Trample my courts no more;
¹³bringing offerings is futile;
  incense is an abomination to me.
  New moon and sabbath and calling of convocation—
  I cannot endure solemn assemblies with iniquity.
¹⁴Your new moons and your appointed festivals
  my soul hates;

Theological Perspective

The name "Isaiah" means "YHWH has saved" or
"YHWH may save." A theological theme recurring in
the book of Isaiah is God's saving sovereignty over
history and all the nations. YHWH is no mere local
tribal deity but one whose glory fills the whole earth
(6:3), to whom all the nations will one day stream,
and who will "judge between the nations" (2:4). In
light of divine sovereignty over all the nations, Isaiah
offers a vigorous critique of empires and their
presumption. History is not left to the powers of
empire. History is in God's hands, and so also are the
hated empires of Assyria and (later) Babylon. Isaiah
urges that Judah should not ally itself with any of
these great powers but, rather, rely upon God in all
things. The idolatries and injustices of these empires
will bring them down. In the meantime, these
powers might well be used as instruments in the
hands of YHWH to carry out a judgment upon
Judah for its own idolatries and injustices. Judah's
best course, then, is repentance and return to
YHWH to offer full allegiance and right worship.
Isaiah extends a hope that "YHWH may save" (a

Pastoral Perspective

Launch the words "Sodom and Gomorrah" at a
group of people, and already your hearers are clear:
judgment is coming. This text comes down like a
gavel in a courtroom—or perhaps more like a
sledgehammer. "Hear the word of the LORD, you
rulers of Sodom! Listen to the teaching of our God,
you people of Gomorrah!" The pastor looking for
words to lure listeners in with feel-good rhetoric will
need to look elsewhere.

This reading comes around during the dog days
of summer, when attendance in some churches is
lagging and limited mostly to the faithful remnant.
Isaiah makes for difficult preaching—who wants to
be the messenger bearing such news as "God hates
your worship"?—but it is possible to preach the
words of the prophet and still attend to pastoral
concerns. In this passage, rough words make way for
sweet promises; the pastor must find ways to remain
faithful to both.

The lection begins with a call for the leaders
("rulers of Sodom") and the masses ("people of
Gomorrah") to hear what God has to say. Modern-

they have become a burden to me,
    I am weary of bearing them.
¹⁵When you stretch out your hands,
    I will hide my eyes from you;
even though you make many prayers,
    I will not listen;
    your hands are full of blood.
¹⁶Wash yourselves; make yourselves clean;
    remove the evil of your doings
    from before my eyes;
    cease to do evil,
¹⁷ learn to do good;
    seek justice,
      rescue the oppressed,
    defend the orphan,
      plead for the widow.

¹⁸Come now, let us argue it out,
    says the LORD:
though your sins are like scarlet,
    they shall be like snow;
though they are red like crimson,
    they shall become like wool.
¹⁹If you are willing and obedient,
    you shall eat the good of the land;
²⁰but if you refuse and rebel,
    you shall be devoured by the sword;
    for the mouth of the LORD has spoken.

Exegetical Perspective

Isaiah 1:1. A three-part superscription introduces the sixty-six-chapter book of Isaiah, a collection of prophetic oracles (and narratives) produced over perhaps four centuries of Judah's history. First, the superscription attributes the following divine "vision" (a generic term that lends a future orientation to the entire work; see also Nah. 1:1 and Obad. 1) to the eighth-century BCE prophet Isaiah ("YH[WH] is salvation"), son of Amoz. Second, it identifies "Judah and Jerusalem" as the vision's principal subjects. Third, it situates Isaiah's approximately forty-year prophetic career within the reigns of four successive Judean kings: Uzziah (783–742 BCE); Jotham (742–735 BCE); Ahaz (735–715 BCE); and Hezekiah (715–687/6 BCE). According to Isaiah 6:1, Isaiah received his call to prophesy in the year Uzziah died. References to these four kings reappear in chapters 1–39, which contain not only all of eighth-century Isaiah's surviving oracles, but also materials dating from later periods.

The book of Isaiah emerged from lengthy and complex processes of composition and redaction.

Homiletical Perspective

Some preachers may take a perverse pleasure in this text, since it assaults worship. We may possess cherished convictions about worship and some valued expertise in its execution, but we may also have resentments. Worship is our job, routinely performed. We know how little difference it seems to make in the lives of most, including perhaps ourselves. We notice that the sermons we labored through and birthed, so that they are like our children, do not change much of anything. To the extent that we are annoyed with the various failings of our congregations, the face presented by the church's worship may seem false. So there may be some of us—frustrated, burdened, and irked—who relish the chance to thunder with God, "I have had enough! . . . When you come to appear before me, who asked this of you? . . . Your offerings are futile. . . . I cannot endure solemn assemblies. . . . Your appointed festivals my soul hates. . . . Though you make many prayers, I will not listen."

The irony, of course, is that we will say these words as part of the church's worship, and we will be

Isaiah 1:1, 10-20

Theological Perspective

possible play on Isaiah's name). Beyond the needed judgment/purification a faithful remnant will return.

Another theological theme prominent in Isaiah is God's concern for justice. Isaiah delivers a prophetic diatribe against the social and political injustice he sees in his society. He denounces the affluent and politically powerful, threatening them with divine retribution (Isa. 2–4), for they are exploiting the poor and oppressed (5:8–13).

Isaiah uses the strongest language possible, addressing the hearers as "rulers of Sodom" and "people of Gomorrah" (v. 10). These cities had become a byword for wickedness in the extreme and divine annihilation. The particular wickedness of Sodom and Gomorrah—contrary to popular assumptions—is a matter of their greed and injustice. The fullest accounting of the "sin" of Sodom and Gomorrah in the Old Testament is in the book of Ezekiel: "This was the guilt of your sister Sodom: she and her daughters had pride, excess of food, and prosperous ease, but did not aid the poor and needy" (Ezek. 16:49). It is not until the Hellenistic period that sexual conduct is even alluded to in connection with these cities. As the cities of Sodom and Gomorrah became bywords for injustice and divine judgment, Isaiah implies, the southern kingdom of Judah now mirrors their condition.

In league with these oppressors are the religious leaders of the state cult. They provide religious legitimation for the unjust social/political system. In fact, the state cult adds its own layer of oppression, by imposing heavy economic burdens on the people. Temple personnel are tax exempt, and providing for their economic support is not optional. The required assemblies (adult males are required to present themselves three times a year at the state sanctuary) and the required sacrifices of cereal and animal offerings are a significant economic burden. The temple personnel are the most likely to benefit from these arrangements and are in a position to manipulate the system. Isaiah questions who *really* requires this "trampling of my courts" (v. 12 RSV) and the burnt offerings and the blood of bulls. There is no delight for YHWH in these things. As they are a burden to the poor, so also they are a burden to YHWH (v. 14).

Worship is perverted by the contradiction between their solemn assembly and their iniquity (v. 13). It may even be termed an "abomination" (v. 13)—an epithet applied elsewhere to idolatrous practices (1 Kgs. 14:23–24). The blood of ritual sacrifice intended for atonement becomes an *un*holy

Pastoral Perspective

day listeners may not be so ready to hear such an accusation; for contemporary hearers, the phrase "Sodom and Gomorrah" often has had overtones of sexual sin in general and homosexual behavior in particular. It may be helpful for the pastor to acknowledge the negative and even explosive history of these words and to explore the true judgment implied in the accusation without overfreighting it with our own cultural neuroses. The first word of this section is "Hear"; it would be a shame if listeners could not do so because of these two words. How can the listener be open to words that ultimately do carry judgment? It is a tough tension to navigate, between not softening the actual prophecy and not making it impossible to hear. Exploring that difficulty with the people may help.

What does Isaiah want his listeners to hear? The words do not get any easier at this point: God hates our worship. The divine speech is laced with harsh and horrible rejections: "What to me is the multitude of your sacrifices? . . . I have had enough. . . . I do not delight. . . . Who asked this from your hand? . . . No more . . . futile . . . abomination . . . iniquity. . . . Your new moons and your appointed festivals my soul hates." Verse 14 would seem to be the withering culmination, but it actually gets worse: "Even though you make many prayers, I will not listen." God will not even listen to prayers. The reason for such absolute rejection is clear: "When you stretch out your hands, . . . your hands are full of blood." God will not hear the pleas of people who come to pray with blood on their hands. This verse makes most plain the source of God's problem with worship—the disconnect between what happens inside the sanctuary and what happens outside of it.

A word such as this does not lose its relevance, because this is always a core problem for God's people—the gap between our practice and our praise. "How can you worship a homeless man on Sunday and ignore one on Monday?" the poster at the homeless shelter asks. The poster may seems glib, but it does point to our perpetual problem: translating our worship into action. Our inattention to injustice delegitimates our praise.

If we want to lift our blood-soaked hands to God, there is only one thing left to do: "Wash yourselves; make yourselves clean" (v. 16). What is required to come clean before God? "Cease to do evil, learn to do good; seek justice" (vv. 16–17). In the broadest terms, it is the turning of a life and the turning of a community of lives. In specific terms, doing good and seeking justice look like this: "rescue the

Exegetical Perspective

Many biblical scholars agree that chapter 1 took shape late in its compositional history (ca. the end of the fifth century BCE) and introduces the entire work. Some of its units likely derive from the eighth-century Isaiah, but others reflect circumstances, perspectives, and themes at home in historically later sections of the book (the exilic Second Isaiah [chaps. 40–55]; the postexilic Third Isaiah [chaps. 56–66]). Isaiah 1:27–28, for example, presents in a nutshell the entire vision's overriding claim.

Isaiah 1:10–20. One cannot analyze verses 10–20 adequately apart from their literary context. Verses 2–9 summon heaven and earth to witness a covenant lawsuit (v. 2a) in which YHWH, the plaintiff/prosecutor, accuses Israel, God's obstinate offspring, of continually rebelling against its divine parent (vv. 2b–4). Why do you keep rebelling (v. 5a), the prophet asks his audience, when repeated beatings leave you bruised and bleeding (vv. 5b–6), your country and cities lie desolate, and strangers devour your land? Only "daughter" Zion, personified as a young, vulnerable female, remains (vv. 7–8). Indeed, YHWH has punished the people so severely that if not for a few survivors, they would have become like Sodom and Gomorrah (v. 9), ancient cities annihilated by sulfur and fire (Gen. 19:24).

Proclaiming YHWH's word was the primary task of Israel's prophets; instructing Israel in God's torah/teaching was largely the responsibility of its priests. In verses 10–20, however, Isaiah assumes this priestly role, quoting a rhetorically charged divine speech that instructs his audience in what YHWH rejects (vv. 11–15) and requires (vv. 16–17) of the people. In two parallel lines, a call to instruction summons Jerusalem's leaders and populace, derisively called "rulers of Sodom" and "people of Gomorrah," to "hear the word of the LORD" and "listen to the teaching of our God" (v. 10). References to Sodom and Gomorrah link this verse to verse 9; here, however, they emphasize the *wickedness* of the former cities' inhabitants, rather than their *extermination*.

In verses 11–15, YHWH vehemently rejects Jerusalem's cultic practices. Why do the people offer sacrifices and other gifts when God cannot abide them? YHWH is sated with whole burnt offerings of rams and the suet of fatted beasts and takes no delight in the blood of bulls, lambs, and goats (v. 11). Whole burnt offerings required that an animal's entire carcass be incinerated upon the altar, its smoke rising to the Deity as a pleasing aroma. Other animal sacrifices permitted officiating priests

Homiletical Perspective

among the worshipers. Whatever may be wrong here, we are complicit, at the very least. We are on the payroll. Isaiah did not speak his words from inside the sanctuary, but we do. Embarrassment is appropriate. As always, although the text may speak from "above" the people, the sermon will have to be preached from among them. To this end, we should allow room for the text not only to accuse the church, but also to ask questions of the church—even if, or especially if, our congregations have desired and pursued exactly the kind of justice demanded by the text.

Truly it is the church, not eighth-century BCE Judah, to whom the text is addressed in our hearing. For us, at least, the cultic practices named by the text are not at issue. Animal sacrifice, incense, and other rituals of temple worship are not the point, nor are the worship practices of any churches different from our own. The target is injustice, oppression, and other evils—and the insidious links between our practice of worship and our participation in these monstrous realities.

That there may really be a link between our practice of worship and our participation in oppression is a shocking assertion. We may assume that the prophet's words on the subject were, and were meant to be, shocking to those who first heard them. The text will not do its work among us if it is not allowed to startle and offend. So we will have to translate, as usual, from the world of the text to the world of our own experience. For the church to hear this text, it will probably need to hear something like: "I hate your worship. Your prayers make me sick. I loathe your music. Your sermons are a sacrilege. Who asked for your offerings? Your Holy Communion stinks. I want none of it."

In our canon, Isaiah is the first of the books of the Prophets, and we are on the very first page of it. This is God's first order of business in the prophetic literature: a withering assault on worship. Writers of recent bestsellers decrying the evils of religion may not have noticed that the Bible is ahead of them. The first and most furious critic of religion is God.

The present attack is on the bizarre disconnect of people praising God while desecrating God's command to love. Does a wife want endearments from her husband when she knows he is cheating on her? Does she want roses that he buys with money he stole from the poor? If he beats the children but tearfully apologizes for tracking mud onto the carpet, can she keep from throwing up, then throwing him out? Worship unconcerned with justice is obscene.

Isaiah 1:1, 10-20

Theological Perspective

thing; the hands lifted up in prayer are "full of blood" (v. 15). There is need not only for the washing of ritual purification, but also for a deeper purification of the life lived—"cease to do evil, learn to do good; seek justice, rescue the oppressed, defend the orphan, plead for the widow" (vv. 16–17).

One of the theological tensions concerns the practice of animal sacrifice, which would have been an ordinary part of all observance of Sabbaths and new moons. The complexity and efficacy of the system of ritual sacrifice in ancient Judaism is much misunderstood in Christian circles. For example, there are different kinds of offerings. Some are understood purely as gifts to God. Peace offerings are meant to signal a reconciled relation with God. Other offerings are intended as expiation for *breaches of ritual committed in ignorance*. Forgiveness of other kinds of wrongs or wrongs done knowingly is never related to sacrifice, but is dependent upon repentance and confession. There is no understanding of divine forgiveness being "purchased" by sacrifice (propitiation).

Christians might avoid misunderstandings of the sacrificial/substitutionary theory of the atonement if they remember its roots in Jewish sacrificial theology and practice that was not propitiatory in nature. One such misunderstanding is the idea that God requires sacrifice (propitiation) offered by someone in order to forgive. More theologically sound is the affirmation that "in Christ God was reconciling the world" (2 Cor. 5:19); the atonement is God's own gracious initiative.

There is in Isaiah and in his near contemporaries Amos and Micah an apparent wariness toward animal sacrifice. In a number of passages like the present one, animal sacrifice is condemned so roundly (Amos 5:21–24; Hos. 6:6; Mic. 6:6–8; Jer. 7:2–7) that it seems to be condemned outright, not simply because it is misused. Some passages (likely postexilic) in Psalms and Proverbs, while they do not disparage animal sacrifice, consistently devalue it in relation to the offering of a pure and holy life (Pss. 40:6–8; 50:7–15; 51:16–17). "To do righteousness and justice is more acceptable to the LORD than sacrifice" (Prov. 21:3).

There is a significant resonance between this text from Isaiah and Christian understandings of true worship as being primarily about how we live our lives before God (see Rom. 12:1–2).

ANNA CASE-WINTERS

Pastoral Perspective

oppressed, defend the orphan, plead for the widow" (v. 17). If the people of God want to lift their hands to God in prayer, they will extend their hands to the most vulnerable as well. Whereas the preceding verses offered strong and challenging words, here is the chance for the pastor and people to play and to dream—to think imaginatively about how the public daily life might rightly coincide with right worship of God. Isaiah sets a good homiletical and pastoral example here, with his list of specific things the people of God do if they want to learn to do good; the pastor might follow suit, crafting with the congregation an extended specific list of ways the people of God might still put worship into action by tending the most vulnerable.

It would be easy to end here—with a list of good things for people to go and do—but the text does not stop. The final word is God's—just as the final action will be—and a famous word it is: "Come now, let us argue it out . . . though your sins are like scarlet, they shall be like snow" (v. 18). The more familiar version of this can be found in the NIV, "they shall be *as white as* snow" which resonates with Psalm 51:7, "Wash me, and I shall be *whiter than* snow." Even if our translations of verse 18 do not include the word "white," many listeners will hear it nonetheless, and the preacher needs to be aware of the racial prejudices that have shaped our hearing of such a phrase. The association of the color white with purity can be problematic and may need to be given thoughtful consideration.[1] However the preacher chooses to deal with this complex and sensitive issue, the last word of the text is the same. Ultimately, whatever washing there is will come from God's hands, not the people's. The only question is whether or not the people—we among them—are willing.

STACEY SIMPSON DUKE

---

1. For a provocative treatment of this issue as pertains to this text, see Randall C. Bailey, "'They Shall Become as White as Snow': When Bad Is Turned into Good," *Semeia* 76 (1996): 99.

and the animal's owner (as well as family and guests) to eat their allotted cuts of meat after YHWH's portions were burned (fat) and daubed/dashed (blood) on the altar.

The rhetorical question, "who asked this from your hand?" (v. 12), functions flatly to deny that God demands these sacrifices when the people present themselves before the Lord at Jerusalem's temple. The negative imperative, "trample my courts no more," orders an end to their offensive cultic practices, including all other offerings and gifts to God, incense, and regular (e.g., new moon, Sabbath) and other cultic rituals and assemblies. Their actions, loathsome burdens to the Lord, are futile. Even their prayers cannot catch YHWH's averted eyes and stopped-up ears, because the hands they raise in a posture of prayer are filled with blood.

The image of bloody hands brings to mind not only animal sacrifices, but also brutality, suggesting that human violence, rather than sacrifices per se, motivates God's present rejection of Judah's cult. This impression is reinforced when, in nine positive commands, YHWH tells the people and their leaders what God actually demands of them (vv. 16–17). The first two imperatives, "Wash yourselves; make yourselves clean," demand far more than skin-deep scrubbing of bloodstained hands, and even the purging of ritual defilement. They also require moral purity—both the radical rejection of evil deeds and the active acquisition ("learn") of what is good, expressed concretely in acts of social/judicial justice ("defend," "plead for") that encompass even Israel's most vulnerable and oppressed folk, its widows and orphans.

In the matter of YHWH vs. Israel, the divine plaintiff/prosecutor has spelled out and substantiated the charges against the defendants, God's rebellious children. One might expect the lawsuit to end with a "guilty" verdict; after all, the Lord is also the judge. Having instructed Israel in its covenant obligations, however, God assumes the role of arbiter, offering utterly to transform (forgive) Israel's transgressions. "Scarlet" sins stir thoughts of bloody hands (v. 15); snow-white wool recalls sacrificial lambs (v. 11). The people can survive: *if* they are willing and obedient (not rebellious!), *then* they will eat (*to'kelu*) the earth's good (things). If they refuse and rebel, however, they will be eaten (*t'ukk'lu*) by the sword—a certainty underscored by the closing formula, "for the mouth of the LORD has spoken."

KATHERYN PFISTERER DARR

It may even establish obstacles to justice. It may bathe us in feelings that carry some sense of completion. The appointment has been kept, a duty discharged, a commitment satisfied—perhaps a catharsis has occurred. Nothing outside the room will likely be challenged, because everything happened already in the room. Even if issues of justice and love are addressed in the room, the seduction of closure may win out. In this and other ways, evil's favorite shelter is a house of worship. The snake slithers into the sanctuary and coils itself around the altar.

None of this obviates the fact that worship is essential for us and requires of us an awed and candid engagement with God that is life giving, community transforming, and world altering. The text does not make this counterpoint, but perhaps awaits it. Preachers, however briefly, must get it said. After all, worship makes it possible to hear this text together; and worship's communal confession may free us to go and do what this word sends us to do; and worship's communal praise may grant us perspective and strength for obedience.

For the sermon, the most famous lines in the text may be the most dangerous, or they could be quite useful. If they are overstressed and oversweetened, the text is gutted; worship is fouled again. It may be strategically useful to place them at the beginning of the sermon, to speak of how soothing it has been for believers, how warmly inviting toward faith— "Come, let us reason together, that's what God says . . ."—then point out that the words follow directly from: "Your hands are full of blood! . . . I will not listen. . . . Cease to do evil, learn to do good, seek justice. . . . [or] you shall be devoured by the sword."

Perhaps we should revisit those famous lines near the sermon's end, having named the grievances of our Critic, the demands and threats of the text, and the offer it makes. There is, in fact, some hope, but we should resist an overhopeful, or wrapped-up, or emotionally moving conclusion. With this text in particular, closure must not happen in the room.

PAUL SIMPSON DUKE

Psalm 50:1-8, 22-23

¹The mighty one, God the LORD,
   speaks and summons the earth
   from the rising of the sun to its setting.
²Out of Zion, the perfection of beauty,
   God shines forth.

³Our God comes and does not keep silence,
   before him is a devouring fire,
   and a mighty tempest all around him.
⁴He calls to the heavens above
   and to the earth, that he may judge his people:
⁵"Gather to me my faithful ones,
   who made a covenant with me by sacrifice!"

Theological Perspective

God can do whatever God pleases. That is the message of this psalm. Some psalms celebrate God's activity as a benevolent, caring presence in the life of the individual and the believing community. Others cry out in protest to God for permitting or ignoring the inequities of life for the people God professes to bless. But this psalm acknowledges God's autonomy, sovereignty, and transcendence. God is not simply "with us." God is not "like us." God cannot be manipulated, and God is on to us. God knows that we think we are in control. God knows that we try to cut deals with each other and with the sovereign Creator of the universe. God is in control, and we would do well to accept that reality. The psalmist makes that clear in this hymn text. Psalmists do not need to be consistent. They are poets and prophets who can be evocative, conformist, demanding, impertinent, aggressive, challenging, winsome, and frustrating in one hymnlike device. They seek to capture the nature of the Divine and make an effort at articulating the impossible.

This psalm is grounded in God's sovereignty. It suggests that God is in control, that religion is dangerous, and that God's ways are past finding out. God does not have to make everything fit, and human beings, at least the religious types (Israel in this case), would do well to understand that fact.

Pastoral Perspective

Accompanied by the tempestuous signs of theophany, the Lord of Psalm 50 speaks, commanding all the people to assemble for judgment. Having already summoned witnesses—earth, the heavens, and the rising sun—the proceedings commence. In this cosmic courtroom, God is prosecutor, judge, and jury. The scene is majestic, impressive, and dreadful.

Whether they believe themselves sinners worthy of hell, or think themselves "good people" with nothing to answer for, most parishioners prefer to avoid the topic of judgment. Some churches omit a confession from their orders of worship, believing that life already heaps enough judgment on us. The confession only reinforces the depressing idea that we are bad and that God is "judgmental." Sunday should be about consolation and encouragement. But others cherish the confession, believing that its omission is evasive, allowing us to cultivate illusions of innocence, emptying grace of its power, and rendering it cheap. Pastors struggle to offer supportive pastoral care consonant with the Bible's witness to the compassion of Jesus and the abundant mercy of God, even as they refrain from giving phony assurances about the reliability of human goodness and humbly proclaim that all have fallen short of the mark.

For people who have already judged themselves—for whom guilt or shame is a dangerous undertow in

⁶The heavens declare his righteousness,
for God himself is judge.   *Selah*

⁷"Hear, O my people, and I will speak,
O Israel, I will testify against you.
I am God, your God.
⁸Not for your sacrifices do I rebuke you;
your burnt offerings are continually before me."
. . . .
²²"Mark this, then, you who forget God,
or I will tear you apart, and there will be no one to deliver.
²³Those who bring thanksgiving as their sacrifice honor me;
to those who go the right way
I will show the salvation of God."

Exegetical Perspective

Although it is separated from the other psalms so attributed (Pss. 73–83), Psalm 50 is the first in the Psalter to bear the attribution "a psalm of Asaph." This attribution refers either to Asaph himself, a chief musician during the time of King David (1 Chr. 16:4–7), or to a guild of musicians following in his tradition (Neh. 7:44). Given the prophetic nature of this particular psalm of Asaph and the prophetic themes reflected in many of the others, it is worth noting that Asaph is referred to as a "seer" in 2 Chronicles 29:30.

Psalm 50 appears in this Sunday's lectionary readings as a complement to the Old Testament reading from Isaiah, both of which are styled as legal cases brought against Israel by God, and both of which discuss the true nature of sacrifice and what constitutes an acceptable sacrifice to God. However, the lectionary editing of the Isaiah and Psalm readings diminishes the connections between these passages. Isaiah 1:2 (omitted) issues a summons to the heavens and the earth as witnesses as in Psalm 50:4 (included), and Psalm 50:9–15 (omitted) more fully addresses the issue of sacrifice discussed in Isaiah 1:10–20 (included).

This observation raises a more encompassing objection to the lectionary truncation of Psalm 50, the division of which disrupts the flow and overall

Homiletical Perspective

YHWH, who called the worlds into being and whose glory blinds and consumes all in its path, whose breath is like a hurricane, who controls the very rising and setting of the sun, is suing you for breach of contract. God will act as plaintiff, chief witness, judge, and executioner—should God just *happen* to win the suit. Oh, and by the way, YHWH is really mad. So what are you going to do now? Why, sing a psalm about it, naturally!

At least that is your response if you are the author of Psalm 50. This whole divine lawsuit thing is a fairly bizarre device. Basically, somebody (God) made a contract (or, if you insist on speaking biblically, a "covenant") with Israel (read: "you"); now God thinks you broke it. What do people do, then as now, when someone fails to uphold their end of a contract? Sue the pants off 'em! Which is just what God does.

Why does God need a court at all? The psalmist spends a fair portion of the rest of this psalm making the point that God is not like humans (v. 21, for example, and the deliciously snide in v. 12, both unfortunately outside this lection). Why place this conversation in the midst of a court of law, or even a royal court, when both are such deeply human inventions? Is God not above such things? Everybody (including you) knows you are guilty before the

Psalm 50:1-8, 22-23

Theological Perspective

Verses 1 and 2 are clear: this is God's world, from sunup to sundown. God can be encountered across the creation. From the psalmist's perspective, God has made clear to the sons and daughters of Abraham that there are some "sacred spaces" in the world that God has made. Zion, the site of the Jerusalem temple, exemplifies the divine presence much as Sinai did for an earlier generation. There are special places where God's presence can be experienced, because God has chosen to be revealed in those earthly locales. All the world is God's abode, but by virtue of God's sovereign choice some sacred places uniquely mediate God's presence.

This spiritual localism is both helpful and destructive. It reminds us that we value and need particular places that convey the Presence in exceptional ways. God has chosen to be revealed in those locales that become sacred through the habitation of the Divine. Space becomes sacred because God is experienced there. Herein is hierophany—the Sacred revealed in the ordinary. Such a Presence can be known in a medieval cathedral or a burning bush "beyond the wilderness" (Exod. 3:1). Hierophany may be experienced in the Holy of Holies on Mount Zion or in the scandalous "Place of a Skull" (Matt. 27:33 and par.).

Thus we learn that the God of the fiftieth Psalm cannot be controlled and is surrounded by a "devouring fire" and a "mighty tempest" (v. 3). This God reveals a Presence that is dangerous, merciful, and terrifying all at once. We seek this God because, as creatures, we long for intimacy with the Creator, yet we are terrified that such a God might turn on us, because we just might deserve annihilation and because God can do whatever God pleases. After all, God "calls to the heavens above and to the earth, that he may judge his people" (v. 4).

Is this sovereign God, this autocratic Deity, also the "God and Father of our Lord Jesus Christ"? We Christians believe that is our greatest hope, even as we confront the varying pictures of God's nature evident in the Psalms. Perhaps Psalm 50:5 could become a bridge between the testaments. The Creator, the transcendent One, is also the God who has chosen to make a covenant with God's own people. Here God asks that the "faithful ones, who made a covenant with me by sacrifice" be gathered to the divine presence. Determining who that people might be is one of the great questions of the world's religions. Again, the theology of that request is at once a potential blessing and a disturbing threat. Who are the "faithful ones"? What is the nature of the covenant, and who can claim it? Is it a covenant

Pastoral Perspective

their lives, and for whom, therefore, the prospect of God's judgment is soul-crushing—Psalm 50 offers reassurance. The defendants at God's bar are not strangers, but God's very own. "Gather to me *my* people," God says, "*my* faithful ones" (vv. 5, 7, emphasis added). The divine judge knows and claims us even as God examines us. Therein lies our hope, for often what threatens us most is not judgment itself, but the fear that once our flawed condition is laid bare for all to see, we will be left bereft, unloved, and alone.

Most people can bear the truth about themselves if they know that they always matter; that God thinks they are worth being examined, known, and judged; that they are important enough to be corrected, forgiven, and restored. If God were not perpetually committed to us, God would long ago have abandoned us to our own self-destruction. To reframe judgment as an affirmation of our eternal importance to God might help fearful parishioners accept the grace that comes from submitting to an honest assessment of their lives.

The charge God brings against the people in Psalm 50 concerns worship. They are accused of believing that God actually feeds on the flesh and blood of sacrificed animals (vv. 8–13, omitted from the lectionary). This is a pagan idea, and the Lord, to whom belong "every wild animal of the forest," and who "know[s] all the birds of the air," rejects it (vv. 10–11). God does not depend on us for survival. God lacks nothing, except perhaps our thanks and praise.[1] So in verse 23, God promises salvation to those who know that God is not like "gods," and whose sacrifice is an homage of gratitude, not an attempt to supply God's needs. There is also a faint echo here of Isaiah's familiar complaint about the falsity of worship unaccompanied by justice and thanks (Isa. 1:11).

Questions about animal slaughter do not weigh heavily on most parishioners' minds today. Many do wrestle, however, with the question of "acceptable" offerings, the role of sacrifice in the life of faith, and the tension between good deeds and divine acceptance. The psalm does not speak to all these questions. By correcting the notion that God needs sacrifice, though, and affirming instead the human need to honor God with thanks, the psalm provides a starting point for engaging them. It also speaks forcefully to the problem of distorted images of God and the ways in which such distortions pervert

---

1. Robert Alter, *The Book of Psalms: A Translation with Commentary* (New York: Norton, 2007), 177.

Exegetical Perspective

message of the psalm. Psalm 50 is clearly divided into four main sections: an introduction (vv. 1–6), a speech about worship (vv. 7–15), a speech about proper conduct within the bounds of the covenant (vv. 16–22), and a concluding statement that reflects both indictments and offers a summary instruction regarding both (v. 23). By essentially ignoring the second speech (only v. 22 remains, which the lectionary connects with the conclusion) and preserving only the first two verses of the first, the lectionary presents this as a psalm only about sacrifice. Even this remaining indictment is weakened by removing the bulk of the argument about the nature of sacrifice. What remains is a legal proceeding that includes no concrete indictment or explanation, only a setup and conclusion.

This is significant, because the form of this psalm is as critical to its interpretation as is its content. Psalm 50 defies the standard classifications typically employed by students of the Psalter and is instead composed as a covenantal lawsuit similar to what is found in Deuteronomistic and prophetic traditions (Deut. 32:1, Isa. 1:2, Mic. 6:1–2). Its cultic function is uncertain, with suggestions ranging from an oracle uttered by a cult prophet, to a sermonic liturgy recalling the covenant of Sinai, to a liturgy sung at a covenant-renewal ceremony. However it might have functioned in the worship life of ancient Israel, the theology of this lawsuit is clear: Israel is held accountable to the letter and spirit of its covenant with God.

The psalm begins with a triple naming of God—*el elohim YHWH*—who is connected to both creation in general and Zion in particular. While the NRSV attempts to bring these together as "The mighty one, God the Lord," it could also be read as "YHWH, God of gods."[1] This alternative might fit better the lawsuit scenario envisioned here, which in the ancient Near East typically involved the summoning of other deities as witnesses or judges. As in other instances of the biblical appropriation of this lawsuit tradition, however, the presence of other deities has been neutralized and replaced by God's summoning the heavens and the earth (both of which are creations of God in the biblical traditions) as witnesses to the lawsuit in which God alone is judge.

Yet even before issuing this summons and initiating the lawsuit, God appears in a mighty theophany of fire and storm that recalls the theophany at Sinai before the giving of the law and the establishment of

1. Mitchell Dahood, *Psalms I: 1–50*, Anchor Bible 16 (New York: Doubleday, 1965), 306.

Homiletical Perspective

hearing even starts, so the whole thing seems a little redundant. While we are asking questions, why are we *singing* about it?

The ancients seem to have enjoyed these courtroom scenes, though, so they are ours to work with, bizarre as they are. The scene does have its own kind of internal logic: if one party is going to sue another, they need someone else, more powerful than they are, to judge the case. If said party is God, God is pretty much stuck with Godself as judge. Of course, everybody on both sides is going to summon the very best witnesses they can; again, God is the best choice God has in the witness department. So really, if God is going to sue someone, acting as judge and chief witness as well as plaintiff is the only way to do it. So it does make sense if you think about it. Sort of. Well, except for the singing part.

Needless to say, there is no way you are going to win the case. That is the point, or at least the place where the point begins. The psalmist uses the all-too-familiar image of a courtroom as a way to lay out, clearly and unmistakably, the charge against Israel (again, that is you): your worship is empty, and you have forgotten your Creator and your contract. You have been confusing religion with a relationship with God. You have gotten caught up in the trappings of your worship, in the bells and whistles and the outfits. You have forgotten that all true worship begins and ends and is shot through with thanksgiving, which is the opposite of idolatry, and that grateful hearts are all that God really asks for.

God's charge invites us to think about the ways we have been spending our own time. God summoned the earth into being, is surrounded by glory, created you from dust, and made the greatest contract in history with you; and *how* much time did you spend raising money for the organ maintenance fund this year? Did you spend *another* whole deacons' meeting arguing about the relative merits of Communion by intinction over sit-and-pass? Do you really believe God cares about your *Book of Order/Book of Common Prayer*/hymnal/favorite Bible translation/<insert your idol here> anywhere near as much as you do? *Really*?

These things are fine so far as they go ("Not for your sacrifices do I rebuke you"), but the point is that you did not really need to go that far in the first place. Simple thanksgiving would have been enough. If you must have all those other things, fine. Just remember that the ones who truly honor God are the ones who play thanksgiving on their organs, the ones whose Communion is thanksgiving, whatever

Psalm 50:1-8, 22-23

Theological Perspective

with Abraham, Jesus, or Ishmael, and who will interpret the boundaries of such an arrangement?

The issue of covenant is no easy question for religionists ancient or modern. Clearly the biblical writers understood the covenant with Abraham as formative, but the covenant always seemed to be under modification—at least in the minds of those biblical and extrabiblical individuals who received new insights into the nature of God's will and work in the world. The prophetic element in Israel, evident in Psalm 50, continually reminds the people of God that the One who keeps covenant with them, revealed to a community of faith, remains the ultimate judge of all creation!

Why is this important to twenty-first-century individuals and faith communities? First, because we moderns (or postmoderns) are prone to think that we are sovereign and that God's word is not a promise of grace but an entitlement to be granted on demand. Worse yet, we democratic idealists often imply that God ought to answer to majority vote in responding to these desires. The psalmist will have none of that. For this ancient writer, God is benevolent, covenantal, and ultimate. Transcendence is essential to the nature of the Deity.

Second, the psalmist also resists that age-old human tendency to shape God in our own image. God's thoughts are God's own. To receive God's self-revelation, to make covenant with God, does not entitle humanity to claim excessive intimacy with the God who can "tear you apart" if you forget the covenant (v. 22).

Third, from a historical perspective, Christians have, in varying ways, attempted to read the poetry of the psalmist in light of the teaching of Jesus of Nazareth, who we believe mediated divine transcendence and immanence with the insights of the Logos, a Palestinian Jew, the Word made flesh. It is no easy task, an old/new covenant worth considering "from the rising of the sun to its setting" (v. 1).

BILL J. LEONARD

Pastoral Perspective

spiritual practice, human relationships, and regard for the world.

Psalm 50 is a highly theatrical text; nonetheless, we are brought up short by the dramatic, even violent tone of God's fury against "the wicked" in verse 22; "I will tear you apart," God vows, evoking the image of a lion ripping limbs from its kill.[2] That is not all. Devastatingly, God also vows that when the hand of retribution begins its gruesome work, "there will be no one to deliver."

Threats like these aim to move God's people to awe, remorse, and conversion, but the God who hurls them will surely strike many people as a Deity begging to be despised. Before such a God, you keep your head down—not to adore, but to avoid detection. How can we reconcile God's vehemence here with the mercy and steadfast love that otherwise characterize the Lord's dealings with humanity in Scripture?

To resolve the apparent contradiction, some pastors explain the divine anger as a time-bound feature of the biblical God's anthropomorphic character. Others try to find a balance in the whole of Scripture between divine justice and divine mercy. Others draw an unfortunate supersessionist distinction between the "angry God of the Old Testament" and the "loving God of the New Testament" in order to reassure the Christian faithful that *their* God would never do such things to *them*.

The ferocity of God's threat in this psalm might instead present an opportunity to explore with repulsed parishioners its metaphorical power when viewed in the context of the vast destructive scope of human sin. One might ask whether this picture of an outraged God is any more frightening than the picture of God's world today—abused, polluted, and despoiled. (Call those witnesses from the creation, let *them* speak!) Is the fury of God more terrible than the fury of human greed, warfare, and genocide? If it can be said poetically that sometimes God feels like tearing us apart, are we who hate one another already showing God just how it is done? The God of Psalm 50 who threatens not to save us does in fact hasten to save us, time and time again. Do our own threats have the same outcome? Are we more in peril from each other than we are from God? Of whom should we really be afraid?

J. MARY LUTI

2. Ibid., 179.

Proper 14 (Sunday between August 7 and August 13 inclusive)

Exegetical Perspective

the covenant (Exod. 19:16–19). The connection to Sinai and the covenant is deepened by God's calling the people "my faithful ones who made a covenant with me by sacrifice" (v. 5). "Faithful ones" here translates *hasidim*, which indicates those who are committed to the covenant, and the allusion to sacrifice recalls the ritual sacrifices that ratified the covenant at Sinai (Exod. 24:3–8). Translated as in the NRSV, this verse invites the people to remember the covenant of Sinai, which defines their relationship to God. An alternative translation brings this out of the past and into the present or future, rendering the underlying Hebrew participle as a "participle of the immediate future," resulting in the following: "those about to make a covenant with me."[2] Such a reading would strengthen the interpretation of this psalm as part of a covenant-renewal ceremony.

Having summoned witnesses and initiated the lawsuit, God now brings two indictments against Israel. The first states that Israel's sacrifices are being made for the wrong reasons. God does not need the sacrifices, since the animals already belong to God and God does not require them for food, as was often the case in ancient Near Eastern understandings of sacrifice. This should not be read as a call to abolish the sacrificial system altogether, however, which is clear from verses 8 and 14. Rather, this psalm suggests that sacrifices should be made as an expression of thanksgiving (vv. 14, 23). This argument is similar to a variety of prophetic critiques of Israel's sacrifices (in addition to Isa. 1:10–20, see Hos. 6:6; Amos 5:21–24; Mic. 6:1–8).

Beginning in verse 16, God calls Israel "the wicked" and issues the second indictment: hypocrisy. Though Israel recites God's laws and speaks the words of the covenant, they ignore these words and act in direct violation of God's commandments. Of particular concern seem to be laws from the Ten Commandments against stealing, adultery, and giving false witness, although these are probably meant to be representative rather than exhaustive.

Rather than offering warnings of specific punishments, as one might expect in a prophetic oracle, the psalm concludes in verse 23 with a teaching: those who offer sacrifices as thanksgiving to God and follow the way of God will know God's salvation.

JOHN W. VEST

Homiletical Perspective

the form, the ones who read only thanksgiving in their *Book of Order/Book of Common Prayer*/hymnal/favorite Bible translation/<insert your idol here> .

Now here is the good news: the court in which God brings suit against you for forgetting God is most decidedly not like any court you have ever known. This is not The People's Court. It is *God's* court, where there is no claim or pretense that what is going on here is human justice. You will not win this case; you lost before you walked in. The exercise was never about winning or losing or justice or punishment. It was always and only about God's love for you—about mercy, about salvation from the small things that we worry about until they tear us apart.

The sacrifices and the organs and the Communion particulars and the worship aids are tools and pointers, symbols and holy gifts God has given for the ordering of our lives and the shaping of our worship. In fact, they are the very means God uses to seal the covenant (v. 5). They, however, are for *us*, not for God, and to think that God is someone like us, who need such things, is to make idols.

The reason God is bothering to go through with this whole (slightly silly) courtroom drama is to remind you who you are: a creature of God, fashioned with God's own hands, filled with God's own breath, reflecting God's own glory. It is to remind your church who it is too: a creation of God, the body of Christ fashioned with God's own hands, filled with God's own breath, reflecting God's own glory. It is to remind you that, for people like you and churches like yours, gratitude is all that is needed to send you out of the courtroom and toward salvation.

Which, you will agree, explains the singing.

QUINN G. CALDWELL

---

2. Peter C. Craigie, *Psalms 1–50*, Word Biblical Commentary 19 (Waco: Word, 1983), 365.

Hebrews 11:1-3, 8-16

[1]Now faith is the assurance of things hoped for, the conviction of things not seen. [2]Indeed, by faith our ancestors received approval. [3]By faith we understand that the worlds were prepared by the word of God, so that what is seen was made from things that are not visible. . . .

[8]By faith Abraham obeyed when he was called to set out for a place that he was to receive as an inheritance; and he set out, not knowing where he was going. [9]By faith he stayed for a time in the land he had been promised, as in a foreign land, living in tents, as did Isaac and Jacob, who were heirs with him of the same promise. [10]For he looked forward to the city that has foundations, whose architect and builder is God. [11]By faith he received power of procreation, even though he was too old—and Sarah herself was barren—because he

Theological Perspective

The dog days of August, roughly midway between Easter/Pentecost and Christmas/Epiphany, often seem a time of spiritual lethargy in churches in the Northern Hemisphere. Thus the lections from Hebrews 11 and 12, assigned for three consecutive Sundays between August 7 and August 27, may be heard as a plea for patience until schools reopen and life gets back to normal. However, the life situation of the readers addressed by Hebrews was considerably more menacing. While it is unlikely that the members of the congregation were facing martyrdom (12:4), some had already been subjected to prison and plunder of possessions, and most had experienced hostility, ridicule, and shame, simply because following Jesus, a crucified savior, set them at odds with the surrounding culture (10:32–39). How does one encourage other Christians to remain steadfast, to persevere through difficult days?

The unknown author of Hebrews approaches the audience through their experience of faith. This book has already reminded the readers that the once-for-all nature of Jesus' sacrifice should bolster their confidence in the realities of faith, hope, and love, sufficient to sustain hope and provoke each other to deeds of love. It has warned them of the judgment that awaits those who have spurned the Lord Jesus Christ (10:26–31) and recalled earlier

Pastoral Perspective

Do we live in an age of faith? There is much talk in popular religious circles about how America is approaching a new awakening in religious fervor.

Religious historians write that the type and fervor of religious belief is often cyclical. The Middle Ages is referred to as an Age of Faith. During this period, intense belief reigned. The Reformation has been called an Age of Revelation, where religious people renewed their emphasis on the revealed Word in Scripture. The seventeenth century began the Age of Reason, with Thomas Paine, Thomas Jefferson, and others arguing for the power of the mind in critiquing religion. The twentieth century has been called an Age of Experience, as charismatic faiths have exploded and modern Americans have looked to experience religion. A well-known writer on the history of U.S. foreign policy stated recently that his next book will be entitled the "Age of Faith," for he believes the twenty-first century will again be a time where intense belief reigns.

As we think about pastoring our congregations through word and deed, few items are more critical than the faith of our people. It is by God's grace, through faith, that we receive salvation. Faith in God is what keeps our people going in the face of life's challenges. Faith is the subject that the author of Hebrews tackles in chapter 11.

considered him faithful who had promised. [12]Therefore from one person, and this one as good as dead, descendants were born, "as many as the stars of heaven and as the innumerable grains of sand by the seashore."

[13]All of these died in faith without having received the promises, but from a distance they saw and greeted them. They confessed that they were strangers and foreigners on the earth, [14]for people who speak in this way make it clear that they are seeking a homeland. [15]If they had been thinking of the land that they had left behind, they would have had opportunity to return. [16]But as it is, they desire a better country, that is, a heavenly one. Therefore God is not ashamed to be called their God; indeed, he has prepared a city for them.

Exegetical Perspective

Hebrews 11 has been described as an encomium (enthusiastic, warm praise) on faith. The theme of faith is announced in Hebrews 10:37–39 with a quotation from Habakkuk 2:3–4 (which is blended with a few words from Isa. 26:20); now chapter 11 develops that theme in some detail through examples. The initial words in Greek of verse 1 are a notoriously difficult challenge for translators. The verse begins with a form of the verb "to be," rendered "is" in most translations, so that the statement reads like a definition in ancient writings, especially philosophical documents. The NRSV reads, "Now faith is the assurance of things hoped for, the conviction of things not seen." Some interpreters suggest translating or paraphrasing "is . . . assurance" with the words "gives substance to" and "is . . . conviction" with the words "offers a proving of." In any case, it is important to understand "assurance" and "conviction" (or alternate words) in the active sense of "faith" that this passage in Hebrews 11 assumes and describes. In brief, the author of Hebrews says that faith gives substance to things that are neither present nor visible. In other words, faith makes real in the present God's things, often thought of as *future*, but more essentially as *eternal*—such as God's own faithfulness (see v. 11).

Homiletical Perspective

These excerpted verses from chapter 11 of the Letter to the Hebrews contain two so-called gems: one of the most frequently quoted verses of Scripture, "Now faith is the assurance of things hoped for, the conviction of things not seen" (v. 1), and a story well worn in its familiarity, the recapped Abraham and Sarah narrative. Preaching on such "old standards" can be one of the most challenging tasks for a preacher. The difficulty lies in making the familiar fresh, in reformulating the biblical wisdom so that it can be heard again. Conversely, some preachers will have the opposite problem—a congregation lacking biblical literacy, who heretofore may have heard this definition of faith only paraphrased outside of its biblical context and who are vague about who these Abraham and Sarah characters are.

It is crucial to consider the working scriptural knowledge of the congregation. Are they acquainted with Abraham and Sarah, and if so, how well? An understanding even of the movement from Hebrew Scriptures to the New Testament before unpacking the actual movements of Abraham and Sarah on their geographic journey will help catch everyone up at the outset. Taking the time to teach the biblical arc is well worth the effort, and an opportunity that is not always so neatly presented.

Hebrews 11:1-3, 8-16

Theological Perspective

occasions of persecution when the congregation persevered by mutually supporting each other. In chapter 11, the author explores yet other dimensions of faith: readers are reminded that what they hope for is intimately connected to their experience of faith ("the assurance of things hoped for") and that they should not expect their faith ("the conviction of things not seen") to be supported by the surrounding culture (v. 1). The writer assures them that God will commend their faithfulness (v. 2) and then begins a litany of heroes who have embodied faith even in the face of disappointment.

Faith is a multifaceted reality, with strange, even paradoxical, features. Born in a revelatory event, it is at once the gift of God's unconditional love and a human response of trust and gratitude that issues in deeds of love and justice. Faith is a way of knowing that constantly seeks understanding, leading to theological reflection and to faith as "belief" in various doctrines about God, Jesus, creation, sin, salvation, and human destiny. Faith is often presented, rightly as here, as that which enables one to cope with the trials and tribulations of life, but Hebrews 11 reminds us of another paradox: faith is also that which has provoked the hostility and ridicule being heaped upon this Christian community.

Despite the claim of 11:1 that faith is not sight ("the conviction of things not seen"), it can be helpful to think of faith as a kind of seeing, at least metaphorically. Many come to faith, for example, by "seeing" something compelling in the life, teachings, death, and resurrection of Jesus or in the communal life of Jesus' followers. Faith, then, is the perception that the way of Jesus is the way to become who I most truly am, a creature in the image of God. Faith includes the awareness that the meaning of life is not to be found in the accumulation of wealth, power, and privilege, but in loving God and neighbor. The "way" of Jesus puts one at odds with the dominant social script, which usually does see the meaning of life in the accumulation of worldly goods.

When faith leads an individual or group to challenge the values of the dominant culture, people are often marginalized and excluded from positions of power and privilege. They may even be regarded as subhuman and thus legitimate targets of hostility, ridicule, and economic discrimination. The refusal of the Christians to worship Caesar or the Roman gods, for example, and their worship of a crucified savior, executed as a traitor to the empire, must have seemed utterly foolish and even subversive to those steeped in worldly wisdom (see 1 Cor. 1:18–25). The

Pastoral Perspective

The Greek word for faith is *pistis*. The apostle Paul used *pistis* frequently in his writings, thirty-five times in Romans alone. *Pistis* had a checkered past in the culture of the early church. In Greek mythology, Pistis was one of the spirits who escaped Pandora's box and fled back to heaven, abandoning humanity. In Luke's Gospel, for example, when Jesus wonders, "Will the Son of Man find faith on earth?" (Luke 18:8), he was speaking to a Hellenistic culture that believed the spirit of Pistis had already left.

The book of Hebrews was written partly to combat such melancholy and to encourage Christians who were having trouble holding onto hope when Christ did not return immediately after his resurrection. In chapter 11, the writer of the book of Hebrews gives us a valuable definition of faith/*pistis*, "the assurance of things hoped for, the conviction of things not seen." The Greek word for "assurance" is *hypostasis*. It is a word that has much to do with our subjective belief. The Bible often relates *hypostatis* to both faith and hope, for our faith is inextricably wed to our hopes.

When pastors conduct pastoral care, we soon realize that within our congregations people all hope for things, yearn for things, and in faith ask God for things. Sometimes their prayers are answered. Children are born. They get the job. The treatment works.

Sometimes things take longer, and like the audience of the book of Hebrews who were waiting for Christ's return, our people are still waiting for an answer from God.

In the Old Testament, Abraham and Sarah also waited a long time for an answer from God. They struggled to have children, something many people in our congregations these days struggle with as well. Abraham obeyed God and stayed true to God so much that he followed God without knowing where God was leading.

It is difficult to follow God when we are not sure where God is leading. When we do not see evidence of action, we begin to wonder whether God is watching over us. We hope that God is watching. We see loved ones grow ill and pray in faith that God will hold their future. Then every once in awhile something positive happens in our faith, something special that restores our conviction, strengthens our hearts, and reminds us why we believe what we believe.

Faith matters. Our faith gives assurance that God has our best interests at heart, knows what we hope for, and holds our future.

We can hope, but in faith we often have to trust God and other people with our future and find our

Exegetical Perspective

Verse 2 is a paradigmatic statement introducing the long series of noteworthy ancients ("ancestors") who in one way or another were approved or attested (by God) in and through faith. In various ways, the faith mentioned here is *trust in God*. Verse 3, in turn, is the first of eighteen sentences in this section of Hebrews (vv. 3–31) that begin with the words "by faith" (vv. 3, 4, 5, 7, 8, 9, 11, 17, 20, 21, 22, 23, 24, 27, 28, 29, 30, 31). In this particular verse, the author tells the readers that faith allows them to apprehend the otherwise unknowable truth that by God's word all creation (NRSV: "the worlds"; literally, "the ages") came into being. Here, there is a striking implicit parallelism: As *by faith* the believers experience the present reality of God's hoped-for future, so *by the word of God* things were brought into being that once had no existence. The implication of this parallel is that God's word is the force or source that acts in faith to bring into existence that which once did not exist. Creation itself offers a model of the workings of faith in the life of the believers.

The next section of material in this lesson comprises verses 8–12. These lines focus on the faith of Abraham and Sarah. Three times (vv. 8, 9, 11) the opening words of a sentence are "by faith," registering the dynamic quality of faith that produces a linear effect (some action) in the life of the person(s) mentioned. In verse 8 the first example of faith in action is Abraham's obeying God when he receives his call to depart from his homeland of Mesopotamia in order to go out to a land that he is promised—without knowing where or seeing what it is. Because of his faithfulness, Abraham becomes heir to a new land. The story of Abraham's call and his obedient response to it occur in Genesis 12.

Verse 9 tells how Abraham sojourns by faith in the promised land. One should recall, however, that he does so without ever possessing any more of that land than the small field near Hebron that he buys from Ephron the Hittite to be a burial ground for his family. Abraham is never the possessor of the land that is promised to him; rather, he wanders on the land and labors there without owning the land. His nomadic existence is recognized by the reference to his "living in tents," and the fact that his heirs continue for some time to live in that same way is registered by the mention of Isaac's and Jacob's living in tents and their being fellow heirs with Abraham to the promise (see Gen. 12, 13, 15, 18, 23, 35).

In verse 10 the author makes a statement that clarifies how and why Abraham is able to live as he

Homiletical Perspective

Another issue for Western, twenty-first-century Christians may be with the working definition of faith found in the first verse, but this is an "issue" that can be an opportunity for the preacher to open up a world of exploration. Both at first glance and by some reputation, the opening lines and the examples of faithfulness offered throughout the reading can seem to lean in the direction of faithfulness as trite certainty. The postmodern mind-set generally rejects such platitudes. Upon closer reading, however, and with attention to the journey motif heavy in the passage, an examination of faith with regard to "things hoped for . . . things not seen" (v. 1) can be quite meaningful for contemporary congregations. A conversation about the mysteries of our world and the movements of God as alluded to in the opening verses will suit the postmodern ethos. Even the secular physicist might agree with the idea that "what is seen was made from things that are not visible" (v. 3).

One other specific issue of sensitivity that recurs throughout the biblical narrative is the recounting of Sarah's miraculous pregnancy following years of barrenness. For women and men facing myriad fertility issues, these stories can be particularly challenging and heartwrenching. In the context of a careful conversation about faithfulness and its fruits, the pastoral preacher will keep in mind that not everyone's prayers are answered. This is, perhaps, always the admonition to the preacher of miraculous healings, but as childlessness is neither a disease nor something that is often publicly discussed, caution bears explicitness.

The recurring theme of journey aids the preacher in approaching this text. Abraham and Sarah "set out for a place . . . and he set out, not knowing where he was going (v. 8)." They live a nomadic existence in tents, setting up no permanent home, but always "look[ing] forward to the city that has foundations" (v. 10). Abraham, Sarah, and their descendants are "strangers and foreigners on the earth, for people who speak in this way make it clear that they are seeking a homeland" (vv. 13–14). Clearly the expedition or crossing as a means of explaining faithfulness has been richly explored. From *Canterbury Tales* and *Pilgrim's Progress* to the writings of Teilhard de Chardin, travelogue and spiritual autobiography are well-matched genres.

The corresponding puzzle piece of this image in the reading is the offering of a homeland; there is a place to which Abraham is called. The item of interest for the preacher is to explore the ramifications for both Abraham and the contemporary hearer of this

Hebrews 11:1-3, 8-16

Theological Perspective

struggle becomes a constant daily effort to sustain an alternative vision amid hostility and ridicule. Here faith presents itself as courage. One should ask whether Christians in North America, who find themselves relatively affluent and holding positions of power and privilege in the dominant culture, can truly identify with the plight of the community of Hebrews. Perhaps one should push further and ask, Have Christians in North America failed to see the difference between being an American and being a Christian?

The recitation of persons and events from the past suggests that faith is not adequately defined by a single individual or community. It must be seen in terms of a larger story that reaches back at least to Abraham, who trusted the promises of God and left his home in Ur without knowing exactly where he was going. None of these ancestors received fully the promise that had been offered. They remained strangers and foreigners, sojourners and pilgrims, even in the land of promise. They died in faith without seeing the promise fulfilled.

What exactly is the promise that the writer of Hebrews holds forth for his readers? Is it otherworldly, simply a matter of going to heaven when I die? The text can be read in this way, for clearly the promise is a "heavenly" country (v. 16) that extends beyond death. It is a "homeland" (v. 14), a place where we can be fully at home, free of the conflicts and contradictions that beset our present existence. Drawing upon images from Jesus' parables about the kingdom of God, one imagines a community of worship, deep friendships between former enemies, a banquet table open to all persons. Strangely, however, precisely because the promise reaches beyond death, it often invades the present through hope, enabling one to see the wondrous beauty already here and inspiring new possibilities for this earthly existence. Perhaps this invasion of hope also renews the courage of faith and enables the faithful to live freely and meaningfully in this beautiful but dangerous world.

JOHN C. SHELLEY

Pastoral Perspective

assurance outside ourselves. We have to have faith that, as the author of Hebrews writes, God has prepared a better place, a "heavenly one," for us, as God prepared for Abraham.

The second part of the definition of faith in chapter 11 is "the conviction of things not seen." The Greek word for conviction, *elenchos*, implies an objective side of faith. It is the proof beyond a reasonable doubt that there is something worth believing in.

Believing in something is what faith is about. Our faith is a gift of God's grace. It comes through God's reaching out through the Holy Spirit to allow us to trust Jesus for salvation.

Faith was so important to John Calvin that there are more words in Calvin's *Institutes* dedicated to faith than any other subject. Calvin thought of faith as the "firm knowledge of God's benevolence towards us," the *elenchos* of faith, the conviction, the certainty, that God cares about us all.

Two centuries ago, in the Age of Reason, when most people lived on farms, made their own clothes, and raised their own food, perhaps one could be an island. Today, however, we have to have faith in the people around us. We have to trust the food prepared at the restaurant, trust the pilot of the airplane, and trust the caregiver at the day care. That is something that many people in our congregations struggle with.

We cannot watch every part of our own lives and those we love. Fortunately, we do not have to, for we know from Scripture and the Holy Spirit that God is watching over us. What gives our faith a firm foundation is that Jesus Christ is Lord and holds our future, come what may on earth. Faith is ultimately a gift of the Holy Spirit. Our opportunity is to respond to God's initiative of such grace.

DAVID E. GRAY

Exegetical Perspective

does: His vision is not strictly earthbound; rather, Abraham looks beyond the temporal binding of his life to the full reality of God and the fulfillment of God's promises ("he looked forward to the city that has foundations, whose architect and builder is God," v. 10). This city of God contrasts with the tents in which Abraham and his family live. God's "place" has a permanence, a security, a stability that goes beyond mere earthly existence.

Verses 11–12 have parallels in Genesis 15, 17, 21, 22, 32. The verses are marked by a serious problem of translation (and textual criticism). Some translations read "By faith Sarah" and others "By faith he [Abraham]" at the beginning of verse 11. More contemporary translations and commentaries take the reading "By faith he" to be the original text for at least two reasons: First, the phrase means "received power to deposit seed," not "received power to conceive"—a reference to impregnating, not being impregnated. Second, verses 10 and 12 have Abraham as their subject, so that taking Sarah as the subject of the statement constitutes an interruption in the flow of the narrative. Sarah is included in the statement, but probably not as the subject of the sentence.

Verse 12 rounds out this section, having parallels to Genesis 15, 22, 32. The magnitude of God's power and faithfulness in promise is registered through the reference to and description of Abraham as being (for the purposes of procreation) "as good as dead"; it is evident that God's power alone, working through Abraham's faith, brings about the miracle of the fulfillment of God's promises to Abraham. In other words, God is faithful to the promise made to Abraham, and in turn Abraham and Sarah by their faith are able to experience God's true faithfulness.

MARION L. SOARDS

Homiletical Perspective

place's being located in this world or in the next. The language is abundant: "the land he had been promised" (v. 9); "the city that has foundations, whose architect and builder is God" (v. 10); "they were strangers and foreigners on the earth . . . seeking a homeland. If they had been thinking of the land that they had left behind, they would have had opportunity to return. But as it is, they desire a better country, that is, a heavenly one. Therefore God is not ashamed to be called their God; indeed, he has prepared a city for them" (vv. 13–16). Meditation on home, city, and the land—both places known to us and those realms about which we merely guess around the edges—can be extraordinarily meaningful to a population that is increasingly transient and in search of connection and rootedness in every sense of the word.

The tension between the journey and the arriving, between the road and the homeland—not to mention the extreme pull between this world and "a better country, that is, a heavenly one"—is grist for much conversation between pulpit and pew. A conversation about our two homes as Christians can be poignant, and our faithfulness in the journey between the two is a gem worth looking at anew. Engaging the sweep of the biblical narrative from our earliest ancestors to the earliest days of the church in one short narrative, we encounter some of the classic motifs of the spiritual life writ large: the mysteries of faith and the journey of a spiritual life. The challenge is to work with the reading without relying on generalities or assumptions.

KATHERINE M. BUSH

Luke 12:32-40

³²"Do not be afraid, little flock, for it is your Father's good pleasure to give you the kingdom. ³³Sell your possessions, and give alms. Make purses for yourselves that do not wear out, an unfailing treasure in heaven, where no thief comes near and no moth destroys. ³⁴For where your treasure is, there your heart will be also.

³⁵"Be dressed for action and have your lamps lit; ³⁶be like those who are waiting for their master to return from the wedding banquet, so that they may open the door for him as soon as he comes and knocks. ³⁷Blessed are those slaves whom the master finds alert when he comes; truly I tell you, he will fasten his belt and have them sit down to eat, and he will come and serve them. ³⁸If he comes during the middle of the night, or near dawn, and finds them so, blessed are those slaves.

³⁹"But know this: if the owner of the house had known at what hour the thief was coming, he would not have let his house be broken into. ⁴⁰You also must be ready, for the Son of Man is coming at an unexpected hour."

Theological Perspective

There is so much to fear: terrorism; war; the economy; global warming; unemployment, hunger, poverty, homelessness; disease and death. It is impossible to escape: walk the neighborhoods, drive the interstates, see the signs all around. If you prefer, stay at home, where newscasters proclaim the bad news from studio sets, texts crawl at the bottom of television screens, information updates flash in Web browsers, and spam e-mails announce that we are doomed if we do not buy the right products immediately. If we were not afraid before, we are certainly encouraged by the media and our culture to be afraid now. Into that fear, across centuries of human experience, Jesus' teaching offers an extraordinary word of comfort in an increasingly threatening world: "Do not be afraid, little flock, for it is your Father's good pleasure to give you the kingdom" (v. 32).

This is not whistling-in-the-dark comfort, but rather the reassurance that what is seen is not all that is, a reminder that the fears attendant upon earthy living need not have the last word in defining one's life. The pericope weaves a tapestry of claims about God (embodied in Jesus and his teaching) around the tenuous thread of human existence. God is "your Father"; God's "good pleasure" is to give the kingdom, a treasure in heaven that is imperishable. These reminders of God's sovereignty and gracious

Pastoral Perspective

Have you ever caught yourself saying, "I never get anything done in my study at church because I am always being interrupted"? Those who preach often suspect that others can sense just when the ideas that shape a sermon are taking form. That is when the phone rings or the knock sounds at the door. To reveal the workings of the preacher's heart, it may be just as honest to admit that it is often when she is on the verge of claiming ordinary words to convey the mystery of God's presence that the preacher blinks. For pastor and people alike, there are many distractions that pull one away from God's word, many projects and pursuits that divert attention from the things of God.

The Gospel text for this week entices the hearer to place first things first. The things of God are to be given the most urgent priority in every Christian's life. Neither fear nor worldly distraction is to lure the children away from God's tender, attentive care. There are no purses, or stock portfolios, of human creation that will not wear out in time. God promises to surprise with the gift of the kingdom those who stand ready and waiting to receive this singular treasure.

There is nothing easy about such waiting in an impatient world. This is especially true when we consider how much of the busyness of parish life is

Exegetical Perspective

The context for these assorted sayings involves ulti-mates. Jesus is in the midst of his journey to Jerusalem to fulfill God's ultimate plan of salvation accom-plished in his death, resurrection, and ascension (Luke 9:22, 30–31, 44–45, 51). In 12:1–3, 8–12 Jesus speaks about that which will ultimately be revealed and how the Spirit will ultimately teach disciples what to say in adverse situations. In 12:4–7 he reminds them who is ultimately in control and therefore should be feared. Subsequently Jesus teaches that riches are not the ultimate concern for one's life (12:13–21), nor should disciples be overly anxious about such penultimate things as life, food, or clothing (12:22–30). Rather, the ultimate concern of life entails being rich toward God and seeking God's kingdom (12:21, 31). The text at hand will build on the theme of ultimates as it involves both possessions and the Parousia.

The text opens (v. 32) with an imperative, an identity, and the underlying reason for each. The straightforward imperative is, "Do not be afraid." This recalls similar imperatives given to Zechariah (1:13), Mary (1:30), the shepherds (2:10), Simon Peter (5:10), Jairus (8:50), and the disciples (12:4, 7). In these instances, fear is a human response impeding one's perception of God's will and ways at work in their lives. In this context, fear entails failing to let go of one's anxieties over the basic necessities for life (vv.

Homiletical Perspective

Who can manage to be ever on the alert—never dozing off or fuzzing out? Calls to alertness do have strategic value in specific contexts. They can command attention to orders issued immediately thereafter ("Listen up!" "Now hear this!"). They can redirect focus from one angle of vision to another ("Look at *that*!" "Observe the following!"). They can snap us to sharp awareness in the face of emergency or imminent threat ("Watch out!"). They can call us back to task when we get weary or lazy in the middle of our watch ("Wake up!"). It is not without reason that duty watches are assigned in shifts; that "red alerts" are issued judiciously by officials charged with protecting public safety. Nobody can remain indefinitely on the alert.

Too much unremitting attention can even be counterproductive to the successful culmination of a creative process. Mathematicians, scientists, artists, composers, authors—even preachers—testify that "breakthroughs" of insight often come when (and only when) they have "taken a break" from extended periods of concentration on the complex challenge they are seeking to address.

All this is to suggest that attempts to employ this pericope as a springboard for exhortations on unending vigilance are not likely to be credible or helpful. Engaging though the Lukan images are, the

Luke 12:32-40

Theological Perspective

protection, along with the promise of the Son's return, serve as antidotes to the human problems of misplaced confidence, complacency, and fear of an uncertain future.

Given the number of reminders not to worry or be afraid that appear in Luke 12, the first hearers of this gospel message must have had reason to fear many things. What about us, about you? Are you afraid of being killed, Jesus asks? Remember that God is concerned even with the hairs of your head (12:4–7). Are you worried about having the right words when you must make a defense of the gospel? Have confidence that the Holy Spirit will give you the words to say (12:8–12). Does fear of an uncertain future cause you to disregard the needs of others and to stash your possessions in a spirit of greediness? Recall that you cannot take it with you at the end of your life (12:13–21). Are you worried about your life, about food or clothing—or, one might add, about organic produce, designer shirts, stylish cars, a fat bank account, or any of the other outward signs that one has "made it" in the eyes of the world? At even a more basic level, are you afraid of starvation and nakedness? Do not let your concern for these things turn you away from what is most important: striving for the kingdom (or reign) of God (12:22–31). It is not necessary to be anxious about life and death (human finitude) or about food and clothing (earthly possessions). These are human means of protection and well-being, but they compare little with God's means. Worrying about them will not make a difference, in one's life or in one's death.

"Do not be afraid, little flock, for it is your Father's good pleasure to give you the kingdom." This is not a God who, after creating the universe, sits back and dispassionately watches it all unfold. This is a God who attends to sparrows, ravens, and lilies, a God whose concern for humankind extends to the very hairs on our heads, a God whose desire is to give the treasure of heaven. These reminders of God's intimate concern can help the preacher to avoid turning the imminent eschatology underlying the passage into one more harbinger of fear. To be sure, one can find passages in Luke that rather easily lend themselves to sermons emphasizing the judgment that is coming or warn of possible punishment (e.g., Luke 19:12–27). However, in this passage, the eschatology focuses not so much on the end times as on the end ways. The consistent message throughout the passage is not, "Be ready so that you will avoid punishment," but, rather, "Be ready so that you will receive blessing." After all,

Pastoral Perspective

rooted in anxiety and fear about the future. What would happen if we really left the future up to God?

Parish programs are designed to keep members engaged. Church activities are targeted for specific demographics, assuming that there needs to be something particularly attractive for each life stage or people will drift away. Much of congregational life gives the impression that Jesus told his disciples to *stay busy* rather than instructing them to have confidence in God's return and to await that day with eager and generous hearts. It is the rare pastor who does not feel similarly compelled to race through the week, running from hospital visit to Bible study to planning session, proving the importance of the pastoral office.

In this week's Gospel lesson Jesus speaks a surprising word of comfort to all whose lives are speeding along at this frantic pace. *"Do not be afraid, little flock, for it is your Father's good pleasure to give you the kingdom"* (v. 32). Simply said, what comes as a gift does not have to be purchased with one's wealth, which the faithful are free to lavish on others in need. Not shame but amazingly tender concern stands at the core of this Gospel text. The pastor's challenge is to help the congregation hear this as an invitation to trust that their future rests in the gracious promises and presence of God.

When anxiety and fear beset a community of faith—which happens everywhere from time to time, snatching away the congregation's confidence like a petty thief—only God can restore what has been lost. This Gospel text offers several surprising images of such a God. The wise pastor will seek a way to set those before the congregation with subtlety and grace.

The first is the image of God's *good pleasure* in giving away the treasure that does not fade or fail. The preacher may invite the congregation to ponder where and when such a gracious God has been encountered in the past. Were there periods of dramatic missional energy and growth earlier in the congregation's history? Was there a time when people were brave, patient, and calm in the face of a crisis? Are there locally known giants in the faith whose willingness to set aside personal gain allowed them to be exemplary in their trust in God's provision for the future? Such specific stories, tapping the congregation's own history and memory, enliven any discussion of this text.

The second image comes in the curious story Jesus tells of the master who returns to his household late at night. To illustrate for the disciples

Exegetical Perspective

22–30a) and forgetting that God is the loving divine provider of our needs (12:30b–32; 11:1–13). The identity Jesus gives to his disciples is "little flock" (v. 32), which reinforces their ultimate dependency on the very care and protection which God provides. The underlying reason members of this little flock are not to fear is that it was God's good pleasure to give them the kingdom in the first place.

Three important points need to be noted regarding Jesus' claim in verse 32b. First, God's good pleasure (or God's delightful decision) to give helpless disciples the kingdom is directly related to the divine pleasure expressed at Jesus' birth (2:14) and after Jesus' baptism (3:22), as well as God's pleasure at revealing ultimate meanings to infants (10:21). Second, in the Greek, the verb expressing divine pleasure (*eudokēsen*) stands in the aorist tense, indicating completed action in the past. In other words, God's delightful decision has already taken place. Thus disciples seek God's kingdom (v. 31) precisely because God already decided to give them this kingdom. Third, "kingdom" does not simply mean eternal life in the sweet by-and-by. Here "kingdom" refers to God's active reign over heaven, which Jesus is now inaugurating on earth through his ministry (1:33; 4:43; 8:1; 9:11; 11:20; 17:20–21). It involves God's lordship over human hearts, minds, values, and actions. God has delightedly decided to include us in this royal rule so that our identity and activity are totally transformed.

This prior divine decision not only grounds the imperative not to fear in verse 32a but also empowers the imperatives to sell, give, and make in verse 33. Jesus' divine investment program turns first-century giving patterns upside down. In that social reality of exploitative reciprocity, one gave only because one expected to receive enhanced status in return.[1] God, however, has already enhanced one's status by giving one the kingdom. Therefore one responds to this divine giving by enacting the values and standards of the kingdom, which here include selling possessions, giving alms, and making purses that contain ultimate, inexhaustible, heavenly treasure. One's heart, then, is not set on getting rich by accumulating human treasure but is set on what God ultimately treasures, which is compassion and mercy for those in need (1:50–55, 72–79; 3:10–14; 4:18–19; 6:27–31, 36; 9:1–6; 10:1–9, 25–37; 12:34).

The text's movement from possessions (vv. 33–34) to Parousia (vv. 35–40) is not as unnatural as

1. Joel Green, *The Gospel of Luke*, New International Commentary on the New Testament (Grand Rapids: Eerdmans, 1997), 495–96.

Homiletical Perspective

simple fact is that neither servants awaiting the return of their banqueting master nor homeowners on guard against thieves can remain on watch 24/7. Fetching though the phrase may be, "expect the unexpected" is problematic both logically and practically.

Furthermore, exhortations to unconditional alertness may not even be in line with the trajectory of Jesus' teaching, as Luke has just deployed it. "Be dressed for action," "Be like those waiting for their master to return"—these injunctions must be orchestrated with those immediately preceding them: "Do not worry about your life," "Do not be afraid, little flock, for it is your father's good pleasure to give you the kingdom" (vv. 22, 32). How ironic if, with the best intentions, today's preacher engendered furrowed-brow fixations concerning the return of the Lord or the advent of the kingdom—fixations not altogether unlike the "possession obsession" that Jesus' teachings have just been at pains to dislodge!

Is there a healthier, more practical (perhaps more faithful) understanding of watchful waiting that a sermon from this text can foster? A possible starting point is reconsideration of *last* week's hanging question, what does it mean to be "rich toward God"? in light of two lines from the text for *this* week: "it is your Father's good pleasure to give you the kingdom," and (describing the action of the master who returns to find his servants alert) "he will . . . have them sit down to eat, and he will come and serve them" (vv. 32, 37).

Presumably the reason Jesus enjoins his disciples to relinquish their possessions is not unrelated to his assessment of the rich man as a fool. The resources his disciples are disposed to preserve (and the resources the affluent farmer is determined to multiply) are dangerous distractions from their "duty watches"—namely, attending to the riches of the kingdom it is God's pleasure to bestow. Being rich toward God is not primarily about putting sizable sums in the offering plate. Making moth- and thief-proof purses is not merely a better business strategy than building bigger barns. What Jesus enjoins, rather, is an orientation toward the whole of life as abundant gift from a generous God—a gift that can, therefore, be given away with abandon.

Neither receiving nor sharing is possible when hands are grasped and fingers clenched. Being "rich toward God" involves (as Ignatian spirituality counsels) a "generosity of spirit" that opens our perceptions toward manifestations of *God's* generosity that are always present, but often at the

Luke 12:32-40

Theological Perspective

those who are ready when the master returns will be the recipients of a heavenly feast (vv. 37–38).

In theological terms, God's providence enables a response that runs counter to the human propensity to be afraid, a response that challenges the tendency to hold on to what one has, in order to protect against what might happen. "Sell your possessions, and give alms" (v. 33), Jesus says, calling on his followers to place their confidence in the imperishable things of heaven, rather than in the moth-eaten things in their own backyards. The passage challenges us with a simple test: Do we want to live lives of taking, or do we want to live lives of giving? The answer we give reveals the truth of our hearts (v. 34) and opens (or closes) us to the blessings that God is prepared to give.

The blessings offered are known most fully by those who are no longer afraid of potential danger, darkness, and death, those who live the sorts of lives that many persons across time and continents cannot begin to embrace or comprehend. Human sinfulness encourages us to believe that giving, instead of taking, will lead to destitution, deprivation, and desperation. The gospel promises, however, that giving from what we have will make us mindful of the God of blessing, and ready to receive the gifts that God offers.

The less we want to have, the less we need to have. This fact is itself one of the blessings God offers, with compound interest. The less we need to have, the less we need to fear. The less we need to fear, the more we know that a life of giving allows us always to live, not on the brink of destruction, but on the brink of blessing, where we can more readily hear the promise that the "Son of Man is coming at an unexpected hour," desiring not to punish but to bless.

AUDREY WEST

Pastoral Perspective

the importance of being ready and waiting, Jesus pictures God's donning an apron and serving a midnight banquet to those found alert and expectant. Can the congregation imagine this scene depicted in a stained-glass window amid the iconography of the worship space? What would it look like to discover God in their very midst, serving an impromptu meal in the fellowship hall?

The great interruption in this week's Gospel text focuses not on the demands of the overly scheduled life but on God, who comes in surprising ways to offer comfort, assurance, and lasting treasure to God's little flock. The pastor's task is to help steward the congregation's imagination toward those things, finally, that matter to such a God.

Unless God is extremely punctual, arriving in time for the weekend service, it may be that God's promised return will come in the midst of the weekly life of those in the parish. Where might the congregation look to see the kind of God who dons an apron and serves those who wait for the things of God? Would that happen in the break room at the nearby office complex, in the cafeteria of the local hospital, in someone's kitchen at home? Where does the simplicity of God's tender assurance intersect with the frenzy and fretting of an anxious world for these particular followers?

The pastor who addresses the certainty of God's return as a gracious event, rather than a cause for panic, may invite the congregation to hear in this Gospel text an invitation to a more playful, expectant reading of ordinary time. Which knock at the door brings the bearer of God's good pleasure? What act of generosity or almsgiving frees one to peek through the door of heaven? What small steps indicate a confidence in God's good future for this particular congregation? All those questions are part of the richness of this week's Gospel fare.

PATRICIA J. LULL

Exegetical Perspective

one might initially suppose. As noted above, the text continues to focus on ultimates. Now the ultimate focus involves Jesus' climactic coming (i.e., his Parousia), at which time God's kingdom (including our lives within this kingdom) will become complete and manifest reality. The immediate concern in the text is not on the delay of Jesus' coming (which will be introduced in 12:45) but the tension between certainty and uncertainty in relationship to his coming. On the one hand, Jesus' ultimate coming is certain; hence the exhortations to full preparedness in verse 35. On the other hand, the exact timing of his coming is uncertain; hence the negative thief-in-the-night illustration in verse 39.[2]

The image of servants awaiting the coming of their master from a wedding banquet helps stress the importance of consistency and constancy in anticipation of Jesus' coming.[3] The servants who are congratulated (v. 37a, 38b) are those whom the master finds vigilant as they actively anticipate their master's certain return, even though they are uncertain of its timing. In a highly unusual, even countercultural move, Jesus declares that their master will take on the role of servant to honor and wait upon such vigilant servants. This role reversal anticipates Jesus imaging himself as one who renders such service in his death (22:24–27). Hence the eschatological reward for diligent watchfulness involves receiving the benefits of Jesus' own servanthood ministry.

What is the ultimate concern of our lives? This text claims that our ultimate concern is God's kingdom, because it was God's pleasure to include us in this divine reign. Consequently what we need, accumulate, and possess in life is transitory, as is time itself. God's delightful decisions for us empower us to use our possessions and our time to enact the values and agenda of God's kingdom in the present as we anticipate its ultimate coming in the future.

RICHARD P. CARLSON

Homiletical Perspective

edges of awareness, easily overlooked when focus gets obsessive.

How, then, does this relate to the image of servants who watch night and day (as contrasted with a homeowner who fails to effectively anticipate the arrival of a thief)?

Being "on high alert" and being "asleep at the switch" are not our only alternatives. We can focus our anticipation, our watchful waiting, in ways that are neither fixated nor fuzzy. We can systematically cultivate tacit awareness, peripheral vision. There is a difference between being *the* lookout and being *on* the lookout. We can sit loose to what we are naturally disposed (or have been long conditioned) to look for ("Seek out this; look out for that—no matter what!"). Rather, we can (in a memorable phrase from homiletician Gene Lowry) "position ourselves to be surprised."[1]

Surprise is surely what the master's servants experience when he at last appears and turns their expectations upside down—serving the very ones who have served him. The kingdom for which we are instructed to strive is presented to us (as the banquet is to them) not as compensation or achievement, but as gift.

Think back to those "creative people" (composer, artist, author, mathematician, scientist, preacher) who, in taking a break, encounter a breakthrough. It does not "just happen." One must carefully nurture disciplined awareness over time. Through that funded awareness, fresh insight comes while (and from where) one "is not looking." Real mastery in any of these disciplines consists in offering oneself in service to "the givens." That is in sharp contrast to a kind of perception that imposes one's deliberate will (or projects one's unconscious fears) on whatever one encounters. An accomplished painter put it this way: "I listen to the colors, who tell me, in good time, and in no uncertain terms, how I must proceed."[2] The painting thus produced is at once a gift *to*, *from*, and *through* the painter.

Perhaps it does not presume too much of this text to surmise that the servants go about their business simply "with an eye to" the one for whom they are working. In contrast, the house owner is "asleep at the switch" when the thief arrives precisely because he has been looking for that thief so long and hard.

DAVID J. SCHLAFER

---

2. Similarly imagery of Jesus coming as a thief in night can be found in Matt. 24:43–44; 1 Thess. 5:2; 2 Pet. 3:10; Rev. 3:3.

3. Note that vv. 37–38 form a chiasm (i.e., reverse parallelism) with the stress being on the center unit, the master's serving.

A   Blessed are those servants (v. 37a)
  B   Master's coming and finding (v. 37b)
    C   Master's serving (v. 37c)
  B'   Master's coming and finding (v. 38a)
A'   Blessed are those servants (v. 38b)

1. Eugene L. Lowry, *The Sermon: Dancing the Edge of Mystery* (Nashville: Abingdon Press, 1997), 95–100.

2. New York artist Charlotte Lichtblau, personal communication.

PROPER 15 (SUNDAY BETWEEN AUGUST 14 AND AUGUST 20 INCLUSIVE)

Isaiah 5:1-7

¹Let me sing for my beloved
    my love-song concerning his vineyard:
My beloved had a vineyard
    on a very fertile hill.
²He dug it and cleared it of stones,
    and planted it with choice vines;
he built a watchtower in the midst of it,
    and hewed out a wine vat in it;
he expected it to yield grapes,
    but it yielded wild grapes.

³And now, inhabitants of Jerusalem
    and people of Judah,
judge between me
    and my vineyard.
⁴What more was there to do for my vineyard
    that I have not done in it?
When I expected it to yield grapes,
    why did it yield wild grapes?

Theological Perspective

To put this text in context, chapters 5–12 pertain to Isaiah's prophecy during the Syro-Ephraimite war in 734 BCE. The parable of the vineyard (5:1–7) and the passage of "woes" that follows it set forth the coming judgment. Isaiah understands all political success or failure to be directly related to the moral condition of the society. The present crisis is directly attributable to the injustice and unrighteousness (v. 7) presented so vividly in chapter 5.

The insatiable greed of the rich and powerful is reflected in their joining "house to house" and "field to field" (5:8). This is, in effect, the sequestering and enclosing of peasant holdings. They are forming latifundia exploited by absentee owners, a practice condemned by Amos (5:11) and Micah (2:2).[1] There is no place left for the dispossessed common people, and they have no legal recourse. In this judicial system, a bribe readily acquits the guilty and deprives the innocent of their rights (Isa. 5:23).

Isaiah employs the parable method, as do Jesus and many other Old Testament writers. The method engages hearers and invites them to judge for themselves concerning the situation. If they have "ears to hear," they find they themselves have been judged in the process. God's indictment of injustice

1. Joseph Blenkinsopp, *Isaiah 1–39* (New York: Doubleday, 2000), 107.

Pastoral Perspective

Every person in the pews is familiar with the anguish of disappointed expectations. The worst disappointments—the pregnancy that never happened, the promotion that never materialized, the romance that turned into betrayal—can almost ruin us with their bitterness. We have all had the experience of having done everything right, only to have our efforts result in no return. It is not hard for a Christian to hear and understand this song from Isaiah, with its disappointed gardener.

The gardener has done everything right. The land was fertile; the work was proper and thorough. The gardener did everything to protect this vineyard and help it grow, so that it would bear sweet grapes for the enjoyment and nourishment of many, but the vineyard yielded wild, bitter grapes with large seeds and very little fruit, as if the gardener had planted nothing at all. What he tasted was disappointment.

The gardener turns now to his sympathetic audience and asks a question: "What more was there to do that I have not done?" (v. 4). The implication is clear—nothing more. The gardener did everything right, but the vineyard failed. He started out singing a love song for his vineyard; now he sings a dirge for a disaster, and it ends on a note of finality: "What more was there to do?" The listener knows the answer: nothing.

340   *Proper 15 (Sunday between August 14 and August 20 inclusive)*

⁵And now I will tell you
   what I will do to my vineyard.
I will remove its hedge,
   and it shall be devoured;
I will break down its wall,
   and it shall be trampled down.
⁶I will make it a waste;
   it shall not be pruned or hoed,
   and it shall be overgrown with briers and thorns;
I will also command the clouds
   that they rain no rain upon it.

⁷For the vineyard of the LORD of hosts
   is the house of Israel,
and the people of Judah
   are his pleasant planting;
he expected justice,
   but saw bloodshed;
righteousness,
   but heard a cry!

Exegetical Perspective

Isaiah 5:1–7, among the eighth-century prophet's best-known oracles, summons its Judean audience to judge the legal complaint of a would-be vintner who lavishes care upon his vineyard, but harvests bitter grapes. The poem conceals the identities of farmer and field until its final verse. Suddenly, the addressees grasp a dreadful truth: YHWH is the vintner; they are the doomed vineyard!

The oracle consists of (1) a two-part introduction, including Isaiah's account of the farmer's exhaustive but futile labor in his field (vv. 1a, 1b–2); (2) the vintner's appeal for judgment, including two rhetorical questions (vv. 3–4); (3) the owner's declaration of his intent utterly to destroy his field (vv. 5–6); and (4) Isaiah's climactic identification of the vintner and his vineyard/pleasant planting, plus two pairs of wordplays emphasizing YHWH's frustrated expectations (5:7).

Isaiah employs an array of poetic and rhetorical devices, including ambiguity and extended metaphor, to engage and ultimately entrap his audience. Uncertainty arises already in verse 1a, two lines that have challenged translators.[1] Who is the "beloved" (*yadîd*)/"loved one" (*dôd*) whose song

1. In the NRSV, Isaiah proposes to sing *his own love song* about his beloved's vineyard. The Hebrew text, however, is better rendered, "Let me sing for my beloved/*my loved one's song* [not a "love song"] about his vineyard" (my trans.).

Homiletical Perspective

How on earth is this a "love song"? It is a futility song—love's labor turns out to be lost. It is a litigation song with a punitive judgment in mind. It promises desertion. Love song? How so, and does this label have implications for how it is preached?

It could be a trick, of course. Isaiah announces a love song, strums a few pleasant chords, and just as the audience leans forward, blows them back with crashing tones. So we can say it is a set-up; as in many other parables, a duplicity is in play. Even the identity of the vineyard owner is withheld until the last sentence. Such a trap cannot likely be sprung in the sermon, especially since the text has already been read! At the very least, a shift in the sermon from brighter tones to darker ones would be fitting.

Still, the use of "love song" to lure us into something that sounds nothing like a love song does not mean that the whole text is not, in fact, a love song. Everything God did for that vineyard (metaphor for bride and metaphor for Israel)—every hole dug, every rock removed, every selection made, every planting done, every protection established (wall, hedge, tower), and every watchful expectation held—was love's eager work. And when it all ended in acres of stinking fruit, the rage that followed was love's other voice. Anger, as C. S. Lewis said, is the

Isaiah 5:1-7

Theological Perspective

among God's people is set in a courtroom scene where a vintner brings charges against an inexplicably perverse and unproductive vineyard. One need only hear the accounting to see the justice of the vintner's case; the verdict is unassailable. Everything the vineyard needs for its flourishing has been lovingly provided, yet it brings forth wild grapes (bitter and useless or perhaps even rotten). The vintner's disappointment, grief, and outrage are palpable in the expressed intention to destroy the vineyard. A vivid accounting of the planned destruction of the vineyard follows in 5:5–6. In case anyone does not make the connection, Isaiah makes it explicit: "the vineyard of the LORD of hosts is the house of Israel, and the people of Judah are his pleasant planting" (v. 7). Chapters 6–10 reiterate the intolerable situation and the consequences that are coming in the form of divine judgment, certain and severe.

The story does not end here, however. This section concludes with chapters 11–12, where promise of a transformation is issued. Although the tallest trees of Lebanon have been cut down, "a shoot shall come out from the stump of Jesse" (11:1). There follow the portrayal of the "peaceable kingdom" and the promise of a new order that is coming, wherein justice and righteousness will be established. A remnant will return. The accounting of their return recalls the exodus. God will "make a way" through the river for the people to cross over on foot. The section closes with a hymn of praise in chapter 12.

An important theological theme in the text is the contrast between God's loving providence and the ingratitude and perversity of humankind. "What more was there to do for my vineyard that I have not done in it? When I expected it to yield grapes, why did it yield wild grapes?" (v. 4.) God's generous provision is met with ingratitude. Good is given; evil returned. The initiatives of love have every reason to expect a response of love, but the response is contempt. The form that contempt of divine love takes is injustice. The love of God and the love of neighbor are inextricably intertwined; so also, contempt for one issues in contempt for the other.

The contrast between reasonable divine expectation and actual human response is sharpened by a wordplay Isaiah employs that does not really come through in the English translation. God "expected justice (*mishpat*) but saw bloodshed (*mispah*); righteousness (*tsedaqah*), but heard a cry (*tse'aqah*)" (v. 7). When these two terms (*mishpat*

Pastoral Perspective

The gardener asks another question: Why? "When I expected it to yield grapes, why did it yield wild grapes?" (v. 4.) Sooner or later, almost anyone facing disappointment comes to this question. In the text, as in life, there is no straight answer. Circumstances crush us, and we have no explanation. We ask why, and we look for good reasons; we find none. Likewise, the gardener gets no answer to the question.

Having pled his case, the gardener makes his decision: he will do nothing more for this piece of land. He will abandon it, let it turn back into a wild field. This sounds right. This is what we counsel people in intractable situations to do: give up, let it go, move on. The gardener will do nothing more.

Now the gardener says one last thing. "I will also command the clouds that they rain no rain upon it" (v. 6). With that, the identity of the gardener is revealed. Only God can withhold rain. This is not just any vineyard owner; this is the divine gardener. One revelation leads to another, and now the identity of the vineyard is revealed as well: "For the vineyard of the LORD of hosts is the house of Israel, and the people of Judah are his pleasant planting; he expected justice, but saw bloodshed; righteousness, but heard a cry!" (v. 7). What started as a song has turned into a parable; now the world of the parable breaks open with a crash. God's people are the vineyard that has not produced, and God has given up.

It would be easy to read this as only a word about Israel in the time of Isaiah, a prophecy of the enemy's military victory over Jerusalem. Isaiah's indictment, however, is as relevant and poignant now as ever: "[God] expected justice, but saw bloodshed; righteousness, but heard a cry!" The accusation is harsh and penetrating. Although Isaiah speaks in the broadest terms, we do not have to look far for examples of bloodshed where justice should be, or cries of pain in place of righteousness. The vineyard is to produce sweet fruit for the nourishment of the world. God nurtures, protects, and tends, yet the world still goes hungry for the gift God's people were meant to bear. Our text is clear: God may give up.

How could this be? Do we not sing psalms about a God whose "steadfast love endures forever"? Do we not gather at a table together and hear again words flung over us like a blanket: "When we turned away, and our love failed, God's love remained steadfast"? Does God really give up? Is it possible to reach a point of no return? Are we already there?

Exegetical Perspective

Isaiah sings? Elsewhere in the Hebrew Bible, the adjective *yadîd* often refers to YHWH's beloved (e.g., Israel in Jer. 11:15; Ps. 127:2, etc.; Benjamin in Deut. 33:12), although never to YHWH as "beloved." In the Song of Solomon, a young woman frequently uses *dôd* to refer to the man she loves (e.g., 1:13; 2:3; 4:16; 5:10). Here, however, neither *yadîd* nor *dôd* betrays the farmer's identity.

Verses 1b–2 describe the owner's care for his vineyard (*kerem*), situated on a very fertile hill (*qeren*). He tills its rich soil, clears it of stones, and plants choice vines. He builds a watchtower to protect it from marauders and even hews out a winepress in it, but his hopes are dashed, because the field produces only worthless grapes.

Thus far, Isaiah's addressees probably assume that he speaks of an actual farmer, his vineyard, and its disappointing harvest. Verses 3–4, however, likely cause them to rethink their assumption. Speaking in the first person, the owner summons the "inhabitant" (singular; better "king") of Jerusalem and fellow Judeans to judge between him and his field. Why would a farmer seek judgment against a plot of land? What, in addition to personal vindication, could he hope to gain from a vineyard he already owns? The implied answers to two rhetorical questions he poses to the "jury" (v. 4) underscore his innocence: the vintner did everything he could; his vineyard's disappointing yield is inexplicable.

Verses 3–4 incline the audience to wonder if both Isaiah and the farmer are using agricultural metaphors—speaking about one thing ("X") in terms suggestive of another (the owner's failed harvest). Israel's poets, including its prophets, frequently employ metaphor to speak about one thing (e.g., Jerusalem) in terms of another (e.g., a rejected daughter [Lam. 2:1] or bereaved mother [Isa. 51:18–20]). Extended metaphors can span many verses, as the metaphorical depiction of Jerusalem, YHWH's adulterous wife, in Ezekiel 16:1–63 demonstrates.

If Isaiah's addressees suspect that he sings of an unidentified subject ("X") in terms suggestive of a vintner's care for his disappointing field, what helps them discern the actual identity of X? Elsewhere in the Hebrew Bible, "vineyard" serves as a metaphor for the female lover in Song 1:6; 2:15; 8:11–12. In Hosea 2, Israel's land appears in the guise of the prophet's/YHWH's faithless wife, who credits her "lovers" (the deities of Canaan) with the fertility she enjoys. On the basis of these and other literary traditions, Isaiah's audience might first "decode" his extended metaphor as follows: the "farmer"

Homiletical Perspective

fluid love bleeds when you cut it.[1] Even the abandonment of the vineyard may be seen as the sad work of love. Promising to take down the hedges and walls and desist from pruning and hoeing is a kind of consent. If safeguards and cultivation are unwanted and meaningless to the people, then withdraw the imposition of safeguards and cultivation; let them have the wildness they want. God knows how it will end, but grants them the autonomy they have asserted.

"Let me sing for my beloved my love-song" (v. 1). This is the banner set above the entrance into the text, proclaiming the theme of all that will follow. The music of it will soon surprise and dismay us, but a love song it remains. In this way the text tells us something of how to preach it. A sad narrative, even with its news of immanent threat, will be offered in the manner and tone, and in the quality of passion, of a song of love. There are other ways to declare judgment, but this is our way, which the text makes hauntingly explicit.

Strangely, God's love for the people may even have become part of their problem, and ours. Like them, we have been well taught on the subject of grace—how God chose, cleared, dug, planted, safeguarded, and undertook a thousand other verbs of loving initiative. Lucky us. We are infinitely loved and assured. We are therefore relieved of heavy obligations, duties, and requirements—and are immune to certain ultimate devastations. In no time, we are lounging in the easiest of all the world's religions, leaning back into the entitlements of grace and an arrogance of heritage.

Love was looking for something else. God's love, it turns out, comes with expectations after all. Three times we read it: God "expected. . . . expected. . . . expected. . . ." (vv. 2, 4, 7). A vineyard is not a plot of geraniums. A vineyard is ground for farming, and the vintner is looking for fruit that refreshes, feeds, slakes thirsts, pleases palates, gladdens hearts, and provides a happy symbol and center for the gathering and sustaining of community. This is why rocks were cleared and holes dug and furrows plowed and hedges put in and walls put up and a watchtower built. The result, however—unexpected and unnatural—feeds no hunger, slakes no thirst, gladdens no hearts, fosters no community. There is, in other words, no justice, no righteousness.

---

1. *Letters to Malcolm, Chiefly on Prayer* (1964), cited in Walter Hooper, *C. S. Lewis: A Complete Guide to His Life and Works* (San Francisco: HarperCollins, 2005), 389.

Isaiah 5:1-7

Theological Perspective

and *tsedaqah*) are used in tandem, the basic connotation is of a society in which the rights of all, including the most marginalized, are respected. This is God's reasonable expectation, given the divine provision.

The human response (like that of the vineyard) is inexplicable. Karl Barth takes trouble to emphasize the *inexplicability*. This perverse human response is an "impossible possibility." It has no ground and no future, either from God's side (for God is unqualifiedly good) or from the side of the creature (for God has created all things good). Proper, authentic creaturehood excludes such a "choice." Human beings "have not to choose between two possibilities [good and evil] but between their one and only possibility and their own impossibility."[2] There is "no place" for this perverse response; it remains absurd. It is better to end up with this conclusion, according to Barth; if one finds a place for evil and explains it, one domesticates it.

A theological tension in the present passage concerns what may be termed the "retributive justice framework" that Isaiah assumes—that suffering can be explained as a judgment upon sin and, conversely, prosperity as a reward for righteousness. Wendy Farley offers helpful insight into this tension.[3] The retributive justice framework is perhaps the dominant one in the tradition. The texts say something to the effect that "Israel did what was evil in the sight of the Lord," and what follow are reports of various catastrophes, losses in battle, and exile. It is as if defeat and destruction are bearable if they are deserved. Although divine punishment is a terrible thing to endure, it reveals a cosmic justice that can be trusted. Many biblical writers seem to prefer this view to the alternatives.

In the writings of Job, Lamentations, and Psalms, however, there is a minority report proposing an alternative reading. The psalmist, for example, proclaims that Israel has been sold "like sheep for slaughter" (44:11), and there is no good reason for it. It is one thing to claim, as Isaiah does, that injustice deserves divine judgment, but quite another to say that all suffering—including the suffering of the marginalized for whom Isaiah pleads—is deserved or divinely inflicted.

ANNA CASE-WINTERS

Pastoral Perspective

Isaiah's words do not offer much hope. There is only judgment in them, and sadness. They picture what happens when a people refuse the care and nurture lavished on them—or accept it, but keep it only to themselves. God, according to Isaiah, will let us have what we want—self-governance, and the inevitable destruction and self-destruction that result.

A prophet can end on a note such as this. The rest of us are usually looking for some good news. If so, we will need to find it elsewhere, beyond these seven verses at least. Later in the book of Isaiah, and later in time, a prophet will sing another song of the vineyard (27:2–6), a happier song, of a pleasant vineyard tended by God, blossoming and putting forth shoots until the whole world is filled with fruit. This song is written after destruction, and is a sort of reversal of what is sung in Isaiah 5. It is not a song composed in optimism and naiveté; it is a song sung from the ashes, after deliverance from horror.

Judgment does come, and punishment; then there will be good news as well. There is hope yet, but first the people must be willing to see the horrible things Isaiah sees (like bloodshed where justice is meant to be) and the terrible things he hears (like cries of pain instead of righteousness). If we can face such devastation, and own our part in it, we might just be ready to submit again to the bruised and aching hands of the master gardener, who still dreams of— and sings for—a vineyard yielding fat, gorgeous fruit for the whole world.

STACEY SIMPSON DUKE

---

2. Karl Barth, *Church Dogmatics* III/3, ed. G. W. Bromiley (Edinburgh: T. & T. Clark, 1961), 197.
3. Wendy Farley, *Tragic Vision and Divine Compassion* (Louisville, KY: Westminster John Knox Press, 1990).

Exegetical Perspective

represents a husband whose relationship with his wife ("vineyard") has gone horribly wrong despite his devotion.

Verses 3–4 demand a judgment from the oracle's addressees, yet they say nothing. Instead, the owner announces his own harsh sentence. Like a husband who casts out his wife, stripping her of the protection and provisions he gave her, he will remove his vineyard's protective hedge and wall, leaving it to devouring, trampling beasts. Abandoned, it will revert to wasteland, neither pruned nor hoed, and overgrown with briers and thorns. Moreover, the vintner will command the clouds to withhold rain, leaving the land desiccated (v. 6b).

Wait! Can a mere human command the clouds? In 2 Samuel 1:21, David curses the mountains of Gilboa: "Let there be no dew or rain upon you, nor bounteous fields!" The farmer's words here, however, are not cast as a curse. So Isaiah's audience likely revisits the poem's extended metaphor, concluding that the owner is actually YHWH!

Verse 7 quickly confirms their suspicion, identifying YHWH of hosts as the farmer and the house of Israel/the people of Judah as God's vineyard/pleasant planting. Like the owner who hopes for choice grapes, YHWH hopes for justice (*mishpat*) but sees bloodshed (*mispah*), expects righteousness (*tsedaqah*) but hears a cry (*tse'aqah*). Though this oracle stops short of a literal announcement of Judah's punishment (described metaphorically in vv. 5–6), both indictment and punishment will appear in verses 8–30.

Scholars have long debated the genre of Isaiah 5:1–7; many conclude that it displays a sophisticated blend of several genres. Introduced as a song, it also contains juridical elements. Moreover, it functions much like the prophet Nathan's parable to King David in 2 Samuel 12:1–15. Following David's affair with Bathsheba and the prearranged death of her husband, Uriah, on the battlefield, Nathan tells his king the story of a poor man's little ewe lamb that is stolen by a rich man to feed his guests. David reacts immediately, insisting that the rich man deserves to die and demanding that he restore the lamb fourfold (2 Sam. 12:5–6). When Nathan responds, "You are the man!" David realizes that he has condemned himself. In Isaiah 5:1–7, the prophet's "jury" does not speak, yet everything about his oracle has inclined them to rule in favor of the "farmer" and against his "field." Not until verse 7 do they fully realize that they, like David, stand condemned.

KATHERYN PFISTERER DARR

Homiletical Perspective

God does not speak the last lines. For four verses the vineyard owner has been speaking, but now it is over. God has gone silent, and the prophet must be the one to finish disclosing what has occurred. Looking for justice, God sees—*bloodshed*! Looking for righteousness—*a cry*! It is a nightmare account. The Giver of joy goes looking for the beautiful feast but finds a spreading river of blood. The love song is ended by the sound of screaming.

The text descends swiftly from the lovely to the horrible. Preachers will need to take seriously what is horrible here. As in all art and in the gospel itself, the dreadful is most powerfully communicated against a backdrop of the beautiful, and vice versa. On this count, our text gives us good guidance. As already noted, the love song banner flying above the text invites us, not only to accent the ardent initiatives and dreams of God, but even when naming our failures and what follows from them, to speak from love's depth.

The text gives good instruction on how to speak two rather difficult words: *justice* and *righteousness*. Although we may love these words, to many people they are rather severe abstractions. Our text knows otherwise. Righteousness and justice are tumbling mountains of delicious, beautiful fruit; they are wine, shared and lifted, for family, neighbors, and strangers gathered in glad, new community. That there should be no such thing among us is truly devastation—it is bloodshed, and a cry.

Any good news? Well, it is a love song. It ends badly. Has God stopped planting vineyards or restoring ruined ones? Has God stopped singing love songs? The bad news is that we can have love sung endlessly over us, and still be useless and a lethal danger to the world and to ourselves. The good news is that Someone still sings, plows, plants, guards, and looks for good fruit. In this is enough hope to set us humming bits of the song at least, and living toward its true ending, Love's own harvest: sweet justice, festive righteousness, a cup of joy in the lifted hands of all.

PAUL SIMPSON DUKE

Psalm 80:1-2, 8-19

¹Give ear, O Shepherd of Israel,
  you who lead Joseph like a flock!
You who are enthroned upon the cherubim, shine forth
² before Ephraim and Benjamin and Manasseh.
  Stir up your might,
    and come to save us!
. . . .
⁸You brought a vine out of Egypt;
  you drove out the nations and planted it.
⁹You cleared the ground for it;
  it took deep root and filled the land.
¹⁰The mountains were covered with its shade,
  the mighty cedars with its branches;
¹¹it sent out its branches to the sea,
  and its shoots to the River.
¹²Why then have you broken down its walls,
  so that all who pass along the way pluck its fruit?

Theological Perspective

Being chosen does not necessarily mean being privileged, at least as the psalmist sees it. In this passage the writer wonders aloud what has happened to the God who claims a special relationship with the people of Israel. Here the singer is both poet and historian, offering both a brief history lesson and a liturgical confession. The first verse captures in one brief couplet the nature of God's transcendence and immanence. The God who is the "Shepherd of Israel," ever present with the chosen flock, is also the God who is beyond all things, "enthroned upon the cherubim," those winged creatures (depicted as a lion's body with a human face) that represent exaltation and distinctive authority.[1] This is no generic God but one whose glory is evident to a peculiar tribal people—"Ephraim and Benjamin and Manasseh" (v. 2).

The immanent God is nowhere to be found. The Shepherd has turned away or, worse yet, gone away, and the sheep are in deep trouble. The psalmist does not hesitate to demand that God intervene as quickly as possible to alleviate Israel's difficulties. Sometimes, when pain is real and God seems absent, worship includes accusation and complaint.

1. W. Stewart McCullough, "Psalms," in *The Interpreter's Bible* (Nashville: Abingdon Press, 1955), 4:432.

Pastoral Perspective

The late summer, when this text is read, is a quiet, pregnant period before the groan and sweat of harvest—a voluptuous season when ruddy farmers lean on neat fences, surveying golden kingdoms with pleasure and pride. Or so goes the idealization. The truth is that we who live in cities burnish this idyll for our own comfort. We have little emotional connection to the land, so we resort to romance. When a freeze destroys a citrus grove in Florida, or disease wipes out the amber waves of grain, we are only momentarily shocked at the loss. Our greatest sorrow is for ourselves, who will soon pay dearly for grapefruit and bread.

We are not so disconnected, however, that we miss the pathos of Psalm 80. Somehow we understand that when a marauder wantonly hacks a flourishing plant to pieces, God's glory is also insulted, trampled down, picked over, and thrown into the fire. This injury is the subject of the psalm.

The splendid planting that once extended from Lebanon to the Mediterranean to the Euphrates has now become an unholy mess, and the reputation of the God who planted it is in question (vv. 11–12). The forlorn vine stands for Israel, overrun by invaders, stumbling economically, lacking security, and humiliated by its comedown. The psalmist raises the obvious question: How has it come to this?

^{13}The boar from the forest ravages it,
and all that move in the field feed on it.

^{14}Turn again, O God of hosts;
look down from heaven, and see;
have regard for this vine,
^{15}the stock that your right hand planted.
^{16}They have burned it with fire, they have cut it down;
may they perish at the rebuke of your countenance.
^{17}But let your hand be upon the one at your right hand,
the one whom you made strong for yourself.
^{18}Then we will never turn back from you;
give us life, and we will call on your name.

^{19}Restore us, O Lord God of hosts;
let your face shine, that we may be saved.

Exegetical Perspective

Psalm 80 is a nearly paradigmatic example of the traditional psalm classification known as communal complaint or lament. It begins with petitions to God to listen to the cries of the people (vv. 1–2). This is followed by a lament over the severity and duration of Israel's current suffering (vv. 4–6) and an allegorical description of this same situation (vv. 8–13). Then comes a plea to God to change this course and restore the prosperity of the people, along with a vow of fidelity and praise (vv. 14–18). This structure is punctuated by a repeated refrain pleading for God to restore the community and bring salvation (vv. 3, 7, 19).

The reference to Israel as "Joseph" and the naming of the tribes of Ephraim, Benjamin, and Manasseh (vv. 1–2) leads most scholars to conclude that this psalm originated in the northern kingdom of Israel during the time before the Assyrian conquest in the late eighth century BCE. Such a northern provenance fits with this psalm's inclusion (in the superscription, not included above) as a psalm of Asaph, which typically reflects northern perspectives. It may even be possible to narrow the time frame of this psalm's origin down to 732–722 BCE, the last decade before the ultimate conquest of the north, a time when the three tribes mentioned were hanging on to their independence.

Homiletical Perspective

It is a perfect metaphor: God as sun, the source of all light and life and warmth, the fount of every energy that enlivens the planet. All that lives, lives because the sun exists. Far distant from our home, yet deeply present, able to warm and grow and nurture life, or to burn and wither and consume it. When it is hidden, the world grows cold and seems strange; nightmares are born. Look it full in the face for a moment, and your eyes will ache; dare to look longer, and you will go blind. Stay in its presence too long, and your face will shine like Moses's, like Jesus'. Its absence would be the death of us all, yet we live with the promise that it will one day grow so large that we will be consumed and the world will either end or be made into a new thing. It is a perfect metaphor.

The metaphor for Israel is nearly as good: the people as grapevine, transplanted and tended lovingly. The vine is rooted deeply in the soil of its homeland, drawing sustenance up through its roots, incorporating the very land into its shoots and leaves and fruit. So long as God's face shines upon it, the vine grows and spreads, reaching out across the land, making shady places in the desert, by its very growth turning and enriching the places where it grows. As soon as God's face is hidden, the vine begins to shrivel and wither, to weaken and turn to tinder for the fire.

Psalm 80:1-2, 8-19

Theological Perspective

Then comes the history. Does this absent or distracted "Shepherd of Israel" need to be reminded of the special history of "my people"? Does God not remember the sacred story? Is worship not a source of memory for people and Deity alike? Israel is the "vine," a metaphor used variously in both testaments by writers who want to accentuate lineage and chosenness.[2] The history of God's destiny with Israel is both a reminder to this distant God and an attempt to reassure a seemingly deserted people.

Verse 8 is itself a theological celebration and dilemma, if not for ancient Israelites, at least for many moderns who revisit the text and its ideas. On one hand, there is the deliverance from Egypt, a journey toward freedom that shaped the nature of the vine itself, but there is a problem. The God who made Israel a vine "drove out the nations and planted it." The psalmist affirms God's participation in the conquest of a new land but rushes past the death and destruction to human life at the heart of the story. Joshua 8:18 says that the Lord told Joshua, "Stretch out the sword that is in your hand toward Ai; for I will give it into your hand." The text reports, "When Israel had finished slaughtering all the inhabitants of Ai in the open wilderness where they pursued them, and when all of them to the very last had fallen by the edge of the sword, all Israel returned to Ai, and attacked it with the edge of the sword. The total of those who fell that day, both men and women, was twelve thousand—all the people of Ai" (Josh. 8:24–25).

In short, the vine began with the massacre of the people of the new land—"heathen" as the KJV calls them (Ps. 80:8)—men, women, and children, all killed in the name of "the Lord." In order for God to plant the vine, a lot of "heathen" had to die. This little verse skips over all the gory details of that slaughter, spiritualizing it as a sign of God's initial care and protection of the people of Israel. Would a similar blind spot occur if a preacher on July 4 were to claim God's chosenness for America without reference to the Middle Passage or the Trail of Tears?[3] Preacher poets then and now would do well to consider that some people's story of liberation and salvation can be for others an account of misery and destruction. Here the story within the story does not get told.

From the psalmist's perspective, however, the divine initiative helped this vine to spread like kudzu

2. Ibid., 434. See Isa. 5:1–7; Ezek. 15–17; Matt. 21:33–42; and John 15:1–8.
3. "Middle Passage" refers to the route of slave ships from Africa to the Americas. The "Trail of Tears" is the name for the forced march required of the Cherokees from North Carolina to Oklahoma in the 1830s.

Pastoral Perspective

Although the psalm speaks of Israel's desolation long ago, it echoes every generation's conviction that it has fallen from former heights and that these are the worst of times. Remember when America was great, men held doors for women, and schoolchildren could write a declarative sentence? Remember when the pews were full, and people in them knew that Moses lived before Jesus? Where have those days gone? This psalm offers much-needed perspective on current laments for the wretched state of one nation under God, traditional values, the declining mainline, the nuclear family. We are not the first to believe that the world is going to hell, or to wonder if because of our failings (or someone else's) God is bringing us low. We will not be the last. A future generation will judge our generation to have been better, and wonder how their generation fell so far from such grace.

The perspective offered by the psalm should warn us of making idols of nation, religion, and policy based on humiliated frustration. It can relativize anxiety about what has been lost, focusing us instead on God's graceful activity in the world, even as the world is always passing away. Freed from nostalgic fears and rooted in gratitude, Christians may more fruitfully engage the demanding practice of discernment, scanning with the Spirit the "signs of the times."

Will God really let the vine rot? God did hard labor for it, bringing it "out of Egypt"—shorthand for the exhausting saga of the exodus. God also "cleared the land" to plant it—more shorthand for the savage war that chased the Canaanites from their own country. How could this same God even be accused of complicity in the vine's demise (v. 12)? Here is an opportunity to explore the vexed question of God's faithfulness, judgment, and correction. Many Christians puzzle over the connections among human offenses, bad events, and divine retribution. When the Twin Towers fell on 9/11, prominent preachers blamed feminists, homosexuals, and civil libertarians for exposing America to "the Lord's decision" not to protect it from attack. Was that the case? Is this the kind of God we worship?

People who recoil from a punitive God may still need to acknowledge that sin has consequences that affect the world. Is there "payback" for human malice and neglect that should send us to our knees with the psalmist in verse 18, bargaining with God and swearing, "Never again!"? Are natural occurrences like tsunamis, famine, forest fires, and the extinction of species wholly natural in character? What is the "divine message" in such events?

Exegetical Perspective

Building on this understanding of the psalm's origin, Zenger suggests that it was updated and appropriated a century later in Judah during the time of King Josiah. According to this theory, the refrains (vv. 3, 7, 19) were added at this time to adapt the psalm as a liturgy for use in the Jerusalem temple. This explanation fits the theology of the refrains, which can be compared to the threefold priestly blessing of Numbers 6:24–26, portions of which have been found in Jerusalem archaeological sites dating to the seventh or sixth century BCE. In this scenario, it is possible that the petition in verse 17 is also a later addition, referring to King Josiah himself. [1]

Zenger goes on to suggest a final stage of development in which this psalm is transformed into a voice of messianic hope in the time after the collapse of the Davidic dynasty. This is supported by a continuation of 80:15 (15b) included in the MT but omitted by the NRSV: "and upon the son whom you have made strong for yourself." This echo of Psalm 2:7, coupled with a more literal translation of 80:17b ("the *son of man* whom you made strong for yourself" instead of "the *one* whom you made strong for yourself"), makes clear how this psalm could have been read in a messianic context. In fact, it is clear from the LXX (which replaces "son" in verse 15b with "son of man") and the Targum (which replaces "son" in this same verse with "King Messiah") that such a messianic interpretation occurred.[2] All of this is neutralized by the omission of 80:15b in the NRSV, which keeps the focus of the psalm on the preexilic king and nation.

Psalm 80 was clearly chosen for this Sunday's lectionary readings because of the vineyard analogy it shares with Isaiah 5:1–7. The verses suggested for reading, 1–2 and 8–19, highlight this connection while passing over the first lament and complaint of the psalm, verses 4–7 (which appear elsewhere in the lectionary). Similar vine and vineyard imagery is also employed in Jeremiah (2:21; 6:9; 8:13), Hosea (10:1; 14:5–7), Ezekiel (15; 17; 19:10–14), and elsewhere in Isaiah (27:2–6).

We have already seen how verses 1–2 contextualize this psalm in both time and space. These introductory verses are also noteworthy for the imagery of God as shepherd and enthroned king. Deities and kings were often referred to as shepherds throughout the ancient Near East, a motif reflected in the Hebrew Bible. However, while there are

1. Frank Lothar Hossfeld and Erich Zenger, *Psalms 2*, Hermeneia (Minneapolis: Fortress Press, 2005), 311–12.
2. Ibid.

Homiletical Perspective

Together, the two metaphors create a rich tapestry of images and sensory experiences through which preachers can follow any number of threads that will lead them to the gospel.

Coming as it does during the hottest time of the Northern Hemisphere's summer, this lection will easily and naturally evoke for many the power and immanence of the sun. Meanwhile, farmers and gardeners of all types will notice that it comes at the beginning of the harvest, when gardens and fields are beginning to burst with ripeness. Images of fully ripened fruit or wasted vines and crops should be vivid symbols at this time of year. Finding themselves placed, like the first hearers of this palm, in the position of the plants they tend may well yield new insights and visions for the hearers.

Likewise, putting the congregation in the place of the vinegrower might yield interesting fruit. Successful gardeners, even houseplant owners, know the work and care that go into rearing plants successfully. They know that over time a successful growth engenders pride, even love, in the grower. Conversely, most people have tried and failed to keep a houseplant alive or a garden thriving. A comparison between us and the divine vinegrower can yield only good news: Where we have failed in our own gardening, God, the master gardener and grafter, will not. Where we have forgotten to water or weed or feed our gardens and plants, God will not. Where we have been lacking, God is full of that knowledge and power needed to bring every plant to fullness of life and fruitfulness of being.

The grapevine image links naturally and evocatively to any number of New Testament stories and images. Parables of vineyards, sowers, and laborers in the field abound, as do references to vines, grafting, pruning, and fruitfulness. Jesus himself claims to be just such a vine as this, and we are its branches.

There are rich possibilities for connecting this parable to Communion, as well. While the juice of the grapes is not technically the "blood" of the plant, perhaps the metaphor can be stretched this far without breaking: If Jesus is a vine such as this, and if a skillful preacher can convince the congregation that the juice of the grapes is something like the vine's blood, does that not add a new layer of meaning to Jesus' claim at the Last Supper that the wine is his blood? If we too have been grafted on that same vine, is not the wine also in some way *our* blood, *our* fruitfulness, and is the act of drinking it in Communion with others not in some way the

Psalm 80:1-2, 8-19

Theological Perspective

through Georgia. A remnant people—with God's blessing—moved across the promised land until, in one of the great lines of the psalm, "the mountains were covered with its shade" (v. 10). Theirs was a grand history born of divine protection and blessing. So what went wrong, the writer asks: "Why then have you broken down its walls?" (v. 12).

Here history takes a turn. The promises seem thwarted if not unfulfilled. The grand protection has been lifted. The "hedges" (v. 12 KJV) have been smashed by God—by God! The people are in trouble. Again the poetic imagery is magnificent: the wild "boar from the forest ravages" the land (v. 13), and the fault seems to lie with God, who has deserted the chosen ones. God let in the enemy; God turned away; God forgot. So the psalmist and the worshiping community sing out for God to come to their aid, "regard" the vine again, and bring retribution on those who have sought to destroy it. The God who planted the vine and cared for it initially is responsible for its continued well-being and sustenance.

This is no hymn of repentance for a people punished for their evil ways. This is the community holding God responsible, hoping to get the divine attention one more time, in order to be rescued from hard times and real enemies. The God who began the story is required to remain faithful to the original covenant. It is less self-righteousness than memory and desperation that prompts the hymn.

Questions abound.

Why do we write some people, especially conquered people, out of the whole story?

Are there times when we hold God, not human beings, responsible for the difficulties and atrocities that beset individuals and communities?

When the boars ravage us, can we, dare we, hold God accountable?

Must we endure the absence of God in our lives and histories, or might we take initiative, even with a bit of an "attitude," to ensure God's return?

BILL J. LEONARD

Pastoral Perspective

The psalmist complains that God's caring intervention has now been replaced by silent indifference. Pastors struggle to respond to questions about God's inaction. Is God biding time? Does God demand moral improvement before aiding us? Are we unable to grasp the larger plan? Or is God sometimes helpless?

Some people find it credible that God chooses to respect human freedom and, like a parent, must live with a permanent sense of things slipping away. The first step toddlers take, after all, is a step *away*. Sooner or later, parents give explicit or tacit permission for them to go. They will go anyway, with or without permission. Moreover, many children grow up to be what their parents never wanted them to be. Eventually they suffer nearly everything their parents labor to spare them. Difficult to stomach at times, this process nonetheless has a mysterious nobility, and one must stay out of it. Pastors might want to introduce the idea—easily misunderstood, but worthy of reflection—that there may be things that for our own good God does not and will not control.

Especially when injustice or the agony of a loved one is involved, God's silence causes untold pain. It puts God's loving reputation in jeopardy. Praying this psalm may help parishioners express their own pain and doubt. Some Christians rarely address God directly with fury or indignant disbelief. Such constraint in prayer may be loosened by adopting the patterns of biblical lamentation. The raw honesty of this genre initially shocks people's sensibilities. It is hard to imagine that God truly welcomes the human fist thrust into the sky, the tortured "Why?" that rises from each global or intimate catastrophe, the boiling anger of the unjustly injured.

Nonetheless, coming to terms with lamentation's impulse to hold God accountable for God's promises lends intimacy to Christian prayer, for at the heart of a believer's rage is longing. In the end, we may yearn not so much for a rational explanation as for tenderness—for God to acknowledge to our grieving hearts that we are often more sinned against than sinning, and that what we need most is not the antiseptic of absolution, but the healing touch of balm for all the gaping wounds that alienate us from our own humanity and divine delight.

J. MARY LUTI

numerous descriptions of YHWH's activities that utilize shepherd language, in only four examples is YHWH actually called "shepherd" (this passage; Gen. 48:15; 49:24; and Ps. 23:1). Moreover, the particular phrase used here, "Shepherd of Israel," is unique to this psalm. The image of YHWH as a deity enthroned on cherubim is related to the ark of the covenant in both pretemple times (1 Sam. 4:4; 2 Sam. 6:2) and in the Jerusalem temple itself (2 Kgs. 19:15; Ps. 99:1).

The allegory or parable of the vine in Psalm 80:8–18 bears many similarities to, yet significant differences from, the song in Isaiah 5:1–7. In both instances, God is the ultimate sovereign over Israel and the nations, responsible for both Israel's establishment and its suffering at the hands of its neighbors. Israel's entire history is represented as a vine that is moved, planted, cared for, and ultimately left exposed by the vinegrower. The difference between the two parables is a matter of perspective. Isaiah 5 represents the perspective of God, who has nurtured Israel, is disappointed with its rebellion, and is punishing the people by removing God's protection against invasion. Psalm 80, the same allegory from the perspective of the people, is presented as a lament filled with anguish and bewilderment.

The ultimate sovereignty and providence of God are highlighted in Psalm 80 by the absence of penitence on the part of Israel. In fact, God is the one who is called upon to repent (the Heb. root of "turn again" in v. 14) and alter the course of events. The appeal is to God's responsibility as planter and tender of the vineyard, not to a sense of reward for the repentance of the people. It is only after God has rebuked the aggressors (v. 16) and strengthened the people and/or the king (depending on how one reads v. 17) that Israel will again praise God (v. 18). It is possible that the vow to "never turn back from you" (v. 18) implies some kind of repentance on the part of the people, but this is by no means clear.

The psalm ends with the refrain, which has been gradually augmented with increasingly specific addresses to the Deity: from "God" (v. 3) to "God of hosts" (v. 14) to "YHWH God of hosts" (v. 19). This refrain provides one last plea to the sovereign God who alone is capable of saving the people.

JOHN W. VEST

closing of a holy circle created, enlivened, and ripened by God?

To take the wine metaphor still further, although in a different direction: winemakers and aficionados know that grapes take up the particular flavors and characteristics of the conditions under which they grew. Geography, soil type, the weather in a given year, the age of vines, and other factors all affect the size, flavor, and aroma of the grapes and of course the wines made from them. Experienced tasters can often tell an astonishing amount about the conditions where and when a particular wine was produced. So what are the characteristics of the place in which your congregation's vine grows? What are the soil and geography, the rain and the climate, like there? With what else must it compete to survive? How much sun has the vine received—or not? Does the congregation feel more like the vine in the psalm, withering from lack of God's gaze, or like a thriving plant?

What particular characteristics has the wine of the congregation taken on? Are there ways that the congregation might be more intentional about taking up the flavors of the place in which it grows? What does this congregation taste like to a new person sipping it for the first time? What about someone who has never tasted wine before? What would it taste like to her? What delights of taste, aroma, texture, and color would an experienced taster discover layered in its life together?

Finally, most importantly, what is it about the congregation that makes God, having planted, tended, and shined upon the vine and harvested its fruit, smack God's lips with appreciation whenever she samples it?

QUINN G. CALDWELL

Hebrews 11:29-12:2

²⁹By faith the people passed through the Red Sea as if it were dry land, but when the Egyptians attempted to do so they were drowned. ³⁰By faith the walls of Jericho fell after they had been encircled for seven days. ³¹By faith Rahab the prostitute did not perish with those who were disobedient, because she had received the spies in peace.

³²And what more should I say? For time would fail me to tell of Gideon, Barak, Samson, Jephthah, of David and Samuel and the prophets—³³who through faith conquered kingdoms, administered justice, obtained promises, shut the mouths of lions, ³⁴quenched raging fire, escaped the edge of the sword, won strength out of weakness, became mighty in war, put foreign armies to flight. ³⁵Women received their dead by resurrection. Others were tortured, refusing to accept release, in order to obtain a better resurrection. ³⁶Others suffered mocking and flogging, and even chains and imprisonment.

Theological Perspective

The reading this week continues the reading from Hebrews 11–12 begun last week. The writer of Hebrews has introduced the idea of faith as the courage to endure, in an effort to stiffen the spines of the little band of Christians struggling with hostility, ridicule, and shame. He has suggested that faith can be fully understood only in terms of the larger story of promise reaching back to ancient ancestors such as Abraham, who were themselves strangers, pilgrims even in the land of promise. The promise seems elusive, not identifiable with anything specific in the lives of the Christians, but nevertheless present in the form of hope, which enables one to live as a stranger in the midst of a hostile culture, reaching for what cannot yet be fully grasped.

What is striking about the present passage, especially 11:29–38, is the fact that faith seems strangely ambiguous. It may lead, on the one hand, to amazing results, such as the crossing of the Red Sea and the fall of Jericho, but it may point, on the other hand, simply to courageous endurance of torture and persecution. The reality of faith cannot be decisively recognized by empirical observation. It is faith itself that perceives the hand of God in the rescue at the Red Sea or in the courageous endurance of martyrs. I have often questioned the author's emphasis on military victories as examples of faith—

Pastoral Perspective

It is not easy being a Christian today. Defining oneself by one's beliefs and faith can be challenging socially. Friends may not understand. Relatives may look with concern. Colleagues may ask why we are willing to give up some of the earthly goods for the sake of something or someone that is difficult to see or experience.

We see a lot of discouragement within our churches today. Mainline Protestant attendance continues to decline. Our everyday challenges can be discouraging.

Today's Christians are not alone. The members of the early church also struggled with discouragement.

What has helped God's people deal with discouragement since the beginning is the knowledge that we are not alone. We follow in the footsteps of people from the earliest biblical times who were unsure of what the future held for them. We follow in the footsteps of saints who along the way chose to trust God anyway. We follow a God who does not abandon us in times of trouble. When we follow the path of staying focused on Jesus Christ our savior, we are able to see the joy in life despite the suffering.

This was the issue faced by the author of the book of Hebrews. The social context of the epistle to the Hebrews was that Jewish Christians were discouraged and demoralized. They felt excluded from the

³⁷They were stoned to death, they were sawn in two, they were killed by the sword; they went about in skins of sheep and goats, destitute, persecuted, tormented—³⁸of whom the world was not worthy. They wandered in deserts and mountains, and in caves and holes in the ground.

³⁹Yet all these, though they were commended for their faith, did not receive what was promised, ⁴⁰since God had provided something better so that they would not, apart from us, be made perfect.

^{12:1}Therefore, since we are surrounded by so great a cloud of witnesses, let us also lay aside every weight and the sin that clings so closely, and let us run with perseverance the race that is set before us, ²looking to Jesus the pioneer and perfecter of our faith, who for the sake of the joy that was set before him endured the cross, disregarding its shame, and has taken his seat at the right hand of the throne of God.

Exegetical Perspective

The reading continues to present yet further sections of the "encomium on faith" that we began to examine last week (pp. 328–33). The larger portion of Hebrews that forms this "praise of faith" comprises 11:1–40. Our lesson falls into distinct segments: 11:29, the people of Israel at the Red Sea; 11:30–31, incidents in the Israelites' conquest of the promised land; 11:32–38, a host of characters from the history of Israel who "through faith" were faithful beyond belief; 11:39–40, a summary statement with regard to those of the past with application to the readers of the letter (to the Hebrews). Then the next section of the epistle, 12:1–2, exhorts the readers to an active life of faith based upon the examples and achievements of those who were faithful in the past, especially Jesus.

In the earlier verses of Hebrews 11 (vv. 1–28) the author comments in some detail on those who are named as being paragons of faith. In the verses of our lesson, the author continues that kind of commentary with the mention of the people of Israel at the Red Sea (see Exod. 14–15), the armies of the Israelites at Jericho (Josh. 6), and Rahab (Josh. 2; 6:22–25). Each of these is introduced with the formula "by faith"; then some words of explanation are given to make clear who these characters are to whom the praise refers. The author seems to realize

Homiletical Perspective

Late August cues a host of different events. For some, it is a continuation or the start of vacation. For others, the return of the academic year or of regular familial routines looms large; agriculturally all kinds of work must be done, depending on the region. The lectionary calendar, meanwhile, does not offer much in the way of feasts this time of year. It might be tempting, therefore, to hear the strains of All Saints humming through this portion of the Letter to the Hebrews, and in this selection the listener really does hear about so many of the saints. The alert congregation may hear in this text names that otherwise go unspoken for years from lecterns, much less pulpits. This, of course, then presents some decisions for the preacher: How much teaching about these biblical characters does my congregation require? How much do I want to do? How much do I need to do in order to make the points I want to make?

Each vignette, captured in a single verse or even less, digests entire stories from the Hebrew Scriptures into neat sound bites, and each vignette could likewise be unpacked to provide material approaching different themes. From the Red Sea and Jericho, both interestingly named by their geography and not by their heroes, to Rahab the dutiful prostitute and David the wayward king, the summary of faithfulness is rich and also complex. Few, if any, of these

Hebrews 11:29-12:2

Theological Perspective

not to mention his inclusion of Jephthah in this list—but his examples do suggest incidents in which God fought for Israel, giving them victory against great odds. This does seem to fit with the earlier mention of Abraham, one "as good as dead," and of course the resurrection of Jesus. The promise is not simply an extension of the present, based on what seems possible at the moment. It is a new creation that invades our present reality and makes the impossible possible.

Christian ethics should emphasize the power of imagination much more than a compendium of moral rules. Often our moral failures are more a failure of imagination than a deficit of good intention and goodwill. We resort to violence because we have been unable to conceive a better way of dealing with conflict. As Glen Stassen reminds us in his study of the Sermon on the Mount, Jesus calls us to imagine "transforming initiatives" in following the way of Jesus.[1]

Hebrews 11:40, especially the phrase "apart from us," has often been cited to support a Christian triumphalism, the claim that, with the coming of Jesus, Christians have supplanted Israel as God's elect. The Holocaust has become a moral imperative for Christians to reconsider their relationship to Judaism, giving particular attention to anti-Jewish passages in the New Testament and two millennia of Christian anti-Semitism. The New Testament does reflect tensions between Judaism and nascent Christianity, and most early Christians probably thought of themselves as a Jewish sect. Hebrews 12:40 may be read in this triumphalist way, as suggesting that God had waited until the coming of Jesus and the establishment of the church finally to deliver on the promises made to ancient ancestors.

It is also quite plausible, however, to read this verse in a spirit of humble gratitude, similar to Paul's image of the church as a "wild olive shoot" grafted into the "rich root of the olive tree" (Rom. 11:17–24). Christians are the beneficiaries of this "cloud of witnesses," not the extraordinary heroes who finally get the job done. A triumphalist reading of any New Testament text calls into question God's faithfulness. If God has reneged on the promise to Israel, how can the church depend on God's faithfulness to the promise made through Jesus Christ?

The mention of "sin" in 12:1 invites reflection on the nature of sin. The singular form challenges our

1. Glen H. Stassen, *Just Peacemaking: Transforming Initiatives for Justice and Peace* (Louisville, KY: Westminster John Knox Press, 1992), 33–88.

Pastoral Perspective

mainstream of society and felt political pressure from the Jewish religious establishment.

Hebrews 11: 29–12:2 sets forth a vision for the church: while living the faithful life has always been a challenge, God's people can trust in their king. The purpose of this passage in its context is to encourage the Jewish Christian community to stay faithful to God in the face of the challenges of life.

Faith allows people to see beyond what is right in front of them, their daily problems, to see what God is doing in their midst, to see what God has done throughout the ages, and to see the future joy God has in store for us.

The writer of Hebrews is writing to a people who are well versed in the Old Testament, so he examines three examples of individuals for starters in the Hebrew Bible who showed great faith in God (11:29–31). The writer contrasts these examples with others who did not have such faith. The Israelites who believed walked through the sea, captured Jericho, and survived. Those who were disobedient in this example perished. This can be instructive when we think about the consequences of disbelief.

The writer of Hebrews includes additional examples from the Old Testament: Gideon, Samson, Samuel, and others who showed great faith in God (11:32–38). In doing so, the writer assumes here that his audience will be familiar with the details of these stories, and so he does not include them. These stories all lead to the same conclusion, that our faith will lead to something joyful in time, even if we cannot now foresee it. As the author of Hebrews puts it, "they were commended for their faith, (they) did not receive what was promised, since God had provided something better so that they would not, apart from us, be made perfect" (11:39–40).

God wants us to depend on God for our salvation. Faith in this passage is not about our trusting ourselves. Trust is outwardly focused. We trust the God who stayed true to our ancestors in faith and will stay true to us.

Hebrews 11 challenges us to endure suffering and to look to Jesus, who endured the cross and is now seated at the right hand of the throne of God. There is a call in the passage not to martyrdom but to endurance. The author writes that Jesus endured the cross and endured suffering for "the joy that was set before him" (12:2). Our congregations also have much to look forward to.

Why should we have optimism about our future? Do we have optimism about the future? Those are important questions for the people in our pews

that such detailed presentation is impossible for the full cadre of faithful persons about to be named.

Thus the author puts together a string of names and references to past models of faith: Gideon (Judg. 6–8), Barak (Judg. 4–5), Samson (Judg. 13–16), Jephthah (Judg. 11–12), David (1–2 Sam.), Samuel (1–2 Sam.), and "the prophets"—perhaps most especially Elijah and Elisha (1–2 Kgs.)—although the other prophets who are named in, or as the authors of, prophetic books of the Bible may be in view as well.

Having identified these figures of faith, Hebrews 11 continues by stating nine achievements attributable to these worthy figures. We read that they (1) conquered kingdoms (see Josh., Judg., and 1–2 Sam.); (2) administered justice (a reference to the general establishment of justice by these figures with special attention to the book of Judg.); (3) obtained promises (a characteristic of many of those named); (4) shut the mouths of lions (Samson [Judg. 14]; David [1 Sam. 17:31–37]; Daniel [Dan. 6]); (5) "quenched raging fires," which seems to recall Shadrach, Meshach, and Abednego (Dan. 3); (6) escaped the edge of the sword (characteristic of several judges, kings, and prophets); and (7) "won strength out of weakness," (8) "became mighty in war," and (9) "put foreign armies to flight" —three phrases reminiscent of many prominent Old Testament (and possibly apocryphal and pseudepigraphical) personalities. The author of Hebrews recognizes these prominent figures and achievements because it is assumed that these persons lived "by faith" and that their accomplishments came about "by faith" and "through faith."

Having essentially cataloged a group of prominent Old Testament personalities and their achievements, the author goes on to speak of "women" and "others." These references seem to point to both canonical (Old Testament) and extracanonical (apocryphal and pseudepigraphical) persons and deeds. First, the mention of the women who received their dead by resurrection may refer to the widow of Zarephath (1 Kgs. 17) and the Shunammite woman (2 Kgs. 4)—although those brought back to life in these stories would more accurately be described as revived or resuscitated than resurrected. In turn, however, the author refers to "others" in verses 35b–38, saying that they were "tortured, refusing to accept release. . . . They wandered in deserts and mountains, and in caves and holes in the ground" (see NRSV for full text). The use of "others" to designate those who by faith were faithful may be a general reference to Old Testament figures, but "sawn in two" seems to be a

characters are flat figures, and our lack of historical proximity to them should not prevent a balanced examination of their well-rounded stories.

The specific heroes and heroines are followed by the generic types of leaders and warriors, women and martyrs. Twenty-first-century Christians living in Western cultures may need an interpreter and guide through the list of "shut the mouths of lions" (v. 33) and "were stoned to death, they were sawn in two" (v. 37). More significantly, the preacher needs to address not just the kinds of persecutions that are included in the reading, but why faithfulness does not exempt us from these situations in the first place. This reading provides an opportunity to combat a worldview, even a theology, that claims that prosperity and blessings come automatically to those who are good and who believe.

Similarly, the passage offers another slightly countercultural viewpoint on the heroes and heroines of the faithful past: "they wandered in deserts and mountains, and in caves and holes in the ground" (v. 38). Amid all the bravery and gore of the earlier verses and before the triumph of Jesus still to come, this is a quiet interlude, but two large ideas are buried in this half verse. First, the faithful are "wanderers," and in some urban, driven, almost manic settings, this word and this concept are worth rediscovering. Secondly, the list of places in which the faithful do their wandering includes places that are quite literally wild. While these places are not lifted up in context as destinations in and of themselves, mention of them does send a message to those whose feet daily touch only concrete and linoleum. Consider Gretel Ehrlich, in *The Solace of Open Spaces*,[1] or Annie Dillard as comrades for more in this way of thinking.

Returning to the list of characters, another approach is simply to reflect on who has been added, or has not been added, to the ranks since the books were closed. Obviously, some churches have kept these lists open, and also obviously, this is a time-honored All Saints' Day tradition. Because the actual qualities that are offered come in opposites—some have military success and some are killed by the sword, some administer justice and some are captured and tortured, some shut the mouths of lions while others are stoned—the new lists we offer should be filled with contradictions. This is also an occasion to seek out the legends, mythology, epics,

---

1. Gretel Ehrlich, *The Solace of Open Spaces* (New York: Penguin, 1985).

Hebrews 11:29–12:2

Theological Perspective

popular tendency to think of sin as a list of acts or deeds that cause trouble and for which one is worthy of blame. If we do think of sin in the singular, it is usually a reference to the basic orientation of the self as one of presumption, arrogance, pride, the will to dominate. Feminist and African American theologians in recent decades have challenged us to consider the dialectical opposite of presumption and arrogance also as sin. Thus sin takes the more "passive" form of despair, apathy, servility, the refusal to accept my responsibility to God and neighbor and to God's future. Is it the case that this more passive form of sin is the bigger temptation for the community of Hebrews? Might it also be the case that this is the more pernicious sin of affluent First-World Christians? We easily accommodate ourselves to the structures and institutions of power and privilege. We eagerly volunteer for work in soup kitchens and other agencies to assist those living in poverty, but we despair of real structural change, realizing just how difficult it is and what it may cost us.

Hebrews 12:2 reinforces the writer's Christology, which seems remarkably Chalcedonian: "Jesus is fully God and fully human." The focus here is primarily on Jesus' humanity and his experience of enduring the cross for the sake of a greater joy, much like the situation facing the community of Hebrews. Jesus' suffering and death are presented, not as a sacrifice for sin, but as his entering into solidarity with all persons, having endured shame, brutal suffering, and death. Jesus, therefore, can identify with the marginalized band of Christians; for that reason they should look to Jesus, "the pioneer and perfecter of our faith." The writer images life as a long-distance race. Jesus is the one who runs ahead, sets the pace, and neutralizes the distractions that entice the runners to wander off course. It seems to be a part of every runner's experience that he or she wonders at some point in the race, "Why am I doing this?" For the small community of Christians beset with shame and hostility, Jesus becomes a reminder that the finite goods of the world, however tempting, cannot finally give life meaning. One must hold out for the ultimate promise.

JOHN C. SHELLEY

Pastoral Perspective

today. When preaching pastorally on Hebrews 11, therefore, we do well to focus on the idea that we have realistic faith for our future because of what God has done in the past. The writer of Hebrews 11 makes this point by including a list of Old Testament individuals who had great faith.

This text from Hebrews encourages our religious practice of prayer and worship. It focuses our lives on staying faithful to the God who is faithful to us. Many in the early church were ready to turn their back on God and return to the more comfortable life of the prevailing Jewish religion. The writer of the epistle encourages God's people to trust God in the future, rather than relying on the past. This text is forward looking. Jesus Christ holds the future of God's people. Those in the Hebrew Bible who were forward looking and trusted God, even if they could not see where God was leading, received their reward.

Christ on the cross was not consumed with the pain of the moment, as great as it was, but kept an eye on the joy that would come when he went to heaven and was seated with the Father. In the same way, we are to look to Jesus Christ, staying in tune with what is going on around us and not ignoring the pain we and others are feeling. However, as Christ looked to heaven, we look to Christ. The text in 12:1–2 calls us to "run with perseverance the race that is set before us, looking to Jesus."

As elsewhere in Hebrews the author argues that Jesus is a superior prophet to those who came before, in this passage he argues that faith in Christ is a better religious tenet than what we have been taught before. Trusting God is the best approach for people in every time and place. Only through faith can one find real joy.

DAVID E. GRAY

Exegetical Perspective

specific reference to *The Martyrdom and Ascension of Isaiah*, and the other descriptions included here in the text of Hebrews may recall 2 Maccabees 6–7, 4 Maccabees, and stories of martyrs of the Maccabean period who suffered severely under the Syrian king Antiochus IV.

Having commended these faithful persons, the author of Hebrews informs the reader that even these individuals did not receive "what was promised," because God had something planned— God's *perfecting* of both the faithful of former generations and the faithful of the author's present-day generation.

In turn, having examined the standard of faith as it was exemplified by the paragons of the past, the author moves on to consider the ultimate embodi-ment of faith, Jesus, who suffered greatly and yet did not lose sight of "the joy that was set before him." Hebrews 12:1–2 opens with a Greek word that is usually translated "therefore." The word is a strong inferential particle that might better be translated "consequently," as it leads into an exhortation to the readers that is based on what went before in chapter 11. The admonition uses the metaphor of a race to urge that readers both be done with sin and also persevere in the face of difficulties. Those called "witnesses" are not observers of the race, but martyrs who have given testimony in faith to God's faithfulness.

An even more significant example (or model) of faith is Jesus himself, who is called "the pioneer and perfecter of our faith." In faith he looked beyond the sufferings of the present to the reality of future "joy." In so doing, he was the "pioneer . . . of our faith." The use of "pioneer" recalls Hebrews 2:10, where it is also said that Jesus is "the pioneer of [God's children's] salvation," who was made "perfect through sufferings." Furthermore, Jesus is said to have "taken his seat at the right hand of the throne of God"—an allusion to Psalm 110 that indicates the completion of his work.

MARION L. SOARDS

Homiletical Perspective

and contemporary poetry which recount the deeds of our shared ancestry.

The shift made at the start of chapter 12 is so powerful that some congregants will forget everything else that comes before it. Rahab and Barak and the wanderers virtually vanish into the "great cloud of witnesses" (v. 1) as the listener receives the new and daunting charge "to run with perseverance the race that is set before us, looking to Jesus the pioneer and perfecter of our faith" (vv. 1–2). Reflecting on the idea of running—as a healthy but sometimes reviled chore, as an endorphin-producing addiction, as a simple part of a game or a recreational activity, as a dire need in an emergency—may produce some avenues worth exploring. Consider too the ability and agility of the listening congregation: fit, sedentary, youthful, aged? A more important word to investigate may be "perseverance," in light of a culture where waiting and long-range planning are foreign concepts.

Finally, we come to the presentation of Jesus in the passage and of the preacher's presentation of Jesus to the congregation. Of the many names and adjectives describing Jesus in the New Testament, "pioneer" stands out. In times and in places where there were still uncharted regions, how would this word have sounded different? After a century that saw human beings land on the moon, what does this word mean? The One who leads the way and opens up new possibilities and also prepares that path for those who come behind, this pioneer still can hold our imaginations. In what realms does our world still see pioneering work being done?

The passage ends with a meditation upon the work and reward of Christ. Contemplation on the balance between future joy and the immediate shame of the cross parallels some of the earlier themes of suffering and blessing; but, while Christ's suffering redeems our human events, no human's story equates to Christ's story.

KATHERINE M. BUSH

Luke 12:49-56

⁴⁹"I came to bring fire to the earth, and how I wish it were already kindled! ⁵⁰I have a baptism with which to be baptized, and what stress I am under until it is completed! ⁵¹Do you think that I have come to bring peace to the earth? No, I tell you, but rather division! ⁵²From now on five in one household will be divided, three against two and two against three; ⁵³they will be divided:

father against son
    and son against father,
mother against daughter
    and daughter against mother,
mother-in-law against her daughter-in-law
    and daughter-in-law against mother-in-law."

⁵⁴He also said to the crowds, "When you see a cloud rising in the west, you immediately say, 'It is going to rain'; and so it happens. ⁵⁵And when you see the south wind blowing, you say, 'There will be scorching heat'; and it happens. ⁵⁶You hypocrites! You know how to interpret the appearance of earth and sky, but why do you not know how to interpret the present time?"

Theological Perspective

The beginning of Luke's Gospel proclaims that Jesus will "guide our feet into the way of peace" (1:79). Near the end of the Gospel, the resurrected Jesus appears among his followers and offers a benediction of peace (24:36). Within this literary framework, how might we understand Jesus' statement that he brings "fire to the earth" (12:49), division and not peace? How can the one who tells a parable of reconciliation between father and son be the same one who sets parents against their children and children against their parents? Did he not bless with peace the sick whom he healed (7:50; 8:48)? Did he not teach his followers to bring greetings of peace as they traveled the country to share his good news (10:5–6)? In light of his own example and the testimony of his preaching, what can Jesus' words of division possibly mean?

Many preachers cringe to see this pericope appearing in the lectionary. Having more than once offered Jesus' message of repentance and reconciliation as a healing balm for fractured communities and shattered lives, we find it hard to make sense of a teaching that claims for itself the outcomes of alienation and division.

Theologians over the centuries are themselves divided about the pericope's message of separation and conflict. Some have used Jesus' words as a warrant for just-war theory in the face of very real

Pastoral Perspective

In legislative meetings, the call for a division of the house is a request to tally by number the votes on each side of an issue. If a pastor were bold enough to ask the congregation whether they preferred to discuss this text or another, seemingly sweeter text, many a hand might indicate a desire for the less challenging story about Jesus.

This lectionary text consists of eight of the toughest verses in Luke's Gospel. The language of division rather than peace, the strident tone of judgment, and Jesus' accusation that those in the crowd are "hypocrites" can be off-putting to visitor and church elder alike. Nevertheless, this Jesus is a Lord worth getting to know. The brave pastor who walks with a congregation through the messiness of this passage claims a rare opportunity to move beyond the saccharine to wrestle with a God of substance and power.

Why should it be so difficult to speak of this Jesus in our churches? In part, the Jesus portrayed in Luke 12:49–56 seems out of character with the Jesus of more familiar texts. What ever happened to the kindly carpenter who healed the man possessed by many demons in Luke 8:26–39 or stopped for supper at the home of Mary and Martha in Luke 10:38–42?

The congregation that has been following the lectionary all summer will know that a decisive turn

Exegetical Perspective

Jesus' words in this text are stark, even shocking. On the one hand the imagery of fire, baptism, and division sounds more like the preaching of John the Baptist than that of Jesus (see 3:7–9, 15–17). On the other hand, these words assert that Jesus has not come to validate human institutions and their values but to initiate God's radical will. The verses just before this lection focus on how disciples are to be attentively prepared for Jesus' incalculable but certain future coming (12:35–48). Now the text shifts to focus on the impact Jesus' mission has on the status quo of human lives.

English translations do not fully capture the vivid language and emphases in verses 49–50. The emphatic opening word in the Greek of verse 49 is "fire," while in verse 50 it is "baptism." Thus the text is highlighting the anticipated results of Jesus' missional advent. Similarly, the pervasive English translation "how I wish" in verse 49 fails to capture Jesus' ardent commitment to implement God's will. In verse 50 the expression typically translated either as "stress" or "distressed" is not meant to show Jesus' anxiety. Rather, the Greek highlights how Jesus is totally absorbed in the mission he has come to accomplish.

Set within the entirety of Luke–Acts, such dramatic language and imagery reinforce Jesus' resolute determination to journey to Jerusalem in

Homiletical Perspective

If, as Gene Lowry suggests, it is fruitful for preachers to approach biblical texts by "looking for trouble,"[1] this pericope provides an embarrassment of riches.

Since last week's lesson, the tone of Jesus' voice in Luke has turned in the direction of shrill. In the intervening material (conveniently omitted by the lectionary) he shifts from talking about servants who are fed supper by an approving master to servants who (for misconduct) are badly beaten (even "cut in pieces," v. 46) by a master displeased with the state of affairs at his unexpected return.

Jesus, who only recently was rebuking James and John for wanting to bring down fire on unwelcoming Samaritans, suddenly declares that he cannot wait to bring down fire himself. (Can you hear James and John complaining, "How come *you* get to when we do not?") Granted, as he confesses, Jesus is "stressed," but it has not been long since he enjoined *them*: "Do not worry" (12:32).

Worse, the one whose birth was heralded by an angelic chorus of "peace on earth" proceeds to announce *not* peace, but *division* and spells that out in assorted vignettes of domestic dispute that sound not at all family-values friendly (vv. 52–53).

1. Eugene L. Lowry, *The Sermon: Dancing the Edge of Mystery* (Nashville: Abingdon Press, 1997), 94–95.

Luke 12:49-56

Theological Perspective

clashes between and among the nations. Others have seen in the juxtaposition of parent and child a description of the division that occurs between believers and unbelievers when these are confronted by the blinding light of the gospel. Both of these views may perhaps be captured in the lines of Julia W. Howe's 1861 "Battle Hymn of the Republic," in which Christ's triumphant return "hath loosed the fateful lightning of His terrible swift sword. . . . He is sifting out the hearts of men before his judgment seat. . . . His truth is marching on."

Still others, influenced by ancient Greek notions of rationality or by the individualistic ideals of modernity, suggest a symbolic interpretation in which the parent-child conflict represents the division within the self between the mind and the passions, as rational thought seeks to overpower the impulses of sin. These varied responses to the apparent contradiction between the declaration of division in this pericope, on the one hand, and Jesus' overarching message of reconciliation and peace throughout the Gospel of Luke, on the other, offer ample justification for the preacher's dilemma.

Not only is the central theological message of the pericope difficult to pin down, but so too are some of its details. Is the fire that Jesus brings a baptism of fire like the Holy Spirit at Pentecost, burning in the hearts and upon the heads of numerous believers, enflaming them to mighty deeds of faithfulness (cf. 3:16)? Is it, rather, the refiner's fire, burning away the chaff of sin or the fruitless branches that do not bear fruit (cf. 3:9, 17)? Is it the fire of judgment, raining down from heaven upon the heads of God's enemies (cf. 17:28–33)?

Perhaps the dilemmas and tensions of Jesus' saying cannot, and should not, be completely resolved. Instead, the pericope is best understood in light of the totality of the gospel story and the interplay between the ways of God and the realities of human history. In that light, one could say that the passage is *descriptive* rather than *prescriptive*. That is, it is not Jesus' purpose to set children against their parents, or parents against their children, but this sort of rupture can be the result of the changes engendered by Christ's work. Indeed, Luke's Gospel, in which this passage appears, includes the Prodigal Son, a parable about a younger son and his father, long estranged by the son's actions, who are reconciled at the end (15:11–32). Even their reconciliation, however, bears the seeds of rupture, as their renewed relationship results in division between elder son and father. Jesus' teaching in our

Pastoral Perspective

occurs in Luke 9:51, when Jesus "set[s] his face to go to Jerusalem." Although mid-August may seem far removed from Holy Week, the proper backdrop for this text rests with those somber, final days leading up to Good Friday. Helping the congregation make that connection through the liturgy and hymns chosen for this week will create a context for understanding the sermon before the preacher even begins to speak.

It may help for the pastor to reflect on ways the strong language of this text might be difficult for some in the congregation to engage if they have experienced judgment or unkind treatment from church people in the past. Only a thin wall separates the sanctuary from the lived experience of the congregation during the week. Those who gather for worship carry with them into worship a lifetime of personal experience, psychological complexity, and sometimes very painful memories from other congregations. That includes awful and shameful things that have been done in the name of Christ's church.

A congregation that lives out Christian practices of inclusive welcome and hospitality will have an easier time listening to Jesus' words of judgment if they do not allow an uncritical emotional reaction to exclusionary practices they have seen in the past. Where issues of family life—including divorce, generational conflict, and the hard work of reconciliation—are often topics for open discussion, it will be far easier to talk about the divided households of Luke 12 than in those parish settings where the challenges of domestic life are simply never addressed. The congregation that regularly makes a common confession of sin and hears an absolution directed to the real-life failures of this generation will be far more likely to know that, beyond Jesus' stern speaking to the crowd, there awaits an equally strong word of forgiveness and God's tender embrace.

This week would not be the time to introduce all those as new initiatives, but the summer months do offer an opportunity to reflect on the faith practices of the congregation. Who is welcome within this gathered community, and how is that word of welcome conveyed in deeds as well as words? What variety of households is represented in the congregation? Are single adults included in all aspects of the congregation's life? Are families without children as likely to find welcome as families with children? Are the divorced, the widowed, the partnered gay or lesbian, and the person estranged from all family members welcomed and tapped for leadership roles according to their gifts?

order to accomplish God's plan through his death and resurrection, as first introduced in 9:22, 31, 44–45, 51 (and subsequently reiterated in 13:31–35; 17:24–25; 18:31–34; 22:14–20, 41–42). Suffering and death will be the baptism into which Jesus will be completely immersed. The fire he has come to cast on earth is not so much eschatological destruction (as John the Baptist envisions in 3:9, 17) but the divided and often hostile responses that the Spirit-inspired proclamation of Jesus' death and resurrection will engender (e.g., Acts 3:12–4:4; 13:16–52). As Jesus' future coming obviates all laxity on the part of his disciples (Luke 12:35–38, 42–47), so too is Jesus fully compelled to accomplish the mission for which he has been sent, so that its results spread to the ends of the earth (12:49, 51; Acts 1:8; 13:47).

Jesus' emphatic words on division in 12:51–53 need to be understood in relationship to core social realities of the first-century world. In that world (whether in Jewish or Gentile realms), the household is the fundamental building block for society. Indeed, the household is regarded as a microcosm of social reality. By claiming to bring not peace but division (v. 51) and then illustrating such divisions in terms of the household (vv. 52–53), the text declares that Jesus' missional advent is not the affirmation of the current social status quo but means its complete obliteration. This is an extension of the radical social reversals first declared by Mary (1:51–55) and Zechariah (1:68–79), and then reiterated in even stronger ways by Jesus (4:16–27; 6:20–26; 7:28–30, 36–50; 8:19–21; 9:46–48).

This imagery of household divisions (echoing Mic. 7:6) carries with it the notion of the complete collapse of current structures as in 11:17–18. Note too that the divisions depicted in 12:52–53 are generational, so that no longer will one's identity, vocation, allegiance, and status automatically be predetermined by family ties. Instead, these will be determined by one's positive or negative stance toward Jesus as first declared by Simeon (2:34–35); also see the depiction of familial upheavals and realignments presented in 9:57–62; 11:27–28; 14:26; 18:28–30; 21:16–17).

Jesus' emphatic denial that he came to bring peace (v. 51) also needs to be considered in relationship to the divine peace that is inaugurated through his advent, as declared by Zechariah (1:79), the angelic army (2:14), Jesus (7:50; 8:48; 10:5–6; 19:42), and his disciples (19:38). The divinely wrought peace that Jesus inaugurates and bestows involves the establishment of proper relationships of

Finally, Jesus starts calling people names again: "hypocrites!" this time, instead of "you fool!" A case can be made for the former name-calling (as we did when discussing that lection); but the apparent invective on this occasion is even more puzzling. What exactly renders a right reading of the weather, coupled with an inability to "interpret the present time," *hypocritical*? Perhaps a brief word about each "trouble" will help to get the sermon process going.

1. The Shrill Sound of Servants Punished or "Cut Off."[2] The behavior severely punished is abuse of other servants, and selfish squandering of food and drink in intemperate orgies. Easy to miss beneath Jesus' graphic language is the additional phrase "put with the unfaithful" (12:46). Failing to rightly administer the gift of the kingdom, intended for all, is ipso facto to put oneself outside the kingdom. (The unfaithful servant by his abuse and misappropriation stands in essentially the same shoes as the foolish rich man.) This has illuminating implications for the kind of "division" that is at the center of the pericope at hand.

2. Fire Brought to Earth by Jesus. There is a significant difference between fire that cleanses and fire that incinerates. James and John envision the latter (9:52–56); Jesus intends the former (12:49). Furthermore, the fire Jesus calls down is a fire he takes upon himself—a "baptism by fire" about which he is "stressed" because it entails his own passion (12:50), voluntarily endured, rather than a holocaust vindictively imposed. It is "the father's good pleasure to give . . . the kingdom" (12:32), but the cost of that gift is Jesus' own self-giving.

3. Family Division Instead of Peace. If what the kingdom God intends is, in fact, a radical common-wealth, then those who insist on keeping its inheritance "within the family" will inevitably find themselves at odds with *other* family members whose vision of a wider "family" is infused by the compassionate fire of Jesus' own radical love. To demand peace (and prosperity) at the expense of those on the margins is to cry, "'Peace, peace,' when there is no peace"(Jer. 8:11). Until we get beyond tribal understandings of "peace in our time" (and on our terms),

---

2. "Cut off" is an acceptable alternative translation to "cut in pieces" in Luke 12:46, and seems more congruent with the direction and intent of the narrative in this parable than "cut in pieces"—if for no other reason than that it would make no sense to "put with the unfaithful" someone who has already been "cut in pieces"!

Luke 12:49-56

Theological Perspective

pericope reflects that same reality. A ministry that reconciles long-standing enemies will inevitably rend relationships that depended on the old status quo.

Humankind does not always appreciate the gospel's great reversals. We do not like it when those we deem undeserving receive the abundant grace promised to all. We want others to be punished for their sin, while we expect to be welcomed into the heavenly home (nobody expects to see their enemies in heaven!). Jealousy, anger, desire for revenge, resistance to change: these can consume us in the face of the gospel, to the point that we find ourselves antagonists against those whom Jesus welcomes.

Jesus' teaching also speaks to the reality of a kinship based not on familial blood ties, but on a covenant of Jesus' blood (22:20). Even among his own people, where he is known as "Joseph's son" (4:22), Jesus becomes an outsider when he announces his mission from God. And when his own mother and brothers try to get close to him, he redefines the familial ties that bind his true family to him: "My mother and my brothers are those who hear the word of God and do it" (8:21). What ties believers together is not the covenant of lineage but the covenant of blood, poured out for those who find fellowship in the family of God.

In art and poetry over the centuries, Jesus is depicted in images ranging from the gentle shepherd to the conquering lamb. Even "The Battle Hymn of the Republic" includes both sorts of images—the one who is born "in the beauty of the lilies" is the same one who "hath loosed the fateful lightning of his terrible swift sword." In theological terms, these twin images represent Christ's mercy and judgment, born out of the reconciling power of God to defeat evil and sin. The passage suggests that—at the opportune time and under the impulse of God—when division begins, the gospel has begun to break in among us.

AUDREY WEST

Pastoral Perspective

How are interpersonal relationships—including the dynamics of family life—addressed in small groups and study opportunities? Has the congregation acquired skills and patience for talking together about issues that often divide families or communities? Is there room for "hot topics" in the congregation's life, or are all divisive issues avoided? Building the capacity to listen to one another on highly charged themes takes time and skill; once established, it is a rare and precious gift.

Where and when are there opportunities for the congregation to stand before God with open hearts, seeking God's forgiveness and the courage to live a Christlike life? Is there hope for those who hear this Gospel text as an accurate indictment of their lives? Beyond formal worship, are there other opportunities for personal confession and reconciliation with God?

The pastor who serves in a congregation where those faith practices have taken root will have a fighting chance of being heard when this Gospel text comes around. Jesus' single-minded determination is a passion we do recognize and often admire. It is like that of the neighborhood activist who goes to work to clean up a block in her city after a child dies in a drive-by shooting. It is similar to the passion of the senior citizen who single-handedly takes on the state legislature to make it easier for elders to purchase at a reasonable cost the prescription drugs they need. It is akin to the zeal of the elementary school student who challenges the congregation to go "green" and is relentless in her presentations to all who will listen. Some things matter so much that only focused attention and strong speech can carry the prophet's message.

A God willing to die for us and for this creation is one of those singular matters. That Jesus has no patience with those who do not grasp the urgency of his pilgrimage to Jerusalem, his mission there, and his life's work. That rests at the heart of this Gospel text. The pastor's task is to help the congregation hear that, finally, as a message of God's grace and mercy. That is worthy work anytime in the year.

PATRICIA J. LULL

mercy, compassion, and justice between God and humanity. Not everyone, however, wants or welcomes this divine peace plan. Hence the initiation of Jesus' peace agenda also triggers contentious disunity and fissures among all facets of society, right down to the societal core of the household. The fact that such divisions include both men and women reinforces Luke's understanding that both men and women will respond either positively or negatively to God's agenda initiated in Jesus' mission and extended through the mission of the disciples.[1] Hence decisive religious decision making is no longer the exclusive prerogative of males.

In Luke 11:16, 29–32 Jesus chastises the crowds for seeking a sign from him to test the validity of his ministry. In 12:54–56 he chastises the crowds for their complete inability to interpret the divine activity now unfolding in their midst.[2] Their interpretive failings are compounded by the fact that though they know how to interpret the harbingers of impending weather patterns (vv. 54–55), they have failed to interpret the harbinger of God's eschatological judgment as it unfolds in the social disruptions caused by the ministry of Jesus.[3]

The harsh sayings and indictments resounding in this text remind us that Jesus has not come to validate the social realities and values we have constructed. Such social realities and values have a propensity to seek a harmony that favors those who hold positions of power at the expense of those who are powerless and expendable. Jesus' missional agenda of compassion, mercy, and justice shatters such a status quo. This is a missional agenda that compels him toward his divine destiny to be accomplished in his death and resurrection. It is the agenda that will result in divisions and contentions on all levels of society, as people are either embraced or repelled by what God is doing through Jesus. It is the agenda that we are called to recognize in the present in anticipation of God's future. It is the agenda that causes us to reinterpret what God is truly about in the person of Jesus, and so to reinterpret who we are and what we are about as disciples of Jesus.

RICHARD P. CARLSON

1. Luke 1:5–25, 26–38, 39–56; 2:34–35, 36–40; 7:36–50; 8:1–3, 40–56; 10:38–42; 13:10–17; 15:1–10; 24:1–12; Acts 1:13–14; 2:17–18; 5:1–11, 14; 8:3, 12; 13:48–50; 16:14–40; 17:4, 12, 34; 18:2–4.
2. Joel Green, *The Gospel of Luke*, New International Commentary on the New Testament (Grand Rapids: Eerdmans, 1997), 508.
3. The reference to "present time" in v. 56 matches the reference to "from now on" in v. 52. Also note crucial time markers in 12:20, 40, 42, 46; 13:1, 9.

the peace on earth proclaimed by angels will remain a peace that "surpasses all understanding" (Phil. 4:7).

4. Good Weather Forecasters but Poor Time Interpreters as "Hypocrites." Classical moral theology distinguishes between "vincible" and "invincible" ignorance. The former is ignorance we are morally responsible to eradicate; failure to do so constitutes "culpable negligence." The latter is ignorance beyond our control, for which we are not held responsible.

If the crowd whom Jesus addresses are involuntarily ("invincibly") ignorant, they will not be held accountable for their failure to "interpret the present time." They will be like the slave Jesus has just described who does not know his master's wishes, and receives minimal punishment. (His negligence is not totally excusable, but his inability to recognize what is required of him serves as a mitigating circumstance.)

The crowd (presumably) is "vincibly ignorant." They have failed to take responsible care for learning from the rich and readily available tradition of Law and Prophets that would enable them to identify commonwealth resource mismanagement and its inevitable negative repercussions in God's economy. They are thus like the slave who, in an attempt to avert just punishment, cries out (fraudulently), "I did not know you were coming or what you wanted me to do."

Such a claim, of course, *is* hypocritical—he (and, by implication, the crowd) *do* know (or are responsible for knowing) that of which they are feigning ignorance. If (as seems plausible) Jesus is charging the crowd with "vincible ignorance," then they are like those who *should* know how to "interpret the present time." To say "we had no idea" is akin to the excuse of bureaucratic servants at all levels of government who protested "how could we have known?" with respect to the devastation wrought by Hurricane Katrina. They *should* have known, and *are* morally responsible for their lack of knowledge.

How tragically, culpably foolish to act in light of what one knows with respect to the patterns and signs of weather, but to claim excusable ignorance with regard to the evident patterns, graceful manifestations, and warning signs of God's kingdom/commonwealth promise! In calling the rich farmer "fool," and the negligent crowd "hypocrites," Jesus does not engage in name-calling; he names what is going on for exactly what it is. That, inevitably though not surprisingly, provokes a sharp division. To gain a hearing, shrill is sometimes needed.

DAVID J. SCHLAFER

Jeremiah 1:4-10

⁴Now the word of the LORD came to me saying,
⁵ "Before I formed you in the womb I knew you,
and before you were born I consecrated you;
I appointed you a prophet to the nations."
⁶Then I said, "Ah, Lord GOD! Truly I do not know how to speak, for I am only a
boy." ⁷But the LORD said to me,
"Do not say, 'I am only a boy';
for you shall go to all to whom I send you,
and you shall speak whatever I command you.
⁸ Do not be afraid of them,
for I am with you to deliver you,
says the LORD."
⁹Then the LORD put out his hand and touched my mouth; and the LORD said to me,
"Now I have put my words in your mouth.
¹⁰ See, today I appoint you over nations and over kingdoms,
to pluck up and to pull down,
to destroy and to overthrow,
to build and to plant."

Theological Perspective

During quadrennial election cycles in the United States, waggish pundits are wont to oil the old political saw: "Whoever desires to be president should be disqualified out of hand." One routine version of this familiar zinger suggests institutionalization, as well: anyone who dares imagine he or she is capable of such responsibility must be as deluded as megalomaniacal, a danger as much to self as to the republic. By this same sardonic reasoning, an individual's reluctance to accept the job—who would refuse the "nomination" should it come—is hailed as the one appropriate, if ironic, commendation.

The Hebrew Scriptures evidence a similar perspective regarding the call and ministry of the prophets. An initial and even ongoing reluctance to embrace the appointed task or speak the divine word can serve to *prove* God's summons, more or less, and legitimize the prophet. Indeed, false prophets are those who most often speak too glibly and eagerly in the name of the Almighty, offering as God's a word that is no word at all, or at least no word they themselves have heard. False prophets speak the pleasing and populist word, the unfounded and optimistic word, the immediately peaceful word, when in fact (as is certainly the case in Jeremiah) there is no quick or lasting peace to proclaim.

Pastoral Perspective

These words from Jeremiah are likely the most familiar of Jeremiah's words for the community of faith, rivaled perhaps only by Jeremiah 29:11, "For surely I know the plans I have for you." Many congregants, even without knowing the exact biblical reference for the words, will recognize the words "Before I formed you in the womb I knew you" as familiar words that have been a part of their vocabulary of faith. It will feel like familiar ground.

The experience of scriptural familiarity in and of itself can bring a sense of comfort and security that may or may not be connected with the actual message of the text. Pastors do well to acknowledge and honor before the people how Scripture is written over time on our hearts and in our consciousness, and how this familiarity becomes a part of the heritage of faith, indeed, the treasury of faith shaping our lives. Where does the congregation recall these verses from Jeremiah first sounding in their regular hearing? Such an examination is a way for pastors to acknowledge before congregants, "Something here is precious for you," and also to affirm for the community the truth that Scripture is precious and treasured in the hearts of the faithful.

In the case of Jeremiah 4:1–10, some of that treasure and comfort for the faithful comes from the

Exegetical Perspective

This passage introduces us to the prophet Jeremiah and begins a series of lectionary readings from the book of Jeremiah. Usually referred to as the call of Jeremiah, these verses show many of the standardized features of prophetic call narratives in the Old Testament:

God's initiating word (v. 5)
Objection (v. 6)
[Chastisement (v. 7), not standard in all call narratives]
Reassurance (v. 8)
Commissioning (vv. 9–10)

This pattern for the narration of call stories is widespread with some variations, but a clearly traditional pattern (cf. Moses, Gideon, Saul, Isaiah, Ezekiel). The shaping of the call story in this pattern suggests a mature prophet looking back on the experience of his call, rather than a narrative of the moment. As in the experience of many of us called into God's service, we understand more fully what we experienced as the stirrings of God's call when we reflect back on the experience, and witness to that call often takes a form we could not have given it at the time.

Homiletical Perspective

This text, like others in the book of Jeremiah, offers a striking glimpse into the intimate, often tumultuous relationship between Jeremiah and the God whose word he uneasily bears. We are moved by this portrait of a vulnerable, reluctant prophet who feels too young and too inexperienced to bear the weight of the divine word. Little wonder that many preachers and congregations, daunted by their own sense of inadequacy for divine service, have treated this text as a mirror of their own experience. If we can see our own vulnerability in Jeremiah's, if we can hear our own reluctance in his protests, maybe we can also take to heart God's assurance that the one who calls will also sustain.

Although certainly there are times to preach this text along these lines, preachers need to be careful not to make this (or any biblical call narrative, for that matter) "all about us." Our angst and ambivalence are real—but, frankly, somewhat beside the point. This text above all stakes crucial claims about the God whose word will come through Jeremiah and about the active, disruptive nature of that word in Jeremiah's day and in our own.

Different sections of the text suggest at least three theological themes for preaching: (1) A sermon based on the divine-human dialogue of verses 4–10

Jeremiah 1:4-10

Theological Perspective

True prophets speak "against the data"[1]—the often displeasing word, the upsetting and foreboding word that will be proven true only over time. Perhaps that very isolating and countercultural dimension of true prophecy is at least part of the true prophet's reluctance: in the short term, the word will be regarded as false and will be unwelcomed, along with its speaker. The word from God will marginalize and even endanger the prophet—and who campaigns for *that* job?

No surprise, then, that when God summons a prophet, the prophet characteristically demurs or even flees. One need think only of Moses and his fourfold attempt to deflect God's claim on his future life and work (Exod. 3:11–4:10). For our present purposes, the fourth of Moses's objections is most salient: "O, my Lord, I am not eloquent, either heretofore or since thou hast spoken to thy servant; but I am slow of speech and of tongue" (4:10 RSV). God's reply is that as Creator—and, it turns out, Redeemer—God is quite as able to refashion as to fashion—whether thick tongues to speak or deaf ears to hear.

Luther's famous benediction regarding Erasmus, "Truth is more powerful than eloquence,"[2] is ripe for application in either the exodus or today's text, but the obvious and acute irony of Moses's call serves as apt background for a consideration of Jeremiah 1:4–10. God's word comes to the young prophet, telling him that God chose him when Jeremiah was younger still. If the language of "setting apart" or "consecration" has a priestly connotation, it may be a tip of the crown, as it were, toward Jeremiah's priestly lineage. Still, he is commissioned a prophet. Jeremiah's objection, "I am too *young*," echoes the objection of Moses.

Moses is not eloquent. Jeremiah is not wise or wizened. Isaiah, for his part, deems himself unworthy: "I am a man of unclean lips and I live among a people of unclean lips" (Isa. 6:5). How shall Isaiah's lips be able to speak a righteous and purging word? Only as God applies to them hot coals from the high altar, of course.

Protests of inadequacy, whether real or imagined, serve to reinforce a basic biblical and theological truth: the actual work of transformation is effected by God alone. Such redemption—often beginning with the prophet, but extending to the situation or nation—is a result of God's word and not any virtue

1. Walter Brueggemann, *Theology of the Old Testament: Testimony, Dispute, Advocacy* (Minneapolis: Augsburg Fortress, 2005; orig. 1997), 76.
2. Martin Luther, *The Bondage of the Will*; trans. J. I. Packer (Peabody, MA: Hendrickson, 2008; orig. 1525), 66.

Pastoral Perspective

assurance that they are known (v. 5). While in the text the prophet Jeremiah reports, "Now the word of the LORD came *to me* saying, 'Before I formed you in the womb I knew you,'" repeatedly the community hears in that a declaration about the all-knowing character of God and deduces that they also have been known before they were even conceived. Other Scriptures also support this deduction for the community of faith (e.g., Ps. 139).

The belief that one is known by God and has been known by God since before one's conception deeply strengthens the hearer's sense of individual worth. It runs contrary to the human angst that in a vast universe our small lives might be meaningless. In the textual declaration, "Before I formed you in the womb I knew you," congregations hear the affirmation that God has known us longer and better even than our own parents and prior to our own consciousness.

The text buttresses for the listener the legitimacy of human dignity and the purpose of individual life. Pastorally this Scripture is often heard on the occasion of baptism, where a person's individual name is called during the sacrament as a way of saying, "This specific person is known and claimed by God through Christ." This verse is also lifted up at confirmations and ordinations and quoted widely in the debate about abortion. Many pastors have found it a helpful text to share in hospital rooms or at funerals, in places where crisis or loss seems to deny what the church has heard the text affirm. It has served as a sort of declaration of faith in the divine assertion of human dignity and worth in moments where the human story seems to send the opposite message.

This is a particularly meaningful text in a world where the lives of so many children—street children, child laborers, children living in the midst of violence, neglected or abused children—appear to assert a different reality. In that sense it is an audacious text that declares for the church an audacious faith in a God who not only affirms, but indeed creates individual human worth and dignity. Pastorally, it is such a deep and significant affirmation that it may be difficult for congregations to hear beyond the first clause of the first verse of this pericope.

The text does go on. It reports the prophet's memory of his being "consecrated" and "appointed" (v. 5). These experiences also will resonate with the listeners. In this text the church and individual parishioners have found language that articulates their own experience of being set apart for a certain task or called to a specific purpose. As with the first

Exegetical Perspective

In that light, several features of his call experience seem clear to Jeremiah in this testimony and now speak clearly to us as we read Jeremiah's witness.

In verses 4–5 Jeremiah seems clear that calling is a divine initiative, and in God's providential purposes far precedes any summing up of human assessment or decision making. God's purposes for Jeremiah precede even his conception and birth. This is less a statement of divine determinism than a decisive witness that a call to God's service is not a carefully considered career choice. Each prophetic call story states it somewhat differently, but all are clear that divine initiative comes decisively from outside of the prophet and requires a response. This divine compulsion precedes any of our careful decision-making processes, often in times and ways that do not fully make sense in human terms.

In Jeremiah's case, and to his astonishment and objection, this call makes itself known to him as a boy (v. 6). How could God want and call someone so young? This text has, of course, been the subject of countless youth-event sermons encouraging the younger members of our congregations that God can indeed call them. This is a legitimate passage to lift up for that purpose. The particular objection of Jeremiah is but one example of the countless objections thrown up to deflect the force of God's call to service. In biblical and contemporary experience the call of God is often counter to what passes for common human wisdom. God often calls unlikely people in unlikely times and circumstances—or so it seems, when measured in commonly accepted human terms.

Since the role of a prophet is to speak God's word, the objection of Jeremiah is that he is too young to know how to speak. Speaking is often the focus in these call-narrative objections. Moses objects that he is unskilled, Isaiah that he is unworthy, Ezekiel that he does not know what to say. In our text Jeremiah argues that as a boy he does not have enough experience. The rebuke to Jeremiah in verse 7 is that the call to proclaim God's word requires reliance on what God gives, not what we can speak by our own power: "You shall speak whatever I command you" (v. 7). This suggests that openness to what God has to say through us is more important than our own facility to come up with clever or inspiring words. Openness, discernment, willingness to be sent mean more than the personal qualities or skills of the prophetic speaker. These may grow, as they certainly do in Jeremiah's career, but a radical awareness that he speaks out of God's

Homiletical Perspective

can emphasize the wedding of divine passion and human passion that bears the word into the world. (2) A sermon might focus primarily on verse 10 to explore the Word that must break as well as build. (3) Finally, if the preacher opts for the longer lectionary selection (including vv. 11–18), the sermon can focus on the two visions of the almond branch and boiling pot, which reveal the God who watches and acts amid human affairs, especially the use and abuse of power.

1. The Wedding of Divine and Human Passion in God's Word for the World. A sermon might focus on what verses 4–10 reveal about God's passionate commitment to speak into every present age, and the essential God-given role of human beings, individually and collectively, to bear God's passionate word into the world.

Verses 4–10, presenting Jeremiah and YHWH in direct, personal dialogue, reveal the characteristic "double agency" by which the divine word is turned loose in the world. Preachers can make a conscious choice to make the fulcrum for proclamation less about Jeremiah's ambivalence and more focused on the driving passion of God to be engaged with God's people. To be sure, one function of these verses is to introduce us to Jeremiah, the uneasy prophet; but more importantly, we find ourselves grasped by a God passionate for the fate of human beings. When we are called as individuals or congregations into the service of God's word and way, God's passion for goodness and wholeness becomes our passion as well, taking shape amid the specific realities of the contexts where we bear witness.

2. The Word That Breaks and Builds. Another approach would be to concentrate on the active verbs in verse 10 ("to pluck up and to pull down, to destroy and to overthrow, to build and to plant"). Destruction, dislocation, exposure, loss: these themes will thunder throughout the book of Jeremiah. The notes of hope will be delayed and subdued.

The word that God sends into the world through Jeremiah is a disruptive word, because it is the word of the covenant-keeping God. Jeremiah is replete with allusions to the Sinai covenant and the tradition of covenant blessings and covenant sanctions.[1] Because the God whose word Jeremiah bears is specifically the covenant partner of the

---

1. See Walter Brueggemann, *The Theology of the Book of Jeremiah* (New York: Cambridge University Press, 2007), 2, 10–16, 23–26.

Jeremiah 1:4-10

Theological Perspective

of the prophet (or other leader, such as Gideon). God equips the called, in other words; God does not call the equipped.

The divine word comes to the prophet unbidden and unmediated; the prophet will henceforth be the mouthpiece of the Almighty, mediating to the hard-eared people an analogously unbidden and most often unwelcome word. Who indeed is either able or eager to put their lips around such a word? Time and again the prophets are uncertain their very human tongues can begin to speak such a mouthful. Who wants to? Certainly not Jonah!

The story of Jonah's call to preach in Nineveh is an ironic twist of the irony. Jonah does not lack eloquence or wisdom as much as willingness. God calls. Jonah resists—but not, like Isaiah, for any *perceived* inadequacy on his own part. Rather, his patriotic disdain of God's universalizing mercy sends him toward Tarshish. As is usually the case, God insists. Soon, damply, Jonah slogs his way across the great city, warning of God's judgment. To Jonah's horror, his (unenthusiastic) preaching occasions the Ninevites' genuine repentance, which in turn cools God's anger, which only stokes Jonah's.

In each case, God rejects rejection to set the prophets on their lifelong if unhappy task. The prophet eventually acquiesces, even embraces (or eats, in the case of Ezekiel) the divine word. Judgment, restoration, or both are ultimately proclaimed, and the spoken word accomplishes what God intends.

Even before the time and call of Jeremiah, the pattern is well attested in the narratives. It is not exhaustive, however. There are some prophets, like Samuel and even Ezekiel, who from their first inklings of prophetic consciousness seem at home with their call, confirmed in their role, eager to embrace their work and its consequences (even when the message they bring is unpleasant). Still, these exceptions go to prove the theological rule, that as surely as God's word comes to a prophet, so does that prophet attempt (at least initially) to demur.

So the theology of this and other call narratives is intentionally ironic. Perhaps the irony of the story is its theology: only the human who knows the impossibility of the task, who may even seek to flee the responsibility, can actually do it.

THOMAS R. STEAGALD

Pastoral Perspective

clause of verse 5, the text seems to have functioned in the community of faith in a way that moves the listener quickly from Jeremiah's experience to reflecting on his or her own experience. The attentive pastor can see that it is for much more than their own ordination that this text is a mirror. Parishioners find in the passage language that resonates with their sense of the Spirit's bringing them to a certain work or task. They report conversations: "Pastor, I just knew I was supposed to be going on that mission trip." "I had the deepest feeling I needed to call and check up on that neighbor." Jeremiah reports being "appointed a prophet to the nations"; his vocation has a global scope. Parishioners find the text articulates their own sense of call and appointment, regardless of the scope and sphere of their own lives and responsibilities.

Jeremiah's report that he did not consider himself up to the task for which he was called mirrors for many persons their feelings in their own experience of God's call. In Jeremiah's words, "Ah, Lord GOD! Truly I do not know how to speak, for I am only a boy" (v. 6), congregants find an affirmation of how they have felt in the face of their own sense of God's call. The text is validation of their own spiritual experience. They find courage in the textual exhortation: "Do not be afraid of them, for I am with you to deliver you, says the LORD" (v. 8).

The dutiful pastor may have to help lead parishioners to reflect on the meaning, for their own faith journey, of Jeremiah's report that his call was not only "to build and to plant" but "to pluck up and to pull down, to destroy and to overthrow" (v. 10). It is likely that part of Jeremiah's call will not resonate as clearly with people's discernment of their own, yet faithful people can find in the prophet a guide to both the promise and the difficulties of serving our God.

JOHN T. DEBEVOISE

power and not his own serves Jeremiah throughout his career, long after he is no longer a boy.

The reassurance in verse 8 is the often-expressed promise of God's presence with those called to lead in God's community. Awareness and trust in God's presence is what drives out fear and brings deliverance. For Jeremiah, this will include fears and dangers from actual enemies who both slander his name and seek physically to harm him. Importantly, this promise of divine presence drives out the inner fear that leads to self-doubt and the temptation to abandon the trust in God at the heart of the call to proclaim God's word. The passionate and poignant passages sometimes called the "confessions of Jeremiah" reveal the extent of inner struggle that plague Jeremiah (e.g., Jer. 20:7–18). To hear and believe that God is with us is central to the leadership of God's people. Trust in God provides the foundation to receive the commission God gives.

Jeremiah's commissioning as God's prophet is first expressed in a physical act: God touches his mouth (v. 9). This parallels the purging of Isaiah's mouth with a burning coal (Isa. 6:6–7) and Ezekiel's mouth filled with the scroll of God's word (Ezek. 2:8–3:3). Again the emphasis is on divine initiative and divine origin of the word one proclaims. The physical act is followed by the direct statement: "I have put my words in your mouth" (v. 9). It is God's word that Jeremiah is to speak, not his own.

The content of verse 10 is the substance of Jeremiah's mission. The arena is not his village of Anathoth but nations and kingdoms. God's call almost always sends those who are called into contexts beyond their own comfortable experience. What follow are six terms that define the content of Jeremiah's preaching. Four suggest a message of God's judgment and the consequences of that judgment for God's people. In Jeremiah's own lifetime, these words of judgment will become reality. The experience of plucking up, pulling down, destroying, and overthrowing clearly relate to the experience of Babylonian exile and the destruction of Jerusalem that Jeremiah will witness in his lifetime. Such judgment is not God's final word, however. Jeremiah will also announce God's intention to build and to plant. God will redeem and renew, and Jeremiah has a word for God's people beyond the reality of exile. The commission to proclaim God's word will not be complete with the declaration of God's judgment. Hope has the final word.

BRUCE C. BIRCH

Jewish people, their God is emphatically *not* the on-call divine patron of whatever self-interested schemes, religious or political, the nation's leaders may devise. Right worship matters. Right treatment of the poor and the stranger matters. When these are neglected, the anguish of the God of Sinai breaks out through God's servants in a potent amalgam of outrage and sorrow.

There is a message here for congregations, especially their leadership. Whatever our role in bearing the word into the world today, we should not be surprised to find ourselves involved in confrontation. God's commitment to right worship, self-giving, and care for society's least has not changed; and God yearns over humanity with a love too profound to turn a blind eye to our self-absorption and self-deception, indifference or intolerance. There will be times when the anguish of God claims us for bold word and action. Only God's promise to sustain us will make such work bearable.

3. The God Who Watches and Acts. The two visions of verses 11–18, the budding almond branch and the steaming pot tilted out of the north, suggest a third homiletical claim: God is not aloof and passive, but on the alert and active amid human power struggles. In Jeremiah, the focus is on power struggle amid nations. God is not disinterested; God watches. (Wordplay connects "almond branch" with the verb "to watch.") Furthermore, God may choose to turn events in this arena to God's own purposes: the tilting pot—a threat from Judah's north—will effect divine judgment.

Warning: there is a major homiletical pitfall here! God is portrayed in this text as allowing the strife of nations to serve divine purposes; but that does not translate into an invitation to the church (or its preachers) to connect world events one-for-one with divine blessing or judgment. What preachers *can* say with confidence on the basis of this text is that God is attentive to our uses (and abuses) of power—relational, economic, social, and political. By working through the lives and voices of individuals and communities, God challenges and influences these vectors of power. Threatened power structures will not take meddling lightly. So to us as to Jeremiah, God says in that so characteristically biblical phrase, "Do not be afraid . . . for I am with you" (v. 8).

SALLY A. BROWN

Psalm 71:1-6

[1]In you, O Lᴏʀᴅ, I take refuge;
  let me never be put to shame.
[2]In your righteousness deliver me and rescue me;
  incline your ear to me and save me.
[3]Be to me a rock of refuge,
  a strong fortress, to save me,
  for you are my rock and my fortress.

[4]Rescue me, O my God, from the hand of the wicked,
  from the grasp of the unjust and cruel.
[5]For you, O Lord, are my hope,
  my trust, O Lᴏʀᴅ, from my youth.
[6]Upon you I have leaned from my birth;
  it was you who took me from my mother's womb.
  My praise is continually of you.

Theological Perspective

Psalm 71 speaks from the perspective of a person of advanced or advancing age. Although the immediate need prompting the address is for deliverance and refuge, the psalm evokes a long history with God going back to the writer's birth. Like any long life, the psalmist's has had its share of "troubles and calamities" and apparent "revivals" (v. 20). While calling for another rescue, the author seems to fear that God will indeed abandon the psalmist, thereby rendering him or her vulnerable to further enemy attack and communal rejection (v. 11). The petitioner asks God to "put to shame and consume" the accusers (v. 13) and promises to continue to praise the divine righteousness.

For a contemporary audience, the text will likely evoke a number of questions about theology in the narrow sense (how we understand God). On the one hand, attributing good and bad to God's hand suggests a strong understanding of divine providence. Many continue to endorse the idea, traditional in much Christian theology, that all is in God's hands, but positing God as the source of both trauma and rescue raises the familiar issue of theodicy. If God is all good and all-powerful, why is there so much evil and suffering in the world? Why, in particular, do the faithful—those who have "leaned on [God] from . . . birth" and praised God

Pastoral Perspective

We know the experience of crying out to God. Sometimes the cry is a curse, a curse that may include taking the Lord's name in vain. At other times the cry is a question: "My God, my God, why have you forsaken me?" (Ps. 22:1). The cry can be a profession of faith: "In you, O Lᴏʀᴅ, I take refuge" (71:1). A cry to God can be a whine, a form of self-pity: "Why me, God?" Cries to God can be a form of prayer called lament. In the Psalms, laments demand that God be faithful, that God live up to God's promises. Laments rise out of trust and confidence, yet also confusion and, sometimes, fear. In a whine, the focus is on oneself; in a lament, the focus is on God. Laments are cries to God that become affirmations of faith.

Confidence and trust, confusion and fear are present in the lament of Psalm 71. The psalmist is confident: "In you, O Lᴏʀᴅ, I take refuge" (v. 1). However, the psalmist is also confused: "deliver me . . . rescue me . . . from the hand of the wicked" (vv. 2, 4). The psalmist is in distress. The psalmist's world is being threatened by unnamed but cruel powers. When confusion creates fear, faith can be both threatened and affirmed.

To hear the lament as an affirmation of faith, we can imagine contemporary situations in which someone would offer a similar cry to God. Imagination is often the first step toward hearing another

Exegetical Perspective

The opening of Psalm 71 delivers a wealth of images of God as an attentive and loving deity who is able to rescue and save those who call on God. The passage also highlights the persistent nature of the relationship between the worshiper and God.

God Our Refuge. The person who prays this psalm is one who is hiding in God, or perhaps trying to hide behind God (v. 1). The image is striking: think, perhaps, of a child who runs to hide behind a parent's legs; or a person in a foreign country who enters an embassy, relieved to be back among the home country's soil, language, and law; or a victimized woman who enters a shelter to gain distance and protection from her abuser. These are powerful images of salvation. Note that the psalm's image does not ask whether the person praying is innocent or guilty; that seems not to matter in the reality of God's willingness to protect and rescue. The psalm asks for protection from "shame," although it is not clear if this should be translated as "let me never be put to shame" (NRSV) or as "let me not be put to shame forever" (my trans.). In other words, the person praying this psalm may or may not have already experienced the shame, and we do not know if the person is asking for protection or relief. This shame may be much more than the feeling of having done

Homiletical Perspective

According to rabbinic tradition, the biblical text is like a garden or an orchard. Those given this text are called to be good stewards of that sacred trust. In this light, a preacher's job is not to provide the "real" or "correct" meaning of the text. Instead, the preacher's task is to cultivate the orchard of the text so that others might enter its domain again and again to join in tending its ground. When the time is right, they can harvest and share its fruit. Some of the ways preachers might honor this responsibility are suggested under the following rubrics, which we may think of as gateways into this sacred grove.

Seeking Refuge, Finding Refuge. As with most biblical texts, one of the gateways into its orchard is provided by the plain meaning of several phrases that frame its recurring plea for refuge. The psalmist declares, "In you . . . I seek refuge. . . . In your righteousness deliver me. . . . be to me a rock of refuge, a strong fortress . . . for you are my rock and my fortress" (vv. 1–3).

An attentive reader may want to point out the initial irony of the text. The refuge sought is already being asserted in and by its liturgical expression. In other words, this prayer is an expression of a relationship that is already sustaining. The plea is

Psalm 71:1-6

Theological Perspective

continually (v. 6)—yet remain vulnerable to unjust attack?

This is a perennially difficult issue for Christian theology, one to which theologians over the centuries have provided various attempts at answers, none of which is altogether satisfactory. The view that dominates in classical Protestantism posits suffering as humanity's collective punishment for original sin. All suffering is deserved, in the general sense; thus God's justice is preserved. Such a view tempts us to explain disaster or disease as divine punishment for sin. Catastrophic storms, AIDS, the horrific events of 9/11—all have been (mis)used publicly as theological morality tales. Doubtless, members of most congregations will have encountered similar interpretations of individual misfortune.

The wounds from such theological arrogance can run deep. Such a perspective offers cold comfort when one faces a terminal illness, the death of a child, or, as appears to be the case for the psalmist, an unfounded but successful assault on one's reputation. Moreover, the psalmist anticipates the personal price to be paid when personal misfortune is interpreted as divine disfavor. The fear of not only abandonment by God but rejection at the hands of the community is palpable here; indeed, they are deeply intertwined. The desire that one's enemies be routed, shamed, and disgraced—doubtless a sentiment familiar to congregants—is tied closely to this twofold fear.

It is noteworthy, though, that the psalmist's invocation of divine providence here does not associate misfortune with sin—either in the past or in this present instance. Good times and bad are part of the ebb and flow of life under God. Indeed, the psalmist witnesses to a lifetime of experiencing the steadfastness of God's presence. The writer does not hesitate to call the current assault unjustified and undeserved—and unqualifiedly so—even as he or she names the very real losses that could result if the enemy wins. Against that fear, the psalmist not only reminds God (and indirectly the community) of a lifetime of model citizenship, but invokes—quite literally—the divine record and the promise of justice and succor.

Here the metaphors used for God are particularly evocative. First, the Deity is imaged as two inanimate objects: a rock and a fortress (v. 3). These images speak to the steadiness, security, and trustworthiness of the divine presence. It is no wonder that these images have found a place in traditional Protestant hymnody ("A Mighty Fortress Is Our God, a Bulwark Never Failing," "On Christ the Solid Rock I

Pastoral Perspective

person. Imagination helps us understand or identify with the speaker's point of view. Who might pray such a psalm in our day? Someone worried about the behavior of a child or a spouse. A person battling a dread disease, a disease that saps strength and hope, a disease that challenges faith. A person of faith caught up in a difficult marriage, a marriage in which one partner seeks to trust God while the other spurns God. A mature person, respected in the community, who has had a moral lapse or suffered an embarrassing defeat. A leader in a church who is trapped by conflict, gossip, or other acts of hostility. Any of these life situations could lead to a lament.

The opening six verses of Psalm 71 invite the reader to imagine the psalmist's life situation. The psalmist is focused upon God: "You are my rock and my fortress" (v. 3). The psalmist testifies to a faith nurtured by time: "Upon you I have leaned from my birth" (v. 6). Time has amazing power to nurture pebbles of faith into bedrock, to turn seedlings of faith into massive trees. The psalmist draws upon memory, memory that reaches back to birth. The psalmist affirms the power of memory and time to create trust in God. Enduring trust leads to hope, the kind of hope that brings forth praise.

When the words of the psalmist stir the imagination, they also evoke memories in the reader. The words "You . . . are my hope, my trust, O LORD, from my youth" (v. 5) bring to my mind a confirmation retreat for about sixty-five eighth-graders. One of the events was a low-ropes course, a physically and emotionally challenging experience that involves climbing and assisting others in completing the course. The exercise was designed to create trust, self-confidence, and fulfillment. The low-ropes course helped the youth discuss what it means to trust God, and to trust others in their journey of faith. The event also created enduring memories, perhaps even sacred memory, the kind of sacred memory we call an epiphany.

As the reader uses imagination and memory, the psalm affirms a trust in God that rises out of sacred experience, even more than out of belief or knowledge. Imagination and memory affirm a trust that can begin with birth. However, for some, trust does not begin with parents or family. Friendship, courses of study (including a low-ropes course), retreats, mission trips, opportunities to serve and to be served, shared worship—all have power, over time, to provide the experiences that can lead to calling God a rock and a fortress. Trust leads to a renewed ability to affirm faith; a renewed affirmation

something wrong; the word in Hebrew may indicate that others have acted or could act in truly evil and destructive ways against the person.

Thus the situation of the person praying cannot be determined. The interpreter needs to be careful, because of this ambiguity, when drawing parallels to modern situations. God's rescue, however, is described with more certainty. God will rescue because of God's righteousness (v. 2). Thus the person's situation may not be relevant at all; God saves because of who God is and because of God's abiding involvement in bringing righteousness, right solutions, and right relationships.

God Our Rock. The psalm prays for God to be like a rock (v. 3). We often think of a rock as something permanent, unyielding, and unchanging. Thus interpreters often consider the image of God as rock to point toward God's permanence, immutability, and consistency. In the Old Testament, however, the image of God as rock almost always carries a connotation not of God's constancy but of God's eager action (e.g., Deut. 32:18; 1 Sam. 2:2; 2 Sam. 22:3; 23:3; Ps. 18:2; Isa. 44:8; Hab. 1:12). God is a rock who saves and rescues. Likewise, this psalm calls God a fortress. Perhaps we should not so quickly imagine the kind of fortress that is entirely defensive, walled up and protected against the outside. This fortress may be more of a fort or fortification, from which power and might can go forth to rescue.

Trust in God. Trust requires a confidence in God's desire and ability to rescue from the negative forces. It implies a past relationship, on the basis of which the person praying has concluded that God can and will deal with the current threat (v. 5). The psalm emphasizes the continuous nature of this long-term belief by stating that this trust has been in place "from my youth" (v. 5) and even "from my birth" (v. 6). Trust takes a lifetime to build.

The person praying places not only trust in God, but also hope (v. 5a). If trust looks backward to the past and concludes that the present can improve on that basis, hope looks to the future and imagines a better possibility than what anyone can see in the present. Hope envisions a way that things could be, in contradiction to the problems and limits of current realities. Hope in God resides in the expectation that God's desires for human life are not limited by what already has been, but instead can transcend the past and create something new in the

that the relationship remain so. The psalmist may be prepared even to undergo victimization for this relationship and the identity it embodies—but not to be cut off from it.

This gateway leads directly to another. The psalm itself can provide the shelter and refuge sought by the worshiper. This would be as true for the earliest congregations who turned to this psalm in prayer as it is for modern congregations who find it giving voice to their deepest needs. Moreover, other psalms provide this kind of sanctuary in ways many will recognize immediately. A preacher sensitive to these dimensions may wish to explore how this psalm and others like it (Pss. 22, 23) can give voice and refuge to parishioners facing difficult times. Indeed, other liturgical texts—hymns, prayers, and other resources like them—can provide similar gifts. How often have those unable to pray found their voice in Jesus' prayers in Gethsemane or in the Lord's Prayer? How often have persons overwhelmed with shame discovered a welcoming sanctuary in singing the Kyrie or in a cherished hymn like Martin Luther's "A Mighty Fortress"?

Should a preacher choose, the initial requests of this psalm could provide opportunities for more extensive thinking about the deeper needs that are faced in times of great difficulty. Preachers who sit with parishioners preparing for their own deaths will know how important this request can be. Indeed, sensitive pastors offer a profound gift when they help someone else maintain their dignity in dying or provide a relationship that is strong enough to endure even the most troubling violations. These are gifts like those the psalmist prays to receive.

Praying with the Psalmist—Praying with Others. No matter how personal the psalmist's prayer is, its lament is not private. It is the shared prayer of a people, even though it is clearly rooted in the mature wisdom of the individual who composed this prayer. That personal history has been made available to a people. The individual voice of one has been given to and adopted by a historic worshiping community.

It has been the practice of corporate Jewish prayer to face people's trials with the prayers of the psalmist. Those trials can be personal experiences of need or the traumatic crises of an entire people. The experiences can range from illness and injury to war and devastation. In the end, praying with the psalm is praying not only with the one who composed it— the psalmist—but also with everyone else who has prayed it before. Praying with the psalmist is joining

Psalm 71:1-6

Theological Perspective

Stand, All Other Ground Is Sinking Sand"). Then, after these images, which conjure a transcendent Deity who shields us behind mighty walls, verse 6 recalls a more intimate encounter with God as midwife: "Upon you I have leaned from my birth; it was you who took me from my mother's womb." The combination of tenderness and toughness reminds us again of the importance, especially in liturgical practice, of calling upon the full range of divine imagery available to us in Scripture and theology.

Too often we treat theology as a set of ideas to which one gives intellectual assent. Theology finds its ultimate home, however, in religious practice. Psalms are more than words on a page that record ideas to be considered; they are scripts to be performed, songs to be sung, prayers to be prayed. They are, in other words, examples of ritual performance. Psalm 71 performs the human-divine encounter in a refreshing way. Too often, Christians approach prayer as they would a formal dinner with a visiting dignitary. One must assume the right position, mind one's language and manners, speak only what will please the visitor's ear. Only if the rules of etiquette are obeyed might one's petition (should one dare to present such) gain a fair hearing.

The author of Psalm 71 models a very different approach to prayer, though. The psalmist feels no compunction in the divine presence about calling injustice by name or acknowledging fears of abandonment and desire for retribution. Out of those fears and desires, the writer literally invokes—calls out and calls on—the God of refuge, succor, and justice known to the author from birth. Ultimately, the psalm also calls to account the community united in faith in this God. Though as vulnerable to rumor and misinformation as any other human gathering, the community of faith is reminded of its obligation to be the place of refuge, succor, and justice for God's people.

ELLEN T. ARMOUR

Pastoral Perspective

of faith leads to praise—and praise is a sign of hope, hope that endures in times of great distress.

As I listen to this psalm, I remember witnesses whose lives affirm the trust of the psalmist. I think of a man in his sixties, the kind of person who has dedicated his life to lay service in the church, who for over fifteen years has cared for his wife, a victim of early-onset Alzheimer's disease. He has taken her to family events, church, even parties. Recently he had to move her from their home to a facility that could better care for her. After they settled in, he danced with her—and her eyes sparkled. I recall the wife whose husband has an incapacitating illness; he cannot speak or move by himself. She has cared for him in their home for more than five years. His children, neighbors, and friends help in quiet ways. Her morning prayer is that she will be able to do what she has to do—with love, joy, and gratitude. A visit to their warm, inviting home, a glance at the radiance in her face, testifies that her prayer is being answered with a bold yes. I see faithful grandparents who pray daily for their two grandsons—one serving in Iraq, the other seeking to accept his homosexuality. The grandparents testify that, in their prayers, they find peace. Through memories of these witnesses, I hear the psalmist affirm faith.

Confidence in God, confusion about the realities of pain and suffering in life, fear that our world may collapse—such moments lead people of faith to cry out to God, to bring forth a lament, not a whine. Laments empower us to be honest with God in ways that bring forth hope, even joy. A lament will not change the world, but such a prayer can change us—change the way we see the world, the way we live in the world.

ART ROSS

Exegetical Perspective

future. God in this psalm is the proper object of both human trust and human hope.

God Who Saves. The person who prays this psalm asks for God's salvation and rescue (vv. 2, 3, 4). This repeated request embodies a core belief that God will save and deliver. This salvation must be more than just providing a refuge. God is not merely a place to hide from the turmoil of the world, or one who would offer comfort and consolation in the midst of life's troubles. God not only rescues people *from* some surrounding and threatening evil; God's salvation delivers people *to* something. The saved person becomes God's herald, announcing God's salvation (vv. 15–16). Perhaps the one whom God saves is sent to the person's own persecutors, to proclaim to them the good news of God's salvation. Through deliverance and salvation, God turns these conflicts of life into opportunities to proclaim the gospel.

God Whom We Praise. Praise is continual, not just a one-time response to the moment of rescue or gain. Here in this psalm, as so often throughout the psalms, a person's praise precedes God's rescue. Praise is not just the response of gratitude for rescue; praise is the natural condition of vital human life. This entire psalm keeps returning to and amplifying these images of praise (vv. 8, 14–16, 17, 18–19, 22–24). In the end, the person praying this psalm is not really hiding behind God. Instead, the person is flaunting God. Through the continual words of praise, this person is constantly making God known and visible to the world. This provocative, praiseful openness may, in the end, be one of the root causes of the opposition that the person experiences. Praise becomes the constant as life moves from birth to death, from youth to old age.

The lectionary includes only the first quarter of this psalm. The other eighteen verses continue to emphasize constant lifelong praise. In particular, the psalm describes old age as one of the situations in which God rescues, so that this person can praise God to yet more generations (vv. 9, 18).

JON L. BERQUIST

Homiletical Perspective

a cloud of witnesses, to borrow a metaphor from Hebrews, but in a way its author could not have pondered. For example, we in the church use this image to place ourselves in the greater worshiping body of Christ that is the church. When we pray with the psalms, we are reminded that as followers of Christ and members of his body we also pray with his people as he did. For twenty-first-century Christians who live and declare their faith in the aftermath of the Holocaust, that recognition carries strong implications about which we should be willing to ask some rather serious questions. When we pray with others who trust these words, we join them in need and solidarity. That could and should enlarge considerably our worlds and the words of any sermon.

To be sure, when we pray this psalm, we are also praying with the church. We are praying with other Christians who are struggling with things that they are facing. Sometimes they have faced much more than we can imagine. Sometimes we are facing things they cannot imagine, but facing them with each other we find strength—refuge. In reaching out, we discover others who have reached out before us and who reach out to us through the psalm.

Still, if we are truly praying the psalms, then we are always also praying with Jews. That insight may be dislocating for some, especially those who see themselves praying for Jews and their conversion. What might it mean for Christians to pray *with* Jews, rather than for Jews? Jews did not give up these historic prayers when Christians adopted them and began to pray with them. We have been linked in this activity over centuries. Only recently have Christians begun to embrace what this common prayer might mean. A sermon willing to address questions like these could itself become a gateway into new relationships between Christians and Jews.

In other words, this seemingly simple psalm is rich with theological nuance and sophistication. Preachers can introduce their congregations to these subtleties and describe ways of praying and thinking that move beyond magical notions of prayer and isolated understandings of their faith.

HENRY F. KNIGHT

Hebrews 12:18-29

¹⁸You have not come to something that can be touched, a blazing fire, and darkness, and gloom, and a tempest, ¹⁹and the sound of a trumpet, and a voice whose words made the hearers beg that not another word be spoken to them. ²⁰(For they could not endure the order that was given, "If even an animal touches the mountain, it shall be stoned to death." ²¹Indeed, so terrifying was the sight that Moses said, "I tremble with fear.") ²²But you have come to Mount Zion and to the city of the living God, the heavenly Jerusalem, and to innumerable angels in festal gathering, ²³and to the assembly of the firstborn who are enrolled in heaven, and to God the judge of all, and to the spirits of the righteous made perfect, ²⁴and to Jesus, the mediator of a new covenant, and to the sprinkled blood that speaks a better word than the blood of Abel.

Theological Perspective

Notice a development in this passage. It begins by lapsing into the somewhat dishonorable Christian habit of favorable self-comparison with Judaism. Christians who do that seek to contrast the Old Testament's God of wrath with the New Testament's God of grace. That betrays ignorance of both testaments. If the New Testament God's mercy is always close to the Hebrew surface, something like judgment is near to Christian texts too. Then we see a thoroughgoing Christian consideration of God that can get pretty scary.

The writer reads the descriptions of religious awe in Exodus as palpable terror. Initially the Christian covenant appears more welcoming—until the writer contemplates refusing it. Then something close to terror surfaces. In both testaments we find a God who is "a consuming fire." Since we cannot escape that fire by leaving the synagogue and crossing over to the church, let us learn what we can about that fire. All American Christians have confronted hellfire. Fire for us means punishment. Either we want it to mean punishment, or we imagine other people do. We have all been scorched by religious fires.

Wherever we stand vis-à-vis the consuming fire—whether we think we are for it or against it—we need to be clear on what biblical writers mean

Pastoral Perspective

We were beginning Watershed, our discipleship class for youth who express a desire to be baptized. The initial meeting was an opportunity for the participants, three seventh-grade girls and a ninth-grade boy, to meet with me, their pastor, and their mentors, adults carefully chosen for each one to accompany them in their faith journey. We met in a pizza restaurant and enjoyed a relaxed meal, hearing what was going on in their lives. Then we asked each of them to share why they were interested in being baptized. A church in the Baptist tradition, we practice believers' baptism by immersion, although we also accept baptisms from other traditions where the individual discerns his or her experience to be the equivalent. In such a case, Watershed serves in the style of a confirmation experience.

Each of the girls shared in her own way her desire to know God better, to be a disciple of Christ, and to be a member of the church. It seemed they were at a point in their faith development where the mentors could walk alongside them, sharing their own faith in appropriate ways, as these young people made an intentional decision to be baptized.

Tim, the ninth-grade boy, listened attentively to the girls as they shared. Then we asked him to share. With a thoughtful look on his face he said, "Well, I

²⁵See that you do not refuse the one who is speaking; for if they did not escape when they refused the one who warned them on earth, how much less will we escape if we reject the one who warns from heaven! ²⁶At that time his voice shook the earth; but now he has promised, "Yet once more I will shake not only the earth but also the heaven." ²⁷This phrase, "Yet once more," indicates the removal of what is shaken—that is, created things—so that what cannot be shaken may remain. ²⁸Therefore, since we are receiving a kingdom that cannot be shaken, let us give thanks, by which we offer to God an acceptable worship with reverence and awe; ²⁹for indeed our God is a consuming fire.

Exegetical Perspective

The author of Hebrews (late first century CE) follows up the extended examples of biblical faith, to which we turned the last two weeks, with an extended warning against rejecting God's grace. There is much more at stake, he argues, in the salvation available in Christ than was at stake in the salvation available to Israel. The presence of God in the heavenly Jerusalem eclipses the terrifying descent of God at Sinai; the benefits of the Christ covenant far surpass those of the Mosaic covenant; the voice of God sounds forth even more emphatically now than it did then. Beware! That is the gist of this challenging passage, and it is well to keep its main points in mind as we help parishioners navigate complexities not easily accessible on first reading or hearing.

From even such a brief synopsis we can see how closely aligned our passage is with the overarching aims and strategies of the book. Hebrews describes itself as a "word of exhortation" (13:22) to Christians with "drooping hands" and "weak knees" (12:12). To reenergize the flagging faithful, it reminds them of the enormity, the incomparable sufficiency, of Christ's saving work. Christ is superior to the Jewish prophets, angels, Moses, Joshua, the Jewish high priests, and the Levitical priesthood (chaps. 1–7). The new covenant is superior to the old, the

Homiletical Perspective

Can you remember the worst thunderstorm of your life? Torrents of rain are lashed about with the wind. Each boom of thunder seems to shake the house to its foundations. Bolts of lightning zigzag fiercely down from the dark heavens. My older sister tells me it is just God taking my picture, but I am not amused.

One can imagine people of old drawing from the imagery of such a terrifying storm to describe in fearsome poetry an encounter with the God of righteousness, holiness, and judgment: "thunder and lightning, as well as a thick cloud upon the mountain, and a blast of a trumpet" coming down on Mount Sinai (Exod. 19:16). Perhaps some ancient prophet had witnessed a volcanic eruption or lived through an earthquake. Speaking of which, how fearfully I remember the 1994 Northridge earthquake in Los Angeles. Before dawn our whole house was wrenching about, crammed with shattering noise and fear.

One has to love Annie Dillard's admonition to the average churchgoer: "Does anyone have the foggiest idea of the power we so blithely invoke? . . . . It is madness to wear ladies' straw hats and velvet hats to church; we should all be wearing crash helmets. Ushers should issue life preservers and signal flares;

Hebrews 12:18-29

Theological Perspective

when referring to God's fire—or the devil's. Is fire punishment? The author of Hebrews, the author(s) of Exodus, the author of the book of Revelation, and our Lord himself would suggest that notion is mistaken. In the Bible, fire is not torture: fire is *purification*.

Fire is used to refine metals. The smelter melts and pours off the gold or silver, then skims off the dross until he can see his own face reflected in the molten metal—not a bad metaphor for God's judgment, now that we consider it. In the book of Revelation, the devil is thrown into a fiery lake. That looks to us like punishment. Yet more likely the writer thinks the lake of fire is a sterile environment in which to prevent the devil from polluting the earth.

The question arises, What gets purified and how? The obvious answer is something like "sin." That is difficult to picture. How can God's fire purify anyone from sin without frying them to a crisp? What would the process look like? Suppose, for example, you are gossipy, or a drunkard, or an embezzler, or a tax cheat. How would God's fire make you different? You would simply be the same old rascal with third-degree burns. No, to be a cogent image, the fire of God must consume something in each of us that goes deeper than our sins. God's fire must purge away the *false self* from which our worst sins arise. The self that God created can emerge only as the self that I construct to retail to others is consumed.

So all the excuses, all the fictions, all the rationalizations, all the "official versions" and self-diagnoses we attempt to sell to others, all the self-adaptations to escape criticism—all that will be consumed in the fire of God's love for God's own authentic creation.

Ironically, religiousness is a target of God's fire. Many of us join a religious group and craft a false self to comply with the group's ideal, taking on manners of speech, dress, belief, even political opinions that fit us into the group. God's fiery love will rescue us from that sort of religiousness as well.

All that happens at the moment when God's presence breaks into our awareness, when we feel ourselves being utterly known, embraced, and accepted. The embraced and accepted self is the *real* self that God created—not our constructs. In that moment, the false self becomes ashes. We discover that the harshest judgment of God's consuming fire is friendlier than our own most lavish self-praise.

In the best of his *Unspoken Sermons*, "The Consuming Fire," the Scots preacher George

Pastoral Perspective

am looking forward to this experience because I have lots of questions. The first one is, 'Why does God in the Bible act as if God had a split personality?' Sometimes God is really kind and loving and forgiving. But then God gets all angry and wants to punish and even hurt people."

After a pause, as we all let his question and the passion with which he asked it sink in, his mentor said, "What a fascinating observation, Tim. You and I are going to have a great time in this process." A lively conversation followed.

Tim could well have been talking about God as portrayed in today's Epistle lesson. Beginning with verse 18, we are assured that we have not come into the presence of God as those who have experienced what Moses did on Mount Sinai, an experience that caused him to tremble with fear (cf. Deut. 4:11–12; 5:22–25; 9:19; Exod. 19:16). The writer contrasts this fearsome encounter with the readers' coming into the presence of God on Mount Zion, which is a "festal gathering" (Heb. 12:22). Jerusalem too is where God lives (Ps. 2:6) and is surrounded by the firstborn (plural) who are there because of their relationship with God's own "firstborn," Jesus (Heb. 1:6).

Just when we are ready to go to the party on Zion, though, the tone changes again with verse 25. Suddenly, we are warned that if we are not careful, this time God will shake not only earth but heaven as well. Then all this is summed up as the writer invites (admonishes?) us to offer to God acceptable worship with reverence and awe, with a further warning that God is a consuming fire. This does not sound like a festive way to worship!

What is the pastoral word for Tim and others who are honest enough to name what they see in biblical texts? Does God have schizoid tendencies? Is God, as Tim asks, sometimes "really kind and loving and forgiving," while at other times "God gets all angry and wants to punish and even hurt people"? Or might this question instead bear witness to our human ambivalence about the nature of God? Texts like this provide a great opportunity for honest dialogue within faith communities.

The author of Hebrews in this passage employs the language of pilgrimage, presenting two destinations along the way: Mount Sinai and Mount Zion. Studying this text in community gives an opportunity to talk about our own faith pilgrimages in honest ways. Where have the Mount Sinais been in your faith pilgrimage? When did God seem like a terrifying presence? Where did you experience God's anger? Where, on the other hand, did you get a

heavenly sanctuary to the earthly tabernacle, the sacrifice of Christ on the cross to that of the priests in the temple (chaps. 8–10). The old prefigures the new; indeed it is a mere shadow-reality in comparison with it (esp. chaps. 8 and 10; also chaps. 9 and 13). To reject all this or let it slip away in lassitude would be a calamity. To embrace all this or reaffirm it would be, to borrow from the Gospels, a discovery of hidden treasure, a pearl of great price. Hebrews is exhortation grounded in expansive reminder—a long homily with theme and variation and reiteration.

The first half of today's reading, Hebrews 12:18–24, hinges on a comparison of Sinai (not explicitly identified) and Zion. It contrasts the theophany experienced by the exodus generation (vv. 18–21) with the revelation of the heavenly Zion/ Jerusalem experienced now by "you," the addressees (vv. 22–24).

The former experience was one of terror (vv. 19b, 22) elicited by fire, darkness, whirlwind, and gloom (v.18; cf. Deut. 4:11–12; 5:22–25; also Exod. 10:21). These palpable signs were accompanied by sounds that only made the terror worse (Heb. 12:21), a trumpet blast (cf. Exod. 19:16), and a voice that left the Israelites begging for relief: "If we hear the voice of the LORD our God any longer, we shall die" (Deut. 5:25; cf. Exod. 20:19). That voice had prohibited human and beast, on pain of death, from encroaching on the holy mount (Exod. 19:12–13), a menacing ban the people had found unbearably severe (Heb. 12:20; cf. Exod. 19:12–13). For all the awesome wonder, this theophany inspired a paralyzing dread.

Not so the revelation of God in the new Zion, the heavenly Jerusalem, which engenders a vibrant promise. The contrast between the revelations is sharpened by the repetition of the word "approach" (NRSV, NIV "come"), first used to introduce the old theophany (v. 18) and now to introduce the new (v. 22). You have not approached Mount Sinai, rather you have approached Mount Zion. At this point the author interjects a riot of images conveying the magnificence of the superior destination (vv. 22–24): it is the city of the living God where we find (a) the festal gathering of angels and those enrolled in heaven, (b) God the judge of all, (c) the perfected spirits of the righteous, and (d) Jesus who mediates the new covenant for the remission of sins through his blood. The author neither explains nor explores these images; he assumes familiarity with them and leaves them to glisten in their vividness.

they should lash us to our pews."[1] More than this! The creator God, one now also understands, is the God of supernovae and neutron stars. Aspects of such divine might and majesty are fearfully alluded to in scene one of this scriptural passage.

Next comes scene two in this drama, which may once have served as the closing exhortation for the Letter to the Hebrews. The second scene also inspires awe and wonder, but now one is awed by the graciousness and hospitality of God's majesty. Now it is Mount Zion and the city of the living God that are envisioned. Here many of the great themes of the letter come to fruition. This is the age of the new and better covenant made possible through the sacrificial blood of the Son and great High Priest. Gathered in festal harmony are uncounted angels to whom Jesus was declared superior in the opening chapter of the epistle. Present in glory are all the righteous who have lived in hope of the heavenly Jerusalem. In response to the vision, there could well be sung "Jerusalem, the Golden": "They stand, those halls of Zion, all jubilant with song, and bright with many an angel, and all the martyr throng."[2]

God, we learn throughout the Bible, is a fierce God of judgment and holiness. God, who is beyond all comprehension, is also a God of nearly incredible mercy and sacrificial love. The coming of the glorious new covenant is contrasted with the old. This is the same God whose graciousness is wondrously made known in "the merciful and faithful high priest" who is not "unable to sympathize with our weaknesses" (Heb. 2:17; 4:15). The same God who "spoke to our ancestors in many and various ways by the prophets . . . in these last days . . . has spoken to us by a Son" who "is the reflection of God's glory and the exact imprint of God's very being" (1:1–3). Through him who "when he had made purification for sins, . . . sat down at the right hand of the Majesty of high" (1:3), the awesome God of power and glory and judgment— of thunder and lightning and earthquake and supernovae—is revealed as the one whose throne of grace may now be approached "with boldness, so that we may receive mercy and find grace to help in time of need" (4:16). The throne of divine power is set in the new Jerusalem. Further song and rejoicing break forth: "Jerusalem, My Happy Home." There

1. Annie Dillard, *Teaching a Stone to Talk: Expeditions and Encounters* (New York: Harper & Row, 1982), 40.
2. Bernard of Cluny (twelfth century); trans. J. M. Neale, 1861.

Hebrews 12:18-29

Theological Perspective

MacDonald described the people of the exodus as follows. When he speaks of sin, understand the *false self* that generates sin:

> While we take part *with* our sins, while we feel as if, separated from our sins, we would no longer be ourselves, how can we understand that the lightening word is a Savior—that word which pierces to the dividing between the soul and the evil, which will slay the sin and give life to the sinner? Can it be any comfort to us to be told that God loves us so that God will burn us clean? Can the cleansing of the fire appear to us anything beyond what it must always, more or less, be—a process of torture? We do not want to be clean and we cannot bear to be tortured. Can we do other, or can one desire that we should do other, than fear God, even with the fear of the wicked, until we learn to love God with the love of the holy? To us Mt. Sinai is crowned with the sign of vengeance. And is not God ready to do unto us even as we fear, although with a feeling and a different end from any which we are capable of supposing? God is against sin. Insofar as and while we and sin are one, God is against us—against our desires, our aims, our fears, and our hopes; and thus God is altogether and always *for us*.[1]

A discordant detail in the parable of the Wedding Banquet (Matt. 22:2–14)—that the king threw out a guest who wore no wedding robe, though the guest had clearly not anticipated attending a wedding when leaving home that day—yields its mystery when we understand that it was up to the host to supply suitable robes to invited guests. This man had refused the offer, likely insisting that he was OK as he was. Invited, yes; fit to be present, not yet.

Think of the consuming fire of God that way: an unavoidable mercy.

GRAY TEMPLE

Pastoral Perspective

glimpse of Mount Zion? When has God provided a joyful welcome for you? Do you experience God with a combination of awe and reverence, yet also tinged with fear?

The Bible is not an instruction book but an invitation to dialogue. Our church has participated in the Youth and Spirituality Project, where we have learned that discipleship training is not so much indoctrination as it is trusting our young people to find God for themselves as we provide companionship for them along the way. As Jesus once pointed out, our children may well lead us to the realm of God.

Troubling passages need not be problems to be solved but may indeed be adventures to be shared. The kind of dialogue in community that leads to transformation begins with an honest acknowledgment of what is there, which Tim was willing to share. There is another troubling aspect of this pericope. That is the subtle, or not so subtle, suggestion that the old, terrifying God of Sinai has somehow been replaced by the mediator of the new covenant, Jesus. This is a frequent problem people encounter when reading Hebrews and reflects a lingering Marcionism in the church we ought to resist. Hebrews is quite clear that the God of Sinai is very much the God of Zion. What does this say about our relationship with the Jewish faith? Here is another great opportunity for community dialogue. Contrast this with Jesus' declaring, "Do not think that I have come to abolish the law or the prophets; I have come not to abolish but to fulfill" (Matt. 5:17).

Over the last few years in his pilgrimage, Tim has wanted to talk about this in his own way. He is very interested in other religions, and he thinks frequently about how the God Christians worship in Jesus Christ is also the God whom Jews know. His elders would do well to do likewise.

LANNY PETERS

---

1. George MacDonald, *Unspoken Sermons: Series I, II, and III* (Sioux Falls, SD: Nu-Vision Publications, 2007; orig. 1867), 17.

Exegetical Perspective

How and in what sense is this goal to which the faithful are drawn also a present reality for them? The author does not say explicitly, but in the second half of our passage (vv. 25–29), devoted to exhortation, he hints that the glories of the new covenant are experienced proleptically in worship: "Therefore, since we are receiving a kingdom that cannot be shaken, let us give thanks, by which we offer to God an acceptable worship with reverence and awe" (v. 28). In the first instance, worship is a metaphor for the sanctified life to which the addressees are to recommit themselves. It is hardly accidental that the chosen metaphor is derived from the shared liturgical experience of the community; that experience, more than any other, gives access to the heavenly Jerusalem.

Such access, however, is not final; the kingdom is still being received (v. 28). In this regard it is instructive to compare Hebrews with the roughly contemporaneous Revelation to John, where the prophet is transported to heaven and the reader swept up with him even into the throne room of God. In Revelation, the reader savors and dwells in this alternative reality, a respite from the harsh conditions of life in the Roman Empire. The tone is consoling. In Hebrews, the reader has the alternative reality in view and is urged to keep moving toward it. The tone is admonitory. The aim in both instances is to encourage, but the way the reader is situated rhetorically differs.

It is appropriate that the second half of today's passage is bracketed by warning: do not refuse God's word (v. 25), an echo of the warning just ten verses earlier not to reject God's grace; and remember, "God is a consuming fire" (v. 29; cf. Deut. 4:24). Once again the author invokes the experience of the Israelites—their disobedience as narrated repeatedly in Exodus—arguing a fortiori against now repudiating God and the unshakable verities God has established (vv. 25b–27).

Preachers and teachers using this text to reinvigorate their own communities might consider (a) the importance of reminder; (b) the challenge of recovering Old Testament references, allusions, and images; and (c) the power of worship to convey the profound realities of the faith and enable people to act on them.

DAVID R. ADAMS

Homiletical Perspective

Thy saints are crowned with glory great;
they see God face to face;
they triumph still, they still rejoice
in that most happy place.[3]

Oh, but there is now yet a third scene in our drama! Do not imagine that the poetry of heaven means that one can forget that this is still the same God—the God of both righteousness and love. Probably many of us would like to emphasize God's mercy nearly to the exclusion of judgment. That would not be the God of Scripture. Nor, when we stop to think, would we be pleased if in the end we discovered that God did not really care about unrighteousness, injustice, cruelty, and evil; that God did not care whether we tried to build at least some aspects of the kingdom here on earth—on earth as it is in heaven. Ultimately God's justice and judgment must be included in God's love. Therefore wrongs are still to be judged by the God of love and mercy, and the imagery of earthquake and consuming fire return.

Moreover, the warning now is more severe, because the word of graciousness has come from the heavenly Mount Zion—not just from Mount Sinai of old. Now there is no escaping when everything on earth and in heaven will be shaken. One hears the haunting song "My Lord, what a morning, when the stars begin to fall." Suddenly I am back in my house the morning of the earthquake. Everything is shaking violently. Things I love may be destroyed. As then bishop in that diocese, I realize many of our churches could be damaged or falling down. The lives of loved ones—even my own life—could be lost.

What is it that Paul tells us? "The only thing that counts is faith working through love" (Gal. 5:6). Many things will come to an end, but "love never ends" (1 Cor. 13:8). What endures is all that has turned to love. What is unshakable is the kingdom of that God who is to be worshiped "with reverence and awe" (Heb. 12:28).

FREDERICK H. BORSCH

---

3. Joseph Bromehead, 1795.

Luke 13:10-17

¹⁰Now he was teaching in one of the synagogues on the sabbath. ¹¹And just then there appeared a woman with a spirit that had crippled her for eighteen years. She was bent over and was quite unable to stand up straight. ¹²When Jesus saw her, he called her over and said, "Woman, you are set free from your ailment." ¹³When he laid his hands on her, immediately she stood up straight and began praising God. ¹⁴But the leader of the synagogue, indignant because Jesus had cured on the sabbath, kept saying to the crowd, "There are six days on which work ought to be done; come on those days and be cured, and not on the sabbath day." ¹⁵But the Lord answered him and said, "You hypocrites! Does not each of you on the sabbath untie his ox or his donkey from the manger, and lead it away to give it water? ¹⁶And ought not this woman, a daughter of Abraham whom Satan bound for eighteen long years, be set free from this bondage on the sabbath day?" ¹⁷When he said this, all his opponents were put to shame; and the entire crowd was rejoicing at all the wonderful things that he was doing.

Theological Perspective

The woman crippled with a spirit for eighteen years and unable to stand up straight does not ask for healing. Instead, Jesus calls to her and sets her free from her ailment by laying hands on her. Her response is to stand up straight and begin praising God. It is striking that she does not ask for healing and no one petitions Jesus on her behalf. Over the years, she has become accustomed, if not resigned, to her long and serious illness, which is attributed to Satan. For eighteen years this unnamed woman must strain to see the sun, the sky, and the stars. For eighteen years she has become accustomed to looking down or just slightly ahead but never upward without difficulty. For eighteen years her world has been one of turning from side to side to see what those who stand upright can see with just a glance. She is used to this, and no one questions her fate. Instead, the leader of the synagogue gets offended that Jesus would heal on the Sabbath.

The focus of this passage is often on the bad behavior of the leader of the synagogue. To our contemporary eyes, he is a poster child for callousness at best and inhumanity at worst. There is much to tempt the preacher to focus on this set of all-too-human interactions. It is important to note, however, that this passage is nestled between the parable of the Fig Tree with its focus on repentance (13:1–9) and the

Pastoral Perspective

One emphasis in the Old Testament concept of Sabbath urges Israel to rest from all work because God crowns creation with a holy day of rest (Gen. 2:2–3). The Lord rests from the work of creation to bless and consecrate the Sabbath; therefore the people of Israel shall not work on the Sabbath (Exod. 20:8–11). In this morning's text from Luke 13, Jesus chooses the other, complementary emphasis of the Old Testament (Deut. 5:12–15), where the Sabbath commandment commands the people of the covenant to observe the day and keep it holy in recognition of their deliverance from slavery in Egypt. In the latter emphasis on Sabbath observance and the practice of holiness, the people undertake a holy work. In either case—of complete rest or of active Sabbath practice—the requirements of life ask what relinquishing work and what active holiness might mean for human beings.

The Pharisees, who emphasize the prohibition of any work, follow the Mishnah's concessions that allow an owner of cattle to take them to water on the Sabbath, provided that the cattle carry no burdens.[1] The communal function of both human rest from work to acknowledge the Lord's sanctification of the

---

1. I. Howard Marshall, *The Gospel of Luke* (Grand Rapids: Eerdmans, 1978), 558–59.

Exegetical Perspective

If we have read the first twelve chapters of Luke and seen Jesus in various contexts healing on the Sabbath and reformulating Sabbath law, the events of this pericope have a familiar feel. Having already declared himself "lord of the sabbath" (6:5) and determined that healing on this sacred day is "to do good" (6:9), we should not be surprised by his actions or his instructions here. Again Jesus finds himself in what appears to his audience to be a quandary. While he is teaching in an unnamed synagogue on the Sabbath, there appears before him an unnamed woman "who has had a spirit of weakness" (my trans.) for eighteen years. Seeing her, he has a decision to make. Will he heal her and violate the oral law pertaining to Sabbath,[1] or will he attend to the Sabbath restrictions and withhold the blessing that she needs? Given his understanding of his mission in 4:18–21, derived from the liberative vision of Isaiah 61:1, his choice seems obvious; although she never even asks, Jesus must heal her.

Luke describes the healing miracle in two parts. Initially Jesus makes a pronouncement in 13:12 that she has been *apolelysai*, "released" or "set free," from

Homiletical Perspective

The miraculous healing described in this story is met with indignation by "the leader of the synagogue" (v. 14). It is well to take care not to suggest that synagogue people are more legalistic than church people. Those in leadership positions in any time and place are supposed to care about the rules! To be in a position of leadership requires bearing the responsibility for understanding the rules in depth and interpreting them as persuasively as possible. An officer of any organization knows how many folks press for exceptions to be made for them. Officers who take their guardian responsibilities seriously try to meet the obligations undertaken when assuming a position of trust. It takes a bit of fine-tuning to distinguish between upholding the rules and allowing for really exceptional cases, particularly when one's trusteeship is under scrutiny. The safest course, usually, is to insist on the rule. It is well to remember that when trying to explain your situation to a representative of the airline or the clerk in the department of motor vehicles!

Noah Feldman writes in the *New York Times Magazine*[1] about his experience of having been educated in a religious school run by a group called

---

1. R. Alan Culpepper ("The Gospel of Luke," in *The New Interpreter's Bible*, vol. 9 [Nashville: Abingdon Press, 1995], 274) notes that this instruction can be found in *m. Yoma* 8.6 (n.147).

1. Noah Feldman, "Orthodox Paradox," *New York Times Magazine*, July 22, 2007, p. 40.

Luke 13:10-17

Theological Perspective

parables of the Mustard Seed and Leaven and their focus on the kingdom or realm of God and how to address discouragement and despair over what we feel we have when we believe we have failed (13:18–21). A more engaging route for the preacher is to consider why a story of healing is found between two parables featuring such uncontrollable elements as mustard (a call for repentance) and leaven (descriptive of the kingdom) that reveal the surprising, invasive character of God's realm.

This unnamed woman can draw our attention to the connection between healing and the dynamic pastoral and prophetic witness to which we are called. As we approach the task of how healing calls forth the pastoral and the prophetic, we must hearken back to the spiritual and social liberation that can help us realize our limits. In doing so, we may well discover that we have moved beyond our limits, but we also see that we have not yet lived into them. The challenges of living into our healing can help us uncover the realities and possibilities in our ministries and also invite others to explore theirs.

Part of the gift of exploring healing is that it can open the doors in the rooms of our lives, and healing encourages us to walk through these doors to discover the grace and hope and judgment that may be inside each room. This, at first glance, may be the last thing in the world many of us want to do in the midst of births and deaths and board meetings. We need to encourage both ourselves and others to develop the ability to assess and reassess our witness, the direction in which it is going, and ask if this is the path of God or the path of ecclesiastical reward, human folly, or grasping at vainglorious shadows. If we do this, we can assure others that we will find more energy and commitment to live the healthy and healing witness that God would have us live.

Theologically, we must insist that people of faith lean into both pastoral and prophetic witness to healing, which is yet one pathway into salvation. It is crucial to point out that there is a rich interrelationship between healing and sin, which this passage also taps into. If we do not recognize the ways in which we walk away from God and from others—sin—then we cannot truly search for genuine healing. At this point the preacher must be both a comforter and an agent of hope, as you point to the ways in which the leader of the synagogue is caught in the all-too-common trap of placing form before substance. When churches are faced with the hard task of discerning the direction of their ministries, helping to draw out the deep kneading of sin and healing, the

Pastoral Perspective

Sabbath and the human activity of observance and keeping the holiness of the Sabbath is to give institutional and communal foundation to both tables of the law: to honor and worship God alone and to render justice to the neighbor. This Deuteronomic understanding of holiness is at the heart of the Old Testament prophetic traditions.[2]

In the account of the crippled woman in the synagogue on the Sabbath, Luke emphasizes the latter understanding of the Sabbath as refraining from work. Jesus elicits rage because the Pharisees control the Sabbath with their work of cumbersome requirements that imprison or enslave people with long-standing bondage. A religious observance that is to remember and honor the liberation of God's people thus becomes in the hands of the Pharisees a means of social control and oppression. A spirit of bondage lives in the woman and restricts her independence and freedom to live in strength and fullness.

Think of the busload of people who leave hell on a holiday to heaven in C. S. Lewis's *The Great Divorce*.[3] One of them, in her earthly life, was a washerwoman in Golder's Green, wringing her livelihood from the soil of the clothing of those who hire her for a pittance. In her life in the kingdom of God, she is herself clothed in a white gown and a tiara, with ladies holding her train and laughing in the bright sheen of God's new day. Most of the people who board the bus for their holiday in heaven away from hell, instead of staying, choose to return to the lower world. The return trip is difficult, because the journey back to hell requires them to find what appears to be a small crack in the expansive green pastures of the realm of the kingdom, and to travel back in a shrinking coach that crushes passengers bent on returning to hell into insufferably cramped quarters until they themselves grow small enough to have wide spaces between them. The crippled woman in Luke, however, stays on holiday.

Jesus challenges the habits of Pharisaic work. Even they lead their ox and their donkey from the manger to water, he says. If the animals are free to drink, then how much more should a daughter of Abraham in the kingdom of God receive freedom for life? She is an heir of the covenant of promise. This freedom from bondage is Jesus' aim in his healing the woman. Satan is the chief spirit of the powers that oppress the earth. Jesus himself confronts the

---

2. Patrick D. Miller, *Deuteronomy* (Louisville, KY: John Knox Press, 1990), 65–70, 79–84.
3. C. S. Lewis, *The Great Divorce* (New York: Macmillan, 1946).

the weakness that has crippled her. Yet the healing is not manifest until Jesus lays his hands on her in verse 13. This seemingly unnecessary second step distinguishes this miracle from the previous Sabbath healing narratives in 6:6–11, where the man with a withered right hand is healed as Jesus commands him to extend his hand, or the narrative in 4:31–37, where the spirit of an unclean demon is cast out as Jesus gives the command. Today's story is perhaps more similar to the account in 14:1–6, where Jesus heals a man with dropsy by *epilabomenos* or "taking hold of him" (14:4), though the touching here may serve a different purpose.

In the present instance Jesus' two-part healing allows him to touch a woman who is unclean, and thereby restore her socially as well as physically. Consider the various instances in Luke's Gospel where Jesus violates Jewish custom and touches unclean people: he touches a leper (5:13), the widow of Nain's dead son (7:14); he is touched by a woman with a dozen-year hemorrhage (8:43–48). Touching that would have conveyed uncleanness, although unnecessary in light of Jesus' ability to heal by command, is a frequent occurrence in this Gospel. Touching says symbolically that Jesus does not care for his own sake that those he heals are viewed as unclean, and that he will not allow the threat of the conveyance of uncleanness to keep him from redeeming the wounded and thus marginalized. In each of these instances, his touch represents fellowship for those whose ailments may have denied them human contact; Jesus' touch is their initial welcome back into community.

The Jesus seen here is also in a familiar position of opposition to the Jewish religious authorities. As with the "scribes and the Pharisees" in 6:7 and the "lawyers and Pharisees" in 14:3, there are present in these healing accounts frequently opponents who are lying in wait to "find an accusation against him" (6:7) or who are silently disturbed by his behavior (14:4). In this pericope, the synagogue leader, described as "indignant," actually argues against healing on the Sabbath (13:14). These figures represent the status quo that Jesus' healings would disrupt; they are the guardians at the gate of an oral tradition that undergirds their societal structure. For them, "doing good" is not the point, for Jesus' good deeds undermine their social order.

The desire to control Sabbath observance is critical for maintaining another social order as well. The slavocracy of the American South was in part maintained by the restriction of "doing good" on the

"modern Orthodox." He reports a school assembly in which a local physician, a member of the modern Orthodox movement, argued that Torah teaches that one might break the Sabbath to save the life of a Jew but not a Gentile, except under particular circumstances. This understanding of the Torah (which, of course, is not unanimously held by Jewish scholars) underlines how seriously observant Jews take the Sabbath. Even if the Sabbath may be broken to save a life, the logic of this view does not permit breaking it to heal an affliction that does not threaten the life of the victim.

The crippled woman in this text is not in mortal danger. Luke tells us that she has borne her affliction for eighteen years. Is it not reasonable to imagine that she could wait another day, or even another week? Of course, she finds herself in quite a different place from the leader of the synagogue. It is easy to counsel someone else to be patient. Rules are more likely to be considered reasonable when they do not affect the rule enforcer. Jesus apparently identifies with the woman rather than the leader, as though her disfigurement were his own, or perhaps his mother's.

Have you noticed how people's tenacity about rules tends to become more flexible when the weight of the rule presses heavily on someone close to them? One can begin to see injustice and even unintentional cruelty in a rule one might ordinarily support. This is true of issues much debated in the church these days. Can you think of examples in your own congregation?

In recent years, some Christians have begun to appreciate the value of Sabbath keeping. They have given up shopping on their designated day of rest, or they turn off phones and let e-mails pile up for a day. We recognize the wisdom in honoring a day of rest and reflection, and we acknowledge the personal discipline required to keep it. Is it possible to respect and honor a rule without permitting exceptions so casually that the rule is sabotaged? Is the key, perhaps, in considering the weight of each potential exception as though it were applied to someone with whom one is especially sympathetic, scrutinizing it with eyes that take into account both the virtues of the rule and the divine compassion as exhibited in Jesus' care for the suffering woman?

Some congregations have no problem with scriptural texts about miracles, while others find them either irrelevant or embarrassing. None of us has the power to get behind the text as though we could make a certain judgment about the event described, nor is such a judgment necessary. The

Luke 13:10-17

Theological Perspective

prophetic and the pastoral, can help set in motion a process that encourages the church (and individuals) to persist in asking questions and seeking answers to those questions about their gifts and abilities. This becomes crucial in our chaotic times. So often churches respond in an either/or manner to chaos—becoming insular and concerned only with the membership of the church, or seeking to answer all the problems and providing all the solutions to those problems through their programming and worship services. The problem arises when neither response calls out the gifts and abilities of people of faith.

We need to remind our congregants and ourselves that we cannot do this alone. It takes nurturing and prodding a community to take on its call, rather than to be content with well-meaning but unfaithful religious hypocrisy. It also means learning to lean on and truly trust God, who is the Spirit and Hope in our lives. This is not always easy to do, but it is absolutely necessary to try to live into.

We are like the woman bent over and unable to look up and see the sun. We know only the dust and dirt underneath our feet. We struggle to see the path before us by straining and twisting, because we cannot look straight ahead. To ask for healing helps us step into Jesus' invitation to mend our souls as we mend creation. There will be times when we will "know" this in ways that are too profound for words or reason. There will also be times when God seems far off and the pathway unclear, but seek healing we must. We are inheritors of the gift of healing of the bent-over woman who stood up straight and began praising God.

EMILIE M. TOWNES

Pastoral Perspective

devil in his temptations (Luke 4:1–13). The crowds come to him for healing from their diseases and freedom from the spirits that trouble them (Luke 6:18; 7:2; 9:1, 37–42).

In the Galilee, the twelve male disciples accompany Jesus, "as well as some women who had been cured of evil spirits and infirmities: Mary, called Magdalene, . . . Joanna, . . . and Susanna, and many others" (Luke 8:2–3) who provide for Jesus and the male disciples with their resources. It is Mary, Joanna, and the other women who accompany him to his crucifixion and bear witness to the male disciples. Here in the lectionary passage for this day, we find that this woman who has been in bondage for eighteen years is a daughter of the covenant made through Abraham with Sarah and that she is one of the many other daughters of Abraham who find freedom from oppression and physical disease in Jesus' exercise of life-giving and freedom-giving touch.

People who witness Jesus' casting out the spirit of bondage and the healing of the arthritic contortion of the woman's body respond in either of two ways. The Pharisees, whose Sabbath practice is to patronize and exercise power over people and at the same time to neglect their burdens, are put to shame. The vast majority of those who witness the new health rejoice at all the wonderful things that Jesus does. The Lord's true Sabbath is God's giving the freedom and rejoicing to such people as the unnamed woman who finds freedom in Jesus' healing touch.

The pastoral theology of the Sabbath in Jesus' practice and teaching implies for us our memory of God's freeing power in Christ over the bondage at work in the world through oppressive burdens on God's people. This unnamed woman becomes a testimony to the freedom of the people of God from demonic oppression and the crippling burden of disease and anything else that robs God's people of full life.

CHARLES E. RAYNAL

Exegetical Perspective

Sabbath. Reflecting on religious practices in the slaveholding South, Frederick Douglass notes:

> It was necessary to keep our religious masters at St. Michael's unacquainted with the fact that, instead of spending the Sabbath in wrestling, boxing, and drinking whisky, we were trying to learn how to read the will of God; for they had much rather see us engaged in those degrading sports, than to see us behaving like intellectual, moral, and accountable beings.[2]

While enslaved Africans desired to worship God and to educate themselves, literally to "do good," they were prevented because their improvement represented a threat to the social system that circumscribed their lives. Although the plantation setting is clearly not a direct parallel to the situation Jesus faces, similar issues of power, control, and order are present in both cases. The control of Sabbath practice in both instances represents a convenient way of maintaining an oppressive system whereby some people are forced to endure perpetual suffering by others who are more concerned with sustaining a system that benefits them than alleviating the burdens of those it cripples.

Jesus' actions challenge that system, as do his words in 13:15–16. Employing a pattern of reasoning familiar from later rabbinic Judaism, Jesus argues from the light to the heavy, or a rhetorical pattern of *a minori ad maius*, as Joseph Fitzmyer notes.[3] If it is permitted to loose (*lyō*) an ox or donkey on the Sabbath, then why is it not permissible to loose (*lyō*) a "daughter of Abraham whom Satan bound for eighteen long years"? Again, for Jesus the care of human beings is itself a religious virtue that takes precedence over rites, rituals, and the social systems they ensure.

What a potent aide-mémoire these words are for us of the danger of allowing institutionalized ritual to shape our understanding of "religion" in ways that curtail "doing good" for those in need in our midst. Like Isaiah 1:10–17 and Micah 6:6–8, Jesus' words here are a requisite reminder that the care for God's people in need is at the heart of our faith.

RODNEY S. SADLER JR.

Homiletical Perspective

bigger issue is to discover how the story functions within the text. For example, what purpose is served by Luke's story about Jesus' healing a woman who has been disfigured by some affliction, perhaps osteoporosis? The heart of the text is theological.

As a theological statement, the story says something about Jesus' identity and authority and about the character of God as revealed in what Jesus does. Jesus does not pray for the woman, as you or I might, but simply calls her over and declares, "Woman, you are set free from your ailment" (v. 12). When he lays hands on her, she is immediately liberated from her crippling affliction. Her healing depends neither on her faith nor on the faith of others—worth noting by all who promise miracles if only everyone will just multiply their prayers or turn up the volume of their faith!

Unlike the Gospel of Matthew, which boldly declares Jesus to be "lord of the Sabbath," Luke leaves it to those who hear the story to identify the one whose compassion becomes manifest in the power to push back against disfiguring illness, and whose authority permits him to do it, despite the fact that it requires the suspension of a perfectly good rule.

This story in Luke's Gospel is immediately followed by two short sayings about the dominion of God. One begins, "[Jesus] said therefore, 'What is the kingdom of God like?'" (v. 18), and the other, "To what shall I compare the kingdom of God?" (v. 20). The story of the afflicted woman seems to anticipate these questions and provide a kind of picture of what the ultimate reign of God will be like. Where Jesus is, the kingdom is. Where Jesus is, things begin to be made right. His ministry provides a foretaste of the coming kingdom. In the reign of God, the world will be repaired. There will be no blindness or loss of hearing, no one broken or disfigured. In the reign of God, there will be no conflicts between what is good for one and what is good for all. If this is the ultimate future God is preparing for us, how might we contribute to some manifestation of it wherever we find ourselves?

RONALD P. BYARS

---

2. Frederick Douglass, "Slaveholding Religion and the Christianity of Christ," in *African American Religious History: A Documentary Witness*, ed. Milton C. Sernett (Durham, NC: Duke University Press, 1999), 105.

3. Joseph Fitzmyer, *The Gospel according to Luke X–XXIV*, Anchor Bible 28a (New York: Doubleday, 1985), 1012.

Contributors

Charles L. Aaron, Pastor, First United Methodist Church, Farmersville, Texas

David R. Adams, Assisting Priest, St. Luke in the Fields Episcopal Church, New York, New York

Stephen P. Ahearne-Kroll, Associate Professor of New Testament, Methodist Theological School in Ohio, Delaware, Ohio

Ellen T. Armour, E. Rhodes and Leona B. Carpenter Associate Professor of Theology, Vanderbilt Divinity School, Nashville, Tennessee

Heidi Husted Armstrong, Interim Pastor, Trinity Presbyterian Church, Tacoma, Washington

Margaret P. Aymer, New Testament Studies, Interdenominational Theological Center, Atlanta, Georgia

Eugene C. Bay, President, Colgate Rochester Crozer Divinity School, Rochester, New York

Jon L. Berquist, Executive Editor for Biblical Studies, Westminster John Knox Press, Louisville, Kentucky

Bruce C. Birch, Dean, Wesley Theological Seminary, Washington, D.C.

Richard D. Blake, Librarian for Graduate and Professional Studies and Health Sciences, Eberly Library, Waynesburg University, Waynesburg, Pennsylvania

Frederick H. Borsch, Professor of New Testament and Chair of Anglican Studies, Lutheran Theological Seminary at Philadelphia, Pennsylvania

Richard Boyce, Associate Professor of Preaching and Pastoral Leadership, Union Theological Seminary and Presbyterian School of Christian Education, Charlotte, North Carolina

Sally A. Brown, Elizabeth M. Engle Associate Professor of Preaching and Worship, Princeton Theological Seminary, Princeton, New Jersey

Robert A. Bryant, Associate Professor of Religion, Presbyterian College, Clinton, South Carolina

Katherine M. Bush, Associate Rector, Church of the Holy Communion, Memphis, Tennessee

Ronald P. Byars, Professor Emeritus of Preaching and Worship, Union Theological Seminary and Presbyterian School of Christian Education, Richmond, Virginia

Quinn G. Caldwell, Associate Minister, Old South Church in Boston, Massachusetts

Richard P. Carlson, Philip H. and Amanda E. Glatfelter Professor of New Testament Language, Literature, and Theology, Lutheran Theological Seminary at Gettysburg, Pennsylvania

Anna Case-Winters, Professor of Theology, McCormick Theological Seminary, Chicago, Illinois

Robert Cathey, Professor of Theology, McCormick Theological Seminary, Chicago, Illinois

John B. Cobb Jr., Professor Emeritus, Claremont School of Theology, Claremont, California

Verlee A. Copeland, Senior Minister, The Union Church of Hinsdale, United Church of Christ, Hinsdale, Illinois

Katheryn Pfisterer Darr, Professor of Hebrew Bible, Boston University School of Theology, Boston, Massachusetts

John T. DeBevoise, Pastor, Palma Ceia Presbyterian Church, Tampa, Florida

Nancy L. deClaissé-Walford, Professor of Biblical Languages and Old Testament, McAfee School of Theology, Atlanta, Georgia

Douglas M. Donley, Pastor, University Baptist Church, Minneapolis, Minnesota

Mark Douglas, Associate Professor of Christian Ethics, Columbia Theological Seminary, Decatur, Georgia

Paul Simpson Duke, Co-Pastor, First Baptist Church of Ann Arbor, Michigan

Stacey Simpson Duke, Co-Pastor, First Baptist Church of Ann Arbor, Michigan

Susan Grove Eastman, Assistant Professor of Practice of Bible and Christian Formation, Duke Divinity School, Durham, North Carolina

Mark D. W. Edington, Rector, St. Dunstan's Church, Dover, Massachusetts

P. C. Enniss, Theologian in Residence, Trinity Presbyterian Church, Atlanta, Georgia

Trevor Eppehimer, Associate Professor of Systematic Theology, Hood Theological Seminary, Salisbury, North Carolina

Richard L. Eslinger, Academic Dean and Professor of Worship and Homiletics, United Theological Seminary, Trotwood, Ohio

Wendy Farley, Professor, Department of Religion, Emory University, Atlanta, Georgia

Kathleen A. Robertson Farmer, Professor Emerita, United Theological Seminary, Trotwood, Ohio

Matthew Flemming, Instructor of Preaching, Columbia Theological Seminary, Decatur, Georgia

Beverly Roberts Gaventa, Helen H. P. Manson Professor of New Testament, Princeton Theological Seminary, Princeton, New Jersey

James Gertmenian, Senior Minister, Plymouth Congregational Church, Minneapolis, Minnesota

Daniel M. Geslin, Pastor, Sixth Avenue United Church of Christ, Denver, Colorado

David E. Gray, Senior Pastor, Bradley Hills Presbyterian Church, Bethesda, Maryland

Douglas John Hall, Professor Emeritus of Religious Studies, McGill University, Montreal, Quebec

J. William Harkins, Senior Lecturer of Pastoral Theology, Columbia Theological Seminary, Decatur, Georgia, and Priest Associate for Pastoral Care, Episcopal Cathedral of St. Philip, Atlanta, Georgia

Elaine A. Heath, McCreless Assistant Professor of Evangelism, Perkins School of Theology, Southern Methodist University, Dallas, Texas

M. Jan Holton, Assistant Professor of Pastoral Care and Counseling, Yale Divinity School, New Haven, Connecticut

Carol E. Holtz-Martin, Pastor, First Baptist Church of Macedon, New York

H. James Hopkins, Pastor, Lakeshore Avenue Baptist Church, Oakland, California

Cynthia A. Jarvis, Minister, The Presbyterian Church of Chestnut Hill, Philadelphia, Pennsylvania

Willis Jenkins, Margaret Farley Assistant Professor of Social Ethics, Yale Divinity School, New Haven, Connecticut

Michael Jinkins, Academic Dean and Professor of Pastoral Theology, Austin Presbyterian Theological Seminary, Austin, Texas

Cheryl A. Kirk-Duggan, Professor of Theology and Women's Studies and Director of Women's Studies, Shaw University Divinity School, Raleigh, North Carolina

Ralph W. Klein, Christ Seminary-Seminex Professor of Old Testament Emeritus, and Editor of *Currents in Theology and Mission*, Lutheran School of Theology at Chicago, Illinois

Henry F. Knight, Director, Cohen Center for Holocaust Studies, Keene State College, Keene, New Hampshire

Steven J. Kraftchick, Associate Professor of the Practice of New Testament Interpretation, Candler School of Theology, Emory University, Atlanta, Georgia

Lisa Lamb, Adjunct Professor, Fuller Theological Seminary, Pasadena, California

Gregory H. Ledbetter, Pastor, Shell Ridge Community Church (American Baptist), Walnut Creek, California

Bill J. Leonard, Dean and Professor of Church History, Wake Forest University Divinity School, Winston-Salem, North Carolina

David J. Lose, Marbury E. Anderson Chair in Biblical Preaching, Luther Seminary, St. Paul, Minnesota

Gregory Anderson Love, Associate Professor of Systematic Theology, San Francisco Theological Seminary, San Anselmo, California

Patricia J. Lull, Dean of Students, Luther Seminary, St. Paul, Minnesota

J. Mary Luti, Visiting Professor of Worship and Preaching and Director of Wilson Chapel, Andover Newton Theological School, Newton Centre, Massachusetts

Thomas W. Mann, Retired Professor of Hebrew Bible and Parish Minister, Winston-Salem, North Carolina

Linda McKiernan-Allen, Minister, West Street Christian Church, Tipton, Indiana

James McTyre, Pastor, Lake Hills Presbyterian Church, Knoxville, Tennessee

Carrie N. Mitchell, Associate Pastor, First Presbyterian Church, Pittsford, New York

Rodger Y. Nishioka, Benton Family Associate Professor of Christian Education, Columbia Theological Seminary, Decatur, Georgia

C. Gray Norsworthy, Chaplain, Big Canoe Chapel, Big Canoe, Georgia

Jeff Paschal, Pastor, First Presbyterian Church, Wooster, Ohio

Bonnie L. Pattison, Independent Scholar, Wheaton, Illinois

Lanny Peters, Pastor, Oakhurst Baptist Church, Decatur, Georgia

Charles E. Raynal, Professor Emeritus, Columbia Theological Seminary, Decatur, Georgia

John Rollefson, Retired Pastor, Evangelical Lutheran Church in America, San Luis Obispo, California

Art Ross, Pastor, White Memorial Presbyterian Church, Raleigh, North Carolina

Rodney S. Sadler Jr., Associate Professor of Bible, Union Theological Seminary and Presbyterian School of Christian Education, Charlotte, North Carolina

David J. Schlafer, Independent Consultant in Homiletical Formation, Bethesda, Maryland

Richard J. Shaffer Jr., Associate Dean, University of Dubuque Theological Seminary, Dubuque, Iowa

Carolyn J. Sharp, Associate Professor of Hebrew Scriptures, Yale Divinity School, New Haven, Connecticut

Richard L. Sheffield, Interim Pastor, Christ Memorial Presbyterian Church, Columbia, Maryland

John C. Shelley, Dorothy Peace Professor of Religion, Furman University, Greenville, South Carolina

Bruce E. Shields, Russell and Marian Blowers Professor of Christian Ministries Emeritus, Emmanuel School of Religion, Johnson City, Tennessee

Matthew L. Skinner, Associate Professor of New Testament, Luther Seminary, St. Paul, Minnesota

Marion L. Soards, Professor of New Testament Studies, Louisville Presbyterian Theological Seminary, Louisville, Kentucky

Haywood Barringer Spangler, Rector, St. Bartholomew's Episcopal Church, Richmond, Virginia

Thomas R. Steagald, Pastor, First United Methodist Church, Stanley, North Carolina

Gray Temple, Gray Temple Consulting, Inc., Duluth, Georgia

Linda E. Thomas, Professor of Theology and Anthropology at Lutheran School of Theology, Chicago, Illinois

James W. Thompson, Robert and Kay Onstead Professor of New Testament, Abilene Christian University, Abilene, Texas

Emilie M. Townes, Associate Dean of Academic Affairs and Andrew W. Mellon Professor of African American Religion and Theology, Yale Divinity School, New Haven, Connecticut

Philip Turner, Interim Dean, Episcopal Theological Seminary of the Southwest, Austin, Texas

John W. Vest, Associate Pastor, Fourth Presbyterian Church, Chicago, Illinois

Thomas W. Walker, Pastor, Palms Presbyterian Church, Jacksonville Beach, Florida

James A. Wallace, C.Ss.R., Professor of Homiletics, Washington Theological Union, Washington, D.C.

Audrey West, Adjunct Professor of New Testament, Lutheran School of Theology at Chicago, Illinois

John E. White, Dean of Students and Vice President for Student Services, Columbia Theological Seminary, Decatur, Georgia

Marsha M. Wilfong, Pastor, First Presbyterian Church, Bellevue, Iowa

Gláucia Vasconcelos Wilkey, Assistant Professor, School of Theology and Ministry, Seattle University, Seattle, Washington

William H. Willimon, Bishop, North Alabama United Methodist Church, Birmingham, Alabama

Scripture Index

Author Index

Bill J. Leonard	Proper 13 PS TP, Proper 14 PS TP, Proper 15 PS TP	Art Ross	Proper 16 PS PP
		Rodney S. Sadler Jr.	Proper 16 G EP
David J. Lose	Proper 7 G HP, Proper 8 G HP, Proper 9 G HP	David J. Schlafer	Proper 13 G HP, Proper 14 G HP, Proper 15 G HP
Gregory Anderson Love	Proper 4 G TP, Proper 5 G TP, Proper 6 G TP	Richard J. Shaffer Jr.	Proper 7 G PP, Proper 8 G PP, Proper 9 G PP
Patricia J. Lull	Proper 13 G PP, Proper 14 G PP, Proper 15 G PP	Carolyn J. Sharp	Proper 4 OT TP, Proper 5 OT TP, Proper 6 OT TP
J. Mary Luti	Proper 13 PS PP, Proper 14 PS PP, Proper 15 PS PP	Richard L. Sheffield	Day of Pentecost NT HP, Trinity Sunday E HP, Proper 3 E HP
Thomas W. Mann	Proper 10 OT EP, Proper 11 OT EP, Proper 12 OT EP	John C. Shelley	Proper 13 E TP, Proper 14 E TP, Proper 15 E TP
Linda McKiernan-Allen	Proper 10 PS PP, Proper 11 PS PP, Proper 12 PS PP	Bruce E. Shields	Day of Pentecost G HP, Trinity Sunday G HP, Proper 3 G HP
James McTyre	Day of Pentecost PS PP, Trinity Sunday PS PP, Proper 3 PS PP	Matthew L. Skinner	Proper 10 G EP, Proper 11 G EP, Proper 12 G EP
Carrie N. Mitchell	Proper 7 OT PP, Proper 8 OT PP, Proper 9 OT PP	Marion L. Soards	Proper 13 E EP, Proper 14 E EP, Proper 15 E EP
Rodger Y. Nishioka	Proper 10 E PP, Proper 11 E PP, Proper 12 E PP	Haywood Barringer Spangler	Proper 7 OT HP, Proper 8 OT HP, Proper 9 OT HP
C. Gray Norsworthy	Proper 4 PS PP, Proper 5 PS PP, Proper 6 PS PP	Thomas R. Steagald	Proper 16 OT TP
		Gray Temple	Proper 16 E TP
Jeff Paschal	Day of Pentecost OT HP, Trinity Sunday OT HP, Proper 3 OT HP	Linda E. Thomas	Day of Pentecost NT TP, Trinity Sunday E TP
Bonnie L. Pattison	Day of Pentecost PS TP, Trinity Sunday PS TP, Proper 3 PS TP	James W. Thompson	Proper 7 G EP, Proper 8 G EP, Proper 9 G EP
Lanny Peters	Proper 16 E PP	Emilie M. Townes	Proper 16 G TP
Charles E. Raynal	Proper 16 G PP	Philip Turner	Day of Pentecost G TP, Trinity Sunday G TP, Proper 3 G TP
John Rollefson	Proper 7 PS HP, Proper 8 PS HP, Proper 9 PS HP	John W. Vest	Proper 13 PS EP, Proper 14 PS EP, Proper 15 PS EP